Monsters, Aliens, and Holes in the Ground

Monsters, Aliens, and Holes in the Ground

A Guide to Tabletop Roleplaying Games from D&D *to* Mothership

Stu Horvath
  Original Photographs by Stu Horvath
  Original Illustrations by Kyle Patterson

The MIT Press
Cambridge, Massachusetts
London, England

The MIT Press would like to thank the anonymous peer reviewers who provided comments on drafts of this book. The generous work of academic experts is essential for establishing the authority and quality of our publications. We acknowledge with gratitude the contributions of these otherwise uncredited readers.

For more information about this book, including notes and praise, please visit the MIT Press webpage: http://www.mitpress.mit.edu/HolesintheGround

Printed and bound in China.
This book was set in ITC Cheltenham, ITC Goudy Sans, Osgard Pro, Duvall, ITC Serif Gothic, Exocet, Rivendell, and Cheee by Derek Kinsman.
Production management by Stu Horvath.

Library of Congress Cataloging-in-Publication Data

Names: Horvath, Stu, author.
Title: Monsters, aliens, and holes in the ground : a guide to tabletop
   roleplaying games from D&D to Mothership / Stu Horvath ; original
   illustrations by Kyle Patterson..
Description: Cambridge, Massachusetts : The MIT Press, [2023] | Includes
   index.
Identifiers: LCCN 2022045208 (print) | LCCN 2022045209 (ebook) | ISBN
   9780262048224 (hardcover) | ISBN 9780262048231 (hardcover) | ISBN
   9780262375450 (epub) | ISBN 9780262375443 (pdf)
Subjects: LCSH: Fantasy games–History. | Board games–History.
Classification: LCC GV1469.6 .H67 2023 (print) | LCC GV1469.6 (ebook) |
   DDC 793.93–dc23/eng/20221006
LC record available at https://lccn.loc.gov/2022045208
LC ebook record available at https://lccn.loc.gov/2022045209

10 9 8 7 6 5 4 3 2 1

Let me tell you of the days of high adventure!

— The Wizard
Conan the Barbarian (1982)

Contents

Introduction

I don't know how I became aware of *Dungeons & Dragons*. There was the all-too-brief Saturday morning cartoon and the wonderfully garish toy line it spawned, but I was never able to catch the cartoon consistently, and I never owned any of the cool toys as a child (though it felt like every kid I knew had one of the bendy hydras). I recall an elementary school book sale where I bought a set of rub-down transfers that contained all manner of *D&D* monsters, along with maybe an Endless Quest book or two. The kid across the street had the *Advanced Dungeons & Dragons* videogame (1982) for his Intellivision. Then there were Steve and Kevin, classmates who had older brothers who played the game. Any one of these, or none of them, could have been my first exposure.

While my parents were broadly supportive of whatever caught my interest as a kid, especially if it involved books, they hesitated to embrace *Dungeons & Dragons*. Their reasoning is a mystery. My dad passed away before I thought to ask, and my mom simply can't recall. I used to think their reaction had something to do with the moral panic around the game. My interest developed in 1985, around the same time *60 Minutes* aired a sensationalized segment titled "Is *Dungeons & Dragons* Evil?" that interrogated a supposed nexus between *Dungeons & Dragons*, devil worship, and suicide.

While that bit of fearmongering worked its way into the concerns of many a parent and teacher, panic wasn't really in the character of my mom and my dad. Instead, I've begun to think that the game's strangeness was the source of their reticence. *Monopoly* this was not and, decades later, it's still no easy feat to explain how *Dungeons & Dragons* works, or even its appeal, to someone who hasn't experienced the game firsthand.

Though the reason is murky, the fact remains: I very badly wanted to learn more about *Dungeons & Dragons*, and my parents were not inclined to oblige. Grandparents are often handy in breaking this sort of embargo. I haven't a clue whether my paternal grandmother was oblivious, motivated by spite for my parents' wishes, or just wanted me to be quiet in the car. Whatever her reason, I came home from the Waldenbooks at the Willowbrook Mall one excellent night with the blue *Dungeons & Dragons Set 2: Expert Rules* box set and module *X10: Red Arrow, Black Shield* tucked under my arm.

If my parents were displeased, they didn't make it known. I suspect any concerns they had evaporated once they saw the rather baffling contents of those products (my mom, who has listened to me rattle on about this stuff for years, and even read the first draft of this book, is still a bit fuzzy on how it all works). Soon after, my dad took me to a local bookshop, Daniel's Den, where I got *Monster Manual II* and a couple issues of *Dragon* magazine (among them was a tattered back issue of #88, with its Jim Holloway cover, depicting an adventurer hiding from an orc war party in a tree—my pick for one of the magazine's all-time best).

If the books on the shelves of Waldenbooks represented *Dungeons & Dragons* at its most respectable, the racks at Daniel's Den hinted at deeper, darker mysteries. Small and cramped, the Den was run by a skinny little hippie with a beard, long hair, and sleepy eyes (presumably named Daniel, though I never asked); it smelled vaguely of incense, and black light posters for bands from the Grateful Dead to Iron Maiden hung from the ceiling. It was the place where I also got my first set of *Dungeons & Dragons* dice, where I bought my first *Wolverine* comic, and where I saw the *Satanic Bible* for the first time (on a tantalizingly high shelf labeled "18+ Only").

For me, the whole vibe of the store contributed to the sense of the forbidden that clings to early *Dungeons & Dragons* products. That intrigued me and helped me understand why, a little later, when I brought the *D&D Basic Set* to a visit at my cousin's, she called it, half seriously, half playfully, "the Devil's Game."

My early collection—an intermediary rule set, a module that was really more of a standalone wargame, the weirder of the two *Monster Manual*s, and a couple of magazines—was not exactly conducive to play. Even after I owned a copy of the *Basic Set*, "playing *D&D*" mostly meant rolling up characters for the sake of it and drawing endless dungeons, sometime with colored pencils. Such was the plight of an only child in the mid-'80s. I was content with *D&D* being a solo pursuit, honestly. I enjoyed reading *X1: The Isle of Dread* over and over, imagining different stories playing out over the blank hexes of the island map.

This state of affairs shifted in 1989, thanks to a product for a game that was not *Dungeons & Dragons*; it was the four-volume *Gamer's Handbook of the Marvel Universe*, a compendium of all the notable (and many forgettable) characters from the superhero comics I was just then getting into. Each of these character profiles was accompanied by various skills and abilities, encoded numerically in a way similar to, but distinct from, *Dungeons & Dragons*. Even without the main rules, it was enough to fuel endless debates among my friends over who would win in a fight. Something clicked during those debates, and it wasn't long before we had TSR's *Marvel Super Heroes* RPG at the table. Soon after that, we were making more serious attempts at playing *Dungeon & Dragons*. I was hooked.

Over the years, *D&D* was the staple, but my group (ever-expanding, shrinking, and reconfiguring) played whatever we could get our hands on: The post-apocalyptic *Teenage Mutant Ninja Turtles* game *After the Bomb*, *Paranoia*, *Tales from the Floating Vagabond*, *Middle-earth Role Playing*, *Nightlife*, *GURPS*, *Pendragon*, and *Call of Cthulhu*. If the local comic shop could order it, and we had the cash in our pocket, we played it. And so it went, for many years. My collection, and thus what I could play, as well as my general perception of RPGs as a hobby and industry, was formed primarily by the vagaries of commercial availability.

For instance: *Call of Cthulhu* products were occasionally on the shelf at the Waldenbooks in the mall. I got my first copy of *Masks of Nyarlathotep* there, but to get anything else in the line required a special order via Infinity Comics, my local shop. And *that* required the knowledge that such things existed. Despite the fact that it was produced by the same company, Chaosium, I never saw a *RuneQuest* product on a store shelf as a kid, and thus an entire branch of RPGs effectively did not exist for me. Anecdotally, I've heard the opposite to be true in other parts of the country, where *RuneQuest* was on shelves, but it was impossible to find *Call of Cthulhu*. Scarcity and distribution were powerful forces in the pre-internet age.

My first glimpse at what I missed came around 2008, in an antique store in Essex, Massachusetts, called the White Elephant. There, on a shelf behind the counter, I found one of the booklets from the original *Dungeons & Dragons* box set, the second volume, dedicated to monsters and treasure. I immediately recognized it as some sort of *D&D* product—though crude, the black dragon on the cover was still clearly recognizable—but I had no idea *what* it was. I didn't know there was an edition of *D&D* before *Advanced Dungeons & Dragons*! It was the box that launched the entire hobby, and I was oblivious to its existence!

I bought the booklet, of course, and eventually purchased a copy of the full box on eBay. Cursory investigation over the next couple of years revealed a much larger world of RPGs than I had previously encountered. Before this point, *Call of Cthulhu* existed for me as a series of paperbacks, but I soon learned there were box sets! And Chaosium put out a lot of other games I'd been unaware of— *RuneQuest*, as I mentioned, but also their adaptation of the *Elfquest* comic series, and Larry Niven's *Ringworld* novels, and the strangely lightweight storytelling game based on the *Prince Valiant* newspaper comic strip. I find that I resonate with Chaosium products, so discovering this larger selection of their catalog meant discovering a wider world of RPGs that felt thoughtful and exciting and mysterious. I discovered that TSR, too, had released a number of products I had never heard of, but these felt more absurd, a kind of trash that had no nutrients but was nevertheless delicious in its absurdity. A version of *Dungeons & Dragons* based on the *Diablo* videogames? That sounds utterly awful: Sign me up!

Wonder-struck, I slowly started adding to my collection, focusing on the prettiest and most perplexing baubles produced by Chaosium and TSR. I was steered by a mix of availability and cheapness—I would never have paid cover price for that *D&D* version of *Diablo*, let alone more, but in an auction lot of random RPG books for fifty bucks, it became a hidden gem. From there, I started replacing books I had previously lost or sold. The profound regret I had for selling my *Middle-earth Role Playing* to Noble Knight Games, coupled by a keen desire to replace them led me to discover the *Shadow World* campaign setting from the same publisher (and in a happy case of irony, Noble Knight now sponsors my podcast). Similarly, replacing lost *Star Wars RPG* sourcebooks eventually led me to West End Games' *Ghostbusters* RPG. There's always one more curiosity to find: A toy, a craft set, a *Sears Wish Book* from 1984.

Box sets hold a particular allure. The use of boxes for RPGs is utilitarian, a way to sell a number of items that are useful separately (such as a player-facing travel guide and a GM-facing booklet filled with a region's secrets) as a single unit, but I've also found them to carry a whiff of mystery, thanks to the likes of Pandora, Lemarchand, and all of the countless treasure chests that wait to be opened in games both analog and digital.

I was also driven by a hunger for new art—I love fantasy art, particularly of the '70s and '80s, and unearthing illustrations I have never previously seen amounts to a kind of aesthetic addiction—but learning the various systems and how they worked and developed became an equal compulsion. A friend of a friend liquidated their collection, and I wound up with hundreds of *Dragon* magazines for fifty bucks. There's a rush of brain chemistry in making a deal that good; mixed with nostalgia, it makes for a potent brew. But it wasn't *just* nostalgia. I felt like an explorer. I was making *discoveries*.

Eventually, I had a significant amount of material and a general willingness to talk at length about what made it so cool, whether it was the art, or some neat scrap of lore, or a clever bit of mechanics. It made sense to put all of that somewhere, so I started the @VintageRPG account on Instagram on April 24, 2017, with a post on *Monster Manual II.* In the beginning, there was no overarching plan, no real criteria, just commentary on interesting RPG products accompanied by cover art and some interior illustrations, one a day, Monday through Friday.

The Instagram posts *did* feel like notes for a bigger sort of project, a book perhaps, but I wasn't seriously considering doing anything about it; it was just a feeling. I had enough books and box sets to post consistently for about two-and-a-half years, three-and-a-half if I included all of the *Dragon* magazines, which seemed like a dubious proposition—surely it would all fizzle out long before then.

It didn't. The project struck a chord with folks. As of this writing, I have over 2,000 posts, accounting for about half-a-million words (this book, by comparison, is about 180,000 words). They've been read by more than 42,000 followers on Instagram and nearly another ten thousand between the associated Tumbler and Twitter accounts, not to mention the listeners of the Vintage RPG Podcast, which I co-host with my friend and game designer, John McGuire. A sort of audio version of the Instagram account, each episode features a discussion centering on a specific RPG or RPG-related product and its place in the larger mesh of history and pop culture. We've also interviewed creators in the industry. The opportunity to chat with longtime creative heroes, like illustrator Tony DiTerlizzi, as well as up-and-coming designers, like Banana Chan, has been both a career highlight and a

valuable resource for continuing my RPG education. We started the podcast in 2018, and by the end of 2022, we'll have released over 200 episodes to a weekly audience of about 3,500 souls.

I now post on my Instagram every day and am working on getting through all of those *Dragon* magazines in chronological order so I can start posting issues of *The Space Gamer, Different Worlds,* and all of the other magazines I've accumulated as my collection continues to expand. After five years, I somehow still have about three years of material to share.

The Instagram allowed me, for the first time, to interact with RPG enthusiasts who I did not play or socialize with. This was, I think, a pretty massive shift in perspective, and it introduced paths of inquiry that would have taken ages for me to find in my flailing, solitary manner. RPGs were always something I played with friends, the product of personal camaraderie. With the Instagram account, though, I suddenly had a view to a larger world I always suspected must exist, and a way to talk to all sorts of folks, both players and designers, about all of the different ways people approach play, the histories of games I never heard of, and the often-surprising ways they fit into the larger tapestry of our culture. There are currents of game design evolution, resonances, and coincidences. RPGs are made through play, by players, for players. The connections and interchanges are simultaneously obvious and obscure, because you can dig in anywhere and find a thread that will lead you *everywhere*. The fact that my venture happened almost concurrently with the explosion of the modern zine scene and all of the experimentation that goes with it seems portentous. RPGs were suddenly in a new golden age that was exciting and productive on a scale that had not been seen for decades, if ever!

When I started the Instagram, I posted what I was interested in at the moment. While that impulsiveness is still the guiding principle of the Instagram feed, it naturally grew into something more cohesive; my impulses were subconsciously leading me down long ruminating paths to conclusions.

Before, I said that the Instagram account felt like notes for a book I had no intention of writing. Well, I changed my mind.

A book is not an Instagram feed, and no matter how much I felt I'd already written the framework for a book in social media posts, an actual book needs criteria and structure if anyone is ever going to get anything out of reading it.

So, what is *Monsters, Aliens, and Holes in the Ground*? The subtitle says it is a guide to roleplaying games. I've arrived at that word after careful consideration. Reflexively, I tend to refer to the book as a history or an encyclopedia, but those are specific sorts of books, with specific requirements that I am uninterested in adhering to.

While there are very many facts in this book and though academics may be interested in it, the book is not only or primarily *for* academics. Rather, think of it as a guided tour across items from my personal collection, which provides a window into a wide, vibrant, yet often overlooked world of tabletop gaming that exists in the shadow of *Dungeons & Dragons*, and connects, in surprising ways, to other facets of popular culture. From old hands who've been playing *Tunnels & Trolls* since it first hit shelves, to first timers who just picked up their 5E *Player's Handbook*, and even to folks who've been curious about RPGs but have never played: There is something new to find in these pages.

The prime source for this book is my personal collection. It consists of over 2,300 conventional RPG publications—box sets, rule books, adventure modules,

and sourcebooks—ranging from the very beginning in 1974 right up to the present day. My collection includes about half of TSR's entire *Dungeons & Dragons* output and just about the entirety of Chaosium's RPG material. In addition to that, as of this writing, I have 465 zines, 686 magazines, 202 board games, 232 gamebooks, 100 RPG-related toys, 218 miscellaneous associated items (like the official *Dungeons & Dragons* yellow vinyl wallet and the introduction letter for Mayfair's *City State of the Invincible Overlord* box set improbably signed by Gary Gygax), and a supporting library of art books and genre fiction that numbers about a thousand volumes. I am constantly adding more, to the sorrow of my shelves.

For this book, I selected games and other products that seemed somehow important to a greater narrative about RPGs. Often, that importance is historical, as is the case with games that embody the hobby's many firsts. There are several games contained here, though, that have little to no impact on the development of the larger hobby, but rather illustrate some common absurdity, a flight of fancy, or a dead end. Innovation isn't always the thing.

Materiality acts as a natural limiter while also giving readers the opportunity to see these products as objects of use. In the photographs, I emphasized their wear, the tears, the warping, and the rubbed edges to show that these books and boxes, particularly the older ones, are not traditional collectibles, but rather tools that bear the marks of their use. There is a beauty in that. When I see my grandfather's hammer, its handle smooth and polished from use, I wonder about all the things he built with it. There is something similar in the dog-eared pages of RPG books—what kinds of adventures did they inspire?

Keeping to products I own also injects a personal element to the book. My conclusions are based on patterns I have discerned through years of reading, researching, and playing the books I discuss. In some ways, this book is a continuation of work I've done as a cultural critic and journalist since 2007. In 2010, I founded the website Unwinnable as a dedicated venue for that criticism, and it has since grown into a monthly publication. One of its philosophical cornerstones is the ferreting out of meaningful connections between games and other facets of popular culture. That's very much a driving force of this book, as well; tabletop RPGs—both as products and in play—draw from and mirror pop culture at large.

As much as there are criteria for inclusion, there are also three potential reasons a given RPG is not included in the book. First, it's entirely possible I've never heard of it! Second, and somewhat related, there are the games I simply don't own. My collection of over 2,300 items is a small fraction of the entire RPG corpus. Back in 1991, *Heroic Worlds* indexed over 250 discrete game systems, but in three ensuing decades of vibrant do-it-yourself scenes and inexpensive printing options, that number has easily exploded into the thousands. I would very much have liked to discuss Meguey Baker's *A Thousand and One Nights*, Julia Bond Ellingboe's *Steal Away Jordan*, or any number of important foreign language RPGs, among them *Mutant*, *Das Schwarze Auge*, *Drakar och Demoner*, and the French version of Chaosium's *Hawkmoon*. In all of those cases and more, I have not been able to lay my hands on copies. Third, there are the books that I am not including for specific reasons—for instance, *Empire of the Petal Thone* (1975).

The game does not appear in this book beyond this mention because, in 2022, the Tékumel Foundation confirmed that creator M. A. R. Barker, using a pseudonym, wrote the novel, *Serpent's Walk*, a sympathetic portrayal of a violent neo-Nazi coup in the near future of the United States.

The book was published in 1991 by the same press that put out the Nazi-themed *The Turner Diaries*. Further, Barker served for many years on the Editorial Advisory Committee of the racist *Journal of Historical Review*, a publication dedicated primarily to denying the Holocaust.

I'm not interested in having the work of a neo-Nazi propagandist on my shelves, and I am certainly not going to give space to one in my book. The same is true for the other creators in the RPG industry who hold a variety of repulsive views—racism, homophobia, transphobia, misogyny, and so on. Knowing what I know about certain creators, if I wouldn't be comfortable having them at my game table, or their products on my shelves, they, too, are absent from the pages of this book. They won't be missed.

That said, I believe it's possible and necessary to untangle some creations from their creators, especially when viewing games or the subject matter on which they draw as historical texts or products of their times. Many pulp and genre conventions are rooted in unsavory beliefs, or were created by those who espoused them, yet they can remain compelling sources of entertainment and inspiration, so long as their problems are acknowledged and confronted. *Call of Cthulhu* is an example of this sort of precarious origin. The RPG comes directly out of the fiction of H. P. Lovecraft, who, for much of his life, held a number of poisonous views. He didn't create the roleplaying game, though, nor does he embody the entirety of cosmic horror as a genre. In fact, many of the designers who worked on the game over the course of its forty years of existence have demonstrated that the motifs of cosmic horror can actively interrogate queer and anti-racist subject matter, *without* absolving Lovecraft of his odious beliefs.

Unlike most other media, players of tabletop RPGs have unprecedented control over the way a game plays out. With rules that are guidelines at best, and a culture that has encouraged tinkering with them since day one, the one truism about RPGs is that there is no single correct way to play them. The same is true of the stories we tell with these games. Find what's cool and interesting and fun, pitch the rest.

While I've made purposeful omissions, a totally comprehensive book of this sort is likely an impossibility. The fact that RPGs are so inextricably tied to these personal experiences of play would likely make a full catalog *feel* incomplete, no matter how many pages or volumes such a venture ran. The adventures that RPGs offer are larger than life; no survey of products could ever hope to capture that immensity of imagination.

Dungeons & Dragons is the first roleplaying game. It's also indisputably the biggest and the most popular—the best known. But it isn't the *only* RPG. Yet, for so many people, *Dungeons & Dragons* is exclusively synonymous with the idea of roleplaying, the same way that Kleenex means "facial tissue" in the common parlance. This is as much the case in 2022, with the game at the current peak of its popularity, as it was in the late '70s and early '80s, when it was the notorious subject of a moral panic. With RPGs though, the gateway, *D&D*, is also often the lone destination.

Rather than reminiscing about familiar experiences, I wrote this book so readers could discover whole new worlds. There are thousands of games out there, differently approachable, catering to all kinds of play, to eclectic interests, to diverse viewpoints. If every reader finds just one game here that they never previously heard of, and considers tracking it down to read or play, I will consider my job more than well done.

Stu Horvath
From somewhere in the
swamps of New Jersey
August 1, 2022

THE 1970S

In which RPGs are born from the embers of war games.
Identity struggles ensue, as game designers stake out the new frontier.
Players confront funhouses, starships, and chaotic caves armed with dice,
random tables, and innovative mechanics.

DUNGEONS & DRAGONS ORIGINAL COLLECTOR'S EDITION, BOX SET, TSR, 1977
GARY GYGAX AND DAVE ARNESON, COVER BY DAVID C. SUTHERLAND III

Dungeons & Dragons (1974)

An interesting fact about tabletop roleplaying games: we can pinpoint the exact moment of their genesis.

In 1968, David Wesely created the *Strategos N* rules and, in 1969, used those rules for a Napoleonic wargame later called *Braunstein*, after the fictional town on which it centered. Unlike other wargames where players controlled a unit of troops or a whole army, in *Braunstein*, each player took the role of an individual in the town.

In 1971, Gary Gygax and Jeff Perren wrote *Chainmail*, a medieval miniatures wargame that included supplemental rules for units inspired by sword and sorcery literature, primarily Robert E. Howard's Conan stories and J. R. R. Tolkien's *Lord of the Rings*. Dave Arneson, who played in some of Wesley's games, brought it all together, using modified *Chainmail* rules to create *Braunstein*-like roleplaying experiences in his homebrew fantasy world of Blackmoor.

After playing a session of Blackmoor together, Gygax and Arneson partnered up to write a game based on these new rules. In 1974, they published the original *Dungeons & Dragons (D&D)* box set, and roleplaying games officially began their public and commercial existence.

The ideas that coalesced into roleplaying games did not appear out of nowhere, however. Storytelling, make-believe, and the dramatic arts are ancient human pursuits. In more recent years, historical reenactments, mock trials, and the live action "creative history" of the Society for Creative Anachronism all play with the idea of acting out collaborative stories in different ways. Tabletop wargaming, which dates back to the late 1700s, sought to simulate the reality of battle by using intricate rules and attributes, with the rolling of dice used to inject the fickleness of luck into the proceedings. All of these things contributed to the creation of tabletop RPGs, but all of these precursors to tabletop RPGs are clearly *not* tabletop

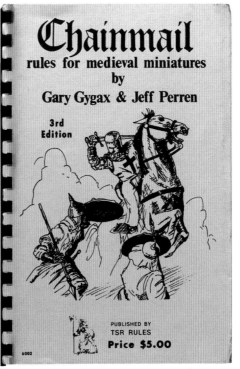

CHAINMAIL, THIRD EDITION, TSR, 1975
GARY GYGAX AND JEFF PERREN, COVER BY DON LOWRY (LIFTED FROM JACK COGGINS)

RPGs, which explicitly combine the act of collaborative storytelling with a framework of rules and an element of chance. When *D&D* first appeared in 1974, there was nothing else like it. It was *new*.

The original run of *Dungeons & Dragons* box sets was hand-assembled and packaged in a box with a faux-wood grain, which sported a crude illustration of a warrior on horseback traced off of a panel from Marvel Comic's *Strange Tales* #167 (in fact, a good number of Greg Bell's illustrations were clearly traced and modified from the art in superhero comic books). Inside were three digest-sized booklets that sketched out the basic framework, not just of *Dungeons & Dragons*, but tabletop RPGs, in general.

Though the definition will change radically over the decades, at the start, an RPG is a system of rules, born out of the Midwestern tabletop wargaming scene, that are used to facilitate a form of

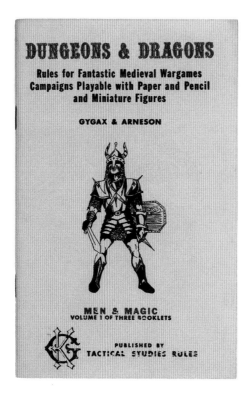

collaborative storytelling for small groups of people. Usually one person, the game master (GM), runs the game, acting as both narrator and adjudicator. The rest of the players take on the roles of individual characters within the story, who are defined by a set of attributes, skills, and abilities. Conflict—that is, anything in which the outcome is uncertain, like trying to connect a sword with the head of a dragon—is resolved by rolling dice, whose results are cross-referenced with the relevant attributes of all parties (and perhaps a chart or two) to determine a result: Failure or success. As in life, roleplaying games can't be won. Rather, the rules exist to ground the story with a certain amount of consistency—think of them as the equivalent of the suspension of disbelief in other storytelling mediums—and that story can go on as long as people care to continue telling it.

Despite a number of printings and cover changes (the biggest occurred in late '75, when the wood grain was phased out in favor of the more widespread white box), in terms of contents there are only two distinct editions of the original *Dungeons & Dragons (OD&D):* Those that were printed from 1974 through 1976 and those printed from 1977 on. The latter version has a malformed starburst on the cover that exclaims, "Original Collector's Edition," in order to differentiate it from the newly released *Dungeons & Dragons Basic Set* by J. Eric Holmes. The 1977 edition also excised terms under copyright by the Tolkien estate. Hobbits became halflings; ents became treants. Nazgul and balrogs were removed entirely, though a pastiche of the latter turned up in the *Eldritch Wizardry* (1976) supplement as the Type VI demon known as the balor. In all other respects, the two editions are identical.

There is much that is rudimentary in *OD&D.* The rules are split across three digest-sized booklets: *Men & Magic, Monsters & Treasure,* and *The Underworld & Wilderness Adventures* (which form the basic template for the trinity of *Player's Handbook, Monster Manual,* and *Dungeon Master's Guide* that *D&D* follows to this day). They're good examples of amateur press publications of the time—well bound, firm covers, clear printing, good paper stock—but a modern reader might flip through and call them quaint or crude. The type is set on a manual typewriter. The illustrations are on the level of idle doodles.

The game system is rough but recognizable as *Dungeons & Dragons,* as it is understood today. There were but three classes for humans—Magic-User, Cleric, and Fighting Man—and three additional races that double as classes—Elves, Dwarves, and Halflings. Each class and race-as-class has abilities that make it unique. Characters are defined by a set of attributes—Strength, Dexterity, Constitution, Intelligence, Wisdom, and Charisma. Experience is conveyed through points gained through actions, with set numbers of points unlocking new levels of personal power. There are magic items and spells and monsters, many of which subvert or break the basic rules. The magic system is often called Vancian, mirroring the way wizards in Jack Vance's Dying Earth stories memorized their spells daily, only to lose them upon their casting. Characters and monsters also have an alignment in the cosmic struggle between the forces of Law, Chaos, and Neutrality, a theme directly adapted from the fiction of Poul Anderson and Michael Moorcock.

Unlike modern versions of the game, however, there is no attempt to make using the books easy for new players, or even explain how they are meant to play. The books seem to be organized to make it difficult to find whatever rule a player is hoping to reference. At first glance, there seems to be no core system for combat—in fact, the game assumes players will use Gygax and Perren's *Chainmail* rules for that. An alternate combat system using a matrix that pits the attacker's level against the defender's armor is included as an afterthought, which eventually develops into *D&D*'s standard combat system. These are not the hallmarks of an approachable game.

The opaqueness of the rules, coupled with the form's newness, made *Dungeons & Dragons* difficult to explain to outsiders who lacked prior experience with wargames. Even the people playing the game were often baffled by it—the desire to "fix" *D&D* is one of the main reasons a larger RPG hobby developed in the first place.

Rules were tinkered with for homebrew games, introducing weather patterns, alternate combat systems, fumbles (which range from the hilarious to the horrifically deadly), critical hits, and more. Enthusiasts crowded at photocopiers to publish their own adventure modules and rules expansions, driven by

their personal passions—a personal favorite, *Authentic Thaumaturgy,* was by a practicing occultist who aimed to rework RPG magic systems so that they were more "realistic."

Lee Gold founded the amateur press association *Alarums and Excursions,* a popular venue for this sort of homebrew experimentation, in 1975, in part, to develop a spellcasting system for *D&D* that used a flexible pool of magic points rather than forcing a Magic-User to memorize their spells each morning. Imitators applied the approach *D&D* took with fantasy to other pulp genres, allowing players to take their stories to the stars, haunted houses, superhero hideouts, high school, and beyond. Designers explored different ways to build rules systems, creating entirely different play experiences that appealed to folks outside of the groups that initially flocked to *D&D*. Conventions sprang up; ideas cross-pollinated. *Dungeons & Dragons* opened the floodgates, but the hundreds of freshly minted fans that poured through redefined what roleplaying games could be by playing the

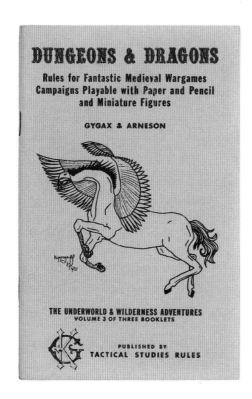

game of *making* games. That player-driven evolution continues to this day.

When speaking with RPG designers for this book, I always asked if they think roleplaying games were inevitable, or if *Dungeons & Dragons* was a unique catalyst. After all, most of the pieces of the puzzle—acting, storytelling, games of chance—were ancient, but no one had arranged them into the proper configuration prior to *Dungeons & Dragons*. Ken St. Andre, the creator of *Tunnels & Trolls,* lays all the credit at the feet of *D&D*'s co-creator Dave Arneson, saying that his work was "a kind of a spark in the undergrowth that turned into a wildfire sweeping across the countryside. Roleplaying was an idea just waiting for its moment to happen, but someone had to do it first. Once the basic idea got into the world it quickly mutated into the vast proliferation of [games] that exist today."

Jennell Jaquays, who penned the classic adventures *Dark Tower* and *Caverns of Thracia,* is less certain.

Typically, with "inevitable things," there are often simultaneous inventions going on. It becomes a matter of who publishes or popularizes things first as to who gains fame or notoriety as the inventor. Would a Ken St. Andre have created *Tunnels & Trolls* without *Dungeons & Dragons* paving the way? Probably not. But would someone in the orbit of Greg Stafford and Chaosium [...] have eventually created a fantasy RPG? I think that's entirely possible. It was a child waiting for the right parents to come along and give birth to it.

James Wallis, creator of *The Extraordinary Adventures of Baron Munchausen,* thinks that is almost certainly the case.

It's clear that there was a lot happening in the 1960s and 1970s. Influences and design traditions from all over the world were coming together and cross-pollinating, the foundations of what would become Eurogames were being laid and wargames were emerging from their military background into recreational forms. So not only were the threads that made *D&D* ready to be woven together, but in a spectacularly mixed metaphor, there was fertile ground ready for it. There was an audience of people who were ready to take on the challenge of a game like that, culturally as well as stylistically, whereas perhaps ten years earlier, before the influence of 3M games and Avalon Hill, and before *Lord of the Rings* had spawned the modern fantasy genre, it would never have found a player base. The time was ripe for it, all the influences were in place.

For Wallis, the remarkable legacy of *D&D* isn't that it created a new, possibly inevitable form of game, but rather that Gygax and Arneson got so much of the framework of the game right from the very start.

Classes and levels, hit points, the way steady power-increases keep people wanting to play, even the genuinely brilliant idea of setting the game in dungeons, because dungeons constrain the players' vocabulary of possible actions and make the [GM's] job easier while they're getting to grips with how the game works and how to run it. That for me is the brilliance of *D&D* and its designers: not that it happened when it did, but that they nailed the formula at the first try.

In successfully capturing that formula, *D&D* became more than just a game. Its essential qualities are the bedrock for an expansive hobby industry that continues to evolve and inspire gameplay and design nearly fifty years later.

Tunnels & Trolls (1975)

When *Dungeons & Dragons* hit the scene, it was like a starter gun going off at the beginning of a race. Even if they didn't realize it, many people were waiting for a game like this, and upon seeing one, they immediately started to tinker, not just with how it was played, but also with how to make other games like it. Many of these folks wanted to play, but *differently*. So, they fiddled with the template *D&D* provided until they found something that suited them. When it comes down to it, anyone who has ever run an RPG is a kind of game designer.

In the '70s, everyone involved in the play and creation of roleplaying games was a hobbyist, even Gygax and Arneson. In fact, that line between hobbyists and professionals in RPGs has long been blurry, with fresh ideas surfacing as often in DIY zines as they do in expensive hard covers (today, some of those hardcovers are published by independent creators or small creative co-ops).

Players pushed the concept of roleplaying games in all sorts of directions, but the first out of the gate was Ken St. Andre, a public librarian from Phoenix, Arizona. In 1975, a friend brought a copy of *Dungeons & Dragons* to a gaming session, but no one could make heads or tails of it. St. Andre decided that the game, though often exciting, was confusing (which, fair), too expensive (what on earth is a 20-sided die?), and too weird (why are "Wisdom" and "Intelligence" different attributes?). To remedy this confusion, he set about making his own game, one that was straightforward, inexpensive, and didn't require anything more than a pencil, some paper, and some 6-sided dice pilfered from whatever board games were around. It took him three days. The result was eventually named *Tunnels & Trolls (T&T)*, but true to the inescapable influence of *D&D*, and despite it having an entirely different feel, St. Andre's group initially called it "Dungeons *and* Dragons" anyway.

Tunnels & Trolls features lightweight rules designed to make the transition from reading to playing as quick as possible. Most of the mechanics involve rolling the dice, adding bonuses from the relevant attributes, and comparing the result, with the higher total determining the winner. This is in clear contrast to the approach of *D&D* and its direct derivatives, which require lots of rules and charts and sometimes a tape measure to account for every conceivable situation. This complexity is in service to the creaky concept of verisimilitude inherited from the wargaming table. A player can pick up *T&T* and have a firm grip on how to play in less than an hour and will be approaching mastery after one session of play.

In *Tunnels & Trolls*, what happens next is far more important than *how* it happens. The cover art by Liz Danforth for the fifth edition conveys the importance of action. There, a monster emerges from the darkness only to be attacked by a group of adventurers in a variety of ways, making for an action scene so dense it is hard to predict what might happen next.

TUNNELS & TROLLS, BOX SET, FIFTH EDITION, FLYING BUFFALO INC., 1979
KEN ST. ANDRE, COVER BY LIZ DANFORTH

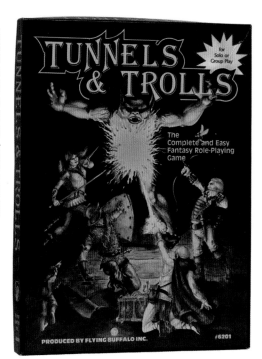

This tension between the relative complexity and simplicity of rules is one of the key philosophical flash points in RPGs. Proponents of complexity, in the service of a kind of mathematical and often illusory realism, have had an edge in the space since the very beginning. Because *D&D* is the first, and its derivative games are the most emulated, players, at large, often equate an encyclopedic, lawyerly knowledge of how those systems and their myriad of loopholes and ambiguities work with mastery. Early critical response to *Tunnels & Trolls* in the hobby magazines like *White Dwarf* and *Ares* illustrates this perceived default, with most characterizing it as too simple, a beginner's game that players would eventually tire of, graduating to systems like *Dungeons & Dragons*.

This critical dismissal overlooks the fact that while play involving complex systems can be deeply satisfying for certain players, others see complex systems as being the biggest barrier, not just to having a good time, but to playing at all. By embracing simplicity, *Tunnels & Trolls* is the first major divergence in RPG design, one that would eventually turn

into a sturdy branch of the RPG family tree, full of stripped down, minimalist fruit. *Tunnels & Trolls* has remained popular and in-print since 1975, despite some critics believing it would be trampled by a succession of ever-more complex RPGs.

This minimalist, action-oriented approach makes sense considering St. Andre had little experience with wargames; he came to RPGs through his love of sword and sorcery fiction. His game design experience before *D&D* centered on creating variations of the board game *Diplomacy*. "*D&D* came directly from miniatures wargaming," says St. Andre, "*T&T* came from literature and comics and fantasy movies." The difference is palpable in the rules, their lightness, and their turn towards action. St. Andre also recognized that after wrestling with complex rules, the next big barrier to playing RPGs is just finding a group of people who are willing to get together to play RPGs. *Tunnels & Trolls* solves this problem with solo adventures, to the extent that many folks think of *T&T* primarily as a solo game.

Solo adventures are prose, but instead of reading through them from start to finish, sections are numbered and arranged randomly. When a moment of decision arrives, the reader chooses between the options presented and proceeds to the corresponding entry to find out the results. This is the same framework as the Choose Your Own Adventure (CYOA) series for young readers (which debuted in 1976). The primary difference is that *T&T* solo adventures also use the RPG's mechanics to resolve certain situations, most often combat. So, where a reader only gets a bad ending in a CYOA book because of a bad decision, a protagonist can die in a *T&T* solo because of a bad roll of the dice.

T&T solos also allow the player's custom character to participate in different adventures, gaining experience and treasure, then bringing them along into new scenarios (or even group play). This approach forms the foundation of the adventure gamebook subgenre of interactive fiction, inspiring series, like *Fighting Fantasy*, *Lone Wolf*, *GrailQuest*, and *Fabled Lands*. In recent years, interest in solitaire RPGs has grown and developed into varied new forms. At a glance, *Tunnels & Trolls* and *Thousand Year Old Vampire* (2019) have very little in common, but deep down, there is an unbroken line of descent.

Looking back, St. Andre admits he had little notion of what might come out of the publication of *Tunnels & Trolls*. He created the game for himself to play and printed it because friends wanted copies, but, "By the end of the year," he says, "I began to have feelings that this roleplaying stuff would turn into my life's work." He never quit his day job at the public library, though.

Bunnies & Burrows (1976)

Yes, this is an RPG about rabbits. One of the many things I love about RPGs is how downright odd they can be without seeming like they're trying too hard. *Bunnies & Burrows (B&B)* is inspired by *Watership Down*, the 1972 novel by Richard Adams—beside the intelligent rabbits, *B&B* also mirrors the cover design of the original UK printing of the novel. These days, *Watership Down* is perhaps best remembered as the animated film (1978) that scarred a generation of kids who didn't expect such horror among fuzzy bunnies in a cartoon (I kid, slightly: Both the book and film are acknowledged, if traumatizing, classics). Back in the '70s, though, the novel was a bit of a sensation, so the idea of it inspiring an RPG isn't entirely off-kilter, especially when compared to some of the licensed games that would appear in the '80s. Given the wargaming sensibilities and many flavors of sword and sorcery aesthetics that dominated the hobby at the time, though, *Bunnies & Burrows* still

BUNNIES & BURROWS, SECOND EDITION, FANTASY GAMES UNLIMITED, 1982
3. DENNIS SUSTARE AND SCOTT ROBINSON, COVER BY JEFF DEE

has an air of the improbable about it.

Players take the roles of intelligent, semi-anthropomorphic rabbits. Bunnies are not powerful critters, by any measure, so the game is largely about avoiding danger. Dr. B. Dennis Sustare (who, along with his co-designer, Scott Robinson, were zoology graduate students at the University of Wisconsin-Madison) believed that RPGs could be about so much more than endless battle, so *B&B* works to shift the emphasis away from combat—*D&D's* specialty—toward puzzle solving and roleplaying. This shift is further facilitated by the setting. It's easier to understand a world of rabbits and dogs and humans and cars rather than one of monsters and magic, because we live in one. That intrinsic familiarity gives players more options at the table, even if, as a rabbit, most of them are some variation of "Run!" "If people were to roleplay rabbits, they had better emphasize speed, concealment, cleverness and trickery over brute force and blind courage," says Sustare. "To roleplay a rabbit, you had better think like a rabbit, in a world of a thousand enemies."

Owing to its early release relative to the

THE WARREN, BULLY PULPIT GAMES, 2015
MARSHALL MILLER

original *Dungeons & Dragons*, *B&B* is credited with a number of design innovations in service of its narrative ambitions. It's the first game to allow for animal characters. It has the first (admittedly rudimentary) martial arts system, which is used to simulate the desperate animal scrabble for survival—messy, tangled, flailing—and is perhaps one of the first times mechanics in an RPG work to mirror the emotional content of the fiction, as well as the physical.

As combat is not the end goal of play, it becomes necessary to provide players something to do that doesn't involve hitting things, which leads to the skill system. *Bunnies & Burrows* has eight attributes (as opposed to *D&D's* six), each with an associated class—Runners depend on Speed, Fighters on Strength, and so on. "And to have something parallel to the magic of fantasy roleplay," says Sustare, "we created a system of herbalism, thinking this might be a reasonable pursuit of intelligent rabbits with their fine noses." The skills are likewise associated with attributes (Dodge with Speed; Jump with Strength, and so on), each with their own rules to use. This is still a way off from what is now considered a skill system, but it's a start.

The creators of *Bunnies & Burrows* try hard to do something different from *Dungeons & Dragons*, but wargaming is still very much in the game's DNA. Despite that basic foundation, *B&B* is the second attempt, after *Tunnels & Trolls,* to move RPGs in a direction that doesn't center on tactical combat power fantasies. There isn't a straight evolutionary line from *B&B* to the narrative-focused storytelling games, like *Dogs in the Vineyard* (2004), that start popping up 25 years later, but *B&B* is the first game to push beyond the fantasy battle boundaries established by *D&D*. This step helps the hobby arrive at the sorts of indie games that focus on collaborative storytelling and lightweight, intuitive rules.

The world was, mostly, not ready. *Bunnies & Burrows,* while well-received, attracted only a modest number of players. Part of the reason was a lack of support from the publisher, Fantasy Games Unlimited (FGU). Mostly, though, *Bunnies & Burrows* came out at a moment in time when everyone was overwhelmingly excited about hitting things with swords, and it didn't have enough swords, or, any swords: "When *Bunnies & Burrows* was released, it seemed as though every genre of RPG was being published," says Sustare. "It was as though a zillion niches were created all at once. Most, however, stuck with the traditional fantasy settings of D&D and others, perhaps because of the allure of the *Lord of the Rings*, and the fine marketing efforts of TSR."

Bunnies & Burrows stuck around, though. "*B&B* never had a huge following," says Sustare. "Over the years, the reaction of D&D players, upon encountering B&B for the first time, was often surprise, wondering why anyone would want to play a rabbit. But if they would try a session, a few of them would come to love it."

The groups of players who cottoned to

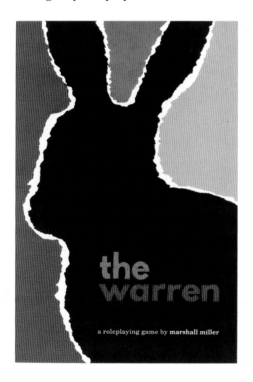

it in the early days grew over time, owing to the game's popularity at conventions. The game found new life in 1992 with an edition of the rules modified for *GURPS* (1986); Frog God Games produced a stand-alone modern edition to warm reception in 2019. Perhaps most interesting, though, is a spiritual successor to *Bunnies & Burrows.* The narrative-focused Powered by the Apocalypse (see page 310) game, *The Warren,* by Marshall Miller, came out in 2015 and helped to expand our modern definition of what constitutes a roleplaying game, just like *B&B* did back in 1976.

Palace of the Vampire Queen (1976)

Some RPG publishers made strange miscalculations about what players were willing to spend money on. The publisher Fantasy Games Unlimited believed for a while that RPGs should be "complete," with everything in one box or book and no supplemental products. That meant that nearly all of FGU's early games, including *Bunnies & Burrows*, were single publications, and, with the exception of *B&B*, most of them have faded into obscurity. FGU's *Chivalry & Sorcery* (1977), on the other hand, *did* have a series of sourcebooks, and because of that, a larger market share and legacy—a new edition came out in 2020.

FGU's allergy has a surprising bedfellow in TSR, the makers of *Dungeons & Dragons.* Though Dave Arneson's *Blackmoor* (1975) contains "The Temple of the Frog," the first RPG adventure ever published, the overriding belief at TSR in the early days was that players wanted to buy *games*, not adventures and campaign worlds.

In retrospect, this is a baffling position, but it also explains a lot of small mysteries in early TSR products, like why there is so little detail on the worlds of Greyhawk and Blackmoor in the books that bear their names—instead, they are almost entirely rules expansions. Or why

PALACE OF THE VAMPIRE QUEEN, FIFTH EDITION. WEE WARRIORS, 1977. FROM THE COLLECTION OF TONY LEGATO. PHOTO BY D. J. ORR. PETER AND JUDY KERESTAN, COVER BY MORNO (BRADLEY W. SCHENCK)

the first stand-alone adventure module, *Palace of the Vampire Queen*, was published by Wee Warriors and sold out of the back of the authors' car, as if they were bootleggers.

There is something kind of beautiful about *Palace of the Vampire Queen* being the first standalone adventure module because it feels similar to the sort of material most folks come up with when designing their first adventure—by which I mean it is bad in the specific, wonderful way, while also being amazing: A Platonic ideal of a glorious mess.

In *Palace of the Vampire Queen,* nothing makes sense. The only context is provided in a one-page background that boils down to a couple of key facts, most of which were already established by the title: There is a queen, she is a vampire, she lives in a palace, and she recently kidnapped a dwarven princess. There isn't even a moody description of the palace exterior.

The palace consists of five levels, each accompanied by a game master's map, a blank map for players, and a chart listing the contents and inhabitants of rooms. Everything is static; the occupants of rooms wait for the players to arrive in order to react. Several rooms have detailed descriptions of furniture and other contents, implying that the rooms labeled "Empty" are literally empty. There are a lot of empty rooms, and there is an alarming number of normal cats just wandering around.

The mix of monsters and other opponents is strange. Many of them hang out on the ceiling. Why do the bandits stick around when five of their gang are in the dining room, stone dead and drained of blood? Why do the werewolves look like ghouls and not werewolves? Why does a vampire keep a garden dedicated to garlic? Why do a balrog, a rust monster, a gelatinous cube, three carrion crawlers, four owlbears, and fifteen gnolls hang out here at all?

There is little evidence in *Palace of the Vampire Queen* of narrative or balance or a sensible dungeon ecology. As with many novice dungeon designs, the palace seems to be populated the way it is because it might be neat, or might be fun, or, in the case of the garlic garden, probably useful for the players. In fact, this energy is baked into the very DNA of RPGs—the term "gonzo" is often used to describe this sort of over-the-top, nonsensical action when it pops up in *Dungeon Crawl Classics* (2012) and *Troika!* (2018), as though it is unusual; but *Palace of the Vampire Queen* (not to mention the natural impulses of many novice homebrewers) proves that extremities of strangeness are really a baseline of the hobby.

For all of its tomfoolery, TSR agreed to distribute *Palace of the Vampire Queen* and three other Wee Warriors publications. About a year later, TSR dropped distribution for all third-party products and were printing modules of their own soon after.

City State of the Invincible Overlord (1976)

As with adventure modules, TSR didn't initially publish materials detailing campaign settings. When Bob Bledsaw and Bill Owen, the newly minted founders of Judges Guild (JG), approached TSR about a license to produce supplemental material for *Dungeons & Dragons*, they were nearly laughed out of the room. TSR granted the license and didn't even ask for royalties. Go ahead and lose money was TSR's response, basically.

Bledsaw and Owen used their experience running *D&D* games for friends to launch Judges Guild and create products that made play easier for GMs. Judges Guild first released a map of a city-state from Bledsaw's campaign, a massive thing printed in four 17-inch by 22-inch sections, bearing little in the way of detail— the idea was that GMs could fill in the map with ideas of their own. The pair, at a card table festooned with a banner, debuted the map at GenCon IX (1976), but the maps themselves were stored in Owen's car. Because they weren't vendors, they

CITY STATE OF THE INVINCIBLE OVERLORD, RETAIL VERSION, JUDGES GUILD, 1977
BOB BLEDSAW AND BILL OWEN

had to bring customers out into the parking lot along the Lake Geneva Horticultural Hall to sell copies. That marks two important RPG products from 1976 that were initially sold from the trunk of a car (see page 11).

A funny thing happened: People kept asking questions about the blank space on the map. They didn't want to create their own city; they wanted to explore the one Bledsaw made. To address this, Owen came up with the idea of a subscription service that would describe the city-state bit by bit. The pair started selling subscriptions on the second day of GenCon, and, across three mailings from 1976 to early 1977, they filled players in on the details of the city-state. In late 1977, the subscription packets were collected for retail sale as *City State of the Invincible Overlord (City State)* and went through several permutations during the life of the company.

City State includes a pile of maps for both the GM and the players, of the city, the under-city, a dungeon complex, and a dwarven stronghold to the north. A booklet provides seemingly endless details—taverns, inns, shops, temples, non-player characters (NPCs), rules for taking out

advertisements, the legal system, random encounters, rumors, and more. It is a brutal, crime-ridden place, ruled over by a remote despot. Adventure lurks, literally, around every corner. There is even an implied narrative path right there in the title: "Invincible? We'll show him—Overthrow the Overlord!"

The city is also a ridiculous place. Across the city, factions that should be at each other's throats mingle amicably on the streets (foreshadowing *Planescape*'s Sigil, perhaps). Shops offer bizarre services—one of my favorites, the Fear Shop, will give characters the worst scares of their lives for the right price. Odd notations abound, like the 16-percent chance of being attacked by angry peasants on Scud Street due to an "insulted daughter." It isn't nearly as absurd as *Palace of the Vampire Queen*, but the emphasis of the material is on making the city-state fun and interesting. Plausibility is never a prime consideration, and that's the source of much of the charm (for proof, check out Mayfair Games' more realistic, and consequently, deadly dull version of *City State* from 1987).

What's more, *City State of the Invincible Overlord* has the feel of having been played in. The sole purpose of the Fraternity for Eradication of Armored Riffraff, or FEAR, is to convince Fighters lower than fourth level not to wear plate armor, because it is "unfair," which likely comes directly from Bledsaw's games. Their methods of encouragement include hurled filth, dousing in yellow paint, and the occasional non-lethal thumping with maces.

The intricate presentation of the city is unprecedented for the time. As Judges Guild continued to put out more books, they also continued to expand the world of the city-state. Other designers, like Jennell Jaquays, got in on the action at Judges Guild, while dozens of small presses sprung up across the country to produce their own worlds and adventures. Up to this point, the hobby defined itself as some kind of wargame variant, or "fantasy adventure games," that featured an adversarial relationship between the players and the GM. With the rise of elaborate imaginary worlds, the idea first posited by *Bunnies & Burrows*—that these were *roleplaying* games—began to permanently take hold.

Judges Guild and their play aids, which TSR was certain would lose money, were immediately successful, so much so that TSR stopped laughing and demanded royalties in late 1976.

Metamorphosis Alpha (1976)

Metamorphosis Alpha (*MA*) is often called the first science fiction RPG. It isn't. Despite some confusion over dates, Ken St. Andre's bawdy *Starfaring* claims that prize. The confusion stems from the fact that *Metamorphosis Alpha*'s foreword is dated July, 1976, and that's often misinterpreted by fans and scholars alike as a publication date. While the game was scheduled to come out at that year's Origins convention, it wasn't ready. Several authorities, including Lawrence Schick, author of *Heroic Worlds* (1991), place the release of *MA* after *Starfaring*. Advertisements in gaming magazines support this timeline, with ads for *Starfaring* running in *The Space Gamer* that summer and *Metamorphosis Alpha* ads first appearing in *Dragon Magazine* that winter.

Starfaring didn't make a big splash, so *Metamorphosis Alpha* became regarded as the first science fiction RPG to capture the imaginations of players, though it only did so modestly before fading from view itself, thanks to a lack of support from TSR.

Is it really science fiction, though? Looking at my shelves, it's worth noting that the vast majority of the RPGs that crowd them are dedicated to some flavor of sword and sorcery fantasy. Even a good number that aren't, like the various cyberpunk-infused games of the '90s, still sneak in a dragon or a magic spell or two. This is a bit perplexing, considering the clear dominance of science fiction elsewhere in popular culture—in 1976, the only major fantasy films of recent note were *The Golden Voyage of Sinbad* (1974) and *Monty Python and the Holy Grail* (1975). In '70s RPGs, the opposite was true: Any science that was present (mostly) took the back seat. This is the case with *Metamorphosis Alpha*.

The game is set on a massive generation ship called *Warden*. Generation ships are a hypothetical solution for interstellar travel at sub-light speed: A vast space ark containing a self-sustaining biosphere that would support multiple generations of passengers through the several thousand years needed to reach their destination. The *Axiom* in Pixar's *Wall-E* (2008) is a contemporary example, but the idea was originally put forth by literal rocket scientist Konstantin Tsiolkovsky in 1928. It's about as hard science fiction as it gets. Tsiolkovsky's theory inspired scads of sci-fi novels, including Robert A. Heinlein's *Orphans of the Sky* (1941) and Brian Aldiss's *Non-Stop* (1958), both of which pondered the potential for social breakdown on a generation ship and both of which directly inspired *Metamorphosis Alpha*.

That's about the last of the science in *MA*. Midway through *Warden*'s journey, it passes through a cloud of radiation that leads to catastrophic mutations in the majority of the ship's flora, fauna, and human population. As a result, the environment isn't just hazardous, it's gone wildly out of control. Years later, as the game begins, human society has slipped into a semi-barbaric state; players are given the option of taking the role of pure humans, mutated humans, or mutated animals. An understanding of the technology on the ship, the robots that maintain it (now mostly malfunctioning, thanks to degrading programming), or even the fact that everyone is *on* a ship, has been lost. *Metamorphosis Alpha*, then, is about survival and regaining lost knowledge. This plays out in a way that feels very much

METAMORPHOSIS ALPHA, TSR, 1976
JAMES M. WARD, COVER BY DAVID C. SUTHERLAND III

like fantasy with strange monsters, crude weapons, deadly combat, and technology so sufficiently advanced it seems magical.

In other words, the world of *Warden* feels very *Dungeons & Dragons*. In one way, this feeling is very mechanical, as the game system is clearly derived from *D&D*. But there is more to it than that. James M. Ward's description of *Warden* is arguably a description of a self-contained world of a campaign setting, the outline of a mega-dungeon, or both. The ship, a 50-mile-long by 25-mile-wide egg, contains 17 levels filled with cities, villages, vast factory complexes, thick forests, rolling plains, mountains, and even an ocean. In between those ecosystems, running through the floors and walls, are a warren of ducts, service tunnels, and engine rooms (all of this, the vastness of it, recalls Larry Niven's *Ringworld*, 1970, which would get its own RPG adaptation from Chaosium in 1984). Players are left to explore the ship, hex by hex in the "wilderness" or square by square in the dungeons of the engineering sectors, all for material rewards (these take the place

of the traditional *D&D*-style experience, with new equipment imparting the new abilities, durability, and heartiness).

These sorts of expeditions are the core of the *D&D* experience and that seems so closely tied to fantasy, for me, that even the presence of laser guns and mutants can't dissuade the association. Rick Swan says it straight in *The Complete Guide to Role-Playing Games* (1990), "Essentially, this is *Dungeons & Dragons* in space." His assessment makes sense, since that is exactly how Ward originally pitched it, though, says Ward, "I have always thought of it as a science fiction RPG." Perhaps genre, like beauty, is also in the eye of the beholder.

Despite being ambitious and distinct, *Metamorphosis Alpha* disappeared, perhaps because it was almost immediately overshadowed by an RPG with a more traditional take on science fiction. Outside of a small number of articles expanding on the game in *The Dragon*, TSR's in-house magazine, it never received additional official support, though it did inspire an important *D&D* module, *S3: Expedition to*

DOOM ON THE WARDEN, GOODMAN GAMES, 2020
JAMES M. WARD, COVER BY STEFAN B. POAG

the Barrier Peaks, and it is a clear spiritual predecessor to Ward's *Gamma World* (1978), another mutation-filled RPG.

1994 marked the final time *Metamorphosis Alpha* appeared in a TSR publication, when a version of *Warden* came out as a self-contained supplement for the short-lived generic RPG system, *Amazing Engine.* Since the turn of the millennium, though, the publication of new editions, reprints, and original material has renewed interest in the game. Ward finally, 44 years later, revealed some of *Warden*'s secrets in the first-ever *Metamorphosis Alpha* adventure, *Doom on the Warden*, released by Goodman Games in 2020.

The retro-modern sheen given to the game by Goodman's stable of artists does much to enhance the mystique of *Metamorphosis Alpha* for contemporary audiences—artist Stefan Poag's striking portrait of a long-dead space captain at once expands the mythology of the game while harkening back to a long visual tradition in sci-fi of sticking skeletons in space suits (the Spooky Space Kook from *Scooby-Doo Where Are You!*, 1969, is arguably the most famous example, but skull-headed astronauts are all over the covers of cheap paperbacks and horror comics from the 1940s on).

Traveller (1977)

Like *Dungeons & Dragons*, the original *Traveller* rules came in a small, digest-sized box containing three booklets. That's about where the comparison ends.

Up to this point, all RPGs have one thing in common: In some way, they emulate or derive from the original *Dungeons & Dragons* design. *Bunnies & Burrows* rearranges the rules to portray a different power dynamic; *Boot Hill* introduces guns; *Tunnels & Trolls* works to make the core rules of *D&D* easier to use. For all of their tinkering, though, they remain *D&D*-esque. *Traveller* is the first RPG that feels like a distinct game, free of *D&D*'s direct influence on its design.

Traveller's first booklet establishes character creation as a solo game unto itself, less interested in attributes (though it does establish them) than it is in creating the broad strokes of a fictional history. This grows out of the character activity mechanics established in Game Designers' Workshop's (GDW) earlier Musketeers-themed game, *En Garde!*. The player enlists the character in branches of the Imperium's military, or for terms of service with the merchant fleet. Dice rolls then determine the results of that service by awarding and increasing skills, abilities, ranks, and salary. In rare cases, a character can even die before ever being played in a group game!

The player can repeat the process, with the character reenlisting or changing careers, so long as they want to pay the numerical penalty for aging four years each go around. Once the character musters out to find adventure, the player has a good idea of what the character has been up to and where their personal interests lie. This knowledge changes play in some important ways. The backgrounds convey a sense of the universe before the game even starts—there is an interstellar empire, a robust military, intergalactic trade, and so on—and establishes the character's place within it.

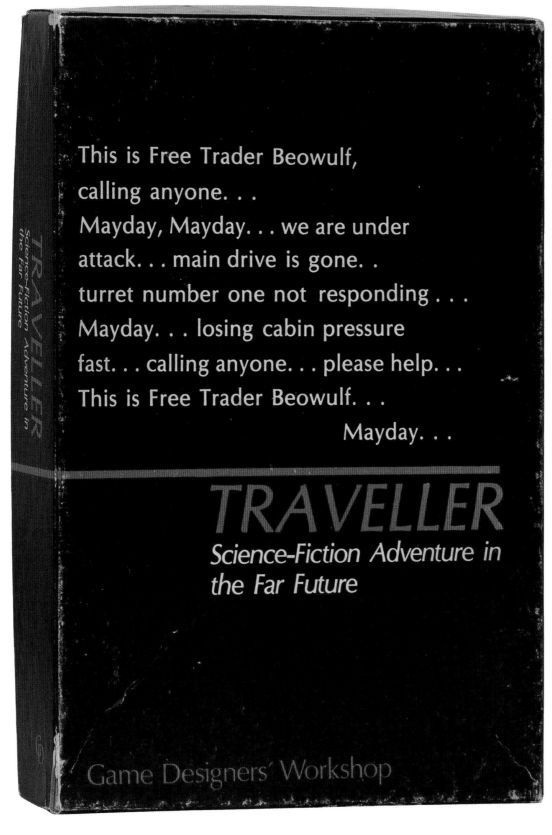

TRAVELLER, Box set, Game Designers' Workshop, 1977
Marc W. Miller

17

Compare this to *D&D*, where a character is defined by predetermined, abstract class characteristics; little, if anything, of the world, or the character's connection to it, is conveyed. *Traveller*'s character creation mechanics represent a significant step in shifting the idea of an RPG character away from a sheet of numbers into something that more resembles a person who might have interests outside of crawling around underground tunnels, killing critters, and stealing treasure.

Traveller's career generator paves the way for approaches to character like *Call of Cthulhu*'s (1981) professions and *Warhammer Fantasy Roleplay*'s careers (1986), or even the optional rules in *Pendragon* (1985) that allow a player to establish the history of their character, their father and their grandfather in order to put down truly deep cultural roots. *Cyberpunk*'s life path system is also direct descendant. All of these examples show how the original iteration of *Traveller* sits at the head of a long line of design developments that emphasize the *role* in roleplaying, pushing the hobby toward storytelling and away from simulation-preoccupied wargaming.

This push continues into the second booklet, *Starships*. The second chapter is called "Starship Economics," and it winds up teaching as much about the universe as it does the rules for space travel. The chapter boils down to the idea that starships of any size are incredibly expensive to build, buy, and operate. That expense centers the *Traveller* experience—a character can't just go off gallivanting; fuel costs money, and so do empty staterooms and cargo holds. Characters have to marry adventure with a little bit of commerce, and that's in the unlikely event that a space bank trusted a player's character enough to extend credit to buy a ship. More likely, a character is part of a larger crew, working for wage or passage and subject to the whims of a captain, or his boss, the actual owner of the ship. All of these layers of fiscal responsibility create narrative friction and sketch in more detail about the universe before players can start plotting their own goals: Who are these other crew members? Is the captain a jerk? What's an interstellar bank like and how serious are they about getting paid on time? Isn't time relative in space?

Again, there is nothing like this in official *D&D* products at this point—no wider world and no pressures of responsibility. Because there is no experience point system or real incentive to fight, *Traveller* opens vistas of potential to *explore*.

Unlike nearly every other RPG ever, *Traveller* imbues its sense of excitement and mystery through text alone. It has almost zero artwork in the core box set or the majority of the subsequent sourcebooks. Instead, the black box cover has words:

This is Free Trader Beowulf, calling anyone...Mayday, Mayday...we are under attack...main drive is gone...turret number one not responding...Mayday ...losing cabin pressure fast...calling any-

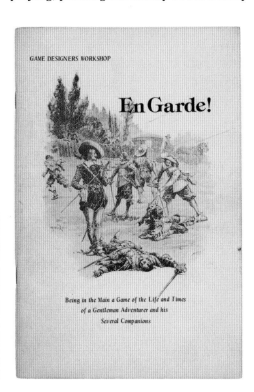

En Garde!, Game Designers' Workshop, 1975
Daryl Hany and Frank Chadwick

one...please help...This is Free Trader Beowulf...Mayday...

Who is attacking the ship? Why? Is there time to save them? The ship's desperate message, printed in stark white letters on a flat black background, does more to excite the imagination than a hundred space battle paintings could.

The mechanics are simple for the time, as well. There is complexity, no doubt—space travel calculations require figuring out square roots and seeing that checkmark symbol in an RPG rulebook evokes the memory of traumatic summer school sessions of algebra class for a certain subset of players (or maybe just me). But the core is an easy roll-to-beat system—roll two 6-sided dice, add or subtract the appropriate modifiers, and hope the result beats an eight. This feels featherlight and straightforward compared to *Dungeons & Dragons*; in fact, it has more in common with modern storytelling RPGs than any of its contemporaries.

Helping all of world building and approachability along is the fact that *Traveller* is the first RPG that lines up with the popular conception of science fiction as laid out in *Foundation, Star Trek, 2001: A Space Odyssey,* and the just-released blockbuster *Star Wars*; there are spaceships to fly, planets to explore, aliens to encounter, and adventures to experience, with plenty of mechanical tools to facilitate their creation. In truth, though, while *Traveller* appealed to fans of space opera, its own inspirations are more firmly rooted in classic 1960s science fiction, like H. Beam Piper's *Space Viking* (1963) and E. C. Tubb's 33-novel Dumarest saga, which began in 1967, among many others. Piper's novel (its importance to the game clearly signaled by the later *New Era* sourcebook, *Star Vikings*, 1994) gives *Traveller* its Sword Worlds, which are named after legendary blades. A number of the game's features spin out of Tubb's novels, but the most notable is the idea of

High, Middle, and Low passage, a key concern for space travel. High Passage is luxurious and reserved for the upper class; Middle Passage is for working crew, and Low Passage is a risky trip asleep in a cryotank, which has a 15 percent chance of resulting in character death!

For the next few years, Game Designers' Workshop released expansions in a series of little black books. Through these and the quarterly *Journal of the Travellers' Aid Society*, GDW gradually filled in the details of their galactic empire. Soon, imperial military personnel were joined by mercenaries, scouts, merchant princes, robots, a variety of aliens, and more, each accompanied by life paths and modular rules expansions. Individually, these expansions allowed players to mix and match options to find a level of complexity that matched their comfort level. In 1983, however, GDW compiled many of those rules into the *Traveller Starter Edition* box set, a decision that proved to be the first step on a road that led GDW to focus on increasingly complex rule systems, starting with the notoriously fine-detailed military RPG, *Twilight: 2000* (1984).

TRAVELLER STARTER EDITION, GAME DESIGNERS' WORKSHOP, 1985 MARC W. MILLER, COVER BY DAVID DEITRICK

1970

1980

1990

2000

2010

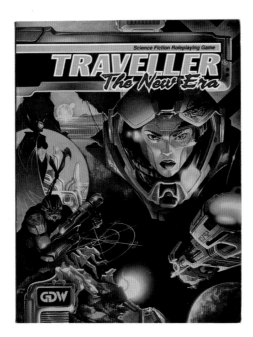

TRAVELLER: THE NEW ERA, GAME DESIGNERS' WORKSHOP, 1993
FRANK CHADWICK AND DAVE NILSEN, COVER BY FRANK ZELEZNIK

the dawn of the hobby, but also to both its scope and the crisp simplicity of its systems. Any game since that involves exploring the stars or interacting with complex technology—*Stars Without Number*, *Coriolis* (2017), *MechWarrior* (1986), *Rifts* (1990), and more—builds on a foundation established by *Traveller*, including contemporary versions of the game, of which there are at least three! Mongoose Publishing (since 2008) and Far Future Enterprises (since 2013) both produce official versions of the game, while Samardan Press released their *Traveller* clone, *Cepheus Engine*, in 2016. *Traveller* even has a ripping heavy metal concept album—The Lord Weird Slough Feg's *Traveller* (2003). How many RPGs can boast that?

Tegel Manor (1977)

Installment L: Tegel Manor was the fourth of Judges Guild's play aid subscription series, following the two mailings that made up the *City State of the Invincible Overlord* and *Installment J: Thunderhold* (which would eventually be folded into *City State* for the retail version). Inside the packet is a 24-page booklet, some mostly-blank player maps, and one of the most labyrinthine dungeon maps ever put into print. A small version of it appears on the cover, but nothing compares to the full-sized, 17- by 22-inches of twisting hallways and secret passages.

The premise is simple. The heir to the manor, Sir Runic the Rump, of the ancient Rump family (this sort of doofy humor is par for the course for Judges Guild), is broke and wants to sell his ancestral home. Unfortunately for him, and the players, it's infested with his undead ancestors—all 100 of them, each possessing a name beginning with the letter 'R'—and he needs help clearing them and the other monsters out. Nowhere in the brief booklet is it explained why no one in the house is named Tegel, nor is it explained

Subsequent editions of *Traveller* were mired in problems. The rules grew dense, and books were riddled with errors, requiring lengthy errata to be playable. Worse, there were narrative missteps. *MegaTraveller* (1987) tried to shake up the setting with the assassination of the emperor and the subsequent splintering of the Imperium into warring factions. *Traveller: The New Era* (1993) pushed the timeline further forward, past the collapse of intergalactic trade and a tentative re-establishment of the Imperium. Both of these advances in the metaplot are interesting, particularly to newcomers, but tended to alienate players who loved the version of the Imperium they were already playing in (witness the success of *GURPS Traveller*, 1998, which consists of more than three dozen books that pretend as if the rebellion never happened). Reactions among remaining *Traveller* players for *The New Era* were particularly mixed, but by then West End Games' *Star Wars: The Roleplaying Game* was the top-selling science fiction RPG. By 1996, financial issues forced GDW to close.

The original *Traveller* still stands as one of the most significant traditional sci-fi RPGs, thanks, in part, to its proximity to how a family of undead rogues produced a paladin, even one so ineffective as Sir Runic. In fact, there are few answers of any kind in the *Tegel Manor* booklet. The room descriptions are terse, usually two sentences at most. That brevity allows the module to get to the table without much preparation while providing enough support for improvisation and enough space for a GM to add their own details, should they desire and so long as they aren't too concerned with the whole romp making sense.

Like *Palace of the Vampire Queen*, *Tegel Manor* is what has come to be known as a funhouse dungeon; that categorization comes with the assumption that making sense is not a primary goal. The very first room in the manor is haunted by the butler, who is the ghost of a balrog named Bertalan. In the stable, a ki-rin (a sort of Asian unicorn) is doing battle with an intellect devourer (a brain with four legs that eats the gray matter of sentient hominids and then camps in their skulls). The building is ten times as twisted as the Winchester Mystery House, a real-life oddity that has just 161 rooms and no dungeons. The result is the creation of an unpredictable environment for players, who are kept guessing at every closed door, and laughing around the play table, even as their characters suffer increasingly improbable demises. This sort of tomfoolery characterizes the "old school" *Dungeons & Dragons* experience for many players, new and old.

With no rules or best practices for design, it makes sense that the anything-can-happen funhouse would be the first type of adventure to appear. They're certainly an easier sort of dungeon to design, and the most immediately gratifying, as every encounter aims to outdo the last. They rather rapidly fell out of fashion, since unabating zaniness often leads players to fatigue and, ironically, boredom. "Naturalist" designs, like Gary Gygax's *Giants*-series modules (see page 42),

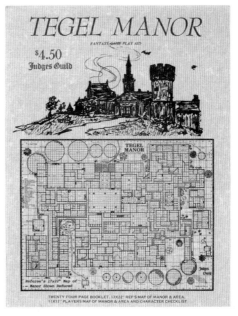

TEGEL MANOR, JUDGES GUILD, 1977
BOB BLEDSAW

quickly overshadowed the funhouse. The later idea of dungeons as a vehicle for narrative, trailblazed by Tracy and Laura Hickman's *Ravenloft*, was the stake through that carefree, funhouse heart, at least until recent years, when the Old School Revival, particularly *Dungeon Crawl Classics* (2014), renewed some interest in the form.

Tegel Manor probably isn't the most well-known funhouse (it is naturally overshadowed by several official *D&D* modules, particularly *S2: White Plume Mountain*, 1979), but it's certainly one of the largest. Owing to the size—nearly 200 above-ground rooms and four underground dungeon levels—this might be the first attempt at a mega-dungeon.

As the name implies, mega-dungeons are huge, nightmare places (usually with a small nearby town serving as a safe base of operations), where a party of characters can spend their entire adventuring careers hacking away without ever entirely conquering. They existed before *Tegel Manor*—Castle Greyhawk, the massive 13-level dungeon of Gary Gygax's homebrew *D&D* campaign, was already a much-discussed legend in 1977—but no one had ever published one before. That meant most people had never seen one, so in this way, *Tegel Manor* was a revelation.

While funhouses fall by the wayside, mega-dungeons became regular fixtures on store shelves, the litany of their names spoken by players in a mix of awe at their treasure and fear at their dangers. Mega-dungeons are also one of the earliest and most enduring tabletop RPG ideas to find adaption in videogames, with *Zork* (1980), *Rogue* (1980), *Metroid* (1986), *Bloodborne* (2015), and many more embracing the concept to varying degrees. *Tegel Manor* (with nearby Tegel Village) isn't quite so arduous or lengthy, but it helped pave the way for all of those other terrifying holes in the ground.

Wilderlands of High Fantasy (1977)

The success of Judges Guild's play aid subscription service meant the need for ever more material. After *Tegel Manor* came *Modron*, which detailed a village, a lake goddess, and rules for underwater exploration. Then came *Wilderlands of High Fantasy,* two booklets and five maps that began to flesh out a larger world.

The approach here is still framed around the idea that GMs are going to want to define the world themselves, so outside of a few key details, the landscape is left roughly sketched. Places of interest are named, and a series of lists give sparse amounts of detail, on par with the brevity in *Tegel Manor* and *City State*. A typical description lists the hex number, the point of interest, and the monsters potentially encountered: "2304 – Altar in cave – 3 crocodiles." That kind of ambiguity works well when dealing with haunted bedrooms or back-alley taverns; small spaces conjured to life with few details. An entire wilderness is not so easily portrayed. Two of the big maps—Tarantis and Valon—are supposed to be full-fledged kingdoms, while barbarian tribes inhabit the regions depicted on the other two. Without any kind of social, cultural,

or historical details, though, the Wilderlands presented here seem vast, ruin-haunted, and empty.

Judges Guild would use *Wilderlands of High Fantasy* as a foundation, filling in details one publication at a time, first with their subscription plan, then in conventional publications. Eventually, this modular approach resulted in the largest, most detailed campaign world available, far more sophisticated than anything produced by TSR for the original *Dungeons & Dragons*. That's all in the future though, and the interesting legacy of *Wilderlands* in 1977 isn't its coming role as a building block for a bigger campaign setting. No, what's keen about *Wilderlands* is all of the wonderful random tables.

Randomness is a key element of RPG design. To understand the how and why of it requires stepping back to wargaming for a moment. The point of most wargaming mechanics is to simulate reality: How much energy does a platoon of musketeers have after crossing a muddy field? How fast is the pull of a trigger relative to the swing of a sword? Simulating the action of a battle, with all of its variables, requires many little mechanical rules systems working in tandem.

To make it a war*game*, though, and not just an exercise in solving an elaborate

WILDERLANDS OF HIGH FANTASY, BOOKLET I, JUDGES GUILD, 1977
BILL OWEN AND BOB BLEDSAW, COVER BY MOHOW AND GIL DEA

mathematical equation, requires two complications: The players' strategic decisions in their roles as generals, and randomness. Rolling dice is still a simulation, but it simulates all of the things the mechanical systems can't account for—a shift in the breeze, the clouds parting to let the sun shine in a soldier's eyes, the gnat buzzing in their ear. That randomness introduces chance, for both catastrophic failure and improbable success. And right there is where it becomes a game.

RPGs make a few small changes to this formula, one of which has explosive results: It seats the player in the role of a single character, instead of as the embodiment of an entire army. This changes everything. As a single character, strategy and tactics recede as the focus of the action, while narrative asserts itself. The GM asks, "What do you do?" *You* aren't an army; *you're* a character with a sword in a weird underground place, and that dragon sure seems angry. *You* better come up with something good. And if the group was playing make-believe, whatever any given player came up with would be good enough, but what makes RPGs special and new is that the course of the story is left, not to the storyteller, but rather to chance, to the die roll, to fate.

There is a sort of intoxicated fascination with randomness in the early days of RPGs. There was no problem a random table couldn't solve, no player's question a random table couldn't answer. *City State* has no shortage of delightfully useless random tables. Roll a 20-sided die to find out why that ruffian decided to start a fight with the players! Roll a 6-sided die to determine how two NPCs are related!

The *Wilderlands* approach to random tables is a bit different overall. They are mostly aimed at populating a location with points of interest. A prime example occurs right at the start, the Ravaged Ruins table, which is actually dozens of nested tables. First, roll in order on Class, Condition, Covering (if applicable), and State, getting something like: Remnants/Large Crater/Rocks/Crumbled & Decayed as the result. Even though there are no definitions to help parse the difference between a "remnant" and a "vestige," a picture of the place should already be coming to mind. Now, roll for Keeper, by which the authors mean the horrible monster that lives there.

These kinds of tables, of which the ones in *Wilderlands* are the earliest, function as tool kits for the GM, providing creative prompts and, given enough of them, a framework for creating large swaths of material for a game session with just a few dice rolls. Gary Gygax applied the same idea to subterranean spaces with the dungeon generator in the *Dungeon Masters Guide*, and similar tables are an important tool in the development of RPG city building. In the wake of the Old School Revival in the twenty-first century, many indie RPGs embraced the tool kit approach and pushed it into new realms of narrative flavoring. The way *Mothership*'s (2018) endless trinket tables flesh out player characters while having no mechanical impact on the game is emblematic of the phenomenon, but there is no shortage of modern RPGs using random tables in surprising ways.

WILDERLANDS OF HIGH FANTASY, BOOKLET 2, JUDGES GUILD, 1977
BILL OWEN AND BOB BLEDSAW

The Fantasy Trip (1977)

While some games were looking for new places to inject randomness, others were trying to minimize it. From the start, character creation was ruled by randomness, often to an extent that felt out of proportion. *Dungeons & Dragons'* rules broadly defined characters through six attributes: Strength, Intelligence, Wisdom, Dexterity, Constitution, and Charisma. Each score was determined in order by the GM, who rolled three 6-sided dice and totaled the result. The values of those abilities, in turn, helped the player decide which classes were viable, with Fighting-Men keyed to Strength, Magic-Users keyed to Intelligence, and Clerics keyed to Wisdom. This method of character creation is meant to reflect the vagaries of natural talents that are determined by birth rather than personal agency, which makes philosophical sense as a design choice, especially if the designer wants certain classes, like the Paladin, to be rare, thanks to the high requirements for multiple attributes. Randomness also ignores the desires of the player and often produces middling or unplayable characters.

It isn't a whole lot of fun to get stuck with a Fighter when a player wants to be a mage, so house rules for rolling characters are the most common. For starters, things might have been different in '74, but I've never heard of someone playing a character for whom the GM rolled the attributes. At the very least, the vast majority of GMs allow players to arrange the scores so their preferred attributes get the highest values. Folks have also come up with alternative systems for rolling, like using four dice and dropping the lowest value, or re-rolling dice that come up as ones. All of these tweaks aim to reduce randomness in favor of giving the player some leeway in creating the sort of character they *want* to play.

In 1977, the wargaming publisher, Metagaming Concepts, launched their Microgame line to provide games that were both cheap to buy and fast to play—the small plastic envelopes usually contain one four-by-seven-inch rulebook, a hex map, and sheets of card stock chits that need to be cut out.

The third MicroGame was designer Steve Jackson's *The Fantasy Trip: Melee*. As the name implies, *Melee* is a simple system for person-to-person (or person-to-monster) combat in an arena setting. It's a lean tactics game more than it is an RPG, in a way that feels similar to Game Designers' Workshop's *En Garde!*. That tactical focus springs partly from Jackson's real-life faux-combat as a Viking during outings with the Society for Creative Anachronism. In *Melee*, characters move around the map and attack each other. The combat is both tactically rich and easy to handle—a rarity—but in terms of gameplay, the fighting is the only action.

The key innovation in *Melee* is the point-buy system for character attributes. It's bare bones here—just 24-points to

THE FANTASY TRIP: MELEE, METAGAMING CONCEPTS, 1977
STEVE JACKSON, COVER BY LIZ DANFORTH

The Fantasy Trip
MELEE

MicroGame 3 $2.95

spend between Strength and Dexterity, but this small shift is the first time that players gained direct control over the creation of their characters, and it amounts to an important mechanical step towards more character- and narrative-driven gaming. In fact, Jackson would make point-buying central to his most ambitious RPG, *GURPS*, while point-buy and similar point allocation systems have become the default for many systems and are options in many others, *Dungeons & Dragons* included.

The Fantasy Trip: Wizard, the sixth installment in the MicroGame line, expands the original *Melee* rules. It adds a third attribute, IQ, and raises the initial point pool to thirty-two. The higher the character's IQ, the more spells they can know and the more powerful they can potentially be. The rest of the main booklet details how magic works tactically, going into far more mechanical detail

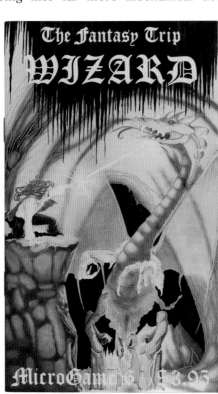

The Fantasy Trip: Wizard, Second edition, Metagaming Concepts, 1979 Steve Jacskon, Cover by Roger Stine

The Fantasy Trip: Wizard, Metagaming Concepts, 1978 Steve Jackson, Cover by Clark Bradley

than other games. Instead of defining rules for magic spell by spell, the way *Dungeons & Dragons* did, *Wizard* establishes rules for each category of spell—control, missile, illusion, and more. The spell descriptions, which are contained in a second, smaller booklet, are short and precise. Compared to the often nebulous spell descriptions in other games that encourage different interpretations, *Wizard*'s magical effects are largely impervious to lawyering.

In addition to expanding the arsenals of the characters, magic also makes the calculation of tactical decisions more complex. In *Melee*, armor provides a reduction of incoming damage at the expense of the character's Dexterity, which determines how likely it is that they'll hit their opponent. There is a call there for a player to make regarding their character's defensive and offensive potential, but it is made before the fight begins. The only decisions the player makes in *Melee* center on how they want to pummel their opponent at any given moment. Magic isn't static the way armor is. Casting a spell drains a character's Strength, which doubles as their character's health. The more spells one casts, the more damage is done to the opponent, but they also leave the caster closer to *their* demise.

This dynamic, in which a character's increasing power proves ultimately corrosive, is central to games like *Call of Cthulhu* and *Warhammer Fantasy Roleplay*. But *The Fantasy Trip* lays out the way to express that danger mechanically, years before those games, and years before it becomes a full-fledged RPG itself, even, with *In the Labyrinth* in 1980.

Arduin (1977)

Where Judges Guild went to the trouble of asking for TSR's permission to publish material compatible with *Dungeons & Dragons*, not everyone followed suit. David Hargrave's series of Arduin zines are in that category.

For instance, they present a suspiciously similar look to the original *D&D* booklets. They're the same digest size and have parchment-colored covers. The printing is inferior, with the typewritten text shrunken to fit on the page, but the art is far better than most of what TSR was publishing at the time (and includes the first published work by Erol Otus, who would soon become an early RPG art icon). They feel like budget imitations of TSR's marginally more professional publications.

Aside from general aesthetics, the substance of the zines is very similar to the *D&D* supplement books. They're collections of house rules created for Hargrave's ongoing *D&D* campaign, set in a world he called Arduin, and intended as modular expansions for homebrew games. Knowing that, though, doesn't make parsing them very easy—Hargrave is constantly referring to a mountain of material, only a portion of which is in any given book.

The "How to Play the Game" section in the first volume is largely devoted to the mechanics of overland travel. The organization is erratic, at best. I had to read through all three of the initial volumes before I understood the concepts to the point that I could incorporate them into a game.

It's worth noting that a designer doesn't need permission to write or publish rules materials for someone else's game—rules systems can't be copyrighted. The problem is that characters and monsters and similar creations with proper names can. More importantly, brand names can be trademarked, which makes signaling to an audience that a product is for someone else's game a bit tricky. This is why today's Old School Revival products have all sorts of oblique ways of cluing players in to the fact that their products work with *D&D,* without ever using the *D&D* trademark: for example, "Compatible with the world's oldest roleplaying game," and similar variations. Hargrave wasn't so cautious and ran afoul of TSR's legal department, which took exception to a passage they saw as advocating for the photocopying of rulebooks, as well as one spell description that appeared to be a direct copy of the *D&D* version. He cut those sections and, to avoid further trouble, all of the direct references to *D&D* in his text. Hargrave initially did so with whiteout, while subsequent printings were properly revised. TSR left him alone after that.

The new classes introduced in *The Arduin Grimoire* set the jam-packed standard: Merchant, Psychic, Barbarian, Rune Weaver, Techno, Medicine Man, and Witch Hunter, all in addition to standard *D&D* classes. While players never gain clear details on what Arduin is like, some topics, like the Techno class that uses salvaged high-tech equipment, imply much about the setting's fusion of sci-fi and fantasy.

There are piles of new treasures, monsters (many silly) and spells, musings on alignment, modified approaches to character creation, and combat (which is ridiculously complex), and a gloss of the 21 layers of hell—and charts! For mist generation, for fumbles, for traps, for character special abilities (some good—natural mechanic!—some bad—bad liar!). *The Arduin Grimoire* establishes not just a precedent for the idea of rules hacking, which is now a thriving staple in the Old School Revival, but a valuable, if jumbled, how-to guide.

The second Grimoire, *Welcome to Skull Tower*, is disorganized along the same lines as the first, collecting a potpourri of new classes, spells, monsters, treasure, rule musing, and helpful random tables. There are even thoughts on best practices for running a game and dealing with problem players. This volume also provides the clearest look at the world of Arduin through a capsule history and a list of tavern and inn names and locations (but no other context, frustratingly). There are no details on the titular Skull Tower either, alas.

Runes of Doom ties up (some) threads left dangling from the other two volumes. Hargrave finally runs down the rules for playing Phraints, humanoid insect war-

Welcome to Skull Tower, Grimoire Games reprint, circa 1984
David A. Hargrave, cover by Morno (Bradley W. Schenck)

riors that are repeatedly mentioned as playable in the previous books, but without any indication as to how play them. There are also mechanics, finally, for the energy weapons used by the Techno class, which cements Arduin's commitment to science fantasy, two years before *S3: Expedition to the Barrier Peaks* saw print. Both of these revelations illustrate how chaotic and slapdash the Grimoires are overall.

Hargrave himself comes through in the third Grimoire, as well. An illustration towards the back is entitled "Attack of the Kill Kittens," which gives readers a sense of his humor, as well as the uncompromising nature of his games. As Lawrence Schick wrote in *Heroic Worlds,* Arduin is "unencumbered by the restraints of conventional good taste," a notion exemplified by the illustration of a topless, ax-wielding female warrior captioned, "Shardra the Castrator."

The Grimoires are a glimpse directly into the late 1970s RPG scene. For better *and* worse, there are many unique ideas but also some crappy, sexist ones, like the "female attributes" chart that translates physical measurements into bonuses

The Arduin Grimoire, Grimoire Games reprint, circa 1984
David A. Hargrave, cover by Greg Espinoza

THE RUNES OF DOOM, GRIMOIRE GAMES REPRINT, CIRCA 1984
DAVID A. HARGRAVE, COVER BY GREG ESPINOZA

and penalties for Charisma. There is a sense of wildness, of no rules, of boundaries undefined.

In some ways, this lack of restraint hints at the genre mixing that would arrive in the '90s with games like *Torg* and *Rifts*. More than that, though, with the Arduin zines, Hargrave plants the first seeds of transgression in RPGs. The zines seem calculated to *shock,* in the same way that some lurid heavy metal album covers sought to fluster squares with cartoon skulls, demons, and blood. That whiff of the forbidden would stick to RPGs for years, and it might be Arduin's greatest legacy.

Dungeons & Dragons Basic Set (1977)

J. Eric Holmes, neurologist and *D&D* enthusiast, pitched TSR the idea of an approachable, easy-to-learn version of the game. Such a teaching box had the potential to lure in a wider, younger audience and mass market distribution. The result was the *Dungeons & Dragons Basic Set*, the first in a long line of introductory *D&D* box sets that continue to crowd shelves to this day.

Holmes worked with the original *Dungeons & Dragons* rules, as well as the first expansion book, *Supplement I: Greyhawk.* The result is essentially a restatement of *D&D* in a clearer, friendlier form. Collating all of the essential contents of four booklets under one cover served as an important step toward streamlining the game; but one of the biggest problems with the original *Dungeons & Dragons* is that understanding the rules doesn't mean a person knows how to play. Holmes bridges this gap by including an example of play and a sample dungeon, both of which illustrate how players put the rules into action. The rules themselves are largely unchanged, though; the "Basic" doesn't refer to some set of mechanical training wheels, but rather to the fact that the box set only supports play for character levels one through three.

This ambiguity makes the existence of the *Basic Set* a bit puzzling, since the original *Dungeons & Dragons* box set was still on the market and represented the whole game, instead of just the first three levels. The *Basic Set* doesn't make sense as a gateway to the forthcoming *Advanced Dungeons & Dragons* system, either (despite protests to the contrary in the text of the book)—that game, while similar, has large mechanical and philosophical differences. Holmes says as much in his 1981 guidebook to the RPG scene, *Fantasy Role Playing Games.* He counsels new players to ignore his box and just go all in on *AD&D*, lamenting, "It seems to me unfortunate that the *Advanced D&D* does not grow smoothly and naturally out of the *Basic Rules*, but it doesn't."

Holmes wasn't alone in his dismay. The schism between *D&D*, which carries on the more flexible, improvisational tradition established by Arneson, and *AD&D*, the more complex, competitive, and tactical game by Gygax, created a sort of brand confusion. This disconnect started, in part, because of friction between Arneson and Gygax, which would come to a head with Arneson suing over, and winning, unpaid royalties in 1979, but it also blossoms into an ongoing headache for *D&D* players for decades to come. The problem pushes beyond mere compatibility issues and into the "Edition Wars," a deeply silly, never-ending conflict in which players argue about which edition of *D&D* is "the best."

Holmes's *Basic Set* contributed to the dominance of *Dungeons & Dragons*, both over the hobby, in general, and, for a time, over Gygax's *AD&D*, as well. Getting the box, with its looming, almost garish dragon, painted by David C. Sutherland III, onto bookstore shelves drove tremendous sales. Although the front of the box clearly states, "the original adult fantasy roleplaying game," it also succeeded in bringing a younger crowd of fresh players. The box set was so successful that it went through seven printings in just four years. Not all of those printings are the same, and the changes reflect quickly evolving ideas about roleplaying.

The original box set included lists of monsters, treasures, and a tool for laying out dungeons, so GMs could make their own adventures. By the end of 1978, after Judges Guild proved there was an appetite for pre-made adventures, TSR was producing its own adventures, so those accessories were replaced by the introductory adventure module *B1: In Search of the Unknown*. In 1980, *B1* was replaced by *B2: The Keep on the Borderlands*, an acknowledged classic and one of the most widely distributed RPG adventures ever, with well over a million copies speculated to be in print (thanks largely to its inclusion in this box set and in Tom Moldvay's 1981 revision).

The *Basic Set* also marks the first time a set of polyhedral dice were included with an RPG. The first sets, up to 1979, contained only five dice: 4-, 6-, 8-, 12-, and 20-sided (the 10-sided die existed in theory, but wasn't in production yet). These were crude, soft plastic dice that wore out quickly (Holmes says, in his book, that most players pitched them in the trash and bought better ones separately). In 1979, thanks to the oil crisis, there was a shortage of petroleum-based plastic dice, so a sheet of numbered cardboard chits was provided to cut up and be used as an alternative, along with a coupon for a set of dice once the shortage abated. The dice were back in 1980 and included a sixth, the 10-sided die, in 1981.

Chivalry & Sorcery (1977)

If the *D&D Basic Set* aimed to make RPGs more approachable and improvisational, *Chivalry & Sorcery (C&S)* achieved the opposite, making rules more esoteric and orderly. Edward E. Simbalist and Wilf Backhaus didn't consider *D&D's* depiction of a medieval world realistic enough, and they sought to correct that problem mechanically.

Realism is an odd dragon to chase in RPG design, partly because most RPGs are lousy with *actual* dragons, but mostly because "realistic" can mean many different things. Simbalist and Backhaus argue that *D&D* provides players dungeons to explore, but little else, and this is a stingy use of simulation. Why not recreate

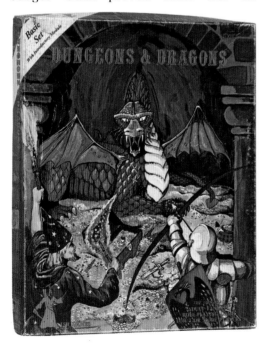

DUNGEONS & DRAGONS BASIC SET, BOX SET, TSR, 1977
J. ERIC HOLMES, COVER BY DAVID C. SUTHERLAND III

CHIVALRY & SORCERY, FANTASY GAMES UNLIMITED, 1977
EDWARD E. SIMBALIST AND WILF BACKHAUS, COVER BY MIKE GILBERT

CHIVALRY AND SORCERY, BOX SET, SECOND EDITION, FANTASY GAMES UNLIMITED, 1983
EDWARD E. SIMBALIST AND WILF BACKHAUS, COVER BY BOB CHARRETTE

an expansive medieval world of laws and customs, economic currents, and family responsibilities with which players can wrestle? This social construction would provide a richer roleplaying experience, expanding the potential goals for characters while injecting players' decisions with more importance as they weigh the risks and rewards attached to character actions. Building a realistic world, one that mirrors our own and is somewhat predictable by those standards, in turn, raises the fictional stakes. Characters are no longer just lists of attributes; they have a place and responsibility in the world and consequences should they fail or fall.

C&S also aims to be realistic in its rendering of the world, the sort of realism we attach to the detail in a photograph. However, the more detail added to an RPG, the more complicated it becomes, requiring more interacting systems and more all-encompassing rules. The owner of publisher Fantasy Games Unlimited, Scott Bizar, brags in the introduction to the game that it, "is the most complete rule booklet ever published. Its very completeness creates problems in the mass of rules to be absorbed." In order to save on printing costs due to this completeness, the type-

written manuscript was shrunk to fit four pages worth of words onto a single sheet.

A great deal of thought and research into the medieval period is on display in *Chivalry & Sorcery*. There is a rule or system for just about everything imaginable, from quantifying social class to measuring incremental success on the battlefield, which is as daunting as it sounds. There is a beauty in complex rules, though, and *Chivalry & Sorcery*'s vividly imply a world in a way few other RPGs, then or now, manage. This implied world was developed in concrete terms in 1979 with two supplements, *Arden* and *Saurians* (though both are roughly hewn by today's standards).

Arden details a sort of Arthurian-style fantasy kingdom, the maps of which combine to be some 38 by 42-inches and cover a region of about 136,000 square miles—the equivalent of the United Kingdom and more than three times the total size of the *Wilderlands of High Fantasy*. The map is painstakingly detailed, but the written matter consists mostly of tables of demographic data, save for a historical and political overview. *Saurians* is the opposite; there's no massive map but also no shortage of interesting cultural and geographical information on the world, a sort of Conan-esque, prehistoric place filled

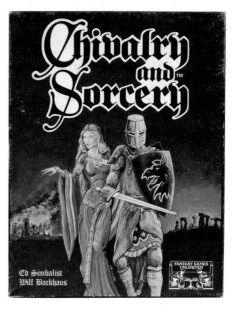

with dinosaurs and reptile people (a curious venue for the concept of realism).

All of this detail encouraged a new kind of focus on roleplaying, certainly, but one that is bogged down by the weight of its rules and their insistence on intricately simulating the world. *Chivalry & Sorcery* is not alone in this focus on simulation. *Fantasy Wargaming* (1981) swaggered into a similar trap, creating a game that is nigh unplayable (but, bizarrely, boasts attributes for God, Moses, and a whole host of Judeo-Christian figures). N. Robin Crossby initially avoided the same fate with his world of Hârn, a wonderfully realized, system agnostic, medieval fantasy world, but then he made the *HârnMaster* rules and embraced a similar zest for expansive mechanics. Though, like *Chivalry & Sorcery*, *HârnMaster* is beautiful in its complexity; *Fantasy Wargaming* is just complicated.

A second Fantasy Games Unlimited (FGU) edition of *Chivalry & Sorcery* appeared in 1983. While it corrected mechanical issues and generally streamlined the system, the industry was increasingly moving toward lighter, faster rule sets. FGU didn't offer much official support—the two *C&S* sourcebooks that were reissued with the second edition were straight reprints, typos and all. Despite FGU's ambivalence, a small but dedicated player base has continued to embrace the game, with the fifth edition successfully kickstarted in 2019 by Brittannia Game Designs (that extra 't' is not a typo).

Monster Manual (1977)

The *Monster Manual* marks the start of a strange time for TSR, *Dungeons & Dragons*, and, to a certain degree, the broader world of RPGs. There is a deeper sort of magic at work here, which makes sense, because a book of monsters is a powerful, imagination-capturing thing.

My entrance into *Dungeons & Dragons* was because of monsters. As a little kid, I loved dinosaurs. A little older, I learned about cryptids, like my own local Jersey Devil and the Loch Ness Monster—is it a dinosaur or a monster? Why not both? A little older, and I had a stack of Daniel Cohen books, like *The Encyclopedia of Monsters* and *A Natural History of Unnatural Things*.

It didn't matter if a monster was supposedly real or entirely fictional, I wanted to know all about it. I was not alone in this. Cohen's books, of which there are many, also covered ghosts, horror movies, and pop culture topics outside the paranormal and were aimed squarely at children. They most often took the form of an encyclopedia, with short entries arranged in alphabetical order, crammed with just the juicy details; there was no room for the boring stuff. This sort of reference book was a common format in the pre-internet days—I have piles of them for kids and adults alike on monsters, mythology, the occult, and general oddness, like Barbara Ninde Byfield's *The Glass Harmonica* (1967) and Rossell Hope Robbins's *The Encyclopedia of Witchcraft and Demonology* (1959).

Most of them are illustrated, the very best strikingly so, like Louis Le Breton's diabolical engravings of Goëtic demons for the 1863 edition of Collin de Plancy's *Dictionnaire Infernal*. While the Victorian era might seem long ago, the origins of this sort of book go even farther back, to the bestiaries. These books, more properly called bestiarum vocabulum, are chronicles of creatures both real and imagined, best known as illuminated manuscripts produced in Renaissance-era monasteries. But the earliest, *The Physiologus*, dates all the way back to the second century and draws from still older sources. Human beings have long been interested in compendiums of monsters, so the emergence of the *Monster Manual* is no surprise, nor is the enduring popular-

MONSTER MANUAL, TSR, 1977
GARY GYGAX, COVER BY DAVID C. SUTHERLAND III

ity of RPG monster books among players.

What is surprising, though, is that, once again, TSR was not the first to release a book of monsters. *All the Worlds' Monsters*, from Chaosium, hit shelves before *Monster Manual,* thanks to printing problems that delayed the latter's release from September to late December. Now, throughout its history, TSR occasionally engaged in poor sportsmanship and aggressive tactics (a well-worn joke I've heard was that TSR stood for "They Sue Regularly"), but the company usually appeared above the fray in public. *All the Worlds' Monsters* seems to have riled the company, though, if TSR vice president of game design, Mike Carr's belligerent foreword to the *Monster Manual* is any indication:

The success of *Dungeons & Dragons* has spawned a considerable number of imitations and spin-off products, perhaps inevitably. Some of these have merit; many, however, do not – and although we may concede their right to exist (however dependent they may be on *D & D*'s audience), we would caution the prospective buyer to consider their true value and not to be confused with those items which bear the *Dungeons & Dragons* or *Advanced Dungeons & Dragons* name and constitute the official *D & D* family of products. As for value, let the others be measured against the standard of quality we have striven for – a hardbound encyclopedia of monsters, for instance, as opposed to a low quality collection which is poorly assembled and bound.

Salty! Fit more for an editorial in *The Dragon* magazine than at the front of the first book in a much-hyped new line, the foreword is entirely odd. The rest of it is one loud toot of *D&D*'s own horn and sounds insecure more than anything. While the low budget *All the Worlds' Monsters* was the first RPG monster book, it was not the touchstone that the *Monster Manual* was about to become, in part, because of what it is: A luxurious, even decadent book.

This is the first hardcover RPG book

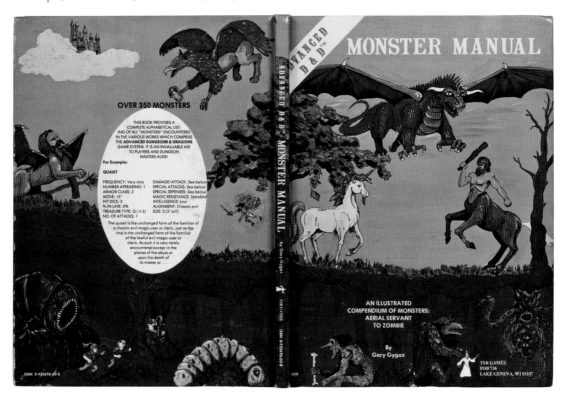

and, until the late '80s, the *Advanced Dungeons & Dragons* line produced the *only* hardcover books in the hobby. That TSR could produce such a book, with its full color wrap-around cover art and interior illustrations on every page (for nearly every monster!), was a testament to their lofty position in the world of RPGs. Those qualities further added to the company's prestige by helping them gain access to the shelves of general bookstores, where they got in front of the eyes of shoppers outside of the tiny gamer niche.

The player response to the *Monster Manual* was overwhelmingly positive (it's the only *AD&D* book that got both a direct and an indirect sequel, for one thing) and a clear contrast to whatever was going on internally at TSR to spur that foreword. Certainly, the book's subject matter of monsters, the most evocative and dangerous component of *D&D*, contributed to its success, as did its scope—over 350 monsters received attributes and descriptions—but I suspect that it was the artwork that cemented its place as an instant classic.

Up to this point, artwork was scarce in RPGs, both because of the small budgets available and printing constraints. What did appear was often crude and amateurish. Even the color cover art of the *Monster Manual*, by David C. Sutherland III, isn't exactly a well-crafted piece by most standards. His interiors are much better examples of his skill, and the final full-page illustration is an exquisitely detailed rendering that implies the garishness of the cover was a measured artistic choice. And there is something compelling in the cover. It always seemed to have a vibe, perhaps due to its cross-section view, that reminds me of a children's activity book. It certainly promises adventure and exploration.

Inside, Sutherland is joined, primarily, by David Trampier, whose clean, precise lines often evoke the feel of medieval

ALL THE WORLDS' MONSTERS, CHAOSIUM, 1977 JEFF PIMPER AND STEVE PERRIN (EDITORS). COVER BY GEORGE BARR

1970

1980

1990

2000

2010

edited by Jeff Pimper & Steve Perrin

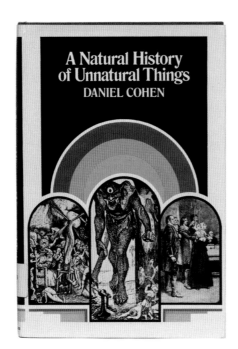

woodcuts. Together, they create a world where green slime drips from the ceiling and treasure chests can come to (hungry) life. RPGs take place in the theater of the mind, but the importance of finally seeing these creatures, often in tableau with unfortunate adventurers meeting their dooms, can't be overstated. Because the illustrations tend towards the cartoonish, these depictions never feel set the way they do in later editions with more detailed, realistic art.

Carr wasn't wrong about *All the Worlds' Monsters*—it was a slapdash affair with typewritten entries and sporadic illustrations of largely arbitrary monsters. *Monster Manual* set the mold for others to follow, including: *Out of the Pit* (1985) for *Fighting Fantasy*, *S. Petersen's Field Guide to Cthulhu Monsters* (1988) and *Malleus Monstrorum* (2003) for *Call of Cthulhu*, *Creatures of Barsaive* (1994) for *Earthdawn*, *The Gloranthan Bestiary* (1988, 2018) for *RuneQuest*, *Galaxy Guide 4: Alien Races* for West End's *Star Wars: The Roleplaying Game*—all embrace a standard of art and detail created here by Gygax and his collaborators.

Players Handbook (1978)

Dungeons & Dragons has inspired the creation of countless works of art over the years, but few are so iconic as Dave Trampier's cover painting for the *Players Handbook*. It's one of the rare pieces of *D&D* art that depicts the events following a battle instead of the battle itself, and it poses endless questions: Why are the adventurers there? Did the lizard people build that place? That idol is going to come to Harryhausen-like life once they pry its eye out, isn't it?

There are distasteful elements openly displayed—the rudely stacked corpses, the naked greed of the looting, and the adventurers seemingly outnumbering the lizardfolk almost four to one. Certainly, no *D&D* painting has been more honest about what players get up to in the game. Yet at the same time, the unseemly qualities of Trampier's adventurers stoke interest. This group of men might not be heroes (almost certainly not, in fact). The whole thing oozes mystery and danger. And there's that sense of the forbidden, as well, that this isn't for kids, that a player has to be prepared for the experience. Save perhaps *Eldritch Wizardry* (1976), this is as transgressive as *D&D* gets. Good or bad, for over forty years, thousands of folks have been reenacting versions of that cover painting with glee.

Despite coming six months after the *Monster Manual*, the *Players Handbook* marks the birth of *Advanced Dungeons & Dragons*. It contains the raw material for constructing and running characters. Fighters get this; Elves get that. Here's a chart with how many spells a Magic-User knows at a given level. There's an alarmingly permissive morality system and a brief rundown of how the entire multiverse works. The subject matter blooms into ever-greater intensity with every passing page, but every player nevertheless needs a copy so they can refer to the small set of pages that explains how their character works. It's clearer and better

PLAYERS HANDBOOK, TSR, 1978
GARY GYGAX, COVER BY DAVID A. TRAMPIER

organized than its predecessor. Though there is no index, it is possible to find topics with relative ease, and they will be stated in something that approaches plain language—except the spell descriptions that take up the bulk of the book; they're written so players and GMs can argue like attorneys over how they work and how much damage they do.

While the original *D&D* seems half-formed and strange to many players who came to the hobby later, much of what is laid out here has become thoroughly codified as *D&D* for years and editions to come. It's both recognizable and familiar, even if the intricacies of specific mechanics (negative armor class is good, actually?) are likely baffling to players who have only played modern iterations of the game.

That recognizable framework was part of Gygax's motivation for creating *Advanced Dungeons & Dragons*: Uniformity. Once *D&D* was in the world, Gygax had little control over how people played the game. Over the first four years of its

existence, it became clear that folks were playing it in all sorts of ways. Some game masters were too brutal, turning dungeons into unrelenting deathtraps. Others were too lenient, giving away treasure as if a dungeon delve was a trip to the mall. Those latter games, which earned the pejorative nickname "Monty Haul," a play on the name of *Let's Make a Deal* host Monty Hall, were particularly vexing to TSR. Tim Kask, TSR's first editor, used the foreword to *Gods, Demi-Gods & Heroes* (1976), an original *D&D* supplement, as an opportunity to shame Monty Haul-style players. "Perhaps now some of the 'give-away' campaigns will look as foolish as they truly are," writes Kask. "This is our last attempt to delineate the absurdity of 40+ level characters. When Odin the All-Father has only (?) 300 hit points, who can take a 44th level Lord seriously?"

To modern players, Kask might seem cranky, at best, and megalomaniacal, at worst, but in the '70s, it was common practice for players to bring their characters from game to game, the same way one might jump into a pick-up game of basketball with whomever is down at the court on a given afternoon. If someone brought a character to a gaming convention, they'd bring any loot they found back to their local game, and no one would think twice about it. Many times, the "home" game master would keep a log of a character's advancement on an index card and give a signed copy to the player to certify to other GMs that the character's abilities and magic items had been legitimately earned through play.

In a world without campaign settings or narrative-focused adventures, where every session is a dungeon or hex crawl, this is the style of play that naturally developed. And even after campaign worlds provided a narrative grounding that tied characters to them, convention play remained competitive well into the '80s. So, with that in mind, this goal of bringing uniformity to *AD&D* play makes sense, in the same way most organized sports have governing bodies and rules commissions. A bit of this comes across in Gygax's approach to the book—there are no introductions or examples of play. This is a book that assumes a certain level of prior experience with the game; it is a reference book, not a "how-to."

Gamma World (1978)

Gamma World is the spiritual successor to James M. Ward's previous game, *Metamorphosis Alpha*. Like its predecessor, it involves mutants and salvaged technology and the mixing of fantasy and science fiction, but instead of the societal breakdown happening on a massive colony ship in space, *Gamma World* is set on our own planet, hundreds of years after a nuclear incident, making it the first post-apocalyptic RPG. That move from ship to planet was at the behest of the players. "We received hundreds of letters asking for a planet-based game," says Ward, "and I delivered *Gamma World*."

Destroying the world in fiction to see what happens next is a tale about as old as human storytelling—looking back to the Bible, everything past the flood is technically a post-apocalyptic narrative. In 1978, while it was already on its way, the post-apocalypse hadn't yet ballooned into the fully-fledged sub-genre it is today. Because of this, *Gamma World's* influences are easy to peg. The foreword name-checks *Starman's Son* (1952) by Andre Norton, *The Long Afternoon of Earth* (1962) by Brian W. Aldiss, *Hiero's Journey* (1973) by Sterling Lanier, and, perhaps most importantly, Ralph Bakshi's 1977 animated film, *Wizards* (which would get its own little-known RPG in 1992).

Beyond those, the 1975 film *A Boy and His Dog* seems like a clear influence, along with the novel *A Canticle for Leibowitz* (1959) by Walter M. Miller Jr., and the *Planet of the Apes* films. There is a tendency for post-apocalyptic fiction to take the subject matter very seriously, as in Cormac McCarthy's *The Road* and the videogame series *The Last of Us,* but that is not the case here. I wouldn't exactly call *Gamma World* a comedy, but it revels in the absurdity of its inspirations and often winds up being far more humorous, though darkly so.

Much of the humor springs from the game's mutations, adapted from *Metamorphosis Alpha*. There are human beings unaffected by the cascades of radiation in the environment but also many new species of flora, fauna, and intelligent humanoids. Basically, any regular animal of our world has a good chance of having mutated into a humanoid version with their own culture and a silly name—like the Hoops, who are eight-and-a-half-foot tall, technology-obsessed rabbit people who can, for reasons unclear, turn metal objects into rubber.

Other animals remain beasts, just of a different sort, such as centisteeds, which are horses with elongated bodies supported by sixteen legs. Random mutation, both physical and mental, (think *Scanners,* 1981), is also possible and rapidly leads to combinations that range from silly, to terrifying, to pitiful. The rulebook is full of lovingly rendered illustrations by Dave Trampier that depict mutants both hopeless and hilarious. Though more restrained, *Teenage Mutant Ninja Turtles & Other Strangeness* (1985) and *Mutant: Year Zero* (2014) both owe a clear debt to *Gamma World*'s mutation mechanics.

The recovery of technology and other items from the old world ("rollerball trophy" is one of the potential "treasures" on the random loot table) provides the impetus for adventure, as well as the method by which characters increase their prowess. While mechanically similar to the original *Dungeons & Dragons,* the key difference is the lack of *D&D*-style leveled character advancement. This leaves characters far more vulnerable to the hazards of the wasteland and keener to scour it for salvage in order to get an edge on survival. Discovering old technology doesn't mean a character will know how to use it, though, even if the player does, so the game uses elaborate flow charts to simulate the fiddling necessary to discern how an object works. Players might spend weeks tinkering with an artifact

Gamma World, Box set, Second edition, TSR, 1983
Gary Jaquet, David J. Ritchie, and James M. Ward. Cover by Jeff Easley

and never figure it out. Imagine the reaction when the treasure they pulled out of the bandit stronghold turns out to be a leaf blower and not a super gun!

The world is both well-defined, thanks to our real-world knowledge and the technology with which we live, and utterly open. The large map of the United States that comes in the box boasts some geographic information—the location of ruined cities, mountains, the new contours of a coast redefined by rising sea levels—but is otherwise empty and left to the GM to fill in. Even though TSR had, by now, warmed to the idea of creating adventures, the blank map remained a pillar of TSR campaign design for years to come, even after Gygax's departure. *The World of Greyhawk* folio (1980), *B4: The Lost City* (1982), *Lankhmar: City of Adventure* (1985), and the original *Forgotten Realms* box set (1987) all use blank spaces as a design feature, for good or ill. *Gamma World* winds up mostly in the good column, thanks to the real-world setting—it is easy enough for a GM to picture their hometown as a post-nuclear hellscape and work from there.

Perhaps the most far-reaching innovation in *Gamma World* is the clutch of secret societies and cults populating the world. Called Cryptic Alliances, each has

GAMMA WORLD, BOX SET, THIRD EDITION, TSR, 1986
GARY JAQUET, DAVID J. RITCHIE, AND JAMES M. WARD, COVER BY KEITH PARKINSON

an exclusive membership requirement and a single-minded agenda. Some are straight-forward, like the Iron Society, which wants to wipe out all non-mutated humans. Some are more byzantine in their construction, like the Ranks of the Fit, a Francophile fascist militia founded by a mutant bear who has read *"Mein Kampf, Animal Farm* and several biographies of Napoleon Bonaparte."* That humanoid bear is pictured with both a Hitler mustache and, improbably, a felt bicorne hat, in later editions. These factions are left loosely defined in the first edition—just a brief list—but it constitutes one of the first codifications of opposed factions in an RPG, something that would go on to become a key component of many games, like *Planescape* (1994), *The Dark of Hot Springs Island* (2017), and, especially, the Orwellian black comedy, *Paranoia* (1984), which fully embraces Gamma World's offbeat sense of humor, if not the mutant-filled wasteland.

Amusingly, the humor in Gamma World was not intentional. "I have a deep dark secret," says Ward. "I never wanted Gamma World to have a shred of humor. All of the other designers working on the game decided humor would be a great element for the game. I was appalled when I saw murder chickens in my game."

Gamma World has left a strange footprint in the history of tabletop RPGs. People loved the game from the second it hit shelves—a rabid fan base persists today—but official support for the game was sporadic and often mishandled. The first edition received just two adventure modules before the 1983 second edition came out, which also received two adventures before fizzling (three counting the scenario that came with the screen). TSR dedicated five adventures to the 1986 edition, but that version was hobbled by atrocious editing and the inclusion of a faddish resolution table imported from the *Marvel Super Heroes* RPG that broke the system. A fourth edition surfaced in 1992 and disappeared within the year. The fifth edition arrived stillborn, in 2000, as a setting for the science fiction RPG, *Alternity,* just one month after Wizards of the Coast announced they were canceling the *Alternity* line. The sixth edition, lacking any sense of humor, was developed by Sword & Sorcery Studio for the *D20 Modern System* in 2003 and went unloved by the *Gamma*-faithful, who preferred a *Gamma*-inspired mini-game called *Omega World,* which appeared in *Dungeon* magazine the year prior in 2002. A collectible card mechanic, widely seen as a cash grab, sank an otherwise exciting seventh edition in 2010. Amusingly, each new edition features a new cause of the world's end.

Despite all that wasted potential, *Gamma World* was clearly onto something that appealed to Cold War-era ideas about what life after the "Big One" might be like. The fusion of science and fantasy in a post-apocalyptic setting bubbled to the surface of pop culture several times in the coming decade, in ways strikingly similar to *Gamma World.* First were the serialized short stories that would become Stephen King's *The Gunslinger* (1978-1981), then the Saturday morning cartoon series *Thundarr the Barbarian* (1980-1981), and then most prominently in Mattel's *He-Man and the Masters of the Universe* (1983-1985), all of which feature their own heady mixes of magic, technology, and mutants. It is hard to say whether *Gamma World* directly influenced any of them (though *He-Man* writer Larry DiTillio, was certainly aware of RPGs and penned many adventures for them, including the classic *Masks of Nyarlathotep)*, but even if it is just a coincidence of zeitgeist, the similarities are striking. While *Gamma World* itself may be in stasis, games, like *Mutant Crawl Classics, Mutant: Year Zero,* and the *Fallout* videogame series (itself inspired by the videogame *Wasteland,* which was designed by tabletop RPG mainstays Ken St. Andre, Michael Stackpole, and Liz Danforth) continue to carry the irradiated torch.

RuneQuest (1978)

Greg Stafford founded Chaosium in 1975 to produce wargames. The first was his own *White Bear and Red Moon,* which took place in a vivid and intriguing Bronze Age world called Glorantha. It would shortly become one of the richest campaign settings in the history of RPGs, but the road to get there was circuitous.

Chaosium toyed with publishing an Arduin game back in 1976, but ultimately passed because it was too complex and too derivative of *D&D*. The company did publish some generic supplements for *Dungeons & Dragons—All the Worlds' Monsters* (1977) and a book about bringing RPG magic in line with real-world esoteric systems called *Authentic Thaumaturgy* (1978)—but it took a couple of years before designers Steve Perrin and Ray Turney struck upon the right formula for the RPG that would become *RuneQuest.* The result was a radical departure from RPG norms. Dana Holm, in a review in *Space Gamer* (September/October, 1978), was fairly baffled, saying *RuneQuest* was, "a strange dicotomy [sic]—different and good."

RuneQuest is one of the earliest games to implement a skill system that lines up with our modern notions, and it was the first one to use percentile dice. Percentiles are an intuitive way to handle uncertain outcomes for most people. The skill system is also robust, with all standard skills open to all characters, to some degree—up to this point, unique skills were usually tied to a specific character class, as with the Thief's ability to pickpocket in *Dungeons & Dragons.* In *RuneQuest,* factors like cultural background and trade might augment a character's skills and abilities, but everyone—including monsters and powerful NPCs—are made of the same basic stuff, plotted into the same matrix. Positioning these attributes as universal makes the notion of character class, a standard at the time, unnecessary.

Class is an odd construction. *D&D* derived the notion from the way military units were defined in wargames. It makes sense in that context—spearmen and cavalry are sensible wargame categories because their skills (spearing, charging) and equipment (spears, horses) are highly specialized for a narrowly defined activity (battle). In a wargame, players don't need to know the pikeman's hobbies. In RPGs, though, class becomes a strange abstraction—a trade of sorts, picked in youth, arranged around archetypal behaviors, requiring rigorous specialty training, and offering a narrow set of abilities that increase in power or effectiveness as the character gains enough experience to "level up."

Every *D&D* class progresses identically—every Magic-User climbs the same ladder in the same way, for instance—which makes class even stranger, because life doesn't play out with every person in a profession progressing in an identical fashion. Considering the obsession with verisimilitude in the early days of RPG design, character class is a set of systems that seems emphatically unnatural.

RuneQuest dispenses with the notion of class and instead finds something more

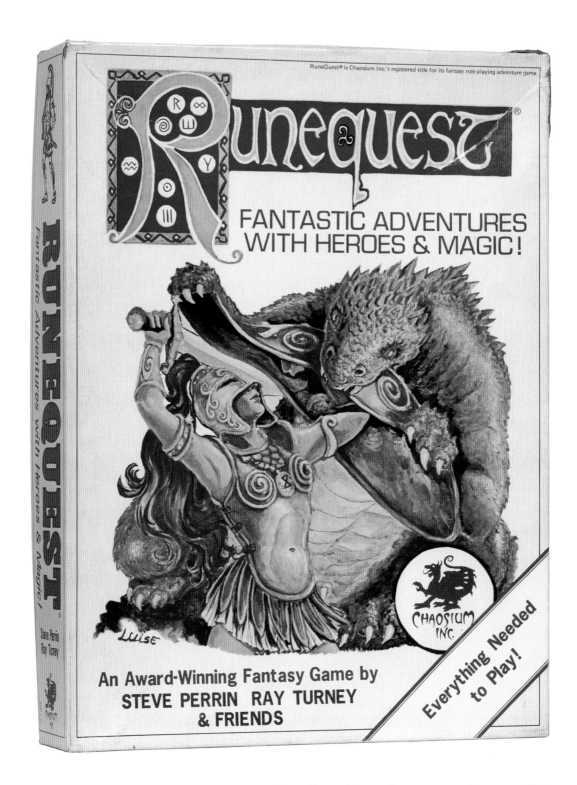

RuneQuest, Box set, Second edition, Chaosium, 1978
Steve Perrin and Ray Turney, Cover by Luise Perenne

naturalistic. Rather than being defined by an archetype, *RuneQuest* allows *players* to define their characters through their choices and actions. Succeed in a skill check, that skill might go up, because the character might have learned something in performing it at that moment. If some activity in the world catches a character's interest, the character can train in it—for instance, the systems of magic in *RuneQuest* are open to anyone who takes the time to study them. Attributes, like Strength, can be trained up, as well.

This level playing field also puts characters in a more precarious spot. Class-based characters generally (and bizarrely) get more hit points every time they level up. In *RuneQuest*, hit points stay the same unless a character invests in some of that physical training to increase their attributes. Static hit points mean characters, no matter their power or experience, are more likely to be grievously wounded or die in combat, which, in turn, makes combat a dangerous measure of last resort. Sure enough, the rest of *RuneQuest*'s combat system, with its hit locations and strike ranks, feels realistic and bloody—it has often been said that it isn't a "real" *RuneQuest* game until someone loses a limb (this being a fantasy world, of course, severed limbs can be put back on with access to the right sort of magic, so dismemberment isn't quite as catastrophic as it sounds). Players uninterested in losing limbs learn to solve problems without swinging swords. In turn, this desire to find non-violent solutions places increased importance on the details of the setting, so as to give players the material they need to overcome adversity through conversation or clever scheming.

There is just enough of Greg Stafford's world of Glorantha in the box to provide stage dressing, but not so much that it is overwhelming. Though there was already a massive amount of lore available, limiting its presence in the box freed players

DRAGON PASS (PREVIOUSLY TITLED WHITE BEAR AND RED MOON, 1975). BOX SET, CHAOSIUM, 1980. ROBERT CORBETT AND GREG STAFFORD, COVER BY RICK BECKER.

from the need for their version of Glorantha to be "correct" or otherwise beholden to the published material. Rather, it signaled that the world was theirs to be used as they wished. "Your Glorantha will vary," is a slogan used in modern *RuneQuest* books in reference to the game's thriving community of fan creators, but it was true from the very start.

More importantly, though, *RuneQuest* is the first game with systems that are thematically reflective of the campaign world, and vice versa. The titular runes form the basis of the game's magic system, but they are also the literal building blocks of Glorantha, the substance of divine creation, that defines the world, its inhabitants, and its many mythologies. Experimenting with how rune magic works on a mechanical level, also, inextricably, teaches the player about how the world works. In this way, *RuneQuest* is an RPG designed specifically for exploring Glorantha. The world is *expressed* by the mechanics.

The G, D, and Q-series Modules (1978)

It took four years for TSR to realize they were leaving money on the table by not publishing their own adventure modules for their games—all of their games languished because of the lack of official expansion. In 1978, to support the new *Advanced Dungeons & Dragons* system, TSR released the G-series modules (G is for *Giant!*), their very first adventures, penned by Gary Gygax (G is also for Gary?).

They feel slight in the hand. *Steading of the Hill Giant Chief* and *Glacial Rift of the Frost Giant Jarl* both come in at a mere eight pages each, while *Hall of the Fire Giant King* is 16. By way of comparison, *Palace of the Vampire Queen* and *Tegel Manor*, neither lengthy by modern standards, are both 24 pages.

Though short, the G-series modules gave TSR the opportunity to showcase the production values that came along with being the big dog in a small industry. The modules have interior illustrations by David C. Sutherland III and Dave Trampier. The outer covers, printed on heavy cardstock, feature monotone color and professionally rendered dungeon maps. Yet, they feel both more and less

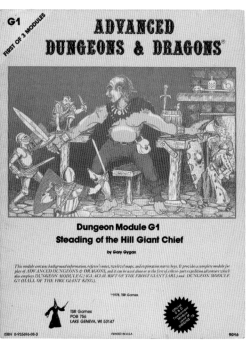

substantial than their competitors. Regardless, the modules set a baseline standard of form for adventure modules that is maintained decades later by some of the Old School Revival publishers.

Gygax took a different approach in the writing, as well. *Tegel Manor* and *Palace of the Vampire Queen* present information in what is, essentially, bullet points, a line or two per room, if that, usually peppered with abbreviated attributes (an approach that has recently come back into vogue, thanks to its usability at the table). Gygax, instead, uses proper prose, describing rooms with full, detailed sentences.

Setting the scene and giving GMs short bits of advice on staging encounters vastly improves the playability of these modules and was especially important at a time when so few people knew how to play an RPG. Gygax's set dressing is almost always tactical in nature. How likely are the room's contents to burn? Can players get the jump on whatever is lurking inside? Will nearby monsters be attracted to the sound of combat? Sometimes, this focus, in addition to overlooking opportunities to roleplay, strays into the downright horrific. One room in *Steading* is occupied by young hill giants. Gygax notes, "noise from here will be

regarded as the 'kids' having fun," and that, "there is no treasure here, but by wearing the young giants' garb, with suitable padding, the party could pass as the youngsters," while entirely ignoring the fact that this strategy likely requires the players to murder a dozen (admittedly large) children. *Dungeons & Dragons* is fucked up sometimes.

There is a semblance of plot, or at least a thin justification for wanton mayhem. An alliance of giants has been raiding the civilized lands in greater numbers, so the adventurers are sent to find out if there is a greater conspiracy afoot (spoiler: there is!), and stop it by killing everything in their path. This strategy, if it can be called that, leads the players to strongholds conveniently arranged in order of increasing strength. Both *Steading* and *Glacial Rift* end in a treasure room where a map to the next fortress can be found alongside a device that, in a move that anticipates the fast travel of modern videogames, literally teleports the group to the next stronghold entrance.

The foregrounding of violence at the expense of all else is a feature here. Who cares about rest and recovery when there are more monsters to kill, right? The answer to this question is that *D&D* is

fucked up sometimes. In the final rooms of the fire giant king's hall, the players encounter the source of the conspiracy, the evil drow—black skinned, white haired subterranean elves that would become the subject of increasing fascination among players of *Dungeons & Dragons* in the ensuing years (see page 220). This marks their first appearance, in which they run away and lead the player into the next set of modules.

The D-series trilogy (1978) consists of *Descent into the Depths of the Earth, Shrine of the Kuo-Toa,* and *Vault of the Drow.* The first is an exploration of an improbable cave complex. In the second, players have the opportunity to ally with a race of evil fish men. The final entry depicts the city of the drow, Erelhei-Cinlu, in an open-ended manner that, in many ways, mirrors *City State of the Invincible Overlord.* The saga of episodic murder exploits concludes with *Q1: Queen of the Demonweb Pits* (1980), in which the players confront and defeat Lolth, the spider goddess of the drow, in her extra-dimensional lair. It may seem odd for players to go up against a literal divinity, in light of Gygax's disapproval of over-powered, "Monty Haul" characters, but in a power fantasy arranged entirely around martial strength

1970

1980

1990

2000

2010

of arms, the violent overthrow of gods seems like the logical end point.

Despite an underdeveloped plot, the overarching narrative distinguishes the G-series modules from their funhouse-style predecessors. Gygax accomplished this distinction, in part, because he attempted to arrange the G-series modules in accordance with a kind of ecological system. *Steading* has Hill Giants and their natural allies in a compound; all of these creatures could be called "earthy"—orcs, ogres, carrion crawlers, and such. *Glacial Rift* then collects a menagerie of cold-themed monsters, while *Hall* takes a similar approach to fire critters (there are trolls there too, despite their noteworthy weakness to fire).

The ecological approach of the G-series is perhaps the clearest example of what James Maliszewski, on his blog *Grognardia*, calls "Gygaxian Naturalism." He argues that there are rules in *Dungeons & Dragons* that, "go beyond describing monsters purely as opponents/obstacles for the player characters by giving game mechanics that serve little purpose other than to ground those monsters in the campaign world." In the *Monster Manual*, for instance, many entries include notes on community sizes and roles, or a per-

centage of time a creature will be found in its lair. These details create a kind of simulation of a world in which the inhabitants go about their own business when not fighting heavily-armed adventurers.

It is an illusion, of course, and often doesn't hold up to scrutiny, as with the case of trolls hanging out in a volcano, or grouping monsters because they all like cold environments (why would frost giants tolerate all of these annoying white puddings hanging around their house?). There is an orderliness to this that seems pleasing, perhaps, but is pseudo-realistic; it's about as plausible as filling a dungeon with monsters that are all the same color. Even the dungeon itself is a conceivable but entirely unrealistic space—part obstacle course, part habitat, part fortress, part tomb. At the same time, though, if a *D&D* game is going well, there is no time for scrutiny; the illusion holds, and, in fact, supports the suspension of disbelief, a fragile thing, but one that underpins much of *D&D*'s design and appeal. As much as detailed campaign worlds are interesting, the G-series demonstrates that an adventure only needs to provide just enough detail to *feel* realistic to keep the game going.

Q1: Queen of the Demonweb Pits, TSR, 1980
David C. Sutherland III, with Gary Gygax, Cover by Jim Rosloff

S1: Tomb of Horrors (1978)

Tomb of Horrors occupies an odd space in the history of the hobby. On one hand, many count it as one of the best *Dungeons & Dragons* adventures ever written. On the other, it is so unlike any other *D&D* adventure, it hardly seems a fair comparison. Beyond taxonomies, *Tomb of Horrors* represents the epitome of a style of play that, if ever it dominated the hobby, has long since been overshadowed. The legend lingers, however.

Gygax originally devised *Tomb of Horrors* for his most experienced players, particularly designer Rob Kuntz and Gygax's son, Ernie. It consists of a relatively small dungeon—33 encounters across 12 pages—that serves as the tomb of the undead wizard, Acererak. The adventure was introduced to the wider world in 1975, at the first Origins gaming convention, as a test for all the folks who bragged about how awesome their *D&D* characters were. It's not like a math test, though. It's more like testing a person for being a witch by throwing them, right thumb tied to left big toe, into a river—if they float, they're a witch, and they get burned at the stake; if they don't, they're cleared, though that also meant they drowned, so it wasn't much consolation.

In direct contrast with the G-series modules, *Tomb of Horrors* isn't a hack and slash sort of jaunt. There are only a handful of monsters. Instead, the tomb is a literal deathtrap, full of dangerous mechanisms and deadly puzzles for players to pit their wits against. The most well-known trap involves the wall with a carving of a great green devil's face, its mouth open—the illustration of which has since become an icon in the hobby for a dirty trick. The darkness within the maw acts as a sphere of annihilation, a magical disintegrator. There is, "plenty of room for those who wish to leap in and be completely and forever destroyed," according to Gygax's adventure text.

Then and now, there aren't many adventures that so thoroughly embrace the notion of running a gauntlet of booby traps, possibly because *Tomb of Horrors* demonstrates how little fun such an experience can be. For starters, in the broadest sense, only one character class in *Dungeons & Dragons*, the Thief, has the skills to deal with mechanical traps, so everyone else is left twiddling their thumbs as the Thief sets to work.

Making matters worse, Gygax's traps are often arbitrary. Players can't puzzle through them like Indiana Jones in the Grail temple; the tomb regularly demands

S1: Tomb of Horrors, TSR, 1978
Gary Gygax, Cover by David C. Sutherland III

they resort to trial and error, or worse, it punishes them for merely walking down a hallway. This sort of invisible danger makes every room a session of Russian roulette and grinds progress to a nerve-wracking snail's pace. Often, players have no idea they've even tripped a trap—the effect happens, and someone dies. There is detailed reasoning for the cause and effect within the adventure text, but it is written more like a legal argument to present to players after the fact, to justify their murder, rather than as a riddle to unravel. If they're lucky, they guess right, and they survive. If not, a new victim takes the lead. Fun? This is the stuff that sets tempers flaring and tables flipping. As with nuclear war and tic-tac-toe in the film *WarGames* (1983), the only way to truly win *Tomb of Horrors* is not to play at all.

There is a natural power imbalance in RPGs. The GM controls the world, most of its inhabitants, and the fickle currents of fate. That power can be wielded in a variety of ways—as an impartial judge, a clue-dropping narrator, an enthusiastic collaborator. The gameplay of *Tomb of Horrors* revels in the full reality-controlling power of a GM unleashed, a deity at their most cruel. The players, whose narrative power is always limited by their character's abilities and the results of the dice, find themselves not so much playing a game but doing battle, at long odds, with the person behind the screen.

In the foreword to *Return to the Tomb of Horrors* (1998), a much expanded and reimagined, though no less deadly version of the tomb, Gygax's language underscores this competitive mindset. The scenario is "demanding." The few who succeeded are "exceptional." "The worst of situations brings out the best in playing ability," he says of one group's clever solution to a trap. He jokes that, if he were meaner, he'd have torn up the sheets of characters who died and "asked for the name and address of their [game masters] so as to pass on the news of the sad loss."

Gygax *didn't* do that, of course, and his tongue seems to be firmly planted in his cheek, camping up the reputation of his most sinister creation and his role as the evil mastermind behind it. After all, the two characters the dungeon was created to dispose of—Rob Kuntz's Robilar and Ernie Gygax's Tenser—both survived to tell the tale. Still, *Tomb of Horrors* was made in an adversarial spirit that seems downright alien today, and as one of the first modules TSR released, it illustrates how central that competitive mindset was in the hobby's early days.

When TSR published *Tomb of Horrors* as the first of the S-series modules in 1978, there were two booklets in the folder. The first is a standard adventure with descriptions of each location within the tomb. The second is a booklet of 32 drawings by David C. Sutherland III and Dave Trampier, making *Tomb of Horrors* the most lavishly illustrated RPG book to date. The illustrations depict key rooms and items found within the tomb, and they're the most memorable part of the adventure.

As much as RPGs are games of imagination, there is always something to be said for seeing the thing. *Tomb of Horrors* is perhaps the first RPG publication that recognizes the power and importance of art. TSR would prove adept at producing piles of iconic art, but other publishers weren't ever far behind. Illustrated booklets of this type were largely out of reach of the budgets of smaller companies, a fact *Dungeons & Dragons* used to excellent effect periodically.

The illustration booklet in *Tomb of Horrors* has a special quality about it, perhaps, in part, because of the interplay between the two artists' styles—Sutherland's is loose and scribbly; Trampier's is as precise as an engraver. Whatever the reason, a sense of mystery and danger abounds. Like tarot cards, there are hidden and often conflicting meanings to be drawn out of the images. It's difficult to say if they are dangling clues, distractions, or temptations. It is unfortunate, though, that figuring out the answer doesn't increase a character's chances of surviving the *Tomb of Horrors*.

Bushido (1979)

Bushido is the first RPG directly inspired by an Asian culture, and in this case, it involves the history and folklore of Japan. It directly influenced the creation of *Oriental Adventures* (1985) for *Dungeons & Dragons*, which, in turn, cemented Asian-themed games as a solid, if small, RPG sub-genre.

The Western preoccupation with Japan isn't entirely accidental. The United States' post-World War II occupation of Japan established a rich, if uneven, cultural exchange between the two countries. Much has been written about the ways in which samurai and cowboy films influenced each other, and *Bushido* draws considerable influence from those samurai movies, particularly Akira Kurosawa's works from the '50s and '60s.

In 1980, Japan's Ministry of Foreign Affairs would start the coordinated exportation of Japanese culture through manga, anime, and other media. Those cultural exports inspired the American film *Enter the Ninja* (1981), which went on to ignite the ninja mania in the United States that would last the rest of the decade and beyond—ninjas everywhere; the Hand in Marvel comics, Stormshadow and Snake Eyes in *G.I. Joe*, the Teenage Mutant Ninja Turtles, every TV show seemed to have its own ninja-themed episode. Japan's government continues this export practice in the present day with the Cool Japan program, an official exercise in soft power that seeks to use the allure of Japanese culture as a way to garner influence abroad. *Bushido*'s release ahead of that pop culture explosion gives the game a stuffy and historically-minded feel, a game by film nerds for film nerds. Perhaps because of this, *Bushido* seems to largely avoid the harmful pan-Asian stereotyping in TSR's slicker, more exciting *Oriental Adventures*.

The world of *Bushido* is not reflective of a single period in historical Japan, but rather, it is a fictionalized Japan referred to as Nippon (that name is the original, Chinese reading of the kanji for Nihon, or Japan), where many historical periods are blended together. This lack of historical rigor gives players a measure of freedom to mimic a range of films that a historical game might not otherwise afford. The inclusion of *yokai* (literally "strange apparitions,") from Japanese folklore expands that freedom even more. Six professions are available for play: Bushi (classic samurai-style fighters), Budoka (martial artists and peasant warriors), Yakuza (professional criminals, not unlike *D&D*'s Thief), Shugenja (Taoist sorcerers), Gakusho (Buddhist or Shinto monks, which combine aspects of *D&D*'s Clerics and Monks), and Ninja, (honorless, stealth-based warriors). Each profession has a suite of supernatural powers fueled by *Ki* (literally "breath;" it's a kind of life force or spiritual energy central to East Asian philosophy). Shugenja and Gakusho also have access to magical spells.

Still, *Bushido* is just lightly fantastic. Each profession has a defined role to play in society, and many of the rules and much of the robust skill system are given over to establishing the aspects of the game that center on social class. Accumulating and maintaining *On*, or honor, is paramount to all characters (except the nefarious Ninja). Being mindful of *On* shifts the focus of the game away from combat and toward roleplaying, especially because earning *On* is just as important to character advancement as combat experience. In fact, obligations weigh so heavily on player actions that the game

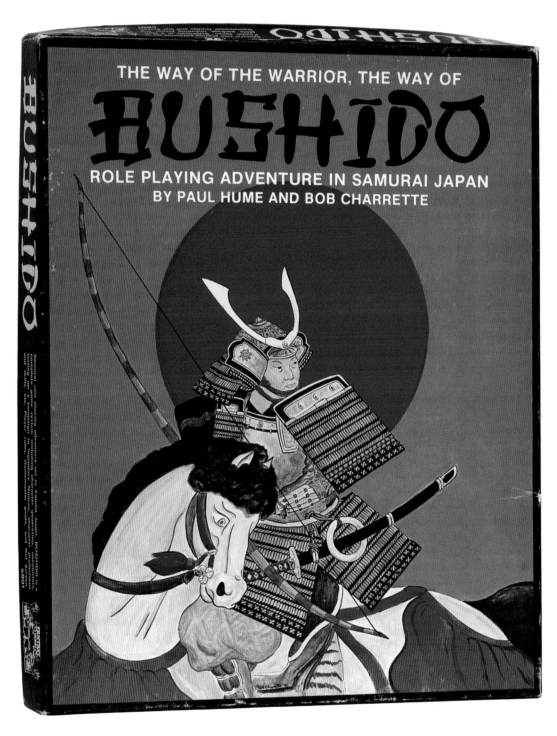

THE WAY OF THE WARRIOR, THE WAY OF
BUSHIDO
ROLE PLAYING ADVENTURE IN SAMURAI JAPAN
BY PAUL HUME AND BOB CHARRETTE

BUSHIDO, BOX SET, SECOND EDITION, FANTASY GAMES UNLIMITED, 1981
PAUL HUME AND BOB CHARRETTE, COVER BY BOB CHARRETTE

recognizes that characters must have a multitude of responsibilities outside of adventuring. It conveys these other activities with "downtime," a variable length of time between adventures during which characters train, study, find jobs, maintain property, potentially marry, and more. All of this social interaction and responsibility grounds the game in a way similar to *Chivalry & Sorcery* and gives characters a sense of greater responsibility beyond chopping up kappa or other critters.

In portraying these social responsibilities, *Bushido* becomes one of the earliest games whose mechanics attempt to both establish and enforce the game's theme, similar to the way *RuneQuest*'s mechanics express the game's world. And it works, despite some issues. Though originally published by Tyr Gamemakers Ltd., *Bushido* fits right in with Fantasy Games Unlimited's slate: The rules are complicated, unintuitively organized, and rough around the edges.

Bushido didn't receive much official support—a single 32-page adventure module, *Valley of the Mists* (1982), was all FGU ever released, which seems a shame for a game with such potential. It does appear to have a surprising legacy in Chaosium's *Pendragon*, a game that, through the use of honor, downtime, and social systems, elegantly marries mechanics, setting, and theme. This connection seems bolstered by the fact that the *Land of Ninja* setting (1987) for the third edition of *RuneQuest* was co-written by *Bushido* co-creator Bob Charrette and brings many of the early game's concepts to *RuneQuest*'s rules. In the years since, the idea of downtime as a mechanic has been embraced by many other games, particularly *Delta Green* and various indie titles.

VALLEY OF THE MISTS, FANTASY GAMES UNLIMITED, 1982. BOB CHARRETTE, COVER BY BOB CHARRETTE

Dark Tower (1979)

While TSR was putting out adventure modules that ran just 12 pages long, Judges Guild was going for distance. Of course, quantity doesn't mean quality: Judges Guild would soon have a dizzying 250 products in print, but to my eye only a small percentage of them rise above mediocrity. Jennell Jaquays's *Dark Tower* is one of the exceptions, a massive, 72-page masterpiece of the early era and her first design for Judges Guild as a full-time employee.

The module lays out a detailed history at the start, establishing a centuries-long struggle between two gods, focused on the region where the adventure takes place. The land was once holy to the good god Mitra—a tower honoring him was built, and a town of growing prosperity sprung up around it. Mitra's rival, the evil god Set, wasn't having it and, like a jerky neighbor, manifested his own tower right across from Mitra's. "The conflict between the two was patterned after the Conan story 'Red Nails,' in which two opposing factions are trapped (largely by their own choices) inside a restricted space to fight each other eternally," says Jaquays.

Calamity and murder between the faithful of both deities followed until a

DARK TOWER, JUDGES GUILD, 1979
JENNELL JAQUAYS, COVER BY JENNELL JAQUAYS

landslide buried everything. Treasure seekers came soon after, establishing a town of their own above their excavations, though they soon fell prey to Set's influence, forming an ageless, murderous cult hellbent on penetrating the secrets of Mitra's tower. Enter the players, hearing of treasure to be found and wanting to find it, who show up and get caught in events beyond their understanding.

This amount of background is unusual, but it sets up the atmosphere and the motivations of the NPCs. Those characters in the village and in the dungeons—and there are many—form a tangle of factions that are at odds with each other. Nearly all of them are quirky to a surprising degree—a bronze dragon polymorphed into a puppy, an evil halfling mage with a menagerie of monsters, a giant stone statue dressed in a ridiculous costume who collects belts. "One of the things I like most in adventures games is exploring and discovering new places," says Jaquays. "The other thing I really enjoy is creating interesting characters. I think both [*Dark Tower* and *Caverns of Thracia*] may have been an attempt to make adventures that felt more like stories than places to just kill monsters and grab their loot." There are many potential

stories here, but no painstakingly laid out plot. That only begins to emerge once the players create their own series of causes and effects that crash through the dominoes Jaquays has thoughtfully set up. The variety of potential player reactions to a giant statue demanding they take off their belts is right up near infinity, I think.

Below the village and between the towers (which consist of six levels each), there are four sprawling dungeon levels connecting all three. Jaquays says,

> The space in between the towers was conceived as being created by "later generations" who carved out spaces and passageways to fit their own needs. This is something that plays through many of my adventure designs. The idea that spaces are built by one person or faction for their purposes and then are converted or added to by subsequent residents. This is how the real-world functions. Game spaces, like real world spaces change owners and use over time. Those changes are either easily recognized by a casual viewer, or carefully hidden by those doing the later remodeling.

It's an elaborate piece of subterranean real estate, decidedly non-linear (both horizontally and vertically) and good for many sessions of play. If *Tegel Manor* and *Metamorphosis Alpha* sketched the outlines of what a mega-dungeon is, *Dark Tower* started filling in the details and establishing the tone. The whole space makes less sense than something designed with Gygaxian "naturalism" in mind, but it doesn't feel as nonsensical as a true funhouse dungeon.

There are these evocative details that imply a richly thought-out world—everyone and everything has a name, even entities that villains can summon, even lowly goblins—but then there are *Tomb of Horrors*-style traps with no basis in reality and villains who seem to do nothing but sit in locked rooms all day (the key to the locked door behind them is inevitably some of their blood or the dust of their bones, which might explain why they stay put). Jaquays makes liberal use of the invisibility spell—chests, gems, written words, walls, and plenty of other critical objects have been rendered unseeable. Meanwhile, illusions conceal important danger signs, such as the snake hair of a medusa (that's a real mean move, honestly). Teleportation is common, too, fouling up the expected traversal. Lots of tricks, lots of gotchas. It's a romp. Clever, compelling, and silly, it never lets players take it too seriously, but it also never ceases to be dangerous. And it is dangerous. Jaquays recommends a party of six to ten characters, ranging from 7th to 11th level.

In 1980, less than a year after the release of *Dark Tower*, *Legendary Duck Tower and Other Tales* hit shelves. While the cover obviously parodies the previous adventure, Jaquays and Rudy Kraft deliver an entirely new scenario inside that is just as complex as the original, but

for an entirely different system—Chaosium's *RuneQuest*.

Ducks, or, more properly, the Durulz, are a race of anthropomorphic ducks that live in *RuneQuest*'s world of Glorantha. As is clear from the cover of *Duck Tower*, they generally appear to have some kinship with Carl Barks's McDuck family. Ducks have also turned up in *Mutant: Year Zero* (2014) and *Symbaroum* (2016). Both of those games share a common ancestor in *Basic Roleplaying* (1980), which is a direct descendant of *RuneQuest*. Legend has it that Greg Stafford put the ducks in *RuneQuest* as a reminder not to take the game too seriously. Jaquays echoes this sentiment, saying, "I don't know why people hate ducks in games. Maybe they're the same people who think fantasy RPGs should be deadly serious." Jaquays and Kraft play the ducks straight; really, in a world that is flat, where some bulls have wings and fly the same skies as dragons, anthropomorphic ducks aren't any different from minotaurs.

Duck Tower is primarily a dungeon crawl in the same vein as *Dark Tower*, with a large, hundred-area complex to explore with flex-keyed encounters—the encounters were defined in the text, but it was up to the GM to place them within the ruin complex, a novel approach for the time. The adventure marked Jaquays's final contribution to Judges Guild as a full-time employee and was turned in unfinished, requiring Kraft's talents to polish it off, a sort of accidental collaboration. Considering the quality on display here, though, it's no surprise that Jaquays and Kraft's next collaboration—an intentional one—would be for Chaosium proper.

LEGENDARY DUCK TOWER, JUDGES GUILD, 1980. JENNELL JAQUAYS AND RUDY KRAFT, COVER BY JENNELL JAQUAYS

THE CAVERNS OF THRACIA, JUDGES GUILD, 1979
JENNELL JAQUAYS, COVER BY JENNELL JAQUAYS

The Caverns of Thracia (1979)

The Caverns of Thracia is another Jennell Jaquays effort for Judges Guild, penned after *Dark Tower*, but before *Duck Tower*. Where *Dark Tower* has a vaguely ancient Egyptian styling, *Caverns* takes on the trappings of ancient Greece. Despite this aesthetic difference, and the fact that *Caverns* was designed for the original *Dungeons & Dragons* system, rather than *AD&D*, the two modules have much in common.

The adventure sees the players discovering the lost city of Thracia, long since reduced to ruins. Beneath, though, some remnants lurk. The Thracians worshiped Thanatos, a personification of death, and their ritual spaces and tombs form the upper reaches of the complex. Beneath that is a large system of natural caves, ruled by the Minotaur King and populated by the descendants of the Thracian's beast men slaves—gnolls, dog brothers, and lizard people who revolted centuries ago. Beneath all of this lie traces of an older reptilian race—think the serpent people who menaced Robert E. Howard's King Kull in Atlantis—who originally inhabited the region and are not quite as extinct as anyone thinks. The caverns are only four levels, but several sub-levels and a variety of paths between them add to the intricacy. A number of spaces are surprising, like the artificially lit expanse of forest, complete with guardian dryads, in the subterranean depths of level three (inspired, perhaps, by C. L. Moore's classic sword and sorcery story "Black God's Kiss," which includes a similar underground wilderness).

Jaquays downplays the funhouse aspects of *Dark Tower*, opting for a more naturalistic approach. There are some strange encounters, like the spirit of death that stalks one area, appearing to characters with three hit points or less to entice them into a final embrace. There are also some living statues. But, by and large, the ecosystem here follows an inner logic that, if it doesn't make any real-world sense, at least feels plausible for a fantasy world.

The consequence of this constraint is that there are fewer zany tricks, and the factions are more difficult to parley with, making the whole thing seem more inclined toward a hack and slash affair, with characters steadily leveling up the deeper they go. The special attraction in *Caverns* is an intricate matrix of random encounter tables that move the inhabitants around the complex, often for specific reasons. This bustle adds to the feeling that these beast men and cultists live there.

There are still moments of weirdness, of course—oracular skulls, a teleportation chamber, a monster that is a door, a clear homage to Tolkien's Moria, and, my personal favorite, Room 102, "The Mysterious Missing Chamber," the entry for which reads, "Look as you might you will not find this room on the map. It never was there and exists only in the mind of the designer, who refuses to admit that she may have made an oversight when numbering her creation and doesn't feel like sticking the number '102' somewhere on the map and letting it go like that."

52

Room 102 captures something essential about the freewheeling production practices at Judges Guild. Jaquays says,

I was mostly freestyling. I let the project decide what it would become and how low it would be. Judges Guild also never really edited anything. The author's words went straight to typesetting. What you see in the printed works is pretty close to the prose I submitted to them. My manuscripts were typed on an electric typewriter on erasable onion-skin type typing paper. Final manuscripts were often cut and paste monstrosities of section of type glued or taped to a carrier sheet rather than reorganizing and retyping the entire document.

This is palpable when flipping through *Caverns of Thracia*, or any other Judges Guild product—they feel somehow precarious, as though they are the product of some barely-survived ordeal, much like the adventurers who make it through them, no doubt.

Along with *Snakepipe Hollow* (1979) and *The Keep on the Borderlands* (1979), *The Caverns of Thracia* share a set of surprisingly similar characteristics, and they represent a kind of culmination of adventure design in the '70s.

Perhaps most importantly, Jaquays's work, in general, and *The Caverns of Thracia,* in particular, are cornerstones of the Old School Revival (OSR) that began in 2004 with the release of Troll Lord Games' *Castles & Crusades*. This style of play started out favoring strange, often illogical environments that create situations to test the ingenuity of players, rather than the skills of their characters. Jaquays's intricate, non-linear spaces are the ideal venue for players to star in stories of their own making. The OSR community has embraced her design sense so thoroughly that Justin Alexander of the game design blog *The Alexandrian* has turned her last name into a verb—"jaquaying" is the act of creating a non-linear (and sometimes non-Euclidean) dungeon.

I find some of the most exciting ideas in the hobby are currently coming out of the OSR community, which has developed beyond merely embracing old styles of play into an increasingly experimental proving ground. Jaquays paved the way for that, though this fact surprises her. "These modules are over forty years old and still in print. That's rare in itself, for any form of media. I don't even consider them my best adventure work."

Cults of Prax (1979)

Cults of Prax is a book of deities, and since the *RuneQuest* system and the world of Glorantha are both intimately connected to the many religions contained within, it is one of the game's most important books. The plains of Prax are both a melting pot and the site of a clash of cultures on an epic scale, so the gods detailed in the book are a cross-section of deities found throughout Glorantha. Several pantheons—those of the native nomad tribes, the invading Lunar Empire, the neighboring Kingdom of Sartar, the city of Pavis, and more—all compete for influence in the region. Playing any edition of *RuneQuest* means getting to know the names of gods like Orlanth, Humakt, Storm Bull, the Seven Mothers, Lhankor Mhy, and Yelmalio very well.

Unlike *D&D*, which features endless deities but few doctrines that matter in terms of the game's mechanics, the cults are *RuneQuest*'s foundation. Most of the cults are set up like the Eleusinian Mysteries of ancient Greece, or similar belief systems in which the faithful are initiated into different levels of mystical secrets over time. Thus, membership in one or more Gloranthan cults acts as a sort of

RuneMasters, Chaosium, 1980
William R. Keyes, Cover by Luise Perrene

Cults of Prax, Chaosium, 1979
Steve Perrin and Greg Stafford, Cover by Steve Swenston

organic character class, bestowing magic and other abilities.

Because the magic and mythology of the cults are alive in the world, they serve a social function, as well as a spiritual one. Worshipers of Ernalda, the earth goddess, help ensure the health of the tribe's crops; priests of Chalana Arroy, the goddess of healing, keep the community healthy; the Storm Bull Spirit Society guards against infections of Chaos (whose own gods received their own sourcebook, *Cults of Terror*, in 1981).

A character's cult shapes their belief system and reflects their culture. As they rise in the ranks of the cult and accumulate more power, their responsibility to the cult, and their community, grows in proportion. So, while players seek the status and power of the rank of Rune Master, attaining it means their character will, for the most part, leave the path of the adventurer. In *D&D*, such a book would only be of use to Clerics and Paladins to expand the available spell list. In *RuneQuest*, religion *is* roleplaying—*Cults of Prax* is a handbook for how all characters (player and non-player) act, both with members of their own cults and outsiders. Learning these customs and how to navigate them is the soul of the game.

It is testament to the monumental

nature of the book that, even though it was originally released in 1979, it has yet to meet its match in depth and clarity. It is a foundational RPG text that breathes life into its core game.

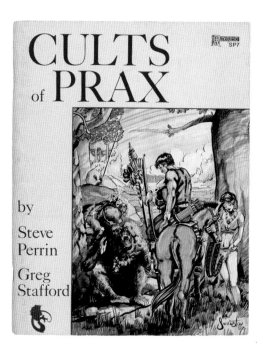

Cults of Prax, retroactively, is the first splatbook. The term came about on newsgroups dedicated to RPGs, specifically in regards to White Wolf's *World of Darkness* games. Each game in the line had a series of sourcebooks that fleshed out the game world: *Vampire: The Masquerade* (1991) had clanbooks, *Werewolf: The Apocalypse* (1992) had tribebooks, *Mage: The Ascension* (1993) had tradition books, and so on.

Since the asterisk serves as an open wildcard in search strings, newsgroups users collectively referred to these sourcebooks as "*books." And because asterisks sort of look like a squished bug or blood drops, or what have you, *book became splatbook. Often, flimsy paperbacks make a "splat" sound when flopped on a table. This etymology is convoluted and silly.

CULTS OF TERROR, CHAOSIUM, 1981
GREG STAFFORD AND DYERS HANDS; COVER BY JENNELL JAQUAYS

Though the terms came about for White Wolf's games in the '90s, *Cults of Prax* shows us that the format has been around for a while. The Player's Handbook Rules series of sourcebooks for *AD&D* Second Edition—*The Complete Fighter's Handbook* (1989), *The Complete Thief's Handbook* (1989), and on, fit the bill. They exemplify what a splatbook is: A sourcebook that is not required for play but expands on or develops a specific aspect of the game world—a character class, a school of magic, a species of monster, a priesthood—and the rules used to play it (an in-universe text isn't technically a splatbook, nor is a setting book, like *City State of the Invincible Overlord*).

Cults of Prax is the first book that fits, retroactively, the established definition. Depending on the player, splatbooks either contribute to the richness of RPGs, thanks to the bounty of options they provide, or are a killer of games, thanks to the unwieldy bloat that comes from having miles of supplemental rulebooks. For better or worse, they remain a staple of RPGs.

Journal of the Travellers' Aid Society (1979)

For the first couple of years of *Traveller*'s existence, Game Designers' Workshop focused on providing additional mechanical options for players—different classes, life path options, rules for building ships. These supplements were similar to toy boxes, giving folks ever more features to play with. That modular, toymaking approach started to change, slowly, in 1979, with *Supplement 3: The Spinward Marches*, which staked out a sector of the Third Imperium that would grow to be central to the game—something to play *in*.

That same year marked the debut of GDW's *Journal of the Travellers' Aid Society* (*JTAS*), a digest-sized quarterly magazine dedicated to all things *Traveller*. Three things of note happen in its pages that prove to be cutting edge developments in what would come to be known as metaplot.

Metaplots rise to prominence in the '80s with *Dragonlance* and become the main vehicle for RPG narratives for much of the '90s before falling from favor after

JOURNAL OF THE TRAVELLERS' AID SOCIETY #9, 181ST DAY OF THE 1107TH YEAR OF THE IMPERIUM, (SUMMER, 1981).
LOREN K. WISEMAN (EDITOR). COVER BY WILLIAM H. KEITH.

the turn of the millennium. Metaplots are narratives that push the story of the world forward independently of the stories that play out in individual adventure modules, and they are told across many different products.

Sometimes, players take part in portions of these larger stories, while other times the stories play out in the background. Sometimes, they make an RPG feel urgent and important, as though players are participating in something greater than themselves. Other times, metaplots drown agency, forcing players to spectate events that are important to the plot rather than to their characters. There are similarities between RPG metaplots and event stories in superhero comics—12-issue DC limited series, *Crisis on Infinite Earths* (1985) is a key example, radically altering the status quo of the shared DC comics universe with sweeping narrative developments, while the lead up to and fallout from that limited series rippled across all of the ongoing series at the time in smaller, more personal ways. The larger, season-spanning story arcs of shows like *The X-Files* (1993-2002) also arguably function as a kind of metaplot.

The first issue of *JTAS* introduces a small but important metaplot detail: The

dates. Rather than list the issue as Summer 1979, like a typical Earth publication, the date is given as 183-1105—the 183rd day of the 1105th year of the Third Imperium. This signals, despite all of the new material and mechanics for the game contained within, that the *Journal* is an in-universe artifact in some small but crucial way.

Issue two follows the dating convention, moving time in the fictional Third Imperium forward 91 days to correspond with the passage of time in the real world. This issue also introduces the regular "Traveller News Service" item, detailing notable events in the Imperium—this issue's brief involves a manufacturing deal in the Spinward Marches. It isn't epic, but just like that, every three months, the universe of *Traveller* is alive and developing in a way that no other RPG was even attempting.

In issue nine (181-1107, or Summer 1981), there is a major development. This issue's news report details the outbreak of war between the Duke of Regina and a new alien species, the Zhodani. Much of the issue is given over to fleshing out aspects of the conflict, which, in the near term, supported the release of *Fifth Frontier War* (1981), a complex wargame re-enacting the invasion. In the *Journal*, though, the war continues, as detailed in the quarterly news briefs, through 1984, wrapping up with an armistice just before the magazine ceased publication. The effects of the war are apparent all over Spinward Marches material for years.

The introduction of this sort of storytelling in *JTAS* is years before TSR would start to experiment with metaplot—the Fifth Frontier War ended as the War of the Lance began. Even later *D&D* metaplots, like the Time of Troubles for Forgotten Realms, feel clunky in comparison; TSR designers often put too much emphasis on the plot. Similar to *Pendragon*, which uses the whole of Arthurian legend as a kind of ongoing metaplot backdrop, the beauty of the Fifth Frontier War is that it plays out in the background of the game, independent of player action. Sometimes, it might crash into the lives of the player characters, but most of the time, it's just flavor that makes the Third Imperium feel like a thrilling place for players to seek their fortunes, however they wish. In that way, it's light years ahead of everyone else.

Dungeon Masters Guide (1979)

Advanced Dungeons & Dragons was born out of Gary Gygax's dissatisfaction with the original *Dungeons & Dragons*. He felt the older game was too free-form and that GMs were too inclined to improvise when making calls about ambiguous rules. The whole game lacked uniformity, a word that comes up frequently in Gygax's preface to the *Dungeon Masters Guide*. "[...] if *Advanced Dungeons & Dragons* is to survive and grow," says Gygax, "it must have some degree of uniformity, a familiarity of method and procedure from campaign to campaign within the whole." A bit further on, he continues:

> Returning again to the framework aspect of *Advanced Dungeons & Dragons*, what is aimed at is a 'universe' into which similar campaigns and parallel worlds can be placed. With certain uniformity of systems and 'laws,' players will be able to move from one campaign to another and know at least the elemental principles which govern the new milieu, for all milieux will have certain (but not necessarily the same) laws in common... This uniformity will help not only players, it will enable [game masters] to carry on a meaningful dialogue and exchange of useful information. It might also eventually lead to grand tournaments wherein persons from any part of the U.S., or the world for that matter, can compete for accolades.

How would he achieve this new, uniform play experience? With rules—lots and lots of them, for every situation that might come up. The more rules, the less chance some rogue GM might make something up on the spot that breaks the game, setting dangerous precedents for *D&D* games everywhere. And so, the *Dungeon Masters Guide* is, in a way, a code of law: A reference for a judge in need of precise information with which to make their rulings. Though the book is massive and features fairly small print, there are limits to how comprehensive 240 pages can be (especially with an incorrect index). The result is not a law library, but an idiosyncratic portrait of Gygax's priorities.

Much of the book makes sense. Clerics will likely need holy water, so there should be rules for how to make it. A lot of the book is odd, like this quote, which constitutes an entire section listed in the table of contents: "It is important for [game masters] to remember that in order to be reflective, a mirror must have a light source." Then there are the bizarrely secretive directives, stemming from Gygax's notion that the entirety of the book be concealed from players, as with the Assassin's class's ability to use poison. "When an assassin reaches 9th level [...] he or she may opt to make a study of poisons," says Gygax. "This decision should come from the player [...] do not suggest it or even intimate that such a study can be undertaken." Confusingly, though, going back to the *Players Handbook,* also written by Gygax, it plainly says Assassins can use poison and can even envenom their weapons without any implication of a level or training requirement (compounding this contradiction, elsewhere in the *Players Handbook*, Gygax also discusses how envenoming weapons isn't possible and cautions GMs against bending the laws of reality to allow it in their games). For a "uniform" game, *Advanced Dungeons & Dragons* sure seems like it's all over the place.

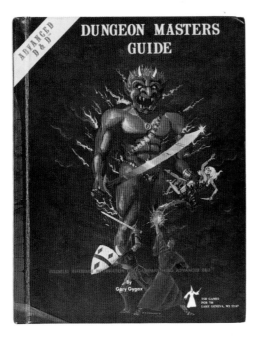

DUNGEON MASTERS GUIDE, TSR, 1979
GARY GYGAX, COVER BY DAVID C. SUTHERLAND III

Lawrence Schick, who became the director of TSR's design studio in January 1979, acted as Gygax's editor on the book. "When I walked in the door, Gary Gygax handed me a cardboard box that contained the typed manuscript for the *Dungeon Masters Guide*," says Schick. "He told me to edit it, organize it and write a few sections that he hadn't gotten around to finishing." In Gygax's preface, he remarks that the manuscript was 1,200 pages. It's a miracle the published book is as cohesive as it is. Even then, it wasn't nearly cohesive enough for some. In the industry gossip column, "A Letter From Gigi," published in Chaosium's *Different Worlds* (October/November 1979), the anonymous Gigi says, "The joke around here is that AD&D *DMs Guide* is what Hamlet was reading when Polonius asked, 'What are you reading, my lord?'" For those not up on their Shakespeare, Hamlet's baffled reply in the play is, "Words, words, words."

The real treasures are the appendices. Most of them form a toolbox of random tables and lists for encounters and for traps. The most robust is the dungeon generator, a descendant of Judges Guild's generation tables in products like *Wilderlands of High Fantasy*, that can be used

along with some dice to create an entire dungeon complex, spelling out room shapes, sizes, contents, and inhabitants. Another set of tables is full of dungeon set dressing. There's a brief guide to gambling and a list of "Herbs, Spices and Medicinal Vegetables." The most widely discussed is "Appendix N: Inspirational and Educational Reading," a collection of fiction that Gygax credits as providing the raw materials of imagination with which he built *Advanced Dungeons & Dragons*.

As with everything else in the *Dungeon Masters Guide*, "Appendix N" is somewhat puzzling. Some of what Gygax includes, like Fritz Leiber's Fafhrd and the Gray Mouser stories, have obvious connections to the sum and substance of *Dungeons & Dragons*. The influence of others, like science fiction, mystery, and horror author, Fredric Brown, remain obscure. Despite the fact that "Appendix N" is not an exact schematic of the primal source of *Dungeons & Dragons*, it created a canon that has taken on a life of its own. The list can be credited with saving some authors from obscurity, like Margaret St. Clair, whose chilling *The Shadow People* (1969) influenced Gygax's creation of the drow, and whose *Sign of the Labrys* (1963) laid out the template for what now might be recognized as a mega-dungeon.

The appendix also forms a sort of archetypal aesthetic for many other games that evolved out of the *D&D* tradition, as is the case with *Dungeon Crawl Classics* (2012), which enthusiastically embraces everything touched by Gygax. Even now, dog-eared vintage paperbacks of books that appear in "Appendix N" routinely fetch surprisingly high prices from collectors.

The *Dungeon Masters Guide* is strange and deeply idiosyncratic. Without a doubt, I believe it's also a masterpiece. Gygax expresses in it a singular vision that feels *true* in a way few other RPG books can ever hope to equal—it is an accidental portrait of the man's brain, circa 1978. Every subsequent edition of

D&D has a *Dungeon Master's Guide,* and every one of them is of dubious utility in comparison. Looking over his subsequent output, Gygax himself never reached this level of clarity again. It's as if he emptied himself out onto these pages.

D&D players get to take the role of all manner of warriors, wizards, elves, and more. But the *Dungeon Masters Guide* gives the GM everything they need in order to play the role of Gary Gygax while they're running their First Edition *AD&D* games, tucked behind their screen, leading their friends into adventure.

The Official Advanced Dungeons & Dragons Coloring Album (1979)

Dungeons & Dragons is the RPG that captured the broader public's imagination. It penetrated all aspects of popular culture—novels, toys, cartoons, movies—in a way that eclipses all other RPGs. That journey into the wider world began with, of all things, a coloring book.

The Official Advanced Dungeons & Dragons Coloring Album was published, not by TSR, but by Troubador Press, an offbeat publisher out of San Francisco. Troubador started printing greeting cards in the late '50s, but in 1967, founder Malcolm Whyte shifted to coloring books and eventually cookbooks, activity books, and art books. Whyte's interest in the underground comix scene (he'd go on to found San Francisco's Cartoon Art Museum in 1984) gave him a knack for pairing upcoming artists with unusual subject matter, resulting in an infusion of countercultural vibes into otherwise square books.

A prime example of Troubador's fusion is *Gorey Games.* In 1979, Larry Evans designed a children's activity book—mazes, word puzzles, hidden objects, matching games—using selections of the eccentric art of Edward Gorey, then best known for his set designs for the Frank Langella revival of the *Dracula* stage play (1977). Troubador's very next book was

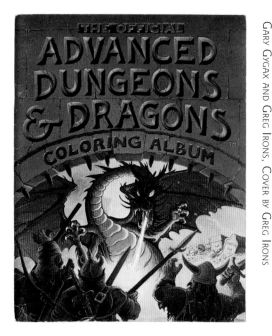

THE OFFICIAL ADVANCED DUNGEONS & DRAGONS COLORING ALBUM, TROUBADOR PRESS, 1979
GARY GYGAX AND GREG IRONS, COVER BY GREG IRONS

the *AD&D* coloring book, a marriage of counterculture and niche nerd culture.

The text of the coloring book is written by Gary Gygax and follows two threads. The first is the main story, which chronicles the jaunt of a group of adventurers through a dungeon. They encounter, among other things, a lich, an umber hulk, a beholder, several demons (including Demogorgon, now famous thanks to *Stranger Things*, 2016), and Tiamat, the queen of evil dragons herself. Several of the adventurers die. Tiamat is called the "Queen of Hell." This is a *children's coloring book*.

The interior illustrations are all done by tattooist and underground comix artist Greg Irons, who previously worked as an animator on the Beatles animated film, *Yellow Submarine.* The first time I saw his work, it left my jaw on the floor—it's intricate yet welcomingly cartoonish with a deep understanding of how the monsters look and what makes them cool to a degree that he outshines many of TSR's own artists of the period. His Tiamat illustration is like something out of Durer. A massive talent, he died too young, hit by a bus in 1984.

GOREY GAMES, TROUBADOR PRESS, 1979
EDWARD GOREY AND LARRY EVANS, COVER BY EDWARD GOREY

The secondary text, printed in installments at the bottom of every other page, is a streamlined, minimalist combat rule-set to be used in the simple dungeon crawl at the center of the book. A player (either alone or with friends) guides four adventurers through the dungeon, fighting monsters with two 6-sided dice while searching for the holy talisman of St. Cuthbert (roll a twelve after killing a monster means the talisman is in the lair!). Each character and all of the monsters have simple attributes and their own special abilities; there is even a scoring system if the mood is competitive. It plays fast and is surprisingly satisfying—I reckon it's the most straightforward game Gygax ever wrote. Except, it turns out that he didn't. While Gygax penned the book's main story, the creation of the game fell to TSR's head of design and development at the time, Lawrence Schick. Authorial confusion aside, along with *Tunnels & Trolls*, this is one of the earliest examples of a pared down RPG system.

There are a handful of products over the decades that capture imaginations and act as gateways into the high adventure of RPGs. Sometimes, as with the "Red Box" *Basic Set*, it's an actual RPG product. More often, it is something just adjacent

to RPGs, like the *Fighting Fantasy* gamebook or the *HeroQuest* board game, fronted with imagination-stoking art. For a person of the right age, in the right frame of mind, a product like that seems to answer a question they didn't know they were asking.

The *AD&D Coloring Album* was the first one of these gateways. When I posted about it on the Vintage RPG Instagram, I got a tidal wave of people messaging me with some variation of, "This got me into RPGs!" A friend of mine, who goes by the name of ZOG, got the coloring book at a garage sale in Minnesota when he was a kid. "On the surface, dragons and monsters and adventurers are low hanging fruit, but I always loved stories and the fact that *Dungeons & Dragons* clearly had some kind of storytelling element was very intriguing even to my young mind," he says. "I loved the map at the center of the book, I remember staring at it and imagining myself as one of the adventurers trying to navigate it." And that was it. He was hooked.

Snakepipe Hollow (1979)

Looking at all of Chaosium's *RuneQuest* material, the vast majority of it consists of source material, like *Cults of Prax,* or large campaigns, like *Borderlands* (1981). *Snakepipe Hollow* is one of only three books that are comparable to *Dungeons & Dragons'* adventure modules in size and format (the others being: *Apple Lane*, 1978, which was included in the second edition box set and *Balastor's Barracks*, 1978, which was a rather crude example in line with *Palace of the Vampire Queen* in terms of overall quality).

That Chaosium put out so few modules is surprising, because *Snakepipe Hollow* is one of the best designed adventures available at the time, even if the cover art of the first edition doesn't inspire much confidence. Speaking of, it is worth mentioning that this is one of only a handful of Chaosium products that received several reprints, a testament to its popularity, so seeing the different covers is a rare opportunity to chart the evolution of the company's design sense and increasing professionalism. It's also worth noting that I bought all of these second hand, so I am not Kalvan the Sinister, though part of me wishes I was.

The creature on the cover of the 1981 reprint bears a mention: It's called a walktapus. Within the context of Glorantha's lore, the creature makes a certain amount of sense: Chaos creates all sorts of abominations, so a bizarre fusion of human and octopus isn't out of the question. The walktapus is also hilarious. I find it hard not to be delighted by such a creature. This kind of nonsense makes early RPGs so wonderful. Conventions of fantasy games weren't so set in stone back then. Designers could get away with a lot more—*RuneQuest*'s ducks stand in testament to this, and there really is no shortage of silliness elsewhere in the hobby— just look at the Jack O'Bear on the cover of *Griffin Mountain* (see page 96). Beautifully, whether or not players take the walktapus seriously, it can mess up even the most experienced warriors, *badly*. That's perhaps the best part—players are

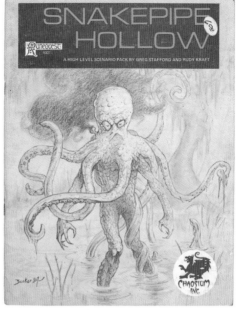

SNAKEPIPE HOLLOW, SECOND EDITION, CHAOSIUM, 1981
GREG STAFFORD AND RUDY KRAFT, COVER BY RICK BECKER

bound to underestimate a monster like this. The journey from silly to deadly is pretty representative of this era of the hobby.

In addition to octopus people, *Snakepipe Hollow* presents a wilderness region and cave system that was once the site of a temple dedicated to benevolent earth deities. In the time before time, a terrible clash between a demigod and a demon riding the Chaos Maggot turned the hollow into a place of horrors. This event is one that is central to the mythology of Glorantha. What begins as a standard dungeon crawl reveals this complex, still-living history to players, culminating in the deepest reaches where evidence of the battle—and the mother maggot itself—can still be found. Once the scenario is finished, players come away with a significant understanding of how Glorantha works and how they fit into a world where myth is real and ever-present. *Snakepipe Hollow* is an adventure, but it is also a teaching tool for future *RuneQuest* games. Few modern adventures can claim to transmit this much world lore to players while still providing a ripping fun time.

Snakepipe Hollow is a dynamic adventure for the time, with several entrances

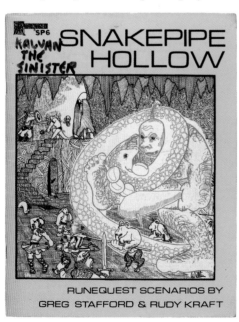

GREG STAFFORD AND RUDY KRAFT, COVER BY WILLIAM CHURCH
SNAKEPIPE HOLLOW, CHAOSIUM, 1979

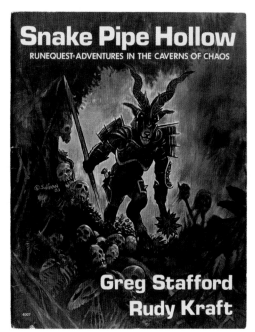

SNAKE PIPE HOLLOW, THIRD EDITION, CHAOSIUM, 1983
GREG STAFFORD AND RUDY KRAFT, COVER ART BY TOM SULLIVAN

and a tangle of possible routes inside—a feature likely springing from Kraft's previous collaboration with Jennell Jaquays. A good variety of creatures populate the hollow, each with their own needs and wants. Together, they form an unnatural ecosystem of sorts, one that makes sense within the fiction, instead of merely providing the illusion of sense, as is the case with many *D&D* modules.

The hollow has existed for centuries and hosted many inhabitants, all of whom have left their marks. It is possible for players to explore it and come to understand its past and current inhabitants, even playing some off against one another, in ways that are often impossible in other adventures. Even the elaborate factions of *Dark Tower* feel comic bookish in the face of the naturalism here. Perhaps most interesting, Stafford and Kraft took great pains to include a selection of plausible reasons for adventurers to visit the hollow, many on behalf of local inhabitants with a variety of agendas, many community-focused. These multiple hooks push against the assumption that exploration will be completed in a single expedition (and that self-enrichment is the only goal). *Snakepipe Hollow* is

meant to be visited multiple times, and to change with each visit. As one might expect from a place called the Caverns of Chaos.

B2: The Keep on the Borderlands (1979)

There were reportedly more than a million copies of *B2: The Keep on the Borderlands* printed; it was included in some printings of the 1977 *Basic Set* and all printings of the 1981 *Basic Set*. It's generally considered one of the best *Dungeons & Dragons* adventures, and despite being written for the *Basic D&D* system, it was used as part of the public playtest package for the Fifth Edition of *D&D* (the most recent descendant of *Advanced Dungeons & Dragons*) as a way to signal to players that the forthcoming game would hold true to its roots (whether it did or not is a matter of spirited debate).

The B-series of modules (B stands for Basic!) was conceived by TSR to reinforce the lessons of *Basic Set* rules, which, broadly, taught folks how to play *Dungeons & Dragons*, a topic broached in surprisingly few TSR publications. The first handful form a sort of core curriculum, introducing situations that require different applications of the rules. As a teaching tool, *Borderlands* is less effective than *B1: In Search of the Unknown*—it certainly lacks that module's odd preoccupation with fungus, which continues to manifest in *D&D* to this day—but it does contribute to the formation of a template for many adventures to come. The titular keep isn't the dungeon, it's the player's base of operations. The dungeon is the Caves of Chaos, an underground labyrinth of caverns populated by many different tribes of monstrous humanoids (and some undead, too, as well as the lizard people in the nearby swamp). The focus on the keep, rather than the caves, is important, as the caves are not meant to be explored in one go. Rather, like *Snakepipe Hollow*, *The Keep on the Bor-*

derlands expects players to make multiple expeditions, testing their opponents' capabilities and, ideally, turning the tribes against each other. This notion of a base of operations becomes more important as dungeons grow ever-larger and more dangerous.

By establishing all of the locations and factions in detail, *B2* lays out all of the dominoes, and the players get to knock them down (or not) in a way that they choose. This approach allows the story to proceed directly out of the actions of the players.

To someone who only played *Dungeons & Dragons*, *The Keep on the Borderland* might look like a massive step forward in terms of the sophistication of its design. In truth, though, *B2* seems to be a culmination of design experiments that were taking place in the industry at large—the massive size of *Tegel Manor*, the unexplored wilderness of *Metamorphosis Alpha*, the rival factions and non-linear spaces of Jennell Jaquays's work, even the naturalism of Gygax's previous G-series modules are all brought to bear here.

Snakepipe Hollow's subtitle is "Adventures in the Caverns of Chaos." Astute readers will note the similarity between that name and the Caves of Chaos, the name of the region of exploration in *The Keep on the Borderlands*. Jaquays's *The Caverns of Thracia* isn't quite so preoccupied with Chaos, but it is otherwise cut from the same cavernous cloth. Structurally, all three modules share similar environments: An untamed wilderness surrounding an elaborate and confusing system of interconnected caves populated by diverse monster tribes that are often at odds with each other. The clear contrast is in the naturalism. *B2*'s caves hew more towards Gygax's illusion of fidelity,

B2: The Keep on the Borderlands, TSR, 1979
Gary Gygax, Cover by Jim Roslof

whereas *Snakepipe Hollow* embraces a sturdier form of realism (as realistic as caves filled with monsters can ever be). *Thracia* sits somewhere in the middle.

This isn't to say that anyone was poaching anyone else, but rather to illustrate a moment of parallel innovation and that this sort of adventure was, perhaps, an inevitable destination for RPG design. A similar confluence would happen again in just a couple of years with all of the same players; there are clear similarities between *The Isle of Dread* for *Dungeons & Dragons* and the Jennell Jaquays's co-authored *Griffin Mountain* for *RuneQuest*. This sort of synchronicity has become rarer, though. From this point on, the patterns are more difficult to see, as more people play their first RPG, more designers join the industry, and ever stranger games hit shelves.

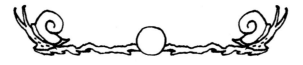

THE 1980s

*In which rapid expansion unleashes an explosion of new material.
Licensed intellectual property ensnares game designers,
and narrative-focused adventure reigns supreme.
Players delve into bustling cities and intricate worlds,
as lightweight rules emerge.*

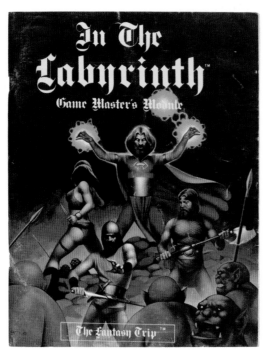

IN THE LABYRINTH, METAGAMING CONCEPTS, 1980
STEVE JACKSON. COVER BY ROGER STINE

In the Labyrinth (1980)

In retrospect, it seems inevitable that *Melee* and *Wizard* would evolve into a full-fledged RPG. That happened in 1980, when Metagaming Concepts released *Advanced Melee*, *Advanced Wizard*, *Tollenkar's Lair*, and *In the Labyrinth*. Together, they form what is known as *The Fantasy Trip RPG*, one of the most intriguing designs from the early days of RPGs.

In line with their titles, *Advanced Melee* and *Advanced Wizard* are vast expansions of the rules that appeared in the MicroGame format a few years earlier—and *Tollenkar's Lair* is a six-level dungeon for use with the game. *In the Labyrinth* charts new territory for *The Fantasy Trip*, serving primarily as the game master's book, with guidance on world building, advice on running adventures, a section on monsters, and rules for character creation, all packed into an 80-page booklet, which indicates a lot about the lightness of the system (especially when compared to the more labyrinthine *Dungeon Masters Guide*, which runs 240 pages).

In the introduction, Steve Jackson says, "*The Fantasy Trip* is not the first role-playing game to be published, but we feel it is the most detailed and playable one yet to appear." I find it hard to disagree! It isn't nearly as approachable as, say, *Tunnels & Trolls*, but it is far more precise and streamlined than *Dungeons & Dragons*, though there is a requisite tolerance for tactics. Even then, the tactical element is playable rather than tedious—*In the Labyrinth*'s slimness didn't give Jackson the room to ramble, so the proceedings are pleasantly concise.

The main innovation here is the introduction of talents, which are skills and special abilities. Both spells and talents are purchased using a pool of points derived from the character's IQ attribute. Wizards and heroes (that is, every character who is not a wizard) have access to both, but wizards can buy talents at double the cost while heroes spend three points to the wizard's one when buying spells. Expanding on its use in *Melee* and *Wizard* for attributes, this arrangement makes *The Fantasy Trip* the first RPG to use a point-buy skill system.

Point-buy allows players direct, fine-grain control over how their character is created and developed over time, adjusting their skills based on what seems important or interesting, rather than having to abide by the strictures of an abstract character class. Want a wizard to swing a sword (like Gandalf), or a warrior who can pick pockets (like Fafhrd)? Want to experiment with a set of skills entirely unlike the established fantasy archetypes? Spend the points!

Jackson's prose is practical and plain-spoken, laying out rules in clear language. He often includes snippets of advice that are rooted in practical theory, like in the entry for "Nuisance Encounters," which are defined as creatures that are not threatening to a healthy group, but might be deadly for a lone adventurer or a group of wounded ones: "The possibility of a nuisance encounter will keep parties from taking safety for granted under any circumstances." Details on a village and a wilderness area round out the guidance. The result is a flexible and intuitive system filled with promise.

The release of *The Fantasy Trip* was eagerly awaited. The buzz can be charted in "A Letter from Gigi," an industry gossip column running in Chaosium's *Different Worlds* magazine. In the June/July 1979 issue, word was that the game could release as a deluxe $30 dollar box set (the equivalent of $117 dollars in 2022!). The following month, Gigi shared speculation that the box set was scaled back to a $20 dollar version (still a hefty sum in 2022 at $78 dollars). Then, in the December/January issue, news came that the game would be issued as four separate booklets at five bucks a pop.

The price for all four wound up amounting to even less at $18, which suited Howard Thompson, Metagaming's owner, well enough—his aim had always been to produce uncomplicated, inexpensive games. The lack of a central release made the game modular, which also benefitted Thompson. Instead of increasing the options available to players, though, the modular release made the game confusing and convoluted. While the color of the titles of the three core rulebooks changed, *In the Labyrinth*, *Advanced Melee,* and *Advanced Wizard* all had identical cover art. As much as I love the groovy disco energy of Roger Stine's figure poses, using the same art on all three books makes telling them apart difficult. Meanwhile, aside from the same typesetting, the yellow and black cover of *Tollenkar's Lair* makes it look like an unrelated product. Taken together, they feel like the contents of a box set, but without the benefit of the actual box.

Complicating matters, Metagaming advertised that *Tollenkar's Lair* could be played using either the advanced rules or the older MicroGame versions of *Melee*

TOLLENKAR'S LAIR, METAGAMING CONCEPTS, 1980
STEVE JACKSON, COVER BY ROBERT PHILLIPS

and *Wizard*. Another line, MicroQuests, launched at the same time, also apparently compatible with both versions of *The Fantasy Trip*. Despite all of this potential confusion, *The Fantasy Trip* was well-received and immediately joined *D&D* and *RuneQuest* as one of the most popular RPGs on the market. Unfortunately, it was undone by bad business practices.

Thompson and Jackson had already been at odds. Thompson thought the game was ultimately too complex and had taken too long to develop. Jackson was upset by the modular release and the fact that he had been cut out of the proofing process. Soon after, Jackson left the company. He bought Metagaming's magazine, *The Space Gamer* and tried to buy the rights to *The Fantasy Trip*, but Thompson wanted more money than Jackson was willing to pay. Lawsuits were filed by both parties over other products. Metagaming released additional *Fantasy Trip* material, but did so erratically, and many announced titles, including science fiction and superhero versions, never surfaced. Not long after the lawsuits were settled, Metagaming closed, and Thompson left the tabletop industry entirely.

The Fantasy Trip was dead, but the point-buy system was here to stay. The superhero RPG *Champions* would use a similar system to great effect, but it was Steve Jackson who, despite losing the rights to *The Fantasy Trip*, used its basic framework to create what is arguably his magnum opus: The *Generic Universal Roleplaying System*, or *GURPS*. And, proving that nothing in RPGs is ever truly dead, Jackson reclaimed the rights to *The Fantasy Trip* in 2017, using a quirk of U.S. copyright law, allowing him to Kickstart a new version of the game in 2018 that reflected his original vision (and, finally, it comes in a box set).

S3: Expedition to the Barrier Peaks (1980)

For as much as *Dungeons & Dragons* asserts a sort of generic fantasy standard, there are many *D&D* modules that subvert that standard, especially in the early days. Few, though, are in the same league as *S3: Expedition to the Barrier Peaks*. Fewer still have gotten stranger with age, but with the gulf between fantasy and science fiction widening in the decades since, the fusion of the two in *Barrier Peaks* might look mighty odd to contemporary audiences. Magic spells and blaster rifles in the same game? Madness!

The trend toward this kind of plausibility in fantasy is arguably thanks to the influence of *D&D* and other RPGs, the mechanical systems of which naturally codify things in the service of play— Steven Erikson and Ian C. Esslemont's *Malazan Book of the Fallen* series spin out of a long-running campaign begun in *D&D* and continued in *GURPS*, for instance. Yet, this codification is simultaneously ironic, because *D&D* was born out of genre fiction traditions that generally shrugged at distinctions between sci-fi and fantasy. A look at "Appendix N" of the *Dungeon Masters Guide* reveals there is no shortage of science. The fact that there isn't information on ray guns in the core *D&D* books is

probably stranger than the idea of freely mixing elements of sci-fi and fantasy in a *D&D* adventure.

Barrier Peaks is the proof. The adventure was originally run at Origins II in 1976, just two years after the emergence of *D&D*. Gygax wrote it to introduce science fiction elements into *D&D* and to generally support *Metamorphosis Alpha* (described by critic Rick Swan as "*D&D* in space"), which was shown off at the same expo.

Barrier Peaks involves a crashed generation ship that is suspiciously similar to *The Warden* from *Metamorphosis Alpha*. The ship's human population is long dead, but the menagerie of alien creatures escaped stasis, and some have flourished in the mountains of Greyhawk (I reckon that this crashed spaceship is far and away the most exciting thing to ever happen in Greyhawk, outmatching decades of published campaign material without breaking a sweat). When the players arrive to investigate the recent attacks by strange creatures at the nearby human settlements, the crash site is completely covered by a landslide and appears, initially, to be nothing more than a natural cave system. Once inside, the truth rapidly becomes clear, though a

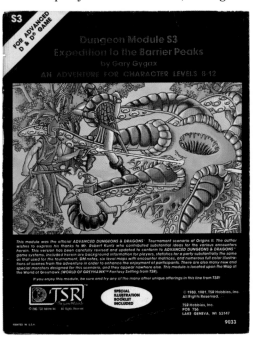

S3: EXPEDITION TO THE BARRIER PEAKS, TSR, 1980
GARY GYGAX, COVER BY EROL OTUS

clever GM can, with careful descriptions, leave players unsure as to whether they are dealing with high magic or high technology, for a while, anyway. In 1976, around the table at a convention using only the theater of the mind, the mystery could probably last indefinitely and GMs wouldn't have to worry too much about having the surprise spoiled. 40-something years later, *Expedition to the Barrier Peaks* isn't exactly a well-kept secret anymore. Even the cover of the 1980 module, which shows a warrior aiming a laser pistol at a Starro clone, gives away the gag.

The published module also includes an art booklet that, like *Tomb of Horrors*, uses illustrations to depict key features of the environment, though this one is far more luxurious. They showcase an all-star roster of artists—primarily Erol Otus, who is joined by Jim Rosloff, Diesel LaForce, Jeff Dee, David C. Sutherland III, and Greg Fleming. It even features four full-color plates, a feat unheard of elsewhere in the industry until later in the decade. The variety of art adds to the vividness of the proceedings, particularly in regards to the monsters. Many of these are new and strange, like the plant people known as vegepygmies, or the wolf-in-sheep's-clothing, a bizarre carnivorous plant that appears, initially, as a cute bunny rabbit sitting on a tree stump. Some are old friends, repurposed into the role of extraterrestrial threats, like the eye of the deep and the mind flayer, who sports an outfit worthy of *Star Wars*, instead of the traditional high-collared robes (interestingly, mind flayers would return to space nine years later in the *Spelljammer* campaign setting). The crown jewel, though, is Erol Otus's froghemoth, the epitome of a B-movie bug-eyed monster, both terrifying (it can swallow people whole!) and hilarious.

The illustration booklet also gives away the spaceship mystery. The fifth illustration is clearly a robot, so the scenario shifts gears, obfuscating details the play-ers would reflexively understand in service of mystifying their characters. The cruelest examples are the guns—some of which fire out of what looks like the back end, some of which look like flat screen televisions—all of which are designed to punish players for trying to interpret the game world with the aid of their real-world knowledge. Using modified versions of *Gamma World*'s item purpose flow charts to discover the proper use of technology further impedes players.

Taken in sum, the invasion of science fiction in *Expedition to the Barrier Peaks* seems like an invitation. If Gygax, who was so often interested in *D&D*'s uniformity, can flip the script with robots and lasers and generally embrace this silly romp for what it is, imagine what typical players can do with *Dungeons & Dragons*: Anything they want.

Greyhawk (1980)

There are several Greyhawks. The first was Gary Gygax's own, created in 1972 as a proving ground for his ideas for *Dungeons & Dragons* and as a funhouse for his kids and friends. This Greyhawk wasn't a world, really, but rather a ruined castle with dungeons so deep and deadly they seemed like a world unto themselves: 13 levels of adventure! If a wider world of Greyhawk existed beyond those dangerous halls, it was only vaguely sketched—an implication of a world.

The second Greyhawk was similar, a mirror image of the massive castle, designed by Rob Kuntz in 1972 so Gygax had a place to play. Even in the '70s, these mega-dungeons, glimpsed in tantalizing tidbits through articles written by Gygax and Kuntz for various gaming magazines, were already the stuff of rumor and legend. People wanted to know *more*.

Gygax was hesitant to oblige. After all, the two Greyhawks were *his*. To publish either of them would mean divulging his secrets to his own players, or having the mysteries of Kuntz's dungeon spoiled for

THE WORLD OF GREYHAWK, TSR, 1980
GARY GYGAX. COVER BY DAVID C. SUTHERLAND III

himself. *Supplement I: Greyhawk* (1975), the first rules expansion for *Dungeons & Dragons*, was fully a dodge—there is nearly no mention of Gygax's world or dungeon among all of the new rules. References to Castle Greyhawk appear in the book just twice: A fountain that spawns endless snakes and a crude drawing of a statue resembling a Moai of Easter Island situated in what looks like a sewer. The caption reads, "The Great Stone Face, Enigma of Greyhawk." No other information is given.

In 1980, perhaps finally conceding that Judges Guild was on to something with their *Wilderlands* setting, TSR published *The World of Greyhawk,* a folio containing a short 32-page gazetteer and a massive 34 by 44-inch map spread across two sheets. Rather than reveal his secrets, Gygax created an alternate universe Greyhawk, similar to, but distinct from, his homebrew campaign world, and a bit vague. Castle Greyhawk gets a brief mention, but mostly, the book is concerned with the various countries, their leaders, a bit of world history, and weather—Gygax was strangely preoccupied with Greyhawk's weather patterns, both here and in

other writings. Jokey references to friends and family (Perrenland, for example, refers to Jeff Perren, who co-authored *Chainmail* with Gygax) makes me doubt Gygax was taking the project entirely seriously. There is a sense that the intent is to provide players with a toolkit they can use to make their own world, but Gygax also seems to be holding back, as though he remains unconvinced that his audience wanted reams of details (they did).

Lawrence Schick, in a brief editorial in *Dragon* magazine (February, 1981) responding to critical reactions to *The World of Greyhawk,* confirms that this lack of detail was Gygax's intent, saying, "[...] it was made deliberately vague in many areas so that individual [GMs] could impress their own ideas and personalities upon it." This results in a world that feels a bit beige. How could it be anything but? The legend of Castle Greyhawk lived unbound in the imagination of players who had spent the last handful of years reading about the truly exciting locales of the world of Greyhawk in *D&D*'s adventure modules. Blurbs on nations, even those populated by villains and evil powers, weren't going to measure up against tombs of horror or vaults of drow.

If one thing from the folio is fixed in the annals of RPGs, it is Darlene Pekul's map. In many ways, it is preposterous—it is immediately obvious that geography just doesn't look like this, but it also isn't worth caring about that sort of accuracy. If I wanted realistic geography, I wouldn't be playing fantasy adventure games. The drawings of the mountains and forests, the repetition of the hexes, the bold bright colors all conspire to create something entrancing. The Greyhawk of that map begs to be explored. It's a shame the gazetteer, and most of the rest of TSR's Greyhawk material, never measured up to that potential.

The World of Greyhawk was expanded into a box set in 1983. It included the much-requested information on the unique deities of Greyhawk. There is also a chapter on trees. That's about it for the third incarnation of Greyhawk. Less than two years after the *World of Greyhawk* box set hit shelves, Gygax was forced out of the company he founded, never to return. Greyhawk went dormant as TSR shifted its focus to concentrate on developing Forgotten Realms as its prime real estate. The last product under the World of Greyhawk banner was *Castle Greyhawk* (1988), which, despite the name, was not the long-awaited mega-dungeon, but rather an elaborate, 13-level parody, filled with villains, like Colonel Sanders, and locations, like Otto's Irresistible Dance Studio. As the back cover exclaims, "The common theme of this dungeon is that no joke is so old, no pun so bad, and no schtick is so obvious that it can't be used to confuse and trip up the PCs!"

The book sinks to that occasion at every opportunity with gusto. Though some fans theorize that the project was conceived by TSR executives as a way to tarnish the departed Gygax's legacy, I remain unconvinced. The book is full of talented freelancers with no obvious axes to grind, and two years seems a long time to wait to execute a character assassination. Still, folks who were waiting to glimpse the legendary dungeon of Castle Greyhawk were not at all amused—the book still routinely appears on lists of the worst *D&D* adventures. The rumors seem more a manifestation of that disappointment than a real controversy—that would explain why no one seems to have any concrete details on the plot, at least.

The fourth Greyhawk belongs, largely, to designer and parapsychologist Carl Sargent. The revival started in 1988, with the hardcover introductory book, *Greyhawk Adventures,* by James M. Ward—Jeff Easley's cover art, with its musclebound griffon rider, always seemed, to me, more

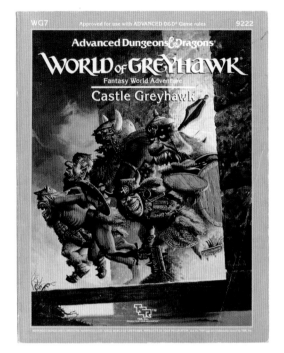

WG7: Castle Greyhawk, TSR, 1988
Dyvers Hands, Cover by Keith Parkinson

in line with *He-Man and the Masters of the Universe* than Greyhawk. Sargent, along with designers Douglas Niles and Rik Rose, retooled the titular free city in *The City of Greyhawk* (1989), a box set that coincided with the release of the Second Edition of *Advanced Dungeons & Dragons* and served as a foundation for a new, forthcoming metaplot.

The box set is long on detail but still short on the excitement found in *Spelljammer: Adventures in Space*, which released around the same time. This version of Greyhawk received five adventures before the new metaplot kicked in, with the two modules leading up to the *Greyhawk Wars* (*Wars*) box set (1991). One of many attempts to fold wargaming back into the *Dungeons & Dragons* experience, *Wars* introduced a new narrative paradigm into Greyhawk. During Gygax's time, the world was on a knife point, with the forces of good and evil locked into a pitched but ultimately uncertain struggle. The fallout from *Wars* tips the balance of power in favor of the forces of evil.

The new status quo was laid out in *From the Ashes* (1992). Evil triumphed and dominates the land. Original Greyhawk

FROM THE ASHES, BOX SET, TSR, 1992
CARL SARGENT. COVER BY JEFF EASLEY

fans tend to hate this period, as it delivers none of the promise of the unreleased Gygax work and reflects little of the disappointing, but by now beloved, material that *had* been released. Long time players have expressed a degree of shock at the betrayal of two mages—Rary and Robilar—who murder two of their fellows—Tenser and Otiluke—in service of the machination of the evil demi-god Iuz. On the other hand, folks who had only recently awakened to RPGs in the late '80s and early '90s, and had no particular attachment to those hoary old NPCs, tend to be more enthusiastic. For me, one of those early '90s players, this is the first time Greyhawk truly feels interesting and energetic as a setting—finally, something was *happening*!

Like so many lines stewarded by TSR, only a handful of products emerged to support the *From the Ashes*-era of Greyhawk before the line was canceled in 1994. Designer Roger E. Moore revived Greyhawk again in 1998, its fifth incarnation, this time under the new owners of all things *Dungeons & Dragons*, Wizards of the Coast. *Greyhawk: The Adventure Begins* is a reset button, restoring the world to the era before *From the Ashes*

(even returning poor Tenser to life). A sixth incarnation emerged in 2001 as a living campaign—a massive, shared, centrally administrated world—for the Third Edition of *Dungeons & Dragons*. Because so much of the material created to support such a massive undertaking was done by volunteers, most of *Living Greyhawk* is considered non-canon. With the launch of the Fourth Edition of *D&D* in 2008, *Living Greyhawk* shuttered, and official Greyhawk material has been scarce ever since.

One more Greyhawk, a seventh, unofficial one, exists. In 1990, during the *Greyhawk Adventures* period, TSR attempted to correct the mistake that was *Castle Greyhawk* with *Greyhawk Ruins*, a serious attempt at constructing a mega-dungeon that fulfilled the requirements of the legend, though it was an original design by Blake Mobley and Timothy B. Brown. Players mostly passed it over. The material was revised and expanded by Wizards of the Coast towards the end of the Third Edition's lifespan, publishing it as *Expedition to the Ruins of Greyhawk* (2007). It was well received as an exercise in nostalgia, but it was overshadowed by legend once again.

In 2003, Gary Gygax announced he was working with Rob Kuntz to produce his original castle and the city design in six volumes under the name Castle Zagyg for use with Troll Lord Games' *Castles & Crusades*. This was to be a massive undertaking, since neither the original city nor the castle was ever finished in any way that was publishable. This makes sense to anyone who has ever written up a dungeon for their ongoing game—my notes never look anything like published adventures, and I'm a professional writer who is uptight about formatting. In the early '70s, Gygax was creating a dungeon level every week or so, and I am sure his notes for at least some were hastily scrawled, if they weren't entirely improvised during the session.

In the end, this new castle was to be a fusion of both Gygax's and Kuntz's separate ruins. And even then, it was left incomplete. In 2004, Gygax had two debilitating strokes. In 2005, Troll Lord Games released *Castle Zagyg: Yggsburgh*, a 256-page treatment of the city, complete with a two-part, fold-out map by Darlene Pekul. It was followed in 2008 by *Castle Zagyg: The Upper Works*, which detailed the above ground portion of the ruins. But, in March of 2008, Gygax died, and his estate fell silent. No more volumes have emerged, once again leaving players to wonder what lurks in those depths.

Dallas: The Television Role-Playing Game (1980)

Despite the many innovations to come, *Dallas: The Television Role-Playing Game* epitomizes a large swath of RPGs that emerged in the 1980s. Up to this point, RPGs were new creations. They weren't necessarily *original*—the vast majority are pastiches that wear their influences on their sleeves, imitating favorite stories, as in the way *Bunnies & Burrows* is an obvious homage to *Watership Down* without actually being *Watership Down*. Over the course of the '80s, licensed games—those based directly on intellectual property from other media—became a key way to make money in the industry. They're everywhere, even when it isn't obvious, as is the case with *Call of Cthulhu*.

Dallas was the first licensed RPG of note. Heritage Models had created a couple of licensed RPGs to support lines of miniatures—*John Carter, Warlord of Mars* (1978) and *Star Trek: Adventure Gaming in the Final Frontier* (1978)—though the systems were rudimentary and neither got much notice. The Barsoom stories were moldy old pulps, 40-years old and already picked over by more successful imitators. The original *Star Trek* series, meanwhile, gained popularity in syndication, even developing a

hardcore cult following, but re-runs are still re-runs. *Dallas*, on the other hand, was a whole different order of magnitude.

A prime-time soap opera revolving around the feuds and fortunes of the Ewing family and their Texas oil company, the TV show debuted in the spring of 1978 as a mini-series and exploded into a 14-season pop culture juggernaut. In the spring of 1980, the show's third season ended on one of the greatest cliffhangers of all time, in which J.R. Ewing (the grinning snake at the center of the show, portrayed by Larry Hagman and seen prominently on the RPG's box cover) was shot by an unknown assailant. People went crazy for it, whipping up an eight-month media frenzy speculating over "Who shot J.R.?"

Hagman, in true J.R. fashion, used the intense public interest as leverage to renegotiate his contract, tripling his per-episode pay from $25,000 dollars to $75,000 dollars. When meeting Hagman at a charity gala, Queen Mother Elizabeth of the United Kingdom said of the mystery, "I won't ask you," which seems to imply she wouldn't have minded if Hagman volunteered the culprit. He demurred. At one point, the script for the episode that revealed the shooter was even stolen. "Who Done It," the episode that resolved the cliffhanger, aired on November 21, 1980, and drew an estimated audience of around 90 million viewers, 76% of all TV viewers in the United States—potentially more people than voted in the Reagan/Carter presidential election earlier in the month. That made it the highest rated single broadcast in U.S. history, until the final episode of *M*A*S*H* took the title in 1983. *Dallas* remains in the number two spot to this day and, in 1980, it was a legitimate phenomenon.

SPI was founded in 1969 and specialized in wargames, though it was always behind Avalon Hill, the company that routinely dominated the hobby. SPI saw the emerging popularity of RPGs and wanted in, producing *DragonQuest* (1980)

DALLAS: THE TELEVISION ROLE-PLAYING GAME, BOX SET, SIMULATIONS PUBLICATIONS, INC., 1980
JAMES F. DUNNIGAN

to compete with *Dungeons & Dragons* and developing *Universe* (1981) to go up against *Traveller*. With *Dallas*, SPI saw a lucrative opportunity to bring RPGs to a wider, mainstream audience and, at the same time, solve the company's chronic cash flow problem.

The game was designed by James F. Dunnigan, a well-regarded wargame designer, military historian, and the founder of SPI. Dunnigan delivered a unique, approachable game that is true to the spirit of the television show. The Director (the GM) sets individual scenes, after which a negotiation phase allows the players, in the roles of their preferred characters from the show, to jockey for advantage using threats and diplomacy. Once a suitable number of ultimatums have been issued, players use their attributes—Persuasion, Coercion, Seduction, and so on—to attempt to make good on those demands, gain control of other characters and organizations, and generally move toward their personal pre-determined victory requirements.

The mechanics are simple by early RPG standards, if inelegant, but probably too complicated at a glance for general audi-

ences circa 1980. A good comparison can be made with TSR's massively successful *All My Children* board game, 1985, which hewed close to the *Candyland* school of game design. The game also assumes all nine characters are in play during any given scenario, which seems like a big group for a family game, while the cut-throat nature of play also seems at odds with the vibe of family game night. Come on, Gran, let's break out *Dallas*, we'll accuse Mom of being a prostitute and sell Dad out to the feds!

Still, even with the clunky math and the mixed messages, playing the game properly delivers an experience not unlike the events of an episode of *Dallas*. For RPGs in 1980, this focus on emergent narratives is really different and exciting—competitive troupe play, whereby acting out roles (rather than swordplay) was the path to victory, is *still* rare in the hobby. There was nothing else remotely like it on the market. The closest cousin might be dinner party games, like *How to Host a Murder*, which debuted a few years later in 1983. It would be some years before similar ideas returned to RPGs, perhaps first with *Ars Magica*, (1987) and growing into the indie storytelling games in the 2000s.

The reason this style of play nearly became a dead end, of course, is because *Dallas: The Television Role-Playing Game* was a massive failure, one of the biggest in the history of RPGs. Despite releasing during the autumn of "Who Shot J.R.?" and at the height of the show's popularity, RPGs were still too strange and too new for the mass market to embrace in 1980. SPI's established audience of wargamers "widely loathed" the game, according to Lawrence Schick in *Heroic Worlds*, and most established roleplayers were so preoccupied with their various genres of adventure games they never even noticed it. SPI's creative director, the late Redmond Simonsen, told Usenet in 1988 that the company printed 80,000 copies. "That was about 79,999 more than anyone wanted. Anyone who is wired on *Dallas* (the TV show) is not also wired on games." Forty years later, the box set can regularly be found, still in the original shrink-wrap.

It has been speculated that *Dallas* dealt SPI a mortal blow. Simonsen disputed that, saying whether or not the game killed the company is beside the point; the important fact is that *Dallas* failed to save the company. That failure also closed off, for a time, an avenue of potential for approachable games that appealed to folks uninterested in swords and laser guns. But it didn't kill the interest in licenses, not by a long shot.

Deities & Demigods (1980)

Back in 1976, TSR published *Gods, Demi-Gods & Heroes*, by Rob Kuntz and James M. Ward. It was the fourth, and purportedly final, supplement for *Dungeons & Dragons*, and aimed to give game masters the tools to incorporate aspects of mythology into their games.

When the *Advanced Dungeons & Dragons* line came around, Ward and Kuntz got to work on a new version: *Deities & Demigods*. The book expresses mythology in terms of *D&D* mechanics, for the gods, monsters, heroes, and artifacts that populate 12 real-world pantheons, from King Arthur's knights to the gods of Olympus. The idea was to give a broad selection of traditions and serve them up to players as examples, so they had guidance for how to create their own—not just a single deity or legendary hero, but a whole web of homegrown mythological stories.

In addition, Ward included three fictional pantheons, derived from Fritz Leiber's Fafhrd and the Gray Mouser stories, H. P. Lovecraft's Cthulhu Mythos, and Michael Moorcock's Elric saga, though these last two were later excised. Rounding the book out were the gods Ward himself created for the various nonhuman creatures that populate the *Monster Manual*, which are perhaps his most beloved and farthest-reaching contribution to *Dungeons & Dragons*. Taken together, these pantheons paint a vivid picture of *D&D*'s understanding and presentation of the divine.

No other *D&D* book has quite the reputation of *Deities and Demigods*. When I first encountered a copy in the late '80s, it was accompanied by the story breathlessly told of how there used to be more pantheons included, but they'd been *removed*. This occurred after the height of the Satanic Panic, but *D&D* still carried a hint of unseemly doings, so the idea of an actual forbidden book was just too delicious. It was made all the more scrumptious when I later learned that Cthulhu and friends were among the disappeared, given that so many of Lovecraft's stories featured mysterious books.

Also exciting was the fact that, owing to youth, the lack of an internet, and the complete ignorance of the existence of RPGs beyond *D&D*, no one had a good explanation as to why the material was cut in the first place. Rumors, spread through word of mouth and probably entirely made up, dominated all conversation about the book, in print, at conventions, in gaming shops, among friends— surely, TSR had done something *evil*, or at least something controversial enough that the people who already thought *D&D* was evil managed to get TSR to censor themselves (and, according to some variant, recall or otherwise ban the original printing). It's no wonder that hunting for a complete first edition of *Deities & Demigods* became my first real RPG-collecting quest. And it wasn't just me: It remains one of the most sought-after RPG books (somewhat erroneously—the book was never recalled, contrary to rumor, and a large number of the first and second printings are out there).

When I was in high school, during the Second Edition years, I started to hear a different narrative, based on the fact that TSR sometimes engaged in questionable

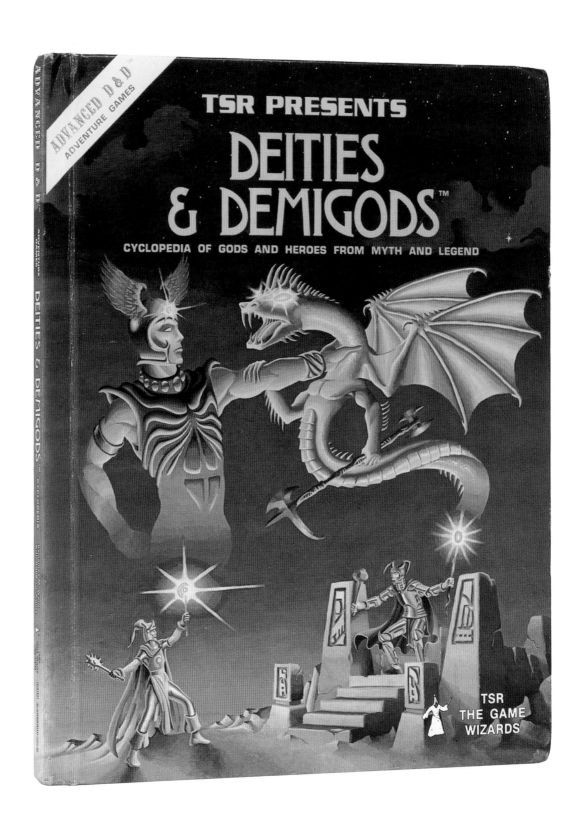

DEITIES & DEMIGODS, TSR, 1980
JAMES M. WARD WITH ROBERT J. KUNTZ, COVER BY EROL OTUS

or predatory business practices. This version of the story goes something like: TSR stole the Cthulhu and Elric material, got sued, and "was forced" to remove those sections. Tellers of this tale are generally vague about who did the suing. Was it Chaosium, makers of *Call of Cthulhu*? Michael Moorcock? Maybe it was Cthulhu itself? In this version, TSR was the villain who was caught red-handed, and, ultimately, justice was served. This "justice," and the erroneous idea that copies of the book were somehow rescued from the pulping machine, made the original edition of *Deities & Demigods* a kind of contraband. Anyone lucky enough to own a copy was surely favored by the gods.

Alas, for all the swirling mystery, the truth of the matter is rather straightforward, even if it is often misunderstood or, sometimes, purposefully distorted. When work began on the book, Ward wanted to include the Leiber, Lovecraft, and Moorcock pantheons, each of which represented major influences on Gary Gygax and *Dungeons & Dragons*. This usage required permission, which he says he diligently got; decades later, the idea that he somehow pilfered Lovecraft and Moorcock's work still chaffs Ward.

Leiber, who Gygax counted as a friend, was easy enough to reach, a phone call away. Ward contacted Moorcock via letter. In a 2009 interview, Moorcock said his permission was given "in the spirit of the '60s/'70s when it seemed to many of us that we were sharing in a common culture." Copyright for Lovecraft's stories is a murkier issue, but Ward nevertheless says he secured permission from Arkham House, a small press founded by friends of Lovecraft with the express purpose of keeping his work in print following his death (whether they had the power to grant Ward that permission, or that he needed it at all, is open to debate, though). Ward recalls in an essay written for EN World in 2019, "They were pleased to get their concepts mention[ed] in the

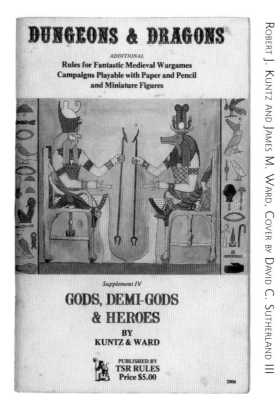

GODS, DEMI-GODS & HEROES, TSR, 1976
ROBERT J. KUNTZ AND JAMES M. WARD, COVER BY DAVID C. SUTHERLAND III

book [...] The book was printed and published in 1980 to wide acclaim." Shortly after publication, though, TSR received a cease-and-desist letter from Chaosium.

Chaosium had secured contracts to develop RPGs based on the works of both Lovecraft and Moorcock—*Call of Cthulhu* and *Stormbringer*, both in development in 1980 and slated for release in 1981. Chaosium didn't want a competitor working with the same properties, and TSR wanted to continue selling *Deities & Demigods*, so the only legal recourse was for someone to sue the licensors, which no one wanted. A deal was struck: Cthulhu and Elric could stay in *Deities & Demigods* in exchange for a "thank you" to Chaosium in the next printing, along with permission to include *Dungeons & Dragons* attributes and trademarks in Chaosium's forthcoming *Thieves' World* box set.

The deal kept all parties happy until the time arrived for TSR to go into a third printing in 1981. This time, Cthulhu and Elric disappeared (though not the "thank you," which lingered for several more printings). The reason why isn't clear. Shannon Appelcline says in *Designers & Dragons* (2014) that TSR removed the material to head off accusations of Satanism in the wake of the James Dallas Egbert III scandal (see page 122), but that doesn't jibe for me. TSR did change the book's name to *Legends & Lore* for this very reason, but they did so in 1985, when the Satanic Panic was at its height. More likely, the removal of the pantheons was a simple bit of business math on the part of TSR's vice president, Brian Blume: Keeping Cthulhu and Elric could potentially lead players away from *D&D* and into Chaosium's arms.

Bizarrely, TSR and Chaosium would find themselves in almost this exact same situation again in 1983, over the works of Fritz Leiber.

Urban legends aside, *Deities & Demigods* is still a beguiling book. Much of its initial promise is delivered in the contours of Erol Otus's epic wraparound cover painting—the palette of purple and green, the comic book colors that often indicate villainy of some stripe, serve as a subtle and accidental reminder of the book's nefarious reputation. In the depiction of the gods and their champions gripped in combat, the painting portrays a relationship between mortals and immortals that is immediate and direct, nearly physical. It is difficult to discern who the proxies are in this drama.

The book doesn't quite deliver on Otus's promise, which verges on something of the metaphysical drama outlined in *RuneQuest*'s *Cults of Prax*. In the previous iteration, *Gods, Demi-Gods & Heroes* (1976), gods were presented as a sort of argument against *D&D* power-gaming along the line of, "How can your fighter have 400 hit points if Thor has 440 hit points?"

That never really worked and, if anything, the profiles presented here, in the style of the *Monster Manual*, made matters worse. It essentially, if unintentionally, equated these divinities with all of the other opponents in the game, nearly all of whom can be bested physically through force of arms. Who can see the detailed powers of Odin's rune wand or Demeter's dragon-pulled chariot and not immediately start to dream up schemes to *get* them? If gods have hit points, they can be hit, and they can run out of them. Of course, killing a god's avatar only sends their spirit back to their divine domain, calling players to even greater heights of adventure (and murder).

In addition to encouraging an uncountable number of attempted deicides, the biggest accomplishment of *Deities & Demigods* may have been in encouraging a generation of players to embrace an abiding interest in mythology. There are three comments I hear repeatedly from longtime *D&D* players via the @VintageRPG Instagram: That it taught them how to write, that it taught them "weird words" (like dweomer or crenellation), and that it sparked a lifelong interest in mythology and folklore. This is true to my experience—I'm guilty of all three!

I had already passed through my obsessive phase with Greek mythology by the time I found *Deities & Demigods*, but it both reignited that enthusiasm and broadened my horizons into other cycles of myth. If the words weren't enough, the illustrations certainly sent me over the edge. I can't imagine someone looking at Diesel LaForce's illustration of the Babylonian demon Druaga and not wanting to know more about what is going on there (turns out the eight-armed, four-legged, tentacle-toed ruler of the devil world was invented for *D&D*, alas). Brian Blume was worried about losing customers to Chaosium, but he never thought about all of the copies of *Bulfinch's Mythology* that *Deities & Demigods* probably helped to sell.

Basic Role-Playing (1980)

Roleplaying games exist as a hobby because of *Dungeons & Dragons*. Not just because *D&D* invented the form, but also because the original *Dungeons & Dragons* box set was so difficult to parse that it inspired dozens of would-be players to come up with their own rules.

Subsequent *D&D* supplements and articles in TSR's house magazines, *The Strategic Review* and *The Dragon*, brought clarity to the rules, but often by asserting that people were somehow playing game incorrectly. Some folks embraced the orthodoxy of those corrections; those who didn't often spun playing "the wrong way" into new RPG systems.

Such was the case for Steve Perrin, who codified his group's house rules and published them as "The Perrin Conventions" in *Alarums and Excursions* (*A&E*), a monthly, RPG-focused amateur press association (APA). Think of an APA as a sort of pre-internet message board: Multiple contributors send their own newsletters and musings to a central editor (in *A&E*'s case, the indefatigable Lee Gold, who started the publication in June, 1975 and has since put out over 540 issues, a truly gob-smacking number), who then prints, collates, and sends the finished copies to subscribers.

An astounding number of RPG designers have published in *A&E* over the years, using the publication as a sort of experimental proving ground. In the early days, it often seemed like a group project to fix *Dungeons & Dragons*—Gold has argued that *D&D* was so successful precisely because it demanded this kind of tinkering. Still, this constant fiddling with *D&D*'s mechanics was something that wore on Gary Gygax's nerves, although he occasionally contributed to *A&E*. *The Strategic Review* (February, 1976), then TSR's house organ, called *A&E*, "an excellent source of ideas, inspirations and fun," but in an extremely cranky essay in *The*

BASIC ROLE-PLAYING, SECOND EDITION, CHAOSIUM, 1981 GREG STAFFORD AND LYNN WILLIS. COVER BY RICHARD BECKER

Dragon (July, 1978), Gygax said that APAs, in general, are,

> beneath contempt, for they typify the lowest form of vanity press. There one finds pages and pages of banal chatter and inept writing from persons incapable of creating anything which is publishable elsewhere. Therefore, they pay money to tout their sophomoric ideas, criticise [sic] those who *are* able to write and design, and generally make themselves obnoxious.

In fairness, alongside this, Gygax was also annoyed about *A&E* contributors sharing photocopies of the *D&D* rules, showing that even contemporary controversies over the sharing of PDFs have their roots in the distant past. And if the APA's similarities to the internet were in doubt, later in that same essay, Gygax says,

> In recent months, I have been the target of some pretty vicious and petty attacks from some of the "APA's." [sic] [...] I've never made any bones about my feelings toward the field: they are unprofessional, unethical and seemingly ignorant

ALL THE WORLDS' MONSTERS, VOLUME TWO, SECOND EDITION, CHAOSIUM, 1979
JEFF PIMPER AND STEVE PERRIN (EDS.). COVER BY TIM KIRK

of the laws concerning libel. Most of the so-called "authors" seem to live in some sort of fantasy world, totally unconnected with the realities of everyday life. A good many of them are incapable of even quoting correctly.

This is about as precise a description of the internet as I've ever read.

The work Perrin produced through *A&E* is just one of many arguments that contradict Gygax's assertions. "The Perrin Conventions" were developed in public on the pages of *A&E*, eventually finding traditional publication in Perrin's *All the Worlds' Monsters, Volume Two* (1977), for Chaosium. That project led Greg Stafford to ask Perrin to design *RuneQuest*, which incorporates the basic shape of "The Perrin Conventions" in its approach to combat.

Once *RuneQuest* was out in the world, Stafford saw the need for an introductory system that was simpler to use while actively teaching the reader how to play—most contemporary RPGs embraced complexity as a point of pride and were ambivalent to newcomers. Stafford collaborated with Lynn Willis to trim down the *RuneQuest* system to the bare essentials. Gone were strike ranks and hit locations. What remained were the bare bones of the percentile skill system, the resistance table for opposed contests, and a combat system that was, fundamentally, "The Perrin Conventions" in a slightly different form.

They called it *Basic Role-Playing (BRP)* and published it as a 16-page booklet, filled with tutorials, a sheet of chits for use in tracking combat, and a very short solo adventure. A version of these rules first appeared in the second edition *RuneQuest* box set in 1980, and the booklet would show up in most Chaosium releases throughout the early '80s. A standalone edition was published in 1981.

Basic Role-Playing gives players a single system that is simple to master and could be used to run any kind of game—it is, essentially, the first generic or universal roleplaying system. Because it is so simple, *BRP* requires customization, though, so just about every game published by Chaosium uses *BRP* as a foundation and introduces specialized mechanics to bring play in line with the theme, like the sanity system for *Call of Cthulhu* or the passion system for *Pendragon*. Since a GM can't really use *BRP* "as-is" to run any sort of game, this leaves room for other games, like *GURPS*, to be *more* generic and universal down the line.

BRP's combat system plays fast and dangerous, which elevates the value of activities outside of combat, like social interaction and investigation, both of which are supported by the skill system. There are no classes, but professions can be used to emphasize sets of certain skills or introduce specialties. It also holds up well to modification from games outside of Chaosium's titles. Kenneth Hite, designer of *Trail of Cthulhu*, reports successfully splicing magic from *Ars Magica* and superpowers from TSR's *Marvel Super Heroes* into his own *BRP* games at different times.

Chaosium expanded *Basic Role-Playing* in 1982 with the *Worlds of Wonder* box set. It contained three worlds—Magic World, Superworld, and Future World—all connected by a sort of inter-dimensional hub, rather like Callahan's Crosstime Saloon. Each world is its own unique RPG.

Magic World is a fantasy RPG in line with *Dungeons & Dragons* that forms the basis for the Swedish RPG *Drakar och Demoner* (1982). Following this Swedish thread provides a dizzying example of *BRP*'s far-reaching influence. *Drakar och Demoner*, translated as *Dragons and Demons*, was published by Äventyrsspel, who would develop another *BRP*-based gamed called *Mutant* (1984). *Mutant*, as befits that name, went through a number

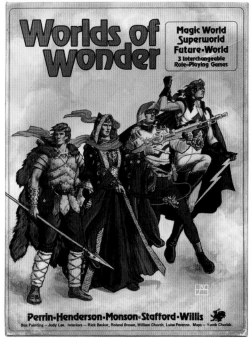

WORLDS OF WONDER, BOX SET, CHAOSIUM, 1982
STEVE PERRIN AND DYVERS HANDS, COVER BY JODY LEE

of permutations, the most recent of which is *Mutant: Year Zero,* (2014), by Free League. That game's system, the Year Zero Engine, powers most of Free League's other games, in a way similar to how *BRP* powers Chaosium's games.

The other worlds don't have lineages quite so impressive. Superworld, Chaosium's answer to *Champion* (1981), proved popular enough to warrant a box set of its own in 1983, followed by a handful of supplements. George R. R. Martin's ongoing *Superworld* campaign served as the basis of the shared universe Wild Cards anthology series, which spans two dozen books (and, in turn, was adapted for Steve Jackson's *GURPS* in 1989 and Green Ronin's *Mutants & Masterminds* in 2008). Future World, which cloned *Traveller*'s concept of character creation through terms of duty, as well as the notion of a vast interstellar empire, made less of an impact—perhaps because, despite the space opera vibe, it didn't have spaceships. Instead, interstellar travel is accomplished through a series of teleportation gates, à la *Stargate*.

After *Worlds of Wonder*, *BRP* lived on primarily through the games it powered,

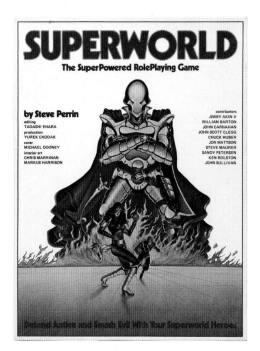

SUPERWORLD, BOX SET, CHAOSIUM, 1983
STEVE PERRIN, COVER BY MICHAEL DOONEY

most famously, *Call of Cthulhu*. In 2008, the core system was recompiled as *Basic Roleplaying: The Chaosium System*, which includes the various specialized mechanics developed for other games as optional modules. That's a long legacy for a game born out of the APAs Gygax said were ruled by "banal chatter and inept writing." I don't too often hear of folks playing *BRP* (though *The Chaosium System* did see a second printing), but the game's importance is undeniable. Take *Basic Role-Playing* away, and the RPG family tree looks bare, indeed.

Call of Cthulhu (1981)

Call of Cthulhu changes everything.

To this point, roleplaying games are nearly united in one way: In some fashion, they are all power fantasies. Characters go someplace, kill some things, find some loot, and maybe gain enough experience points to unlock their hidden personal potential in the form of some new spells or a new power. It may be easy for a character to die, as in *RuneQuest* or *Tunnels & Trolls*; characters can even potentially die during character generation, as in *Trav-*

eller. Danger aside, RPGs are about daring deeds and the accumulation of wealth, of knowledge, of power. In the end, there may be death, but always in the service of glory. There is a lone exception to this power fantasy: *Bunnies & Burrows*, in which survival is the name of the game. While the desperate lives of rabbits may be the stated theme, though, the system, which takes inspiration from *Dungeons & Dragons*, is still arranged around these notions of gain and improvement.

Call of Cthulhu is the first horror RPG. Horror, as a genre, is generally concerned with powerlessness. Even swaggering horror films bristling with guns, like *Aliens* or *Predator*, spend much of their runtime removing the reasons why the characters swagger, showing how ineffective the guns are at keeping the characters safe. That *Call of Cthulhu* is inspired by the works of H.P. Lovecraft amplifies this natural mechanic of horror. In his nihilistic cosmos, the universe is populated with mind-unraveling blasphemies older than time. Players are used to villains who hate them, but Lovecraft's gods don't even know or care that they exist.

In a complete inversion of the power fantasies of other RPGs, characters in *Call of Cthulhu* are doomed. The real-world setting means they are people of typical proportions and talents. They are fragile. Anyone with a gun (which, depending on the model, can do up to ten points of damage before bonuses) poses a significant risk to a character's health and well-being (most characters have around ten hit points). An outré monster, then, with a myriad of claws and tentacles, represents a nearly impossible physical challenge. In addition to mechanics for tearing and rending soft investigator bodies, though, *Call of Cthulhu* introduces mechanics for sanity—exposure to the supernatural preys on the mind. By merely seeing something unnatural, characters stand to lose sanity points. Lose enough, and a character will be

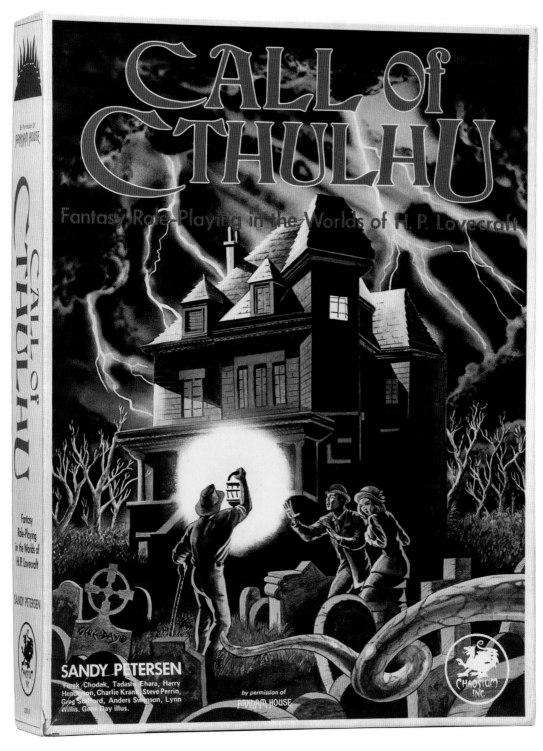

CALL OF CTHULHU, Box set, Chaosium, 1981
Sandy Petersen, cover by Gene Day

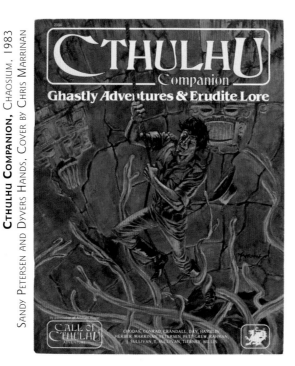

CTHULHU COMPANION, CHAOSIUM, 1983
SANDY PETERSEN AND DYVERS HANDS, COVER BY CHRIS MARRINAN

mechanics, but none were so thorough, nor so successful as *Call of Cthulhu*. Even today, when effective horror RPGs are more abundant, few rival the way *Call of Cthulhu* expresses the debilitating nature of starring in a horror story.

Like most Chaosium games, *Call of Cthulhu* uses the *Basic Role-Playing* system. The primary difference from the base system is Sandy Petersen's sanity system, which effectively mimics the states of mind present in Lovecraft's stories, modeling insanity as a plot device rather than striving for a nuanced depiction of the realities of mental illness.

In the game, sanity drains away from seeing monsters, reading occult books, learning unsettling facts, and witnessing horrible sights, like disfigured corpses. A single large shock might result in temporary irrational behavior (cleverly, in the face of such a shock, a character can fail an Intelligence check in order to block it out, thus preventing the loss of faculties). A large amount of sanity winnowed away

plagued by psychological traumas. Lose them all, and the character becomes irrevocably insane and is removed from player control.

In the rules, characters are referred to as investigators. Encouraged by the robust skill system and the physical frailty of the characters, the act of investigation is an entirely new mode of play for the hobby. *Call of Cthulhu* gives characters access to the one thing they can accumulate to their advantage: Knowledge. Investigators are bound together because they have glimpsed the true and terrifying system of the world that lurks, unseen to most, beneath the veneer of civilization. Each brush with magic or monsters, every case they work, adds to that knowledge, which makes them more effective opponents of the supernatural, for a time, even as it erodes their sanity. In this way, the death of a character is, perhaps, a kind of release—a goal.

Unlike every other RPG up to this point, the mechanics of *Call of Cthulhu* function in a way that is corrosive to characters. They rob them of power and are designed to destroy them in interesting ways. Previous RPGs sought to marry theme with

FRAGMENTS OF FEAR, CHAOSIUM, 1985
SANDY PETERSEN AND DYVERS HANDS, COVER BY TOM SULLIVAN

over a short period of time results in indefinite insanity, which usually leads to a phobia or a similar disorder derived from the experience that marks the investigator from that point forward. Finally, dropping to a sanity of zero leaves an investigator hopelessly, incurably insane, which removes them from play to spend the rest of their days in a sanitarium, or, perhaps, to use all of their accumulated eldritch knowledge to serve the obscene powers they once opposed.

Sanity mechanics reduce a real and complex struggle for many people to a series of dice rolls and roleplaying cues. Doing so is inherently trivializing, especially when the mechanics incorporate real disorders. In light of this issue, the most recent edition of *Call of Cthulhu* makes significant changes to how sanity is handled, characterizing it in a broad sense as a loss of personal control in the face of terrifying events involving knowledge and supernatural creatures that are poisonous to human consciousness. Small losses of sanity represent a momentary lapse, a gasp, a shudder. Larger losses result in greater outbursts, like fits of rage or panicked flight. Rather than assigning mental disorders as a mark of "permanent insanity," the rules encourage GMs to edit the details of an investigator's background sheet, warping the noted ideologies and twisting meaningful relationships.

It's also worth noting that, despite H. P. Lovecraft's unsavory views, the creators of (and designers working with) *Call of Cthulhu* largely avoid the overt bigotry that crops up in a number of Lovecraft's stories—this isn't to say that the game is free of insensitive material. Rather, to my eyes (which are admittedly biased), these missteps—particularly in the scenarios published in the '80s—seem like a symptom of a designer tying an adventure too closely to real history or leaving some troubling pulp stereotype unexamined. These are easy enough to discard in play.

Pulp Cthulhu, Chaosium, 2016
Mike Mason and Dyvers Hands. Cover by Victor Manuel Leza Moreno

The majority of official *Call of Cthulhu* sourcebooks and adventures sidestep the topic of racism entirely, focusing on narratives that cast clearly inhuman foes, like fungus people from outer space, rather than terrestrial threats.

In recent years, Chaosium has moved to become increasingly and explicitly anti-racist, disavowing Lovecraft's bigotry in public statements. This move has resulted in a re-examination of the *Call of Cthulhu* corpus, inspiring projects, like the thorough revision of *Masks of Nyarlathotep* (2018), which rehabilitates that campaign's lingering pulp stereotypes, and Chris Spivey's *Harlem Unbound* sourcebook (2017), which centers play on the experience of Black characters. LGBTQIA+ perspectives are brought to the fore in *Berlin: The Wicked City* (2019), a sourcebook and set of scenarios for Weimar Germany. All of these books serve as a heartening barometer for how RPG audiences are becoming more inclusive and attracting a more diverse audience.

BERLIN: THE WICKED CITY, CHAOSIUM, 2019
DAVID LARKINS, WITH MIKE MASON AND LYNNE HARDY, COVER BY LOÏC MUZY

CALL OF CTHULHU STARTER SET, BOX SET, CHAOSIUM, 2018
MIKE MASON AND FRIENDS, COVER BY VICTOR MANUEL LEZA MORENO

The success of *Call of Cthulhu* is massive. It has won piles of awards and is regularly cited by virtual tabletop services, like Roll20, as one of the most-played RPGs worldwide, which must be gratifying considering the headaches it caused Chaosium early on with *Deities & Demigods*. That enthusiasm may seem surprising for an RPG set on annihilating its characters, but I find *Call of Cthulhu* unabashedly fun, despite the scares and the despair. Horror can be a perplexing genre for folks who don't naturally gravitate to it, but for those who do, all of that darkness and terror tends to be rather cathartic. I laugh harder and more often when playing *Call of Cthulhu* than with other games and, anecdotally, my reaction aligns with the experiences of other players I've spoken with. Maybe I'm just laughing the nerves away. Still, whether fun or scary, the designers of *Call of Cthulhu* must be doing something right—Chaosium released seven editions over four decades.

Unlike *D&D*, there aren't significant differences between *Call of Cthulhu* editions. The most dramatic changes are aesthetic—packaging, boxes, books, the art,

and layout. The rules change slowly and, for the most part, imperceptibly. Petersen's initial version of the rules was issued in three editions of box sets—all of which look, essentially, identical—with only minor changes. The fourth edition (1989), the first issued as a softcover book, was expanded to include material from the *Cthulhu Companion* (1983) and *Fragments of Fear* (1985). The fifth edition (1992) received a significant revision and reorganization by Lynn Willis that was tweaked continually through a 5.5 edition and a formal sixth. The seventh (2014) marked a significant overhaul by designers Mike Mason and Paul Fricker, bringing the game in line with advances in contemporary design (Mason would go on to become the line's creative director). The current edition is further supported by the *Call of Cthulhu Starter Set* (2018), one of the best starter boxes on the market today.

Acknowledging that horror is not bound by time or place, Chaosium has produced a gigantic library of sourcebooks for different time periods and regions—a series of nightmare vacation guides. Want to know where to go to get

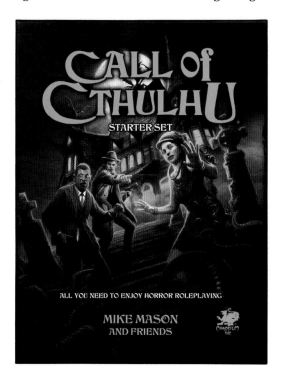

eaten in Tibet, or the best spots to see sights no one was meant to see in Australia? There are sourcebooks for both of those destinations and more. The series of Lovecraft Country sourcebooks from the early '90s is a classic of the form.

Players can also lose their minds in ancient Rome, the Dark Ages, during the French Revolution, in Sherlock Holmes's London, during the Cold War, right now, or centuries in the future when the sun is about to go out. And if the horror is too great, they can embrace the two-fisted, weird science-fueled pulp fiction of the *Pulp Cthulhu* (2016) rules, which can either stand alone or work modularly with other versions of *Call of Cthulhu*, depending on their fancy.

Beyond Chaosium, *Call of Cthulhu* has inspired plenty of other RPG makers. Pagan Publishing's *Delta Green* (1997) is a novel take, mixing modern-day *Call of Cthulhu* with a sort of paramilitary version of *The X-Files*. Before renovating *Call of Cthulhu* proper, Mike Mason and Paul Fricker did interesting work at the helm of *Cthulhu Britannica* for Cubicle 7 (2009), which also produced an odd fusion of war story and cosmic horror with their *World War Cthulhu* line (2013). Perhaps the most notable is Kenneth Hite's investigation-focused Call of Cthulhu remix, *Trail of Cthulhu* (2008). There's also the ultra-minimal *Cthulhu Dark* (2012) and the time traveling, post-apocalyptic *Fate of Cthulhu* (2021), not to mention all of the plug-in sourcebooks that introduce Cthulhu into otherwise "un-Cthulhu-y" games, like *Sandy Petersen's Cthulhu Mythos* (2019), which unleashes eldritch horrors to either *Pathfinder* or *D&D* 5E, depending on the version. The slumbering god is certainly one of the strangest of pop culture canonizations, but there seems to be an endless appetite—and deep wallets—for all things Cthulhu. So long as that remains true, the Great Old One will continue to loom large over RPGs.

Champions: The Super Hero Role Playing Game (1981)

As with science fiction RPGs, it isn't the first superhero RPG that made the biggest splash, or even the second, or third! *Champions* is the fourth superhero RPG, after *Superhero: 2044* (1977), *Villains and Vigilantes* (1979), and *Supergame* (1980), but it is the first one to bring the genre to life (and the only one to keep chugging on uninterrupted for 30 years).

There is something special about the cover art that speaks to the game's intentions—Mark Williams works magic drawing off-brand superheroes and villains. Those characters, who are often blatant, winking imitations of recognizable figures from the Marvel and DC universes, never fail to capture something of the boundless energy of the four-color world. They're also delightfully bizarre—for example, the cover image is a mix of Bronze Age comic sensibilities (1970-1985), but the villain is a disorienting blend of Magneto, Cyclops, and the low-rent villain, Constrictor, from the Marvel stable, with a color palette that seems to reference the original Bob Kane Batman design (from early 1939, before the character first appeared in that May's issue of *Detective Comics*). That's a whole library of comic book lore transmitted in a single image.

The game grew out of some tinkering with new powers for *Superhero: 2044*, but started to come together as its own game once the authors encountered *The Fantasy Trip*. *Champions* is the first entirely new game to embrace the idea of non-random character generation through a point-buy system, and it marks a significant expansion of the concept.

Champions lets players spend their 100 points on just about everything: Attributes, skills, equipment, and, most importantly, powers. Unlike *The Fantasy Trip*, and later, *GURPS Supers*, players aren't purchasing pre-fabricated abilities. Rather, they can customize their powers

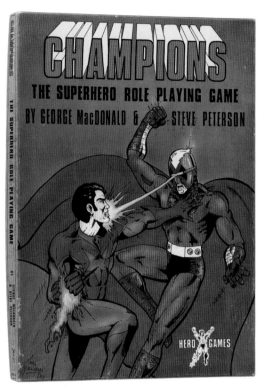

CHAMPIONS, SECOND EDITION, BOX SET, HERO GAMES, 1982
STEVE PETERSON AND GEORGE MACDONALD, COVER BY MARK WILLIAMS

JUSTICE, INC., BOX SET, HERO GAMES, 1984
AARON ALLSTON, STEVE PETERSON, AND MICHAEL STACKPOLE, COVER BY BRIAN K. HAMILTON

with modifiers, advantages, and limitations, all of which affect the final cost, for better or worse—instead of getting an ice ray that works like everyone else's ice ray, a player can design one that can pierce armor and explode, but can only be used three times a day. The downside of the point-buy system is that it introduces quite a bit of bookkeeping, but the upside is that a given character is tailor-made to the player's exact specifications. The character sheets even provide a mannequin-like figure on which to draw a cool superhero costume (something *Superworld*, 1983, Avalon Hill's *RuneQuest*, 1984, and other games would embrace in the future).

Champions also introduces the idea of disadvantages. Similar to the way that ice ray costs less because of a limitation, a player can select an interesting flaw, restriction, or character note in exchange for more points to spend on other powers or advantages. Vulnerabilities offer a range, dependent on rarity—Superman's weakness to Kryptonite would only net him five more points to spend,

but taking the classic secret identity puts 15 additional points in the player's pocket, enough for an extra limb with points to spare!

Disadvantages would become a key feature of *GURPS*. Also anticipating *GURPS*, Hero Games used the success of *Champions* to spin the Hero System into other genres. *Espionage!* (1983) was about, well, espionage; *Justice Inc.* (1984) tackled all flavors of pulp, and *Fantasy Hero* (1985) did the sword and sorcery thing; nowadays, *Champions* is really more of a genre sourcebook for the broader Hero System than it is a standalone game.

That genre flexibility makes the Hero System a fairly universal or generic system, though one that is a close cousin of Chaosium's *Basic Role-Playing*—each genre has special mechanics that prevent crossing over characters without some conversion. Like Chaosium, Hero Games was also open-minded about licensing and collaboration. Steve Jackson's *GURPS Autoduel*, Chaosium's *Superworld*, and FGU's *Villains and Vigilantes* were just some of the games that cross-pollinated with *Champions*. The line even survived financial troubles in the mid '80s by forming a long-term partnership with Iron

Crown Enterprises—after all, team-ups and crossovers are a key part of the superhero comic experience.

Thieves' World (1981)

The history of pop music is littered with supergroups, collaborations that draw together already famous musicians to cut an album. Think: The Highwaymen, which consisted of Johnny Cash, Willie Nelson, Waylon Jennings, and Kris Kristofferson, or the Traveling Wilburys, which gathered together George Harrison, Tom Petty, Bob Dylan, Jeff Lynne, and Roy Orbison.

These sorts of groups tend to represent a specific moment in time, an intersection of careers that produces one or two albums, then dissolves as the artists move on to other projects. *Thieves' World* is the roleplaying game equivalent of a supergroup, a moment of amazing promise that attracted a huge nexus of talent, delivered an amazing product, then dispersed as if it never happened at all.

Thieves' World (1979) was the first fantasy anthology to embrace the notion of a shared world. It was conceived by Robert Lynn Asprin, Lynn Abbey, and Gordon R. Dickinson in 1978. Since world building acted as the most significant hurdle to writing fantasy fiction, why not provide authors with a ready-made world in which to tell their stories? Those stories would, in turn, fill in the details of that world.

They came up with Sanctuary, a recently conquered city, primarily characterized by its thriving criminal underworld. Out of the invasion unfolds a larger drama—the gods of the new empire struggle against the original gods for control, and mortals are regularly swept up in their rivalries. The concept attracted an all-star roster of writers, including Poul Anderson, C. J. Cherryh, Philip José Farmer, and more, who contributed to a dozen anthologies between 1979 and 1989. Several authors spun their own novels out of their *Thieves' World* work, and there

THIEVES' WORLD COMPANION, CHAOSIUM, 1986
LYNN WILLIS AND DYVERS HANDS, COVER BY WALTER VELEZ

was even a series of graphic novel adaptations in the mid '80s (which was now-iconic comic artist Tim Sale's first big break). The series was successful enough that similar shared-world series appeared in its wake, like C. J. Cherryh's Merovingen Nights, George R. R. Martin's Wild Cards, and Janet Morris's Heroes in Hell.

The anthologies were a massive success among RPG players. With their ensemble cast of characters and interwoven narratives, they feel like RPGs, a feeling that would grow as the editors overturned the status quo with setting-wide events, like the collapse of the Rankan Empire, with which both characters and authors would have to reckon. Chaosium snagging the *Thieves' World* license was a coup—almost everybody wanted to play in Sanctuary.

Smartly, that's exactly what Chaosium delivered: The ability for anyone to visit the city, no matter their preferred game system. Abilities and guidance for all of the major inhabitants of Sanctuary were provided for in *Adventures in Fantasy, Chivalry & Sorcery, DragonQuest, The Fantasy Trip, RuneQuest, Tunnels & Trolls,* and even the science fiction RPG, *Traveller!* Thanks to

THIEVES' WORLD, BOX SET, CHAOSIUM, 1981
LYNN WILLIS AND DYVERS HANDS, COVER BY WALTER VELEZ

the *Deities & Demigods* kerfuffle, Chaosium got both versions—advanced and basic—of *Dungeons & Dragons* in the mix. What's more, the conversions were written, in most cases, by the designers of those games—Dave Arneson, Lawrence Schick, Marc Miller, and Ken St. Andre all have credits on the front of the box. Chaosium even brought in pinch hitters for what is arguably the core of the box—the city itself—tapping Midkemia Press to develop the streets and alleys of Sanctuary.

Taken all together, for the world of role-playing games, the *Thieves' World* box set represents unprecedented star wattage, a once-in-a-lifetime, never-to-be-repeated collaboration—and Chaosium's best selling box set up to that point. It's the "We Are the World" of RPGs, if, you know, "We Are the World" was actually a good song.

Midkemia Press was formed out of a group of *D&D* enthusiasts at the University of California, San Diego that started publishing RPG materials in 1979. Today, Midkemia is best known as one of the set-

CITIES, MIDKEMIA PRESS, 1979
STEPHEN ABRAMS AND JON EVERSON, COVER BY STEVE ABRAMS AND RICH SPAHL

tings of Raymond E. Feist's long running series of novels, *The Riftwar Cycle*, some of which draw on that long ago RPG campaign. But, in the late '70s, the name was associated with cutting edge RPG city design. Their first book, *Cities: A Gamemaster's Guide to Encounters and Other Rules for Fantasy Games* (1979), takes the Judges Guild method of creating a city experience through nested random tables and refines it, creating a massive set of potential street encounters.

The process is split between two parts—first, the GM rolls on the table to determine the part of town the characters are in to learn who is on the street, then the GM rolls on the corresponding chart to see what those people are doing. Many of these encounters are just bustle—a character bumps into X. Some offer hooks for impromptu adventures—X is looking to hire someone to do Y. Some are complications or dramatic scenes, like an assassination attempt. And the intent is to roll often, like every 15 minutes or so in real time.

These rapid-fire, but often inconsequential encounters, create the illusion of a metropolitan churn, where player characters are but a handful out of thousands of

CITIES, SECOND EDITION, MIDKEMIA PRESS, 1981
STEPHEN ABRAMS AND JON EVERSON, COVER BY RICHARD BECKER

THE CITY OF CARSE, MIDKEMIA PRESS, 1980
STEPHEN AND APRIL ABRAMS. COVER BY APRIL ABRAMS

inhabitants, all with their own agendas. A series of rolls opens many avenues for emergent storytelling. Picture a party trying to get somewhere fast, but city guards have set up a checkpoint that is snarling traffic (roll one), and while they try to get through, a drunken warrior starts trying to hire the party's thief for a job (roll two), while a succession of people bump into the mage (rolls three, four, and five). The players are just walking down the street, and already, they're trapped in the best kind of chaos that keeps compounding the longer they're out.

Cities was followed by *The City of Carse* (1980) and *Tulan of the Isles* (1981), both of which applied the earlier, generic concept from *Cities* to predefined cities from the Midkemia homebrew game, tailoring the random tables to each city's distinct character and providing details for every building.

The second edition of *Cities* (1981) returns to randomization, providing tools similar to the street encounter tables in order to flesh out the city, building-by-building, business-by-business, and arranged to yield believable results (no one wants their mansion in the district with all of the butchers, after all).

Midkemia joined these two tools—random tables for street encounters and city building—to capture the gritty urban feel of Sanctuary, as established in the anthologies. There are 15 pages of tables that account for everything, from time of day, to street size, to neighborhood; they make *Thieves' World* feel alive, on the fly, and guarantee that no two trips through Sanctuary's streets ever feel the same, just like a real city.

Midkemia Press released a few more products before closing during the industry downturn in 1983. Chaosium reprinted several of their books in the mid '80s, though: A third edition of *Cities* (1986, which also received a *RuneQuest*-specific version through Avalon Hill in 1988), *Carse* (1986), and *Tulan of the Isles* (1987).

In 1986, Chaosium revisited *Thieves' World* with the *Thieves' World Companion*, which accounts for the events of the anthology's volumes three through six. The miracle of cooperation from 1981 had passed, though; the only non-Chaosium systems appearing in this volume are Iron Crown Enterprise's *Role Master* and *Middle-earth Role-Playing*. Says writer Lynn Willis in the introduction, "Like Sanctuary and its mythos, the hobby of roleplaying also evolves. Several of the game systems which our original supplement embraced have, for various reasons, fallen by the wayside. Others are not usable by us at this time."

Dungeons & Dragons B/X (1981)

The Holmes *Basic Set* was intended as a brief introduction to *Dungeons & Dragons*, so it only supported play for levels one through three. The idea was that when players hit that cap, they would graduate, either to the original *D&D* box set or to the more complex *Advanced Dungeons & Dragons* rulebooks (despite the fact that *AD&D* was a different, albeit similar, system).

This plan worked for a while, but when TSR stopped printing the original *D&D* box set in 1979, it became clear that the *Basic Set* needed a follow-up. But first, the *Basic Set* itself needed some sprucing up to bring it in line with four years of new developments in game design. Tom Moldvay headed up this significant revision, essentially rewriting and expanding the original *Dungeons & Dragons* rules. The result is something far more polished and better organized than the previous iterations, one that also draws a clearer distinction from *AD&D*—this is, emphatically, a standalone game.

Perhaps most importantly, Moldvay leans into Holmes's idea of teaching people how to play by reading the rulebook, something the original *D&D* and *AD&D* do not attempt. Moldvay's sample dungeon, a haunted keep, is a bit better suited to this introduction than Holmes's nebulous cavern complex. *B2: The Keep on the Borderlands*, also included in the box, then reinforces all the lessons of the rulebook.

Ultimately, this *Basic Set* is the same, but also different. A key difference is the art. Erol Otus leads the way with the box cover, the neon green dragon plays off the bright magenta of the box sides in a wonderfully garish fashion. That brightness downplays the mystery and danger of earlier core *D&D* products and moves the focus to fun.

Inside, a murderer's row of TSR artists—Otus, Jeff Dee, Bill Willingham,

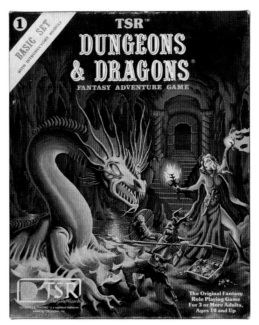

DUNGEONS & DRAGONS BASIC SET, BOX SET, TSR, 1981
TOM MOLDVAY, COVER BY EROL OTUS

and Diesel LaForce—deliver pages of evocative illustrations. The box also marks the first appearance of the key for dungeon mapping by LaForce, TSR's future full-time cartographer. Making dungeon maps is, for many GMs, one of the more enjoyable and satisfying parts of *Dungeons & Dragons*. LaForce's icons helped countless folks discover the joy of map-making while also providing GMs with a wellspring of inspiration for their homebrew dungeons (this GM spent the bulk of fourth grade drawing elaborate, color-coded dungeons on graph paper instead of paying attention to math lessons).

Stephen R. Marsh and David "Zeb" Cook took on the *Expert Set*, which covers rules of play for levels four through 14 and features another wonderfully gaudy Otus piece that spies on the action of the *Basic Set*. While that box set focuses on delving into underground dungeons, *Expert* handles the hazards of wilderness exploration, supported by *X1: The Isle of Dread*.

True to the history of *D&D*, in general, the mystique of dungeons, and thus the *Basic Set*, is stronger and lives more in the general imagination than the surface

world. This fact can be glimpsed in the map key—LaForce's hex symbols are great, but don't excite the imagination in the same way as the dungeon symbols. Still, the *Expert Set* marks the formal introduction of the Known World, specifically the Grand Duchy of Karameikos.

The setting is derived from the homebrew world created by Moldvay and Lawrence Schick in the mid '70s, and, like Greyhawk, large swaths would be further developed through the line's adventure modules. Unlike Greyhawk, the Known World received steady support through the mid '90s, thanks to the Gazetteer series of sourcebooks, making it, perhaps, the most detailed TSR campaign setting after Forgotten Realms. TSR eventually produced a version for *AD&D* under the name Mystara.

Together, these box sets would come to be popularly known as *B/X D&D*, and they're well regarded as the most playable versions of all of the early *Dungeons & Dragons*—simpler than *AD&D,* more welcoming than the original *D&D* or Holmes's *Basic Set,* and lacking some of the stranger flourishes of Frank Mentzer's *BECMI* (see page 107). *B/X* has since become a standard for Old School Revival hacks, first

with *Labyrinth Lord* and more recently with Gavin Norman's streamlined restatement of the system, *Old-School Essentials* (2019). As ever, the past, present, and future of RPGs intertwine.

X1: The Isle of Dread (1981)

X1: The Isle of Dread was my first *Dungeons & Dragons* module, owing to its inclusion in the *Expert Set* box set. (as a kid, I had the blue box from 1983, so all of my nostalgia dopamine comes from the 1983 version of *X1* with the orange cover). It's important for a number of reasons, but for me, its true power lies in a single page: The map of the island—its shores charted, its interior blank. There are few things in RPGs as tantalizing as a blank map. All of those empty hexes are a challenge, and the imagination leaps to fill them.

A hex crawl is the primary way wilderness areas are handled by RPGs and, in a way, they render geographic areas into dungeon-like spaces (though dungeons tend to be, at least, semi-linear and constrained, while the wilderness is, well, wide open). Each hex on the map is defined by a specific type of terrain. As they travel through, players might stumble into random encounters or specific points of interest, which can be anything from an NPC with a problem, a ruin, or a strange rock formation, so long as it contributes to the player's understanding of the place. Hex crawls often lack concrete plots—players explore, uncover information about the region, set their goals, and make their own stories. That blank map might be all the encouragement the players need.

Hexes have a long history of portraying terrain for wargaming for two primary reasons—they allow more directions for maneuvering than a square, and, unlike the octagon, they interlock. Hexes have a tactical relationship with troop chits in wargames: How fast can they move? Do they have cover or high ground? But, in games like *Outdoor Survival* (1972) and *Source of the Nile* (1977), hexes are used to facilitate exploration and potential hazards—this is a more direct touchstone for how they're used in RPGs.

Outdoor Survival was listed as necessary equipment for playing *D&D* in the original box set, so there was always an expectation that GMs would use hexes in some capacity during play. TSR assumed that GMs would be making their own worlds and hexes. While the hexes of *World of Greyhawk*'s overland map was the first seeming indication that TSR was softening that stance, *The Isle of Dread* is the first time *D&D* ventures out of the underground and into the hexagons of the wilderness in an official published adventure. Others, like Judges Guild's *Wilderlands* books, were already traipsing around the hills and dales, but TSR getting in on the action meant the hex crawl was going mainstream.

There isn't a lot of plot in *The Isle of Dread*. Rather, there are secrets to discover and plenty of factions with their own interests; players can embrace those interests or cross swords over them, as they fancy. The island is clearly inspired by *King Kong* (1933) and Ray Harryhausen's films—there are dinosaurs, psychic squid monsters, pirates, giant clams, terror birds, intelligent giant spiders, and more to run afoul of, and that's not even accounting for the native populations of humans, phanatons (a sort of intelligent combination of a monkey and a raccoon), and rakasta (cat people). No gigantic ape appears, alas.

Those psychic squids, creatures more properly called kopru, are the faction causing the most trouble for everyone else, and they live in a secret temple hidden in the volcano at the center of the island, but that discovery comes at the players' pace, not the GM's. A climactic battle in the heart of a volcano feels like a decent consolation prize for the lack of a gigantic ape, and, if it's not, there's noth-

X1: The Isle of Dread, TSR, 1981
David "Zeb" Cook and Tom Moldvay, Cover by Jeff Dee

ing stopping a GM from adding one (conveniently, there is a profile for one in Gygax's *WG6: Isle of the Ape*, 1985, which is essentially a direct translation of *King Kong* into a *D&D* adventure).

Hex crawls naturally encourage world building, on the hex-to-hex level of the adventure, certainly, but also in terms of the campaign world. The island needs to exist somewhere, after all, a place to sail to and from, a home for when the expedition is over. The *Expert Set* introduced the Grand Duchy of Karameikos, a nation of the Known World, likely the point of origin for an expedition to the island; the module itself brings in the larger campaign world. Again, it is through a map that the introduction makes its biggest splash with the strange names of countries and cities inviting further exploration. Players would get their chance to explore these mysterious locales over the course of the X-series modules and beyond.

The Isle of Dread is one of those adventures that echoes through RPG design, even in recent years. It's less about anything specific in the module. Players might remember Tim Truman's illustration of the hydra attacking a boat more

X1: THE ISLE OF DREAD, TSR, 1983
DAVID "ZEB" COOK AND TOM MOLDVAY, COVER BY TIMOTHY TRUMAN

vividly than anything laid out in the text—there's potential here, but it requires a bunch of players stomping around to come together, and many of the escapades spin out of the personalities around the table rather than the prompts in the book.

The format of those prompts, though, is classic. Similar to the way *The Keep on the Borderlands* is seared into the brains of tens of thousands of *D&D* players because of its inclusion in the *Basic Set*, so too is the approach to wilderness adventures (put forth in *The Isle of Dread*) because of the tens of thousands of *Expert Sets* TSR sold with *X1* packaged inside.

The module makes something like *Griffin Mountain*, a much larger, elaborate, and detailed wilderness campaign, seem ponderous, not because of the disparity in size, but because of the layout. *The Isle of Dread* nails the presentation, to the extent that I wouldn't be surprised if some of its DNA could be involved in videogames that deal with open world wilderness exploration. *The Dark of Hot Springs Island* feels so much like a perfect hex crawl, in part, because it improves on *X1*'s faults while keeping the same basic approach—it even has a volcano!

GRIFFIN MOUNTAIN, CHAOSIUM, 1981
RUDY KRAFT, JENNELL JAQUAYS, AND GREG STAFFORD, COVER BY JENNELL JAQUAYS

Griffin Mountain (1981)

Like *X1: The Isle of Dread*, *Griffin Mountain* is an attempt to define a vast wilderness for roleplaying. As with the trio of chaotic caverns in 1979—*The Caverns of Thracia, Snakepipe Hollow*, and *B2: The Keep on the Borderlands*—this is one of those moments when talented designers were independently investigating the same ideas at the same time, producing results that are both surprisingly similar and wildly disparate.

Griffin Mountain joins Greg Stafford and Rudy Kraft, authors of *Snakepipe Hollow*, with Jennell Jaquays, author of *The Caverns of Thracia* (and who previously collaborated with Kraft on *Legendary Duck Tower*). It was initially developed as a generic "gateway" *RuneQuest* adventure by Kraft and Jaquays, but Stafford was so impressed by the depth of detail in the manuscript that he decided to import the region into his world of Glorantha, naming it Balazar and placing it north of Prax. Fascinatingly, the entire book was written without the trio ever meeting in person—a common enough occurrence in the twenty-first century, but one that

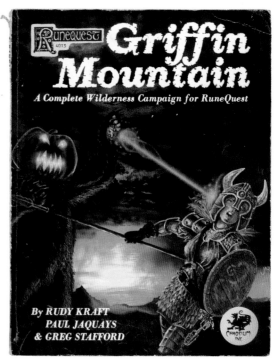

seems onerous and impressive in an era when communication over distance was limited to phone calls and snail mail.

While *The Isle of Dread* is a longish module, *Griffin Mountain* is massive—a 200-plus-page campaign that follows in the footsteps of Judges Guild's *Wilderlands*. Unlike that setting, which was defined over the course of many books and supplements, *Griffin Mountain* marks the first time an RPG campaign packed this amount of information into a single product. Readers not only get the history and geography, but also the religion, politics, important personalities, notable settlements, adventure sites, and even the weather patterns for a 500-square-mile wilderness.

There's so much detail, in fact, that it is challenging to imagine getting a good enough handle on it all to run it for a group. The intention here is to let players off the leash to wander through a great big sandbox of interesting locations, adventuring and getting into trouble as they see fit. Even now, not many campaign books feel so complete or so open. That freedom, and the relative wildness of the region, also give players the opportunity to make a real impact. A couple of successful sorties is enough to gain some notoriety and set rumors swirling in the taverns and along the caravan routes. In a short time, a savvy party can become a powerful force in local affairs.

As with many of Chaosium's best products, *Griffin Mountain* takes an intricate approach to its world—one that focuses on players experiencing a different reality, rather than only centering on tactical combat. Some unique methods imbue Balazar with much of its charm: First, because so much of the region is spread out, with pockets of civilization lining caravan routes, it is possible (and encouraged) to work across the wilderness as guards, messengers, monster hunters, map makers, and more—while stopping at every tavern along the way to carouse,

GRIFFIN ISLAND, BOX SET, AVALON HILL, 1986 RUDY KRAFT, JENNELL JAQUAYS, AND GREG STAFFORD, COVER BY STEVE PURCELL

of course; second is the elaborate rumor system. Factions, important NPCs, and some locations, like taverns, all afford opportunities to purchase information. Sometimes, that information can give players valuable insights into the world— if players are going to cull the griffin population, or clear the Festering Island, they're going to need some intelligence from those in the know. Sometimes, the information leads directly to a new adventure or a site worth exploring. Sometimes it even results in a map—there are six hand-drawn ones, including one to a gold mine! Rumor charts have become a mainstay of RPG scenarios, but it is unusual to encounter ones this robust. By simulating the constant conversation and gossiping that happens on the road or in places where travelers gather, Balazar starts to take on a life of its own.

Avalon Hill reprinted *Griffin Mountain* when they licensed the game for their largely disastrous third edition in 1985. It was one of only a few of Chaosium's *RuneQuest* products that received the treatment—would that it wasn't so.

Avalon Hill envisioned *RuneQuest* as a generic fantasy RPG. Glorantha was still included in the core box set, but it was presented as one of two options, the other being a fantasy version of the real-world. When the company reissued *Griffin Mountain* as *Griffin Island*, they stripped all of the references to Glorantha. Most of the details stayed the same—the people, the settlements, the adventure sites—but the mountain was relocated to an island, and a bunch of orcs and lizard people moved in. Removing the Gloranthan lore carves out the campaign's uniqueness, rendering it indistinct from other products of the period.

Where *Griffin Mountain* feels cohesive and whole, *Griffin Island* feels disjointed and broken. It also takes itself a bit too seriously. The original cover art, by Jennell Jaquays, with the ridiculous yet somehow terrifying Jack O'Bear, does much to set expectations for the boozy bar crawl that *Griffin Mountain* is at heart. The Avalon Hill cover painting of a warrior squaring off against a lizard person is rather tame in comparison. The fact that neither really features a griffin (there is one silhouetted by the moon on the cover of *Griffin Island,* at least) is an amusing oversight.

The reprint did one thing right, though—shades of *The Isle of Dread*, Avalon Hill provided a large, mostly blank map of the island for players to fill in as they explored, complete with (possibly erroneous) annotations from previous owners. It is the only exciting thing in the box.

Stormbringer (1981)

Stormbringer brings the world of fantasy author Michael Moorcock's most famous character, the haunted anti-hero Elric, to roleplaying games. That world is rich, strange, and doomed.

The Elric stories are some of the most important in the body of twentieth century fantasy writing, constituting a clear break from earlier traditions and a foray into territory decidedly grimmer and more psychedelic. Elric is very much the opposite of Conan or Aragorn, a portrait of frailty who is addicted to terrible drugs. His weakness makes him a pawn in the eternal struggle between Law and Chaos, where he traffics in dangerous magic and makes himself a prisoner of the soul-stealing sword, Stormbringer. He does harm, intentionally or not, to everyone around him. More often than not, his achievements are accomplished, not by his own prowess, but through his exploitation of pacts made between his ancestors and a variety of supernatural entities. He saves no one. In the end, he heralds the destruction of his world. This grim trajectory affords the RPG the opportunity to offer a play experience quite different from the ones most players were used to.

Stormbringer is arranged around the idea of high-powered play and accomplishes this through a new magic system that focuses on the summoning and binding of demons and elemental spirits. Everyone with the requisite attributes can use demon magic, and the art's main application is the creation of magical items infused with the essence of the entities thus imprisoned.

Using demon items, characters can reach superhuman levels of prowess—*Basic Role-Playing* games normally allow skills that range from 1-percent to 100-percent, but a demon sword, say, might raise a character's attack skill to 112-percent. This value means, short of a roll of 100, which always indicates a fumble, that

STORMBRINGER, Second edition, Box set, Chaosium, 1985
Ken St. Andre and Steve Perrin, Cover by Frank Brunner

99

DEMON MAGIC: THE SECOND STORMBRINGER COMPANION, CHAOSIUM, 1985
LARRY DITILLIO, KEVIN FREEMAN, MARK L. GAMBLER, AND ARNO LIPFERT, COVER BY DAN AND DAVID DAY

STORMBRINGER, FOURTH EDITION, CHAOSIUM, 1990
KEN ST. ANDRE AND STEVE PERRIN, COVER BY MICHAEL WHELAN

character cannot miss. Demons and spirits can be bound into other objects, as well, augmenting other abilities.

It's through the magic system that *Stormbringer* most captures the essence of Moorcock's stories. Like any deal with the devil, the power derived from these bargains comes with the potential of paying a high personal cost, from crippling ailments, to the risk of possession, to the loss of free will should they become an Agent of Chaos (this is, perhaps, a net positive for some players, who will thrill at throwing themselves into melees screaming, "Blood and souls for my lord Arioch!" over the course of their very short lives). These costs infuse the game with an overriding sense of doom: Eventually the bill comes due for even the greatest hero. This fate is reflected explicitly in the campaign setting—at the point in Moorcock's fictional chronology where players find themselves, the world is ten short years from ending.

To this point, with the exception of *Call of Cthulhu*, RPGs offered progression that was based on the gradual accumulation of power over time. In Elric's world, however, power is there for the taking. *Stormbringer* is about the price of that power.

The genius of the game is the way the mechanics numerically express power. A character will never miss another sword swing. A character will never suffer damage from an enemy's attack again. A character cannot be outwitted. A character is immune to poison. *Stormbringer* seduces players by offering a way around the randomness that so often frustrates their ambitions and, in giving them that power, sets their fate and damns them. It is a rare thing for a *Stormbringer* character not to be utterly consumed by their choices in the end, just like Elric.

The first three editions of *Stormbringer* box sets, like *Call of Cthulhu*, are largely interchangeable, receiving only minor adjustments to rules and format. The fourth edition, a softcover book featuring an amazing painting by Michael Whelan, compiles the best material from various companion books.

The *Stormbringer* line has no shortage of great art, mostly from professional comic book artists. Frank Brunner, who had previously adapted Elric stories for

Heavy Metal, contributed what amounts to an entire portfolio of Elric pieces to the box set, including its cover painting. Steve Purcell (*Sam & Max*) did the cover of the adventure *Black Sword* (1985). All three Day brothers also worked on the line, with Gene (*Star Wars*, *Master of Kung Fu*) contributing the cover of the *Stormbringer Companion* (1983), and Dan and David delivering the cover of *Demon Magic*, along with much of the interior art.

In Moorcock's fiction, Elric is but one aspect of the Eternal Champion, around whom swirl the conflicts between Chaos and Law in their local pocket of space and time. Chaosium intended to expand *Stormbringer* with a series of box sets based on Moorcock's other champions, but the only one that materialized was *Hawkmoon* (1986), an adaptation of the Moorcock's Runestaff stories set in the Tragic Millennium, a time far in our future, after nuclear war and plagues forced the world back to a pseudo-medieval period. Mutants abound, and the line between science and magic is blurred. It didn't catch on in the US, but it took on a life of its own in France; a new edition became the subject of a Kickstarter campaign in 2021. A few other

HAWKMOON, BOX SET, CHAOSIUM, 1986
KERI CAMPBELL-ROBSON, COVER BY FRANK BRUNNER

Stormbringer products carried the odd little bicycle-like Eternal Champion logo, then faded into history.

Fiend Folio (1981)

Unlike the previous *D&D* core books, *Fiend Folio* isn't a groundbreaking book. The last of the five *Advanced Dungeons & Dragons* hardcovers to feature wrap-around art, it is a bit of a black sheep, born out of a troubled production and destined for an unenthusiastic response and a quiet repudiation.

It's a monster book, like the *Monster Manual*—a sequel of sorts from the United Kingdom, mostly compiling monsters submitted to the "Fiend Factory" feature in Games Workshop's *White Dwarf* magazine. It was originally supposed to be released by Games Workshop under license—GW was distributing and reprinting TSR products for the UK market so successfully that the two companies considered merging. They didn't, though, and the fallout from that failed deal led GW to slow walk production on the book. *Fiend Folio* was meant to come out in 1979—as evidenced by the date in the foreword—but didn't hit shelves until 1981. When it did, TSR, not Games Workshop, published it, and they used the book to launch their own UK division. Awkward!

The book is a mixed bag. Though the term "crowd-sourced" didn't exist at the time, *Fiend Folio* bears some of its hallmarks. The quality of the monsters is uneven, with many feeling like thinly veiled imitations, variants, or combinations of creatures that appeared in the *Monster Manual*. Others are downright silly, like the infamous flumph, a sort of intelligent, Lawful Good, airborne jellyfish that flies by farting and attacks by excreting a noxious fluid, or the adherer, which is like a mummy covered in glue. There is also a concentration of undead creatures that are essentially interchangeable skull-faced creeps. Many of the monsters lack any sort of depth. Ed Greenwood, creator

FIEND FOLIO, TSR, 1981
DON TURNBULL (EDITOR), COVER BY EMMANUEL

of the Forgotten Realms, lambasted the book in a four-page review in TSR's own *Dragon Magazine* (November 1981), saying it marred the beauty of *AD&D* and undermined its "sought-after consistency." Reactions elsewhere were lukewarm, and, in 1983, when TSR reissued the original *AD&D* books with new covers by Jeff Easley—the so-called orange spine editions—*Fiend Folio* was the only one not to get reprinted.

Despite this initial negative response, the *Fiend Folio* opened a door for a specific sort of weirdness to creep into *D&D*. A number of critters detailed in the book hail from realms outside of human perception—negative energy fields that feed on human suffering, strange creatures that project themselves onto the astral plane. The githyanki, a sort of evil and mystical offshoot of humanity, would become favorite villains for designers in the coming years, showing up everywhere from the Forgotten Realms to *Dark Sun*. These creatures and more pave the way for far-out *D&D* campaign settings, like *Spelljammer* and *Planescape*.

There are also more conventional icons, as well. Without the death knight

introduced here, the Dragonlance saga would lack one of its most beloved villains. Shadow demons, bullywugs, and hook horrors, all of which first appeared in the *Fiend Folio*, would soon show up in the 1983 cartoon series. The grell—a giant floating brain with a squid-like beak and tentacles—was improbably immortalized with its own toy and remains a classic monster of the game (and is probably my all-time favorite).

And while *Fiend Folio* was largely a dead-end for *AD&D*, it is a glimpse into the future of a behemoth of a different sort. Omitting the book from the 1983 reprints, coupled with the ridiculous moral panic surrounding *D&D* in the '80s, lent the book a certain mystique, something that was compounded exponentially by the art. It *is* grimmer, certainly, with so many adventurers suffering grisly fates among its pages—eaten by rat things, throats torn out by flying heads, garroted, disemboweled, eaten whole, carried off by crabmen.

This violent vibe is completely different from the rest of *Dungeons & Dragons* and the sense of danger is due primarily to the heavy black ink of illustrator Russ Nicholson. Nicholson's work grounds even the most ridiculous creatures, like the odd hell bird called the achaierai, giving his world a gritty weight. His striking, full-page illustrations of the githyanki and the grell fixed those creatures in the imagination of players (in the case of the githyanki, he was helped along by Emmanuel's strange cover art depicting them on the shimmering astral plane). Nicholson expands the aesthetic foundation of the British interpretation of fantasy that was already established, in part, by Ian Miller and the weekly *2000 AD* comics. All of these aesthetic choices would coalesce in the years to come in the Fighting Fantasy series of adventure gamebooks and in the many faces of Games Workshop's gore-flecked, heavy metal-influenced *Warhammer* franchise.

Borderlands (1982)

The premise of *Borderlands* is simple, verging on generic. Prax, the great expanse of plains that form the primary setting of early *RuneQuest*, has been conquered. An exiled duke has been tasked with establishing a frontier settlement and civilizing the region to the standards of his imperial masters. To do that requires mercenaries. Enter, the players.

Contracts are signed, terms of service are established, and in a few hours, the players go from shiftless vagabonds to gainfully employed peace keepers with roofs over their heads and a community to serve. The campaign plays out over seven episodes, and many of them feel very much like jobs—there is no real connective thread, no secret conspiracy, no sinister plots. There are daring rescues and plenty of dungeons, but this is not high adventure, not really. Despite the Chaos monsters, the box set all feels rather mundane, especially if workaday routines are established between the main episodes—trips to Horn Gate for supplies, minor diplomatic incidents with the local tribes, perhaps, a special trip to Pavis for a holiday. Over the course of the contracted year, though, something magical should happen: The players *should* naturally and organically become invested in the fate of the people among whom they live.

Prax is a complicated place. *Borderlands* teaches players the region's rich history, and, through that, they should learn how to navigate that complexity. This is land under imperial occupation (the Lunar Empire is generally positioned as antagonists in published *RuneQuest* material). Are the players the boot on the neck of the oppressed population? Is the exiled Duke *really* serving his masters? Would rebellion serve the peoples' interests? Answering those questions, and others, is not easy, but they are straightforward compared to the swirl of conspiracies and politics players will find in

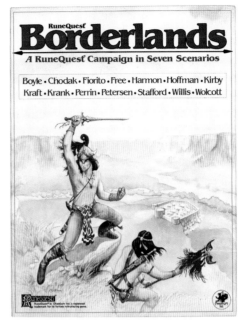

BORDERLANDS, BOX SET, CHAOSIUM, 1982
STEVE PERRIN AND DIVERS HANDS, COVER BY LISA A. FREE

Pavis. *Borderlands* prepares them for the larger world of Glorantha.

Borderlands is yet another entry on the list of RPG products coming in rapid succession that provides an experience totally unlike anything else available on the market at the time. Certainly nothing else makes room for daily life or teaches as much about the world as this box does so elegantly. Even *Griffin Mountain*, released for *RuneQuest* the year before, doesn't feel so well lived-in (interestingly, the final scenario in *Borderlands* provides a potential transition to *Griffin Mountain*, should the players feel ready to move on from the homes they've established). Taken with that book and the Pavis-centric box sets, Glorantha of the early '80s was the richest, most detailed campaign setting on the shelves.

1970

1980

1990

2000

2010

Star Frontiers (1982)

With a couple of different flavors of mutant or post-apocalyptic science fiction under their belt, TSR took a surprisingly long time to develope a space opera RPG. In doing so with *Star Frontiers*, they managed to create something that wasn't a direct rip-off of *Traveller*, the game it would primarily compete with, nor was it another version of "*Dungeons & Dragons* in space." It doesn't even feel overly similar to *Star Trek* or *Star Wars*. Looking back on it now, *Star Frontiers* feels very much like its own sort of sci-fi and anticipated many ideas used in the *Mass Effect* series of videogames (and, since some clear influences on *Mass Effect*—'90s space operas, like *Babylon 5* and *Farscape*—appear after *Star Frontiers*, the potential connection feels especially portentous).

In *Star Frontiers*, humans, along with three alien species, independently develop what amounts to hyperdrive technology, meet in the Frontier Sector, form a federation, and find themselves embroiled in a violent conflict with yet another mysterious species of alien. In *Mass Effect*, they're giant mechanical squids; in *Star Frontiers*, they're sinister intelligent worm things that occasionally ride dinosaurs.

Those villains, the Sathar, head up a group of unusual alien designs that actually *feel* alien, a distinct contrast to the run-of-the-mill, humanoid-in-a-Halloween-mask sort that populate so many science fiction settings (including, quite literally, *Star Wars*).

The Vrusk are long-bodied, many-legged insectoid ultra-capitalists; Dralasites are giant sentient amoebas with offbeat senses of humor; Yazirians are enthusiastically impulsive gliding apes (one features prominently on the box art). Different races usually render down to a few stereotyped traits once they hit the gaming table—elves are flower children, dwarves are Scottish. *Star Frontiers* makes

a genuine effort, and mostly succeeds, at creating aliens that are strange enough to resist stereotyping while still maintaining characteristics players can latch onto in order to develop personalities and motivations. Someone loved all four species, enough that they all appear, albeit with different names and modified abilities, in the *Spelljammer* campaign setting, four years after *Star Frontiers* went dark.

The game runs on a straightforward percentile system that's robust and flexible for the time, especially for a TSR game that displays "from the makers of *Dungeons & Dragons*" prominently on the box cover. Combat is often strangely non-lethal, and medical tech provides the same level of service as healing and resurrection magic in fantasy settings. Players either love this hardiness or hate it, and house rules for increasing the severity of damage are fairly common.

Strangely, *Star Frontiers*, a science fiction game about space exploration, went two years without rules for spaceships, which wasn't a big deal, at first, since the initial adventure modules presented a story line about being marooned on a strange planet. Ships were introduced in the *Knight Hawks* box set (1983), which

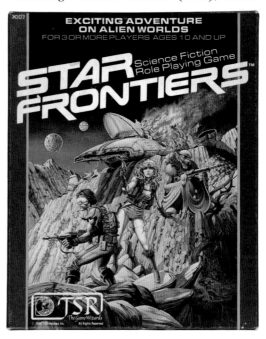

delivers a suite of information on both star fighters and larger capital ships. Combat is resolved using a tactical hex-based wargame, which might seem dull, but is a step up from *Traveller* in terms of ease and excitement. The combination worked well enough that West End Games' *Star Wars* RPG launched with a tactical wargame as a core part of the line a few years later.

In 1985, TSR released *Zebulon's Guide to Frontier Space*, which was meant to be the first volume in a series of sourcebooks that overhauled and expanded the *Star Frontiers* line. The significant change is the implementation of the Action Resolution Table, which is basically a simplified version of the Universal Table used in TSR's *Marvel Super Heroes*. That system worked well enough for superheroes, but TSR shoehorned it into *Star Frontiers* and *Gamma World*. Players of those games hated it. There are good rules expansions in *Zebulon's Guide*, too, but good, bad, or otherwise, it's all moot. Beware the doom invited by putting "Volume One" on the cover of an RPG book: *Zebulon's Guide* was the last supplement for the game. The second volume, which was to include the second half of the rules revision, never appeared, making the whole reboot incomplete and arguably unusable. So it goes, I guess.

No one seems to know exactly why TSR decided to scuttle *Star Frontiers*. I often see folks on Instagram assume that it was to make room for the ill-starred *Buck Rogers XXVc* (1990), but that came out five long years later. I have a theory, though: I think TSR ditched *Star Frontiers* on the hubristic assumption they could outbid the competition for the *Star Wars* RPG license. In *Defining a Galaxy: Celebrating 30 Years of Roleplaying in a Galaxy Far, Far Away* (2018), Bill Slavicsek says that in the mid '80s, FASA Corporation convinced Parker Brothers to give up the hobby games portion of the *Star Wars* master game license so they could snap it up and

develop *Star Wars* wargames. Unfortunately for them, a sales manager let the details of the deal slip during a convention, setting off a bidding war.

Slavicsek notes that negotiations between Lucasfilm and West End Games over *Star Wars: The Roleplaying Game* were ongoing in 1986, which leads me to believe the bidding war started during the summer convention season of 1985. In the 2016 *Rolling Stone* article, "How a Pen and Paper RPG Brought *Star Wars* Back from the Dead," Greg Costikyan is quoted as saying, "[West End Games] made a bid of $100,000. We later learned that TSR had tried to get the license too, but they only bid $70,000." Could TSR have pre-emptively canceled the *Star Frontiers* line in a run-up to their unsuccessful bid for the *Star Wars* license? I wouldn't be surprised; that's exactly the sort of inept foot-shooting that was the specialty of TSR's business side.

Fighting Fantasy (1982)

The US approach to interactive fiction comes out of Edward Packard's Choose Your Own Adventure series (1979) of gamebooks and features narratives that snake in a non-linear way through numbered passages, with the reader choosing between the possible paths. TSR's Endless Quest books used this format. The British approach is essentially the same but with the addition of light RPG elements, often dice-based, for character creation and management of inventory, combat, and magic. Often called *adventure* gamebooks to distinguish them from their American cousins, they spring directly out of American tabletop RPGs, using the format established for *Tunnels & Trolls* solo adventures.

There are many beloved series—Joe Dever's Lone Wolf (1984-present), J. H. Brennan's GrailQuest (1984-1987), and Dave Morris's various series—but the adventure gamebook phenomenon all starts with Steve Jackson and Ian

THE WARLOCK OF FIRETOP MOUNTAIN, PUFFIN BOOKS, 1982
STEVE JACKSON (UK) AND IAN LIVINGSTONE, COVER BY PETER ANDREW JONES

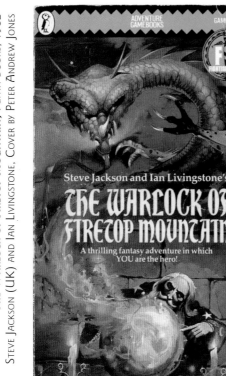

FIGHTING FANTASY: THE INTRODUCTORY ROLE-PLAYING GAME, PUFFIN BOOKS, 1984
STEVE JACKSON (UK), COVER BY DUNCAN SMITH

Livingston's Fighting Fantasy series, which kicked off in the UK with *The Warlock of Firetop Mountain* in 1982.

With American RPGs expensive to import and British-designed RPGs still a few years off, the UK-published Fighting Fantasy was the easiest and least expensive way for Brits (and Canadians and Australians) to dip their toes into the fantasy RPG experience. This situation suited Jackson and Livingston just fine, as they (along with John Peake) were the founders of Games Workshop, which reprinted a number of American RPGs for the UK market. When Fighting Fantasy readers were ready for the full experience, Games Workshop was waiting.

The Warlock of Firetop Mountain stamps out the basic template for the series. The book is a straightforward dungeon crawl, with the reader entering the lair of the Sorcerous Overlord Oldoran Zagor with a mind to kill him and claim his treasure; it's straightforward, if a bit morally bankrupt. The 6-sided die-based system is simple and sturdy with three attributes—

Skill, Stamina and Luck—just enough to give the proceedings some tooth without bogging it down.

The book has two distinct parts. Livingstone wrote the first, which proceeds along a set course, propelling the reader and forcing them to make decisions basically at random. The second, penned by Jackson (not to be confused with the Texan behind *The Fantasy Trip* and *GURPS*), is a maze that allows for free (and often circular) exploration. The two parts are unified by the fact that there is one single, optimal path through the book; and the idea is that it should take multiple attempts, accompanied by maps and notes, to learn what it is (this notion of finding the optimal path is a central one for many British adventure gamebooks).

Rooms filled with bizarre inhabitants and weird traps liven up the proceedings. Livingstone's method would win out for the majority of the Fighting Fantasy line, as well as most other similar gamebooks; but Jackson used his open world approach in his Sorcery! series (a sort of Fighting Fantasy spin-off), which I regard as some of the very best adventure gamebooks ever written.

The Fighting Fantasy series is lavishly illustrated, usually by Games Workshop's pool of artists. The narcotic strangeness of Peter Andrew Jones's cover sets an unusual tone—is the warlock conjuring or napping; is the dragon a thing of flesh or a fever dream? Echoing the *Fiend Folio*, *Firetop Mountain* is ornately illustrated by Russ Nicholson, whose work here is equal parts gorgeous, gruesome, and mysterious. His depiction of Zagor, lean, bearded, imperious, bedecked in elaborate robes and intricate jewelry, is unlike any mage seen before, both decadent and diabolical (and so intriguing that even though he dies in this book, he comes back at least two more times in the course of the series). The illustration of a decomposing ghoul with a face full of worms pushed the limits of acceptability for what was then regarded as a children's book and got the series into some hot water with evangelical groups, similar to what *D&D* was dealing with stateside (see page 122).

The moral panic didn't dent sales. *The Warlock of Firetop Mountain* and the Fighting Fantasy series proved to be a massive on-ramp for bringing new players into the RPG hobby, particularly in the British commonwealth, to a level that is on par with the *D&D* red box and *HeroQuest*. *Firetop Mountain* alone was reprinted five times in 1982, ten times in 1983, and seven more in 1984, eventually selling well over two million copies and inspiring a popular board game to boot. It's the anchor for a series that ran 59 volumes and has been revived three times. There are videogames and regular, non-interactive novels. The game system would be expanded into an RPG of sorts in 1984, with *Fighting Fantasy: The Introductory Role-playing Game* and more robustly in 1989 with *Dungeoneer* and the Advanced Fighting Fantasy line of books. That system later formed the basis of Melsonian Art Council's absurdist RPG, *Troika!*, one of the key contemporary indie RPGs.

DUNGEONEER, PUFFIN BOOKS, 1989
MARC GASCOIGNE AND PETE TAMLYN, COVER BY JOHN SIBBICK

Dungeons & Dragons BECMI (1983)

If there is a quintessential *Dungeons & Dragons* product, it's the "Red Box" version of the *Basic Set*. It could be found on store shelves for nearly a decade and likely marks TSR's greatest success in penetrating the mainstream marketplace. If someone had even a passing interest in *D&D* in the '80s, they probably owned, or knew someone who owned, or otherwise desperately wanted, a Red Box. Through this gateway passed untold thousands of new players.

The box is the most professional looking trade dress on a *D&D* product to this point. The bright red catches the eye, and the painting by Larry Elmore holds it: All the years of *D&D*, past, present, and future, seem captured in that image—the courage of one warrior, the ruined architecture, the terrifying dragon, the mortal combat, the *treasure*. The painting accomplishes this summation, despite (or perhaps because of) some odd compositional choices—the warrior's awkward thrusting stance and the dragon's single

DUNGEONS & DRAGONS SET 1: BASIC RULES, BOX SET, TSR, 1983
FRANK MENTZER, COVER BY LARRY ELMORE

horn both feel disorienting or atypical in a way, even after all of these years. The rest of the graphic design is sharp, legible, and in the mode of the decade. This box, and the rest of the line, looked great on bookstore shelves and in magazine ads, in a way the previous *Basic Set* boxes did not. It's packaged to sell.

The rules inside are designed to be played. This is the third iteration of the basic rules, revised by Frank Mentzer, and it is the leanest, most approachable version yet. It teaches through easy-to-follow solo adventures, introducing players to the nefarious wizard Bargle the Infamous, and the beautiful, doomed Cleric, Aleena. There is even a rust monster, so players can start getting used to the idea of playing with jerky GMs who use monsters to ruin their sweet kit (rust monsters turn metal to dust).

The presence of Larry Elmore and Jeff Easley's work in the interior illustrations signals a larger shift in aesthetic directions, as well—their clean, realistic styles are bright and welcoming in contrast to the darkness of Dave Trampier and the weird psychedelia of Erol Otus. One interior illustration by Elmore—a warrior, lantern held high, approaching the gloomy entrance of a dungeon—is a new, perfect encapsulation of the *D&D* experience.

DUNGEONS & DRAGONS SET 2: EXPERT RULES, BOX SET, TSR, 1983
FRANK MENTZER, COVER BY LARRY ELMORE

DUNGEONS & DRAGONS SET 3: COMPANION RULES, BOX SET, TSR, 1984
FRANK MENTZER, COVER BY LARRY ELMORE

The *Basic Rules* serves as the "B" in *BECMI*. As with the *B/X* boxes, the Red Box was part of an effort to put a new coat of paint on the introductory boxes while also expanding the line. The bold blue *Set 2: Expert Set* received a similar buff and polish by Mentzer, though the result isn't nearly as dramatic as the Red Box; it still focuses on wilderness adventures, but it also sketches out the Known World with more detail.

Elmore's interior art continues to be epoch-defining here. Towards the back of the book is an illustration of a party of adventurers—Fighter, Magic-User, Dwarf, and Elf—gathering their loot. Another bit of *D&D* quintessence: The otherwise frail-looking wizard finds the strength to heft a coffer overflowing with gems and jewelry; coins rain down on the Dwarf, who has sunk to his knees and looks on the verge of tears.

The first new box in the series—"C" is for *Set 3: Companion Rules*—came out in 1984. Where *Expert* topped out at level 14, *Companion* expands to level 25, five more

DUNGEONS & DRAGONS SET 4: MASTER RULES, BOX SET, TSR, 1985
FRANK MENTZER, COVER BY LARRY ELMORE

DUNGEONS & DRAGONS SET 5: IMMORTAL RULES, BOX SET, TSR, 1986
FRANK MENTZER, COVER BY LARRY ELMORE

possible levels than a character can achieve in *Advanced Dungeons & Dragons*! The theming starts to get wobbly here, though. Where the Red Box tackled dungeons, and the Blue Box tackled the limitless wilds, the Teal Box (odd color choice, honestly) tackles property ownership. Not exactly the stuff of high adventure, it comes with the responsibilities of vassalage and the potential for political entanglements and mass combat (the box has rules for both).

In essence, the *Companion Rules* are about the transition from adventurer to ruler, mirroring the fortunes of Conan, but the book never comes right out and says it, perhaps because Mentzer was worried that responsibility is a drag (King Conan definitely thought so, just look at Arnold in the epilogue of the movie, all gray and bored!). Eventually, the characters become so powerful that it is difficult to envision how they live in the game world—an inherent problem in level-based rules systems. In most cases, retirement seems preferable to roleplaying a king.

The game starts to get *very* strange in *Set 4: Master Rules* (1985) where the level cap is raised to an astounding 36. Much of the book still seems unsure about what

characters of this level are supposed to be doing. The Master experience boils down to ruling ever larger domains and fighting bigger wars (a surprising number of pages are devoted to siege engines). But space is also dedicated to tantalizing ideas, like anti-magic, powerful artifacts, the multiverse, reality shifts, and immortality. That last is particularly interesting.

In the Known World, the gods are heroes who have, through their legendary feats, ascended to divinity, and *Master Rules* lays out the four paths to achieve a similar destiny, one for each class. They're all ridiculous. The Cleric, for instance, must first find a time traveling artifact and use it to manipulate events so that three kings of different periods retain and expand their dynasties. Then, the Cleric must preside over a realm of at least 50,000 people and build a new capital. Finally, they must found their own dynasty, ruling over it for 20 years and resolving four crises that threaten their country. Then, they become a god?

The paths for the other classes are just as preposterous. The Fighter has it the worst, needing to live additional lives as each of the other classes for extended periods. All of these requirements feel

strange in the context of *D&D* and don't seem suited for typical play. And, even in the unlikely event that a character can somehow succeed and achieve immortality, the rules advise that immortal characters be retired into the custody of the GM.

That's pretty rich, considering the "I" in *BECMI* stands for *Set 5: Immortals Rules* (which hit shelves in 1986, the same year that *Highlander* hit theaters, so queue up Queen's song "Princes of the Universe" before continuing reading). Despite all of those wild requirements for godhood in the *Master Rules*, the arc of the M-series modules provides a shortcut to immortality in *M3: Twilight Calling*, 1986.

Immortals Rules details what happens next. At this point, the concept of levels is dumped, along with the entire previously established progression system. Instead, accumulated experience points are converted to power points, which are used to vastly enhance a character's powers while maintaining their divine rank, which can be raised by competing in Olympics-style god games!

Instead of dungeons and castles, much of a character's time as an immortal is spent creating their own plane of existence and wearing a loin cloth. It is apparent that a good deal of thought went into conveying the experience of a kind of godhood. The box set probably amounts to something like a magnum opus, and it is a delight to read in many ways. I just can't imagine playing it. And apparently neither could TSR; only three modules supporting the *Immortals Rules* were released, and they don't represent the promised experience well. The strangest of them is *IM1: The Immortal Storm*, where brief visits to New York City and Chicago somehow feel more disorienting than a plane of reality inhabited by sentient musical notes.

Star Trek: The Role Playing Game (1983)

On one hand, *Star Trek* is one of the most recognizable franchises in science fiction, which makes it a no-brainer property to license into an RPG. In fact, the very first licensed RPG was a *Star Trek* RPG. *Star Trek: Adventure Gaming in the Final Frontier* (1978), a joint venture between Heritage Models and Gamescience, was essentially a vehicle to sell miniatures and went unsupported beyond the initial rules. It faded away soon after release, which left the license ripe for someone with a fresh take to snatch up. That is exactly what FASA Corporation did after a couple of years spent producing material for other games, like *Traveller*.

On the other hand, the humanism of *Star Trek*'s creator, Gene Roddenberry, imbued the original television series with a strong anti-war stance, making it a strange fit for an RPG in the landscape of the early '80s, when the influence of wargaming was still so strong. This war footing was made clear during the RPG's development.

FASA farmed out the design to four freelance design groups, each of which delivered a prototype that was too combat-focused. The fifth and final design team avoided this pitfall, but the pull of wargaming would prove too strong for the

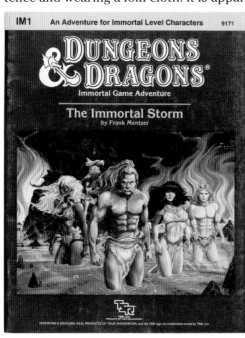

IM1: THE IMMORTAL STORM, TSR, 1986
FRANK MENTZER, COVER BY LARRY ELMORE

STAR TREK: THE ROLE PLAYING GAME, BOX SET, FASA CORPORATION, 1983
GUY MCLIMORE, GREG POEHLEIN, AND DAVID TEPOOL. COVER BY MITCH O'CONNELL

game's ship-to-ship combat component in the long run.

The way the game initially handled space battles is novel and facilitates a lot of roleplaying. The general action of the game is structured to mirror the action of the original TV series, with the players, who are at the helm of the ship in various officer roles, visiting alien planets and solving problems. In ship-to-ship combat, each character takes the position on the bridge that matches their duties as an officer—the helmsman maneuvers the ship and fires the weapon systems; the navigator maintains shields; the captain issues orders and coordinates the various stations.

There are combat roles for everyone, down to the communications officer (they track casualties), which introduces many potential complications and roleplaying into what would otherwise be a straightforward turn action in wargame. It's an unusual way to manage space combat and is one of the earliest examples of play that encourages live-action roleplay in a way that feels reminiscent of kids playing make-believe—I can easily see people in a living room, arranged with chairs and small folding tables as if they were on

the *Enterprise* bridge, facing a "view screen" bulletin board displaying the battle hex map.

That make-believe quality speaks to the game's overall approachability. FASA wisely designed *Star Trek: The Role Playing Game* with an eye toward attracting new players. It uses a skill system that is, at its core, a simplified clone of *Traveller*. Like that game, characters are defined by their service, accumulating specific skills and experience through tours of duty.

The core box set assumes that characters have a prior career in the various branches of Starfleet, but other products expand the potential character histories, allowing players to come up through the Romulan and Klingon navies. *The Orions* sourcebook (1987) gives players the option of pirate backgrounds, and there is a sourcebook for merchants. Or players can just take the roles of the classic characters from the show; that's fine, too.

Star Trek aired for three seasons before its cancellation in 1969. A long and popular run in syndication followed, and a rabid cult following developed over time. Despite the fact that, starting in 1979, *Star Trek* lived on in the feature film series, fans were starved for *Trek* content—novels, comics, magazines, games—Trekkies didn't care; they wanted *more*.

In our current moment in history, one filled with intellectual properties that weave narratives across multiple forms of media and that are painstakingly cataloged in fandom wikis, it seems like an unimaginable position for a company to take, but through most of the '80s, Paramount was inconsistent in maintaining a *Star Trek* canon. This lack of oversight put FASA in the position of being, not just a creator of *Star Trek* canon, but its primary cataloger (a position West End Games would also find itself in later in the decade with *Star Wars: The Roleplaying Game*, though in that case, Lucasfilm actively encouraged and embraced the developing RPG canon, for a while).

FASA created huge swaths of material as needed, including dozens of ships, some Klingon language fundamentals, and a lawless area of space called the Triangle that remained unclaimed by the Federation, the Klingons, or the Romulans. The Triangle was designed as the central playground for the RPG (similar to the Spinward Marches in *Traveller* and the Outer Rim territories that would be developed later in the *Star Wars: The Roleplaying Game*) where games that centered on merchants or pirates played out without having to deal with pesky restrictions, like laws.

The Triangle expanded on the idea of the Neutral Zone, first introduced in the original TV series in "Balance of Terror" and destined to be explored at great length in *The Next Generation*. FASA also embraced some existing *Trek* lore, like the novel, *The Final Reflection* (1984), by John M. Ford, which sought to build a plausible Klingon culture out of the very little information presented in the original TV show. Ford then wrote *The Klingons* supplement (1983) for the RPG, which, along with the novel, had some lasting impact on *Star Trek*'s on-screen depiction of Klingons as protagonists, despite the details being ultimately judged non-canon by *Trek* creator Gene Roddenberry.

FASA also developed the Romulans over several sourcebooks, making them as formidable as the Klingons (despite having appeared in just a handful of episodes in the original series). FASA was on to something there, as *The Next Generation*, and, later, *Deep Space Nine*, would also take a keen interest in the Romulans. With Roddenberry the ultimate authority on canon, FASA's Romulans eventually went out the window.

Despite their best efforts, FASA couldn't shake their martial impulses.

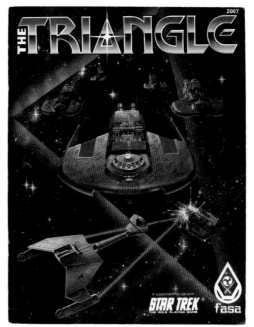

THE TRIANGLE, FASA CORPORATION, 1985
GUY MCLIMORE, GREG POEHLEIN, AND DAVID TEPOOL, COVER BY DAVID MARTIN

Designers kept combat in the spotlight of *Star Trek: The Role Playing Game*, with violent solutions to problems coming up again and again. The second edition of the game gave into wargaming and provided an optional strategy system to resolve ship-to-ship combat.

Eventually, Roddenberry had enough. He was particularly upset when he learned of a Trek-themed ground combat strategy game and a scenario in which the Federation initiates a war with the Klingons and the Romulans; coupled with Paramount Marketing's disappointment in FASA's handling of the sourcebooks for *Star Trek: The Next Generation*, this was enough to justify pulling the license in 1989.

That pissed off a lot of fans of the RPG! After six years and a substantial pile of books and magazines, players were invested in this version of the *Star Trek* universe. When *The Next Generation* came out, some fans were genuinely angry to see creator Gene Rodenberry disregarding the FASA canon in favor of his own. When Paramount Marketing revoked the license, some fans even speculated Rodenberry was to blame. This might sound familiar: A similar drama would unfold a decade later involving *Star Wars* and the expanded universe founded in the West End Games RPG.

Star Trek, after all, *did* promise to boldly go.

James Bond 007 (1983)

Where SPI rushed into the RPG market and spontaneously combusted for their trouble, Avalon Hill took their time wading into the pool. When the wargaming company did, their first foray was through a subsidiary company, Victory Games, ironically staffed by former SPI designers.

Victory Games primarily developed SPI-style wargames, but they also held the license for super spy James Bond, for which they developed *James Bond 007: Role-Playing in Her Majesty's Secret Service*. Espionage games weren't new. Merle Rasmussen's *D&D*-derived *Top Secret* had been around since 1980 (though it feels more like a commando game than a spy game), and with Hero Games' *Espionage!* and Flying Buffalo's *Mercenaries, Spies & Private Eyes* both hitting shelves in 1983, *Bond* had company. Regardless, brand recognition propelled *Bond* to the top of the heap, though it didn't hurt that the game was easy to pick up and play.

Character creation is handled with a point-buy system, complete with disadvantages (here called weaknesses, like Bond's weakness for beautiful women), no doubt thanks to *Champions'* success in illustrating the method's flexibility. Skills are tested using percentiles, with the target determined by cross-referencing the skill value against a difficulty level determined by the GM. This is done with a resolution table; for a task of average difficulty, a player looks at the central column. An easier task might shift down a number of columns; a more difficult task would shift up—a clear inspiration for the Universal Table in *Marvel Super Heroes*, and perhaps, in a way, for the adjective ladder in *Fudge* (1992).

If a player succeeds in their roll, they check the result on an additional table (so many charts in the '80s!), which determines their level of success. Up to this point, resolution in RPGs was pass or fail. *James Bond 007* introduces four degrees of success—acceptable, good, very good, and excellent—that color the results. Each skill has different success requirements. Encoding a message with Cryptography requires a good success. Interrogations, on the other hand, yield different quantities and qualities of information depending on the success level. An acceptable result might be, "There are guards ahead," whereas an excellent result might be, "There are three guards ahead in a reinforced checkpoint with a machine gun, but if you stick to the right wall, you'll be in their blind spot." This graduated approach to resolution would go on to become a popular design feature in other games.

Bond is also unusual in its focus on the player character. The rules explicitly state that, unlike most other RPGs, GMs should give every advantage to the players, letting the dice determine their failures rather than plot contrivances, some-

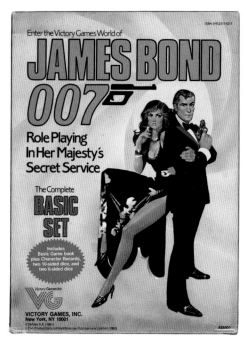

JAMES BOND 007 BASIC SET, Box set, VICTORY GAMES, 1983
GERARD CHRISTOPHER KLUG, COVER BY JAMES TALBOT

thing mechanically supported by the tiers of success. Tipping the balance toward player success leads to a game that is snappy and cinematically action-oriented (if perhaps a bit overpowered—designers would later learn that complicating gradations of failure are often more interesting and fun than degrees of success). A luck mechanic using Hero Points amplifies the power fantasy by allowing players to alter outcomes at a cost (the cinematic approach and luck points would both figure prominently in *Star Wars: The Roleplaying Game*).

Owing to its embrace of the effortless heroism of Mary Sues and Marty Stus, *Bond* is designed for small groups; it never says so explicitly, but the rules are well-suited for duet play—one player and a GM. That arrangement shouldn't be that surprising coming from a company that specialized in two-player wargames, but the game does shine a spotlight on individual characters (and puts more pressure on the player) in a way that most RPGs do not.

Several sourcebooks give GMs ample tools to create their own adventures. The most notable are *Thrilling Locations* (1985), a compendium of setting details and floor plans, which anticipates the *Shadowrun* tool kit, *Sprawl Sites*, and the *Q Manual* (1983), a guide to all of the glorious gizmos. Primarily, though, the line consists of adventures, all but two of which are based directly on the books or films (the outliers are sequels to *Goldfinger* and *You Only Live Twice*).

Cleverly, the adventures change the details of the plots to keep players guessing. One of the biggest swerves is the absence of iconic Bond villain Ernst Stavro Blofeld and his organization SPECTRE, thanks to a decades-long rights dispute involving the film, *Thunderball* (1961). Instead, the game introduces Karl Ferenc Skorpios, his pet greyhound, and his tarot card-themed organization T.A.R.O.T. (Technological Accession,

Revenge, and Organized Terrorism), which is arguably superior. Cats are obviously more villainous than dogs, but the tarot card theme and its implied hierarchy is a good deal spookier than SPECTRE, which, unfortunately, has nothing to do with actual ghosts.

Ravenloft (1983)

From the moment he crept out of his crypt, Count Strahd von Zarovich proved to be one of the most enduring characters to spring from *Dungeons & Dragons*. He was born in 1978, created by Tracy and Laura Hickman, to serve as the villain of their homebrew adventure. They playtested the scenario every Halloween for five years before pitching it to TSR, who published it as an official module, *I6: Ravenloft*. It's a groundbreaking module, with an emphasis on story that would lay the groundwork for the *Dragonlance* saga and narrative-focused scenarios for the next decade.

Ravenloft embraced the aesthetics of gothic horror stories, which immediately made it stand out among the Frazetta-influenced visuals of most *D&D* modules—Strahd is depicted in a tuxedo while the generic adventurers in Clyde Caldwell's illustrations look like, well, generic adventurers clad in armor; it's an unusual juxtaposition. The mix of eras somehow works, though, telegraphing that despite the gothic setting, the adventure is still fantasy at its core (much the same way *The Isle of Dread* is still a very standard *D&D* experience despite the trappings of *King Kong*).

Ravenloft also used a gothic framing for its narrative. Long ago, in the realm of Barovia, Strahd loved a woman named Tatyana, who, in turn, loved his younger brother, Sergei. Blaming her rejection on his age, Strahd resorted to necromancy to restore his youth, and, on the day of the wedding between his brother and Tatyana, he murdered Sergei. Tatyana, horrified, took her own life, and Strahd, now a vampire, retreated to his castle to

I6: RAVENLOFT, TSR, 1983

TRACY AND LAURA HICKMAN, COVER BY CLYDE CALDWELL

brood after killing the traitorous guards who attempted to assassinate their corrupt lord by riddling him with arrows. It doesn't get more gothic than that.

While that history remains true, the staging of the module changes with each play. Several key factors are determined by the draw of tarot cards during a fortune-telling session before reaching the castle. Four cards determine locations—of Strahd himself, of his diary (which details the love triangle), and of two powerful magic items that can result in his undoing. The fifth card determines one of the Count's four potential motivations, the most interesting of which is his desire to use the presence of the players as a way to seduce the burgomaster's adopted daughter, Ireena, who bears more than a passing resemblance to Tatyana.

Aesthetics and narrative tricks aside, *Ravenloft*'s reputation as a classic sits squarely on the shoulders of Strahd himself. In many ways, he's the first genuine *Dungeons & Dragons* villain. The lich at the heart of *Tomb of Horrors* is really more of a trap than a character, while the trio of chieftains from the Giants-series of modules are merely big piles of hit points with names. These, and others, have grown in stature and detail over time and with the release of new products, but Strahd is different. He is a fully fleshed out character from the start: He has an agenda and an inner life. And, perhaps most importantly, he is present throughout the module, taunting the players, and testing their mettle in skirmishes and feints, rather than waiting for them in the final room of a dungeon.

Part of Strahd's character is conveyed in an unlikely way: Mechanically. Player characters and monsters were built out of similar but distinct systems. Strahd marks the first time in *Dungeons & Dragons* when the two systems merge. He is a monster, with the vampire's full suite of powers, but he is also a tenth-level Magic-User with the accompanying selection of spells. The combination makes him a formidable opponent, but it also imbues him with a sense of history and personality.

Ravenloft proved so popular that TSR commissioned a sequel, module *I10: Ravenloft II: The House on Gryphon Hill* (1986). Though attributed to Tracy and Laura Hickman, it was completed after Tracy left TSR, with the writing done in sections by David "Zeb" Cook, Jeff Grubb, Harold Johnson, and Douglas Niles. Unlike the elegant *Ravenloft*, *Gryphon Hill* is a confusing mess, with parallel realities, a machine that swaps personalities, and two Strahds (one being a sort of heroic, Frankenstein-like alchemist who is not a vampire at all, maybe). I've never quite grasped the module on its own terms, let alone the option to muddy the waters further by running it in conjunction with the original (three Strahds?).

Despite its failings, *Gryphon Hill* expands the gothic world surrounding Strahd and provides the rough outline of what would eventually become the campaign setting *Ravenloft: Realm of*

Terror (1990), even introducing the lich, Azalin, who is arguably the setting's main character. The box set reveals the Dark Powers who, using magical mists, spirit away especially evil people and their lands in order to add them to a cursed collection of interconnected domains of dread. These evil souls become Darklords, and, though powerful, they suffer curses that reflect their evil deeds back at them forever.

The campaign setting is a mixed bag. On the one hand, it is a wonderful exploration of gothic horror. *Dark Sun*, with its striking artwork by Gerald Brom and Tom Baxa, is often credited as the first aesthetically-driven campaign setting, but this unfairly overlooks how the massive body of gloomy artwork by pulp artist Stephen Fabian defines *Ravenloft*, with its foggy streets, cluttered studies, and haunted visages.

On the other hand, the power-accumulating mechanics of *D&D* make a poor machine for horror, even with the box set's fear mechanics. Both are based on saving throws versus paralysis, and, while less clunky than the fear mechanic in *CB1: Conan Unchained*, they still don't function as elegantly as *Call of Cthulhu*'s

RAVENLOFT: REALM OF TERROR, BOX SET, TSR, 1990
BRUCE NESMITH AND ANDRIA HAYDAY, COVER BY CLYDE CALDWELL

sanity system. There is a vexing lack of clarity in the core theme of the setting, as well—why have the Dark Powers assembled this zoo of evil? Is it to punish the Darklords? That would seem to be the case, with their various curses. But then why bring innocents, like the player characters, into the mists, as well? Conceivably, the domains of dread could function as a massive battery for existential suffering, but if this is the case, the box set never explores it.

Nevertheless, Strahd is the first Darklord, with the mists claiming him and Barovia shortly after Tatyana's suicide. The Dark Powers gifted him with complete dominion over Barovia, but once a generation, Strahd meets a woman who appears to be the reincarnation of Tatyana, and history repeats. He languishes there still. In practical terms, Strahd is both central to the *Ravenloft* campaign setting, but also removed from it. He is the subject of several *Ravenloft* novels, and his presence is felt all over the support materials; but, he is far too powerful and too important to the setting to be challenged by a party of adventurers like those who might have once bested him in the original module.

I10: RAVENLOFT II: THE HOUSE ON GRYPHON HILL, TSR, 1986
TRACY AND LAURA HICKMAN, COVER BY CLYDE CALDWELL

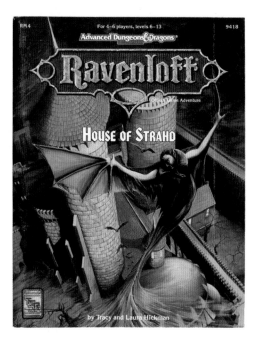

Strahd's new position as a cosmic lynch pin didn't stop TSR from reprinting the original module as *House of Strahd* (1993), updating the source material to take into account *Ravenloft*'s unique rules while aligning it with Strahd's new power level as a Darklord. The result is strange. The once cutting-edge module now feels strangely old fashioned among the more narrative- and exploration-focused *Ravenloft* campaign material. Strahd had grown too large for his once mesmerizing and mysterious castle.

In 1999, TSR issued a Silver Anniversary version of *I6*, which was a direct update of the original module to *AD&D* Second Edition rules without including the additions from the *Ravenloft* campaign setting. In 2006, Wizards of the Coast updated the original module again, this time to the 3.5E rules, as *Expedition to Castle Ravenloft*, by Bruce Cordell and James Wyatt. This version distinguishes itself by expanding the source material, fleshing out Barovia, and providing additional adventure material outside of the castle. For these books, Strahd remains largely the same.

A decade later, Wizards once again returned to Castle Ravenloft with *Curse of Strahd* (2016), updating the module for *D&D* 5E. This version maintains the basic approach, expanding the Barovia that Cordell and Wyatt introduced, but jettisons their details. Instead, the Hickmans returned to brainstorm new ideas. This Strahd feels different somehow—colder. His dark romanticism has been drained out, and his ambition is largely replaced by boredom. He kills, and terrorizes, and corrupts because it is the only way he can divert his attention from an unending existence.

In many ways, Strahd is a vessel for the audience's relationship with an ever-changing and evolving vampire legend. While a character in his own right, he is broadly drawn, so every group of players can make him their own. There are many Strahds, each defined by the tastes of the people at the table.

Strahd has surprisingly little in common with the Dracula of Bram Stoker's novel—most obviously, he lacks the mustache, but also the feral impulsiveness and much of the psychosexual subtext. Stoker's biggest influence on Strahd is actually found in the one facet of his character that popular culture has most often ignored: The implication that Dracula was a practitioner of the black arts and an enthusiastic devil worshipper. From this comes Strahd's status in *D&D* as a Magic-User, his obscene necromantic experiments and his compact with the Dark Powers. The two original modules, when combined, also mirror the settings of the novel, with *I6: Ravenloft* depicting a version of Castle Dracula in Transylvania and *I10: Gryphon Hill* standing in for the English countryside.

In terms of fashion sense and temperament, Strahd has more in common with Lugosi's debonair, calculating Dracula, as well as the refractions of that interpreta-

tion of the character that have bounced through popular culture since 1931 (so much so that the box art for the original NES *Castlevania II: Simon's Quest,* 1987, itself a conglomeration of Dracula tropes, lifts Clyde Caldwell's iconic cover painting for *I6: Ravenloft* and it doesn't look at all out of place). *Curse of Strahd,* meanwhile, gives a nod to Anne Rice's vampire novels. Here, Strahd's previous consorts are women, and he has a new obsession with a possibly reincarnated Tatyana, but the most recent object of his affections, Escher, is a man—a gesture to the bisexuality of Rice's Lestat.

The clearest antecedent of Strahd, though, is Barnabas Collins, the vampire that dominated ABC's soap opera *Dark Shadows* from 1966 to 1971. Like Strahd, Collins is cut from the same cloth as popular conceptions of Dracula, but it is in Collins audiences first see the synthesis of the vampire legend and the reincarnation romance of Boris Karloff's *The Mummy* (1932). Like Tatyana, the object of Collins's affection leaps off a cliff to her death rather than become his lover and, a century later, the vampire is obsessed with a woman who resembles her. This idea captured the popular imagination so thoroughly that it has been included in

many subsequent adaptations of *Dracula* (beginning in 1972 with *Blacula* and, in my view, forever cemented in 1992's *Bram Stoker's Dracula*), to the point that most people assume it was part of the original novel.

More than anything, it is the Collinsesque cycle of reincarnation that defines Strahd, beyond the confines of any one adventure module and into the realms of the meta. In the *Ravenloft* campaign setting, the Dark Powers force Strahd to relive his lowest moment, reintroducing him to the woman who he can't help but drive to her death, again and again. Even if a group of adventurers should triumph in *House of Strahd,* those Dark Powers will bring him back to unlife and start the cycle again.

Thanks to *Ravenloft*'s status as a classic, and its numerous reprints, this cycle holds true in real-world play, as well. I have killed Strahd three times, and even though the most recent time was the likely the last for me, he will live again, and be killed again, for other groups around other tables, for as long as people gather together to play *Dungeons & Dragons.* Fun for the players, but for Strahd, it is an endless torment.

The Dark Powers are truly cruel.

HÂRN REGIONAL MODULE, BOX SET, COLUMBIA GAMES, 1983
N. ROBIN CROSSBY, COVER BY N. ROBIN CROSSBY

Hârn (1983)

For some, the exercise of creating detailed, "logical" imaginary worlds just for the sake of it—not for a novel or an RPG—is a deeply rewarding intellectual endeavor. This practice has given way to, at least, two beloved realms—Forgotten Realms and Glorantha—both of which predate the existence of RPGs. Another is Hârn, N. Robin Crossby's world. Unlike the others, though, when Hârn was introduced, it wasn't bound to a set of rules. It was just a world, fit for any system—the first truly system-agnostic setting.

Confusingly, Hârn debuted in 1983 in three different forms: A box set called *Hârn Region Module* and two folios, one simply called *Hârn*, the other called *Hârn Master Module*. This confusion has continued into the present, with Columbia Games issuing *Hârn* products in all sorts of oddball formats, like loose-leaf binders and clamshell corrugated cardboard boxes.

All three versions contain the same two books and a map. The first book, *Hârnview*, is an overview of the continent (Hârn is but a portion of a larger world), its kingdoms, religion, history, and economics. There is also a set of guidelines for making characters with histories suitable for the world, along with a suggestion for a pre-game session that allows players to make formative decisions (and experience their consequences) for their character's life before becoming an adventurer, á la *Traveller*.

This gloss on a pre-game session is vague, all in all, but this nevertheless is the first mention I've seen of what is now referred to as "session zero," a set-up session in which players and GM hash out boundaries, homebrew rules, and generally establish the tone of the game together.

The second book, the *Hârndex*, is an alphabetical reference book full of fine grain details of Hârn. This is where Crossby's intricate world comes to life. It is a mere 64 pages, but it's packed with information of all kinds. Hârn is a low magic, medieval fantasy world unlike any other, largely because of the thought that went into creating a plausible cluster of competing cultures—it feels very much at the opposite end of the spectrum from "gonzo" games, like *Dungeon Crawl Classics*. It *is* slightly dry, but still manages to be compelling, because it seems so realistic (at least, as realistic as a world with orcs can be). More than any other RPG book I've ever encountered, this feels like a history book about a region in the real-world I'd never previously heard of.

Subsequent books take a similar approach. From 1983 to 1987, more than 30 supplements came out for *Hârn*. Every kingdom got a book, and there is a 16-volume encyclopedia (totaling around 400 pages) that was issued monthly from 1984 to 1985. *Cities of Hârn* (1983) takes an approach that provides building-by-building detail while also giving GMs the tools to fill in large swaths of the cities with their own ideas, in many ways anticipating *Lankhmar: City of Adventure*. Religion is covered in *Gods of Hârn* (1985); it is up to the GM whether the gods actually exist, though, and if they're worth their salt, they'll never tell. Major castles were next. The pace at which Crossby worked meant he ran out of areas of Hârn that needed detailing rather fast, so he soon moved on to the other continents.

The art is a significant contributor to the world's sense of cohesion, a secret truth of RPG world building. Crossby's maps and Garry Steinhilber's floor plans are detailed; Steinhilber's map key is as inspiration-stoking as the one Diesel LaForce developed for the *Dungeons & Dragons Basic Set*. Meanwhile, Eric Hotz provided just about every illustration for every *Hârn* product produced from 1984 to 2000, creating a remarkably consistent visual representation of the world through sepia toned drawings that alternate between gritty realism and a

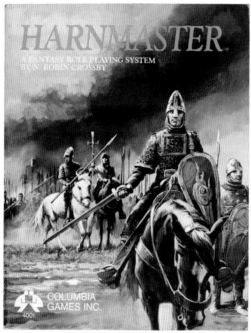

HÄRNMASTER, COLUMBIA GAMES, 1986
N. ROBIN CROSSBY, COVER BY MICHAEL CODD

flattened, faux-medieval style—a clear forerunner of the single artist approach to campaign settings that TSR would adopt in the '90s. Most RPGs focus on epic clashes, but Hotz routinely favored domestic scenes and depictions of everyday objects that do so much to breathe life into the world.

All of this material is methodical and internally consistent. Nothing else in the mid '80s, and a good deal after, right up to now, comes close to providing the amount of detail in *Hârn*. Depth and breadth. There are like a million Forgotten Realms books, and it is still no contest.

After several good years of publishing Hârn as a system agnostic setting, Crossby created a system called *HârnMaster* (1986). A realistic, nitty gritty world deserves a realistic, nitty gritty rule set. The combat system uses 18 hit locations—that's more than *RuneQuest*, but far less than a game like *Aftermath!* (1981), which has 30. A lot of folks say it is derivative of *RuneQuest*; the framework of abilities and a percentile skill system support that claim, but I feel that spiritually, it is more in line with something like *Chivalry & Sorcery*, where the complexity of the systems is meant to bring richness to the imaginary world.

HârnMaster does have a nicely developed magic system, which consists of six elemental attunements, likely inspired by Iron Crown Enterprises' *Spell Law* (1981). The arrangement of attunements in opposition to each other is a forerunner of the Second Edition of *AD&D*'s schools of magic. A mage begins attuned to one element and gets bonuses for spells involving it, penalties for the opposite, and diminished effects for the rest. If a mage grows powerful enough, they can go "gray," transcending the bonuses and penalties of elemental opposition. It's neat, and it effectively echoes real-world magical traditions while also feeling unique.

HârnMaster increasingly monopolized Crossby's time, taking him away from working on the world. In 1994, he stopped writing new material entirely as tensions grew between him and Columbia Games. He split with Columbia permanently in 1997 and started producing *Hârn* content under the moniker Kelestia Productions. Columbia continued to release their own supplements, and legal disputes between the companies continue to this day. Crossby, sadly, passed away in 2008 at the age of 54. His death feels like a kind of robbery, but his eldest daughter Arien, along with a rich fan community, continue to keep *Hârn* alive.

DragonRaid (1984)

In 1979, a student at Michigan State University named James Dallas Egbert III disappeared. The 16-year-old computer science major was a child prodigy who struggled with parental pressure, feelings of isolation, depression, and substance abuse. After being hired by the Egbert family, private detective William

Dear learned about Egbert's enthusiasm for *Dungeons & Dragons* and theorized to the press that it was connected to his disappearance. Students were rumored to play live-action versions of *D&D* in the university's underground complex of steam tunnels, and the fear was that Egbert was hurt or lost within them.

In reality, he had fled for New Orleans after an intentional, near-fatal overdose. There, he worked, for a time, on an oil field before Dear tracked him down and brought him into the custody of his uncle. In 1980, Egbert died by suicide.

The controversy carried on, though. The press had seized Dear's hypothesis that Egbert's disappearance was connected to *D&D*, sensationalizing the theory even after Dear discarded it. Dear explains in his memoir of the case, *The Dungeon Master* (1984) that he regrets ever making the connection, for all the good that does. From here, the idea of the troubled young man who plays *D&D* and cannot distinguish its fiction from reality entered the public imagination.

By 1981, the Egbert case evolved into a full-blown urban legend, featuring impressionable children sneaking into subterranean places en masse to play a game that, by the public standards of the day,

SUPPLEMENT III: ELDRITCH WIZARDRY, TSR, 1976
GARY GYGAX AND BRIAN BLUME, COVER BY DEBORAH LARSON

was strange. In 1981, two authors used the Egbert case as the basis for novels—Rona Jaffe penned *Mazes & Monsters,* and John Coyne delivered *Hobgoblin* (Coyne improbably claims not to have been influenced by the Egbert story, however).

Though fiction, many read these novels as accurate portrayals of the effects of *D&D* on impressionable players. They're both garbage books, but they caught a zeitgeist that continued to trouble *D&D*, specifically, and RPGs, in general, for years to come. The awful made-for-TV movie adaptation of *Mazes & Monsters* (1982)—Tom Hanks's first leading role—only worsened public perception. Although the quality was only a step above an *Afterschool Special*, the film exposed many viewers (particularly moms) to RPGs for the for the first time.

Egbert's disappearance, both real and fictionalized, fed into a larger moral panic that was spreading primarily in the United States, which alleged that nefarious forces were secretly corrupting young people through the culture they consumed. *Dark Dungeons* (1984), an

DRAGONRAID, BOX SET, ADVENTURE LEARNING SYSTEMS, INC., 1984
DICK WULF, COVER BY R. J. WATSON

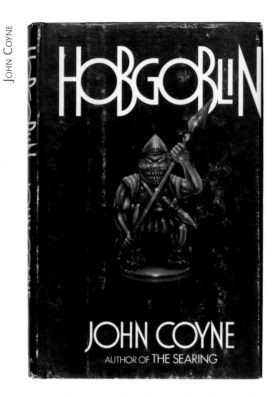

HOBGOBLIN, G. P. PUTNAM'S SONS, 1981
JOHN COYNE

extremist evangelical comic book tract by Jack Chick, depicted *Dungeons & Dragons* as a gateway to actual magical powers. A 1985 segment on *60 Minutes* entitled "Is *Dungeons & Dragons* Evil?" did little to assuage parental fears. Gary Gygax appears as the game's primary defender, claiming the game is the subject of a witch hunt. While accurate, he comes off as dismissive and arrogant, the unwitting villain of the piece. All of this simultaneously imbued *D&D* with a palpable sense of danger and, ironically, fueled sales.

MAZES AND MONSTERS, DELACORTE PRESS, 1981
RONA JAFFE

The existing moral panic and evangelical demonization of *D&D* makes the 1984 release of *DragonRaid*, the first Christian roleplaying game, all the more improbable. Conceived by author Dick Wulf as a tool for teaching and proselytizing the gospels, the game casts kids as holy warriors who clash with monsters representing a smorgasbord of sins in order to memorize Bible passages and learn to

keep the Gospel in their daily lives. The text on the box conveys the game's overall tone: "The exciting new adventure for courageous Christians;" "Building warriors for spiritual battle;" "Will you fight the good fight?" Whether or not it succeeds in those aims is immaterial, producing a game like this in 1984, at the height the Satanic Panic, when both players of RPGs and evangelicals were bound to find common ground in hating it, was both brave and a massive misreading of the marketplace.

The use of massive in this case is literal. The box set is three inches deep and jam-packed with stuff. There are seven books—a player primer, a rulebook, a player's handbook, a GM's guide, and three adventure modules. There are two pads, one of character sheets, one of supplemental sheets for optional skills (like Hatred of Evil, Righteously Mingle with Evil, and, that old favorite, Resist Torture), along with a bunch of character counters, dice (though they are never called dice because of what I suspect is a religious proscription of gambling implements; the player 10-sided dice are StarLots, and the GM's 8-sided die is the Shadow Stone), battle grids, and a

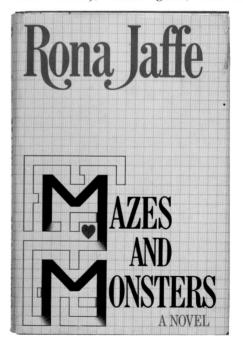

124

tape cassette, which the back of the box promises to be "a dramatic introduction to *DragonRaid*, explanation of the basic rules and player briefing for The LightRaider Test."

There isn't much interior art, but the color cover illustrations by Christian artist R. J. Watson are rather warm and welcoming in an old-fashioned, Sunday school workbook sort of way. All of the components are high quality for the time; it is one of the heftiest RPG products in my collection.

The system is simple and uses what is essentially a resistance table for unopposed contests—the ability value (itself an average of several attributes) is cross-referenced with a difficulty level to provide a number to beat using the dice (er, StarLots). Combat requires opposed rolls in which, interestingly, the enemies use the 8-sided Shadow Stone, which puts them at a disadvantage to the players' 10-sided StarLots—this advantage addresses one evangelical criticism of *D&D*, namely that it places good and evil on even footing. A more involved combat system with critical hits is optional. The most curious thing about *DragonRaid* is what amounts to the magic system, which is based on the idea of WordRunes, essentially Bible quotes that must be recited from memory to, well, create magical effects. This kind of transparent "teaching" tool is easy to make fun of, of course, but it is also an extremely early example of the dialogue-as-mechanic ideas that would crop up in storytelling games and more narrative-based RPGs years later. Is the verb/noun system in *Ars Magica* so different?

DragonRaid was a failure. When I learned of the game's existence in 2019 from an ad in an old issue of *Dragon* magazine, I received a copy direct from the publisher, who was selling box sets assembled from original components that had been sitting in storage since the '80s, which seems like a predictable outcome based on where the RPG industry was at

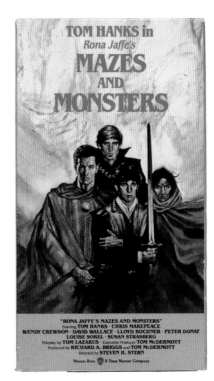

MAZES AND MONSTERS, WARNER HOME VIDEO, 1986
VHS CASSETTE SLEEVE

in 1984. Entrenched RPG players resented the game's blatant fundamentalist Christian themes (folks I have talked to who were forced to play it at religious retreats are particularly acidic in their appraisals), and evangelical Christians thought it was misguided and ultimately just as evil as all the other roleplaying games. In 2018, Lightraider Academy began work on reviving the line. Maybe they'll have better luck this time around.

CB1: Conan Unchained! (1984)

CB1: Conan Unchained! is a great example of an unenthusiastic attempt at a licensed RPG product. The strangely blurry film still of Arnold Schwarzenegger is right there on the cover, fuzzily letting the reader know that this is a marketing tie-in for his *Conan* movies. Released in 1984, *Unchained!* lines up with the box office run of the lesser of the two, *Conan the Destroyer*. Aside from Jeff Butler's interior art, done in the vein of Marvel's *Conan* comic magazines of the '70s and '80s, the rest of the module is a disappointing cash-in.

Designer David "Zeb" Cook makes a valiant effort. He introduces a fear mechanic to account for Conan's uneasiness with the supernatural. He also presents luck points as a way to account for Conan's legendary good fortune. Alas, neither of these systems is straightforward.

Every magical object, creature, and effect has its own fear value, and in order to determine whether a character is scared, the player multiplies that by the value of the character's Wisdom score—a bit more cumbersome than *Call of Cthulhu's* simple subtractive sanity system. Luck, meanwhile, is a resource hidden from the players—they don't know how many points they have, nor how many points a given action will cost, making them rather less useful than the player-controlled luck pools in games like *James Bond 007* or *Ghostbusters*.

Neither of these modifications go very far in making *D&D* feel more suited for Conan's world. Hyboria is a place of little magic, few monsters, and a level of violence that *D&D's* power fantasy mechanics struggle to convey. There *is* a monster in this module called a manotor (predictably, it's a centaur with bull horns,

which is actually a step up from the design of the one that appears in *Conan the Barbarian* King-Size Annual, July, 1978) but it feels more like a joke than anything requiring a fear mechanic. I doubt TSR initially set about to create a plausible Conan roleplaying experience, though, when capitalizing on Conan's popularity was demonstrably easier—witness TSR's *Conan Role-Playing Game*, 1985, which is actually built on the *Marvel Super Heroes System*.

The adventure spends rather long stretches with the characters captured and enslaved by a group of raiders, during which not much happens. Eventually, the players have the opportunity to attack a sorcerer in his tower—but even that feels generic. Worse, the adventure is designed for pre-generated characters, and, since only one of them is Conan, three of the four players are likely to be disappointed when they're cast as the sidekicks.

Conan Unchained! illustrates a significant interplay between *Dungeons & Dragons* and popular culture. *Conan the Barbarian* (1982), *Conan the Destroyer,* and *Red Sonja* (1985)—who had her own tie-in *D&D* module, *RS1: Red Sonja Unconquered* in 1986—were part of a larger revival of interest in sword and sorcery films, born out the second wave of Tolkien popularity that took hold in the late '60s and culminated in the animated movie adaptations in the late '70s: the Rankin/Bass *The Hobbit* (1977), Ralph Bakshi's *The Lord of the Rings* (1978), and the Rankin/Bass *Return of the King* (1980).

This trend continued on and off throughout the '80s. Some of the films were good, or at least interesting, like *Black Angel* (1980), *Excalibur* (1981), *Krull* (1983), *Ladyhawke* (1985), *Legend* (1985), and *Willow* (1988). Most were not, like the countless barbarian movies that sought to cash in on *Conan the Barbarian*'s success. Disney even got into the act, with the live action *Dragonslayer* (1981), which is great, and the animated adaptation *The Black Cauldron* (1985), which, lamentably, is not (though Lloyd Alexander's *The Chronicles of Prydain* novels, upon which it was based, are excellent and criminally underrated).

Dungeons & Dragons naturally benefited from this popular interest in fantasy. Folks who came out of theaters wanting more sword swinging and spell slinging would find it on the shelves of the bookstores in the malls, under a large cardboard dragon display. This was not a one-way relationship—*D&D* existed as part of a larger tradition of fantasy storytelling, both drawing from and informing the very things that went into the movies.

There is a scene in *Conan the Destroyer* when Conan and his companions are trying to sneak into the palace but find the tunnel blocked by steel bars. As his companions (who fit the *D&D* classes of Thief, Magic-User, and Acrobat suspiciously well) squabble about what to do next, Conan leans into the bars and, straining with all his brute strength, bends them wide enough for the group to pass through. The shot looks alarmingly similar to David C. Sutherland's illustration in *B1: In Search of the Unknown* of a barbarian bending bars (an actual ability tied to the Strength attribute in *Advanced Dungeons & Dragons*), surrounded by his companions, who include a thief and mage.

In the introduction to his fiction anthology, *Appendix N: The Eldritch Root of Dungeons & Dragons* (2020), Peter Bebergal writes that Gary Gygax's "Appendix N" is not, "a map to *D&D* rules, monsters or gameplay." The same is true of *D&D*'s outward influence. There is likely no way to prove that *Willow* or *Krull* sprang from sessions of a *D&D* game, but they display enough aspects of the game—the way a group of adventurers comes together, for instance—that it feels like *D&D* had a part

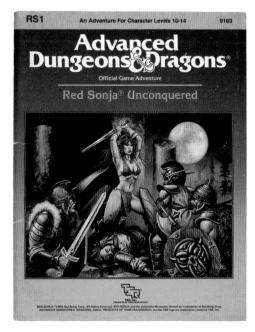

RS1: Red Sonja Unconquered, TSR, 1986. Anne Gray McCready, Cover by Clyde Caldwell

in its creation. And whether it actually did or not is immaterial.

Marvel Super Heroes (1984)

It's interesting to see the gulf of quality between *Marvel Super Heroes: The Heroic Role-Playing Game* and *CB1: Conan Unchained*. Where *CB1* feels like the work of a good designer trying desperately to salvage a corporate cash grab, *Marvel Super Heroes* is a fun and functional reflection of the source material in roleplaying game form.

The game, often called FASERIP for the acronym created by its attribute names, is straightforward, using percentile dice and the Universal Table to resolve conflict. The Universal Table is a color-coded chart; cross-reference the skill value and the die roll, get the result. Green is good; yellow is really good; red is devastatingly good, and white is bad. The table matches the bombastic energy of the comics of that era: Big risks, big results. It's a bit tedious to resolve every roll using the table, but it is a clear system for beginning players, especially kids, at whom the game is emphatically aimed. It moves fast and scales nicely to account for the

MARVEL SUPER HEROES, BOX SET, TSR, 1984
JEFF GRUBB AND STEVE WINTER, COVER BY JEFF BUTLER

different power levels of various characters, allowing a street level character, like the Punisher, with no superpowers, to hold their own against a powered character, like Spider-man, and still contribute without being annihilated if someone with cosmic powers, like Galactus, shows up. The art, delivered by artists from the Marvel Bullpen, helps sustain that four-color energy, too.

There is a brief section for players to create their own heroes, but it's an empty gesture. The intention here is for players to take the roles of existing Marvel characters—why make a *Champions*-style faux-Wolverine when actually playing Wolverine is an option? Eschewing character creation means *Marvel Super Heroes* lacks the versatility of other super hero games, but that's a fair trade when players can finally find out whether Punisher can take on Galactus in a fight (it's doubtful, but heck, nothing is certain until the dice start rolling).

The *Marvel Super Heroes* line is TSR's most successful work with a licensed property (not that competition is thick on the ground). It's certainly their most expansive, receiving many support products across two editions. There is a palpable energy and enthusiasm that shines through the material, both in the official products and the monthly feature "The Marvel-Phile" in *Dragon* magazine, which detailed a new corner of the Marvel Universe in game terms most months, from 1984 until the line ended in 1993.

In 1986, the company released the *Marvel Super Heroes Advanced Set*, which so significantly expands the game that it functions as a standalone game—it doesn't require the 1984 yellow box to play. If *Marvel Super Heroes* is a beginner's game, this is an intermediary level one, much expanded and more in line with a

general RPG experience, but still easy to grasp. The system was overhauled; the Universal Table grew to allow for more results—the box is full of more possibilities. Unlike the original set, the creation of custom characters is front and center (though the system produces characters that feel underpowered compared to their colleagues from the comics), and there are neat rules for building a team headquarters. For even more superpower options, there's *The Ultimate Powers Book* (1987), an exhaustive catalog of powers from the comics with nearly 300 to choose from.

A large number of sourcebooks (and adventure modules) were released as TSR set to work converting the whole of the Marvel Universe into an RPG. An entire box set was devoted to mutants; another laid out Marvel's version of New York City, complete with the Sanctum Sanctorum of Dr. Strange on Bleecker Street (a starburst on the cover of that box claims it is "the most detailed city-setting ever created for a superhero role-playing game," which is exactly the sort of overblown claim that might appear on the cover of any given Marvel comic of the era; it doesn't come close, for the record).

The eight-volume Gamer's Handbook of the Marvel Universe series, a sort of character index modeled on the Official Handbook of the Marvel Universe comic series (1982), translated hundreds of heroes, villains, and supporting characters into game terms. The series is a Marvel universe time capsule, capturing all of its glory and ridiculousness from 1988 to 1992. There are classic characters and obscure, each with detailed biographies. There are annual updates to run down who was killed and who changed costume. This is how I expect the biggest RPG company to do a licensed RPG: Completely and with no restraints.

Toon: The Cartoon Roleplaying Game (1984)

Toon was born out of a conversation among designers at a convention about genres that would be difficult to adapt into RPGs. Jeff Dee (designer of *Villains and Vigilantes*, 1979, but best known for his illustration work, particularly in *Deities & Demigods*) submitted cartoons, specifically the reality-bending ones produced by Warner Brothers, for debate. Whether zany cartoons can make for a good RPG is a reasonable question—RPGs are built with rules, while *Looney Tunes* are entertaining because they break *all* of the rules: Bugs Bunny looks out the screen at the viewer, gravity stops working, death is impossible, angry lions can be pulled out of a bag, and the animator can change the details of the world with a swish of a brush. All of the designers at the table agreed: An RPG based on cartoons was impossible.

This judgment stuck in game designer Greg Costikyan's craw apparently, and a few years later, he designed *Toon*, seemingly, to see if it could be done. He submitted the result of the experiment to *Fantasy Gamer* magazine as an article, but editor Warren Spector liked it so much that he developed it for stand-alone publication. At the time, Spector was editor-in-chief of

TOON: THE CARTOON ROLEPLAYING GAME, STEVE JACKSON GAMES, GREG COSTIKYAN, COVER BY KYLE MILLER

TOON: THE CARTOON ROLEPLAYING GAME, STEVE JACKSON GAMES, 1984

Steve Jackson Games, but he is now best known for developing the videogames *Deus Ex* (2000) and, germane to the current topic, *Epic Mickey* (2010).

There are indeed rules in *Toon*. For the time, they were extremely simple: A 6-sided die-based system with four attributes (Muscle, Zip, Smarts, and Chutzpah), 23 skills, and a choice of special ability, called a Schtick (like hypnotism, or a bag with everything inside). Plot points are the nomenclature for experience; they can be spent to improve abilities. The mechanics of the game seem beside the point—there to keep everyone on some semblance of the same page. Other rules seem to hint that there are no rules at all: Characters can't die; they just Fall Down and three minutes later (literally: time it), they get back up again. In fact, there are two truisms presented at the start of the book that may be the only real rules of the game: "Forget everything you know," and "Act before you think." If those two rules are followed, play focuses on pushing the story forward and entertaining the other people around the table. All of the other rules can take a hike.

David "Zeb" Cook, in his essay on *Toon* for James Lowder's *Hobby Games: The 100 Best* (2007), says, "*Toon* was an evolution in roleplaying and it helped us — players, GMs, and especially designers — to see more clearly the essence of roleplaying." Compared to every RPG I've covered so far, and a good deal to come, *Toon* seems like the anti-RPG. It is practically impossible to run long-term campaigns (a later supplement, *Son of Toon*, 1986, attempted to rectify that, with ambiguous results). Even long sessions seem to be a stretch— there is a real risk that players will be exhausted from laughing so hard after about an hour or two, which makes sense considering most *Looney Tunes* shorts wrap up after ten minutes.

But, as Cook observed, *Toon* was pointing the way to something new. While other games had been funny before now, *Toon* was also the first game entirely focused on comedy. More importantly, it was the first in a wave of rules-light games that flew in the face of the accepted design doctrine that RPGs needed complex rules systems to be fun or satisfying. The games that followed in the wake of *Toon,* like *Paranoia*, *Ghostbusters*, *Star Wars*, *Prince Valiant*, and on, many of them by Costikyan, many of them intentionally funny, in turn, lead to modern storytelling and indie games. Those games, which often have rules so simple they seem not to be RPGs at all, focus on strong themes and collaborative, entertaining narratives, both serious (*Sorcerer*) and silly (*Fiasco*).

Skyrealms of Jorune (1985)

Skyrealms of Jorune is one of the most relentlessly strange and difficult to pronounce RPGs ever made. Andrew Leker created the world of Jorune as a student for a high school writing assignment and later used it as the basis for a roleplaying game (originally a hack of *Metamorphosis Alpha*). He self-published the first, rather rough version, in 1984.

A year later, Leker and his sister, Amy, took another crack at the game, reorganizing and streamlining everything,

resulting in the better-looking 1985 box set (sort of: A printing delay meant components were sold without the box at GenCon 18; actual boxed copies didn't appear until 1986). Leker supported the game with an aggressive ad campaign— ads for the game, decorated with the game's unusual art, were a staple in *Dragon* magazine in the late '80s.

The system is clunky and skill-based, full of inconsistencies, and peppered with reference charts that border on terrifying. The gamemaster notes explicitly focus on roleplaying rather than combat, perhaps in a tacit admission that the system is junk.

What *Skyrealms of Jorune* demonstrates, though, is that system isn't everything. The draw here is the world. Jorune is an alien world colonized by humans in the remote past. War and cataclysm followed, returning civilization to the stone age. Thousands of years later, society has crawled back to a medieval level of technology, but ancient artifacts (read: Laser guns and power armor) can still be found in the oldest ruins.

Some aliens can also tap into the Isho, a sort of crystal-fueled magical energy field not unlike the Force from *Star Wars*. The result is an intriguing mix of fantasy and science fiction that becomes stranger and more genre-defying the more it is investigated. Players are on a Tothis, a kind of ritualized pursuit of citizenship that requires sponsorship, which is earned through the performance of tasks, like exploring the ruined world for ancient Earth-tec or hunting impressive beasts. This arrangement is a natural set-up for adventure and sets the stage for organic exploration of the strange world.

What *Skyrealms of Jorune* succeeds at, better than any other RPG setting, is an aggressive pursuit of alienness. The unabating use of in-world language, while making for a fascinating atmosphere, also becomes a significant hurdle for a basic comprehension of the setting. The glossary runs two-and-a-half pages, with two columns, and very small print! From the back of the box, a place of prime importance from a marketing perspective: "Jorune is a place where names like Iscin and Maytrish inspire admiration, where the thailiers of the huge Corondon are cast into blades, where Shanthas rule a technology invisible to humans. The referee is not the absolute controller of the players' fate." Right, exactly, I agree entirely. It rather reminds me of Rick Moranis's speech to the horse in *Ghostbusters* (1984).

Where *D&D* is almost inherently familiar, drawing on well-established fantasy touchstones, everything in *Skyrealms* is unusual. Much of the box is devoted to making the various bizarre societies and cultures seem cohesive, yet they remain unlike anything sword and sorcery conventions have prepared players for. The best I can compare it to are the animated film *Fantastic Planet* (1973) and maybe *Barlowe's Inferno* (1998).

Much of that bizarreness is thanks to the fabulous work of illustrator and co-designer Miles Teves, whose realistic style gives Jorune an uncanny verisimilitude. It is on display in his painting for the front of the box, a tableau in a Renaissance style, depicting the "Death Scene of Sho Copra-Tra, Sholari of Tashka." I don't know what that means, but the painting still transmits great emotional weight, despite the aliens. That weight is true of *Skyrealms of Jorune* in a broad sense, as well—no matter how weird the setting, with its floating islands and eyeless, phallic creatures, the painstaking attention to detail always manages to ground it.

The layering of detail creates a kind of self-reinforcing veracity out of the collage of fictional facts. Hârn does this, as well. Similarly, *Ars Magica* and *Vampire: The Masquerade* both start out fairly realistic despite their fantastic elements, only to take on ever more vibrancy, thanks to their scores of sourcebooks. This approach to world design is most reward-

Skyrealms of Jorune, SkyRealms Publishing, Second edition, Box set, 1985 Andrew Leker and Miles Teves, Cover by Miles Teves

ing when building worlds that are far outside the bounds of what genre conventions teach players to expect, as with Jorune, or later, with Talislanta, and the world of Barsaive in *Earthdawn*. Details have the power to transform worlds that should be baffling into worlds that are endlessly intriguing.

Masks of Nyarlathotep (1984)

Stephen King may have made a fortune selling horror novels that double as doorstops, but the genre was born in the short story. Edgar Allan Poe, M. R. James, Ambrose Bierce, Arthur Machen, Algernon Blackwood, Robert W. Chambers, and H. P. Lovecraft built their reputations as masters of the genre, in part, because brevity is the soul of terror. This rule of thumb might create the expectation that *Call of Cthulhu*, the first horror RPG, would work best using single session scenarios played with the assumption that most, if not all, of the characters would be dead or insane by the end. In practice, however, this is not the case!

Call of Cthulhu was a whole new style of RPG, and most of the early scenarios are

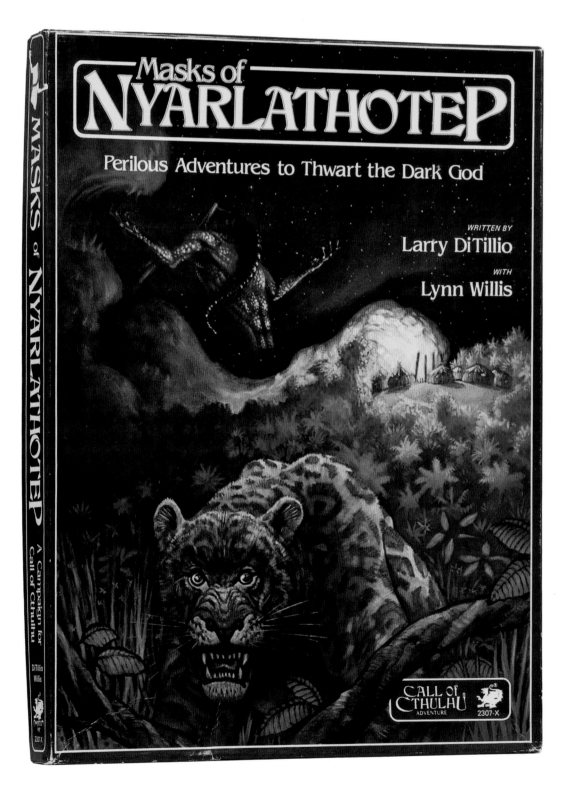

MASKS OF NYARLATHOTEP, BOX SET, CHAOSIUM, 1984
LARRY DITILLIO AND LYNN WILLIS, COVER BY TOM SULLIVAN

underwhelming; because of that newness, many foundational scenarios just never manage to be scary. Others hew too close to *D&D*-style dungeon crawls, leading investigators into caves or sewers where large groups of monsters that can't be defeated lie in wait. The fun of a *Call of Cthulhu* one-shot is in the sense of impending doom, not so much the doom itself, which is final and tends to mark the end of the night. While this flow of gameplay is clear now, it took years of trial and error before designers found the right formula and began pumping out memorable one-shots.

In the meantime, *Call of Cthulhu* found its footing in sprawling, long-form campaigns. The first, *Shadows of Yog-Sothoth* (1982), is about an international occult conspiracy to wake Cthulhu from his eons-long slumber a little earlier than planned. In terms of a horror story, it's often bizarre, and there's time travel, but it all manages to hang together somehow. It's also extremely deadly.

Chaosium has a knack for putting together compelling campaigns, as material, like *Borderlands*, demonstrates. In that campaign, and most others like it, satisfaction comes from seeing how the characters grow over time. *Shadows of Yog-Sothoth* established that a *Call of Cthulhu* campaign is something else entirely, a march to the gallows, where every character shines brightest in the moment of their demise. Just like the gag that a *RuneQuest* adventure isn't complete until someone loses a limb, it isn't a real *Call of Cthulhu* campaign until all of the characters who start the story have been killed off and replaced by fresh investigators, like a fleshy, terrified Ship of Theseus.

Judging from the sheer number of high-quality *Call of Cthulhu* campaigns that have seen print, like *Horror on the Orient Express* (1991), *Beyond the Mountains of Madness* (1999), and *Tatters of the King* (2006), to name a few, along with the praise these campaigns have earned from critics and players, the perverse delight in seeing character after character devoured by the cosmos never seems to lose its charm. But truly heady heights were reached with the 1984 release of *Masks of Nyarlathotep* (*Masks*).

There's something special about this box. It puts forth a thrilling, globe-trotting adventure that begins with a murder and, by inches, reveals a vast, international occult conspiracy (there are a lot of these in *Call of Cthulhu*, actually) to open a gate for the Great Old Ones. Chapters take place in New York, London, Cairo, Kenya, Shanghai, and Australia (this last chapter was cut from the original for space, released as a stand-alone scenario in the Australia sourcebook, *Terror Australis: Call of Cthulhu in the Land Down Under*, 1987, and finally restored to create *The Complete Masks of Nyarlathotep* in 1996). Where *Shadows of Yog-Sothoth* links together seemingly disparate scenarios, each with their own beginning, middle, and end, the chapters of *Masks* are contiguous and make up a massive sandbox. Players can move around the world at will, chasing threads as they please, so long as the doomsday clock still has time left on it.

That mix of horror and exotic locales naturally draws comparisons to *Indiana Jones and the Temple of Doom* (1984). Both came out around the same time, so there is a bit of pop culture zeitgeist at play between the two. The game's blasphemous rituals certainly function to strike a tone similar to the famous heart-grabbing temple scene of the film, and Mola Ram's cackling evil would certainly be at home at the feet of Nyarlathotep (unfortunately, *Temple of Doom* and *Masks of Nyarlathotep* both rely on a similar sort of cultural stereotyping to flavor their pulp—predominantly white characters visit exotic foreign locales to confront fictional regional practices that native inhabitants are unwilling or unable to end on their own). There is also potential for players to lean into the madcap in *Masks of Nyarlathotep*. Despite the titular temple of doom having curtains made from human flesh, the film also delights in over-the-top slapstick. Likewise, the RPG campaign offers ample opportunities for the ridiculous and, as a testament to its flexibility, the latest edition includes room for the (slightly) more lighthearted *Pulp Cthulhu* (2016) rules.

Whatever the tone, the stakes are high—the various cults of Nyarlathotep are nearing the completion of schemes that have been in motion for thousands of years, and the fate of the world is at their mercy. While the scale of the story is global, the horror remains intimate and immediate—yes, there are powers at work beyond my comprehension, but I am a bit busy dealing with this fellow trying to murder me with a machete at the moment, thanks.

When players aren't doing their best to avoid dying at the hands of cultists, the immediacy of the campaign is maintained, in part, by plentiful player handouts, designed with an eye toward tactile realism: The newspaper clippings have period advertisements on the back; the handwritten notes are actually handwritten; the mysterious matchbox from a bar in Shanghai can be folded up into an actual matchbox. These objects ground the proceedings, and, while other RPG products have had handouts before and since, those in *Masks* have taken on a special life of their own. There is a long tradition of GMs creating elaborate homemade props for this campaign. In 2018, the H.P. Lovecraft Historical Association took this impulse to charmingly absurd heights, creating a box packed with elaborate props for the revised edition of the campaign; a $900 dollar deluxe version even comes complete with statuary and cultist robes.

Masks was my introduction to *Call of Cthulhu*. I had read Lovecraft before I first

played, but I was surprised by how hopeless his themes seemed within the context of an RPG. All of the murder, insanity, and human sacrifice in *Masks of Nyarlathotep*, much of which was visited upon players, seemed almost cruel. For me, *Masks* finally fulfilled that promise of transgression that early *Dungeons & Dragons* always seemed to hold. Something about this campaign—the open world, the handouts, the pulpy tone, the elaborate mystery, the apocalyptic stakes, the horrible deadliness, or some combination of it all, captured imagination and attention in a way few other RPG products ever have. As a campaign, it remains nearly unmatched in both scope and scale, by anyone, including Chaosium.

Masks of Nyarlathotep isn't perfect. Without a doubt, it is a wide-ranging, detail-oriented investigation, and that means it isn't easy for newcomers to run. There wasn't much of an understanding for how to support a GM in running such a large campaign in 1984, and there likely wasn't room in the box even if such advice was available. Much of the problem is inherent to a sandbox approach that is so strikingly different from other campaigns. At any given moment, players can decide to go anywhere, regardless of whether or not they're prepared. Many encounters and NPCs are only roughly sketched, and some threads are left open, or they explicitly lead outside the bounds of the campaign. All of this open-endedness means copious amounts of notes and a level of flexibility that was unprecedented for the time. Running the campaign is still a big ask, even now.

Back in 2015, fans of the campaign successfully kickstarted the *Masks of Nyarlathotep Companion*, a massive collection of material that seeks to fill in the blank spots and generally help a GM run the campaign. I have never witnessed an RPG campaign inspire such a comprehensive project. The *Companion* is exhaustive, and it's exhausting in its depth of love and thought. There are extra scenarios, NPCs, pages of historical information, a detailed accounting of every book and artifact found over the course of the game, and more. It is a complete deconstruction and reconfiguration of the source material that runs approximately 500 pages longer than the original campaign; yet, it still manages to leave some questions unanswered.

Masks of Nyarlathotep isn't easy on players, either. Those new to roleplaying, in general, or *Call of Cthulhu,* in particular, are probably out of their depth. Even experienced investigators risk getting lost in the tangle of red strings on the cork board. It's also unrelentingly deadly. Every chapter ends in an orgy of violence and insanity. Only the most prepared—or luckiest—investigators will survive.

Perhaps strangest of all, *Masks of Nyarlathotep,* as written, doesn't have a climactic finish. This is also a side effect of the sandbox approach—if players can go anywhere, then the site of the potential crescendo is *everywhere.* Everything a GM needs to build a dramatic ending is there. Remember, nearly every chapter ends with a terrible, mind-rending event, so all that's left for the GM to do is make the ending that much more terrible. The lack of real guidance on how to accomplish this feels like an oversight, though. The book's primary suggestion is that the real world is the one in which the heroes failed—that the Great Depression, World War II, and Reagan are all the result of Nyarlathotep's gate opening, which, ha, yea, that's clever, I guess, but it's also an unsatisfactory way to end a campaign that a group probably played for over a year.

More seriously, *Masks* also has trouble navigating the inherent pitfalls of playing through a story modeled after the work of

MASKS OF NYARLATHOTEP, SECOND EDITION, CHAOSIUM, 1989
LARRY DITILLIO AND LYNN WILLIS, COVER BY LEE GIBBONS

H. P. Lovecraft and other pulpsmiths during the 1920s. There is an obvious gender imbalance, a good portion of the villains are clichéd dark-skinned foreigners, and there are some tasteless depictions of sex rituals. These missteps feel like a product of the '80s, a time when these sorts of problematic depictions remained prevalent and often entirely unexamined.

Thankfully, in 2018, *Masks of Nyarlathotep* received a complete and official revision to bring it in line with the seventh edition *Call of Cthulhu* rules, and the new version goes to great lengths to correct the faults of the original. For starters, it includes a new, explicitly anti-colonialist prelude chapter in Peru in which the villains are literally undead conquistadors that suck the fat from their victims. The overarching conspiracy involves a group of white people co-opting the existing indigenous cults to enact their own schemes and creates explicit friction between the groups. Race issues were particularly troublesome in the New York chapter: The cultists are based in Harlem, largely made up from African immigrants, and they are the only Black characters encountered in the original version of the chapter. Chris Spivey's *Harlem Unbound* showed how ridiculous this presentation is, especially considering the ongoing Harlem Renaissance, and the new edition of *Masks of Nyarlathotep* addresses the problem by including a subplot involving a wrongful conviction for murder, corrupt cops, and Harlem residents working against the cult.

The campaign is otherwise thoroughly modernized and reorganized to provide support and ease of use to GMs with all levels of experience—it is split across two volumes that come in at a beastly 666 total pages. It even has a genuine ending that clearly lays out the requirements for success, partial success, and failure, with definitive consequences for all. Those consequences are essentially what the original campaign led players to expect, but it is validating to see them in print. About the only thing the new edition doesn't change is how incredibly deadly the campaign is, but then, dying in *Call of Cthulhu* is half the fun.

Middle-earth Role Playing (1984)

Iron Crown Enterprises (named, presciently, after the iron crown of the Witch-king of Angmar) got its start like so many other RPG companies: Publishing rules that expanded on, changed, or otherwise fixed the official *Dungeons & Dragons* rules published by TSR.

Their very first product was *Arms Law* (1980), a robust percentile-based combat system that could replace the existing combat system of just about any game. In time, it would become the cornerstone of a whole new RPG system called *Rolemaster* (1982). The idea was to offer players more detail by way of elaborate systems that could be tinkered with endlessly. Players would find that a love of math was helpful. As befits a game jokingly called "Chartmaster," the original edition of *Arms Law* is a 24-page booklet perched atop a pile of loose-leaf charts, including

the infamously and deadly critical hit matrix that killed, in grisly fashion, countless player characters.

Arms Law originally sprang out of a homebrew game based on Middle-earth, so, after experimenting with the publication of an original adventure module—*The Iron Wind* (1980), set in what would eventually become known as the Shadow World campaign setting—Iron Crown approached Tolkien Enterprises (a company distinct from the Tolkien Estate) about licensing Tolkien's world for an RPG and other tabletop games.

Surprisingly, Tolkien Enterprises granted the license without issue. The fact that this tiny company, new on the scene, managed to snag what was arguably the biggest license in fantasy RPGs will never cease to boggle the mind; it's made all the more astounding by the fact that no other RPG company prior to that even tried!

Iron Crown's approach to the license was novel. While simplified attributes were included for their *Rolemaster* system, detailed notes on conversion were provided, essentially making the early Middle-earth sourcebooks system agnostic. This was intentional on Iron Crown's part: They assumed, correctly, that these books would appeal to and should be marketed primarily to players of *Dungeons & Dragons*.

Most of these early products, like *Isengard and Northern Gondor* (1983) and *Southern Mirkwood: Haunt of the Necromancer* (1983) detail important locations from the books that were sure to appeal to even casual readers. Even after the company published *Middle-earth Role Playing* (*MERP*), a dedicated, "simplified" version of *Rolemaster*, a significant portion of Middle-earth sourcebook sales continued to come from *D&D* players and casual readers.

MERP is a glorious mess. The ruleset, the sourcebooks, all of it—mess.

There is no reason to adventure in Middle-earth using *MERP*. Along with the fact that the sourcebooks are essentially system-agnostic, the system Iron Crown offered feels radically out of sync with the themes and aesthetics of Tolkien's world. The magic is too present and too powerful for a world in which the supernatural is draining away. The combat is too gruesome and deadly for a series of novels about a nearly bloodless war against the forces of evil. Other RPGs were modeling their systems to reflect their themes at this point, but *MERP* makes no such attempt.

Another source of chaos is Iron Crown's choice of era in which to place *MERP* products. Era is admittedly a difficult aspect of the setting to establish—the most identifiable moments in Middle-earth's history are also those set most firmly in stone. To set the game during the War of the Ring is to either tediously reenact the books, or to reduce the players to the role of Middle-earth's janitors, cleaning up the minor messes left in the wake of the worthies.

To avoid diminishing the players' potential impact on the world, *MERP*'s default setting is 1,500 or so years before the War of the Ring, during the Witch-king's slow conquest of the kingdoms of Dúnedain. This period of Middle-earth history is ripe to explore, with many important events happening while much else is left open ended. For instance, during this time, the city of Minas Ithil is conquered by Sauron, becoming Minas Morgul; players can experience the city in its twilight, participate in its doomed defense, and witness its corruption. That's pretty great!

The problem is that *MERP* rarely stuck to that period. Most adventure modules feature scenarios set in many eras. *Hillmen of the Trollshaws* (1984), one of the first I owned, has adventures set in Third

MIDDLE-EARTH ROLE PLAYING, BOX SET, IRON CROWN ENTERPRISES. COLEMAN CHARLTON, COVER BY CHRIS WHITE

Age 164, Third Age 1671, and an unspecified year in the early Fourth Age, after the War of the Ring. What is a GM supposed to do with three scenarios set across nearly 3,000 years?

Another problem is that Iron Crown's Middle-earth is a fever dream version of Tolkien's world. Similar to how the galaxy of the film version of *Star Wars* needed to be expanded in order to become a viable setting for an RPG, so too did Iron Crown need to flesh out Middle-earth. The main difference is that, despite the staggering amount of creative energy poured into the process, the result is a world that feels somehow strange and wrong.

Because I was a naïve kid when I first encountered the *MERP* sourcebooks, I thought they were spun out of some secret Tolkien material—unpublished notes or perhaps drawn from Christopher Tolkien's seemingly endless series of books analyzing his father's creative process. Despite the many regions and histories detailed in the sourcebooks only briefly appearing in Tolkien's writing, it all seemed somehow *authentic*, and the material that felt the most true lent credence to details that might have otherwise seemed dubious.

For instance, there are nine Nazgûl, the human kings corrupted by Sauron with

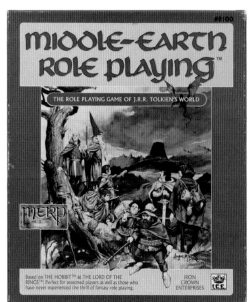

MIDDLE-EARTH ROLE PLAYING, BOX SET, SECOND EDITION, IRON CROWN ENTERPRISES, 1986
COLEMAN CHARLTON, COVER BY ANGUS MCBRIDE

ROLEMASTER, BOX SET, IRON CROWN ENTERPRISES, 1982
TERRY K. AMTHOR, COLEMAN CHARLTON, PETE FENLON, AND DYVERS HANDS, COVER BY MATTHEW J. JORGENSEN

lesser rings of power, and Tolkien gives a proper name to just one: Khamûl the Easterling (in material published as *Unfinished Tales*, 1980). One named Ringwraith just wouldn't do for an RPG, though, so the folks at Iron Crown not only named the rest, but also gave them elaborate backgrounds (even including a corrupted queen, Adûnaphel the Quiet).

All of this world building is weaved through existing Tolkien lore thoroughly enough to feel plausible—so much so that plenty of online "wikis" list the name of the Witch-king of Angmar as Er-Mûrazôr, despite it being entirely made up for *MERP* (it looks cool *and* has *two* circumflexes so surely it is real, right?). Ringwraiths aren't great villains for an RPG, though—they're obscenely powerful, and readers know that they remain undefeated until the Battle of the Pelennor Fields, so a selection of lesser nemeses was required to harry the player heroes.

Across all of the *MERP* supplements, the servants of the Dark Lord take varied forms. The coolest are in *Gorgoroth* (1990), a book that details much of Sauron's military. Among these lieutenants are the Angûlion, a sorcerer who gave up his eyes for magic gems and looks out through the needle-like teeth of his dragon head helmet, and Tónn Vathkûr, a warrior who wears a flaming helmet fashioned from a bull skull. *Dark Mage of Rhudaur* (1989) has a character who wears a cape made of human ears! Alone, these blackguards, and many others, feel about as Middle-earth as the cackling henchmen of Cobra Commander or Skeletor, but presented as they are, just one step removed from the Ringwraiths and with plenty of their own circumflexes in their names, they gain a dim legitimacy. The riveting realism of Angus McBride's cover paintings and Liz Danforth's delicate character studies bolster this plausibility through their beauty and consistency.

Discovering this faux Middle-earth was similar to the brief period of time when I believed Lovecraft's *Necronomicon* was a real book (don't judge). During that time, I tracked down and read the Simon *Necronomicon* (1977), a hoax grimoire cobbled together from Babylonian mythology and a poor understanding of the Cthulhu mythos. It was obviously a fraud, but it was also such entertaining trash that I found myself reluctant to admit the book was a fake.

Unlike the Simon *Necronomicon*, though, *MERP* books aren't trash. They conjure a world in vivid, exacting detail. It

INCLUDES:
- A full color 24" x 36" poster map of Middle-earth, including the wild lands — north, south, and east — and a superimposed reference grid.
- Descriptions of the principal inhabitants of Middle-earth, including: a language tree and linguistic data; cultural notes; and an in depth time line.
- Maps and notes on Middle-earth's topography, climate, trade routes, and population centers.
- Guidelines for incorporating Middle-earth into any major role playing system.
- Produced and distributed by IRON CROWN ENTERPRISES, Inc. Stock # ME2200.

may often feel like fan fiction, but it is so internally consistent that it is difficult not to love. Each book takes a region and runs down the flora, fauna, history, current factions, and all of the locations of interest and potential adventure sites. Taken together, even with the odd gaps (how is there not a sourcebook for Barad-dûr, the seat of Sauron's power?), it stands as one of the most intricately portrayed RPG worlds ever created, even if only a small portion of it is recognizable from Tolkien's works.

The ambition to create a massive world was there from the very start. Iron Crown's first *Middle-earth* product, *A Campaign and Adventure Guidebook for Middle-earth* (1982), is a sort of stage-setting sourcebook for the world at large, answering all of the burning questions players had about weather patterns and ocean currents. The book is a bit whatever; the real selling point of the guide is Iron Crown co-founder Peter Fenlon's gor-geous map of Middle-earth. It isn't a recognizable Middle-earth, though. Tolkien's map accounts for less than a fourth of the area Fenlon presents, all of which is full of new places, strange geography, and countless stories untold.

And many of them remain so. Over the course of 17 years, Iron Crown produced over 80 sourcebooks and adventures, but many details of the expansive world were left unrevealed. Further exploration was cut short when Tolkien Enterprises, sensing Tolkien properties were about to become significantly more valuable, thanks to the imminent Peter Jackson films, pulled the RPG license from Iron Crown in order to resell it at a profit in 1999. Already in dire financial straits due to the collapse of the collectible card game bubble, being forced to shelve in-production designs and pulp their existing *MERP* inventory drove Iron Crown into bankruptcy.

PETE FENLON'S EXPANSIVE MAP OF MIDDLE-EARTH, FROM THE BACK COVER OF *A CAMPAIGN AND ADVENTURE GUIDEBOOK FOR MIDDLE-EARTH* (1982).

Dragonlance (1984)

I6: Ravenloft focused *D&D* on story and character over traditional catacomb crawling (though there was still plenty of dungeon in which to delve and slashes to hack). Building off of that module's success, TSR embarked on a grand experiment in multimedia RPG narrative with the Dragonlance saga. The idea, initially conceived by *Ravenloft* creators Tracy and Laura Hickman, was simple: 12 linked adventure modules, each focusing on a different type of dragon. Instead of being confined to underground spaces, these modules used an entire fantasy world to tell an epic story of good and evil.

Tracy Hickman assembled a number of TSR writers, editors, and artists to work on developing the concept. TSR's "Big Four" artists—Larry Elmore, Clyde Caldwell, Jeff Easley, and Keith Parkinson—functioned like the art department of a film, cranking out design concepts, defining the look of the world, and staging important scenes. As the scope of the story broadened—gods return, a war breaks out—it became apparent that there was potential for more than just a series of adventure modules. Inspired by the success of TSR's *Endless Quest* series of youth-oriented gamebooks and an unquenchable desire to crowd ever-more shelf space in mainstream bookstores, the *Dragonlance* team decided to tell the story in a trilogy of novels, as well.

The DL-series of modules would eventually encompass 16 publications—the 12 adventure modules that chart the course of the War of the Lance, two anthologies of shorter adventures, a sourcebook, and a wargame. Taken as a whole, the result is more interesting than good.

The main adventures use a massive cast of pre-generated characters with established backstories—the same that appear in the novels—which puts an unusual emphasis on the *role* of roleplaying. There isn't much room for interpretations of characters that stray from their portrayals in the books, particularly regarding the stubborn knight, Sturm Brightblade, and the sickly and tormented mage, Raistlin Majere, who would later emerge as the saga's fan favorite (this novel-first strategy is doubly strange, considering that, for at least the first few modules, a book wasn't even out yet).

Meanwhile, the action is mostly on rails. There is a goal; there is one way to achieve it, and players move from "Point A" to "Point B" in order to do so, usually with a bit of pointless dungeon exploration in between. This framing strangles the events of many of the modules, even when a more relaxed approach was possible, as is the case with *DL3: Dragons of Hope* and *DL4: Dragons of Desolation*, which depict events that don't even occur in the original three novels.

At other times, when a GM might expect the narrative to be unyielding, the modules opt for ambivalence, like when *DL8: Dragons of War* skips over the death of Sturm, an event that is arguably the central point and certainly the emotional heart of the entire second novel. In the game, Sturm can saunter on through the very end of the story, oblivious to his destiny in the books.

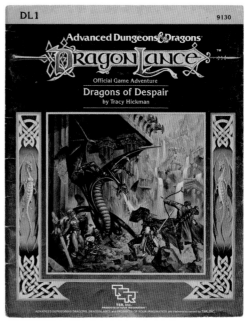

DL1: Dragons of Despair, TSR, 1984
Tracy Hickman, Cover by Clyde Caldwell

There are reasons for this unevenness. For starters, no one had ever attempted directed storytelling on this scale in an RPG. There were already big campaign stories and small metaplots, but a serialized epic about a world embroiled in war, told across 12 installments in two years? That's ambitious as hell, and the result is often equal parts compelling innovation and awkward mess.

The novels further complicated the proceedings. The original author hired to write them didn't work out, so Tracy Hickman and Margaret Weis took over, but this change meant that the first novel, *Dragons of Autumn Twilight*, was written after the first four DL-series modules. Mapping a novel to the framework of the modules proved challenging, hence the divergence in plot between the novel and the modules. For the rest of the saga, the novels were written first. Designers then weaved the modules around the plot of the novels, often tackling, in detail, events that wound up being resolved with a few lines of dialog in the book; that makes for better novels, but messier modules. Sometimes, the mess inspired clever solutions. *D8: Dragons of War* handles a large transition from the previous module by including a travelogue that uses an inter-

DL8: DRAGONS OF WAR, TSR, 1985
TRACY AND LAURA HICKMAN, COVER BY KEITH PARKINSON

active, pick-your-path format, which is a brilliant way to zoom out on the action of the story to move the action along in a way that benefits both the narrative and the mechanical level. But later in the same module, the designers bungled the climactic battle. The GM can either play it out as a wargame, which minimizes the agency of the individual characters, or they can resolve the whole conflict with a single modified die roll, essentially a coin toss, which annihilates that agency.

In the end, there are too many plates to keep spinning. The designers had to follow the novels without spoiling them, while keeping up the dragon-of-the-month theme, maintain the basic *D&D* formula—environment exploration coupled with dungeon diving—and deal with two divergent storylines across a multi-part modular series in order to make it all work with a strange cast of pre-generated characters that, by the end, includes at least one person who should be dead. It's too much.

The original *Dragonlance* saga has moments of brilliance, but it never really delivers on its promise of world-shaking high adventure. And underwhelming though the DL-series may ultimately be, it is also the high point of the setting. Future

DL4: DRAGONS OF DESOLATION, TSR, 1984
TRACY HICKMAN AND MICHAEL DOBSON, COVER BY KEITH PARKINSON

DRAGONS OF WINTER NIGHT, RANDOM HOUSE, 1985
MARGARET WEIS AND TRACY HICKMAN, COVER BY LARRY ELMORE

efforts to continue or reboot *Dragonlance* were an exercise in false starts. The *Time of the Dragon* box set (1989) introduced a whole new continent that received scant support. The idea here is to provide a play area that wasn't encumbered by the events of the War of the Lance and, while it was an unusual and engrossing exercise in world building, it didn't actually feel like *Dragonlance*.

The *Tales of the Lance* box set (1992) returned to classic *Dragonlance* and attempted to address ballooning continuity issues. It stands as, perhaps, the definitive *Dragonlance* RPG product, but it struggled to attract attention among TSR's other '90s offerings. Another version—this one for use with the card-based SAGA System—emerged in 1996 and failed to gain much traction; the attempted revival in the new millennium met a similar fate. This lukewarm legacy seems to point at some intrinsic flaw; time will tell if the new iteration for the Fifth Edition of *Dungeons & Dragons* finds and corrects it.

TIME OF THE DRAGON, BOX SET, TSR, 1989
DAVID "ZEB" COOK, COVER BY ROBIN WOOD

Despite the shortcomings of *Dragonlance* as a campaign setting, it was an important sea change for TSR and RPGs. With the initial release of *Dragonlance*, TSR seemed to be acknowledging how dramatically the landscape of RPGs had changed in their ten years of existence (and this is true again a decade later with the SAGA System's experiments using the sorts of lighter, diceless play that was emerging in the '90s). There were dozens of games that now allowed players to take all sorts of roles that had nothing to do with killing monsters and hauling treasure out of holes in the ground.

The contrast is clear in the art: The clean, heroic figures in the paintings of the Big Four have little in common with the grimy killers in Dave Trampier's cover of the *Players Handbook*. *Dragonlance* marks a clear break with that past. From this point forward, *Dungeons & Dragons* increasingly embraces epic, heroic fantasy above all else. That shift was not welcomed by everyone, marking *Dragonlance* as one of the earliest points of friction that would ultimately result in the Old School Revival movement two decades later.

Silly as it may sound, *Dragonlance* also taught TSR the value of dragons. Despite the name, *Dungeons & Dragons* was light

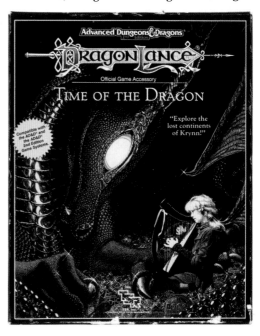

on the big beasties before *Dragonlance*. After, they suddenly appear on far more of the covers. It turns out that people really like dragons and enjoy buying books about them!

The DL-series also positioned narrative as the new holy grail, not just of TSR, but of the RPG industry. Competition modules become rarities as the possibilities of metaplot are explored. Metaplots of varying complexities support just about every *D&D* campaign setting from here on out—*Forgotten Realms* has more than one.

Outside of *D&D*, *Torg*, *Shadowrun*, and each of White Wolf's World of Darkness games all have significant metaplots. When the Time of Judgment effectively ended all of the various metaplots in White Wolf's games, signaling the decline of the metaplot in general, it was two decades after the DL-series first appeared—an eternity in RPG terms. Even after interest in metaplots faded, large narratives still played out in *Dragonlance*-inspired ways, as with Paizo's *Pathfinder* adventure paths—sprawling, modular plotlines that played out in *Dungeon* magazine for the third edition of *Dungeons & Dragons* and later in dedicated products for *Pathfinder*.

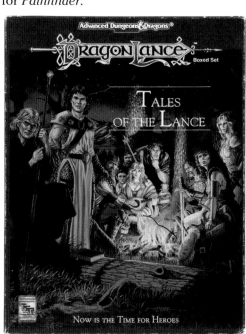

Despite all of those ups and downs in the roleplaying sphere, *Dragonlance*'s real legacy is the novels. There are, astonishingly, over 200 *Dragonlance* novels, making it one of the largest and most popular shared fictional worlds. They aren't great works of art. The original trilogy loudly echoes Tolkien's *The Lord of the Rings*, to the point that it sometimes verges on fan fiction, while subsequent core books feel like a multigenerational soap opera. As the number of books grew, no character or event was left undeveloped. Looking through the list of titles, I am slightly surprised that the bartender from the first inn doesn't star in his own novel. Just about everyone else does.

In an acidic, unsigned review of *Dragons of a Fallen Sun* (2000), *Kirkus Reviews* states, "Kirkus, having previously remarked on the inexplicable popularity of the Weis-Hickman combo, has nothing to add." That anonymous critic isn't necessarily wrong, but they are certainly missing the point of the *Dragonlance* novels and the uncomplicated escapism they provide—their popularity is tied directly to their predictability.

I loved reading these books when I was 12. I lost my mind over them. I read at least 20 of them in short order and dare not revisit them for fear of ruining the cherished memories. Even as a 12-year-old, I saw Sturm Brightblade's death coming, but I was still profoundly upset when it happened, so much so that I carried *Dragons of Winter Night* around in my school bag for months, refusing to finish the book, but also refusing to give up on it. I've read better books, but not many are as world-shaking (or *fun*) as a *Dragonlance* novel for a nerdy kid of precisely the right age.

Harold Johnson and Dyvers Hands, Cover by Larry Elmore

Tales of the Lance, Box set, TSR, 1992

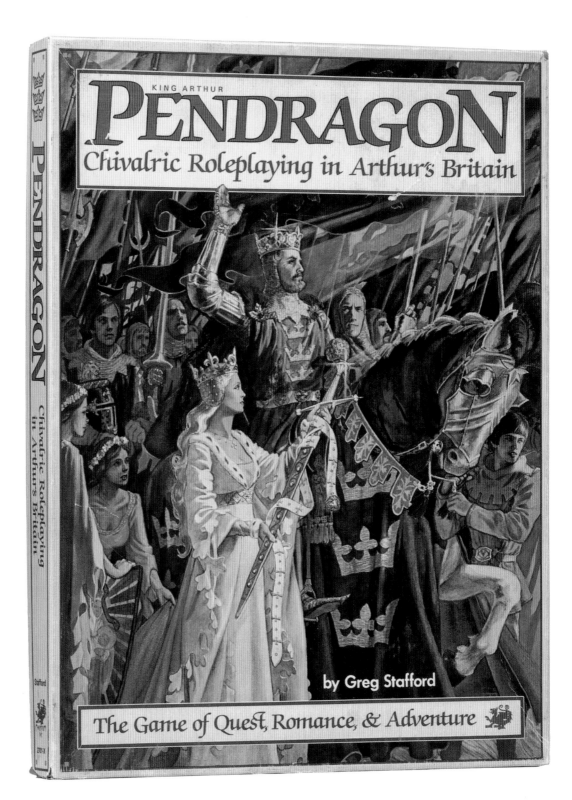

KING ARTHUR PENDRAGON, BOX SET, CHAOSIUM, 1985
GREG STAFFORD, COVER BY JODY LEE

Pendragon (1985)

Pendragon (1985) Looking at the RPG market over time, it is common to see a number of designers executing their particular take on a specific genre or property. There are, for instance, many games about ninjas, or Cthulhu! Many RPGs incorporate Cthulhu in some form, either directly or as a pastiche, now that he seems to be in the public domain.

It might seem strange, then, that there aren't shelves full of King Arthur RPGs, seeing as how Arthurian legends are widely known, in the public domain, are often adapted in other media, and are foundational to fantasy literature, with which so much of the RPG industry is preoccupied. *Pendragon* is the reason: Greg Stafford's game is so definitive an Arthurian experience that no one has ever succeeded in rivalling it.

The game is the product of a deep love for the Matter of Britain, as that body of medieval lore is sometimes called, and wide-ranging research. Stafford's background material draws, not just on the medieval romances, but also on the customs and culture of England from the post-Roman period to the end of the Middle Ages. The myriad of pop-cultural iterations of Arthur also find themselves in the weave—Boorman's film *Excalibur* (1981), Mary Stewart's Merlin novels (1970-1979), *The Once and Future King* (1958), the *Prince Valiant* comic strip (1937-present), and so on—and contribute just as much as Malory's *Le Morte d'Arthur* (1485), though they provide more to the atmosphere of the game rather than its details.

Pendragon's origins reach back to the late 1970s when Stafford hired author Phyllis Ann Karr to help him research the many threads of Arthurian lore as background material for his board game, *King Arthur's Knights* (1979). That research eventually became the exhaustive and entertaining encyclopedia, *The King Arthur Companion* (1983). Karr essentially takes all of the Arthurian stories and tries to reconcile them into a cohesive whole—no small feat considering the endless variety of versions and contradictions. With *Pendragon*, Stafford continues that synthesis of stories and crafts them into an interactive fictional history.

The fictional history forms up a massive creative undertaking. It started out as a 12-page timeline in *The Pendragon Campaign* (1985), covering the first 25 years of Arthur's reign and promising to cover more in future volumes. Under the title *The Boy King* (1991), Stafford revised and vastly expanded the timeline to cover, in 136 pages, the first 37 years of a now 80-year campaign, including important events, battles, characters, and melodramas. He completed the project in 2006, releasing it as *The Great Pendragon Campaign*, a massive 429-page accounting of the full 80-year campaign that begins with Uther Pendragon's wars to unite England and ends a few years after Arthur's death.

The bulk of the book is concerned with plotting out the entire Arthurian story—pulling the sword from the stone, the love triangle between Arthur, Guinevere, and Lancelot, the scheming of Mordred, the hunt for the Grail, and the seemingly endless wars—along a workable RPG timeline. This story is not meant to *be* the game, but rather a rich tapestry that functions as a backdrop to the players' adventures, giving them greater context and thematic meaning.

Year by year, the glorious and tragic tale of King Arthur unfolds. Sometimes, players may witness key events; sometimes they will play a key role, but mostly, these events are the stage dressing—the players have their own legacies to forge. Taking into consideration that, setting aside multi-session adventures (there are over 100 adventures included in the *Great Pendragon Campaign* alone!), every session is supposed to roughly coincide with one year of the chronology, it

THE KING ARTHUR COMPANION, RESTON PUBLISHING, 1983
PHYLLIS ANN KARR, COVER BY JODY LEE

becomes apparent that *Pendragon* is a truly massive game.

This endeavor, of course, is not for everyone. If a player has no interest in the legends of Arthur or the romance of knighthood, *Pendragon* will likely bore them to tears. Much of the action is caught up in politics, military campaigns, and affairs of the family. The latter is a central focus for a game in which players will ideally play several characters from the same bloodline during the full campaign—they'll be spending more time siring heirs and tending the estate than going off on foolhardy quests.

Further, the game's system judges actions from a twelfth century standard, which can be a bit baffling to the modern moral mind. In fact, there are multiple codes of honor that are directly and frustratingly contradictory. This is often the point: How a person navigates those contradictions reveals much about their character. Glory is paramount (and unbound by matters of honor); the game uses it as a sort of experience system. Virtues and vices exist on a binary scale, swinging back and forth between extremes. At the start of the campaign,

everyone is a brute. As Arthur rises to power, he civilizes England, so there is a natural struggle among players to look after the interests of their characters while adapting to the new chivalrous standards of behavior. Actions lauded as heroic at the start of the campaign might be regarded as a knavish by the end.

As with nearly all of Chaosium's games, *Pendragon* is a modified version of the *Basic Role-Playing* system. Those modifications, which form the heart of the game, are an attempt to portray a character's state of mind through RPG mechanics—specifically, a medieval state of mind. This mode of behavior is expressed in two ways.

First are Personality Traits: 12 opposed pairs of virtues and vices, like Merciful and Cruel. As one value rises during play, the other falls. A knight who embraces virtue receives mechanical bonuses, though which trait is the virtue and which is the vice is determined by a character's cultural heritage and their religious beliefs. Second are Passions, which are strongly held, emotional beliefs.

For most starting characters from the Salisbury area, whose families have suffered at the hands of Saxon invaders for decades, "Hate (Saxons)" is a common passion—in a riff on *Traveller*'s method of resumé-as-character-creation, later versions of *Pendragon* derive many starting attributes by determining the history of a character's father and grandfather through the use of elaborate charts. Loyalty to your lord, love of your family, and various flavors of envy are also common.

These Passion attributes rise and fall during play, depending on how a character behaves. If justified by the situation, they can be rolled, with a successful check indicating that the Passion has been inflamed; this conveys bonuses for skills, usually in combat. A knight who is overcome by his hatred of Saxons while fighting Saxons is a force of unbridled destruction. Passions, left unchecked, can also lead to madness, the way that Lancelot's love of Guinevere left him, for a time, a violent hermit.

Anyone familiar with Arthurian legends will recognize the moral struggles over loyalty, honor, and love that are at the core of *Pendragon*. The combination of Passions and Personality Traits show how a character feels and acts. They provide a framework of roleplaying cues, charting both how a character has acted in the past and how they will likely act in the future. They can also compel action. A gluttonous knight at a sumptuous feast might be called on to roll their Gluttony if they are trying not to eat—a successful check means they must partake in the meal.

Used properly, this mechanical representation of personality reinforces roleplaying. If that feast is taking place on the Other Side and has been prepared by Faeries, a player might perceive the danger of eating that the character would be oblivious to, thus the Gluttony roll would encourage the character to act according to their nature (the score of which, again, reflects the character's previous behavior and decisions). Most importantly, though, these mechanics encourage players to push their play closer to the spirit of the source material, even if they aren't very familiar with it (or if it is downright bizarre by modern standards).

Arthurian legends are driven by uncontrolled emotions, by good people committing terrible deeds then seeking impossible atonements. *Pendragon* is about extreme, often irrational behavior pushing characters to heroic heights and tragic ends. There is very little daylight between the mechanics of the game and the narratives it encourages, which is why *Pendragon* is a perfect game, *for what*

King Arthur Pendragon, Nocturnal Media, 2016
Greg Stafford, Cover by Jamie García Mendoza

it aims to be: A recreation of the Arthurian romances in an interactive form, with a focus on simulating knighthood as it developed over the course of Arthur's fictional reign. That is an extremely narrow definition of perfection. And yet, I can think of no other roleplaying game that so deftly marries theme, system, and source material.

Oriental Adventures (1985)

In 1984, TSR was in trouble, thanks to financial mismanagement (spending money on everything from a fleet of employee cars, to purchasing an arts and crafts company, to raising a shipwreck). Gary Gygax, who had been in Los Angeles attempting to secure a movie deal for *Dungeons & Dragons*, returned to Wisconsin and saved the company with *Unearthed Arcana* (1985), a new *Advanced Dungeons & Dragons* rulebook.

Consisting mostly of material collected from Gygax's *Dragon* magazine articles, it significantly expanded the game with new character classes, races, and other rules. The book was strewn with errors, and the new races and classes were overpowered—if Ed Greenwood thought *Fiend*

ORIENTAL ADVENTURES, TSR, 1985

GARY GYGAX, FRANCOIS MARCELA-FROIDEVAL, AND DAVID "ZEB" COOK, COVER BY JEFF EASLEY

Folio blew up *D&D*'s cherished consistency, I can't imagine what he made of *Unearthed Arcana*. Nevertheless, the book saved the company and ushered in a sort of half-step to a new edition of *D&D* (this pattern of producing half-editions repeats across *D&D*'s history). Inspired, in part, by *Bushido*, *Oriental Adventures* was the second installment of the rules expansion.

The book is essentially a new *Players Handbook* for *AD&D* dressed in Asian trappings—the idea being that if *D&D* is a pastiche of Western culture, history, and folklore, *Oriental Adventures* would expand the canon to include those of the East. There are ten classes, chief among them is a revamp of the original Monk class from the *Players Handbook*. Joining them are a nomadic Barbarian, Kensai (weapon masters), Wu Jen (hermit sorcerers), Bushi (professional soldiers), Sohei (warrior priests), Shukenja (wandering holy folk), and Yakuza (gangsters). Samurai and Ninja need no explanation, though it is worth noting that Ninja must take another class as their cover for daily life.

There are also three new races—Hengeyokai are intelligent, shapeshifting animals; Korobokuru are a sort of dwarf; Spirit Folk are the embodiment of natural

forces. A host of spells, new equipment, and a martial arts system round out the book. The main mechanical contribution to the larger *D&D* ecosystem comes from the introduction of non-weapon proficiencies—a sort of abstracted skill system—that would be revamped just a year later by Douglas Niles for the *Dungeoneer's Survival Guide,* and again in 1989, by Cook himself for the Second Edition of *AD&D*.

Quite a lot of space is given over to a campaign setting called Kara-Tur, a fictionalized conglomeration of Asian geography and culture. This material was meant to form a second continent in the world of Greyhawk, but after Gygax's exit from TSR at the end of 1985, the plan changed, and Kara-Tur found itself bolted onto Ed Greenwood's Forgotten Realms a few years later. Ironically, it is exactly the sort of real-world-inspired setting material that Greenwood avoided in his homebrew version.

By all accounts, *Oriental Adventures* was wildly popular, most likely fueled, in part, by America's pop cultural preoccupation with all things Asian during the '80s. It was TSR's biggest seller in 1985.

If the exotifying title of the book alone wasn't a red flag, the text from the back cover certainly is: "...The mysterious and exotic Orient, land of spices and warlords, has at last opened her gates to the West." As much as *Oriental Adventures* is inspired by chambara and kung fu films, that single sentence demonstrates that the book is influenced just as much by lurid pulp stereotypes, Yellow Peril propaganda, and the lingering specter of European imperialism. The notion of an insular, xenophobic Eastern society protecting its wealth of spices from Western traders is about as literal an echo of real-world colonialism as a game can have.

Problems plague the inside of the book, too. There are two new systems to convert established stereotypes into mechanics. There's Comeliness, a new attribute that measures beauty and social grace, literally translating the act of objectification into *D&D* game terms. This attribute has troubling implications considering the long tradition of Western audiences fetishizing Asian women ("opened her gates?") and feminizing Asian men. Honor, meanwhile, measures a character's worth. Separate from alignment, it complicates the already dodgy morality of *D&D* by allowing evil characters to have high honor, or vice versa, playing specifically into the stereotype of the Asian trickster and generally contributing to the underlying idea that Eastern modes of living are fundamentally strange and somehow Other.

In *Orientalism* (1978), one of the several ways Edward Said defined the term was as a kind of flattening or reducing of the complexity and variety of the many Asian cultures into a singular, imaginary potpourri, by Western "authorities," for Western audiences; there is no clear distinction between Asian cultures. The bulk of *Oriental Adventures* is inspired by feudal Japan, with elements of the Three King-

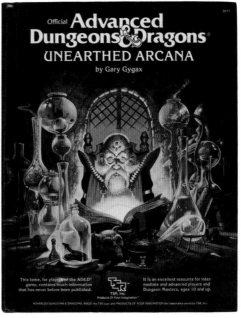

Unearthed Arcana, TSR, 1985
Gary Gygax, Cover by Jeff Easley

doms period in China and the Golden Horde grafted on for variety. It's a kind of monolithic mush of fantasy "Asianness" that verges on parody. This isn't a book for Asian players; it practically says as much right on the back cover—the intended audience is Western tourists, come to pry out well-kept Eastern secrets. *Oriental Adventures* seems to spring from a kind of willful ignorance fostered by decades of colonialism and exoticization that have made trafficking in these stereotypes a reflex for Westerners.

The book's release was the start of a cycle. *Oriental Adventures* was met with praise and high sales from an audience that was predominantly white. Seven years later, TSR took the same approach to the Middle East and compilation of Middle Eastern folk tales, *One Thousand and One Nights*, creating the Orientalist *Al-Qadim: Arabian Adventures* (1992), another expansion of the Forgotten Realms campaign setting. It received a whole line of a dozen more products over the next two years, despite a modest reception among an audience that was, still, predominantly white. Shockingly, *Oriental Adventures* was released again in 2001, updated for the third edition rules.

Al-Qadim: Arabian Adventures, TSR, 1992
Jeff Grubb, Cover by Jeff Easley

It won an ENNIE Award, a fan-voted industry award, for Best Campaign Setting. The audience? Still predominantly white.

The audience for RPGs is slowly becoming more diverse, but attitudes are changing much faster, thanks to efforts like Agatha Cheng and Daniel Kwan's *Asians Represent!* podcast, which has thoroughly deconstructed the tropes of *Oriental Adventures* and, through that, contributed to making the hobby a more welcoming place (and won back-to-back ENNIE Awards of its own, for Best Podcast, in 2020 and 2021).

Thus far, there hasn't been an *Oriental Adventures* released for the fifth edition.

Dragonroar (1985)

By the mid '80s, most wargame publishers were experimenting with producing RPGs. In the states, SPI had put out *DragonQuest* and *Dallas,* while Avalon Hill developed *James Bond 007* and licensed *RuneQuest* from Chaosium. In the United Kingdom, Standard Games, best known for medieval-themed wargame, *Cry Havoc* (1981), got in on the action with *Dragonroar*, which somehow beat *Warhammer Fantasy Roleplay* to market, becoming the first major British-created fantasy roleplaying game (the first playable Brit RPG, in general, was likely the small press version of the superhero RPG *Golden Heroes*, 1982).

Not everything is going to be a classic. Sometimes the absurd deserves a little celebration. *Dragonroar* is pretty absurd. The system is simple; it's really more of a stripped-down tactics game than a fully-fledged RPG; there are no mechanics for anything outside of combat. That combat is clearly intended for play with miniatures (unsurprisingly, the back cover of the rulebook features a full color photograph of the *Dragonroar* miniature line within a diorama, mimicking the action of the cover). It's firmly for beginners and provides a solid, if martially inclined, introduction. The tone is light and cheer-

ful, and the explanations are clear. Like *DragonRaid*, there is an audio cassette; the first half walks players through the book's contents, and the second half features narration for a solo adventure that seems equally mortifying and helpful. The book also contains a more traditional GM-led adventure. There are character chits and environment floor plans. All of this is fine: Players could do a lot worse for an introductory RPG box set in 1985.

War hedgehog, though. There's a war hedgehog on the cover, right there, under the decidedly un-aerodynamic dragon. "These are giant intelligent hedgehogs," says the book. "They normally stand 8' tall. They do not wear armor as they are well protected by spikes [...] Less than 10% of hedgehogs practice magic. Most prefer to be warriors, using giant double headed axes."

The war hedgehog is one of the most amazing things I've ever seen, and it could only exist because of RPGs. I can't imagine any other media suffering something so goofy to live. And while they aren't featured on the cover, the game's listing for killer penguins is equally wonderful. "They live mainly on fish, but some groups that live near shores or major

DRAGONROAR, BOX SET, STANDARD GAMES, 1985
PETER O'TOOLE, COVER BY PETER DENNIS

shipping routes like to supplement their diets with manflesh," the book says, explaining that they affix metal blades to their beaks. The hell with orcs, give me a fantasy world full of homicidal mutant penguins and giant ax-wielding hedgehogs any day.

Teenage Mutant Ninja Turtles & Other Strangeness (1985)

Debuting in May of 1984, Kevin Eastman and Peter Laird's *Teenage Mutant Ninja Turtles* (*TMNT*) comic series was an instant sensation. Looking back on it now, this success was probably inevitable: The premise was something new that excited comic book readers while bridging the gap between mainstream superhero stories and the more adult indie comix scene. At the same time, it consciously built upon the more serious strains of superhero comics from the era, specifically Frank Miller's *Ronin* (1983-1984) and his legendary run on Marvel's *Daredevil: The Man Without Fear* (1978-1983)—without naming names, the first issue of *Teenage Mutant Ninja Turtles* explains how the same chemical that blinded Matt Murdoch also mutated the turtles. On top of all of its connections to superhero comics, *TMNT* also tapped into the persisting ninja-mania, which was kicked off by the film *Enter the Ninja* in 1981.

Collectors who, at the time, saw comics as a potentially lucrative investment created a speculator's market around the book. The independently produced, black-and-white comic, printed on newsprint and in small quantities sparked a feeding frenzy, driving up prices, making copies scarce, and sparking a boom in similar black-and-white indie titles. An instant legend in the world of comics, the popularity of *TMNT* didn't immediately explode outside of that realm, though.

Palladium Books, founded by former small press comic creator Kevin Siembieda, purchased the rights to produce an

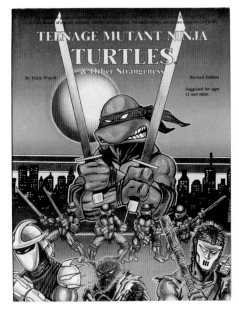

TEENAGE MUTANT NINJA TURTLES & OTHER STRANGENESS, PALLADIUM BOOKS, 1985
ERICK WUJCIK, COVER BY KEVIN EASTMAN

RPG based on the turtles almost immediately after the comic debuted. Palladium had already experienced some success with superhero RPGs; *Heroes Unlimited* also hit shelves in 1984. Simpler and with a broader appeal, thanks to the growing popularity of the comics, *Teenage Mutant Ninja Turtles & Other Strangeness* provided a convenient introduction for *Heroes Unlimited* and other Palladium games, all of which use the same core mechanics that would eventually be called the Megaversal system.

TMNT & Other Strangeness appeals to players by translating a world unseen in the comics into a world that can be inhabited and explored. There are details on the characters from the comics, of course, not to mention plenty of art by Eastman and Laird, but the star attraction is the mutation rules. They're robust, accounting, not just for a wide range of potential mutant animals, but also for degrees of mutation (in other words, how human-seeming the character appears, which can be very much so) and the potential for mental powers, as well.

This variety of choices coupled with an ambiguous alignment system gave *TMNT & Other Strangeness* a sense of freedom and maturity that few other games could

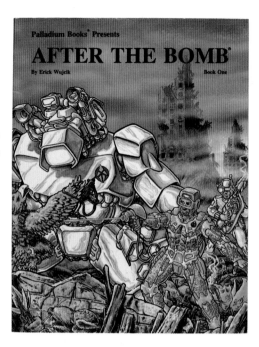

match—it wound up serving as an important introduction to RPGs for many players, particularly ones who haunted comic shops, and it was proof of a vibrant RPG world beyond *D&D* for many others. Despite the inherent silliness of martial arts-trained mutant animals, the street gangs, violence, and urban decay all feel serious, a vibe that RPGs, like *Cyberpunk*, *Shadowrun*, and *Vampire: The Masquerade* would embrace into the next decade. In this way, *TMNT & Other Strangeness* feels ahead of its time.

Teenage Mutant Ninja Turtles & Other Strangeness was Palladium's first big hit. Instead of immediately producing more branded *TMNT* supplements, Palladium next released *After the Bomb* (1986), a setting book developed out of *TMNT & Other Strangeness*'s mutation mechanic, a system that was not covered under the terms of the comic license. This was a clever move, freeing the setting from the constraints (and royalties) required of *TMNT & Other Strangeness,* even though the roster of *TMNT* comic artists contributed quite a bit of art to the line, making it recognizable as *TMNT* without *being TMNT.*

After the Bomb presents a post-apocalyptic world where the Eastern seaboard of the United States is ruled by warring factions of mutant animal people who have renamed everything with punny animal names—Philadelphia is now Filly; New York is N'Yak.

Regular humans still exist, though in smaller numbers, and they are almost always cast as gun-toting technocratic imperialist villains, which, is fair. The second installment, *Road Hogs* (1986), moves the action to the West Coast and flips that script. Here, the human Americorps are the heroes, and the villains are an army of mutant bikers. It's basically *Mad Max 2: The Road Warrior* (1981), but with anthropomorphic animals. There's a pile of new mutant types, including aquatic animals (mutant whales?) and a lengthy section on vehicles that includes rules for combat and building new rides, vastly expanding player options. Further books explore Australia, the Yucatan, and a very strange parody of Arthurian England that involves a re-awakened Merlin.

Despite a number of sourcebooks that made the game ever stranger, introducing space travel, aliens, and time travel, the *TMNT & Other Strangeness* line peaked in the late '80s—a victim of irony. Palladium used their work on *TMNT* in order to

secure the license to produce a game based on the *Robotech* anime. The agent who brokered that deal, Martin Freedman, was so impressed by the *Teenage Mutant Ninja Turtle* property that he went directly to Eastman and Laird to sell them on developing other merchandising opportunities, which eventually led to the cartoon series, the toy line, the films, and the turtles' ascension into the ranks of pop culture icons. The cartoon jettisoned the comic's grim and gritty atmosphere in favor of more kid-friendly fare. According to Kevin Siembieda, the massive success of the cartoon and subsequent toy line evaporated the cool factor for teens who had been playing the game. The RPG line disappeared soon after.

World Action and Adventure (1985)

"For the accomplishment of writing the *World Action and Adventure* series, five departments at San Diego State University awarded Gregory L. Kinney fifteen units of credit: English, Sociology, Zoology, Psychology and Multicultural Education," so declares the back cover of the main *World Action and Adventure: The Realistic Role-Playing Game* rulebook, right next to a photo of the author in a sharp suit, skinny tie, and matching pocket square. The other two volumes of the trilogy of rulebooks feature the same quote, but the photo of Kinney changes. In one, he's dressed for a bit of yachting, like a preppy villain in an '80s college comedy; in the other, he looks like an Indiana Jones cosplayer.

Everything about this RPG is startling—its naiveté, its scope, its production values, its ambivalence to playability, its *poetry*. *World Action and Adventure* is a universal system, calibrated to reality, that is, to simulating the world in which we live. If it exists, or existed, on planet Earth, *World Action and Adventure* purports to represent it in game terms, which diminishes its universality—*GURPS* this is not.

The core book is brimming with charts and tables that *do* attempt to exhaustively catalog the contents of our world: Life expectancy by era, lists of animals, lists of business types, minimum hours of sleep, a matrix for determining the outcome of a trial, a list of diseases with 64 entries that notes, "these lists cover just about all the diseases." A set of tables for important events in a character's year includes a sub-table for embarrassment—at a party, with a friend, many people around, hundreds watching.

I'm not even getting into the more robust collection of animals and careers in the supplemental books. Why play something exciting, like an explorer or daring military commander, when a player can roll up a mail carrier or a notary public? As for the play itself, there is a system here. Some of it is informed by *D&D*, though it is much more simplified. Some of the action is intended to be resolved using the multitude of tables and charts, assuming the GM can find the correct one for the situation. RPGs tend to be made out of small systems of mechanics that interact with each other in compelling ways. Most of the systems of *World Action and Adventure*—and there are dozens of them—don't seem to interact at all. They just generate facts that have no mechanical impact.

And yet the game *is* charming, almost sweet. Lawrence Schick, in *Heroic Worlds*, calls it, "without doubt, the *nicest* RPG ever published." *World Action and Adventure* is a portrait of the world painted by someone whose view has not yet been complicated by that world. Kinney conveys a real "can-do" attitude in his preface, too. He thanks everyone who helped with the project (particularly his mother, who, judging from the name of the publisher, founded a company expressly to put into print these three sturdy hardcover books, which are easily the highest quality RPG books on the market in 1985).

While the game captures something of

WORLD ACTION AND ADVENTURE OFFICIAL GUIDE, M. S. KINNEY CORPORATION, 1985
GREGORY L. KINNEY

Lankhmar (1985)

Fritz Leiber's Lankhmar stories chart the key misadventures of two rogues, the big barbarian Fafhrd and the skulking thief Gray Mouser, as they make their way in a strange and decadent world, winning fortunes, losing them again, then celebrating (or commiserating) with a drink (or ten). Most of the tales center on Lankhmar, the City of the Black Toga, but some range into the wider world of Nehwon. Magic is in this world, but it is corrupting and remote—its practitioners shunned. By keeping the focus on more pragmatic matters, like boozing, city living, and the pursuit of gems the size of one's head, Leiber renders more nuanced characters and a more complex world than those portrayed by earlier authors. Conan often seems a kind of demi-god, whereas Faf and the Mouser are decidedly and delightfully fallible, ruled, as they are, by desires that are all too mortal.

Leiber's influence on the sword and sorcery genre runs deep—he coined the term "sword and sorcery," after all! Out of all of the authors and works Gary Gygax included in "Appendix N," his bibliography of D&D inspirations, the Fafhrd and the Gray Mouser stories stand out for having some of the clearest influence on the game. The entire Thief class owes much to them, as does the idea of a thieves' guild. Leiber didn't invent the notion of a thieves' guild—there's plenty of historical precedent for them; Miguel de Cervantes introduced them to Western literature in his short story, "Rinconete y Cortadillo" (1613), and the concept expanded in the early 1700s with the introduction of the *One Thousand and One Nights*—but he did much to crystallize it into a concept that would turn up again and again in fantasy literature. He centered taverns and the taprooms of inns as haunts of adventurers. Perhaps most importantly, Fafhrd and the Gray Mouser provide a template for what play-

the do-it-yourself ethos of the hobby, a time-honored RPG tradition, these acknowledgements reveal how much help a team of one often needs, no matter how much inspiration and stubbornness they have on tap. It takes a village: Even his grandparents took part in the play tests (and it had play tests, which is more than can be said for a number of *D&D* publications). Kinney wanted a different sort of game from what *Dungeons & Dragons* was delivering, so he made it (with help). Even if it comes off as an oddity 35-years later, it's an admirable artifact.

And sure, there is a poem at the front of the book, 20 verses long, that sings the praises of all sorts of adventure. It's possible to make fun of it (though, is it really any worse than the multiple songs included in the *Dragonlance* modules?); at the end of the day, Kinney had to get credit for his English class—that's a unique design constraint for an RPG.

> "With *Word Action and Adventure* there is one thing that is sure in any time and every place it's here for all the human race."

ers might be—not just as individual characters, but as companions. Although ruled by self-interest, they are true friends nonetheless. Before Leiber's knaves, fantasy heroes were largely lone wolves.

Using Lankhmar as a setting for *Dungeons & Dragons* seems almost inevitable because of Leiber's outsized influence. In fact, *Lankhmar: City of Adventure* is arguably the third campaign setting in *D&D*'s history. Greyhawk was first, then the Known World, introduced in the Expert box set. Owing to the large pool of source material to draw from, Lankhmar feels more comprehensive and thought out than those others.

The book, which is relatively brief at 96 pages, crams an astonishing amount of detail from Leiber's stories—personages from the books (even some dead ones, like the necromancer, Hristomilo, and Krovas, the grandmaster of the Thieves' House, get their due), endless guilds, monsters, and factions. Despite the name, it even finds space to describe Nehwon, the world beyond Lankhmar's smoky walls.

In all, it is a vivid recreation of Leiber's source material. However, the Lankhmar tales are just one ingredient in the stew that is *Dungeons & Dragons*. Many features that *D&D* players may take for granted seem out of place in Leiber's gritty, low magic world, so play in Lankhmar requires significant adjustments to the *D&D* system. The most noticeable is the removal of elves, dwarves, and other non-human races, which is a smart design choice that does much to preserve the feel of Leiber's stories. In terms of classes, magic-using characters see the most changes; the only options available are Black Wizards—a combination of the traditional Magic-User class with the Illusionist—and White Wizards—a combination of the standard Cleric and Druid classes.

Everything about spellcasting is slowed down; casting times stretch into hours and days, while spells are regained

LANKHMAR: CITY OF ADVENTURE, TSR, 1985
BRUCE NESMITH AND DOUGLAS NILES, COVER BY KEITH PARKINSON

after a week of rest, instead of a night's sleep. Magic items are vanishingly rare. Of the martial characters, Paladins and Rangers are available, but seem a bit like sore thumbs, thanks to their rigid and largely unselfish pursuits. This is a world meant for Fighters, Thieves, and Assassins. Dropping magical demi-humans but leaving Magic-Users feels like a half-measure, but *D&D* is going to *D&D*.

The approach to the city itself is the real star of the book, holding its own even against TSR's deluxe *City System* (1988) box a few years later; it is likely the best presentation of an RPG city until *Night City* in 1991. It accomplishes this urban feat in three ways.

The first method is modeled on Flying Buffalo's approach. Their *Citybook* series (launched in 1982) detailed unique businesses, their location, and their proprietors (and their problems), in a format ready to drop into any homebrew city. *City of Adventure* doesn't have the space for such detail, but it does give a rundown on every important building and

FRITZ LEIBER'S LANKHMAR: THE NEW ADVENTURES OF FAFHRD AND GRAY MOUSER, BOX SET, TSR, 1996
SHANE LACY HENSLEY AND STEVE MILLER, COVER BY ALAN POLLACK

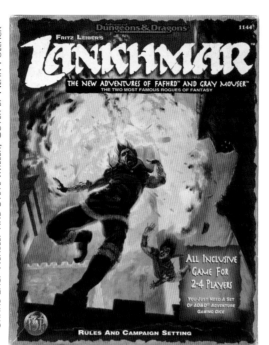

establishment in Lankhmar, which is enough for most GMs to work with.

Secondly, *City of Adventure* takes a page from Midkemia's city design playbook, providing a few pages of random tables for generating buildings and NPCs. There is no encounter matrix, so this city never really comes alive with the bustle of commerce, but a number of short encounter seeds adequately make up for that shortcoming.

The final method is the most interesting. Looking at the poster map of the city, players will note Lankhmar is dotted with blank white squares. These squares represent the tangled backstreets of the city, intimately known only to neighborhood locals. When players leave the main avenues and take to the alleys, the GM uses one of 12 provided map squares (or one of their own devising) to fill in the location. These modular blocks introduce a sense of randomness and an element of the unknown to the city. A devious GM who changes the square each time players visit might even create a sense of mystery and disorientation. Lankhmar certainly changes fast!

The best part about the creation of *Lankhmar: City of Adventure*, though, stems from another licensing screw-up and has nothing to do with roleplaying games at all, but helped Leiber himself in his waning years.

The death of Leiber's wife, Jonquil, in 1969 affected the author profoundly. Glimmers of his mindset can be seen in the 1970 novella, *Ill Met in Lankhmar*, which chronicles the second and most portentous meeting of Fafhrd and the Gray Mouser. In that story, the rogues' lovers meet a grisly end at the fangs of a swarm of rats. The pair exact a bloody revenge on the culprits—a necromancer and the thieves' guild that employed him—then abandon their home city to embark on new lives as drunken vagabonds.

As far as I know, there was no violent revenge for Leiber, but he did retreat from a comfortable life in Los Angeles as a professional writer of fiction to a seedy one-room apartment in a San Francisco residential hotel, where his manual typewriter was perched over the sink. There, he traded his 12 years of sobriety for three years of booze and barbiturates. He eventually eased, but never entirely relinquished, his substance abuse. Despite his spartan accommodations, he traveled frequently to science fiction conventions, and visiting writers reported that he was well stocked with books.

Another work of fiction, Leiber's novel *Our Lady of Darkness* (1977), might have some insight. In it, Franz Westen struggles with his alcoholism and the loss of his wife, who haunts him as a human-shaped pile of books that he's arranged on one side of his bed. Westen, an obvious self-insert, appraises both his substance abuse and his desire to find ways to reconnect with the world outside of his hovel in a forthright manner. Fiction is often neater than real life, but the novel seems to indicate Leiber neither regretted nor was embarrassed by his choices.

Along with genuine affection, Gary Gygax might have empathized with Leiber's struggles during TSR's early collaboration with Leiber on the wargame *Lankhmar* (1976); he even hosted the author for a week following Leiber's stint as a guest of honor at GenCon X in 1977. The author's struggles also likely contributed to the decision to include elements from the Fafhrd and the Gray Mouser stories in *Deities & Demigods*, as well. Greg Stafford of Chaosium was also a fan and friend of Leiber. In 1982, through Leiber's agent, he arranged a license to develop an RPG based on the Fafhrd and Gray Mouser stories—a deluxe box set, like *Thieves' World*, containing details on the city, a system for solo play, and new fictional elements created by Leiber.

The problem: Leiber, unbeknownst to the other parties involved (including, possibly, himself), sold the same license to TSR a few months later. Learning of this situation, TSR, under the leadership of the Blume Brothers, resolved to sue Leiber. Though Chaosium stood to retain the license when the dust settled, a lawsuit would likely have been devastating to both Leiber's finances and his state of mind. Further, TSR was undeniably the larger company, with a wider web of distribution than Chaosium. A *Dungeons & Dragons* product set in Lankhmar would generate far more money for Leiber than one from Chaosium, something that was clear from the advance payments Leiber received from both companies—TSR's $3,000 dollars was 12 times the $250 dollar offering from Chaosium, and came with the promise of renewal for the same amount in three years' time, in addition to royalties. Leiber was resigned to honor his original deal with Chaosium, but Stafford didn't want to see the author be sued, so he cancelled the contract, even though doing so meant losing over a year of design work on the box set. He did ask

Leiber for (and received) the return of the initial $250 dollar advance, though.

Leiber lived comfortably on the royalties from *Lankhmar: City of Adventure* and the rest of the *D&D* line for nearly a decade, until he passed away in 1992.

Warhammer Fantasy Roleplay (1986)

Due to the high cost associated with importing books into the United Kingdom from the US, much of Games Workshop's early business involved reprinting American RPGs for the UK market, including *Dungeons & Dragons,* for a while, then *Stormbringer*, *Traveller*, *RuneQuest*, and *Call of Cthulhu*, among others. All of these titles leave a clear mark on *Warhammer Fantasy Roleplay* (*WFRP*), Games Workshop's first original RPG.

Warhammer is a skill-based percentile system with tactical combat tuned for the use of miniatures. The rules start to shine when they get into the character careers, which paint over a *D&D*-style class system with the trappings of trade in a way that is informative of the world and reflective of realistic life experience, à la *Traveller*.

The careers, which range from the expected, like Merchant, to the delightfully odd, like Rat Catcher, give a window into the setting of the Old World (which it shared with the miniature wargame *Warhammer Fantasy Battle*) and help define characters for roleplay. They also have exit ramps to other careers—that Rat Catcher, with some hard work and gumption, can eventually work their way up to become a Grave Digger—so they serve as the primary tool for character progression, again rooted firmly in the fiction of the world.

That world is the real treat. Much of the lore is laid out in the book, but it comes alive through the way it is reflected in the game's systems. The Old World is roughly analogous to a high Medieval, early Renaissance Europe. There are guns and

WARHAMMER FANTASY ROLEPLAY

WARHAMMER FANTASY ROLEPLAY, GAMES WORKSHOP, 1986
RICHARD HALLIWELL, RICK PRIESTLY, GRAEME DAVIS, JIM BAMBRA, AND PHIL GALLAGHER, COVER BY JOHN SIBBICK

dwarves; magic is incredibly dangerous. Chaos is a constant, reality-unraveling threat. Much of the world has a veneer of civilization, but it's thin and easily scraped away to reveal a reality that is impoverished, violent, and brutal.

In contrast to many of Games Workshop's later exercises in the grim and dour, *Warhammer Fantasy Roleplay* embraces gallows humor and anti-authoritarianism in a way that mirrors, albeit dimly, the anti-Thatcher sentiment that comes through in British comic books during the late '80s (for further proof of this connection, one has only to look to *Judge Dredd: The Role-Playing Game*, 1985, which was adapted by Games Workshop from the popular comic strip in *2000 AD* about a dystopic police state and uses a modified version of *WFRP*'s ruleset).

The art does quite a bit of world building. John Sibbick's iconic cover sets the stage well, with a double dose of mohawks telegraphing a certain amount of "in-your-face" punk rock attitude inside. Tony Ackland fills out the world with traditional illustrations that emphasize the grime. Just as important are Dave Andrews's

building diagrams and floor plans. As much as their utility for the miniature-centric portion of the game is self-evident, seeing these workaday buildings gives life to the world in a way that most other city books before and since lack.

Artwork has traditionally been important to Games Workshop's approach to world building—it was already a key part of the success of the *Fighting Fantasy* adventure gamebooks series. The roster of artists for *Warhammer Fantasy Roleplay* products soon grew to include Ian Miller, Russ Nicholson, John Blanche, Martin McKenna, and Will Rees, and goes a long way toward cementing the company's unique aesthetic for years to come.

It's impossible to talk about *Warhammer Fantasy Roleplay* without also talking about *The Enemy Within*, the episodic campaign often ranked as one of the best ever produced. The first volume, *The Enemy Within* (1986), is essentially an in-depth sourcebook of the Empire—a sort of fantasy version of the Hapsburg Holy Roman Empire—detailing its history and its political factions. This is the foundation material for the campaign, which kicks off with the brief scenario, "Mistaken Identity," in which one player is falsely thought to be an agent of a Chaos cult.

"Mistaken Identity" leads the players into the second volume, *Shadows Over Bögenhafen* (1987), where a diabolical plot is nearing completion. A powerful local merchant sold his soul to a demon, and the time is nearly up for him to make good on his end of the bargain. In an attempt to wiggle out of the deal, he has bamboozled other powerful local merchants into performing a ritual—he thinks it will save his soul, and they think it will make Bögenhafen the economic seat of the Empire. They're all wrong and, hopefully, the players can unravel the mystery

158

and stop the plot before catastrophe strikes. It's an excellent yarn, short on combat but long on *Call of Cthulhu*-style investigation and growing dread, as Chaos exerts itself into the town.

Death on the Reik (1987) follows, thanks to a letter found in Bögenhafen that leads the players to travel through the Empire on a river boat as they seek to reveal the forces of Chaos secretly at work in the land. The Reikland is presented as a waterborne sandbox with several seemingly discreet adventures loosely connected by the underlying interests of Chaos. There's a goblin-infested mine, an expedition into a Chaos-blasted wasteland, a kidnapping to foil, and an abandoned observatory to explore. The largest section is devoted to Castle Wittgenstein, which is a terrible place to visit. The castle and its town are well detailed and, like the rest of the box set, there is no firm course for the plot. The action is driven by player choice, and the campaign materials are written to support the GM in determining the consequences—throughout the series, the books repeatedly encourage GMs to lie to the players or to juke the rules in order to keep the game on track and fun. It's a very open and sophisticated design for 1987.

Power Behind the Throne (1988) is the thrilling conclusion to *The Enemy Within* campaign. Technically, there are two more installments, *Something Rotten in Kislev* (1989) and *Empire in Flames* (1989), but the former is a tonal digression that leads into the latter, a disappointing climax that is no longer considered canonical. It is worth noting that Cubicle 7's lush, 10-volume modernization of the campaign (2020-2022) completely replaces *Kislev* and dramatically overhauls *Empire*, which is a welcome course correction. And anyway, *Power Behind the Throne* feels like the finale.

It brings us to Middenheim, where Chaos has infiltrated the highest levels of government and, through a punitive tax

SHADOWS OVER BÖGENHAFEN, GAMES WORKSHOP, 1987 GRAEME DAVIS, JIM BAMBRA, AND PHIL GALLAGHER, COVER BY WILL REES

scheme, is close to taking over the city entirely. I know "tax scheme" sounds about as thrilling as the "trade negotiations" in *The Phantom Menace* (1999), but it actually serves as an excellent entrance into the intrigues of the people in power. Much of the book is stage setting, devoted to the week-long, city-wide festival taking place during the adventure and detailing a few key locations. During that week, the players are on their own, investigating as they see fit and generally attempting to garner influence among the city's ruling class. The major NPCs are presented in alarming detail, so GMs know exactly what they do and how they will react to key events and player petitions. *Power Behind the Throne* is very much focused on roleplaying; very little action takes place until the last night of the festival when everything balances on the knife point. Its plot is well-thought-out and devious, with a failsafe that cleverly insulates it from being cracked open too early, while still providing plenty of weighty threads for players to keep busy with until the end.

And, strangely, that's basically it. A few additional titles come out, then Games

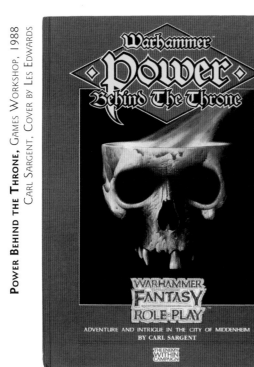

POWER BEHIND THE THRONE, GAMES WORKSHOP, 1988
CARL SARGENT, COVER BY LES EDWARDS

Workshop quits the RPG business to focus on its various miniature wargames. For a brief time, Games Workshop shunted *Warhammer Fantasy Roleplay* over to a much-abused subsidiary, Flame Publications, before Hogshead Publishing picked up the license, keeping the game alive through 2002. Other editions and variants have since been produced by a number of companies, including another Games Workshop imprint called Black Industries, but none of have quite recaptured the feel and character of the original. Even Cubicle 7's fourth edition, which honors its forebears with gusto, feels distinct in its modernity. The grim and the sardonic, all wrapped in colorful motley, it seems, was the product of an all-too-brief moment in time.

Dungeoneer's Survival Guide (1986)

The *Dungeoneer's Survival Guide* continues the informal 1.5 edition of *Advanced Dungeons & Dragons*, following *Unearthed Arcana* (1985) and *Oriental Adventures*. The book and its companion, the *Wilderness Survival Guide* (1986),

DUNGEONEER'S SURVIVAL GUIDE, TSR, 1986
DOUGLAS NILES, COVER BY JEFF EASLEY

seem to be a reaction to the contemporaneous movement to lighten rules (à la *Ghostbusters*, for instance), offering ever more layers of optional systems to frustrate players and slow play.

The focus is on simulating the drudgery of navigating perilous underground spaces. This *can* be fun and interesting—*Torchbearer* (2013), *Goblinville* (2019), and the *Call of Cthulhu* campaign *Beyond the Mountains of Madness* (1999) all use inventory management and the traversal of hazardous terrain in different ways but to thrilling effect. The rules in *Dungeoneer's Survival Guide*—for moving, climbing, jumping, falling, *breathing*—seem expressly designed to get players to whine, "When do we get to hit things?"

Most of these rules fall away or are otherwise handwaved as *D&D* evolves. The only mechanic with any lasting power is proficiencies, the clumsy skill system that would be integral to frustrating players of *Advanced Dungeons & Dragons* Second Edition for years to come. The real legacy of the *Dungeoneer's Survival Guide* lies towards the back, in the "Dungeon Master's Section." There, amid black-edged pages, it introduces one of the core concepts that *D&D* strives to arrange itself around from this point forward.

Dungeons are strange places. For many people, the first association of the word is with a sort of underground jail in a castle: Stone walls, iron grates, dripping ceilings, rats, and the like. For the most part, though, this characterization is a fabrication of nineteenth century gothic novels and amateur historians who mistook storage rooms for oubliettes.

Dungeons in RPGs are not prisons. Sometimes, they are ruins. Sometimes, they are caverns beneath inhabited places, like a fortress or a city. They have their own ecologies and economies that darkly reflect the lives on the surface. They're metaphors made to manifest, and therefore, they don't truly align with anything humanity has made or experienced. Perhaps the most impressive dungeon entrance in the real-world is in Italy—the Orcus mouth in the Gardens of Bomarzo, but that hellmouth leads to a small dining room, not a realm of adventure (though it might be fun to play *D&D* there).

There are plenty of wondrous caverns in the world, like Carlsbad or the Grotta Gigante, but no monsters or evil sorcerers lair there, lining the tunnels with traps. The Paris Catacombs is perhaps the closest real-world equivalent—part tomb, part sewer, largely unmapped—in 2004, police discovered a movie theater and restaurant in a previously uncharted section of the complex, a find that wouldn't feel out of place in White Plume Mountain. While rare in the real-world, in literature and mythology, the human imagination has often insisted that the secret places underground are full of terrors and treasures. The land of the dead, be it Hades or Dante's infernal circles, is often situated là-bas, *down there*, as is Daedalus' maze, his prison-labyrinth that is also the home of the Minotaur.

The clearest antecedent, though, appears in Margaret St. Clair's *Sign of the*

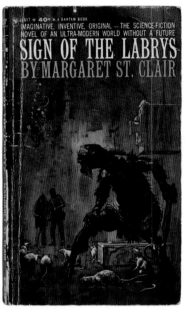

SIGN OF THE LABRYS, BANTAM BOOKS, 1963 MARGARET ST. CLAIR, COVER BY WILLIAM GEORGE

Labrys (1963): A vast post-apocalyptic bunker, filled with living quarters, subterranean forests and oceans, traps, a plethora of fungi, laboratories, bizarre factions, and unexpected connections (a door in the bottom of an autoclave?) between ever deeper levels. That subterranean realm is man-made, but St. Clair also covers the idea of a vast system of natural caves inhabited by cannibalistic elves in her novel, *The Shadow People* (1969). Both of these complexes feel halfway between a dream and an acid trip. It's no surprise that Gygax included both books in "Appendix N."

There are lots of dungeons in *Dungeons & Dragons*, of course. Many are published, and many more are created by GMs as needed. With the adventure module *D1: Descent into the Depths of the Earth* (1978), Gygax implied the existence of a deep place much larger than a dragon's cave or a lich's tomb. In *Dungeoneer's Survival Guide*, it gets a name, "the Underdark." The *Survival Guide* describes a small section, called Deepearth, which contains outposts for many of the major Underdark factions, but the implication is that the wider vastness is populated by an endless variety of creatures and cultures. Some of those, like the brain-eating mind flayers, are inimical to surface dwellers. Others, like the deep gnomes, are merely wary. But none so thoroughly capture the imagination of *D&D* players as the drow, the treacherous, spider-worshiping evil elves. The concept of the Underdark and its alien inhabitants is simple, but it represents a massive shift in paradigm: A vast subterranean realm of caverns and tunnels and cities and seas; a world-dungeon in the hollow earth that is every bit as vast and varied as the sun-touched lands.

GURPS (1986)

When I was a kid, some of my favorite toys were the knock-offs from the supermarket or the five-and-dime. They resembled the designs of the big-name lines, but they were obviously not official. I loved these toys because they broke the narrative rules presented in the tie-in cartoons. I could have some Warduke impostor as a lieutenant of Cobra Commander, heading up of a squad of monster men from some Hong Kong line. It didn't make sense, and it was glorious.

GURPS is kind of like that.

Intermittently, throughout the history of RPGs, the idea of a unified or universal game system has been an ambition for a certain sort of GM and player. For many years, Chaosium's *Basic Role-Playing* (*BRP*) came closest; it provides a universal core system, but requires modifications before it can deliver specific sorts of play experiences. Despite the fact that *RuneQuest* and *Call of Cthulhu* both use *BRP* rules at their core, they are not compatible with each other. If a GM wants a character to walk from 1920s Massachusetts through a magical portal into Glorantha, it is going to require converting their attributes. With a fully universal system, that transition is seamless—a player might need a rules module to handle specific facets of the setting or genre, but the essential underlying mechanisms of play remain unchanged, no matter where the action goes.

Steve Jackson was thinking about a universal system as early as 1981, but only announced *GURPS* in 1983, then an acronym for *Great Unnamed Role-Playing System*. In 1985, players first glimpsed the game in *Man to Man*, the standalone publication of the combat system for what is now called the *Generic Universal Role-Playing System*, and *Orcslayer*, which introduced a fantasy setting. The first box set hit shelves in 1986.

GURPS is exactly what it says it is—generic and universal. A GM can use it to run anything their heart desires. The system is easy to understand and is derived from the point-buy mechanics Jackson developed for *The Fantasy Trip*. Characters are created by spending a set number of points across abilities, skills, advantages, and disadvantages (which net more points to spend, similar to *Champions*). Conflicts are resolved using 6-sided dice. The game scales nicely; if a GM is running a realistic spy game, players start with fewer points to spread around than if the GM is running a superhero game.

Much of the appeal of tabletop RPGs lies in the exploration of richly realized fictional worlds. *GURPS* offers the opposite—an entirely blank slate. A *GURPS* campaign can be about anything the players want it to be, thanks to the frankly massive line of *GURPS* sourcebooks that allow players to plug in the specific rules they want to use. Looking to run a game about high-tech time traveling rabbits who hunt demons? *GURPS* has it covered. The astounding number of sourcebooks run the gamut from practical, like *GURPS High-Tech* (1988), a collection of equipment, to the bizarre, like a setting sourcebook for the 1967 psychedelic British television series, *The Prisoner* (1990). There are even *GURPS* conversions for other RPGs, like *Vampire: The Masquerade* (1993) and *Bunnies & Burrows* (1992).

Perhaps thanks to Jackson's tongue-in-cheek predilection for conspiracy

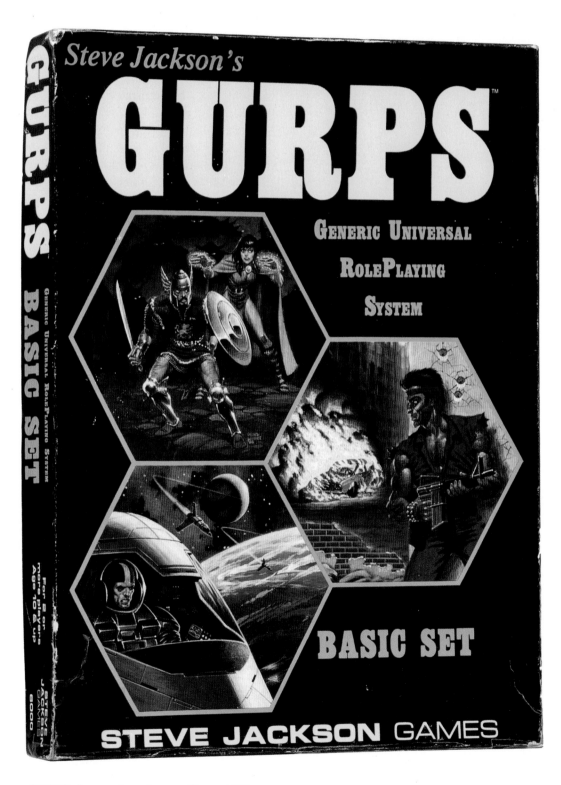

GURPS, Box set, Steve Jackson Games, 1986
Steve Jackson, Cover by John Zeleznik

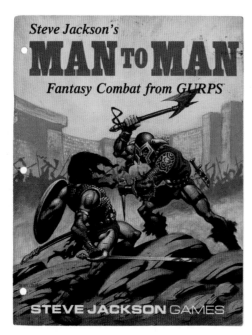

STEVE JACKSON'S MAN TO MAN, STEVE JACKSON GAMES, 1985
STEVE JACKSON, COVER BY DENIS LOUBET

part of the fun of the comics is the unexpected mix of genres. The core sourcebook is *GURPS Supers* (1989), but unlike most of the *GURPS* sub-lines, this one received support with a fair number of additional supplements (and its own trademark). In an amusing quirk of licensing, George R. R. Martin's shared universe superhero fiction anthology series, *Wild Cards*, which was born out of an ongoing campaign of Chaosium's *Superworld* RPG (1983), received its own *GURPS* sourcebook in 1989.

Others have since tried their hands at crafting universal systems. *Fudge, Fate, Savage Worlds,* and *Universalis* all come to mind. Some are lighter, more flexible, and more modern. The unified d20 System that spun out of the third edition of *Dungeons & Dragons* went on to essentially conquer, and nearly destroy, the entire RPG industry. Despite the successes of those other games, *GURPS* still feels unmatched in many ways. In the modern era, where one flop of a sourcebook can potentially kill a company, no other universal game can afford to be anywhere near as rich or as varied as the world the *GURPS* line invites players to create.

theories in games like *Illuminati* (which also received a *GURPS* sourcebook in 1992), the manuscript for *GURPS Cyberpunk* (a 1990 sourcebook covering the sci-fi subgenre, not a *GURPS* version of the R. Talsorian RPG of the same name) was seized by the Secret Service, who alleged that it was a guide for computer crime. The incident was, in part, the catalyst for the creation of the Electronic Frontier Foundation, and it became their first high profile case—considering that organization's long and storied history of safeguarding digital civil liberties, *GURPS Cyberpunk* has, perhaps, one of the most far-reaching real-world influences of any RPG. Ultimately, nothing came of the charge except a delay in publication, but Jackson *was* able to market the book as "seized by the FBI." Another surprising *GURPS* influence: Interplay initially used the system for the original *Fallout* videogame before deciding to develop their own *GURPS*-like system called SPECIAL (an acronym of the game's attributes, as with *Marvel Super Heroes*' FASERIP).

Because of the way it scales and can account for just about anything, *GURPS* is a natural system for a superhero game;

ORCSLAYER, STEVE JACKSON GAMES, 1985
STEVE JACKSON AND WARREN SPECTOR, COVER BY DAVID MARTIN

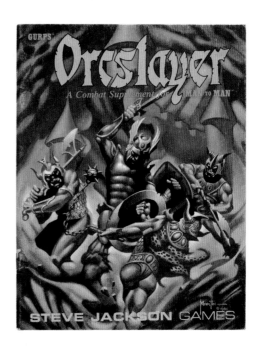

Phoenix Command (1986)

1980 saw the release of *Aftermath!* and *The Morrow Project*, two games with complex systems that aimed to realistically simulate combat in a post-apocalyptic world. For a certain sort of player, the idea of weighing the small mechanical differences between firearms or tracking blood points, which simulate bleeding to death (a feature of *The Morrow Project*), represent a kind of wonderland. Meanwhile, pop culture was increasingly fascinated by guy-with-gun action movies, like *Rambo* (1982)—but really the more bombastic 1985 sequel, *Rambo: First Blood Part II*—*Red Dawn* (1984), and *Commando* (1985). These two threads—the rise of the action movie and realistic combat simulation—combined to form the military RPG. The highest profile game of this sort was GDW's near-future *Twilight 2000* (1984); a close runner-up was Leading Edge's *Phoenix Command* (1986), the cover of which features a delightful collision between Rambo-style commando aesthetics and '80s-era clip art design.

The latest in a series of modular combat systems developed by Leading Edge into a sort of house system, *Phoenix Command* is devoted to modern military small arms. It is dismaying in its detail, chronicling the many possible ways to shoot guns (and be shot by them) with excruciating precision. There are 35 possible body locations for bullets to hit in *Phoenix Command* (admittedly down from the 60 in Leading Edge's first system, *Sword's Path: Glory*, 1982). While the proliferation of military RPGs in the '80s is evidence that there are players who find this sort of chart consultation exhilarating, it beggars belief that these sorts of systems saw regular play without significant simplification through house rules.

The three licensed games Leading Edge released as modular expansions of *Phoenix Command* are where this subgenre gets interesting. While each is a complete, standalone RPG, they all use the same simplified (though, ultimately, complicated) system, and because of that, there is an implicit potential for crossover play, which is just astonishing.

The first game makes perfect sense considering Leading Edge's history and inclinations. In 1989, the company released a tactical board game based on James Cameron's *Aliens* (1986). The board game was a success to the degree that its profits handily funded the company's other lines. *Aliens Adventure Game* (1991) was an attempt to cash-in on that success a second time, selling the same basic experience of the board game in RPG form.

The system's focus on firepower and tactics makes it a good fit for reenacting the events of the film, with players taking the roles of hardened Colonial Marines. And while the continuing appeal of such a game initially seems limited, there is a surprising amount of material in the book that expands the universe of the franchise, along with a wealth of stills from the movie. Additional star sectors are sketched out; new alien species are presented, all of them hewing, in some way, close to the xenomorphs of the film—injecting just the right amount of variety

PHOENIX COMMAND, BOX SET, LEADING EDGE GAMES, 1986. BARRY NAKAZONO, COVER BY SCOTT MILLER

into the formula of marines shooting monsters in close quarters. One sector even lives on beyond the Leading Edge RPG. Tartarus, with its burrowing Harvester aliens, is included in Free League's recent *Alien: The Roleplaying Game* (2019).

The line begins to get bizarre with the next game: *Bram Stoker's Dracula Role Playing Game* (1992), released to coincide with the Francis Ford Coppola film of the same name. The core concept is interesting enough—the events of *Dracula* actually happened, and the RPG takes place in the aftermath, when a whole host of vampire activity begins in the wake of the big guy's death and continues on through the modern day (so while readers might be expecting a Victorian-era sourcebook, there's still information on helicopters and modern military materiel).

As it turns out, vampires also pose a similar tactical challenge to xenomorphs. The RPG arranges vampires into secret households that mix thralls and vamps of varying ages and power levels. Because they are discrete, these households can be located anywhere and in any sort of configuration, which, in turn, leaves the action open to an endless variety of strategies. Less inspiring is the clue points system that reduces the investigative narrative to pure mechanics, with players accumulating points relative to the amount of time they spend investigating; then random tables reveal what they've learned or found, which accumulates more points, which leads to more rolls, until the nest is found.

Leading Edge followed *Dracula* with one of the strangest licensed RPGs ever produced: *The Lawnmower Man Virtual Reality Role Playing Game* (1993). The film (which is terrible and so removed from the Stephen King short story it purports to be based on that King successfully sued to have his name removed from the cover of the VHS), involves virtual reality, experiments on chimpanzees, and, eventually, an intellectually challenged handyman, Jobe, who is downloaded into a mainframe where he becomes a cybergod.

The game picks up after the movie ends, with CyberJobe having taken over the DataNet and waging the War for Virtual Reality. Players take the roles of various agents who set themselves in opposition to CyberJobe and his minions, both in a murky techno-conspiratorial real-world and the brand new virtual one, which only a fraction of player characters can enter, annoyingly. The book has some 50 pages of guns, which, I am sure, are very handy in virtual reality.

Ghostbusters (1986)

Everything about the *Ghostbusters* RPG is improbable. As with *Bunnies & Burrows* and *Toon*, a common reaction I've observed when people learn of its existence is, "Wait, they made *that* into an RPG?" Yes, they did! And it is pretty great, but it only gets stranger from here.

Though published by West End Games, *Ghostbusters* was designed by an all-star team from Chaosium—Sandy Petersen, Lynn Willis, and Greg Stafford. Despite a string of important and influential games,

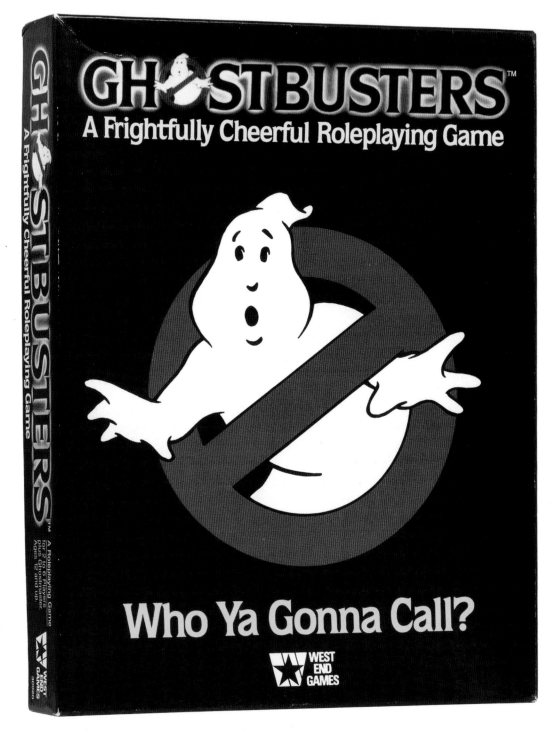

GHOSTBUSTERS, WEST END GAMES, 1986
SANDY PETERSEN AND LYNN WILLIS, WITH GREG STAFFORD

167

Chaosium was in rocky shape, thanks to a general downturn in the RPG industry and an unfulfilling partnership with Avalon Hill for *RuneQuest*'s third edition. *Ghostbusters* results from Chaosium's experiment to see if they could hire out their services as a design house. The result of that experiment is unclear. On the one hand, Chaosium never attempted such an arrangement again. On the other hand, they invented a new style of RPG mechanic that would not only dominate the hobby for the next decade or so, but also lead to the creation of one of the only games that ever seriously challenged *Dungeons & Dragons*' dominance of the industry. Not bad for showing up to a freelance gig, right?

That mechanic is the dice pool. Select the appropriate skill and roll a number of dice (in *Ghostbusters*' case, a 6-sided die) that corresponds to the skill's level. If the total beats a difficulty number set by the GM, the player succeeds in whatever they are attempting. If it is lower, they fail. There is a wrinkle: One of the dice has the *Ghostbusters* logo on it in place of the 6—if that comes up on a roll, it counts as a 0, and something bad happens.

While not codified in the *Ghostbusters* rules, it is easy to see how to modify rolls further by adding or removing dice to reflect circumstance, helpful equipment, help from pals, and any reason at all, really. Designers instantly recognized the potential at the heart of this flexibility. Greg Costikyan (who consulted on *Ghostbusters* and streamlined the systems Chaosium delivered) made the mechanic the heart of West End Games' *Star Wars: The Roleplaying Game* in 1987.

Shadowrun would use a slightly different dice pool method. Instead of totaling all of the dice, each individual die can be a success or a failure; the more successes, the better the result of the action. *Mutant: Year Zero* and its derivative games follow this path. However, it is the effect that *Ghostbusters* had on Jonathan Tweet

and Mark Rein-Hagen, the designers of *Ars Magica*, that made the biggest impact. The pair was so impressed by the dice pool system that they began experimenting with the mechanic, which, for Tweet, resulted in *Over the Edge* and for Rein-Hagen, *Vampire: The Masquerade* and nearly the entire catalog of White Wolf games. The RPGs that define the '90s basically spring right out of *Ghostbusters*—a long shadow for a quirky comedy game to cast.

Brownie points, used by the game in numerous ways, add another "X" factor. When something bad happens to a character, they lose brownie points. Characters can lose them for screwing up a job or from falling out of a window—there is no health system or real risk of death in the game, so brownie points stand in as hit points. Players can gain brownie points, usually at the end of the adventure, for succeeding at tasks. They can spend them too. 30 brownie points allow a player to raise one of their character's traits. Most importantly, similar to *James Bond 007*, spending one on a roll allows a die to be added to a skill check, giving the player a chance to exert some control over the narrative. West End Games would use this idea for their *Star Wars* RPG, calling them Force points, and they have, as luck points, become a standard feature in RPG design in the decades since.

All of that mechanical stuff is well and good, but is *Ghostbusters* a good game about bustin' ghosts? Yup! Folks tend to look back at *Ghostbusters* and see it as a designer's game in the same way a music aficionado might call Frank Zappa or underground hip hop artist MF DOOM a musician's musician. That characterization undersells its popularity, though. "*Ghostbusters* was considered a success pretty much out of the gate," says Bill Slavicsek, who was working as a game designer for West End Games at the time. "And its success led the company to pivot from a board game company to an RPG company."

The game does a good job of channeling the source material. It's funny, and the humor works on many levels, though, despite *The Real Ghostbusters* (1986-1991) cartoon airing concurrently, the RPG isn't geared toward kids—sex is a primary character motivation. There are essentially two version of the game in the box. The first is stripped down, and players take the roles of the film's characters for unconnected one-shots. Campaign play is more complex (though it is still easy compared to pretty much every other RPG on the market at the time) and involves custom characters setting up their own Ghostbusters franchise (an idea that, interestingly, floated around for a long time as the potential basis for the long-awaited third film).

There's a lot of paperwork included to make running a franchise feel suitably authentic. While much of the game feels like it's meant to be taken as a slapstick version of *Call of Cthulhu*, it is, in many ways, (like the original film) a zany small business comedy. This working stiff theme comes through in the list of characters in the campaign section, which collects petty irritants, like surly hot dog vendors, along with more serious threats, like criminals, lawyers, and demons. My inner five-year-old thrills at the idea of running a character who has a proton pack to shoot at ghosts, but I have to admit that my adult self sees the appeal of aiming one at my accountant.

It is easy to pick up and play right out of the box, which is not something that many games, even Chaosium's own relatively approachable ones, could claim at the time. *Ghostbusters* flies in the face of the idea, dominant though dying well into the '90s, that *real* RPGs need to be mas-

sive and complex. It opens the door to different approaches, like the cinematic role-playing of *Star Wars* or even the story-telling of *Prince Valiant*. *Ghostbusters* has a clear inheritor in the rules-light indie game *InSpectres*. Considering the broad appeal of the *Ghostbusters* movie, the fact that the *Ghostbusters* RPG and its dice pool descendants appealed to all sorts of folks outside of the usual RPG demographic should come as no surprise.

Star Wars (1987)

Dungeons & Dragons may be the best-known RPG, but it isn't the one that has made the biggest impact on popular culture.

After the release of *Return of the Jedi* (1983), most subsequent Star Wars material—the Marvel comic book series, the *Ewoks* (1985–1986) and *Droids* (1985) cartoons, the two Ewok TV movies (1984, 1985), all of dubious quality—was aimed directly at children in the interest of supporting a long merchandising tail. By 1986, even the comic series had wrapped up. The *Star Wars* saga was effectively over. I was eight years old in 1986, so I am an unimpeachable authority.

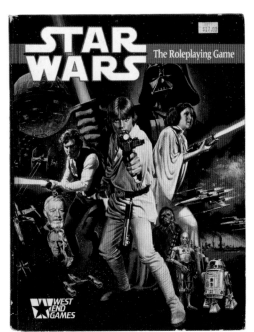

STAR WARS: THE ROLEPLAYING GAME, WEST END GAMES, 1987
GREG COSTIKYAN, COVER BY TOM CANTRELL

It wasn't until 1991, with the release of Timothy Zahn's *Heir to the Empire*, the first in a trilogy of well-regarded novels set five years after the events of the movies, that the spark of more serious interest was reignited. Zahn's novels paved the way for the multimedia extravaganza of *Shadows of the Empire* (1996)— a novel, videogame, toy line, soundtrack, and pretty much everything *but* a new movie that aimed to fill the gap between *The Empire Strikes Back* (1981) and *Return of the Jedi* (this wasn't a new phenomenon for *Star Wars*, though—the audio drama *Rebel Mission to Ord Mantell*, 1983, bridges *A New Hope* and *Empire*, for instance). That experiment lent considerable momentum to the idea of new films, which culminated in the release of the first prequel film, *The Phantom Menace* (1999), and the full reawakening of the *Star Wars* franchise as a multimedia juggernaut.

None of that would have been possible without *Star Wars: The Roleplaying Game* (*Star Wars: TRPG*) from West End Games. And still, the decision to adapt *Star Wars* into an RPG was perplexing to some. Bill Slavicsek, who oversaw the RPG line in its first year and went on to become West

End Games' creative director, recalls, "One editor at Marvel who I worked with at the time even told me, '*Star Wars*? Why'd you take that license? That property is dead.'"

If *Star Wars: TRPG* was just a token licensing effort that kept the fire burning, that would have been enough. "It was a growing market that would provide Lucasfilm Ltd. with new products while also being niche enough that if we totally screwed it up, it probably wouldn't harm the overall property in the least," says Slavicsek. For several years, the RPG was the only place to find high quality stills and production materials from the movies, like Ralph McQuarrie's now legendary concept art, much of which had never previously been published. That alone fed an appetite: The last art books, story books, and sketch books for the franchise saw print in 1983. They were hard to track down in the pre-internet era, and reissues wouldn't hit shelves until 1994.

In the original rulebook, some of the art received the full color treatment on 16 pages. Outside of a few TSR and Games Workshop products, color interiors were unheard of for RPG books, but these were certainly a boon for *Star Wars* aficionados. A full-color arms race ensued in the RPG industry. Slavicsek says in his short memoir, *Defining a Galaxy: Celebrating 30 Years of Roleplaying in a Galaxy Far, Far Away* (2018), "At GenCon the year after we released the two hardcover books, Jim Ward [...] complained to [West End Games' game designer] Curtis Smith that because of what we did, he had to go and make the Second Edition of *Advanced Dungeons & Dragons* a full-color hardcover book." Full-color has since become an industry standard.

The *Star Wars* RPG is about a whole lot more than color pages and neat movie art, though. It is also a great game on its own—an all-time classic. Designer Greg Costikyan expanded on the dice pool mechanics originally used for *Ghostbusters*, creating a fast and exciting game. Characters are created from templates, many of which are familiar to fans of the movies—Failed Jedi, Brash Pilot, Smuggler, Young Senatorial, Wookie—but the focus is on creating new adventures, so unlike *Star Trek: The Role Playing Game*, the beloved characters from the movies are strictly in the realm of the GM.

The game also took steps towards embracing the language of film—the introductory adventure uses a pre-written script for a mood-setting scene that includes an opening text crawl like the films. Leaning on the way that the first film opens with a scene in which a massive Star Destroyer chases the rebel cruiser, the rules advise that scenarios jump right in and start *in media res*. This sort of cinematic approach to play would be fleshed out further in Bill Smith's second edition of the rules, which counsels the GM to cut away from the action to describe scenes the characters can't possibly know about but which raise the stakes of their situation.

Everything about the system is arranged around building momentum to a climactic finish, and it joins *Toon* in actively encouraging GMs to throw rules out if they endanger the flow of the action and the story. It all comes to life, for both the players and the GM, thanks to the rich, shared experiences provided by the films. As much as the mechanics of *Star*

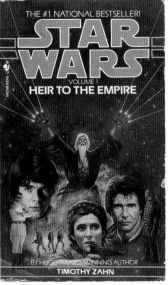

HEIR TO THE EMPIRE, BANTAM BOOKS, 1992
TIMOTHY ZAHN, COVER BY TOM JUNG

Wars: The Roleplaying Game were designed to encourage anyone to pick them up, the movies were the true leveler.

Star Wars has a specific *feel*, in the way that characters run headfirst into danger, or how the galaxy is at stake but there's always room for a quip, a hare-brained scheme, or a cool pose. Embracing that is more important than rolling dice or knowing the mechanics, and the rules recognize the truth of that pursuit. "Just like our general sense of fairy tales and medieval fantasy primes us on how to play *D&D*, *Star Wars* is part of the general culture. Remember, most of our early adopters were fans like me," says Slavicsek. "They had seen the three movies multiple times, whether in the theaters or on VCRs. That's all we really had and we devoured it over and over. And yes, it was a conscious design decision to set the game during those movies. We did our best [to portray them], and then the magic happened."

In addition to keeping the franchise alive in the public imagination, *Star Wars: The Roleplaying Game* expanded the universe in ways makers and custodians of

REBEL MISSION TO ORD MANTELL, BUENA VISTA RECORDS, 1983
BRIAN DALEY

the *Star Wars* movies could scarcely anticipate. By the time the RPG line folded in the wake of West End Games' bankruptcy in 1998, it consisted of more than 130 products, all contributing to an ever-richer fictional universe. West End's approach to this galaxy building is typified by the volume that launched alongside the core rulebook: *The Star Wars Sourcebook*. Says co-author Bill Slavicsek in *Defining a Galaxy* (2018), "We were just trying to get it done on time and make it look as good as we possibly could. We had no idea it would be influential."

The *Sourcebook* was a compilation of existing information culled from the movie scripts, novelizations (though not *Splinter of the Mind's Eye*, 1978, which was already considered out of canon), the art books, and trips to the Lucasfilm archives. The idea was to distill the clearest depiction of ships, aliens, characters, and other items that appear in the films and then, if necessary, create new material as needed to fill in the details of a plausible universe. A good, simple example of a needed addition is the section on passenger liners. None appear in the films, but it isn't wild speculation to assume that somewhere in the *Star Wars* universe, people take luxury space cruises.

It became clear, though, that many details necessary for an RPG just didn't exist in the *Star Wars* archives: What is the name of the shipyard that produced the X-Wing starfighter? Or any of the iconic ships, for that matter? What do the hammerhead aliens call themselves? Surely not "Hammerheads," as the packaging for the action figure claimed. The audience doesn't need to answer such questions when watching a movie, but players do when creating a believable RPG world. Without official answers, Slavicsek and Smith had to make them up.

This state of affairs is remarkable in a few ways. First, unlike Paramount's ambivalence regarding *Star Trek*'s canon, Lucasfilm took a keen interest in what West End Games was creating. There were topics the RPG was not allowed to expound upon, mostly regarding the Clone Wars and other events, long speculated about, that preceded the original films. "They'd never let me delve too deeply into Yoda's background or describe his species and planet of origin," says Slavicsek. "I was disappointed at the time, but seeing how that has developed over the years, I understand why they held fast to that. I wish they would have let me go deeper into stormtroopers, though. I was sure they were clones and some sort of remnant of the clone wars, but they wouldn't let me do more than hint at that back then." There was also an approval process. Sometimes that went well, resulting in "Ithorian" becoming the proper name of the hammerhead aliens. Sometimes, it didn't: Lucasfilm wouldn't budge on the very silly "Mon Calamari."

Secondly, charting out this universe grew to be a huge undertaking. The *Sourcebook* covers everything needed to get started. It conveys a strong sense of the Empire's capabilities, the different sorts of ships and tech available, a rundown of key alien races, and robust character biographies with piles of new

172

details. Want to know how Han and Chewie became friends? That's in here. Want to glimpse a depiction of the Tusken Raiders as a multifaceted culture instead of mere savage brutes? That's in here, too, surprisingly.

But 144 pages just isn't enough space for *everything*. The *Sourcebook*, then, is a cornerstone for a massive storehouse. The vast majority of the *Star Wars* RPG line is sourcebooks. West End Games issued a dozen *Galaxy Guides*. They start off focused on the films—just about every character that appears on-screen has a profile, a full body illustration, and a block of skills and abilities. There's the droid (R5-D4) that short circuits before being sold to Owen Lars (and Owen Lars, for that matter), random Imperial officers whose names were previously unknown, and a ton of background aliens from the Mos Eisley cantina and Jabba's palace.

That's just scratching the surface. The profiles flesh out the characters while attempting to fill some plot holes from the movie that surface when a person thinks about it too much (as would happen when writing a book like this). Why didn't the Death Star gunners annihilate the rebel attack force? Because some nimrod Imperial admiral broke up the crack gunner groups and assigned staff alphabetically, forming new, untested groups. It's a thin explanation, but also one that seems like something the Empire would do. Later *Guides* would tackle aliens, bounty hunters, ships, scouts, criminal organizations, and other aspects of the galaxy not touched on in the movies.

Beyond the *Galaxy Guides*, handbooks were released for both the Imperial and Rebel military forces, planets, star ports, fugitives, and even a technical manual for the Death Star. As time went on, the rapidly expanding universe grew recursive. When Timothy Zahn began work on the Thrawn trilogy, Lucasfilm gave him a box of West End Games sourcebooks for reference, which he used to great effect.

GALAXY GUIDE 4: ALIEN RACES, WEST END GAMES, 1989
TROY DENNING, COVER BY BILL SELBY

As his novels hit shelves, West End, in turn, produced sourcebooks about *them*, and every other major piece of media in the *Star Wars* expanded universe, good (*Tales of the Jedi Companion*, 1996), bad (*The Truce at Bakura Sourcebook*, 1996), and weird (*Dark Empire Sourcebook*, 1998). When West End Games started to falter in the mid '90s, their detailed universe was re-canonized for non-roleplayers in Del Rey's *Star Wars: Essential Guide* (1995-2012) series.

Most of the *Star Wars* universe, as detailed by West End, is no longer canon—sort of. In 2014, after purchasing the franchise, Disney redefined the *Star Wars* canon to only include the six films and *The Clone Wars* (2008-2020) cartoon series, in an effort to clear the slate in advance of new projects. But, while vast swathes of the expanded universe are "gone," a whole language of *Star Wars*, created by West End Games, lives on.

Bill Slavicsek, in *Defining a Galaxy*, thrills to hear Finn say the word "medpac," a term Slavicsek coined in the *Sourcebook*. "Twice. That was pretty cool." He expanded on this to me, saying there were no guarantees anything created for the RPG would live on beyond the RPG, "Lucasfilm made it clear that

George Lucas was not beholden to anything we wrote, even though we were getting everything approved along the way. So, imagine my delight and surprise when names and concepts I helped create began showing up in the prequels, the *Clone Wars* animated series and other places."

West End games codified a feeling. The vibe is in Zahn's novels, because they drew directly from West End Games' sourcebooks, but there have been whiffs of it in some of the Disney *Star Wars* media, as some of the old canon gets reintroduced. *Rogue One* (2016), *Star Wars Rebels* (2014-2018), and *The Mandalorian* (2019-present) all have aspects that will make someone familiar with West End Games' *Star Wars* RPG point at the screen in delight. Slavicsek certainly has. "A lot of the heart of what I created appears in those shows in almost every episode," he says. For people not familiar with the RPG, it may just seem like more *Star Wars*—but that's about as grand a legacy as an RPG can ask for.

Forgotten Realms (1987)

From the release of the G-series modules, Greyhawk was the de facto campaign setting for *Advanced Dungeons & Dragons*, even though there wasn't much commitment to the idea of Greyhawk *as* a setting. While the modules were nominally set in Greyhawk, the expectation was that players would ignore that and drop the dungeons into their own homebrew worlds. Players were genuinely interested in the details of Gygax's world, but the *World of Greyhawk* folio and box set didn't deliver on their expectations. When Gygax left the company in 1985, TSR retained the rights to Greyhawk but were no longer beholden to it. With a new edition of *Advanced Dungeons & Dragons* in the works, TSR wanted a new, unified game world to serve as its home, something free of the shadow of Gygax and more open-ended than *Dragonlance*.

Ed Greenwood's Forgotten Realms was an obvious choice. Greenwood created his imaginary world when he was eight, as a setting for his fiction. He was introduced to *D&D* in 1975, but it wasn't until he got a copy of the *Monster Manual* in 1978 that he was truly hooked. "I twisted my existing-for-my-own-fiction-only fantasy world to 'match' *AD&D* when the first *Players Handbook* came out," he says. Regular play in the Realms began soon after, run at Greenwood's local library.

His first article in *The Dragon* magazine, detailing creatures called "the curst," appeared in October, 1979, and a steady stream of Forgotten Realms material, keenly devoured by readers, followed in subsequent issues. When TSR decided to shelve Greyhawk for something new, Jeff Grubb approached Greenwood. "Jeff contacted me to see if I had a complete, detailed fantasy world at home, or if I just made things up as I went along (I answered 'yes' to both questions)." TSR acquired the Realms in exchange for a modest sum of money and a new computer.

After the box is opened, the first thing that is apparent about *Forgotten Realms* is how massive the world is; the *DM's Sourcebook of the Realms* shows the continental United States looking tiny in relation to the Realms. Large portions of the world are left for the GM to fill in with their own material, while the rest is detailed by Greenwood and company with an eye toward giving players and GMs a little bit of everything. "The Realms was the land of a thousand-thousand stories, so it fit [TSR's] needs," says Greenwood, "To be able to accommodate *Arabian Nights*-style adventures, pirate adventures, jungle adventures, frigid ice country adventures and so on, all in one setting."

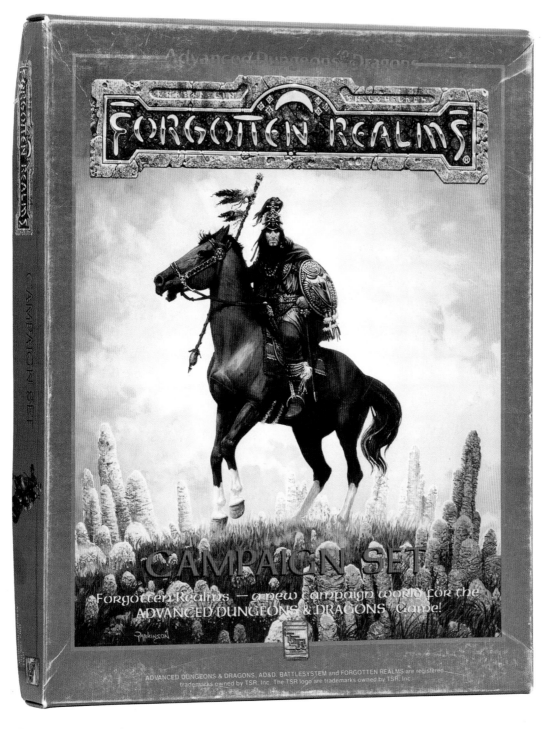

FORGOTTEN REALMS CAMPAIGN SET, BOX SET, TSR, 1987
ED GREENWOOD, COVER BY KEITH PARKINSON

CITY OF SPLENDORS, BOX SET, TSR, 1994
ED GREENWOOD AND STEVEN SCHEND, COVER BY FRED FIELDS

Forgotten Realms does everything *BIG*. The crown jewel of early *Forgotten Realms* was the city of Waterdeep, which TSR endeavored to make the biggest fantasy city ever detailed. It was introduced in the 1987 sourcebook *Waterdeep and the North*, but that was the tiniest appetizer compared to the *City System* box set that followed the next year.

It is, basically, a box of maps. Ten of them fold out and fit together to depict Waterdeep on a street-by-street level. Laid out, it measures a massive nine-feet by five-and-a-half-feet. The 11th map provides an aerial view of the city, while the 12th depicts Castle Waterdeep with a comical level of detail. The accompanying book outlines the particulars of 282 city buildings, leaving the GM to determine the nature of the rest using random tables. The result is a city that feels strangely empty.

City of Spendors (1994) updates and improves upon both *City System* and *Waterdeep and the North*, though it doesn't have 45-square feet of maps in the box. And I'm not even getting into Undermountain, the mega-dungeon underneath Waterdeep; that's covered in over ten different books and box sets over the years (and editions) and, even with all of that

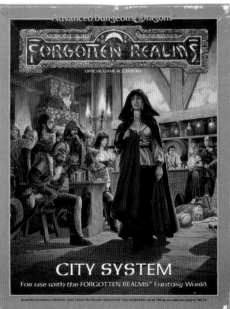

CITY SYSTEM, BOX SET, TSR, 1988
KAREN S. BOOMGARDEN, COVER BY LARRY ELMORE

content, I am fairly certain there are parts that remain uncharted.

As with Greyhawk, there are two Forgotten Realms: Ed Greenwood's personal one, glimpsed through his *Dragon* magazine articles, in which he still runs regular games, and the public facing one published by TSR. That world almost immediately took on a life of its own. It first saw print in a novel, not an RPG product: *Darkwalker on Moonshae* (1987) by Douglas Niles. The isles he described were actually part of a setting he had pitched, called Albion. TSR preferred them to Greenwood's Moonshae Isles, so they just replaced them with Niles's version.

Greenwood has professed that his own Realms are grittier and that he prefers to avoid clear equivalents to real-world cultures, something TSR had no compunctions about, turning the Realms into a sort of fantasy Epcot. To their folly, the pan-Asian *Kara-Tur*, 1988, and the Arabian themed *Al-Qadim*, 1992, have been fairly criticized for their Orientalism in recent years, while *Maztica*, 1991, a *D&D*-ified retelling of the Spanish conquest of Mesoamerica, sinks under the weight of its unexamined imperialism.

These missteps are overwhelmed by the sheer size of the ever-expanding body

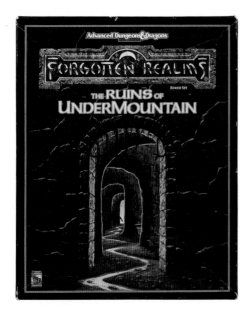

THE RUINS OF UNDERMOUNTAIN, BOX SET, TSR, 1991
ED GREENWOOD, COVER BY GERALD BROM

of work that is the Forgotten Realms. The sourcebook line for third edition *D&D* included 20 volumes! Despite, or perhaps because of, a certain generic quality in the original box set, the campaign setting has become an ongoing success for *D&D*, with thousands of players exploring the Realms for decades now, through the RPG material, but also through novels (the fictional footprint of the Realms is larger than *Dragonlance*, with well over 300 different novels in the line) and videogames (of which there are dozens, though the *Baldur's Gate* series is particularly well-regarded and has a new installment forthcoming). I shudder to think at how many linear feet the decades of RPG books and boxes stack up to.

Greenwood admits it is odd to have so many other people working on the Realms over the decades, but also delightful. "Your own campaign world simply can't ever surprise you, if you're the sole creator," he says. "Some, like Bob Salvatore, who created Menzoberranzan, have brought to life wonderfully dark things I would never have thought of; others, like Elaine Cunningham, *got* Waterdeep so well that I was convinced she must have been reading my mind!"

Ravens Bluff, The Living City (1987)

The Role Playing Game Association (RPGA) was founded in 1980 by Frank Mentzer to support the official use of TSR products for tournament games at conventions—these consisted of four-hour games with pre-generated characters, one of whom was, through a system of scoring or GM discretion, selected as the winner (whatever that means), at the end of the session. A large number of official *D&D* modules were written for the tournament scene, which gives them a distinct quality that imparts the sense of taking an exam. The old school ideal of adventures testing the ingenuity of players, rather than players inhabiting a character in a way similar to an actor, is tied to the tradition of tournament play.

A yearly RPGA membership fee gained a body access to the tournaments and other official functions (many members formed local clubs) and, after 1981, a subscription to the quarterly *RPGA Newsletter*. It was a sort of low fat, nerdier version of *Dragon* magazine, full of short scenarios and material for all sorts of games in the tournament rotation, even some that weren't published by TSR. By issue four, the newszine was renamed *Polyhedron*.

LC1: GATEWAY TO RAVENS BLUFF, THE LIVING CITY, TSR, 1989
JEAN RABE, COVER BY KEITH PARKINSON

Despite the advertisements that were included in just about every TSR product encouraging players to join, the RPGA seems to have been a rickety operation. *Polyhedron* notoriously arrived late; support for members was spotty, and the organization itself was perilously under-staffed. It often seems a miracle *Polyhedron* came out with any regularity at all. Flipping through any given issue from the first six years or so generally brings to mind the agonizing final act of William Friedkin's *Sorcerer* (1977) during which Roy Scheider trudges through the jungle on foot with a load of unstable dynamite on his back.

By 1987, membership was dropping off and, in the face of more narrative-focused adventures and the increasing popularity of persistent campaign settings, tournament play was slipping out of fashion. To right the ship, *Polyhedron* introduced the Living City, Ravens Bluff, in March of 1987. In an early use of crowdsourcing, the plan was to create a city of member-submitted locales and characters, then use it as the setting for future adventures. This submitted material appeared regularly in the newszine—for instance, the September, 1987, issue details the Open Scalery, a fish

market. Later magazines include short scenarios set within the confines of Ravens Bluff, as well as previews of significant events on the horizon.

Eventually, the locations and characters were collected in the LC-series accessory books—*Gateway to Ravens Bluff, The Living City* (1989), *Inside Ravens Bluff, The Living City* (1990), *Nightwatch in the Living City* (1991), and *Port of Ravens Bluff* (1991). The covers are surprisingly second rate for what amounted to a new and exciting way to play *D&D*. Despite being set in the Forgotten Realms, the cover of the first book is a re-purposed painting of Caramon and Raistlin Majere, heroes from the *Dragonlance* setting, and it isn't even one of artist Keith Parkinson's best. It's difficult to image Kevin Ward's bizarre cover art of a vagrant assaulting a minstrel on the front of *Inside Ravens Bluff* inspiring any sales. The best of the lot is Robin Wood's delightfully overjoyed thief, but *Nightwatch* is the least interesting of the books—more a traditional adventure than an expansion of the Living City concept.

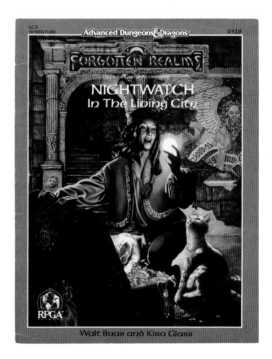

Walt Baas and Kira Glass

Despite the chintzy packaging, living games represent a type of play only a company the size of TSR (and later, Wizards of the Coast) could effectively facilitate. Even with members generating lots of material and volunteers organizing games on the local level, the effort still required a huge amount of official support, especially considering that adventures in the Living City continued until the release of the Third Edition of *D&D* in 2000. The resulting experience is unique: In a way, living games deliver on the vision Gary Gygax laid out in the *Dungeon Masters Guide*, of a uniform set of *D&D* rules that allow players to move characters from game to game seamlessly, but it is doubtful he imagined anything on the scale of Ravens Bluff.

Characters were created using a standardized point-buy method, rather than the traditional random generation. This kept everyone on even footing, but there were downsides. "Most characters ended up being identical to each other and were only differentiated by roleplaying personality," recalls Andrew Whitmore, a regular visitor to Ravens Bluff. There was also an

THE CITY OF RAVENS BLUFF, TSR, 1998
ED GREENWOOD. COVER BY JEFF EASLEY

abundance of record keeping. Gold was carefully tracked, and provenance for magic items and other special equipment was logged. "Most people kept their characters in binders in plastic sleeves. I get nostalgic every time I smell cheap dry erase markers like the ones people used to track hit points," says Whitmore.

Games took place regularly at official events, where organizers split players up into tables by character level, so players often played with folks they didn't know. Sessions were designed to run for four hours, followed by bookkeeping. And a player could take their character anywhere, across town, to another state, to a convention.

There were also real consequences to the games, which gave them a special weight. Results for key components of the adventures were tallied and sent to the RPGA, with the majority result changing the state of the city and affecting future adventures—if the majority of players knocked down a building, cured a plague, or killed an important NPC then that became the new status quo. There were also drawbacks to massive groups of strangers playing *D&D* together, too. "There wasn't just a rules lawyer, it was

LC4: PORT OF RAVENS BLUFF, TSR, 1991
JEAN RABE AND SKIP WILLIAMS. COVER BY ???

LIVING GREYHAWK GAZETTEER, WIZARDS OF THE COAST, 2000
GARY HOLIAN, FREDERICK WEINING, ERIK MONA, AND SEAN K. REYNOLDS, COVER BY WILLIAM O'CONNOR

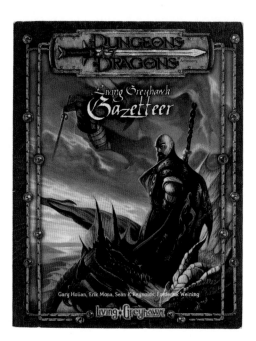

Rules Law Firms and Supreme Court," says Whitmore. "The minmaxers were insane. The improv comics were to the max. Then mix in the social element to *D&D* and the drama was through the roof. This isn't to say the social aspect was all bad," he adds. "I know people who met their roommates, spouses and soulmates through Living City."

The RPGA replaced the LC-series with *Living Greyhawk* in 2000. It functioned similarly, though with more character creation restrictions. Rather than just one city, *Living Greyhawk* brought a world to life.

Mirroring Gygax's original Greyhawk, which was a map of the United States with the names changed, *Living Greyhawk* divided the real-world up into meta-regions (similar to the Society for Creative Anachronism's kingdoms, a meta-region scheme that has been in existence since the mid '60s). Different adventures were available in each region, with different rewards. At the start of the calendar year, a player received 52 time units. Playing

sessions in a player's home region cost one unit, and two if visiting from another region (like at a convention). Time units could also be spent on downtime activities, like crafting items. Once a character ran out of units, they couldn't be played until the next year—all of their time in Greyhawk had been accounted for.

"Where I live, Phoenix, Arizona, was represented in Greyhawk as the Kingdom of Nyrond," says player Cody Eastlick. "While I played in Living Greyhawk I moved to Wisconsin for a time and was able to take part in adventures in the Highfolk region. It was a really immersive way of playing, the whole *Living* thing made sense." Another resident of the Kingdom of Nyrond, Dylan Myers, admired the quality of the game sessions. "[They were] very tightly written and only seldom did they feel railroad-y," he says. "My games were often sprawling and disorganized, [so] I was impressed at the epic-feeling adventures that could be introduced, run and wrapped in four hours (more like four and a half)."

In its eight-year run, *Living Greyhawk* produced more than a thousand adventures—each region was receiving one adventure each week. Those adventures were played by tens of thousands of players worldwide. It's impressive that the game runners maintained such a critical mass of play over such a period of time. While *Living Greyhawk* was ongoing, Wizards of the Coast also ran a Living Force campaign for their *Star Wars Roleplaying Game* (2000), and the fourth edition of *D&D* had a Living Forgotten Realms campaign; but with the advent of the fifth edition of *D&D*, the concept of a living world was scaled back for the *D&D Expeditions* program and largely disappeared when that was discontinued in 2016.

Ars Magica (1987)

Ars Magica (1987)
Over the course of the '80s, the power of story was on the rise: *Ravenloft* shifted *D&D*'s focus from hack and slash, and the *Dragonlance* saga played out in literal novels; *Pendragon* and *Lankhmar* created roleplaying experiences out of literary sources; *Call of Cthulhu* de-emphasized the importance of individual characters by making them so fragile. And then there is *Ars Magica*, a crystal ball that offers an opportunity to glimpse the future of narrative in RPGs, not least because it leads directly to the game that dominates narrative design for the next decade.

Considering that, on its face, *Ars Magica* is a game about wizards, in practice, it has very little in common with its fantasy contemporaries. Rather, many of its design choices are more in line with story games that emerge in the new millennium. The central location of the game world, the covenant fortress where the Magi live, is defined, not through edicts of the GM, but through collaboration, with all players contributing details. In fact, *Ars Magica* is one of the first games to flirt with the idea of totally eliminating the role of a GM. There *is* one, but there is no assumption that the same person takes the GM role session-to-session. Players aren't expected to play the same character session-to-session, either.

Ars Magica outlines what it calls a troupe style of play, which encourages players to create a Magus, as well as an assistant, who can be played when the Magus is busy with research or otherwise preoccupied. The fortress also has a large population of servants, warriors, and such, a sort of shared pool who can also be controlled by individual players. This variety of options encourages players to emphasize the importance of the overall story, deploying the character best suited to move it forward, rather than centering the development of one favored personage. As there is no expectation of game

Ars Magica, Second edition, Lion Rampant, 1989
Jonathan Tweet and Mark Rein-Hagen, Cover by Doug Shuler

balance, with magus characters effectively as powerful as the players desire them to be, there isn't any incentive to play them exclusively in the name of self-improvement. Other games, like *RuneQuest* and *Pendragon*, assume that players will control multiple characters due to responsibilities or healing, but no other game has embraced the troupe style so thoroughly. It didn't really take off in the wake of *Ars Magica*, either—later editions have downplayed the concept, a fact that seems like a missed opportunity.

The world of *Ars Magica* is one that resembles our own, a Europe of the Middle Ages, just before the dawn of the Renaissance (the presence of art by Eric Hotz, who so thoroughly defined Hârn, goes a long way to imbuing this "mythic Europe" with a grounded sense of realness). The main difference is that all of the mystical, religious, and superstitious assumptions about the world that circulated during the medieval period are true: God seeks to raise humanity up; Satan strives to bring humanity down; the realm of Faeries hides from, feeds on, or is fascinated by humanity, in turn. Magi seek to avoid or combat these supernatural factions (as well as human political factions that can prove to be an even more imminent danger) in order to pursue their Hermetic arts.

Magic is open-ended and freeform. At the core of the system are 15 arts—five techniques and ten forms that, together, form the verb/noun mechanic. The techniques are the verbs (in a distortion of Latin, of course): Creo, I create; Intēllego, I perceive; Muto, I transform; Perdo, I destroy; Rego, I control. These are combined with the nouns, which cover all the stuff of creation—the four elements, the body, the intellect, animals, plants, among others. These arts can be combined and spoken to create just about any magical effect imaginable (I can't help but think of the spoken Bible verses of *DragonRaid*'s word runes). Some spells are already formulated; others are created by the Magus in the moment. Both require die rolls and skill scores to determine success. An elaborate laboratory system allows for improving skills, researching spells, and creating implements to aid in this process. This work takes place during seasonal sessions when the character is unavailable for conventional play.

Magic is not simple! As the rulebooks says, "True magical prowess requires native talent, long term theoretical study, years of practice, a comfortable familiarity, intuitive understanding, high confidence in one's skills and much courage." It is unclear whether it is referring to the fictional magic of the world or the mastery of the game's magic system.

Reflecting the complexities of Hermetic magical systems in our own world, *Ars Magica* developed a bedrock of rich lore and history to act as the foundation of the game and its magic. The Order of Hermes, to which every magus belongs, is divided into 12 houses. Each house, linked to a specific region of Europe and its customs, has their own distinct character and ambitions. This nexus of societies presents a massive tangle of politics and intrigues for players to navigate, all of which was first broadly detailed in *The Order of Hermes* sourcebook (1990), though greatly expanded on in future editions of the game with the series of Tribunal books. This framework, consisting of history, faction details, and cultural predilections, is largely sans mechanics and represents what has come to be known as a splatbook. The Lion Rampant approach to this sort of sourcebook would shortly take over the RPG market.

After the departure of co-designer Jonathan Tweet (he left to get a regular job, though it didn't stick), Mark Rein-Hagen merged Lion Rampant with the Weick brothers' *White Wolf* magazine to form White Wolf Game Studio (with Rein-Hagen and Stewart Weick using their pay from writing *Galaxy Guide 6: Tramp Freighters* for the *Star Wars: The Roleplaying Game* as seed money).

With a fresh company, Rein-Hagen set to work on a series of interconnected games, known collectively as the World of Darkness. The first game was the massively successful *Vampire: The Masquerade*, which used an expansive line of splatbooks to expand the game's lore. Early ones focus on the various vampire clans, one of which, Tremere, started out as a house of the Order of Hermes. Not content to just gaze backwards to the past, *Mage: The Ascension* (1993) goes on to reimagine many of the core concepts of *Ars Magica* for a freshly modern, though often mind-boggling context.

Talislanta (1987)

Dragon magazines from the late '80s were peppered with ads for *Talislanta* that declared, "No Elves!" That is a true statement. There's no room for them with all of the other races creator Stephen Michael Sechi dreamed up.

Talislanta is weird, like *Skyrealms of Jorune* weird. Inspired largely by the writing of Jack Vance, the world is rich in magic, thanks to the ancient race of sorcerers called the Archaens, whose powers mirror our own scientific achievements, creating wonders, like spaceships and even something that sounds a lot like virtual reality. Their experiments resulted in many strange races and eventually led to the Great Disaster, which changed the face of the continent. The result is a land of many regions, each unique in character. Some might call this tonal inconsistency, and that is true, to a degree, but the result is so varied and strange a world that it is easy to forgive its silly bits. How can a player be upset with a game that offers 84 types of characters to play right out of the gate?

Those 84 types are pre-generated character templates—pick one, modify a couple values, and they're ready to play. The core of the game is surprisingly lightweight. Skills are compared in different configurations to provide bonuses or penalties to a die roll, which is resolved on a simple table that determines degrees of success or failure. There's more nuance to be found, but the core mechanics run just 12 pages (these were even reimagined in 2005 as a generic, multi-genre system that would eventually be called the Omni System).

The mechanical lightness of the rules lets players focus on what makes *Talislanta* special: The seemingly endless creative thought that went into the campaign setting. There's a kind of spectrum for fantasy settings. On the far left are the landscapes rooted in our world and its stories, "realistic" games, like *Call of Cthulhu* and

A NATURALIST'S GUIDE TO

TALISLANTA

By Stephan Michael Sechi

Illustrated by P.D. Breeding

FANTASY ROLE PLAYING GAME SUPPLEMENT

A Naturalist's Guide to Talislanta, Bard Games, 1987 Stephen Michael Sechi, Cover by P. D. Breeding-Black

Pendragon sit out there. Dead center, there are standard fantasy trope settings, like the Forgotten Realms or even the Third Imperium of *Traveller*. Moving right, the horizon becomes stranger, passing Athas and Glorantha and Barsaive and eventually arriving at the edge, where Jorune and Talislanta live.

Talislanta is neither tidy nor gestalt. It never feels entirely cogent, and the tone is all over the place. What *Talislanta* is, though, is fresh, even 30-years later. The world jumps off of the page. It has a cousin, perhaps, in *Rifts*, in that it seems like a massive outpouring of creativity without any apparent limits imposed by its creator. It feels like every impulse Sechi had is sitting right there on the page. It doesn't really make sense. How could it? If he tried to curate this world, it wouldn't be half as glorious.

There is very little of the standard issue fantasy for the neophyte to grab onto. Not only are there no elves, there aren't any orcs or minotaurs either. Instead, there are the spooky black savants, the reptilian araq, shaitans, winged apes, and void beasts. There are some dragons, though. Dragons are inescapable, I guess.

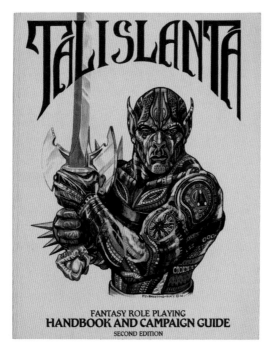

FANTASY ROLE PLAYING
HANDBOOK AND CAMPAIGN GUIDE
SECOND EDITION

Like Jorune, Talislanta owes a debt to its artist, P. D. Breeding-Black, who accomplishes feats of world building through her illustrations, which establish a unique, consistent visual style across all of the books in the line—the colorfully tattooed Thrall warrior on the cover effectively shows how *Talislanta* often manages to feels simultaneously familiar and exotic. In this way, it seems to be a prime influence on *Earthdawn*.

Despite this feast of ideas, *Talislanta* never set the world on fire. Bard Games folded after two editions. A modest third that included the game's first adventure modules and a campaign by designer Robin D. Laws was published by a young Wizards of the Coast. That edition gave up the ghost in 1994, and the license bounced around a number of small publishers, none of which experienced any particular success.

In 2010, Sechi, who retained the rights for all Talislanta material produced to that date, opted to publish digital versions of all five editions, on *Talislanta.com* under the Creative Commons license, making it entirely free for players to read and play. And there are still no elves.

Cyberpunk (1988)

Cyberpunk—the science fiction sub-genre—is a slippery thing formed out of a laundry list of influences: New wave sci-fi by Moorcock, Dick, Ellison, and Ballard, hardboiled detective novels by Dashiell Hammett and Raymond Chandler, punk culture, the nascent hacker movement, and more. It is difficult to pin down exactly when it coalesced into the sub-genre recognized today. The term was coined by Bruce Bethke for the title of his story "Cyberpunk," which appeared in 1983, but I tend to think of the release of William Gibson's 1984 novel, *Neuromancer,* as the moment it came into its own. The 1982 film Blade Runner offers another reasonable point of cyberpunk's pop culture inception.

Cyberpunk tends toward the dystopian, tackling themes of alienation and a technological class war between the lowlifes on the streets and the corporate elites in the high-rise penthouses above. In some ways, it's incredibly prescient as a genre in predicting social and technological changes (the ever-increasing wealth gap, class warfare, the internet), while in other ways, it misses the mark entirely (smart phones, e-cigarettes, issues of race).

As with Bethke's short story, the first cyberpunk RPG cut right to the chase with its name—*Cyberpunk*, by Mike Pondsmith, the first prominent Black RPG designer. Amusingly, the first edition is now referred to as *Cyberpunk 2013*, as the progress of time's ceaseless march required adjustments to the setting; the 1990 second edition moved the setting's date to 2020, the 2005 third edition moved it to the 2030s, and the current edition, *Cyberpunk RED*, which came out in 2020, takes place in 2045.

The game cites some unexpected sources of inspiration in Roger Zelazny's *Damnation Alley* (1969) and Walter Jon Williams' *Hardwired* (1986), both of which involve tank-like vehicles in a

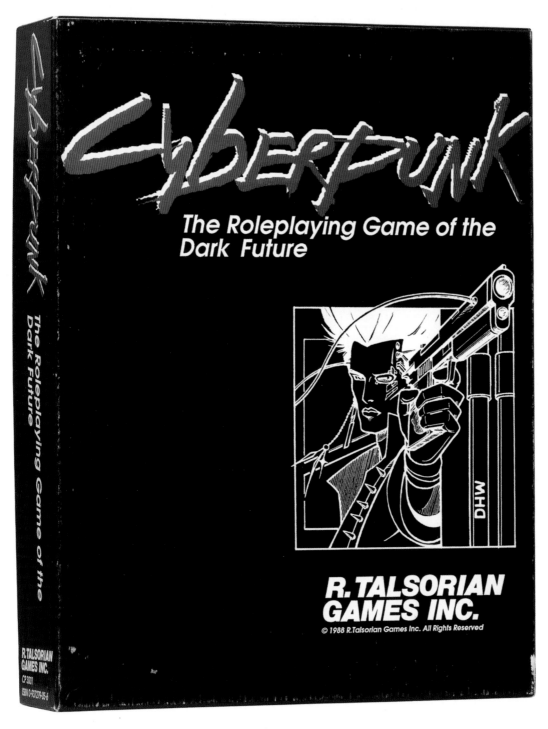

CYBERPUNK, BOX SET, R. TALSORIAN GAMES, 1988
MIKE PONDSMITH, COVER BY SAM LIU

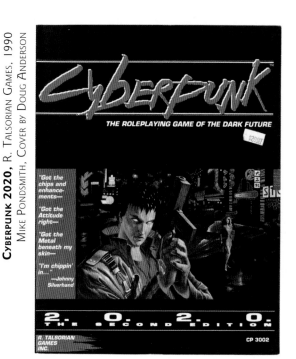

CYBERPUNK 2020, R. TALSORIAN GAMES, 1990
MIKE PONDSMITH, COVER BY DOUG ANDERSON

There is an emphasis on heavy combat materiel, even for professions that seem less inclined to combat, like the band-fronting Rockerboy. The combat system, called Friday Night Firefight, is straightforward, tactical, and lethal—no matter how experienced a character may be, a single bullet always has a chance to splatter them. All of these systems are rudimentary in the initial release but see a significant upgrade in the next iteration of the rules—everything is expanded and polished; the Lifepath system has more options, and everything fits together better. The world of *2020* feels real and plausible where in *2013,* it seemed a bit jagged and indistinct.

As cold and empty as *Cyberpunk* can sometimes feel, it reflects the prevailing attitudes of an era that was, at large, embracing style over substance. The game often plays with a very '80s pre-occupation in the illustrations, many of which affect something of Patrick Nagel's style or channel the chaos of Max Headroom, but with more references to unusual tech and many, many more guns.

Sometimes, though, there are flashes of an unexpected vibrancy, as in *Night City* (1991), which details the central setting

post-apocalyptic wasteland (the latter, which eventually got its own sourcebook for *Cyberpunk*, involves a mercenary who can drive a hovertank with his mind, thanks to a cybernetic interface). *Cyberpunk* still embraces the genre's high tech/low life urban aesthetic, but these novels account for a certain amount of ultraviolence and military fetishism that don't appear in most other cyberpunk stories. In fact, the three pillars of *Cyberpunk,* as laid out in the rulebook, are: "1. Style over substance. 2. Attitude is everything. 3. Live on the edge." The result is a flashy, deeply cynical world where calibers are high and life expectancy is low.

This ethos is reflected in the game's systems. Character creation springs from the Lifepath system that, similar to *Traveller,* defines a character through their history. Skills are profession-based and are improved individually through use or augmented via cybernetics ("chrome," in the parlance of the game world, and don't get too much, or a character risks losing their grip on their humanity—the cyber part of cyberpunk as a genre also has trouble navigating issues around disability and personhood).

NIGHT CITY, R. TALSORIAN GAMES, 1991
MIKE PONDSMITH AND DYVERS HANDS, COVER BY DOUG ANDERSON

for the game with energetic entries and a digital facade—as with many *Shadowrun* books, the graphic design incorporates elements that mimic an internet browser interface; it's easy to imagine the isometric city maps rising out of a tablet screen as a kind of hologram. *Night City* is often silly (the name, for instance, isn't slang; the place was founded by a guy whose last name was Night, a fact sure to set some eyeballs rolling) and gritty to the point of parody, but it also begs to be explored, even if doing so means the serious risk of a player having their character's face blown off by a population bristling with ordnance.

Cyberpunk springs from a moment in time that reflected grim and gritty themes, particularly in comic books, where a readership that grew up on superheroes was getting older and craving weightier stories. *Watchmen* (1986-1987) and *The Dark Knight Returns* (1986) both came out just two years prior, *Hellblazer* launched in January of 1988, and *The Sandman* showed up in November, signaling a shift toward mature themes and counterculture concerns that would only grow in the '90s. This darkening is true of *Cyberpunk*'s place in RPGs,

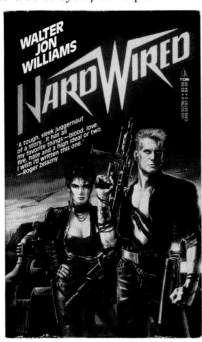

as well. The moral ambiguity introduced here eventually becomes a significant part of the language of urban science fiction and fantasy, paving the way for games, like *Shadowrun, Nightlife, Vampire: The Masquerade, Unknown Armies,* and more in the edgy '90s.

Bullwinkle and Rocky Roleplaying Party Game (1988)

The Adventures of Rocky and Bullwinkle and Friends (also known as *Rocky and His Friends, The Rocky and Bullwinkle Show,* and other various configurations, depending on who was syndicating the show or producing the DVDs) was a television cartoon series that ran from 1959 to 1964. It was structured like a variety show; each episode contained several short tales with their own dedicated cast of characters. Thus, Rocky the flying squirrel and Bullwinkle the moose squared off against the spies, Boris and Natasha, over and over again; the Canadian Mountie Dudley Do-Right was always foiling Snidely Whiplash; Mr. Peabody and Sherman were always off on a new time traveling adventure, and so on. The animation was crude, the jokes "punny." A good deal of the show was satirical, but nearly every character was about as smart as a bowl of pudding, so it appealed to both adults and kids in equal measure.

The show has a long legacy of influence in the art and development of American animation, but as a kid who grew up in the '80s, I mostly knew it as the weird cartoon that I sat through when I woke up too early to watch the good stuff on Saturday morning. In a nutshell, this disconnect between the content and the audience is why the existence of the *Bullwinkle and Rocky Roleplaying Party Game* (*B&R*) is so perplexing. It isn't quite in the same league as *Dallas*, but it is a head-scratcher nonetheless: Who is this game *for*?

Surely, it isn't for children, who in 1988 were being treated to shows like *Pee-wee's*

Hardwired, Tor Books, 1987
Walter Jon Williams, Cover by Luis Royo

1970

1980

1990

2000

2010

187

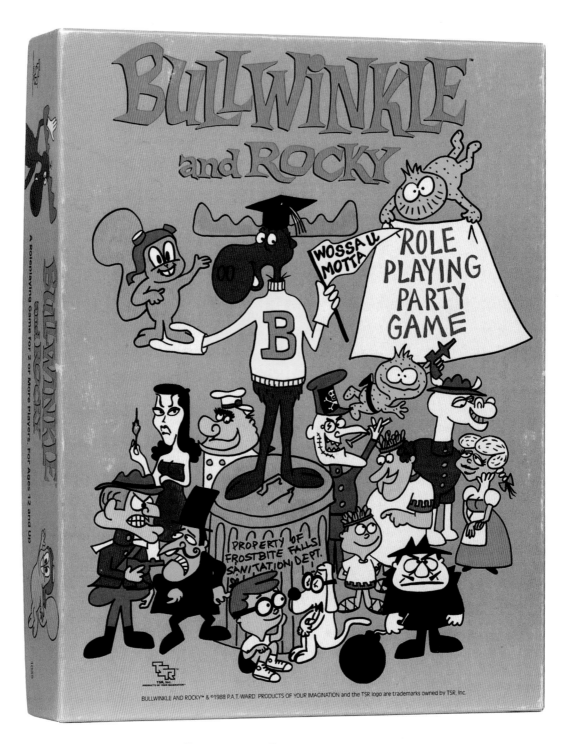

BULLWINKLE AND ROCKY ROLEPLAYING PARTY GAME, Box set, TSR, 1988
DAVID "ZEB" COOK, COVER BY SUE MYERS

Playhouse (1986-1990), *Teenage Mutant Ninja Turtles* (1987-1996), and, bizarrely, a cartoon series based on the R-rated film *RoboCop* (1988). Looking back, it feels like a sort of cosmic accident that I am familiar with Rocky and Bullwinkle at all. Was there a segment of the adult population who were hardcore Wossamotta U alumni, clamoring for a silly moose-fronted party game to break out on a Saturday night? I guess anything is possible. Were people who played *D&D* supposed to turn to this when not everyone in the group could make it? That seems the most improbable of all the possibilities.

And yet, the game does indeed exist, exuberantly. The cheerful orange box is packed with doo-dads—spinners for resolution, big fold-up character cards for reference, novelty diplomas as rewards for winning (from Wossamotta U for heroes and the Ukrainian Safe-Cracking Academy of Pottsylvania for villains), and plastic hand puppets (for no reason at all)—all for the low price of $15 American dollars.

B&R has very little in common with other games produced by TSR, or any other RPGs that were available at the time from any publisher, with one exception: The similarly themed *Toon* (perhaps unsurprisingly, Warren Spector worked on both). Like that game, *B&R* is a lightweight game about cartoon comedy. The rules in the box are centered on getting laughs and little else. There are so few rules, in fact, that Lawrence Schick, in *Heroic Worlds*, wonders if it is even technically an RPG at all.

There are three variants of play in the box. The first outlines a card-driven collaborative storytelling game. The group chooses a story from the included booklet, reads the introduction to see how it starts, and then reads the end to see where they need to wind up. Then, each player narrates in turn, incorporating one of the words printed on their cards. Once they play a card, the next player can interrupt and take control of the narrative, playing one of their cards, and so on. When everyone is down to a single card, they all throw it onto the table—the player whose card is at the bottom gets to narrate the end. These are essentially the same mechanics *Once Upon a Time* would use five years later.

The second variant adds complexity and competition into the mix. Here, the story being told uses specific characters and settings from the cartoon, re-enacting what could be the plot of a Dudley Do-Right segment. Players are arranged into teams of heroes and villains, with each character having a special ability and a specific goal. If they accomplish the goal in the final round, they lead their team to victory. Conflict is handled with spinners and is rigged in favor of the villains, who tend to succeed much more than the dim-witted heroes. On the other hand, failure tends to be funnier than success, so if laughter is the ultimate goal, then the inverse is true. When it's a player's turn to narrate, they are essentially in control of the world (like a traditional RPG GM) until they play their card, and the game encourages players to use that power to stack the deck for their team. As soon as they play their card, though, the next player can steal the narrative and all of its associated power.

The third variant is much the same as the second, but it allows for custom characters. These are interesting because they are defined, not by numbers, but by descriptive words and phrases. Examples are given using established characters: Mr. Peabody has Brains, Natasha has Pretty Good Disguises, Bullwinkle is Dumb Beyond Belief, and so on. These traits are entirely free form and are as versatile as a player can argue them to be, anticipating games like *Over the Edge* and *Hero Wars*.

All of these things—collaborative storytelling, failing forward, rotating GMs, and keywords as attributes—are now staples of indie and storytelling games that began to emerge in the '90s and came into their own after the turn of the millennium. And that's what is exciting about *Bullwinkle and Rocky*: It was years ahead of its time, but no one noticed because it was wrapped in the dusty trappings of an old cartoon.

HeroQuest (1989)

HeroQuest blew countless minds when it came out. A joint venture between Milton Bradley and Games Workshop, it distills the most adversarial RPG concept—gamemaster versus players—into an asymmetrical, tactical dungeon crawl board game. It spins out of a tradition of adventure board games that started with *Dungeon!* (1975); games like Games Workshop's *Talisman: The Magical Quest Game* (1983), the board game adaptation of *The Warlock of Firetop Mountain* (1986), and Chaosium's *Arkham Horror* (1987) followed, but *HeroQuest* overshadows all of them.

It plays as much like the videogame *Gauntlet* (1985) as it does a rules-light introduction to RPGs. One player is the evil sorcerer Zargon, the others pick one of four archetypes—Barbarian, Wizard, Elf, and Dwarf—and use little character sheets to track their progress. They then venture into the dungeon to hack apart monsters and find loot, which they can carry over (or sell to purchase new items) between games. The base game has 14 or so scenarios with different board layouts, objectives, and hints of narrative to play through. Combat is simple—roll hits and compare them to the shields rolled by an opponent, plus their defense attribute, with the difference going toward damage.

The game encourages the players to cooperate against the GM. A group using even minimal teamwork will make short work of the dungeons—there is power in fighting as a unit. Everything is skewed to favor the heroes, and their improvement between games, through equipment upgrades, exacerbates this problem. Monsters are slow and have no ranged attacks, so smart players learn early that they can stack up at doorways to turn the

HEROQUEST, BOX SET, MILTON BRADLEY, 1989
STEPHEN BAKER, COVER BY LES EDWARDS

bottleneck into a meat grinder. When this happens, there isn't a whole lot the GM can do to make things more dangerous. While these are problems for adults and experienced tabletop gamers, this game is calibrated for kids and, despite claiming to be cooperative, it truly shines with chaotic chemistry when a bunch of gloryhound eleven-year-olds resort to backstabbing each other to be king of the hill.

The game, though, is largely secondary to the bits. *HeroQuest* has wonderful bits. There are the miniatures, of course, a big pile of them. Player characters appear in red plastic, undead—ghouls, skeletons, and mummies—in white, humanoids—goblins, orcs, and fimir (a sort of one-eyed ogre)—in green, and Chaos—warriors, priest, and the mighty gargoyle (some assembly required!)—in gray.

Miniatures have been used in RPGs for as long as there have been RPGs. They are part of the older wargaming tradition, and their assembly is an entire hobby on its own, with unique barriers to entry. Painting RPG miniatures requires specialized equipment, like tiny brushes, putty for filling gaps in the sculpt, holders, primer, paint, patience, and a modicum of talent. The inclusion of miniatures in *HeroQuest*, with their different colored plastics, shifts the perception of miniatures from being some rarefied gaming implement or artwork to something more easily identified as a toy to be played with, like molded plastic army men.

For many Americans, *HeroQuest* also represents their first exposure to the Games Workshop aesthetic, an enticing mix of grim and cartoonish that contrasted with the prevailing "realistic" sensibility peddled by TSR, which was excellent for hooking kids who were increasingly courted by grittier entertainment, like *Indiana Jones and the Temple of Doom*, 1984, or *The Dark Knight Returns*, 1986. This tone is perfectly encapsulated by the cover painting, by Les Edwards, which depicts an overblown tableau that

can be seen as very serious or very comical, depending on the viewer's inclination.

Often overlooked but equally important are the pieces of furniture. Everything, from the tombs, bookcases, and even doors, had a little 3D component made of cardboard and plastic to place in the appropriate spot in the dungeon. There are even little plastic rats and skulls to decorate the torture rack. These objects worked to define the space in a way that was entirely foreign to RPGs of the time, which played out largely in the theater of the mind. Terrain is a part of wargaming, of course, but requires even more effort than painted miniatures (and space!). The furniture in *HeroQuest* serves as a tantalizing taste of immersive tabletop gaming environments. Ever more elaborate experiments, from modular modeling kits to cardstock floor tiles to 3D-printed structures, have sought to feed that appetite in the ensuing decades.

Taken all together, *HeroQuest* represents an unprecedented gateway into RPGs and associated hobbies, though, like lightning in a bottle, it is one suited for a unique moment in time and difficult to reproduce (many similar games failed to do so). It is far more enticing than the *D&D* coloring book or the red box *Basic Rules*, both of which acted as similar entry points.

After a decade of basic sets and beginner rules that tried to teach stripped down versions of complex games, *HeroQuest* clarifies and distills the whole experience of *D&D*-style RPGs on both sides of the game screen, simply by being an approachable, standalone game. And perhaps most importantly, the game was heavily advertised in comic books and on television ahead of the holiday season. As 1989 came to a close, *HeroQuest* was inducting a whole new generation of tabletop RPG players at the dawn of the '90s.

Advanced Dungeons & Dragons Second Edition (1989)

After a decade, *Advanced Dungeons & Dragons* was growing creaky. It wasn't the most organized game to begin with, but the rapid expansion of rules beginning with *Unearthed Arcana* (1985), while bailing TSR out of dire financial straits, led to rulebook bloat—too many rules, many of which unbalanced the game, were spread across too many books. It fell to David "Zeb" Cook to take all of those rules, streamline them, reorganize them, put a proper index on them, and cobble together a straightforward set of books that would bring *D&D* into the next decade.

The Second Edition of *Advanced Dungeons & Dragons* offers something that is recognizable but also new. What Cook understood about *D&D*, and what has been mostly overlooked by subsequent editions, is that *D&D*'s simulation—the basic mechanics of the game—don't need to be balanced. They need to be sturdy. They need to trudge along like workhorses even when spells and magic items and unexpected player superpowers subvert and break those rules—*especially* when—this havoc is what makes the magic magical. The rules are solid, a bit dull, but they can be driven off a cliff and they will still pretty much work.

There are, of course, controversies. Second Edition removed a number of classes and races. Gone are Monks, Assassins, and half-orcs, as well as all the character options introduced in *Unearthed Arcana* and *Oriental Adventures*. Cook also either fixed or irrevocably broke the Bard, depending on who is asked. Proficiencies, introduced in *Oriental Adventures* and refined in the *Dungeoneer's Survival Guide* as an optional skill system, became a core mechanic in Second Edition, a kind of low-rent skill system that is broken, confusing, and often ignored.

There was a general sense among players that TSR was sanitizing the game in the wake of the controversies of the '80s. They weren't wrong! The target demographic kept getting younger, so the packaging became more family friendly. Demons and devils were missing from the *Monstrous Compendium*, and when they returned a few years later, they were no longer called demons and devils. Naked breasts were covered by chainmail bikinis. The removal of Assassins and half-orcs smacked of similar self-censorship.

An oft-overlooked feature of the Second Edition of *AD&D* is that it is entirely, smoothly compatible with First Edition material. So, all of that material that the worriers at TSR removed and all of those broken classes from *Unearthed Arcana*? Players could still use them just fine. Unfortunately, facts are often no match for the power of belief.

If the game master was the star of the show in the First Edition, the Second Edition shines the spotlight on the players. It's all about options. By the time the edi-

PLAYER'S HANDBOOK, TSR, 1989
DAVID "ZEB" COOK, COVER BY JEFF EASLEY

tion collapsed under the weight of its endless rulebook expansions, players could use 15 character class and race handbooks, four Wizard spell compendiums, three for Priests, and three more volumes of optional rules to flesh out their characters. There was also a four-volume encyclopedia collecting every magic item ever published by TSR—one of the best *D&D* supplements ever published—that is ostensibly for the GM, to dole out to their players.

It's a massive amount of material, grown organically over the game's lifespan, and it would provide the raw materials for the third edition's avalanche of customization options a decade later. These options naturally shift the power center away from the GM, continuing a process begun by the wildly powerful character classes in *Unearthed Arcana*, reducing their omnipotence, re-framing the session as a collaboration between both sides of the screen. The game moves away from the idea of the GM as a judge making rulings on obscure game laws and starts to embrace the idea of rules as guidelines for play. This, in turn, opens *D&D* up, however awkwardly for its stab-centric mechanics, to new modes of play that focus more on character and story than combat.

Game masters get new toys, too. More than any other edition of *D&D*, this is the edition of the monsters. The initial approach, the *Monstrous Compendium*, was novel: A big loose-leaf binder, one monster per side of a sheet (sometimes two), with a picture and a lengthy description that gives the GM everything they need to know, from tactics to behaviors, to social structures, and more.

The use of a binder is important. I find there is, for one, significant overlap in the Venn diagram between people who love running RPGs and the people who are enthusiastic about office supplies. There's a tactile component, as well—the process of selecting monsters, removing

DUNGEON MASTER GUIDE, TSR, 1989
DAVID "ZEB" COOK, COVER BY JEFF EASLEY

their sheets, and compiling them with adventure notes feels a bit like choosing weapons for a duel. Most importantly, a binder seems to say, "This book isn't finished." Unlike the *Monster Manuals*, the *Monstrous Compendium* promised *more*.

Over the next four years, TSR released a second binder and a dozen appendices filled with ever-more monsters, and that doesn't count the many compendium sheets that were included in the back of adventures or at the bottom of box sets. In 1993, alas, TSR abandoned the binder and returned to traditional books with the *Monstrous Manual*. Seven setting-specific appendices would follow in short order, along with four annuals collecting monsters published individually in products or magazines. It is a mind-numbing number of monsters.

Unearthed Arcana proved, decisively, that rulebooks were the biggest money maker for *D&D*. It sold like gangbusters, which makes sense: The necessary mechanical division between the one person running a tabletop RPG and those

MONSTROUS COMPENDIUM, VOLUME ONE, TSR, 1989
DYVERS HANDS, COVER BY JEFF EASLEY

playing it means that the bulk of the products—the screens and monster manuals and campaign box sets and adventure modules branded with "Game Master's eyes only"—call to the wallets of only one fraction of the audience. Core rulebooks, on the other hand, are marketed to both GMs *and* players, the whole audience. But there is a limit. Gygax, ever the innovator, had stumbled upon a roleplaying publishing paradox: Game companies need to publish rulebooks to make money, but the more rulebooks they publish, the more unwieldy and unwelcoming the game becomes. This is both a function of time (to learn several books worth of rules) and money (with which to buy them).

TSR launched a streamlined Second Edition of *AD&D*, in large part, to avoid rules bloat. Despite that promising start, the Second Edition would fast outstrip the original in terms of published material. That staggering number of optional rulebooks of questionable quality eventually contributed to TSR's bankruptcy and sale to Wizards of the Coast. The cycle of slimming down, followed by a gradual expansion of rules would repeat, with some variation, for both the Third (2000) and Fourth Edition (2008) of the game.

Second Edition is what I played in my teens, which means it is the edition that I devoted the most time to and, consequently, the one I know best. It is also the one I love most. Anecdotally, this accident of birth seems to be true for many players I've spoken with—the edition of *D&D* in which they immersed themselves from about ages 12 to 16 seems to be the one they'll always carry a torch for. Meanwhile, I've got a bonfire.

Second Edition produced plenty of stinkers, but it had just as many gems, and not just the conventional sparklers—Second Edition is downright bizarre, a consequence of the huge number of talented designers required by the breakneck production schedule. In hindsight, it's pandemonium—not just the rules, but also the settings, the dead-end experiments, the endless resets and reboots, and product lines that just trickle off into obscurity. It's challenging to determine what's an inspired design and what's a cynical corporate cash grab. In almost all cases, the truth is somewhere in between. But that's hindsight. In the moment, caught in the swirl of endless new *D&D* books, an impossible number to keep up with, even with a dedicated group of friends building a library together, the sheer avalanche of books made Second Edition and the years I spent playing it exhilarating—and exhausting.

Spelljammer (1989)

If *Metamorphosis Alpha* was metaphorically *Dungeons & Dragons* in space, the *Spelljammer* campaign setting is entirely literal in bringing high fantasy to the outer reaches. The result is gloriously bewildering.

Space travel is made possible in the *D&D* universe by means of magical artifacts called Spelljamming helms—a spellcaster sits on it and vroom, off they go. The setting depicts space using a clever mix of superseded scientific theories. Planets are contained within crystal spheres, a sort of literal interpretation of Ptolemy's celestial spheres. Those spheres are connected by a flammable

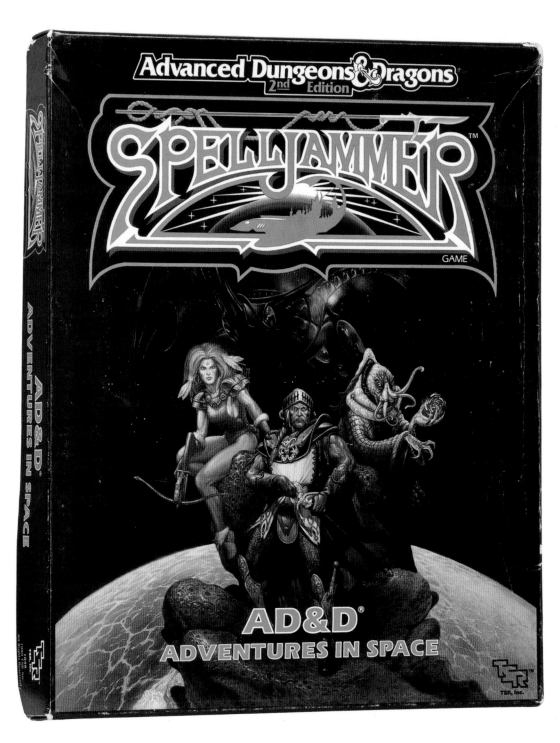

SPELLJAMMER, BOX SET, TSR, 1989
JEFF GRUBB, COVER BY JEFF EASLEY

THE LEGEND OF THE SPELLJAMMER, BOX SET, TSR, 1991
JEFF GRUBB, COVER BY JEFF EASLEY

elemental gas called phlogiston (a substance originally posited by Johann Joachim Becher and formalized by George Ernst Stahl to explain combustion and oxidization). Phlogiston serves as a kind of interstellar ocean.

It is a friendly sort of void—there is no killing vacuum, objects maintain envelops of their own breathable atmospheres, and gravity always pulls in the most sensible direction. Dozens of races sail the spaceways, each with their unique (and often silly) ships themed in some way to reflect the core of their being. Elves have biomechanical craft that mirror plants and insects, mind flayers sail nautilus-like ships, and the ships of the slave-taking neogi resemble mutant spiders. *Spelljammer* might have even been called "steampunk," had the term been widespread at the time, but the strong influence of adventure writers, like Jules Verne, Robert Louis Stevenson, and Patrick O'Brian keep the more psychedelic aspects of the setting from getting too far out of hand.

Spelljammer was a hugely ambitious campaign setting that launched alongside the Second Edition of *Advanced Dungeons & Dragons* as an example of the game's bold new direction. So much so that,

despite many requests to relaunch the line over the years, it remained a relic of that bygone age, perhaps too much a product of its time. Recently, however, Wizards of the Coast announced a revival that will introduce Spelljammer to the Fifth Edition of *D&D*. Exciting though that may be, I can't imagine something so weird as the original coming out today— the new version already seems different, a little less odd, a little more formulaic.

Conceived by Jeff Grubb, one of the key design goals of *Spelljammer* was to connect all of the existing TSR campaign settings—thus, *Dragonlance*'s Krynn, *Forgotten Realms'* Toril, and *Greyhawk*'s Oerth are all places *Spelljammer* characters can hail from and visit. This idea is novel, but the original box is entirely dedicated to traversal through the vastness of space; there are no destinations unique to Spelljammer and no central space hub for players to call their home. It is less a campaign setting than it is a campaign conduit.

Legend of Spelljammer (1991) partially addresses this misstep in describing the massive manta ray-shaped ship that holds a city on its back (its silhouette is visible in the line's logo). If this was a traditional sci-fi setting, *Spelljammer* (the ship) would function as a kind of massive spaceport, not unlike Deep Space 9, that is dotted with strongholds held by all manner of spacefaring races who live together in something resembling peace. That gives players plenty to explore (and a potential place to live) while pursuing the central mystery—who the heck runs the ship?

The Astromundi Cluster (1993) provides a space wilderness to explore (though one that cannot be easily escaped once entered), in what amounts to be a very strange asteroid field, a free-wheeling zone of danger and daring that often borders on the psychedelic. Here is possibly where the brain-eating mind flayers originated. There are floating pyramids and sentient (and hungry) asteroids, and plenty of taverns in which to drunkenly recount triumphs and tragedies.

Neither of these quite corrected the feeling of aimlessness that was accidentally established in the initial box set. Still, *Spelljammer* was TSR's first real high concept campaign setting, and it paved the way for the box sets, like *Ravenloft Campaign Setting* (1990), *Dark Sun Boxed Set* (1991), and *Planescape Campaign Setting* (1994). That last sprang directly from the ashes of the *Spelljammer* line, replacing it as the central hub between *all* of the TSR worlds.

Prince Valiant: The Story-Telling Game (1989)

In *Heroic Worlds* (1991), Lawrence Schick laments the difficulty of defining what roleplaying games are, as there are lots of "games and books that are almost, but not quite, RPGs." *Prince Valiant: The Story-Telling Game* is one of the first games to explore the other side of that coin: How much can be chopped out of a game—in this case *Ghostbusters*—in order for it to still be recognized as an RPG? *Prince Valiant* answers this question by arranging its minimal system around coin tosses.

There are only two character attributes: Brawn governs physical activity, and Presence deals with matters of communication. Players must split seven points between them. After that, nine points are distributed among six skills. These values equate the number of coins tossed—sometimes the players test an attribute; sometimes they combine an attribute with a skill. Heads count as successes. If more coins come up as heads than the GM's challenge number, the player succeeds. And that's about it: An ultra-simplified dice pooling game, in essence.

There are extended contests for important fights and a slightly more complex set of advanced rules, but at their core, the rules are so minimal that they are distilled on a single page (admittedly in a font size smaller than the rest of the book). Because of this simplicity, conflicts can be laid out and resolved rapidly, with no need for exhaustive system knowledge, so the rules encourage the role of the GM to be shared from scene to scene. It's an excellent introductory game for teaching newcomers about the basics of the hobby and, though not marketed as such, it's a perfect first RPG for kids or families.

Or, it would have been if it was based on anything other than the *Prince Valiant* comic strips. There is no denying Hal Foster was an illustrator of staggering talent. The book is full of his illustrations, and they are astounding accomplishments of composition and detail. Speaking as a kid once obsessed with both comics and King Arthur, though, and who saw the comics section of the Sunday paper as the lone refuge from the rest of the day's punishing boredom, *Prince Valiant* deftly resisted all of my attempts

PRINCE VALIANT: THE STORY-TELLING GAME, CHAOSIUM, 1989
GREG STAFFORD, COVER BY HAL FOSTER

to understand it, let alone love it. It was musty and dusty, and all of the haircuts and mustaches were preposterous. Greg Stafford's love of the legends of King Arthur is well known, and his admiration for Hal Foster glows bright in the pages of the *Prince Valiant* rulebook, but, similar to *Bullwinkle and Rocky,* this was not a property that people were going to go wild for. It sold slowly.

Of course, commercial success is no measure of quality or importance. In the coming decade, RPGs would move away from elaborate systems of simulation and become interested in encouraging narrative in a variety of ways. Some games embraced the pool mechanic, like *Vampire: The Masquerade,* which uses a system literally called the Storyteller System. Others, like the myriad of storytelling games that emerge in the new millennium, concentrated on finding new ways to strip out or otherwise minimize rules in order to lower barriers to collaborative storytelling. These games might not owe a direct debt to *Prince Valiant,* but *Prince Valiant* was nevertheless at the forefront of a new style of play.

Shadowrun (1989)

Shadowrun is an interesting nexus of a game, a culmination of many threads of RPG design from both the '70s and '80s. The designers were old hands. Bob Charrette and Paul Hume had designed *Bushido* and *Aftermath!* (1981), while Tom Dowd had contributed to the second edition of the superhero game, *Villains and Vigilantes* (1982). The result is both the first and most restrained of the big cross-genre RPGs (*Rifts* and *Torg* both came out in 1990).

Shadowrun expands on the look and tone of *Cyberpunk* and lifts much of its jargon and core technological concepts directly from William Gibson's novel, *Neuromancer* (1985), while also anticipating what *Vampire: The Masquerade* (1991) would eventually do aesthetically.

Mechanically, *Shadowrun* and *Vampire* have a shared ancestor in *Ghostbusters,* as both use the variant comparative dice pool mechanic (instead of totaling all of the dice rolled, each individual die is counted as a success or failure). Finally, it is also one of the first RPGs to present a new system and distinct visual presentation in one core book, complete with color plates for character archetypes, a format that became a standard for many games in the '90s.

All of these various strands came together to make *Shadowrun* one of the biggest and most enduring RPGs of all time, sparking not just a massive line across seven editions, but also novels, videogames, and one extremely unfortunate promotional video.

Tim Bradstreet (who would shortly go on to define the visual stylings of *Vampire: The Masquerade*) and Jeff Laubenstein also deliver some stellar, street-level illustration work. Janet Aulisio comes on board for the second edition, providing deep shadows through which to skulk. It is Jim Nelson who exemplifies *Shadowrun*'s overwrought urban look. Nearly all of the art is complimentary, though, working together to create a varied, gritty world; even Larry Elmore, whose work is normally glistening, gets in on the grime.

Much of *Shadowrun*'s appeal comes from this worn-out world, a near-future version of our own, in which a series of events caused massive unrest and political changes, culminating with the return of magic and, with it, elves, orcs, trolls, and dragons. Of course, it being created in 1989, *Shadowrun* often embraces ideas that ring troubling today—like using Native American traditions as plot devices, or using stereotyped fantasy races as an opportunity to interrogate real-world oppression, or even the fact that there is a character class called Street Samurai (though that term comes from slang in Gibson's *Neuromancer*).

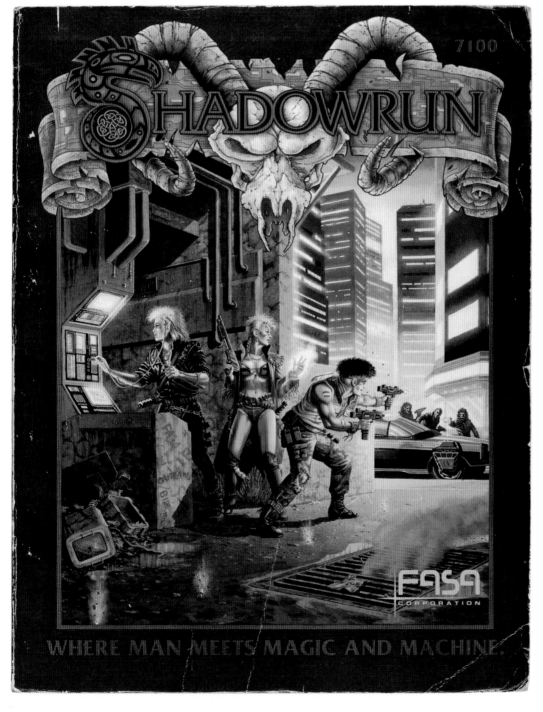

SHADOWRUN, FASA CORPORATION, 1989
BOB CHARRETTE, PAUL HUME, AND TOM DOWD, COVER BY LARRY ELMORE

199

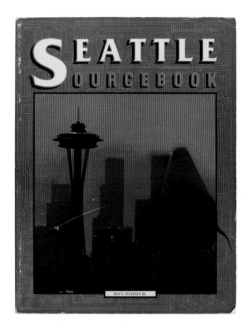

SEATTLE SOURCEBOOK, FASA CORPORATION, 1990
BOY F. PETERSEN JR., COVER BY DANA KNUTSON

Shadowrun might have been bigger still if they nailed it from the start, but the first iteration of the rules was less than streamlined. FASA corrected some of that with the second edition, in 1992, which gave the game a much-needed polish. Even then, unified mechanics only appeared, gradually, in later editions, so players had to navigate unique systems for each category of character. Combat-based characters, what the game calls physical adepts, use a straightforward skill system, modified by magic, drugs, or cybernetic enhancements (though magic tends to bounce off cybered characters).

But then there are three types of magic-users—Mages, Shamans, and Adepts (a sort of mystical monk)—as well as hackers, called Deckers in the game's parlance, and Riggers, who can control technology like vehicles and security systems with their minds. All five of these have their own specialized mechanics. An added wrinkle, imported from *Cyberpunk*: A lot of decking (if hackers hack, Deckers deck) takes place during combat, with the decker playing their own mini-game inside the matrix while their companions protect them from harm. Mages who pull a Doctor Strange and astral project find themselves in similar situations.

None of these different systems are a problem for a player, who only has to contend with the one set of mechanics that pertains to their character. It's another story for the GM, who has to manage all of these systems on top of their usual duties. *Shadowrun* asks a lot from GMs, but those up for the challenge find great narrative rewards, as well.

Anti-capitalists will be pleased, though: While governments fragmented, corporations consolidated power and are, in true cyberpunk fashion, the primary villains of the setting. Players take the roles of lowlifes and criminals—failed Mages, Street Shamans, Mercs, hackers, and gangsters. The titular shadowrun is a mission of corporate espionage during which a small team steals from or otherwise incinerates the interests of a megacorp (which inevitably reveals their involvement in some kind of labyrinthine conspiracy that threatens to destabilize the multiverse).

For all of the pitfalls, *Shadowrun* is a game with a heart. The fantasy elements counter the coldness of the game's science fiction, encouraging characters to have beliefs and ideals. Those convictions give stakes to everything in the game, which, in turn, make the world come alive. Characters don't run covert ops on dangerous corporate interests in order to maintain the status quo; they do so to change life for the better (a theme that *Underground* will pick up in a few years). It isn't perfect, but after *Cyberpunk*, with its '80s-style lionization of greed and self-centeredness, it's a running jump in the right direction.

SPRAWL SITES, FASA CORPORATION, 1990
JOHN FAUGHNAN, BOY F. PETERSEN JR. AND MICHAEL STACKPOLE. COVER BY STEVE VENTERS

A trio of books that came out shortly after the *Shadowrun* core rulebook are foundational, both for *Shadowrun* and the larger landscape of RPGs in the '90s.

The first is *Shadowrun*'s very own city sourcebook, the *Seattle Sourcebook* (1990). The default setting was an interesting choice, part of a larger pop culture moment for a city about to become the center of the grunge and alternative scene once Pearl Jam's *Ten* and Nirvana's *Nevermind* hit airwaves in 1991. The sourcebook takes the form of a paper version of a hyperlinked web guide (that, format-wise, anticipates a lot of user interfaces for smart phones and tablets) long before that sort of display really existed online. There are even little scroll cursors in the layout—it imparts an immediate sense of how it would work even though it doesn't *work*.

The bulk of the book includes entry after entry detailing countless restaurants, clubs, and other locations of interest. Each entry has a straightforward block of information, followed by flavorful comments and reviews by shadowrunners and other Seattle denizens, sort of like a cyberpunk Yelp, which was founded in 2004, nearly 15 years after this book came out. True to its form as a faux travel guide, it feels largely like a data dump. A year later, *Cyberpunk 2020* would take the same basic approach with *Night City* and elevate it to a masterpiece.

If the *Seattle Sourcebook* sketches out the macro, *Sprawl Sites* (1990) is concerned with the micro. Less a sourcebook than it is a toolkit, the book lays out sets of encounters (over 130 of them!), modular world pieces, and NPC archetypes. Everything needed to throw together a scenario on the fly is here. The locations are probably the most useful—in addition to floor plans, they also include notes on who or what might be in the establishment, as well as how they work. Most GMs will already have a good idea of what a restaurant is like, but they might be at a loss for what a Talismonger shop entails.

In this way, *Sprawl Sites* contributes much to the lived-in feel of the *Shadowrun* world. The same is true of the contacts. The brief rundowns, accompanied by Jim Nelson's portraits, are interesting, encourage creativity, and possess a clear place in the ecosystem of the world. With this and the core rulebook, a GM can run *Shadowrun* forever. Unfortunately, no one seems to have lifted the toolkit format for other RPGs.

Finally, there's the *Street Samurai Catalog* (1990), which is exactly what it says it is: A catalog of equipment geared toward Street Samurai, one of *Shadowrun*'s conventional combat archetypes. Tech books and equipment catalogs, like this, give a subtle glimpse at the nature of the world, a sort of environmental storytelling. *Chromebook* (1991), for *Cyberpunk 2020*, is another great example, but many games would adapt the format. This one is an explicitly in-universe document and shares the same tablet interface layout as the *Seattle Sourcebook*—it's designed for players to use as an actual catalog, which makes sense—flip through it, get some ordnance, hit the streets, and blow up some megacorp offices. Just leave the mall katana at home.

+HE 1990S

In the looming shadow of the new millennium,
the metaplot gains favor amid genre mixing and expanding lore.
Game designers explore "mature" themes, often wrestling with
tensions in our world and beyond. On the horizon,
the first glimmer of an indie movement shines through the grit.

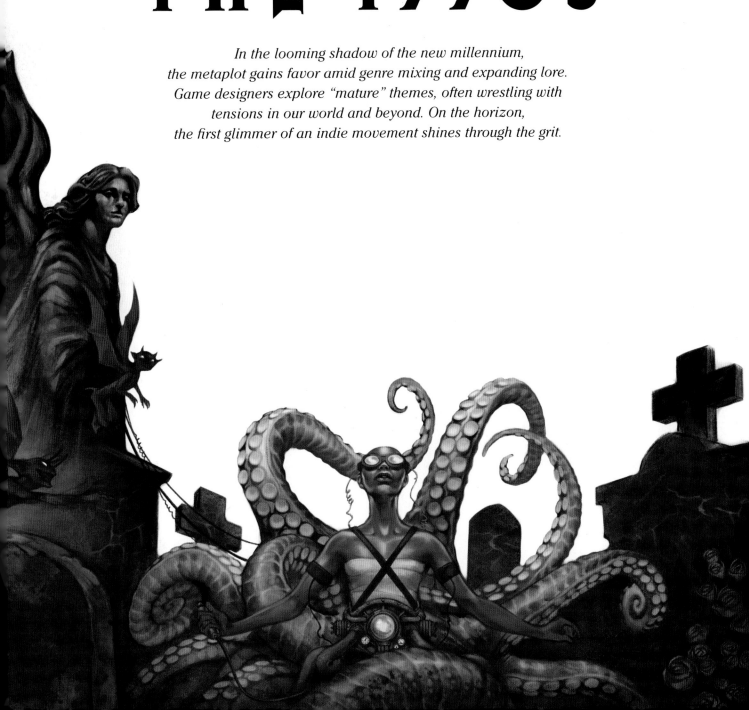

ROLEPLAYING THE POSSIBILITY WARS™

TORG

™

THE BATTLE FOR A REALITY-TORN EARTH!

Torg: Roleplaying the Possibility Wars, Box set, West End Games, 1990
Greg Gorden and Bill Slavicsek, Cover by Daniel Horne

Torg (1990)

With narrative increasingly becoming the cornerstone of role-playing, genre becomes a significant focal point of the '90s. Early in the decade, all of the genres were crashing into each other, giving rise to large multigenre games, like *Shadowrun* (originally published in 1989, though the vast majority of its supplements came out in the '90s), *Torg*, and *Rifts*, both of which were introduced at Gen Con 1990. As the decade wears on, the bombast of the multigenre games fades and gives way to games that are pre-occupied with deconstructing, or otherwise playing with, genre conventions. But that's later.

Torg sits in the middle of the spectrum, neither aiming to be as hypothetically plausible as *Shadowrun,* nor as full-on everything-is-exploding as *Rifts*. Earth is the subject of an interdimensional invasion, with huge regions of the world changed to reflect the nature of those interloping realities, expressed in game terms as degrees of Axioms: Magic, social, spiritual, and technological. These Axioms define how reality works in a given dimension. Our own is low on magic and spirituality, but high in social and technological.

Six realities took part in the initial invasion—Victorian horror overlaid a portion of Southeast Asia; a primal dinosaur land, complete with reptilian humanoids, emerged in several regions of North America; a *D&D* reality subsumed the United Kingdom and Northern Europe; France became dominated by the Cyberpapacy, a repressive medieval theocracy that accidentally merged with a cyberpunk reality on its way to invade earth; the Nile region was overwritten by a pulp reality full of masked mystery men and weird science; finally, Japan was invaded by Nippon Tech, a racist caricature born out of '80s era fears of Japan as a corrupt, world-buying hyper-capitalist technocracy. These all have a variety of Axiom levels. The Living Land, which invaded North America, has no magic, low social and tech, but high spirit, meaning that in those regions, guns don't work, everyday people have trouble communicating, and miracles are fairly common.

Players take the role of Storm Knights, people who have been fundamentally changed by the energies of the invasion. They can be from our world or from elsewhere, but they are united in their opposition to the invading high lords. As with West End's *Star Wars* RPG, characters are template-based. The initial box set offers 24 templates, and additional templates were included in the sourcebooks that detail the various invading realities, so a party of players could consist of a cop, a werewolf, a cyborg, a wizard, and an intelligent giant starfish. Unlike regular folks, Storm Knights carry their own pockets of reality with them, so a cyborg Storm Knight doesn't keel over when crossing over into the low-tech Living Land. Much of the fun for players of *Torg* is to be found on the borders of realities, messing with Axioms, and generally by seeing what they can get away with.

The Possibility Wars, at large, played out in a metaplot that stretched across novels, many adventure modules, and the Infiniverse products—first newsletters, later sourcebook compilations of important plot points that function like a living campaign. The metaplot gave players an intriguing power through the use of rumors. These were presented in modules and in the newsletters, and players voted on whether or not they were true. The results spawned further adventures, which contained more rumors, and continued on, creating a sort of a massive group choose-your-own adventure.

These expansive possibilities both make *Torg* attractive to players and stifle its playability. Many of the basic mechanics are wonderfully cinematic, encouraging play that embraces action and high adventure. Defeats almost always end in incapacitation rather than death. Successes, meanwhile, can shake reality.

Torg uses a 20-sided die to resolve actions, rolled to beat a target number—if the player rolls a 10 or 20, they can roll again, adding the result to their total. This can go on indefinitely if the player keeps rolling 10s and 20s, potentially resulting in awesome totals (this re-rolling is often called an "exploding" die and, indicative of *Torg*'s lack of restraint, most games that use the mechanic only have a die explode on the roll of one specific value, not two).

This bombast is augmented by the Drama Deck, used by both players and the GM. Each card has values that provide potential advantages, complications, or special sub-plots. The Martyr card, for instance, allows a player to defeat an opponent at the cost of their character's life; others might penalize skills or cue a villain's monologue. The cards evoke the dramatic turns of fortune that occur in action movies—the rulebook frequently references the *Indiana Jones* movies to make its points.

All of these mechanics are light and fast, but each reality adds more weight, even if they are all a *kind of* unified system, despite the absence of many necessary rules from the core box set. To play a magic-using character from Aysle, the *D&D* reality that overwrote England, the Aysle sourcebook is needed; a Nippon Tech martial artist requires the Nippon Tech sourcebook. Seemingly every new *Torg* book introduced a new system, decentralizing the game's mechanics and raising the overall power level. Coupled with the rapidly advancing metaplot, *Torg* was expensive to jump into and dizzying to keep up with.

Torg was uneven in other ways, too. Take the name of the game, for example. What's a Torg? It's a codename that stuck. When the game was in development, the folks at West End referred to it as "The Other Roleplaying Game" to differentiate it from *Star Wars*. They couldn't think of a better name come time for release, so they just called it *Torg* and performed a quick narrative retrofit, making Torg an in-game title, a sort of high lord of high lords that the game's ultimate villain, the Gaunt Man, aimed to be. This impromptu origin says a lot about the foundation on which the game is built.

The production values are also surprisingly low. The box set is adequate, but many subsequent books have inferior illustrations, which distinctly disadvantage *Torg* when compared to the strong aesthetics of *Rifts* and *Shadowrun*. Even the box art, a perfectly acceptable effort by Daniel Horne, sends mixed messages about the experience of playing the game—the pairing of the kick-ass cyberpunk woman and the middle-aged priest has me asking all sorts of questions, none of which include, "How can I get some of that high adventure?"

The Nile Empire, West End Games, 1990
Ray Winninger, Cover by Daniel Horne

The various game products have an inconsistent tone, as well. Many play it straight, but others are full of puns and others questionable humor. The finale of the metaplot, *War's End* (1995), features Jeff Mills, an in-universe RPG designer and the seemingly fictionalized version of *Torg* designer Greg Gorden (who had left West End years earlier). Mills (or more accurately—disturbingly—his death) is instrumental in the module's events, an ill-conceived twist playing on the reality-bending finale of Grant Morrison's classic run on the comic book series, *Animal Man*, in which the creator and the creation collide.

Worst of all, the clash of genres is often also a clash of cultural stereotypes. Nippon Tech is the worst offender, but the Cyberpapacy's secret creation of an artificial AIDS virus isn't far off. Other stereotyping plagues the portrayal of the Southeast Asian inhabitants of Orrorsh and the North African people in the Nile Empire.

In many ways, *Torg*, with its cinematic style and promising Drama Deck, seemed like the cross-genre RPG with the most promise, but by 1994, only the most dedicated of the die-hard fans were still playing. In 1995, West End Games discontinued it.

Rifts (1990)

Palladium Books had used the same core rule system for nearly every game it published in the '80s—fantasy worlds, cyborgs, *Teenage Mutant Ninja Turtles*, superheroes, mechs, Lovecraftian horrors, commandos, and more had been powered by the same, growing system. *Rifts* is that system's apotheosis, unifying all of the rules that came before into one massive, scaling mega-system that bridges the various worlds associated with those rules. The result isn't merely a universe, it is the Megaverse.

Like *Torg*, the world of *Rifts* is one like our own, but several centuries in the future, after surging arcane energies at

Rifts, Palladium Books, 1990
Kevin Siembieda, Cover by Keith Parkinson

the nexus points of ley lines tore interdimensional holes in reality—the titular rifts—allowing other realms of existence to bleed through: Gargoyles rule France; vampires have a kingdom where Mexico used to be; the Federation of Magic conquered Chicago; Atlantis is back, and the creature that may one day devour the world is growing in the Mariana Trench.

To survive against this swirl of supernatural forces, humanity has developed ever more powerful weapon systems, like the Glitter Boy power armor complete with rail guns or the—well, there's other wild technology, but players seem to only ever want to get Glitter Boy armor. And sometimes low-tech options are the most effective, like the startling new innovations in (holy) water guns detailed in *Vampire Kingdoms* (1991).

The announcement ad in *Dragon* magazine (August, 1990) declares, "There is so much to tell about *Rifts* that we don't know where to begin." That was true then, and it is just as true now. *Rifts* is the RPG born out of dumping all of the toys out into the middle of the room and making them fight—G.I. Joes in TIE Fighters, He-Man fighting M.A.S.K., the rubber great

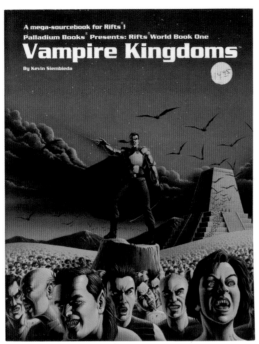

VAMPIRE KINGDOMS, PALLADIUM BOOKS, 1991
KEVIN SIEMBIEDA, COVER BY KEVIN LONG

white shark inexplicably flying through the air to hunt ThunderCats. The game aims to answer every variation of the comic book store question, "Who would win?" No wonder creator Kevin Siembieda was keen to distribute the sourcebooks *to* comic books stores.

Rifts fires on every cylinder ever created. It caters to players who want to fight deranged giant robots *and* demons *at the same time* with the biggest explosions possible. Its arcane rules system is built for bombastic, over-powered play. Each new book in the line juices the power levels higher, with little concern for balancing with earlier titles, a terrifying escalation considering the line consists of more than 80 books (this was a problem for *Torg*, but for some reason, it feels like a selling point for *Rifts*).

The perfect example of *Rifts*' unbound power levels are its treatment of health and damage. As with most RPGs, characters start out with a modest number of hit points that represent their bodily health. *Rifts* tops out at 30, initially, but that number can increase with time and experience. Above this value is the character's structural damage capacity (SDC—*Rifts*

loves confusing abbreviations), which represents physical conditioning. Incoming damage reduces SDC first. It is painful, but not actually life-threatening (similar to how a cut on the hand is not a killing wound, no matter how many stitches it might need). Most starting characters have between 10 and 40, or so, SDC.

Then there is mega-damage capacity (MDC), which is a gauge of high-tech armor. 100 points of SDC equals a single point of MDC (usually—there is some inconsistency in the conversion across the *Rifts* product line), which conveys the terrifyingly destructive power of mega-damage. When unarmored, the rules say, "a mega-damage weapon will blow you to atoms." That Glitter Boy rail gun can do up to 180 points of mega-damage, the equivalent of an astounding 18,000 points of SDC. Buildings tend to fall over regularly in *Rifts* combat.

Given this over-the-top, anything-goes approach, it is no surprise that the game found its initial audience among comic book-reading teenagers who had never previously played RPGs (and continues to be popular among those seeking a nostalgic hit for those lazy, comic-reading teenage days). There is something about *Rifts* that seems unleashed, or unrestrained, like it's the product of a never-ending brainstorming session where everything becomes increasingly bigger and badder and, generally, covered in skulls.

It should be a mess, but the art holds it all together. Keith Parkinson, an iconic '80s *D&D* mainstay, delivered many of the best covers for *Rifts* books, including the core rulebook, and it is gratifying to see the game's weirdness fuel the artist's expansive vision. His cover for *World Book 16: Federation of Magic* (1997) exemplifies how *Rifts* pushed his art well beyond the fantasy standards of *D&D*. The real star of *Rifts*' art, though, is the clean, technical line work that Kevin Long provided for the game's first five years. He does a masterful job making all of the disparate elements seem cool and cohesive—magic and tech and high tech and super-high-tech and psionics and animal people and faction after faction—and so many skulls!

Lovecraft Country (1990)

The release of the fourth edition of *Call of Cthulhu* (1989) sparked a golden age for the line that would continue through Lynn Willis's fifth edition (1992) and well into the '90s. Classic scenarios long out-of-print were repackaged and reprinted while exciting new material emerged, both from Chaosium (like the epic campaign *Horror on the Orient Express*, 1991) and from independent publishers, like Pagan Publishing; their magazine, *The Unspeakable Oath*, launched in 1990, was indispensable for serious *Call of Cthulhu* players and would eventually spawn *Delta Green*. The moment reached an intoxicating peak early, in 1990, with the launch of the Lovecraft Country sourcebooks.

There are four—*Arkham Unveiled* (1990), *Return to Dunwich* (1991), *Kingsport: The City in the Mists* (1991), and *Escape from Innsmouth* (1992)—and together, they form a playable literary landscape that accounts, not just for the stories of Lovecraft, but also for many of the writers who have visited in his sandbox—August Derleth, Lin Carter, Robert Bloch, Clark Ashton Smith, Brian Lumley, and Ramsey Campbell among them. And when those worthies proved lacking in necessary details, Keith Herber and Kevin A. Ross filled in the gaps with their own imaginations. The result is a massive collection of secrets and horrors. A natural progression from Chaosium's earlier city designs, like *Pavis* and *Big Rubble*, there isn't another RPG sourcebook project that is quite on the same scale as Lovecraft Country.

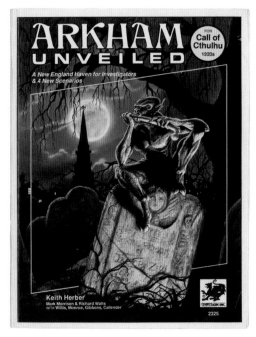

ARKHAM UNVEILED, CHAOSIUM, 1990
KEITH HERBER, COVER BY LEE GIBBONS

Herber's *Arkham Unveiled* formed the template, detailing, block by block, H.P. Lovecraft's famed, witch-haunted town of Arkham, Massachusetts, home to Miskatonic University, where there is no shortage of terrible mysteries. It's an ambitious book that details every noteworthy building, person, and lowdown within the city limits (and beyond), while also providing plenty of real estate in which GMs can fix their own particulars.

As some liberty has been taken with the dates, players never know what to expect from hazards with a literary pedigree. Herbert West, Reanimator, is dead and gone, his macabre legacy now an urban legend whispered by medical students at the university. Meanwhile, the poor mathematician Walter Gilman is dreaming in the Witch House, and the poet Edward Derby is imprisoned in Crowninshield Manor with his wife, Asenath Waite—their dooms not yet upon them. If players wander onto the blasted heath, they'll find themselves in the middle of the denouement: The Gardeners are dead, but the reservoir is still hypothetical, and the "colour out of space" still lurks in its well. To encounter these stories in their various states of

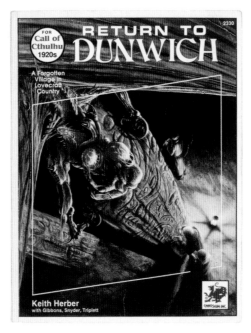

RETURN TO DUNWICH, CHAOSIUM, 1991
KEITH HERBER, COVER BY LEE GIBBONS

KINGSPORT: THE CITY IN THE MISTS, CHAOSIUM, 1991
KEVIN A. ROSS, COVER BY JOHN T. SNYDER

progress gives this Arkham a sense of familiarity, but also danger—and those are just looking at the details players might know about from reading Lovecraft's stories. There are plenty of other dangers, too, like the ghouls in the cemetery, long dead sorcerers, and secret members of Keziah Mason's witch cult lurking in all walks of Arkham's life.

Return to Dunwich, also by Herber, marks a significant improvement on *Arkham Unveiled*. It brings readers through the rambling hills northwest of Arkham, to the decaying village of Dunwich (pronounced "dunnich"). Dunwich oozes a rich, rural strain of horror, soaked with poverty, degeneracy, black magic, and ancient mysteries. Herber deepens those mysteries considerably, revealing that the region was twice settled in the past, once by the pre-human Hyberboreans and, later, by renegade Druids. Both groups vanished after running afoul of something that lurks beneath the land, something that promises paradise but is also the source of the region's decay. Ruins and relics from both cultures are strewn across the countryside—pyramid-like hills that never frost over, massive stone heads sunk in the swamps, standing

stones. Artist John T. Snyder excels in depicting the remains.

Return to Dunwich is set just a few months after the events of Lovecraft's story "The Dunwich Horror." In, perhaps, Lovecraft's pulpiest tale and the one most aligned with the feel of a *Call of Cthulhu* scenario, a group of professors from Miskatonic University uncover a terrible truth—that Wizard Whateley mated his daughter with an extradimensional entity, producing two grandsons: A vaguely human one named Wilbur and another who *takes after the father*. After Wilbur's demise, his monstrous, invisible brother runs rampant through the desolate hamlet, until it is banished by a heroic librarian named Henry Armitage.

These two threads intertwine to create a free-form campaign. Armitage hires the player characters to tie up some loose ends from his adventure, which requires an investigation of the region and its inhabitants. How the dozens of interviews and the endless hikes through the bleak countryside play out is up in the air—*Return to Dunwich* details over 200 residents and a vast area of over 100-square miles, both above and below the surface. There are countless interconnected threads of history, family secrets, and ancient hor-

rors to untangle over dozens of sessions. The sheer amount of material is only half as impressive as Herber's ceaseless creativity and his control of the atmosphere, which is consistent throughout. This is likely his masterpiece.

With *Kingsport: The City in the Mists*, Kevin Ross took over the writing duties while Herber moved to the editor's chair. As with the other books in the series, this is a deep dive into a city and its inhabitants. A picturesque seaside town, Kingsport is the least famous and defined of Lovecraft's imaginary Massachusetts locales. This lack of fictional detail gives the Kingsport of the RPG the chance to become something intriguing in its own right.

Ross uses Lovecraft's story, "The Strange High House in the Mist," as a jumping-off point. In that story, the house in question, high above the city on the promontory of Kingsport Head, sits at a junction between worlds, namely this one and the Dreamlands, Lovecraft's medieval fantasy realm. Ross uses that proximity to the sleeping world to infuse the entire city with a kind of dreaminess. The cosmic recedes while horrors more Romantic and Gothic step to the fore.

The dream threads of the book crescendo with Ross's scenario "Dreams and Fancies," in which the suicide of a young poet leads investigators into dreams based on poems by an obscure Romantic, concluding with them confronting their wickedest selves. It is a nightmare, but it's also beautiful in its construction, full of loaded, highly metaphorical imagery, brought to delightfully creepy life by Jason Eckhardt's illustrations. There is also a scenario involving undead pirates, a clear homage to John Carpenter's *The Fog*, and Kingsport receives its own cult dedicated to a sentient green

flame. It is still a place of terrors, but the essence is unique when compared to the bulk of *Call of Cthulhu*'s material.

Finally, there is Ross's *Escape from Innsmouth*, which is, in many ways, the culmination of the Lovecraft Country sourcebooks. Based on Lovecraft's masterpiece, *The Shadow Over Innsmouth*, Innsmouth is a fishing town in destitution, largely abandoned, where half of its xenophobic residents are half-human hybrids of the fish men—Deep Ones—that live beneath Devil's Reef off the coast. The deal between the two groups was made generations ago with gold and sorcery, but lingers on now as a curse of the blood.

Ross brings the same level of detail as the other books, but because the town is so depopulated, there's room for a short two-part campaign that ranks among *Call of Cthulhu*'s very best. The first part takes place after Lovecraft's story and partly reenacts it—players visit the town looking for a disappeared grocery clerk and wind up having to escape when the hybrids come for them in the night. The second acts out the raid mentioned in the denouement of Lovecraft's story, where the federal government takes military action against the town and its Deep One allies. The raid has multiple strike teams with numerous objectives occurring concurrently—players shift roles from their own characters to stock soldiers as the action cuts cinematically back and forth, like the climax of a *Star Wars* film, but with more tentacles. In terms of construction, the scenario is a hall of famer.

The book's art is fantastic, as well, if subdued. Jason Eckhardt has a special talent for drawing gloomy, derelict buildings, and his drawings provide much of the rich atmosphere for the first half of the book. Meanwhile, John T. Snyder's line work creates evocative portraits and horrific moments of action. It is one of Chaosium's best-looking books and provides the raw inspiration for one of the better Lovecraftian videogame

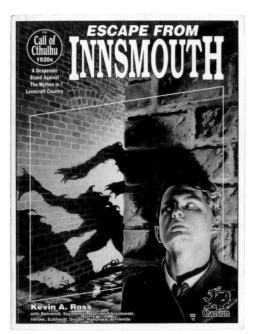

ESCAPE FROM INNSMOUTH, CHAOSIUM, 1992
KEVIN A. ROSS, COVER BY JOHN T. SNYDER

adaptations, *Call of Cthulhu: Dark Corners of the Earth* (2005). The raid on Innsmouth, as described here, is a formative event for *Delta Green,* as well.

Summed up, the four books paint a vivid nightmare version of New England to explore over many, many hours of play, along with the three collections of scenarios explicitly tied to Lovecraft Country—*Tales of the Miskatonic Valley* (1991), *Adventures in Arkham Country* (1993), and *Dead Reckonings* (1998). The local focus is a contrast to most other *Call of Cthulhu* material up to this point, which usually involves international travel and at least a hint of Indiana Jones-style derring-do. Having so many horrors in the backyard plays into one of the key, if often overlooked, ideas behind *Call of Cthulhu*: Once the curtain is peeled back and the truth of the Cthulhu Mythos is understood, characters realize it is everywhere, soaked into the very ground, and they wonder how there was ever a time they couldn't see it. Chaosium's Lovecraft Country books make explicit the idea that there is an eldritch horror around every corner, if an investigator knows where to look for it.

Nightlife (1990)

Despite a fixation on monsters in tabletop roleplaying games—with book after book just full of 'em—there isn't much opportunity to *play* a monster. The vast majority of the time, monsters are the opponent, the obstacle between the players and their goal.

Up to 1990, the only game purposely designed to let players walk a mile in a monster's shoes is Ken St. Andre's third game, *Monsters! Monsters!* (1976)—John Gardner's *Grendel* it is not. The sole point of St. Andre's game is to turn the tables on those pesky heroes and eat them. It's mayhem, rather than moral nuance.

Nightlife has similar deficiencies—philosophically it is more The Sisters of Mercy than Sartre—but it, at least, attempts to convey some depth in its '90s-style angst. A variety of monsters, known as the Kin, secretly live among us, with their own agendas, factions, squabbles, and turf wars. In fact, the two worlds would likely never mix if not for two reasons: Kin need humans (whom they call the Herd—cute) to feed on, and they have an abiding interest in the various music and subculture club scenes in New York City, hence the title.

A surprising amount of space in the equipment section is devoted to jewelry and fashion items, to the point that an advertisement for Trash and Vaudeville wouldn't feel out of place. A later sourcebook, *In the Musical Vein* (1991), is devoted to encouraging player characters to form a band and go on tour. It even introduces resurrection music, a genre created by the Kin that combines jazz, rap, and speed metal (weird as that may sound, it does kind of anticipate nü-metal or acts like The Dillinger Escape Plan that would start to appear later in the decade).

There are seven playable types of Kin: Vampyres, Werewolves, Ghosts, Daemons, Wyghts, Inuits, and Animates. Vampyres, Werewolves, and Ghosts adhere to traditional definitions; Daemons are summoned extradimensional creatures (though not necessarily infernal); Animates are essentially Frankenstein's monsters; Wyghts are a sort of catchall undead category; and Inuits are, well, probably a mistake. In the real world, the word Inuit refers to a group of indigenous peoples who live near the Arctic circle in Greenland, Canada, and Alaska.

As described, the authors likely meant to use the word manitou, which refers to a spiritual manifestation of the world's life force in the theology of some Native American groups, particularly the Algonquian peoples in the New York region. Ultimately, the category of character is on shaky ground; like many RPGs of the period, *Nightlife* is careless with cultural appropriation, exotification, and racial representation.

There are more sorts of Kin, many strange and interesting, but these seven are the only ones complex enough to merit play. Each character is a collection of powers, Edges, in the game's parlance (perhaps unintentionally anticipating the modern notion of edginess being cringeworthy) and Flaws. Some of these abilities and weaknesses line up with folklore in expected ways—Vampyres can shapeshift, but are vulnerable to garlic—while some are surprising—Werewolves can feed on the psychic emanations caused by human pain, instead of just feeding on humans, though there isn't anything stopping them from doing both.

Additional Edges can by learned later, but at the cost of the character's humanity. Literally! Humanity is an attribute that ranges from zero to 100, the higher the number, the greater their hold on their psychological humanity. Characters start at 50. Using Edges, feeding, killing, or injuring indiscriminately lowers their Humanity while showing mercy and being pleasant raises it (there are, obviously, far more opportunities to burn off Humanity in a game than to gain it). The lower a character's Humanity, the more difficult it

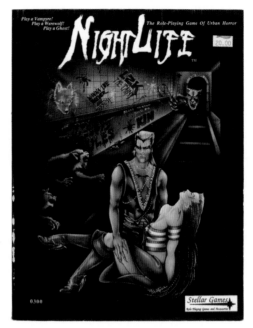

NIGHTLIFE, STELLAR GAMES, 1990
BRADLEY K. MCDEVITT, L. LEE CERNY, AND WALTER H. MYTCZYNSKYJ, COVER BY PAMELA SHANTEAU

is to increase Edge powers, and the more susceptible they become to their Flaws.

In the broad strokes of *Nightlife*, there is a possible case of parallel evolution in Clive Barker's *Cabal*, which portrays a secret, underground society of monstrous people. The novella came out in 1988, and the film version hit screens in 1990, along with a comic book adaptation, the same year as *Nightlife*. It's the similarities between *Nightlife* and *Vampire: The Masquerade*, though, that bring to mind the phenomenon of twin films, the surprisingly frequent and slightly maddening occurrence of two movies with similar subjects releasing in close proximity, as with *The Prestige* and *The Illusionist*, both of which came out within months of each other in 2006.

Vampire calls its children of the night Kindred, who live secretly among us, enjoy the club scene, and have to maintain their Humanity attribute lest the inner beast take control. That dual, conflicted nature follows through most of the *World of Darkness* games. What *Nightlife* lacks that the *World of Darkness* has in spades is lore and factions, but, ironically, *Nightlife* provides a system that allows all sorts of different night creatures to

213

interact, a cross-over that the various original *World of Darkness* games, frustratingly, never quite managed.

The real pleasure of the game is its depiction of a '90s New York City before so much of the rock subculture got sucked out of it. The game city is a rich setting full of gangs, corporations, secret societies, oddballs, weirdos, clubs, bars, and just about anything else imaginable—a large portion of the rulebook's 250-pages is given over to it. Because fashion, art, and music are central to the game, it functions a bit like a time capsule of the city in the '90s, the same way the film *The Warriors* does for the late '70s. Lacking photos, *Nightlife* concentrates on and succeeds in capturing the essence of the era.

The World of Darkness (1991)

With its single rose laying on green marble, the cover of *Vampire: The Masquerade* looks utterly unlike any other RPG book on shelves in 1991. Instead, it channels aesthetics from outside the hobby. Primarily, it evokes a funerary sense of mourning and mausoleums. Perhaps the clearest pop culture resonance is with the cover art of Ministry's 1983 album, *With Sympathy*, but there is also a hint of romance, as well, a topic much overlooked in RPGs up until now. And sure enough, *Vampire* and the suite of

World of Darkness games that followed, enjoyed unprecedented success in the '90s, thanks to that conscious attempt to appeal to an audience outside of traditional tabletop players. To this day, *Vampire* remains the only RPG to seriously threaten (and even briefly overtake) the primacy of *D&D*.

It is, as the name shouts out, a game about vampires, but not dusty old undead creeps, like Dracula and Strahd. Rather, these are vampires in a thoroughly modern mode, springing as much from Andrew Eldritch's mirror shades and Robert Smith's careful dishevelment as they do from Anne Rice's *Vampire Chronicles* series or the films, *The Hunger* (1983), *Near Dark* (1987), and *Lost Boys* (1987).

Here is a complex, world-spanning society of vampires existing in the shadows of our world. Players take the role of young vampires—that is, less than a century old—as they attempt to find a place in a world dominated by antediluvian forces while dealing with their own appetites. There is a lot of angst, leather, and lace, and maybe a bit of bad poetry. A surprising fact: White Wolf trademarked the term "Gothic-Punk," explaining in the rulebook that,

> the Gothic aspect describes the ambiance and institutions of mortal society [...] The Punk describes the way people live [...] Rock, punk and rap are even more of an escape and release, and rebellion is codified in styles of dress and speech. All in all, the world is more corrupt, more decadent and less humane than any suburbanite would like to believe.

The game itself is focused on narrative—all of the *World of Darkness* games run on the Storyteller System, a skill-based system that uses a comparative dice pool mechanic derived from *Shadowrun* for resolution. Games seem to take one of two paths—ones that focus on the

WITH SYMPATHY, ARISTA, 1983
MINISTRY, COVER BY ALBERTO RIZZO

VAMPIRE: THE MASQUERADE, SECOND EDITION, WHITE WOLF PUBLISHING, 1992
MARK REIN-HAGEN, GRAEME DAVIS, TOM DOWD, LISA STEVENS, AND STEWART WEICK, COVER BY MARK PACE **215**

MILWAUKEE BY NIGHT, WHITE WOLF PUBLISHING, 1992
DUSTIN BROWDER, COVER BY JANET AULISIO

day-to-day unlife of the characters (perhaps anticipating Jim Jarmusch, decades before *Only Lovers Left Alive*, 2013), or ones that dive headfirst into the vast web of political machinations of the 13 major clans, their derivative bloodlines, and the countless secret societies and factions.

For players who love lore, *Vampire* delivers with its massive metaplot, so much so that a sizable audience exists only to devour the piles of lore books with no intention of ever playing the game. I appreciate the commitment to both the scope of the world building and the devotion to the fine details, especially since a vast majority of it seems to be of dubious utility for running a game.

There are sourcebooks for *everything*— every clan, every secret society. There are about a dozen sourcebooks for cities, as well, which are key to running a game. Most of the cities are big, cosmopolitan ones, like New York, Chicago, and Los Angeles; New Orleans, so important to '90s goth culture, received one and Montreal, "the New Orleans of the north," received one too. So did Milwaukee? And not only did Milwaukee get one, but it came second after Chicago. Every city has rats, so every city is going to have

vampires; it just seems preposterous that *Milwaukee by Night* (1992) would not just beat *New Orleans by Night* (1994) to shelves, but that it would do so by two whole years.

This approach to world building proved to be a popular (if expensive) one for all sorts of RPGs for the duration of the decade. The formula *Vampire* struck upon, though, was unmatched. Intricate and stretching back to the dawn of humanity (and peppered with Tim Bradstreet's gritty, world-defining illustrations), the world hews close to our expectations while also radically re-imagining vampires. And while talking about a history that spans millennia, it still manages to strike the tone of a catty gossip session, the sort of scuttlebutt folks chat about in the back of the club while the DJ spins "How Soon is Now?" for the millionth time.

Because of the game's natural inclination toward soap opera-style stories of high melodrama, its modern setting, and its fashion sense (which encouraged just enough of a sense of playing dress-up without having to resort to foam swords or wizard hats), a lively live-action roleplaying community developed. Play was often public and organized locally and on a large scale, with many city groups having their own vampire "courts," full of secret signs, elaborate politics, and fake fangs. In this way, life imitated the fictional Masquerade. They may not have been real vampires, but for a time, a secret world mingled with a mundane one in the goth clubs of the '90s.

Vampire: The Masquerade often refers to itself as a game of personal or urban horror. As with *Nightlife*, players take on the role of monsters who struggle with their natures and the things they must do to survive, but at the end of the day, players are taking the role of immortal, romanticized monsters with magic powers. Because of these traits, *Vampire* (and the other *World of Darkness* games) often feel more like a low-power superhero game than a horror movie.

There is a good deal of political commentary, too. Vampire society is rigid and hierarchical. Power and prestige are closely associated with the vague accidents of age and bloodline. Despite the fact that the ruling organization, the Camarilla, is characterized as "good" and desires to co-exist unseen with humanity (hence the "masquerade"), while the Sabbat, a cabal of violent lunatics who want to bathe the world in blood, are characterized as "evil," the desire to burn it all down *is* appealing. Especially if players decide to read the Camarilla as a rich, upper class, wielding tradition like a weapon against a young working class that is sick of it all (this is the explicit ethos of the Anarchs, another, non-lunatic vampire sect). Besides, Sabbat is basically the RPG equivalent of *Near Dark*'s Severen (portrayed by Bill Paxton)—psychopathic, covered in blood, unrestrained by social compacts and exactly the sort of vampire most folks *want* to play, even if they don't want to admit it.

Severen's brand of vampirism is always lurking in the background. Most vampire clans want to keep on hiding and scavenging on humanity, because largely, some semblance of their humanity is still intact. This restrain is expressed through mechanics, as well as narrative—player characters need to take care against increasing their power, which erodes their humanity, lest they succumb to the beast and are removed from play. Later sourcebooks dedicated to the Sabbat would make room for players who wanted to embrace their inner beast, but only in a restrained way. So, like Jesse Hooker (portrayed by Lance Henriksen) in *Near Dark*, Severen, alas, remains out of reach.

Vampire was followed in 1992 by *Werewolf: The Apocalypse*, which is set in the same world yet remains strangely separate. While the systems are the same, in theory, crossing over vampires and werewolves never feels quite right. This awkwardness is true of all of the Monster: The Noun games—the inability to have a monster team-up à la *The Monster Squad* (1987) or *Abbott and Costello Meet Frankenstein* (1948)—was a problem that the original *World of Darkness* never solved satisfactorily.

While the basic construction of the systems is similar, the two games differ greatly in philosophy and theme. Werewolves are, on the one hand, trying to protect humanity's connection to nature (the game features a strong message of environmental consciousness) while, on the other hand, trying to prevent a supernatural apocalypse at the hands of their own large metaplot and an entity called the Wyrm.

Like *Vampire*, there is a complex mythology at play, involving numerous werewolf tribes and other shapeshifters. While *Werewolf* claims to also embrace a gothic-punk aesthetic, in execution, it is more representative of a combination of internet furry art and urban primitivism, though despite my opinion on the looks of game, the die-cut slashes in the early editions of the core rulebooks are undeniably evocative. It simultaneously manages to sustain a stronger atmosphere of horror than *Vampire* while also feeling like more of a superhero game in play.

Werewolf also reveals a larger problem with the secret histories of *World of Darkness*. The Masquerade in *Vampire* is a conspiracy aimed at convincing the world, at large, that vampires don't exist. By introducing werewolves, with their own rich history, the shadows in which everyone is supposed to be hiding suddenly seem

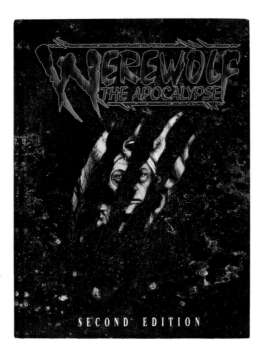

WEREWOLF: THE APOCALYPSE, SECOND EDITION, WHITE WOLF PUBLISHING, 1994

MARK REIN-HAGEN, WITH ROBERT HATCH AND BILL BRIDGES, COVER BY CHRIS MCDONOUGH AND TONY DITERLIZZI

The complexity and flexibility of the mechanics are fascinating, and made more so by the fact that, like *Ars Magica*, the framework for the game extrapolates from real-world esoteric traditions. It is also extremely complex to play, particularly for the GM, who has to have a working knowledge of multiple traditions, each with their own unique mechanics. The power levels are also off the charts and *Mage*, ultimately, demonstrates why the various original *World of Darkness* games shouldn't cross-pollinate (Adepts win all of the fights, even the unfair ones).

In *Wraith: The Oblivion* (1994), players take the roles of the recently dead. In temperament, it is like *Beetlejuice* (1988) but without so much as a drop of humor. It's all "Big. Dark. Room," and no "Banana Boat." Players seek transcendence (entry to Heaven, basically, though that place may just be a rumor), while trying to avoid oblivion. Players can check in on the lives they left behind, but that is technically illegal in the bureaucratic empire of the dead.

Wraith is a horrific nightmare of a game, and I honestly have a hard time believing anyone ever played it. It is relentlessly dour. Also, slavery is an essential component. The hell-bureaucracy of the afterlife's entire economy is dependent on it. Worse, everything "physical" in the afterlife is made from souls. If a character needs something, they buy some slave wraiths, smelt them down, and forge them into whatever they need, literally rendering sentient entities into inanimate objects. Basically, to do anything in *Wraith* is to participate in or profit from slavery, which is a hideous concept and one impossible to excise, thus making it unplayable from my perspective.

There is a mechanical idea in the game that bears mentioning, though it further complicates play. Player wraiths draw their power from their connections to the living world, the pursuits they were passionate about, the people they cared

crowded. The overstuffed feeling becomes downright comical as the *World of Darkness* continues to expand.

Mage: The Ascension (1993), the modern re-imagining of *Ars Magica*, comes next. Unlike the previous games, which explore the idea of player-as-monster, *Mage* casts players as spiritually awakened practitioners of mystical arts who are seeking to either wake the masses of humanity or keep them slumbering.

The main attraction is the open-ended magic system. In brief, the world is a reality defined by consensus. Magic is the process by which the awakened can alter or subvert that consensus through force of will. If that magical effect is too exposed to the consensus (basically, if enough regular people witness it and recognize it as breaking the laws of reality) then reality will re-assert itself, and the mage will experience blowback called Paradox, which generally involves the mage getting their face melted off. So, the idea is for the player to choose the effect they're looking to achieve, pick the type of magic they're going to use, and come up with a clever way to pull the wool over reality's eyes so their character doesn't disintegrate or explode.

about. There exists within a wraith, though, a self-destructive id-like force, called Shadow, that pushes them to the release of oblivion. That sabotaging Shadow is played by another player at the table. This arrangement sounds either amazing or disastrous, depending on the maturity of the group, but mechanically, it anticipates much of the experimental spirit of play that comes out of the indie movement in the following decade.

Wraith is also interesting because its metaplot wrapped up so conclusively that the final book in the line revealed all of the remaining secrets, and the whole shebang was put to bed after, finished, final, forever.

There are more games, each more improbable than the last. *Changeling: The Dreaming* (1995), with its fae-souled humans living in both the real world and the fantasy land of the dreaming, seems inspired by the issues of Neil Gaiman's *The Sandman* that were drawn by Charles Vess. There's *Hunter: The Reckoning* (1999), *Mummy: The Resurrection* (2001), and *Demon: The Fallen* (2002). I feel somewhat cheated that there was never a *Creature from the Black Lagoon* game, *Gillman: The Snorkeling*.

For all of the innovation and great ideas on display across all of the *World of Darkness* lines, there were problems from the start. The first version of nearly every game in the series was ugly and semi-broken, followed soon after by the second edition, which attempted to salvage the games with corrections and tidier production values. Given that White Wolf books had a habit of physically falling to pieces in short order, this is, perhaps, a feature and not a bug.

World of Darkness also once again proves what attracts people to an RPG—in this case, mountains of lore and intri-

GUIDE TO THE SABBAT, WHITE WOLF PUBLISHING, 1999
BY JUSTIN R. ACHILI, WITH W. H. BOURN, AND DYVERS HANDS, COVER BY BILL SIENKIEWICZ

cate metaplots—is also most likely to destroy it. There is simply too much. *Vampire* alone has a dizzying number of books, but the additional lines and the inexorable metaplots formed a non-stop avalanche for devoted players. New players coming to the game a year or two into a line were quickly alienated by the unceasing flow.

The *World of Darkness* was also of its time, a manifestation of pre-millennium tensions. Once the new millennium came, and Y2K failed to send the world back to the stone age, and the four horsemen didn't ride, all of these brooding '90s games about imminent apocalypses of various flavors all seemed a bit silly and self-indulgent. The dreary *Wraith* metaplot wrapped up in 1999, sending shockwaves through the metaplots of the other *World of Darkness* games that revived the various remaining game lines for a couple of years; Time of Judgment concluded the story entirely in 2004.

Nothing can keep a good monster down, of course. The whole *World of Darkness* line rebooted in 2004 with the well-regarded *Chronicles of Darkness* games, and 2018 saw the release of a controversial fifth edition of *Vampire: The Masquerade*. Neither of these recaptured the height those lines reached in the early '90s, though—the world has mostly moved on, and the Camarilla probably likes that just fine.

Drow of the Underdark (1991)

In 1987, R. A. Salvatore was working on *The Crystal Shard*, the second novel set in TSR's Forgotten Realms, after Douglas Niles's *Darkwalker on Moonshae* (1987). Forgotten Realms as a product line barely existed at that point, so the only reference material Salvatore received was Niles's novel, which led him to believe the Moonshae Isles *was* the Forgotten Realms. From that perspective, it made sense that this new novel would mention some of Niles's characters and events—the Moonshae Isles are rather small, after all. So, Salvatore settled on the idea of having one of Niles's characters act as a sort of sidekick for his new hero, Wulfgar of Icewind Dale. Once Salvatore realized the size and scope of the Realms, and TSR decided they'd rather not have authors sharing characters, as they did with the Dragonlance novels, Wulfgar was relocated a thousand miles away, to his native Icewind Dale. This change also meant he needed a new sidekick. And Salvatore needed to come up

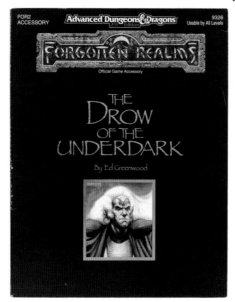

DROW OF THE UNDERDARK, TSR, 1991
ED GREENWOOD. COVER BY JEFF EASLEY

with one *right now*, because his editor, Mary Kirchoff, was heading into an important meeting about the book. On the spot, Salvatore created a drow ranger named Drizzt Do'Urden. Asked if he could spell that, Salvatore recalls in a Facebook post that his response was, "Not a chance."

So much for Wulfgar being the star of the show.

Drizzt was an instant fan favorite for many of the same reasons kids often gravitate to Batman. He has a cool back story, forsaking the evil ways of his people to live among the inhabitants of the surface world, though they often misunderstood him. He lives by a strict code of honor, and it always guides him down the right path. He can do *anything*, and he often does it with minimal effort and an excess of panache (with a little help from his two magical scimitars and his magic panther friend who is also a cute statuette in her downtime). He overshadows pretty much everyone in the known universe.

If Drizzt was a player character in a *D&D* campaign, he'd be a power fantasy nightmare (and that player might be the most flagrant cheater who ever lived). He was so popular that once the Icewind Dale Trilogy was complete, Salvatore's next series went back in time to explore the ranger's early life in the Underdark. Those books marked the true start of an ongoing saga that has stretched across an astounding 37 novels, making Drizzt the most recognizable character to come out of *Dungeons & Dragons*.

Before Drizzt, many people were fascinated by the idea of the drow (also known as dark elves), thanks to the cryptic reference to their existence in the first *Monster Manual* and then their subsequent turn as villains in the G, D, and Q-series modules. *Unearthed Arcana* (1985) made drow a playable race, and that certainly appealed to the sort of players who enjoyed taking on the role of Assassins and other evil characters. After Drizzt, though, *everyone* was begging to play a good drow (or, at the very least, a ranger who duel-wields scimitars and who scrambles to claim any figurine of wondrous power the party finds).

There are many reasons not to let players take the role of drow. For one, they have too many special abilities—the innate power to summon darkness, levitation, unnatural stealthiness, just to name a few—that throw off the balance of the game in their favor (even a game not particularly interested in balance, like the early iterations of *D&D*). They are also evil to the core, a society born of and reveling in darkness; Drizzt was the notable lone exception. The marching orders during the early years of *AD&D* Second Edition were to avoid controversies, so having a legion of pre-teens pretending to be spider-worshiping assassins was not an ideal outcome. Thus, *Drow of the Underdark*, by Ed Greenwood, feels like the first of many attempts to dissuade players from playing drow by detailing how awful and unrelentingly evil they are. Though, there are mixed messages: That's Drizzt on the cover. Greenwood provides a detailed appraisal of their poisonous culture and beliefs that probably made folks *more* inclined to play evil drow characters because of all the nifty magic items they get. *Menzoberranzan* (1992), the box set detailing Drizzt's deeply unpleasant hometown, detailed more of the same.

Drizzt and the drow seem to very much embody a swirl of contradictory currents in *D&D* during the early '90s. They are both edgy (at least for the young audience TSR was courting at the time), but safe (compared to other, increasingly adult-oriented RPG products available over the course of the '90s). Salvatore is immensely popular—Drizzt books routinely show up on the best-seller lists, and he's sold more than ten million books over his career—but Drizzt, as he appears here, in Jeff Easley's paintings, a refugee from *Elfquest* with big hair and mutton chops, feels like a relic from another time. And this is true, too, of *D&D* at the time.

Despite the success of *Dark Sun* with its BDSM visuals and the imminent goth/industrial envelope-pushing of *Planescape*, vast swaths of *D&D* were showing the game's age. Inside the bubble, in which *D&D* is the only RPG, and the Big Four paint their clean, heroic tableaux (see page 140), it was difficult to see how creaky and dated the whole game had gotten. From the outside, though, with games like *Vampire: The Masquerade* staking out new, complex frontiers, the old power fantasies look dusty, tame, and spent.

D&D carries on, of course, with Drizzt and the drow along, in a flurry of products throughout the '90s. In the 2000s, they appear regularly in the various *D&D*-licensed videogames, like *Baldur's Gate II: Shadows of Amn* (2000), *Icewind Dale II* (2002), and *Neverwinter Nights: Hordes of the Underdark* (2003). Drizzt was recently immortalized in plastic with his own action figure (complete with his two magic scimitars and his magic panther friend). He doesn't have mutton chops anymore, though.

The idea that drow (except Drizzt) are irredeemably evil is fraught and represents one facet of a much larger problem in the treatment of race within the context of fantasy and science fiction—namely that race, which in the real world is a social construct, is made obviously and biologically real within the fiction. This approach goes back farther than RPGs—essentialism is present in both *The Lord of the Rings* and the Conan stories, to name two formative fantasy founts.

This flawed portrayal of race, which often leans on stereotypes and "inherent" behaviors, is widespread in *Dungeons & Dragons*. It's further exacerbated by the game's rigid alignment system and, inconveniently, the existence of Drizzt himself.

The noble figure of the drow ranger moved to good deeds contrary to his nature brings clarity to an issue that might have otherwise remained obscured.

Alignment is the *D&D* framework for morality. There are nine flavors, mixing all possible combinations of good, evil, law, chaos, and neutrality. The intention was, in most cases, for a character's alignment to be an aggregate—a person acts may ways in a day, or a year, or a lifetime, but mostly, they wind up *aligning* with one particular pattern of behavior. In practice, though, especially when dealing with "monsters," alignment became an absolute. The tactical focus of *D&D* naturally encourages this perception (it can be seen in other ways, too, as with the option for parley gradually slipping out of the core play experience). As *D&D* is a game of combat, not philosophical discussion, it is expedient (and self-reinforcing) to downplay any sort of moral nuance: Thus, all drow are evil, so I hit them with my sword, and because I hit them with my sword, all drow are evil.

Players would never say all humans are Lawful Evil, or even regular elves (though Gygax did write them to be inherently untrustworthy)! Yet, players generalize nearly all drow as depraved, except those handful who, like Drizzt, come to the sur-

face world and embrace *our* ways. And that's the crux of the problem: With elves and humans, the similarities outweigh the differences, but with drow, the inverse is true. They have jet black skin (often portrayed as gray or purple, due to the difficulties in painting jet black skin) and shock white hair. They live in darkness, in a brutal subterranean world. Their culture, revolving as it does around the exaltation of a spider demon, twists and debases drow from birth, making them debauched, treacherous, and capable of casual mayhem. Drizzt lives his life as a force for good, because he escaped that world. Had he remained, he would have become a horror.

Given the way *D&D* is structured and the way drow have historically been portrayed, they are bound to a binary: A drow is like Drizzt and is a credit to their race, or they are a psychotic killer and an exemplar of their race. Either way, they are explicitly Other, not us, *them*, and probably not to be trusted, even if they seem acceptable by *our* standards. This fallacy dovetails with the colonial structure of the game—"discover" a place and despoil its inhabitants.

Gary Gygax says as much on the Dragonsfoot forum when discussing the behavior of the paladin, a Lawful Good holy warrior, "[...] as I have often noted, a paladin can freely dispatch prisoners of Evil alignment that have surrendered and renounced that alignment in favor of Lawful Good. They are then sent on to their reward before they can backslide." His post is punctuated by a laughing emoji. Later in the same thread, he says, "If the foes of these humanoids are so foolish as to accept surrender and allow their prisoners to eventually go free and perform further depredations, your 'Good' forces are really 'Stupid.'"

Fractal-like, this repeats through all of *D&D*, and many other RPGs. Whenever a "race" of Others, like orcs, goblins, or kobolds are labeled as inherently evil,

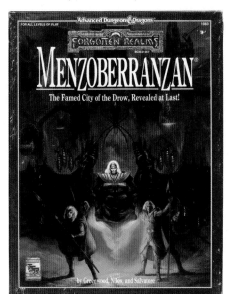

MENZOBERRANZAN, BOX SET, TSR, 1992
ED GREENWOOD, DOUGLAS NILES, AND R. A. SALVATORE, COVER BY JEFF EASLEY

players are given permission to harm them without consequence and, in doing so, malignant abstractions of real-world racism, prejudice, and oppression are overtly reinforced. Awareness of this cycle has grown in recent years, accompanied by attempts to change it.

The Fifth Edition of *Dungeons & Dragons* makes attempts to be more actively inclusive, but progress is slow and often seems to end with lip service. These problems of alignment regarding orcs and drow were a topic of serious discussion on Twitter in 2020, and Wizards of the Coast promised to address concerns in a "meaningful" way in *Tasha's Cauldron of Everything* (2020), a supplemental rulebook. That fix took up a single page in a 192-page book and amounts to some vague, optional rules about personal backgrounds.

As usual, prospects look more promising outside the bounds of the official *D&D* universe. Players have long had a habit of fixing *D&D* before the designers. Eugene Marshall's zine *Ancestry & Culture: An Alternative to Race in 5E* (2020) goes a long way in showcasing a solution by replacing the *D&D* concept of race with two concepts: Ancestry and Culture. Ancestry is largely aesthetic, determining basic appearance and defining the inherited traits of size, speed, age and any inborn special abilities, like the Dragonborn's breath weapon. Culture determines everything else—ability scores, alignment, and language—signifying the primacy of society over the vagaries of birth in shaping a character's lifestyle and beliefs. Wizards of the Coast should take note. And outside of *D&D* entirely, games like *Spire*, about drow revolutionaries battling their oppressors, radically re-imagine the dusty old paradigms.

Dark Sun (1991)

Spelljammer was the first high concept campaign setting for *Dungeons & Dragons*, asking "What if *D&D*, but in space?" Soon after, *Ravenloft: Realm of Terror* (1990) asked, "What if *D&D*, but with Universal monsters?" and let a single artist, Stephen Fabian, define the setting's aesthetic. I'm not clear on why—perhaps Fabian's work was too gloomy, or drew too clearly on visual elements, both gothic and macabre, that were already well established in the real-world—but *Realm of Terror* didn't capture imaginations based on aesthetics alone. Then, *Dark Sun* came along and tossed all of the traditional fantasy trappings in the trash.

Dark Sun's high concept question comes in several parts: "What if *D&D*, but heavier in tone, harsher, and colored, not just by elements from the dying earth sub-genre, but also by those straight out of a *Mad Max*-style post-apocalypse?" The art of fantasy illustrators Gerald Brom and Tom Baxa tie together this aesthetic-first high concept—not just visually! Unlike just about every *D&D* product that came before, with the possible exception of *Realm of Terror*, the art of Brom and Baxa distills and transmits the themes of the setting without players having to read a single word of the box set.

The art both poses and answers the high concept question and many of the minor questions that follow, unspoken, in its wake. Brom's paintings, many of which were composed before the details of the setting were decided, evoke an alien landscape that seems dry, harsh, and strangely sexy (when life is a struggle, passions burn hot and fetish-friendly, I suppose). Baxa's interiors add to this a jagged, mutated sensibility. Together, they fix the world of Athas as blasted, red, parched, sweaty, and hostile in the minds of players.

Athas is indeed a brutal place. Water is scarce, and the land has been drained of vitality through corrupt magic. Power is

DARK SUN, BOX SET, TSR, 1991
TIMOTHY B. BROWN AND TROY DENNING, COVER BY GERALD BROM

consolidated into the hands of a scattering of sorcerer-kings, each ruling their own city-state with an iron fist. Genocide has depopulated the world. Slavery is widespread. Contrasting with vanilla *D&D*, psionics are common, gods are absent, and arcane magic is a blight on the environment. In addition to *Mad Max 2: The Road Warrior* (1981), obvious inspirations for the setting include *Spartacus* (1960), *Dune* (1965), Edgar Rice Burroughs's John Carter of Mars stories (1911-1964), and Jack Vance's Dying Earth books (1950-1984).

Dark Sun is perhaps TSR's most obviously political product. Coming as it did in 1991, a year after activists brought the 20th anniversary of Earth Day to the international stage with a multi-million-dollar awareness campaign, it is difficult not to read the campaign setting as a grim warning (especially now, decades after the warning was largely ignored and extreme weather has become the disturbing norm).

The sorcerer-kings are remote despots who care only for their own comforts. Their subjects are entirely disposable, and wide swaths of them are systematically exploited to their deaths. Wild green spaces are unheard of (finding just one is a plot point in the metaplot novels). Most sorcerers literally suck the vitality out of the world. 30-years later, *Dark Sun* still feels relevant as a cautionary fable about unchecked power and a disregard for the environment.

To express the hazards of life on Athas mechanically, new characters start at level three and have at least one mental power. In a classic example of TSR extortion, a beige box on the back cover stresses that, "In order to explore the world of *Dark Sun* you must have a copy of the *Complete Psionics Handbook*."

Truly: Players can explore Athas just fine without it.

In addition to a higher level, attributes have a boost, rolling for a possible range from 8 to 20, instead of the usual 3 to 18, and with additional bonuses as well. New races and classes also add to the hardscrabble atmosphere.

Two races—the half-giants and the half human/half dwarf muls—are distasteful studies in fantasy eugenics, specially bred in the slave pits to provide efficient laborers in the case of the former and prized fighters for the arenas in the latter. The third, the fan-favorite thri-kreen, are mantis-people that bring a delightful dash of *Star Frontiers*-style alienness to the proceedings. Gladiators battle for the blood lust of the crowds; Defilers drain the land of life for their own magical power, and scheming Templars serve the mystic will of the sorcerer kings. *Dark Sun* is still *D&D*, but it's tweaked just enough that it also consistently lines up with the themes of the setting in ways that feel surprising. This alignment is satisfying to see in action and one of only a few times a heavily customized *D&D* works effectively. And, of course, thirst is just as deadly as monsters and politics on Athas, so all of

DUNE TRADER, TSR, 1992
ANTHONY PRYOR, COVER BY GERALD BROM

DRAGON KINGS, TSR, 1992

TIMOTHY B. BROWN, COVER BY GERALD BROM

those old, seemingly pointless rules for inhospitable environments finally have some use, too.

Dark Sun's initial adventure modules (one in the campaign box, then seven more individual releases across two separate story arcs) have a novel design innovation. Instead of the familiar booklet with all of the necessary details for the GM's eyes only, these are housed in a pair of spiral-bound flip books that can be stood up like an easel on the table. One contains the information needed to run the game; one is full of maps and illustrations of the action for the players to take in at the appropriate moment, which is very reminiscent of the art handouts from the S-series modules. They certainly provide space for numerous additional visuals, fulfilling one of TSR's central goals for the setting.

Those adventures are a prime part of *Dark Sun*'s metaplot. From the outset, the world is less a sandbox and more a series of carefully plotted set pieces. The box set represents a start state for the campaign world, and Troy Denning's five-novel series, the Prism Pentad, immediately upends that status quo with slave

rebellions, regicide, and the death of the setting's singular, corrupting dragon.

These same events provide the backdrop for the initial set of adventures. *Dark Sun* favors custom characters over pre-generated ones, but the trade-off is that, at least in the first few adventures, the characters are relegated to the role of janitors, making minor contributions to the great deeds of NPC heroes and generally tidying up loose ends. By the end of the arc, the players are free of the fetters of the novels, forging their own destinies into the second series, which culminates with an invasion from the astral plane by the githyanki (which, sure, why not?) in *Black Spine* (1994).

There were interesting ideas on the outskirts of the metaplot. *DSR2: Dune Trader* (1992) introduced an entire new class and reimagined the campaign setting as one ripe to explore the triumphs and tragedies of a mercantile existence. Sadly, the idea received no support outside of this one book. More ambitious is *Dragon Kings* (1992), a hardcover rules expansion that takes characters through level 30.

Early in its development, *Dark Sun* was called War World, and it is easy to see how these high-powered options might have carried over from that earlier version of the setting. There are creepy war machines made out of giant undead beetles and rules for mass combat (yet another example of TSR trying, and failing, to weasel the *Battlesystem* wargame rules into *D&D*). Perhaps most central to the campaign setting, it details the process by which a Defiler wizard can transform into the ecosystem-destroying Athasian version of a dragon (or, the angelic, life-fostering avangion, for Preservers). Unfortunately, like the merchants of *Dune Trader*, these ideas received no further support.

By 1995, the metaplot was scattered all over the place, and the setting kept becoming more sci-fi in character, so TSR issued a revised and expanded box set to reel it all in. Hitting the reset button derailed the train. Longtime fans didn't cotton to the new version, and TSR abruptly shut down in 1996. In 2010, the setting was revived for the Fourth Edition of *D&D* and was even the setting of a two-year living campaign, Ashes of Athas. Periodically, rumors swirl about a revival for the current Fifth Edition, but for now, it seems the sun has set on one of *D&D*'s harshest campaign settings.

Amber (1991)

Roger Zelazny's *Chronicles of Amber* (1970-1991) is a series of ten novels that pitch genre out the window. The first few chapters of the first novel read like Dashiell Hammett, but the whodunnit soon gives way to swords and spells, weird technology, and psychedelic swirls of parallel realities. Yet, even when manticores and demons take center stage, a hint of the hardboiled remains in the air, thanks to the labyrinthine plots laid out over the course of the saga.

The cycle came out in two, five-book phases. The first ran from 1970 through 1978 and features Corwin in his quest to claim his late father's throne. The second series ran from 1985 through 1991 and features Corwin's son, Merlin, as he comes into his own as a Prince of Chaos. As delightful as the fast-paced, intricate story is, the game focuses primarily on the fiction's unique setting.

Amber, the only real city, is situated at the top of existence, both fundament and firmament. At the bottom is Chaos, constant, roiling, diabolical change. Between the two, an infinity of other worlds exist, all of which are shadows cast by Amber itself, a Poisonville projected through a prism and splashing all across the vast multiverse. Our Earth, where large swaths of the action take place, is one of these shadows.

The royal family of Amber are reality-bending, semi-immortal sorcerers (as are members of the Courts of Chaos), who

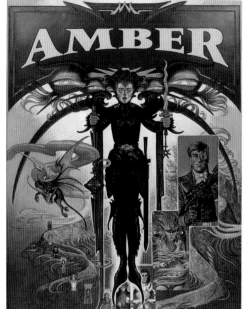

can travel through Shadow, manipulating it and taking advantage of time differentials to master skills and weave elaborate, murderous plots. Over the course of the series, all manner of things wind up at stake—lives, legacies, thrones, magical power, sanity, the fate of all realities—with various family members arrayed in equally varied and ever-changing allegiances around them.

Eric Wujcik, designer of *Teenage Mutant Ninja Turtles & Other Strangeness*, founded Phage Press specifically to develop an RPG based on the Amber novels. In an effort to make the game as grand and audacious as the fiction it was based on, he made a bold design decision: As it says right on the tin, *Amber Diceless Role-playing* doesn't use dice, or any other randomizer.

Amber aims to simulate the fiction as closely as possible. In this, fellow players are both friends and foes, in turn, and often simultaneously. It is one of very few RPGs that not only assumes players will battle others players, but also arranges the entire game around that competition. From the very start, at character creation, the knives are out.

Characters are made of just four attributes—Psyche, Strength, Endurance,

SHADOW KNIGHT, PHAGE PRESS, 1993
ERICK WUJCIK, COVER BY MICHAEL KUCHARSKI

and Warfare—the values of which are purchased in auction, using a pool of 100 points. Yet, purchases are complicated by a variety of factors. For one, unlike other auctions, points aren't refunded for a losing bid, and for another, attributes are ranked.

In the books, Corwin often speaks of his many siblings in terms of absolutes: Benedict is the best general, Gerard the strongest, and Fiona the most powerful sorcerer. In games terms, this means that the character with the top ranking will always defeat the lower ranking characters in a fair contest, with the gap between the scores signifying how long the contest lasts—big gap, quick contest. These absolutes make the auction system a prolonged, treacherous affair, with players jockeying, blustering, making deals, and otherwise trying to manipulate their way to their preferred outcome. It is unlikely that everyone gets what they want, but highly likely that rivalries will form, and grudges will be nursed. In this way, players make characters, but also organically simulate, after a fashion, their long history of scheming against each other before play even begins.

Once the public auction is finished, any surplus of points can be spent in private. Attributes can secretly be raised (though only to the level of an existing rank—they can't exceed the top rank, and, even if they did, purchased attributes are always a little less reliable than ones gained in auction). Special powers and equipment, like swords and armor and magic bits, are also on the market, as are allies (steeds, valued retainers) and custom-made realms in Shadow where a character may securely brood and plot. There are no skills—Amberites can master any skill seemingly overnight by practicing it in the right region of Shadow, thanks to time differentials (time passes faster the further one moves from Amber).

Taking all of these factors into account, the shape of the game starts to become clear. While the attributes determine a clear victor in a fair contest, the point of *Amber* is never to do battle on even ground. If a player is sure to lose a contest of Strength, they need to go to great lengths to change it to a contest of Endurance—stack the deck, devise treacherous diversions, forge alliances with brethren, and betray them when they are at their weakest. The very fabric of reality is at the players' beck and call in *Amber*—success lies in exploiting it to the fullest.

With everyone at the table playing the same devious, high-stakes game, uncertainty comes from the unpredictable actions of fellow players. In the face of that, dice seem less than trifling.

There hasn't been an RPG quite like *Amber*, before or since. Bold though it was, the game didn't do very well commercially. The lack of dice became a flashpoint of controversy, with dice enthusiasts dramatically swearing off the game. That's a bit ridiculous, but it does get at a key hurdle *Amber* faced: People *like* rolling dice. They've been doing it for thousands of years and a significant part of the appeal of RPGs is giving dice, often in sparkly colors, a toss.

Phage published just one other book for the system, *Shadow Knight* (1993), which expanded the rules to cover material in the Merlin-centric novels. There was also a magazine—*Amberzine*—which ran intermittently, accumulating 15 issues from 1992 to 2005. Despite this spotty support, *Amber* developed a devoted following; thanks to its hardboiled heart and the focus on interpersonal interaction, it was a natural fit for live-action players. Annual *Amber*-centric conventions continue to the present day.

Dice aficionados needn't have worried—the future of RPGs wasn't diceless. Still, *Amber* was an important, experimental step in character-focused, narratively creative game design that opened many doors for future indie and storytelling game designs. At the end of the decade, another important game, *Nobilis*, would opt to forgo dice entirely, while others, like *Everway*, would use cards as optional randomizers, and more games would try unusual methods of resolution after the turn of the millennium.

Kult (1991)

A repeating motif in '90s RPGs is the notion that there are two versions of reality. The first is the one we all perceive day-to-day and generally take for granted. The other reality is secret, or hidden, and somehow deeper, or more *true*. This phenomenon wasn't unique to RPGs—it's at the core of *Twin Peaks* (1990-1991, 2017) and *The X-Files* (1993-2002, 2016-2018), two of the decade's defining television shows, and perhaps achieved its clearest expression on the big screen in *The Matrix* (1999).

Call of Cthulhu was the first RPG to play with the idea, and it comes up again and again—*Nightlife*, *Vampire: The Masquer-*

Kult, First English Edition, Metropolis Ltd., 1993 Gunilla Jonsson and Michael Peterén. Cover by Peter Andrew Jones

ade, *Over the Edge*, *Underground*, *Planescape*, *Delta Green*, *In Nomine*, *Unknown Armies*, and *Nobilis* all place players in the role of characters who somehow have the inside scoop on existence. I could even argue that *Torg* and *Rifts*, with their intruding, overwriting realities, depict worlds in which the secret has been explosively made manifest. As the millennium approached, American society collectively braced for grand revelations and transmitted our anxieties about how the paradigms might shift to popular culture.

None of those games commit to the bit quite so thoroughly as *Kult*. Here, reality is an illusion maintained by the Demiurge, a sort of false creator entity, to keep humanity from realizing its own inherent divinity. Perceived reality is, essentially, a prison (a concept that will be familiar to students of Gnosticism or fans of Philip K. Dick's *VALIS*, 1981).

The Demiurge disappeared under unknown circumstances at the end of the nineteenth century, and the entity's illusion has begun to unravel. That doesn't afford the opportunity of a great escape, however. Unlike *The Matrix* or *VALIS*, both of which position their enlightened characters as shepherds who will lead the rest of humanity out of bondage, there are no greater purposes in *Kult*, just desperate survival in the face of ever more existential precariousness. Beyond the comfortable illusion is the Metropolis, the ruined ur-city that contains all other cities, the fires of Inferno, and a host of entities that want to bring an end to all of creation.

Kult is, after all, a horror game. In this vein, it takes its cues from Clive Barker (*The Hellbound Heart*, 1986, is obvious—the rulebook even makes clear references to the Lament Configuration—and *The Great and Secret Show*, 1989, seems likely), and perhaps, the *Hellblazer* (1988-2013) comic series. There are deep veins of bleakness and misanthropy mined here. As with many other '90s RPGs, *Kult* strives to tackle mature themes, but often feels lurid, shocking for the sake of shock. Despite this sensationalism, there is a surprising lack of moral judgment about the paths characters take to enlightenment.

Much of this philosophical journey plays out in the mental balance mechanic. *Kult* is derived from Chaosium's *Basic Role-Playing*, so mental balance is the game's answer to a sanity mechanic. A value of zero represents a regular person, centered and stable. Advantages purchased in character creation (like a sixth sense) and positive in-game events (adopting a puppy, say) add points, increasing stability. Disadvantages (anything from being a rationalist to having phobias), negative events (a death in the family), or encounters with the supernatural, subtract points, decreasing stability. Characters with high values in either direction (+/-25) appear strange to their "normal" neighbors and with good reason: They're on the path to Awakening, or reclaiming their lost divinity. At +/-100, the character's shadow gains autonomy and attempts to halt their progress! At +/-500, the character transcends, but the

process is grueling; the path so long that it is much more likely the character will be consumed by their appetites and ambitions (or murdered by their shadow) long before they reach their destination.

This frailty is partly a reflection of the fact that the world of *Kult* is dangerous, but also partly because characters are vulnerable by design. Most come from a lower social stratum—criminals, starving artists, cops, reporters, drifters. Beyond that, the characters all harbor sordid secrets that range from enduring supernatural curses to being the subject of medical experimentation to being possessed by a demon. These secrets taint the characters and, most likely, provide the means for their eventual destruction.

Unsurprisingly, the original Swedish edition of *Kult* proved controversial, with the game being spuriously connected to several cases of murder and suicide. These rumors spurred a broad anxiety in the country about RPGs and their appropriateness for children. Considering that Sweden is currently a hotbed for cutting edge game design, that anxiety must not have amounted to much.

Kult was imported to the US in 1993 by Metropolis Ltd., a company co-founded by Terry K. Amthor (one of Iron Crown Enterprise's co-founders and one of the first openly gay creators in the hobby) specifically to produce an English language version of the game. On the back cover is a warning, explaining that some might find the game disturbing and that it isn't recommended for players under the age of 16, a clever bit of marketing copy that likely increased the game's appeal in the eyes of 14- and 15-year-olds.

Over the Edge (1992)

Where *Kult* is most often mentioned in the same breath as Clive Barker, *Over the Edge* seems inextricably tied to William S. Burroughs, particularly his novel *Naked Lunch* (1959) and Cronenberg's film adaptation (1991). Like many '90s RPGs, it is preoccupied with conspiracies, and its attempts at tackling mature subject matter are evenly split between thought-provoking and sophomoric. It advertises edginess right there in the title, but the transgressions found within come from a starting point of perplexing naiveté. The game is not without its charms, however.

Mechanically, *Over the Edge* springs, surprisingly, from *Star Wars: The Roleplaying Game*. After moving on from *Ars Magica*, Jonathan Tweet and Mark Rein-Hagen were both inspired by the dice pools in *Star Wars*. Rein-Hagen was further inspired by *Shadowrun*'s comparative mechanics and came up with *Vampire: The Masquerade*. Tweet stuck with the additive dice pool, and *Over the Edge* was born. Roll the number of dice, add them together, and compare the total to a target number to see if a test succeeds or fails.

Instead of laying out an exhaustive skill system, characters are made out of keywords (or short phrases) that describe the character; one primary (which rolls four dice), two secondary (which roll three), and a flaw (which subtracts a die from the pool whenever it applies). Keywords are freeform and made up by the player, with their applications implied rather than made explicit. So, a character with the primary keyword "pit fighter" and the secondary keywords "tough" and "philosophical" already creates a vivid picture of the character.

Using those keywords is a matter of arguing the plausibility of their appropriateness to a situation in order to take advantage of their additional dice (a baseline proficiency is assumed in most tasks, giving players two dice to roll when their keywords don't apply). Thus, the broad umbrella of skills implied by the term "pit fighter" likely includes all manner of violence, but it would be a stretch to argue that umbrella could be used to drive like a professional in a car chase. There is a great deal of untapped potential in these

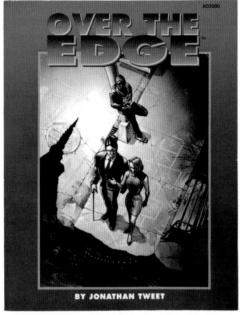

OVER THE EDGE, ATLAS GAMES, 1992
JONATHAN TWEET AND ROBIN D. LAWS, COVER BY DOUG SHULER

keywords, which other designers would mine, in time, including *Over the Edge* co-designer Robin Laws, who would develop the concept further for his *Hero Wars/ HeroQuest* system.

The system is designed to fade into the background and facilitate freewheeling play, a feature that, no doubt, inspired indie game designers in the next decade. The setting, with all of its hooks and suggested mysteries, is the main attraction, less as a place to explore and more as a venue to inflict that system upon, like a firing range or a tropical atoll.

Players are let loose on a small Mediterranean island called Al Amarja, particularly its main city, a cosmopolitan metaphor called The Edge. It is an exotic place, repeatedly conquered and colonized until its original culture and creeds have largely melted away. Replacing them is an enthusiasm for plots, debauchery, violence, and all manner of weirdness. On Al Amarja, rock stars are worshipped with religious fervor, Satanists lurk everywhere, used nooses are favored fashion accessories, and secrets seethe under the surface. It aims to recreate certain aspects of Tangier, Morocco, as described by Burroughs—libertine and brimming with drugs—as well as Interzone, its drug-addled, looking glass version, a nightmare place of secret agents, indiscriminate murder, and bizarre narcotics. There is also a touch of Philip K. Dick in Al Amarja, as well as Robert Anton Wilson's *The Illuminatus! Trilogy* (1975).

Unlike its counter-cultural inspirations, though, Al Amarja feels strangely safe (compared to, say, the Blue City of *Lacuna Part I. (second attempt)*, 2011, which feels wildly dangerous with just a fraction of the pages and detail). There is plenty to do and plenty of clues to gather for a variety of potential plots, teased through the book's GM section, but those mysteries often don't amount to much or are guiltlessly discarded. In fact, play often mirrors the cut-up technique Burroughs popularized, with game narratives becoming a collection of vignettes, shifting priorities (and venues), as dictated by the whimsies of the players at the table.

If conspiracies are *everywhere*, it doesn't matter how a GM rearranges the intertwining tendrils. Naiveté adds to this ungrounded feeling. There is just one nightclub in all of The Edge, and it is a mobbed-up jazz joint done up in art deco trappings. Where are the throbbing discos and the dank rock clubs? References to casual drug use abound but with little apparent understanding of the reasons that drugs (and alcohol abuse) often fuel nightlife and counterculture, nor is much made of their consequences.

In *Naked Lunch*, junkies seek out the Black Meat, a noxious substance ground from the flesh of giant aquatic centipedes that leaves its devotees in a rapture of vomitous delirium. There are giant black centipedes on the cover of *Over the Edge*, but nothing so horrific as the Black Meat lurks in its pages. With the exception of a strip club and a brothel (both catering to straight men), Al Amarja is also nearly sexless (a noticeable absence in the game's cousin, *Vampire: The Masquerade*, as well—despite the long association between vampires and voracious sexual appetites, the *Vampire* rulebook explicitly states their bloodsuckers have zero sex drive). There is no mention of fetishes of any sort or even nods to musical subcultures, like punk and goth, which are common in other '90s RPGs. Displays of queerness are also absent, despite queerness saturating Burroughs's literary work. For an island that professes to be so interested in excess and freedom from conventionality, the details all seems oddly square.

Fudge (1992)

Before *FUDGE* there was *SLUG*.

Steffan O'Sullivan posted on the rec.games.design newsgroup on November 17, 1992, asking if anyone wanted to help him design what he called a "freeform RPG." The post laid out a series of design requirements:

> A loose character creation system that can be as brief or detailed as the player wants. [...] A single, easy to remember, non-chart-bound game mechanic to handle all actions that need resolution, including combat. [...] A way to incorporate supernormal abilities (magic, psi, cyber, etc.) without unbalancing the game. [...] A smooth and logical way for the character to grow in experience.

Then O'Sullivan (who had previously written four *GURPS* books, like the adaptation of *Bunnies & Burrows*) laid out the rough rules for a game that meets those requirements, which he dubbed *SLUG* (*Simple, Laid-back Universal Game*).

Folks jumped in to help, and *SLUG* quickly became *FUDGE* (*Freeform Universal Donated Gaming Engine*). This collaboration is a landmark moment. For one, this is the first time an RPG was developed by a public community on the internet—the credits list 24 primary contributors beside O'Sullivan. Because of its digital conception, *FUDGE* is also one of the first RPGs to be distributed for sale digitally; Grey Ghost sold copies of the rules on disk. Another involves that word "donated" in the name—the idea was to release the basic version of *FUDGE* for free on the internet, forever, and this plan has remained true even though print and PDF versions have since been made available commercially. Even more of a crystal ball, the game also comes with an early sort of open-source license, nearly a decade before Creative Commons or the Open Gaming License, which allows other creators to make and publish derivative works so long as certain conditions are met.

FUDGE next became the *Freeform Universal Do-it-yourself Gaming Engine*, then dropped the acronym entirely to become, simply, *Fudge*, as in: "Just fudge it," a philosophical cornerstone of a game that encourages players to let the rules take a backseat to the story.

But what the heck *is* it? *Fudge* is less an RPG system than it is a toolkit for creating your own RPG system. The players and GM collaborate to hash out which attributes define a character, how to organize skills, which special abilities to use— every facet of the game is modular and adjustable, allowing players to dial in the exact level of complexity they desire. Some complexity can even vary from player to player, depending on preference. This modularity is a big shift from what players were used to, and it proved to involve a whole lot more work for something that ultimately aims to be light system.

Even the loosest RPGs to this point were full of constraints (that characters have some sort of health gage, like hit points, or that they have numerical attributes at all), many of which players had internalized so thoroughly that they no longer felt the fetter. The wide-open freedom *Fudge* offers can be paralyzing, like climbing out of a dark crawlspace only to emerge in the blazing sunlight at the top of a tall tower without a railing in sight. It

FUDGE, SECOND EDITION, GREY GHOST PRESS, 1995
STEFFAN O'SULLIVAN, COVER BY JEFF KOKE

also requires a great deal of trust between the players—the rulebook never tells the player "no," so topics like power limits need to be set through group consensus.

The only elements of *Fudge* that aren't optional are the adjectives and the dice. Echoes of FASERIP, all of the skills and attributes and powers in the game are rated on a seven-level ascending scale of adjectives: Terrible, Poor, Mediocre, Fair, Good, Great, and Superb (though even this array isn't set in stone—GMs can add more adjectives to the scale to make a more complex system and remove them for a higher-powered game). Challenges and tasks are rated on the same scale. A character might have the climb skill or the dexterity attribute rated at Good, but if the GM says climbing the sheer cliff face is a Great challenge, the character is sunk, right? Nope, that's where the dice come in.

Fudge uses a set of four custom 6-sided dice. Each die has two blank faces, which change nothing, two faces with minus signs, which lower a rating, and two faces with plus signs, which raise it. To test a skill, a player rolls all four dice. In the case of my climbing example, a roll of two pluses, a minus, and a blank would move the character from Good to Great and scampering up the cliff, while a plus, a minus, and two blanks would mean they'd have to find another way up. *Fudge*'s core resolution is fast, easy, and scales to everything. And if someone doesn't want to buy the custom dice, they can do it with regular 6-siders (1-2 is a minus, 3-4 is a blank, 5-6 is a plus), or cards and coins can be used, or the game can be played completely diceless—guidance for those options are all in the book.

Most folks didn't see it at the time, but *FUDGE* marks a fundamental change in RPGs. Simultaneously a system of rules and a treatise on game design theory, it questions many of the methods and mechanics that are taken for granted about roleplaying and reshapes those assumptions, paving the way for other games to continue pushing into new forms in the coming decades. Not the least of which is *Fate*, a refined version of *Fudge* that further spotlights roleplaying and collaborative storytelling while reducing the role of dice.

Earthdawn (1993)

There is a series of RPGs that feel both strange and plausible, thanks to their relentless commitment to adding ever more detail to the setting. First comes *Skyrealms of Jorune* then *Talislanta*. *Earthdawn* feels like the culmination. Further, *Earthdawn* marshals those details to reimagine fantasy stereotypes while also providing reasonable explanations for odd player behaviors and other elements most games take for granted, like the existence of dungeons.

Earthdawn takes place in Barsaive, a region of a prehistorical alternate earth that roughly lines up with what is now the Pripyat region of Ukraine, complete with a horrible place called the Blood Wood that corresponds to Chernobyl's zone of alienation. There is powerful magic here, but it is cyclical. The tides of magic come in, allowing for wonders but also opening the doorway for Horrors, vast supernatural entities that ravage the land. The world has just endured a high-water mark, the Scourge: 400 years in which Horrors stalked the surface, and mortals fled to subterranean cities for their survival. Players emerge from underground as the tide goes out, sweeping away most of the Horrors and revealing a new, ruined landscape to explore. While many of the underground settlements reemerged to form a network of vibrant, independent city-states, not all survived. Those broken refuges, cracked open like oysters, are the dungeons—within are treasures and dangers to discover in turn.

Or perhaps, one might even find a left-over Horror. Not all of them vanished with the downturn of magic, and they represent a unique challenge in the world of *Earthdawn*. Casting a spell incorrectly or discovering a particular artifact might attract their attention. Even talking about them or just *thinking* about them can bring them forth. They can mark a character, haunting and hunting them for obscure reasons, and once a character's been noticed, killing the Horror is the only solution. That's no easy feat.

There are plenty of conventional dangers, as well. Factions and conspiracies are thick underfoot—everyone has an angle to play. There is very little here that is predictable—every step players take in navigating the world leads to surprises. For instance, humans are a minority. The Scourge greatly diminished the human empire of Thera, which is a better fate than they deserve since they're a rotten bunch of slavers. The power vacuum they left in Barsaive was filled by the dwarves, perhaps because the elves now spend all of their time bleeding and screaming. Meanwhile, trolls have air ships. There are lizard people and rock people and tiny fairies; everyone has magic; the entities that pass for gods are petty and often insane.

With this mix of fantasy, cosmic horror, and the post-apocalyptic, *Earthdawn* is another '90s RPG that freely mixes genres. It comes by it honestly, though: The setting was envisioned as a sort of bookend to the near future world of *Shadowrun*, the original genre-mixing RPG, and shares many of that game's approaches to magic and fantasy races.

Surprisingly, though, it doesn't share *Shadowrun*'s varied approaches to system. *Earthdawn* is much more unified, with all characters Adepts who use a magical discipline called Thread Weaving to access special abilities tied to their class (so, an Illusionist uses Threads to cast their spells, while a Sword Master engages them to perform unbelievable feats with their blade). Threads are also used to attune characters to magical items, which, unlike most RPGs, are all unique and grow in power over time, use, and research (compare this to *Dungeons & Dragons* or *RuneQuest*, where a large percentage of enchanted equipment is generic and static). Tasks are all resolved using a unique, "stepped" dice pool—in brief, the various skill levels, "steps," correspond to different combinations of dice that, when rolled, have a 50-percent chance of resulting in the value of the skill or higher. While every player is using what amounts to the same core mechanic, the applications vary from character to character, and from action to action, with the large-scale manipulation of the Patterns woven from Threads becoming proportionally complex to resolve.

Though cumbersome, Threads bind the game to the setting, echoing *RuneQuest*'s portrayal of a world in which magic is common and everyone can access it, to some degree. While most RPG systems are geared toward instilling a sense of adventure, the majority of *Earthdawn* seems configured to convey a sense of place and culture. There are the miles of written lore, of course, but so much is accomplished with the art. That is true of RPGs, in general, but especially

EARTHDAWN, FASA CORPORATION, 1993
GREG GORDEN, COVER BY RICK BERRY

so here. The duty roster is a long one and shares many of *Shadowrun*'s key artists, like Janet Aulisio, Jim Nelson, Rick Berry, and Jeff Laubenstein, who also acted as the art director. Most of the illustrations are portraits, and none seem generic. I find it impossible to look at them and not start building my own narrative around them. Aulisio, an enigmatic figure who largely vanished from the industry later in the decade, delivers some sublime work for the setting. In previous games, her work is characterized by deep shadow. This is true here, but she also showcases an astounding sense of color and pattern—her portrait of the Obsidiman merchant, in striped pants and patterned textiles, lounging against a mosaic wall, in many ways, sums up the complex visual language of the entire line.

In a fantasy world, one of the most difficult tasks is conveying that sense of the fantastic. The design of *Earthdawn*, through its careful presentation in both art and text, gives players the necessary details to bring to life a world of wonders as easily as they might conjure a game set in the real-world. Once there, players can go forth and forge their own legends.

Underground (1993)

The obvious influences of Mayfair Games' satirical, ultra-political RPG *Underground* give potential players a fair idea of what they're getting into: There are comic books, particularly Pat Mills's *Marshal Law* and Alan Moore's *Miracleman*; there are the social upheavals of the time, like the Los Angeles riots of 1992; there's the cult classic animation of *Aeon Flux*; and don't forget the music of Public Enemy and Rage Against the Machine.

Artists Geoff Darrow, Peter Chung (creator of *Aeon Flux*, fancy that), and more depict a world that is demonstrably violent and awful. The year is 2021, and everything is completely *fucked*. President Daryl Gates and Vice President Rush Limbaugh of the Plutocrat party have just left office. Scientologists have turned Germany into a theocracy. South America is the wasteland battlefield for countless wars perpetrated by corporations (the Cola Wars are literal wars in *Underground*).

This is where the players come in. The corporations use technology salvaged from a crashed UFO (and its dead alien crew) to give their soldiers low-level super powers. However, this genetic modification results in serious psychological

UNDERGROUND, MAYFAIR GAMES, 1993
RAY WINNINGER, COVER BY GEOFF DARROW

strain, so the corporations develop a superhero comics-themed virtual reality environment called Dreamland, which eases the psychosis of the subjects while programming them to kill.

With the wars over, the soldiers have returned to a society that neither wants nor trusts them (just like Vietnam). Players take the role of these deprogrammed, psychologically fragile, superhero-themed veterans, and try to find their way in a society on the brink. Some don't fare well, becoming criminals, murderers, psychopaths, cannibals, and politicians. For others, the black-and-white morality imparted by living in a simulacrum of the golden age of superheroes leads to a kind of clarity: The world is bad because those in power are villains, and someone needs to stop them.

Satire is easy to misread. Off the top, about a third of *Underground* hits sour notes, born largely out of the conflation of shock value with the perception of maturity and a conscious desire to cut against the omnipresent notion of political correctness, a very '90s-era pitfall. The world of *Underground* is legitimately horrible in just about every way. It was terrible when I read the book in 1993, but in 2021, it feels eerily prescient in many ways, a collage of *Onion* headlines mutating and taking on a life of their own—over the top, yes, but still holding up an unnerving mirror.

The game's saving grace is in its encouragement of players to be more than nihilistic cyberpunk assholes. Rather, the world of *Underground* is unrelentingly awful, specifically to get a reaction out of players. They're supposed to get so upset about something, anything, in the fictional world that they focus the purpose of their character's existence on changing it, usually by blowing stuff up, which feels uncomfortably close to domestic terrorism—*Underground* is far from perfect! The depiction of mental illness and the effects of trauma as vectors for ultraviolence are insensitive and largely incorrect, and, while much is also said about class, little is said about race, reinforcing a common blind spot in the cyberpunk of the '80s and '90s. Pitfalls aside, something about the angry spirit of the book seems dead on about the future of society.

Underground uses a modified version of the Mayfair Exponential Games System, also known as MEGS, a logarithmic system that served as the backbone of the *DC Heroes* RPG (1985). As with TSR's *Marvel Super Heroes*, the system was designed to allow characters with a wide range of power levels to interact without the "normals" getting smeared. It's a system that requires a rearranging of brain synapses, but once a player gets it, it's kind of genius.

It uses a sliding benchmark scale, where each value of units is equivalent to a variety of stuff. One unit is 125 pounds, 12 feet, five seconds, 64 cubic feet; four units is double that: 250 pounds, 24 feet, etc. Because players have all of these equivalencies, they can add and subtract units related to different categories in order to obtain meaningful results. For example: Say a character with a Strength of 25 wants to throw a car that weighs 15 units (a ton and a half). Subtract 15 from 25, and apply the ten leftover units to distance—about 100 feet. The scale can be applied in all sorts of interesting ways. Neat, right? I am, by no means, a math person and writing these sentences hurts my head a little bit, but I have to admit, understanding it feels like I now know magic.

While MEGS powers most of the play, the real interesting system in *Underground* is Parameters. Parameters are seven attributes that define groups and locales at a glance—Wealth, Safety, Government Purity, Quality of Life, Education, Necessities, and Take-Home Pay—each valued between one and 20, with values above 15 indicating social stability.

Locations scale, so a GM can devise Parameters for a city, a neighborhood, a high-rise, a corporation, a government department, or a decentralized social group. The Parameters are also the means by which the characters can effect change in the world—just move the Parameters to the goal numbers set by the GM. To do this, players spend reward points (earned, like experience points, at the end of scenarios), as required by the size of the group or location—a neighborhood requires 20 reward points to move a Parameter a single point, but altering the status quo on the state or national level requires far more. In addition, there needs to be a narrative justification. If the players are trying to stop a developer from bulldozing a commune, they need to do something in the world that represents a change in the mechanical abstraction, like throwing the corrupt official from the permitting office out of a window in order to raise the Government Purity value by one. In this way, the changes the players wish to make inspire the actions of their characters and provide the framework for the game's scenarios.

There are two complications: Because nothing happens in a vacuum, for every Parameter raised, one other Parameter goes up, and another goes down in set and predictable ways; every corrupt permitting person that a player throws out of a window is going to raise Government

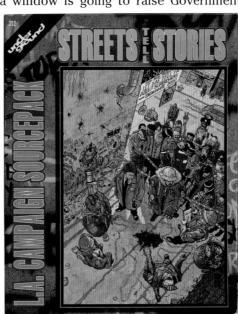

STREETS TELL STORIES, BOX SET, MAYFAIR GAMES, 1993 CHRISTOPHER KUBASIK AND RAY WINNINGER. COVER BY COREY BARBA

Purity *and* Take-Home Pay while decreasing Safety. Second, reward points are also used to improve a character, so players are explicitly putting the needs of the community before their own.

The potential of the Parameters system is on full display in *Streets Tell Stories* (1993), the Los Angeles campaign setting box set. Inside, players get a neighborhood-by-neighborhood breakdown of the Greater Los Angeles area; this is a helicopter's eye view—it communicates the character of the neighborhood, how it fits with the rest of the city, and leaves plenty of room for players to incorporate their own individual ideas. The central concept is that all of the player characters live in, protect, and generally look to improve their home neighborhood. For all of the poor taste, wobbly satire, and ultraviolence in *Underground*, I can't think of another RPG with a system so explicitly focused on making the world a better place, one block at a time.

Once Upon a Time (1994)

In 1993, Wizards of the Coast released the first collectible card game (CCG), Richard Garfield's *Magic: The Gathering*. CCGs are deck-building games—a player begins with a standardized starter deck and add to it with booster packs of randomized cards, tweaking the effectiveness of a given deck to align with different strategies. *Magic* is styled as a game of arcane duels—players take the role of powerful sorcerers called Planewalkers, summoning creatures and marshaling cosmic energies to combat an opponent.

It was an instant success, selling out its entire stock by the end of the year; by the end of 1994, the game sold over a billion cards, and through 2016, that number grew to 20 billion. RPG publishers took notice of the game's fantasy trappings, its hinting approach to the lore of its universe, and, mostly, its runaway financial success.

Seeking to capitalize on the fact that Wizards of the Coast couldn't meet demand, competing CCGs flooded the market. 1994 saw the release of the *Dungeons & Dragons*-themed *Spellfire*; Wizards of the Coast licensed *Vampire: The Masquerade* for *Jyhad* (which they later renamed *Vampire: The Eternal Struggle,* to distance it from the Arabic word and its connotations) and developed one based on *Over the Edge*. CCGs based on *Kult* and *Middle-earth Role Playing* followed in 1995. Chaosium was late to the party in 1996 with the *Call of Cthulhu*-themed *Mythos*. Dozens more—based on TV shows, videogames, movies, comic books, and original concepts—poured in besides.

At the same time, a handful of games experimented in using cards in different ways, replacing or supplementing dice-based randomization with them, or using them to tell a story. *Once Upon a Time*, which debuted at the same GenCon as *Magic: The Gathering*, isn't an RPG, but looking back nearly 30-years later across a landscape now dotted with storytelling RPGs, it is difficult not to view *Once Upon a Time* as one of their earliest progenitors.

James Wallis, who joined the project as a designer after Richard Lambert came up with the concept of *Once Upon a Time*, and Andrew Rilstone made it into something playable, believes it's an important touchstone for storytelling in games. "It hasn't created a genre of storytelling card games as such," he says. "I think its influence is more about demonstrating that story and gameplay don't have to work on separate levels [...] that characters and theme aren't just something to be pasted on top of some mechanics, and creating a story is as satisfying as playing through a pre-written one."

The idea of the game is to collaborate to tell a fairy tale. Each player is dealt a hand of cards containing story elements that the player discards once they incorporate them into their narrative. These are things, like wolves, princesses, and stepmothers—the stuff of fairy tales. They also get a secret Happily Ever After card, which describes the ending a player is driving toward. Once out of cards, players conclude with that ending and win the game. There are, of course, complications. Hesitating, or just plain running out of inspiration, means drawing a card and passing the narrative off to the next player. Control of the story can be stolen, as well—mention something that appears on a card in another player's hand, and they can play it to hijack the tale. Finally, the overall thrust of the story has to make sense, as decided by the consensus of the other players.

And, that's it! The game is straightforward, charming, plays fast, and, because almost everyone is familiar with fairy tales, it is welcoming to players of all experience levels. The improvisation required by some later storytelling games can result in something akin to stage fright—this was an issue for players of *The Extraordinary Adventures of Baron Munchausen*, a direct descendant of *Once Upon a Time*, and the problem crops up again and again. Here, though, the cards mitigate storytelling paralysis by guiding players to the words they need to use.

Familiarity with the game adds strategic complexity, as well—a player can fake out their opponents once they know the different Happily Ever After endings, and they can try to weave their story around the prompt cards they can remember. That'll serve them in two ways: It will prevent their story from being hijacked by another player, and it will lead to the telling of ever more strange and entertaining stories. Then, everybody wins.

Planescape (1994)

In systematizing everything, *Dungeons & Dragons* accidentally stumbled into some complex metaphysical questions. In the context of the game, the behavior of mortals isn't just a matrix of impulse and need, it is naturally *aligned* to one of nine polarities—Lawful Neutral, Neutral Good, Chaotic Evil, and all of the other possible combinations. Those alignments have corresponding harmonies, in the world, in magic, in the divine. A whole cosmology springs from them: As above, so below.

This multiverse is the Great Wheel, first presented in *The Dragon* (July, 1977) and expanded upon in increasing detail in the *Players Handbook*, *Deities & Demigods*, and, exhaustively, in *Manual of the Planes* (1987). Inspired, in part, by the shifting realities of Roger Zelazny's *Amber* novels, the Great Wheel accounts for all of the known energies and spiritual forces in creation, arranging them into a unified, clock-like scheme reminiscent of an orrery, those gilded contraptions of gears and gemstones that model the scale and movements of our solar system.

Taking the form of a series of concentric circles, in the very center is the Material Plane of mundane existence, as well as all of the parallel realities that cascade out of every path not taken. Surrounding that is the Ethereal Plane, a sort of membrane that connects the Material with the elemental planes, the sources of primal elemental energy, like Fire and Water.

PLANESCAPE CAMPAIGN SETTING, Box set, TSR, 1994
David "Zeb" Cook, Cover by Robh Ruppel

Similarly, the silvery void of the Astral Plane connects the Material to the Outer Planes—the Nine Hells, Elysium, Pandemonium, and on—that house divinities, afterlives, and the raw powers of belief.

Manual of the Planes establishes that all of these realms are inhabited and can be visited by mortals who are powerful enough or clever enough to navigate the magical portals between the worlds. That book, however, reads like a particularly heady set of stereo instructions, so while it was clear players *could* travel the planes, it remained difficult to imagine why they would want to and just what they'd find there if they did. Nearly a decade later, *Planescape* provides those answers.

In *Planescape*, players live and adventure among the infinite planes of existence and their bizarre inhabitants, which include the spirits of the dead who've met their great reward (or are suffering their well-deserved punishment). Ideas and convictions are as much weapons and armor on the planes as anything forged from steel.

And, perhaps most ambitious of all, it connects all of the other campaign settings TSR produced. As a crossroad, it is a clear successor to *Spelljammer*, which connected *some* of the established *D&D* campaign settings. That setting, with its weird spaceships, was arranged around traversal and lacked a strong central hub for characters to use as their base of operations. *Planescape* has a hub and a half with the city of Sigil, which hovers above an impossibly tall spire in a spot that is as close to the center of the multiverse as a series of interlocking infinite spaces can allow.

Often called the City of Doors because it contains countless portals to other places, it's also called the Cage because it can be hard to escape—unlike other cities, it doesn't have roads or bridges or any conventional exits. The city is essentially built on the inside of a tire: There is no horizon, just more streets, always curving up. If a resident looks straight up and is lucky enough not to have the "sky" filling with smog, they can see the streets and buildings of the other side of the city inverted above them.

Spread through the wards are the various bizarre civic buildings, as well as temples, homes, factories, taverns, public spaces, slums, and markets full of every commodity in existence. Civil workers speak in rebuses, buildings are covered with razor sharp vines, and the rats are smarter. Angels and demons and all of the other entities coexist in tense peace here, thanks to the power of the mysterious Lady of Pain, the city's nominal ruler, whose visage forms the line's menacing logo.

Most importantly, Sigil is home to the factions, 16 organizations the box set likens to "philosophers with clubs." David "Zeb" Cook, the setting's designer, says they are "people devoted to their completely crazy ideas. I created the drunken barroom equivalent of philosophy class and really tried to take the ideas to the outer edges." If the planes are each a monolithic idea taken to its most extreme conclusion and arranged in opposition, then the factions, with all of their eccentric partisans and their odd notions, are the endless, metaphysical shouting matches over the true nature of the universe.

The Dustmen claim we're all already dead; the Believers of the Source think we're all gods in the making; for the Athar, divinity is just a big con, and the Bleak Cabal believe that nothing means anything at all. And a dozen more besides all of them are sure that they're right and the other folks are wrong. And they *are* right, or they could be, because if enough people believe *a thing* on the planes, that *thing* has a habit of being true. So, they

MANUAL OF THE PLANES, TSR, 1987
JEFF GRUBB, COVER BY JEFF EASLEY

curry favor, recruit to their cause, and consolidate power. Each faction runs its own civil service, guarding their turf, hoarding their influence, girding for metaphysical war. If that wasn't enough, in a distinctly meta turn, most factions also map to a broad caricature of a style of *D&D* play, so as players page through the faction descriptions, they will likely see themselves and their styles of play dimly reflected back.

If there is a problem with *Planescape,* it would be its vast strangeness. There's a lot to explain and not nearly enough space to fit it all in. Where something like the Forgotten Realms is endlessly detailed, it doesn't need to be—the *Forgotten Realms* original box set left swaths of territory for the GM to fill in because the designers were confident that GMs had the capability. This is not so true of *Planescape.*

In addition to the initial box set, it took three more box sets to detail the Outer Planes—*Planes of Chaos* (1994), *Planes of*

Law (1995), and *Planes of Conflict* (1995)—while the Inner Planes, the Astral, and the Ethereal each received a guidebook. A whole box set was also devoted to the Blood War, the eternal battle between the devils of the Nine Hells and the demons of the Abyss. Players got two guidebooks, one of which, *The Planewalker's Handbook* (1996) is nigh indispensable. Sigil was fleshed out across three. Taken together, all of that material barely feels like a good start.

The art picks up where the words leave off. *Planescape* is the apex of the aesthetic-driven, high-concept *Dungeons & Dragons* setting. Dana Knutson developed all of the concept artwork for the setting, which Robh Ruppel turned into covers, and Tony DiTerlizzi used to fill out the interiors.

DiTerlizzi shifted the look of fantasy RPGs—no exaggeration. To this point, *D&D* (and therefore, the rest of the fantasy-minded folks in the industry) were escalating a sort of clean, tightly rendered, and classic realism. Larry Elmore is probably the most prominent exponent of this school, but even an artist like Gerald Brom grounds his BDSM imagery and dramatic poses with a similar realism.

DiTerlizzi is entirely different. He goes back farther for his inspiration, to the golden age of illustrators, like Arthur Rackham and Howard Pyle, though hints of modern illustrators, like Alan Lee and Brian Froud, or filmmakers like, Terry Gilliam or Jim Henson, are apparent. Like all of those artists, his work has elements of realism, but also leaves plenty of space for the whimsy and emotion afforded to the cartoonish and strange. His loose watercolors wash over ink, subverting expectations and changing the way many players saw fantasy in their mind's eye.

Planescape was truly weird. Nothing else looked like it with its rusty metal, industrial typefaces, and odd marble squiggly things decorating the text. The philosophy was thick. There were goths.

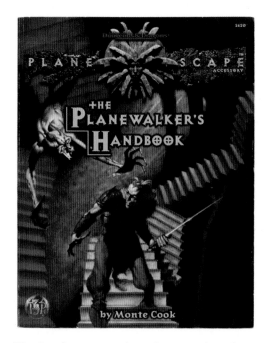

THE PLANEWALKER'S HANDBOOK, TSR, 1996
MONTE COOK, COVER BY ROBH RUPPEL

The books were written in a canting slang that made fun of characters from other *D&D* campaign settings for being clueless. Combat in *Planescape*, where power differentials were off the charts, was never a great idea; words always made for better weapons. Yet, even then, *Planescape* often feels built for something besides conflict—the art, the philosophy, and the infinite reaches encourage exploration in a way few other *D&D* settings do: Characters are encouraged to just walk off into the multiverse until they find something to wonder at.

Aria (1994)

Aria: Canticle of the Monomyth is a perhaps the apogee of the high concept RPG. It attempts to forge a game out of complex subjects, but winds up more interesting to read than to play. In fact, it is uncertain that playing Aria is a real possibility.

The monomyth in question is the notion that there is, deep down, just *one* story at the core of *all* myths, legends, and folklore, a fountainhead from which all other stories flow. The word comes from *Finnegan's Wake* (1939) by James Joyce, but was popularized by Joseph Campbell's idea of the hero's journey that he presented in *The Hero with a Thousand Faces* (1949).

Similar ideas had been proposed earlier by Sir James George Frazier in *The Golden Bough: A Study in Comparative Religion* (1890) and Robert Graves in *The White Goddess: A Historical Grammar of Poetic Myth* (1948), but it was Campbell who captured the popular imagination, in no small part, thanks to the influence he exerted over George Lucas and the *Star Wars* franchise. Campbell himself was influenced by Carl Jung's ideas about archetypes and a collective unconscious, believing that not only did the monomyth underpin all the world's stories, but also, if looked upon closely, the narratives of our lives. As with *The Golden Bough* and *The White Goddess*, there is plenty of scholarly evidence that the hero's journey is the product of cherry-picked examples and ethnocentrism, but that hasn't stopped it from becoming one of the most-used tools among storytellers in the decades since.

The appeal is understandable. It speaks to a universal human experience, that despite all of the differences, there are fundamental human characteristics. When human beings create *anything*, Campbell argues that they inherently draw on this shared foundation. There are only 12 musical notes, but there are an unlimited number of songs. The monomyth says the same is true of stories.

Aria recognizes that the monomyth is a product of all human endeavors, a manifestation of cultural structure, perhaps its keystone. As such, the idea behind the game isn't to just create some characters and tell stories. Rather, it seeks to excavate the monomyth by creating all of the worlds, cultures, and histories that shape those characters and stories.

Players don't play a single character; they play many characters across the timeline of the game world, as well as the role of countries, factions, towns, and

1970

1980

1990

2000

2010

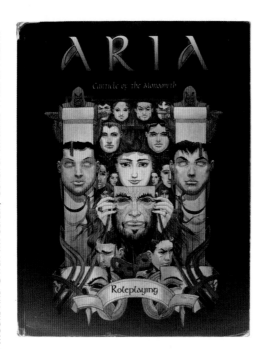

ARIA: CANTICLE OF THE MONOMYTH, LAST UNICORN GAMES, 1994
CHRISTIAN SCOTT MOORE AND OWEN M. SEYLER, COVER BY MICHAEL WILLIAM KALUTA

ARIA: WORLDS, LAST UNICORN GAMES, 1994
CHRISTIAN SCOTT MOORE AND OWEN M. SEYLER, COVER BY MICHAEL WILLIAM KALUTA

cultures, zooming in and out as the grand history demands, with consecutive sessions dealing with situations potentially centuries apart. Back in the '70s, designers like Greg Stafford and Ed Greenwood, created elaborate fictional worlds as an intellectual exercise. *Aria* attempts to make an entire roleplaying game out of this exercise. It goes without saying that this is hugely ambitious (and perhaps unsurprising—Last Unicorn Games is probably best known for its ill-fated RPG adaptation of Frank Herbert's science fiction series *Dune*, which features a universe no one has ever accused of being streamlined or simple).

The game certainly matches its industry to its ambitions. The rulebook is massive with over 500 pages dedicated to a series of meticulous, intertwined creation systems. An additional book of similar size fleshes out the world creation further. Everything has seemingly endless gradients of variables, each exhaustively discussed. Does the character have a curse, a doom, a doomed destiny, or are they haunted? On a scale from "Very Fair" to "Very Dark," what is their complexion, and what is the effect of that complexion on the available range of hair and eye colors?

The need for this level of detail is questionable and made more frustrating by the dense use of specialized jargon throughout the book. It isn't a campaign, it's a canticle; they aren't characters, they're personas. Sentences creak under the weight of capitalized game terms. And this is just the creation portion of the game. Running *Aria* is a daunting prospect, even when setting aside the pressure to make all of the realistic details *mean* something. Though the game only uses a single 10-sided die, the way these systems mesh together often requires the consultation of multiple charts or the use of formulas to calculate a result and the myriad repercussions.

Aria doesn't know if it is a tool or a game, and the two polarities of its existence constantly get in each other's way. As a tool, it anticipates projects, like Kevin Crawford's *Stars Without Number*, which is of similar size and is interested in a similar level of detail. That game has none of *Aria*'s pretension, however. All of *Aria*'s creation takes up so much time and results in characters and environments so bespoke and bejeweled that one has little to no idea what to do with them. If they were physical objects, they might be placed on a shelf. As imaginary things, it

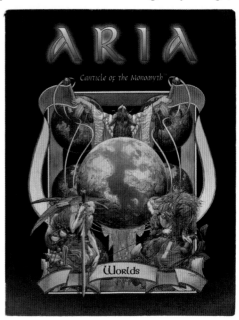

is nearly impossible to fathom this game being played with them.

And yet, the sort of experience *Aria* strives to provide *is* possible. Ben Robbins's games *Microscope* and *Kingdom* are both collaborative storytelling games. *Microscope* is concerned with history, and players fill in the details and play out scenes within an established timeline. *Kingdom*, on the other hand, is about communities at a crossroad in their history. These two games, which can be combined, are interested in many of the same ideas as *Aria*.

They also function as tools in many of the same ways—many a *D&D* campaign world has been created out of the stack of index cards that remain after a game of *Microscope*. There are two main differences that speak to their success. First, with *Aria*, the creation is prelude. For *Microscope* and *Kingdom*, it's part of the play, with everyone contributing to the story. Second, they're far easier to handle. Both run 80 pages, which detail mechanics that are easy to grasp. *Kingdom* follows its rules with an additional 80 pages of helpful advice on ways to play. Both books provide support—they want people to play! That is more than can be said for *Aria*, a game of intriguing ideas that never speaks plainly enough to truly let players embrace them.

Castle Falkenstein (1994)

Considering the level of cynicism in Pondsmith's earlier game *Cyberpunk*, the energetic steampunk world of *Castle Falkenstein* is a surprising contrast. Here be dragons, high adventure, and clear lines between good and evil. In a grim and gritty decade of moral dilemmas, in many ways, inspired by *Cyberpunk*, *Falkenstein* is a startling (and perhaps lone) splash of bright, uncomplicated color.

Color plays an unusual role in the presentation of the book, as well. The first half is in full color and, unlike most RPGs, is entirely dedicated to detailing the world of the game in one-page increments without any discussion of mechanics. Those appear in the back, in black and white—a utilitarian framework supporting a world of wonders.

That world is an alternate version of ours, circa the Victorian era, in which faerie magic is rampant and has combined with the steam-powered industrial revolution to produce many technological marvels. The world is literally right next door to our pedestrian existence—the conceit of the game is that a game designer, Tom Olam, was ensorcelled into this other reality, *A Connecticut Yankee in King Arthur's Court*-style, where he was caught up in the Great Game of politics, plots, and empires, a situation inspired primarily by *The Prisoner of Zenda* (1894).

All the world is familiar, but seen through a sooty lens. Instead of dying in 1886, Ludwig II is now the king of a realm that extends from his native Bavaria into the twilight lands of Faerie. Jules Verne is France's Minister of Science, and Karl Marx is the head of a secret anarchist brotherhood. Dracula, the Invisible Man, and Phileas Fogg aren't fictional. The titular Castle Falkenstein is a magic construction and a kind of nexus of worlds, where Tom Olam now resides. And through playing the game, which is supposedly cobbled together out of a journal Olam sent back to our world, players will somehow share his adventures? Help him? Prepare for the eventual revelation that the forces of evil have invaded our reality? The text is unclear, but the details aren't important when buckles are in need of swashing.

Character creation begins with the selection of a template. Sticking to the framework of the Victorian melodrama, there is the Heroic Hero, Tragic Hero, or Flawed Hero for the gents, and Innocent Heroine, Clever Heroine, Tragic Heroine, or Fallen Heroine for the ladies (though there is nothing stopping a woman from being Heroic or a man from being Fallen).

CASTLE FALKENSTEIN: HIGH ADVENTURE IN THE STEAM AGE, R. TALSORIAN GAMES, 1994
MIKE PONDSMITH, COVER BY WILLIAM C. EAKEN AND MARK SCHUMANN

The templates define the broad strokes of the character and their arc—it is clear that the Tragic Hero is going to fall off of a cliff at some point. Then, the player selects an archetype, which fills in many of the details of their lives, with anything from Journalist to Faerie Lord on offer. Unlike most other RPGs, neither the template nor the archetype has a mechanical purpose for humans (faeries and dragons have their own sets of rules, but they're the exception). Rather, this framework serves as the foundation for a key narrative portion of the game: A character's diary.

Following a series of prompts, a player writes the first entry as the character. Through this exercise, they generate a picture of how their character looks and acts, along with their motivations, their enemies, their goals, all laid out in prose but distilled to keywords. Once this is done, the player selects a handful of skills they are good at, one they are great at, and one they are poor at. To improve those skills, players log their character's efforts during play in the diary and work with the GM to determine when the effort merits results. All of this journaling comes out of epistolary novels of the period, like Bram Stoker's *Dracula* (1897)

and Wilkie Collins's *The Moonstone* (1868), and clearly anticipates writing games, like *De Profundis* and *Thousand Year Old Vampire*.

Also unusual is *Castle Falkenstein*'s use of playing cards instead of dice. Players begin with a hand of four cards. To perform a skill, a player has to beat a difficulty number assigned by the GM, using the value of the skill—a poor skill is 2, and good is 6, for instance—and the value of a card from their hand. Complicating matters: Every skill is associated with a suit—heart skills are in the realm of emotions, diamonds for the mind, clubs for the physical, and spades for matters of status—and the skill and suit have to match in order to gain the full value of the card. If not, the card only counts as a one, no matter the face value.

A player can use multiple cards, which is helpful, but the GM has their own hand of cards that they can play in opposition, which is decidedly unhelpful to players. Combat works in a similar fashion, with red cards representing attacks and black cards defense. Spellcasters use a second deck, drawing a card during every two minutes of game time until they gather the requisite power, represented by the total value of the cards, in order to unleash their sorcery.

Cards were in the air in the mid '90s (though hopefully not weaponized, like Ricky Jay's), and *Castle Falkenstein*'s use of cards was, undoubtedly, influenced by the success of *Magic: The Gathering* (1993). By using cards, it felt of the moment without having to be a competitive card game; further, the use of cards leans into the Victorian notion that dice are vulgar and likely sinful. More importantly, the relatively simple card-based system allows the game to focus on its world and its narrative themes, which, like *Once Upon a Time*, wind up being some of the few bright and sunny patches in a gritty decade of overcast skies and steady drizzles.

Everway (1995)

With the success of *Magic: The Gathering*, it makes sense that Wizards of the Coast would try their hand at a card-based RPG. Jonathan Tweet's *Everway*, with its cascade of realities and the Spherewalkers who move between them, also seems like a remix of *Magic*'s themes (which is a bit curious, considering Wizards was developing an RPG set in the world of *Magic* at the same time, although it never saw release).

The CCG isn't the only influence on the game, of course. The name of the game is shared with a central city in the fiction, filled with gates and strangeness that hearkens back to both *Planescape* and Tweet's earlier RPG, *Over the Edge*. The mix of mythologies and cultures recalls Neil Gaiman's *The Sandman*. There is, perhaps, a whiff of the videogame *Myst*'s (1993) puzzling surreality, as well. Despite sharing many of those touchstones with many games released in the '90s, *Everway* stands as a wholly unique RPG in its execution—even today.

Much of the game verges on the abstract and is intentionally open-ended, something made abundantly clear by the fact that the central mechanics use a deck of cards—the Fate Deck—that resemble the Major Arcana of the tarot. Each card features ambiguous, symbolic art that depicts the polarities of an archetypal concept. Thus, the Death card, as with our real-world tarot, represents change (if drawn obverse) or stasis (if drawn inverse), whereas the evocative card, Drowning in Armor, unique to *Everway*, represents protective measures turned dangerous (obverse) or true protection (inverse). The deck is, at once, a prop used in-universe for fortunetelling, a tool for character creation, and the primary way the game resolves tasks.

Players take the roles of the aforementioned Spherewalkers, who are defined by their relationships to the four classical elements. Earth is endurance, both physi-

Everway, Box set, Wizards of the Coast, 1995
Jonathan Tweet, Cover by Susan Harris

cal and mental; Air is the intellect; Fire is power; and Water is intuition. Each element is assigned a value from a pool of 20 points, and, as with *Amber*, they function as absolutes. A character with an Air of five is always going to out-think a character with a four.

Special powers can be purchased, as well. Similar to *Over the Edge*, they're defined by a descriptive phrase—loyal steed, sharp tongue, made of vines—and the cost is determined by whether the attribute described is Frequent, Major, or Versatile. Being made of vines would likely count as all three, thus costing three points. Magic is also an option, but like *Ars Magica,* it is freeform, and each magic-using character must design their own system for its use, a daunting task. Cards are drawn to frame out a character's back story and determine a vice, a virtue, and a conflict. Finally, players select a name that, in a very Neil Gaiman-like fashion, reflects *what* they are. In the rulebook, NPCs sport names like Rarity, Wonder, Greatheart, and Favor.

That completed, the players are ready to embark on their adventures. These exploits are entirely narrative in nature and governed by three open-ended laws. The first is the Law of Karma, which demands that powers, abilities, and attributes be applied logically. The second is the Law of Drama, which demands the story progress—so, the clue must be found, the rumor told, the hidden path revealed (Robin Law's Gumshoe System, which powers games, like *Trail of Cthulhu*, takes this law to heart). The final law is the Law of Fate, which dictates that uncertainty be resolved with the Fate Deck, which, ironically, guarantees very little certainty, as it turns the game into a kind of extended tarot reading. For example, when characters who evenly matched in their fire attribute are brawling, the GM draws a card: War, inverted, which indicates "Effort Misspent"—but whose?

This ambiguity is the main problem with *Everway*. It is gorgeous (the list of artists who contributed their art to the cards includes Ian Miller, Rick Berry, Hannibal King, Jeff Miracola, and more), it is intriguing, and it seems so simple to dive into—but it's not. Simplicity, it turns out, isn't always so simple. Where the cards in *Once Upon a Time* propel the game forward and keep it grounded, the cards of *Everway* are like a prism, splitting potential paths and splashing them in all directions. Spontaneously marshalling the potential outcomes of the cards into a coherent narrative seems a challenge for the best gamemasters, even 25-years later, with a large field of storytelling games lowering the barrier to entry for this sort of play. Surely, playing *Everway* with Jonathan Tweet is a dream, but for most groups left to their own devices, I suspect a session of the game would be a nightmare.

Deadlands (1996)

Let me unfurl the '90s RPG checklist: A rulebook in the *Shadowrun* style, containing all that's needed to run the game in a single volume? Check. Color plates for the character archetypes? Check. Lots of bespoke, interacting systems that make the various archetypes, like mad scientist and huckster, feel unique, but also require extra effort on the part of the GM to manage? Check. A mix of genres, in this case horror, western, steampunk, and the weird? Check. A world full of lore, factions, bizarre history, and a robust metaplot, conveyed through dialect-heavy prose? Check ("varmint" gets thrown around quite a bit, which is either a blessing or a curse depending on how the reader feels about Yosemite Sam). A manifestation of pre-millennium tensions conveyed through edgy aesthetics and themes of anxiety about social and cultural upheavals? Check, check, and check.

Strict adherence to this list isn't meant to imply that *Deadlands* is bad or rote, just that its construction and broad themes are extremely of its time. It is difficult to criticize a game that came out in 1996 for being too emblematic of '90s RPG design, but it's also hard to discuss the game without constantly pointing out just how '90s it is.

For example, like many other games that appeared in the '90s, the prime inspiration for *Deadlands* is likely a comic series, Joe R. Lansdale and Tim Truman's *Jonah Hex: Two-Gun Mojo* (1993) and its follow up, *Jonah Hex: Riders of the Worm and Such* (1995), a highlight for the weird west sub-genre at the time. In *Designers & Dragons* (2014), Shannon Appelcline cites Gerald Brom's cover painting for the *Wraith: The Oblivion* sourcebook, *Necropolis: Atlanta* (1994), as providing the immediate inspiration for creator Shane Lacy Hensley (to the point that the *Deadlands* rulebook also sports a Brom painting on the cover), but it seems preposterous to me that Hensley, Brom, and the art department at White Wolf were all unaware of the Vertigo series, especially given the out-sized influence that mature audience comics had on RPGs at the time.

The history of the world of *Deadlands* is the same as ours until 1863, when, like *Shadowrun*, a Native American ritual unleashed powerful supernatural forces into the world. Unlike *Shadowrun*, those supernatural forces keep a low profile, since they feed on fear, and a full-scale invasion would leave their prey jaded and ready to fight. Still, 13-years later, when the game is set, the world is a pretty unpleasant place to live.

The land has twisted; parts of California have fallen into the sea; the Civil War drags on, and the invading spirits are closer to their goal of creating a Hell on Earth. A good deal of the material is clever, as with the Hucksters, a spellcasting class that comes into their powers by deciphering the occult secrets encoded in *Hoyle's Book of Games* (a fictitious reimagining of our real-world Hoyle's *Rules of Games*, 1949). Some portrayals, like those of Native Americans and the use of the Ghost Dance as a plot device, seem ignorant—another trait *Deadlands* has in common with *Shadowrun*.

Jonah Hex: Two-Gun Mojo #1, Vertigo Comics, 1993
Joe R. Lansdale, Timothy Truman, and Sam Glanzman, Cover by Timothy Truman

Perhaps inspired by its steampunk cousin, *Castle Falkenstein*, but definitely owing to its Wild West setting, *Deadlands* makes use of some novel mechanics (and terminology—the GM is the Marshal, and the players are a Posse). Characters are created using a deck of poker cards; each card indicates the sort of die the player will use to test the associated trait—a two of any suit will see them rolling a 4-sided die, an ace gets them a 12-sided die.

The dice balance out interestingly, because in *Deadlands* they can "explode"—roll the highest value, roll again, and add the result to the total, continuing as long as the player keeps rolling the highest value. So, a 12-sided die has the potential to put up a big number in a single roll, but a 4-sided die has better chances of exploding (annoyingly, the game mixes metaphors and refers to this as "rolling an ace").

Players will need a few more decks of cards, too. One goes to the marshal and another to the posse to track combat initiative. The spells of Hucksters and

Deadlands, Pinnacle Entertainment Group, 1996
Shane Lacy Hensley, Cover by Gerald Brom

NECROPOLIS: ATLANTA, WHITE WOLF PUBLISHING, 1994
SAM CHUPP AND JAMES A. MOORE, COVER BY GERALD BROM

FADING SUNS, HOLISTIC DESIGN, INC., 1996
BILL BRIDGES AND ANDREW GREENBERG, COVER BY JOHN BRIDGES, JAY MARSH, AND KARL HAWK

inventions of Mad Scientists also require decks, with poker hands determining the success and power of the endeavor. Oh, and every player gets a pool of poker chips that can be cashed in to modify die rolls or avoid harm—unused chips are cashed in at the end of a session for bounty points, which are used to improve characters. Regardless of whether this saloon-style theming comes off as charming and immersive, or just plain grating, it all works together well as a system. After all, *Deadlands* remains one of the most popular of the Wild West-themed RPGs. Granted, most of the competition isn't worth talking about, but there are way more competitors than one might expect, including *Dogs in the Vineyard*, which wraps its mechanics in the trappings of poker, to similar, if more measured, effect.

Fading Suns (1996)

As the '90s progressed, the popularity of space opera science fiction games was eclipsed by gritty, street-level cyberpunk. By the end of the decade, *Traveller* and *Star Wars: The Roleplaying Game*, two massively successful RPG fran-

chises, were defunct. It was a dicey moment for spaceships. *Fading Suns* sought to avoid the same fate by embracing many genres.

Echoing *Warhammer 40,000*, *Fading Suns* primarily fuses space opera and fantasy. Comparisons to Frank Herbert's seminal novel *Dune* (1965) and David Lynch's film adaptation (1984) are warranted. *Stargate* (1994), Isaac Asimov's *Foundation* (1951), and Gene Wolfe's *The Book of the New Sun* (1980-1983) novels also come to mind. Perhaps there is a hint of *A Canticle for Leibowitz* (1959). There is also a good deal of horror to be found in *Fading Suns*; cosmic entities lurk in the black spaces between the stars, and debauched occultists devote themselves to calling up demons.

The game takes place in the far future, long after humanity found alien technology that allowed for interplanetary travel by using Jumpgates, which were constructed by the mysterious Anunnaki—I'd bet someone who worked on the *Mass Effect* videogames was a *Fading Suns* fan.

Technological booms and busts followed, and an interstellar empire rose to power, but that empire has now grown decadent and superstitious. Medievalism

runs rampant. Noble houses plot against each other and clamor for prestige, but all of their designs are nothing compared to the will of the all-powerful Universal Church of the Celestial Sun. The tension between science and faith is immense—many sophisticated technologies, like artificial intelligence, are forbidden by the Church. There are interesting aliens, deadly politics, psychic powers, and more. And, as the name *Fading Suns* implies, the stars are going out, and the end of all things is likely near. The sum of it all is weird and moody and expansive, a deft combination of disparate inspirations.

There is much lore to digest (though the metaplot it fueled never resolved). The library of sourcebooks focuses on the game's many factions, particularly the great noble houses—House Hawkwood (a stand-in for *Dune*'s House Atreides), House Decados (essentially *Dune*'s Harkonen), The Hazat (space Zorro), House al-Malik (space Caliphate), and House Li Halan (holy space samurai)—all of which feature painstakingly developed histories that span centuries.

The political struggles of those houses form the major backdrop for the campaign, but the roleplaying experience of *Fading Suns* feels very personal in how it examines and tests the way player characters fit into the universe. The *Players Companion* (1997) puts this perspective

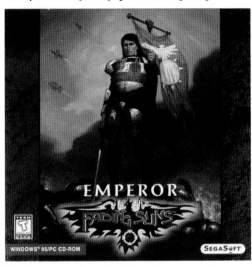

in focus. Every major character type—Noble, Merchant, Alien, Priest, and on—receives one page detailing a generic day in their generic life. Reading through this section provides insight into the universe of *Fading Suns*, more so than all of the histories and genealogies.

This arrangement feels akin to *World of Darkness* in many ways: In its philosophical approach, in the way the line of books breaks into lore-heavy, mechanics-light sourcebooks, and even the aesthetics, which, with all of their piercings and goggles, embrace the gothic and the punk. This sense of similarity is for good reason, since the game's designers, Andrew Greenberg and Bill Bridges, were important staffers at White Wolf before working on *Fading Suns* (Bridges would later return to oversee the relaunch of the *World of Darkness* line in the next decade). This White Wolf-style approach to lore and aesthetic mixed with science fiction themes would cast a long shadow. In addition to *Mass Effect*, there are glimmers of *Fading Suns* in other science fiction videogames, like *StarCraft* and the *Dead Space* series.

This interplay is interesting for two reasons. First, as the capabilities of videogames grew more impressive over the course of the '90s, they were able to offer experiences that were similar to tabletop roleplaying games but different in that they were accompanied by exciting visuals. There was much anxiety at the time regarding how games, like *Diablo* (1997), *Ultima Online* (1997), and *Everquest* (1999) were potentially luring tabletop players away from RPGs. Second, Holistic Design *started out* making videogames; their third videogame was a strategy game called *Emperor of the Fading Suns* (1997).

The videogame places the player at the head of their house (chosen among the five) and lets them explore more than 40 planets of the galaxy, each consisting of huge terrain maps. Most of the game is

EMPEROR OF THE FADING SUNS, HOLISTIC DESIGN, INC., 1997
COVER BY GERALD BROM

FADING SUNS PLAYERS COMPANION, HOLISTIC DESIGN, INC., 1997
BILL BRIDGES, ANDREW GREENBERG, AND DYVERS HANDS, COVER BY GERALD BROM

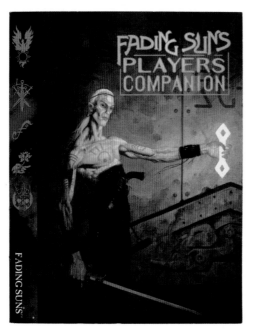

concerned with exploration and combat in this context, which is similar to hex-and-chit tabletop wargaming. There are additional layers of systems—a great-for-the-time diplomacy engine, commerce, a frankly vast tech tree, and a political system that determines the victor (the object of the game is to be elected Emperor).

All of these systems were simultaneously intriguing and opaque. One of my favorite disasters: The church would periodically declare forms of technology heretical (sometimes thanks to bribes and lobbying), which could, in turn, invoke the wrath of inquisitors and zealots, rapidly unraveling all of my hard work (until I could find the right church official to bribe).

Emperor of the Fading Suns was intended to see release simultaneously with the tabletop game. Instead, it came out early in 1997, and it was, unfortunately, a buggy mess. Like the RPG, though, it found the embrace of a sizable fan community that has supported it with homemade modifications and fixes ever since.

Delta Green (1997)

When Pagan Publishing's quarterly *Call of Cthulhu* fanzine, *The Unspeakable Oath* (*TUO*) appeared in 1990, its keen understanding of the game turned a lot of heads. The first issue was almost entirely comprised of the work of John Tynes, but the level of quality was so high, and the ideas on display so interesting, that it caught the attention of folks at Chaosium.

Soon, the magazine's pages were filled with a rich mix of *Call of Cthulhu* designers and energetic new writers. The success of fanzine had the effect of creating two sorts of *Call of Cthulhu*—the mainstream books published by Chaosium that maintained a consistent PG-13 tone versus the underground publishing house that pushed boundaries and was expressly R-rated, with a maturity level oscillating between *The Exorcist* (1973) and *The Toxic Avenger* (1984), depending on the article. *The Unspeakable Oath* injected a transgressive allure into what was already shaping up to be a golden period for the game.

TUO's most important contribution to the world of horror roleplaying came in the Fall 1992 issue, in the shape of "Convergence," a short scenario by Tynes set in the modern day that involved weird science, sentient fungus scientists, and those classic UFO pilots, the Greys.

The scenario is half of the CyberCthulhu cross-over that sought to mix *Call of Cthulhu* with *Cyberpunk 2020*—the second scenario, concerned more with the physical trappings of the sub-genre, appeared in the *Cyberpunk*-centric fanzine *Interface* (1990-1992). The *Call of Cthulhu* part experiments with tone. There are no megacorps or netrunners, but the scenario has a big dose of hopelessness, systemic corruption, trans-humanism, government overreach, and wide-ranging conspiracies. Most importantly, it casts players in the role of FBI agents who are also part of a secretive, unofficial government program called Delta Green.

DELTA GREEN, PAGAN PUBLISHING, 1997
DENNIS DETWILLER, ADAM SCOTT GLANCY, AND JOHN TYNES, COVER BY BLAIR REYNOLDS

CTHULHU NOW, CHAOSIUM, 1987

SANDY PETERSEN AND DYVERS HANDS, COVER BY TOM SULLIVAN

In 1987, Chaosium released a sourcebook for playing *Call of Cthulhu* in the modern era, *Cthulhu Now*, but the book was largely devoted to scenarios. The rules portion was under 30 pages, most of which were given over to equipment and firearms. They do little that would redefine Lovecraft's cosmic horror for the contemporary period; they just give players bigger guns. John Tynes initially came up with the idea of Delta Green in order to provide a richer narrative framework for his own modern-era games. This framework would eventually expand into the first *Delta Green* sourcebook, published by Pagan Publishing under license from Chaosium.

Delta Green operates on a set of assumptions. Lovecraft's stories (as well as those of select writers, like Robert W. Chambers and Ramsey Campbell, and even some key Chaosium scenarios, like *Masks of Nyarlathotep*) are essentially historical accounts documenting events that actually happened. Additionally, *Delta Green* extrapolates the repercussions of these events into a rich tapestry of history, conspiracy, and horror.

The saga starts when Robert Olmstead, the protagonist of Lovecraft's classic story, *The Shadow over Innsmouth* (1936), flees the horrible fish people of Innsmouth, Massachusetts, and convinces the federal government that action must be taken. The feds raid the town and encounter creatures they can't explain, so they send a submarine to drop depth charges on *something* off the coast. These events, which form the denouement of the story, pose a tantalizing question: What happens when the United States government finds clear proof of existential supernatural threats?

Delta Green offers an appropriately complicated answer. Some in the government ignore the truth, others try to bury it, a very small group tries to understand it, and those with firsthand knowledge of the terrors that lurk in shadowy places are highly motivated to see them annihilated.

Artifacts are destroyed, ancient grimoires torched, and cultists are disappeared into off-the-books prisons or shallow graves—when all else fails, try high explosives. Thus, Delta Green was formed, receiving its name when it was folded into the OSS during World War II as a psychological warfare group. After the war, it was disbanded and revived multiple times, which taught the group's leadership to insulate its mission from the fickle tides of politics and ambition. After a botched mission in Cambodia in 1969, Delta Green becomes a conspiracy, a decentralized network of government officials who siphon agents and money out of legitimate programs to fund black ops against known supernatural threats.

Of course, where one government goes, so go the rest. The original sourcebook details the Nazi occult program called the Karotechia, which Delta Green fought in a secret war. Readers also learn about similar occult bureaus from Imperial Japan, the Soviet Union, and the UK. After the Roswell crash in 1947, Delta Green even finds a rival within the US government, the UFO- and weird science-obsessed Majestic 12, a purported federal agency that figures prominently in many of our real-world conspiracy theories. Government outfits are only the tip of the factional iceberg, though. There are criminal organizations, cults (and sometimes criminal organizations that are also cults!), UFO fanatics, tabloid television shows, terror groups, and alien invaders.

While based on the literary bedrock of a constantly evolving shared universe, the *Call of Cthulhu* RPG never had a meta-plot. Perhaps because the rich fiction from which it drew felt like enough, or maybe because the fatalism so perfectly conveyed in the mechanics made an expansive narrative seem unnecessary—characters just burn up too fast in the friction of the game.

Delta Green successfully argues the opposite: A rich narrative web increases the horror for the players, even if the characters don't experience the full story. There is a thrill to combing through the histories and timelines, making connections, and developing theories. This emergent storytelling works particularly well when players discover a reference to something, like *Masks of Nyarlathotep* or another Chaosium-produced 1920s-era scenario—so many artifacts and books that were briefly owned by player investigators once again sit in the storehouses of cultists and madmen, and it is exciting (and perhaps a bit cosmically disheartening) to see more of that history laid out. It also makes the nightmare world seem somehow more immediate. And because the lore is largely limited to just four books—*Delta Green*, *Countdown* (1999), *Eyes Only* (2007), and *Targets of Opportunity* (2010)—the designers avoid the oppressive weight of a constantly expanding metaplot in the vein of *Vampire: The*

THE UNSPEAKABLE OATH ISSUE 7, PAGAN PUBLISHING, 1992
COVER BY BLAIR REYNOLDS

Masquerade. *Delta Green* intrigues and provides endless possibilities, but it doesn't overstay its welcome.

Perhaps most cleverly, this secret history also removes a hurdle for players. *Call of Cthulhu* treats the supernatural as a revelation that occurs for characters in the course of play, and while that is often interesting and fun, it overlooks the fact that players of a Cthulhu-centric game have probably read some Lovecraft. This knowledge can present a challenge when it comes to playing characters who do not know the secret truth of the universe. In *Delta Green*, though, the knowledge the players may have of Lovecraft's stories—vague recollections of strangeness, gleaned from dusty pulp fiction pages—is often equal to what the characters know—vague recollections of strangeness, gleaned from dusty after-action reports.

Introducing spycraft and politics into a game of cosmic horror complicates matters. Members of Delta Green are generally law enforcement, military, or intelligence operatives, all of which come with

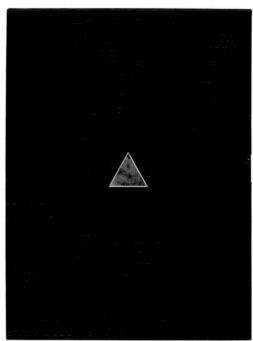

Delta Green Slipcase Set, Arc Dream Publishing, 2018
Dennis Detwiller, Shane Ivey, and Dyvers Hands

their fair share of real-world baggage. The sourcebooks never shy away from the problematic aspects of those careers, nor do they pass judgment on them. Delta Green missions routinely ask characters to resort to measures that go far beyond the legal without judging those decisions (though it does recognize that Delta Green agents are criminals). Navigating the moral maze of accountability is a job for the players.

In 2016, Arc Dream Publishing released a new *Delta Green*, this time as a stand-alone system (though one still inspired by the *Call of Cthulhu* system). The modifications shine a spotlight on the moral and psychological toll the supernatural takes on agents and their families.

Each character receives a certain number of Bonds, determined by their profession. These represent the people who matter to the agent—wives, husbands, children, partners, squad mates, support groups, and so on—and they start with a value equal to the character's Charisma attribute. Sanity works in a way similar to *Call of Cthulhu*, with exposure to violence, helplessness, and the unnatural whittling away the attribute's value.

In the heat of the horror in *Delta Green*, though, players can opt to save their character's sanity by letting the value of a Bond relationship deteriorate instead. Narratively, this decision manifests as an increasing distance between the character and their loved ones as they wrestle with the traumas induced by their work. If a Bond's value drops to zero, the relationship is lost, and with it, potentially more of a character's sanity as they become increasingly isolated.

The cost of losing Bonds is balanced by downtime, short scenes in which an agent's life at home can be navigated, offering the opportunity to repair old Bonds and form new ones, bolstering the character's sanity (alternately, players can opt to have their characters lean into their investigative obsessions, corroding their relationships further in exchange for benefits once the scenario resumes). They can also attempt therapy (a dodgy prospect, considering the source of an agent's problems and therapy's relationship with the unvarnished truth), improve their skills, commune with nature, or embrace the work at the cost of all else.

Of course, characters can still confront a sanity blasting monster and run off, cackling, into the night, never to be seen again. But *Delta Green* more often pits players against other humans, rather than monsters, which, in turn, places an increased value on examining the human toll of the missions. This approach, as with *Unknown Armies*, seems like an attempt to probe something essential about characters and their relationships to their trauma. It doesn't always ring true, but it represents a vast improvement over sanity systems that feature pulp-inspired caricatures of mental health.

In Nomine (1997)

For enthusiasts of the Vertigo line of comics, the film *Dogma* (1999), in which two fallen angels attempt to exploit a loophole in order to sneak back into Heaven, feels very much like a love letter (or fan fiction) from director Kevin Smith to Neil Gaiman's *The Sandman* and Garth Ennis's *Preacher*. Those same comic readers might have similar feelings when confronted by *In Nomine*.

In that game, players take the role of angels and demons who have incarnated in human form to fight a kind of cold war for human souls. Flipping through the book instantly brings to mind the "Season of Mists" storyline (1990-1991) from *The Sandman*, in which Lucifer shuts down hell, as well as John Constantine's many encounters with the First of the Fallen in Garth Ennis's *Hellblazer* run (1991-1995, 1998).

Gaiman's short story "Murder Mysteries" (1992), which recounts the investigation into the murder of an angel in a time before the Fall, and the film, *The Prophecy* (1995), in which the angel Gabriel (a bizarrely cast, scenery devouring Christopher Walken) attempts to find a metaphysical weapon that will turn the tide in a second war in Heaven, are two other likely sources of inspiration for the game.

Except, the Steve Jackson Games' (SJG) version of *In Nomine* is an American import of a French game in two volumes: *In Nomine Satanis* for the demon-centric campaign and *Magna Veritas* for the angels' side of the conflict. They first came out in 1989 and, like *Shadowrun*, they so accurately predict vast swaths of pre-millennium tension and pop culture obsession that it is downright unnerving. None of the comics of movies about angels and demons *inspired* the American version *In Nomine*; rather their successes indicated there was a receptive audience in the States for an import of an RPG with similar themes.

Unlike the French version, the default American scenario seems to want players in the roles of angels. Demons are still supported, but they are less mechanically interesting—they don't have to answer to anyone, and their redemption is not tied to their actions. Angels, on the other hand, are part of a collective, each a single voice in a larger celestial choir. Musical metaphor saturates the game—demons are arranged into bands, all of creation is called the Symphony, and the actions of both groups are either resonant or dissonant with their essential natures. When angels act against their nature, they acquire dissonance. Too much dissonance can turn an angel into an outcast or it might precipitate their Fall, a very real concern when running covert missions—it's difficult to fight a secret war without resorting to some decidedly un-angelic skullduggery.

Also, unlike the French version, the SJG version takes itself rather seriously. The world of *In Nomine* is surprisingly, emphatically rendered in shades of gray. In the broadest sense, Heaven seems to desire a universe that is incrementally better, while Hell would prefer it incrementally worse. In practice, though, "better" and "worse" have many different definitions.

There are 13 archangels and 14 demon princes marshaling their forces. Each has their own ambitions and agendas. Hardly any actually like each other. This tangle of cross-purposes is further complicated by the various Judeo-Christian religions—some angels are champions of the Catholic church, some favor Islam, and some seem curiously ambivalent. The game never chooses a side—good and bad outcomes are a matter of perspective. The relentless mechanical nature of the resonance/dissonance system, which removes all context from the action in question, is bound to make players question the righteousness of their cause at some point, no matter their allegiance. A

IN NOMINE, STEVE JACKSON GAMES, 1997
DEREK PEARCY, COVER BY JOHN ZELEZNIK

good angel doing bad things is a demon, and vice versa.

This moral precarity and unfairness is undercut, somewhat, by the game's cheeky D666 system, a hold-over from the more light-hearted French version. To resolve conflicts or test skills, players roll three 6-sided dice. The first two are totaled and compared to a target number to determine success or failure, while the third determines the margin of success or failure (a refinement of *James Bond*'s qualities of success). Rolling all ones results in a divine intervention that benefits the interests of Heaven, while rolling all sixes marks the intercession of Hell. And that's it. Given the number of powers available to players, the simplicity of the system makes for fast, muscular play, a stark contrast to the careful political balancing acts the game world is arranged around.

In Nomine won some awards and was a modest success but, tellingly, once the millennium turned and all that particular sort of existential anxiety vanished, *GURPS In Nomine* came out (2000), essentially discontinuing the company's lone non-*GURPS* RPG and incorporating it into the larger *GURPS* ecosystem.

Unknown Armies (1998)

Like *Planescape*, *Unknown Armies* springs from the idea that belief is the key building block of reality (a notion that underpins much of real-world Western occultism, in which magic is a manifestation of personal will). As might be guessed from the cover, though, *Unknown Armies* takes the concept in a decidedly grimmer direction. The game posits that it isn't just a run-of-the-mill belief that changes the world, but rather a specific sort of personally obsessive, self-destructive belief that does the trick.

To get a sense of the occult underground the RPG seeks to create, though, I need to start at the top. Throughout its history, humanity has generated avatars, people who are so thoroughly what they are that they become something *else*. The rulebook offers eight examples of archetypes characters might embody, some familiar, some not—the Demagogue, the Executioner, the Flying Woman, the Fool, the Masterless Man, the Merchant, the Pilgrim, and the Savage—but there are many, many more.

Several people might embody an archetype to varying degrees, expressed in the game through a percentile skill value, but the lone person in the entire world who achieves 99-percent becomes the living embodiment of that concept (similar to *Nobilis*). At least, until someone knocks them off the top of the hill. People who are larger than life, whose talents seem almost supernatural, whose accomplishments thunder across the ages, they might be an ascended avatar—Jimi Hendrix, Shakespeare, and Alexander the Great all fit the bill.

There is an upper limit, though. Should there ever be 333 ascended avatars at the same time, they merge into a new godhead, the world ends, then resets, and the cycle begins again, forever. Of course, lots of folks don't want to see that happen, so in addition to the jockeying between avatars to be king of a given hill, various factions (not all of them natural) plot and scheme to make sure the tipping point never comes, or it happens sooner. Conspiracy, murder, and all manner of nefarious doings follow.

The play of the game takes place far downhill from the lofty metaconcepts, on the outskirts of society, in the sewers and back alleys and abandoned factories. Players can take the roles of prospective avatars. They can also be Adepts, who channel their obsession through the game's magical foci—history, alcohol, sex, money, clockwork, and entropy— each of which gives with one hand while taking with the other. Players can also take the role of a normal person caught in the occult undertow; maybe they're destined to become an avatar or an Adept down the line; maybe they just heard the wrong whisper in the wrong back room and are trying to survive one more day. Regardless of what a character is, bad things are going to start piling up around them, even as they attempt to use their powers to change the world for the better. It isn't an easy trick to pull off.

Unknown Armies uses a simple percentile-based skill system—role under the character's value—that is generally reminiscent of *Call of Cthulhu*, which makes sense considering co-designer John Tynes's pedigree with that game. There are some interesting nuances, though. For starters, there are eight free skills, like Lie and Drive. All characters have a basic aptitude for them. The rest of the skill system is free form, like *Over the Edge*, in which players select a key word or phrase—Firearms, Horseback Riding, Appear Vulnerable, and so on.

With these, players not only get to perform the action, but also gain access to what the game calls the penumbra, a set of associated skills and knowledge. Echoing the example from the rules, the Firearms skill primarily allows a character to shoot guns, but it also enables them to take care of guns, know about gun culture,

UNKNOWN ARMIES, ATLAS GAMES, 1998
GREG STOLZE AND JOHN TYNES, COVER BY THOMAS MANNING

and have a set of contacts related to guns, all in proportion to the level of the skill. So, someone with a 30 would know folks at the local gun range, or maybe a hood who specializes in Saturday night specials, while someone with an 80 likely has an international arms dealer in their cell phone (or Rolodex, this being the '90s).

Characters are built to go to extremes. In addition to an obsession and its associated skill, each character has three passions: One that inspires fear, another that inspires rage, and one the evokes their better angel. Passions rule rational life, but also fuel a character's eventual deterioration—the more one succeeds in their endeavors, the deeper they'll sink into the occult underground. The cover art is a good indicator of how that is going to ultimately turn out. Mechanically, these powerful connections mean a player can flip-flop their rolls—switching a 74 to a 47, say, or outright re-rolling if switching doesn't lead to a success—once per session for skill tests associated with a passion and any time they test the skill associated with their obsession.

As might be expected from a game that is essentially about enduring trauma, *Unknown Armies* has a sanity system, one that was certainly the most nuanced available when it first came out. There are five stress meters that measure a character's susceptibility or resilience to violence, the unnatural, and situations relating to helplessness, isolation, and identity. Whenever a character is confronted by something that pushes against their sanity, a player rolls against their Mind attribute. Success hardens a character, and failure causes irrational responses—panic, frenzy, or paralysis—in both the short- and long-term.

Hardened characters are increasingly unphased by the awful situations that they confront, which is beneficial in the short-term, but leads to a deadening of their human emotions. A character with all five meters fully hardened loses all interest in their passion (and the mechanical benefits it bestowed). Meanwhile, a character who maxes out their failures on a given tract always becomes irrational when faced with that sort of horror. They also develop permanent disorders that exacerbate their passions and obsession. Either way, touched as they are by the supernatural, each success and failure moves the character by degrees to the edges of normal society. Regular people recognize that they are somehow different, while the characters themselves are unable, or no longer desire, to connect in the usual ways. Unlike *Call of Cthulhu*, no matter the status of a character's sanity, they stay in play, with a framework provided to guide players through their character's behavioral changes.

Sanity systems in horror games have the difficult job of portraying the corrosive effects of the supernatural on the human mind without trivializing real-world issues of mental health. Distilling such a nuanced topic into mechanics is always going to be fraught, but *Unknown Armies* improves upon the archaic and often offensive system of the past. The system feels grounded in first-hand experience and missteps can be balanced by

the fact that the group collaborates to set parameters for the story, giving players more control over what might befall their characters than in other games.

In fact, what *Unknown Armies* leaves out is telling: The rules explicitly state that multiple personality disorder and schizophrenia are not included as possible consequences of failed sanity checks because including them would trivialize those conditions. This sort of discussion of sensitive topics and how to approach them in a game wasn't really happening before this point. At best, there might have been a catch-all warning that a game was intended for mature audiences, which more often gave designers the license to push all of the envelopes instead of protecting players from upsetting content. By frankly explaining their reasoning in the text of the rules, the designers of *Unknown Armies* were inviting further discussion, and that conversation is still going on more than two decades later.

The Extraordinary Adventures of Baron Munchausen (1998)

Like *Fudge*, there is not much precedent for *The Extraordinary Adventures of Baron Munchausen*. It came out of nowhere, seems preposterous on its face, and winds up signaling a massive paradigm shift. Unlike *Fudge*, some might argue that *Munchausen* isn't actually a roleplaying game. To those people, I say: Pistols or swords?

A little history before I demand satisfaction on the dueling grounds. Baron Munchausen is probably best known, either thanks to the Terry Gilliam film adaptation of his exploits (1988), a noted box office bomb, or as a plot device in countless medical and police procedural television shows (Munchausen Syndrome, named for the Baron, is a sort of attention-seeking hypochondria, though its veracity as a diagnosis is, appropriately, uncertain). His origins go further back, however. He was apparently a historical figure (though, with everything involving the Baron, keeping a cautious shaker of salt nearby is wise), a soldier known for telling tall tales about his time fighting for the Russian Empire against the Turks.

These anecdotes inspired writer Rudolf Erich Raspe to anonymously pen his own outrageous stories attributed to a Baron Munchausen in 1785. Much to the real Baron's embarrassment, Raspe's tales were of an entirely different order of magnitude, with the fictional Baron flying on a cannonball, traveling to the moon, and somehow using tree branches to repair a horse cut in half. After the initial publication, the stories took on a life of their own—more than two centuries later, adaptations, re-imaginings, and cameos by the Baron in other tales number in the hundreds.

A few details of the original stories are important to the shape of the RPG. For starters, the Baron narrates the tales himself, and, while his manner is friendly, his tales are told with an objective tone. Everything about his presentation is designed to feel plausible. It is only because the events themselves are so categorically absurd that they are clearly fabrications. And even then, the Baron often expresses surprise at the events he describes, which serves to make the reader unsure of the truth. Finally, while not true of the first edition, later versions by Raspe have the Baron being most insistent that everything he says is true, no matter how preposterous or inconsistent.

Raspe's Munchausen stories don't actually recount wild adventures. They recount a man recounting; it is a story about telling stories (or, uncharitably, about a man lying through his teeth), so the *Baron Munchausen* RPG is a game

THE EXTRAORDINARY ADVENTURES OF BARON MUNCHAUSEN, HOGSHEAD PUBLISHING, 1998
JAMES WALLIS, COVER BY GUSTAVE DORÉ

about telling stories (or, players lying through their teeth).

As such, the book is a mere 24 pages, written by the Baron himself, and, even then, it is accompanied by much of his trademark digression. The rules themselves amount to half-a-page. They dispense with most of what is taken for granted in an RPG. "The rules came in a sudden rush during a shower," recalls creator James Wallis, "but that was after years of noodling around the idea of a conventional RPG about the Baron and his exploits, which did not work at all."

Play commences around a table at the tavern of the players' choosing. Everyone has a purse in front of them, filled with one coin for each player at the table. The last person who bought a round begins by asking the person to their right to tell a story and delivers a prompt, such as, "So, Baron, tell us the story of the time you fed the entire city of Luxembourg bacon from a single pig."

The storyteller then weaves a five-minute tale, heaping on as much ridiculousness as possible, and finishes with a vow of their truthfulness. Other players can complicate the story by putting one of their coins in the center of the table and offering a suggestion: "But Baron, wherever did you find a frying pan the size of Versailles?" The storyteller can either accept the coin and add the embellishment or deny the coin and insult the questioner. The questioner, in turn, can add another coin, raising the stakes further, take back their coin like a coward, or challenge the storyteller to a duel (or three rounds of roshambo, for those squeamish about violence), with the winner taking all of the coins.

Once a story is finished, the teller invites the person to their right to share a story, and around it goes until everyone has had a chance to weave a tale (or has begged off, buying the group a round as punishment). At that point, every player takes the coins in front of them and gives them to the storyteller they think told the best story. The person with the most coins is the declared the winner to the cheers of everyone at the table, and uses their winnings to buy the next round.

This is about the most minimal set of rules to see release so far, but there are rules, so it is definitely a game with strategy. The rules explicitly instruct players to aim to outdo the previous storyteller, so the final storyteller (the person who initiates the game!) has a vast advantage in terms of winning, due to their position within the order—they know exactly what needs to be topped, and, even if they fail to top it, they benefit from having told the most recent tale. The only way for other players to minimize that advantage is through the judicious use of the interruption wagers, which, if used properly, can derail the current storyteller while reminding the listeners of the derailer's own tale.

"*Munchausen* is absolutely about improvisation—it's inspired and driven

by it—but it is not about improvising the rules," says Wallis. "The rules and the structure are absolutely solid, and have to be for the game to work. I have had people tell me that it's not a real game, which I utterly reject—it has a fixed endpoint and a winner, it's much more of a game than 99% of RPGs."

And roles are being played. In some way, all of the players embody Baron Munchausen himself when they are telling their story. Even if the Baron isn't in mind, the players are still encouraged, in a meta fashion, to take on the role of a fictional storytelling gentleman of some stripe.

This tale-telling mirrors the format of club tales established with Lord Dunsany's Joseph Jorkens stories. The framing device for which, inspired by the Munchausen tales, is that Jorkens is telling them to his fellows at a London gentleman's club. The Jorkens stories (the first of which, "The Tale of Abu Laheeb," appeared in in 1926) went on to inspire many similarly formatted collections—L. Sprague de Camp and Fletcher Pratt had *Tales from Gavagan's Bar* (1953), Arthur C. Clarke had *Tales from the White Hart* (1957), and Spider Robinson had *Callahan's Crosstime Saloon* (1977), which even received its own GURPS sourcebook (1992). RPGs had flirted with the club tale before that, too. The pop culture spoof RPG, *Tales from the Floating Vagabond* (1991), takes the format and remarries it to the expository excesses of the Baron, to great comedic effect.

Floating Vagabond reveals a curious paradox, though. While a fairly simple game, it nevertheless has far more rules to manage than *Baron Munchausen*, yet, in many ways, it's a simpler game to play. *Munchausen* demands much of its players for all its pared down simplicity. They must be willing to improvise wildly, often at the drop of a dime (literally, thanks to the wagering system), while injecting ever more absurdity, a talent for which there is definitely a knack. As with *Fudge,* a sort of paralysis can set it, or worse, apathy, both of which are more likely the responses of players with long histories of traditional roleplaying. Storytelling is hard enough on its own without turning it into a competition!

Still, *Baron Munchausen* represents a sea change—it's visible right on the cover. Hogshead Publishing, which had, up until now, made its money publishing *Warhammer Fantasy Roleplay* products under license from Games Workshop, calls *Munchausen*, "a role-playing game in a New Style," a term that indicates a self-awareness of its innovation. It was true! Other New Style games followed. There are two satirical games, *Puppetland/ Power Kill* (1999) and *Violence*, both of which question assumptions RPGs make about violence. *Puppetland* (published in the same book as *Power Kill*), *De Profundis*, and the five mini-games contained in *Pantheon* (2000), all toyed with the ways RPGs handle narratives. Many of these ideas and conventions are taken further in the next decade by games like *Sorcerer*, *Universalis*, and the broader indie/storygame movement.

"At the time I was working on the game I did not feel that I was creating anything particularly different or radical or new,"

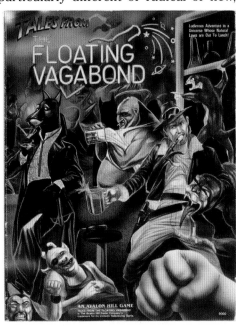

says Wallis. "I just thought it was a cool idea with a couple of good jokes, so in hindsight it seems that I initiated the story-game movement by accident."

Nobilis (1999)

The first edition of *Nobilis* is a small, pinkish hardcover book. Perhaps because of the cover art, a painting by Alphonse Mucha ("The Seasons: Winter") that is in the public domain, it looks more like a blank journal that might be found near the cash register in small bookstores than an RPG.

Inside is a densely written, mesmerizing game that would, if not for the greatly expanded and polished second edition from Hogshead Publishing, likely have faded into obscurity. Where the first edition seems to shrink from the eye, the second edition demands attention; a bright, white, nearly 12-inch square book of 300 pages, it glows among the dark covers of its RPG brethren. A luxurious tome, it was the first RPG book to be priced north of $40 dollars.

On its cover is the beguiling sculpture, *Le Sphinx Mystérieux* (1897), by Charles van der Stappen, a choice that imbues the book with a sense of authority and greatness, like a piece in a museum or a monument. With the first and second editions straddling the turn of the millennium, *Nobilis* does stand as a kind testament to the previous decade.

At this point, '90s RPG design decisions are almost a catechism. *Nobilis* embraces many of the tenets. The game concept is sky high. There are two worlds, a magical one hiding under the surface of a prosaic one. The influence of Neil Gaiman's *The Sandman* is palpable. Lore and factions abound. Like *In Nomine*, the wars fought in *Nobilis* are cold and quiet. Like *Amber*, there are no dice, nor any randomizers (chance has no place in a game of divinities). The system and its focus on narrative are deceptively simple—the game's heady concepts are the reason it is so

TALES FROM THE FLOATING VAGABOND, AVALON HILL, 1991
LEE GARVIN, NICK ATLAS, AND JOHN HUFF, COVER BY JAMES HOLLOWAY

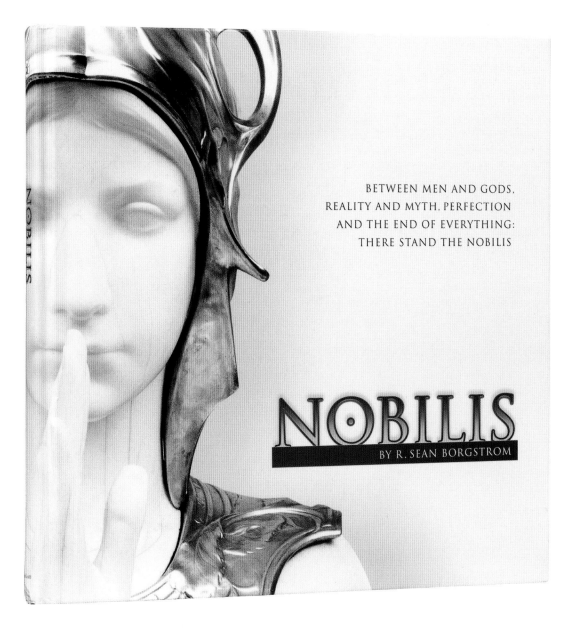

BETWEEN MEN AND GODS,
REALITY AND MYTH, PERFECTION
AND THE END OF EVERYTHING:
THERE STAND THE NOBILIS

NOBILIS
BY R. SEAN BORGSTROM

NOBILIS, SECOND EDITION, HOGSHEAD PUBLISHING, 2002
JENNA K. MORAN, COVER BY CHARLES VAN DER STAPPEN

fascinating, but they also make playing it seem like a challenge. It is, indeed, a '90s RPG!

Players take the role of Sovereign Powers, regular people who have been given a dual nature by a powerful celestial entity called an Imperator. In the mundane world, they're (mostly) regular humans, but in the mythic world, which they can enter at will, they embody a concept from the real-world, in a manner reminiscent of a god. These concepts can be grand, like the Endless from *The Sandman*—Delirium, Desire, Destruction, and on—or they can be pedestrian, like, well, Walking, Waffles, Summer Breezes, or whatever captures a player's imagination.

As in the world of the ancient Greeks, where everything contained a guardian spirit, every idea in the game's reality has a spiritual representative that cares for and is generally responsible for it. In normal times, Imperators handled a collection of these metaphysical estates themselves, but the war with the Excrucians—entities from outside existence who seek to unravel creation, not unlike the Nothing from *The NeverEnding Story* (1984)—has required them to delegate.

Imperators come in several varieties; there are angels and devils and intelligences that map to mythological deities, all arranged in a dizzying feudal hierarchy that is largely incomprehensible by design—these are cosmic forces outside of the limited human experience, after all. While players take the roles of entities that approach divinity, they remain half human, which keeps them comprehensible—and unpredictable.

A large portion of the book is devoted to creation. Characters consist of four attributes—Aspect, which accounts for anything physical; Domain, which represents how entwined the character is with the concept they embody; Realm denotes their degree of control over their Chancel (more on that in a moment); and Spirit, their magical aptitudes—each of which

are assigned a value through a point buy system. These values are absolute, as in *Amber*, so a character with a four in Aspect always beats a three in a physical contest. Each attribute has a pool of five or more miracle points that can be spent to change the foregone outcome of that contest. They can also be used to power various miracles—a sovereign power of wine might spend four miracle points to fill the cups of everyone in their city, for instance. Added to this are gifts and handicaps, and the character is essentially done, but the work of creation is not.

Players must also collaborate to define their shared Imperator, the Chancel (a sort of highly thematic pocket dimension that acts as a sanctuary), and a heraldic crest of flowers that represents the family (in the mythology of *Nobilis*, every aspect of creation is defined by a flower planted in Heaven, thus flowers have many symbolic meanings and magical uses in the game).

This collaborative part of the process is the crystal ball that allows players to glimpse the shape of the coming storygame movement. Defining the game world through collaboration is one of the key tenets of *Nobilis,* and it is one of the first games to encourage the GM to always say "yes" to players whenever possible (*Dogs in the Vineyard* further codifies the Rule of Yes). *Nobilis* is also one of the earliest games to devote space to discussing and setting boundaries, and to look after the comfort of players, something that *Sorcerer* embraced concurrently to the *Nobilis* second edition (which was accompanied by a handbook for live action players, *The Game of Powers* (2003), where such boundaries are especially important).

These are design philosophies that tend to be associated with modern games that require little or no preparation and have low barriers to entry for newcomers to the hobby. Yet, *Nobilis* feels intimidating. The physicality of the book is part of it—large, starkly beautiful, full of strange illustrations. It's difficult to hold and makes the reading a formal affair—sit up straight, book flat on the table, no slouching, and certainly no lounging on the couch. It feels difficult, the same way silent movies and Victorian literature can, regardless of whether or not they *are*. They have an air of burden, thanks to their age and status. So, too, does *Nobilis*—presented with formality and a certain poetic flare, it's a type of game that was strange by the standards of the day; and for its trouble, it's gained a reputation of impenetrability. This characterization is unfair, and the long line of approachability-minded storygames that have followed in the wake of *Nobilis* demonstrate that a reappraisal is warranted.

Violence (1999)

The slang term "murderhobo" first appeared in 2011 as a portmanteau or blending of "murderous hobo," which had been in use since 2007. Both originated on the message boards of RPG.net, and both are used to dismiss a specific style of *D&D* play in which players are rootless deathmongers, wandering the land in search of plunder and violence.

While the terminology is recent, the style of play is quite old. I've already discussed how Trampier's iconic cover of the *Players Handbook* is a tribute to murder hobos. The style of play is, perhaps, one of the very first, judging from the descriptions of Gary Gygax's early playtests exploring Castle Greyhawk. If *Violence* is any indication, the murder hobo style was not only widespread, but perceived as a default for *D&D*.

Violence is a satirical RPG and one that Designer X (a barely-there pseudonym for Greg Costikyan) clearly expected no one to actually play—the subtitle is "The Role-Playing Game of Egregious and Repulsive Bloodshed." Designer X describes the game, the third in Hogshead Publishing's New Style series:

Violence™ is a lot like *Dungeons & Dragons*® by that other company. You and your friends play characters in an imaginary world. You wander about a maze, kicking down doors, killing whatever you find on the other side, and taking its possessions. The main difference is this: The world isn't some third-rate fantasy writer's drivel about elves and dwarves and magic spells, but the world of today. The doors you kick down aren't those of a subterranean dungeon—unless you're in the subway—but those of decent, honest, hard-working people who merely want to live their lives. The things you kill aren't cardboard "monsters" whom the game defines as okay to kill because, well, they're *monsters*—but fellow human beings, with families and friends and hopes and fears and highly developed senses of morality—far better people than you, in fact. And the things you steal aren't "magic items" and "gold pieces" but stereos, jewelry, and whatever other items of value you can lift.

Indeed, you yourself are a monster: a monster in the true sense, not the "fantasy" one. You are a degraded, bloodthirsty savage, the product of the savage streets, a Jeffrey Dahmer, a droog, a character out of Brett Easton Ellis. You delight in pain and blood and mayhem. You won't live long, I promise you, but you'll leave a trail of mangled corpses in your wake.

The New Style games were meant, on one hand, to be innovative. "*Violence* is the one that doesn't really fit in the New Style range because [...] its structure is fiercely traditional," says James Wallis, owner of Hogshead, "but I regard it like the Situationist manifesto that was bound in sandpaper to destroy the books it was shelved next to. Once you've read *Violence*, you can't look at old-school *D&D* the same way again."

Since satire is often mistaken for endorsement by the folks being satirized, Costikyan goes so far over the top to get his point across that he's in low orbit. The book is grotesque, sneering, and snide, explicitly calling itself disgusting and questioning the moral fiber of anyone willing to read it. It's often quite funny but also gets at a deep frustration regarding the centering of violence in all sorts of play—tabletop games, videogames, make believe. Questions about that particular intersection would shortly become the focus of national attention in the wake of the Columbine High School massacre in April of 1999.

Costikyan finds room to skewer other topics, as well, like sexism in hobbyist spaces and unrestrained police violence—there are explicit, outraged references to the murder of Amadou Diallo by New York City police officers, which had occurred in February of that year. All of these problems, sadly, still feel just as topical and unresolved as they did 22-years ago, perhaps more so.

Whenever social criticism is aimed at *D&D* and similar games, one of the most common responses is, "But it's fantasy!" When chainmail bikinis are criticized for catering to straight male players? But it's fantasy! Appropriating Asian culture? But it's fantasy! Questionable portrayals of race? But it's fantasy! *Violence* reveals the lie. By changing just one detail of the *D&D* experience—transitioning from a fantasy

VIOLENCE, HOGSHEAD PUBLISHING, 1999
DESIGNER X (GREG COSTIKYAN), COVER BY CLINT LANGLEY

world to our own modern world—it becomes clear that much of the player behavior that is taken for granted in *D&D*, and is reinforced by the mechanics and aesthetics and on, seems downright anti-social when it plays out in the context of an apartment building or a suburban neighborhood.

Reading *Violence* is a revelation. Even if *D&D* can provide a multitude of experiences beyond that of the murder hobo, even if the mechanics are tweaked to encourage non-violent solutions and social adventures, even if strides are made to make the game more inclusive and diverse, even then—whenever I pick up a *D&D* book, I hear Designer X whispering his ugly truths in my ear.

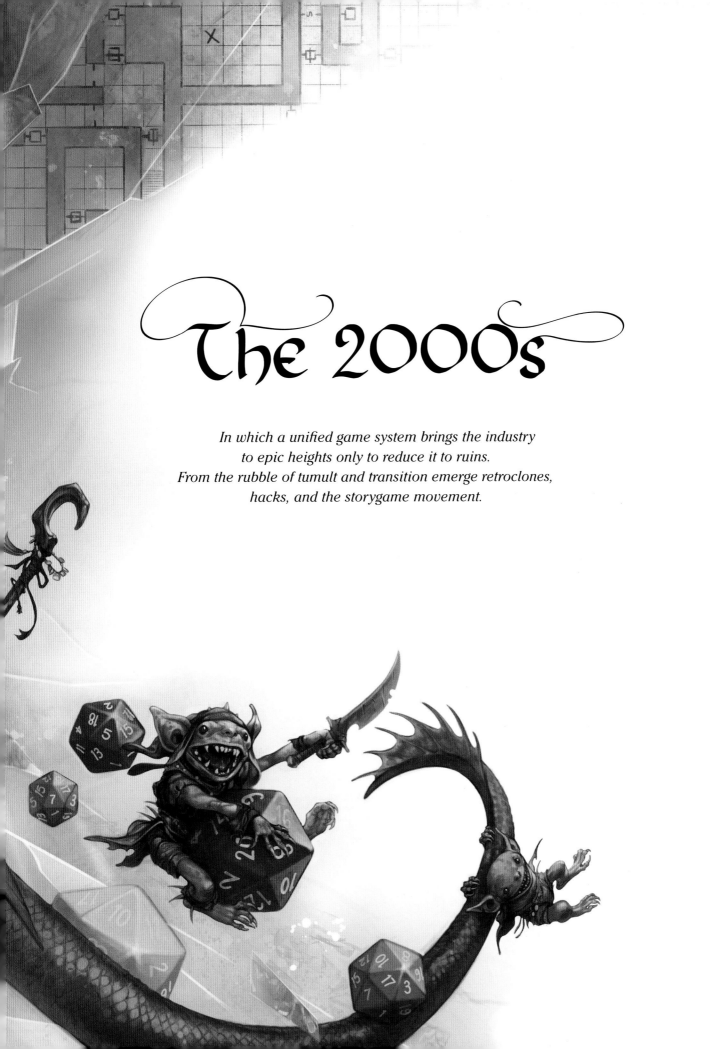

The 2000s

*In which a unified game system brings the industry
to epic heights only to reduce it to ruins.
From the rubble of tumult and transition emerge retroclones,
hacks, and the storygame movement.*

Dungeons & Dragons Third Edition (2000)

From the earliest moments following the birth of *Dungeons & Dragons*, there has been endless, fractious, quixotic debate over how to play the game correctly. It exists in the forewords to the supplements of the original *D&D*, imploring GMs to be measured in rewarding players, lest they have ridiculously overpowered characters. It's apparent in the ongoing debates in *Alarums and Excursions* about how to correct systems people saw as broken, debates which helped create a larger RPG industry. It inspires the partisans of every iteration of *D&D*. The original players think everyone else plays wrong; the First Edition players think *Unearthed Arcana* broke the game (they aren't wrong, but that doesn't make it any less fun to play), and those 1.5E folks think the Second Edition is a heretical watering down, a bloated cash grab, or both. Moldvay did it right—no, Arneson, no, Holmes, no, Mentzer.

The Third Edition is born out of this din, with its origin stretching back to the Second Edition of *Advanced Dungeons & Dragons*. In the wake of the nonsensical accusations that *D&D* was somehow spiritually and psychologically dangerous, a decision was made to excise certain controversial elements from the new edition. Assassins, half-orcs, devils, and demons were all removed.

In an op-ed for *Dragon* magazine (February 1990), James M. Ward explained that the makers of *D&D* wanted to avoid the wrath of angry mothers. At the time, many players saw this as an unfair capitulation to irrational antagonists that resulted in a sanitized game. Although Zeb Cook's rules for the Second Edition of *Advanced Dungeons & Dragons* are entirely compatible with Gygax's original rules—meaning players could easily put Assassins and demons and whatever right back in—this perceived sterilization became a source of simmering resentment for the better part of the decade. Half measures, like bringing back devils as Baatezu and demons as Tanar'ri, further stoked the fires of discontent rather than fostering reconciliation.

For some folks, when TSR went out of business, it seemed a well-deserved comeuppance for long-remembered wrongs. Wizards of the Coast, who purchased TSR in 1997, were seen as liberators, restoring the game to its former glory. There is a noticeable, gleeful turn in latter day Second Edition products once designers no longer had to worry about what the moms thought. Many publications returned to old stomping grounds, literally, as with *Return to the Tomb of Horrors* (1998) and more obliquely, with Monte Cook's *A Paladin in Hell* (1998), which is inspired by a beloved illustration from the First Edition *Player's Handbook* and formally returns the terms "devils" and "demons" to the game with a heavy metal attitude.

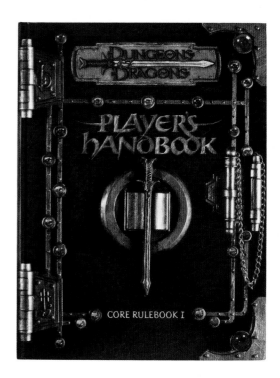

PLAYER'S HANDBOOK, WIZARDS OF THE COAST, 2000
MONTE COOK, JONATHAN TWEET, AND SKIP WILLIAMS, COVER BY HENRY HIGGINBOTHAM

For better or worse, the Third Edition of *Dungeons & Dragons* was forged, in part, by the goodwill generated in those last days of Second Edition. While, on some philosophical level, it was marketed as a return to its roots, on a mechanical level, it was a complete overhaul.

The idea was to create a totally unified system that used a 20-sided die to resolve all conflicts. Half-orcs returned as a player character race (though Assassins did not return as a class). A new spellcaster, the Sorcerer, ditched the old pick-and-memorize spell mechanic in favor of spontaneous casting, like the Cleric. Combat was greatly expanded and made highly tactical. Feats replaced the old non-weapon proficiency skill system and functioned more like special abilities, and prestige classes offered unique specializations at higher levels.

There was a new focus on character customization through mechanics, with *every* new book introducing ever-more rule options—so much so that it feels like there was an intent to publish a rule for every potential situation and outcome. Because the rules were so comprehensive, the idea of character builds emerged,

MONSTER MANUAL, WIZARDS OF THE COAST, 2000 MONTE COOK, JONATHAN TWEET, AND SKIP WILLIAMS, COVER BY HENRY HIGGINBOTHAM

a notion that there are optimal fine-tuned customizations that give players greater advantages in play. To the surprise of no one, the system was a massive success.

Prior to the release of the Third Edition of *Dungeons & Dragons*, Wizards of the Coast released two licenses. The first was the Open Gaming License (OGL), which supposedly made the mechanics of the Third Edition, as expressed in a system reference document, open for commercial use by any publisher (this is a bit of a fib, see page 295). The second license was for the use of an official d20 System trademark, designed to signal that products developed under the OGL were all compatible.

The reasoning behind this licensing scheme was purely economic. Core rulebooks retain their market value longer over time, while profits from supplemental material diminish. In releasing these licenses, Wizards of the Coast effectively outsourced the development of the expanded *D&D* line. Many publishers

DUNGEON MASTER'S GUIDE, WIZARDS OF THE COAST, 2000 MONTE COOK, JONATHAN TWEET, AND SKIP WILLIAMS, COVER BY HENRY HIGGINBOTHAM

BOOK OF VILE DARKNESS, WIZARDS OF THE COAST, 2001
MONTE COOK, COVER BY HENRY HIGGINBOTHAM

jumped at the opportunity; Troll Lord Games, Goodman Games, Green Ronin, and Mongoose all got their start by producing supplemental sourcebooks and scenarios for the Third Edition of *D&D*. Wizards also released the d20 *Star Wars Roleplaying Game* (2000) and *d20 Modern* (2002) to expand the d20 System into other genres. Hundreds of products hit the market.

There were some unforeseen consequences, however. No one predicted how many companies would be willing to develop new games for, or convert their existing games to, the d20 System. Chaosium's *Call of Cthulhu* (2002) and White Wolf's *World of Darkness* (2007) both got the d20 treatment, for instance. In a short period of time, huge swaths of the RPG industry had been converted into the d20 System industry. This was a precarious overcommitment.

Three complications came together to topple d20's supremacy. The first problem came to light thanks to the *Book of Erotic Fantasy* (2003). The riot of demons and old school revelry that happened at the tail end of Second Edition continued into Third Edition with one particular book, the *Book of Vile Darkness* (2002), a

mature audiences title that strove to imbue as much gross awfulness into *D&D*'s portrayal of evil as possible. There's nudity, graphic depictions of sadomasochism, and demons galore; the book is an orgy of questionable taste and prudish kink shaming, masquerading as a transgressive reaction to a decade of perceived self-censorship. And because it was published by Wizards of the Coast, it was an acceptable addition to the *D&D* canon. The *Book of Erotic Fantasy*, on the other hand, introduces all manner of material involving sex into the d20 System, including conception, birth, and sexually transmitted infections. Regardless of whether players want to include material like that in a game, it seems rather tame in comparison to the unhallowed excesses of *Book of Vile Darkness*.

Since Wizards had already published *Vile Darkness*, opening the door for mature content, the company's swift reaction to the third-party published *Book of Erotic Fantasy* was unexpected. As soon as the book was announced, Wizards revised the d20 license to include a standard of decency. This forced Valar Project, the book's publisher, to drop the d20 trademark, as well as all references to *D&D*, and to publish the book under the OGL, instead. Wizards of the Coast's display of discretionary power made other publishers understandably nervous.

The second problem was *D&D* 3.5 (2003), a comprehensive revision of the core *D&D* books that sought to address complaints and correct numerous minor errors. The corrected edition was released at Gen Con, taking d20 System publishers by surprise and rendering many forthcoming books outdated before they even hit shelves.

The final issue was one of success. There was just too much product flooding the market without enough quality control. Many d20 books were obvious cashins. After a brief but lucrative boom period, the d20 brand was rapidly devaluing in the opinion of players. By the end of 2003, the boom turned into a bust. Because so many publishers had committed to the d20 System, the sudden collapse of the market caused a massive drop in sales and sparked a disaster, devastating the industry. Many companies went out of business, and for a moment, it looked like the whole industry might fall apart.

It survived, but just barely.

Many of the remaining publishers looked for alternatives. Some dropped the d20 brand but stayed committed to the underlying system, publishing under the OGL. Green Ronin's *Blue Rose*, which used their house version of d20, called True20, is one example. Others hacked or otherwise experimented with d20, like Troll Lord Games' *Castles & Crusades*. Still, others looked back to earlier editions, creating retroclones and kicking off the Old School Revival. Some noteworthy products still came out under d20, despite the downturn. Those are often characterized by and noted for their sheer size. The groundbreaking *Ptolus: Monte Cook's City by the Spire* (2006) from Malhavoc Press provides over 600-pages of luxurious detail for urban adventuring; even that massive book is outmatched by the over 800-page *The World's Biggest Dungeon* (2004) from Alderac Entertainment Group. Slimmer books saw print too, like *Dark•Matter*. Originally a conspiracy-themed setting for TSR's *Alternity* line (1999), it was converted to d20 Modern as a standalone game (2006) and served, for many players, as an introduction to horror roleplaying. Designers, like Sean Richer, whose *Terror of the Stratosfiend* (2019) pushes those boundaries even further, carry those influences into the modern day.

The Third Edition of *D&D* soldiered on for several years, growing volume by

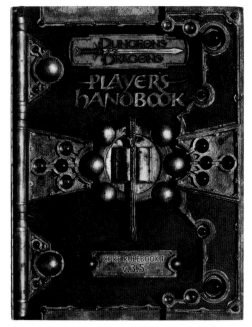

PLAYER'S HANDBOOK V.3.5, WIZARDS OF THE COAST, 2003 MONTE COOK, JONATHAN TWEET, AND SKIP WILLIAMS, COVER BY HENRY HIGGINBOTHAM

volume, straining shelves, the system groaning under its own weight. By 2007, there were 12 core rulebooks and well over 50 sourcebooks, each of which added new rules, races, prestige classes, monsters, magic items, and spells to the game.

While continuing to play such a sprawling game was undoubtedly daunting, the announcement of a forthcoming new edition nevertheless pissed off many players, who felt their piles of books would soon be rendered worthless. They were invested and, true to their fears, the Fourth Edition of *D&D* (2008) proved to be radical overhaul of the fundamental systems; it offered no compatibility with previous material and no nostalgia-centered marketing to smooth over the ruffled feathers. The new edition was a financial hit upon its release and was supported by a line nearly as big as its predecessor, but that success was fleeting—the game lasted just four years. More importantly, it marked a point of fracture that left a significant number of players behind: Those who stuck with the Third Edition and those who moved on to *Pathfinder*.

Hero Wars (2000)

Back in the early days of Glorantha, Greg Stafford coined the term "heroquest:" An in-universe metaphysical practice by which religious initiates could perform elaborate rituals and literally take on the aspect of a god to relive the events of important myths. Doing so could bring blessings to the community in the form of good crops, say, or personal power to the participants, in the form of strong magic or relics; or the participants could stray, finding new mythways or becoming lost forever in the Godtime.

This metaphysical pursuit was intended to form the core of an RPG—if *RuneQuest* is a game about exploring the physical world of Glorantha, *HeroQuest* was envisioned as a way to explore Glorantha's living mythology. Though long promised, it never materialized, and Stafford eventually let the trademark lapse. Milton Bradley snatched it up for their beloved board game of the same name, and, for many years, that was the end of the story.

Meanwhile, a series of business-related complications unfolded for Stafford. Chaosium licensed *RuneQuest* to Avalon Hill (1985), resulting in an ill-fated third edition of the game that never made the kind of money on which both companies were banking.

Chaosium hadn't licensed Glorantha, though. Those rights stayed with Stafford, who had final approval over anything Avalon Hill produced that was set in his world. Avalon Hill disliked the extra hurdle to publication, so it initially marketed *RuneQuest* as a generic fantasy system. Glorantha was in the core box, but so was a mythic Europe, and the first wave of products were setting agnostic. Some Glorantha material saw print in the late '80s, but stopped in 1989 (and resumed in 1992, then stopped again in 1994 when the line folded). All the while, Stafford was publishing system agnostic Glorantha material through Chaosium. In 1996, Chaosium found itself in some dire financial straits, thanks to the collapse of the collectible card game market, prompting Stafford to spin Glorantha and its associated trademarks off into another company, Issaries, Inc. The obvious next step was to make a new Glorantha RPG.

To do that, Stafford devised a fan donation scheme that anticipated the crowdfunding publishing models that currently dominate the industry. Fans could purchase shares of Issaries for $100 dollars. When the sold shares amounted to $50,000 dollars, the company would start work on a new RPG, which would be delivered to market in 18 months. This was in 1997, a dozen years before Kickstarter was founded, and there were, predictably, issues to work out—using the term "shares," instead of "patrons" or "backers," invited regulatory headaches in all 50 states and would have forced the company to publicly report its earnings. Issaries ironed out the scheme into something resembling our modern crowdfunding models in 1999. The following year, *Hero Wars* hit shelves.

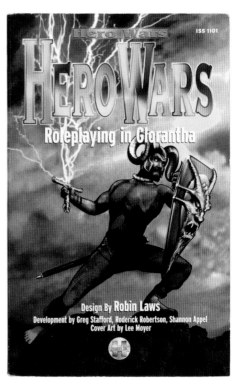

Hero Wars marks a culmination of narrative-focused RPGs up to this point in time. As much as the industry spent the previous decade-and-a-half trying to free itself from complex mechanical systems and simulation, it was a messy divorce. The difficulty of this process can be seen most clearly in *D&D*'s clumsy narrative experiments, but most games of the '90s that had sprawling metaplots also had similarly sprawling systems to navigate. Meanwhile, freeform games over-corrected, providing less structured experiences that were highly improvisational and often challenging to comprehend for long-time traditional players. Some of those, like *Nobilis*, were philosophically ambitious—they weren't concerned with simulation, but they had to account for narrative possibilities across several realities, resulting in games that could be as complex as *D&D*, just in different, non-mechanical ways. These RPGs remained *BIG*, trading one kind of encumbrance for another.

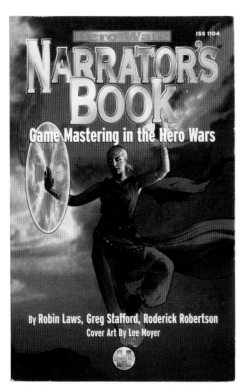

HeroQuest: Roleplaying in Glorantha, Steve Jackson Games and Issaries, Inc., 2003 Robin D. Laws and Greg Stafford, Cover by Lee Moyer

This complexity is true for *Hero Wars*. Designed by Robin D. Laws, it is very much a natural evolution of his work on *Over the Edge*. Characters aren't created so much as described, and their keyword-based skills and attributes are then derived from those descriptions. The keywords imply much—for instance, every character is going to come from an ethnic group, and that keyword broadly covers the group's cultural norms and treats them as skills. So, a character from Prax will be good at riding, hunting, desert survival, and such, while a Sartarite likely knows farming, herding, and how to survive in the forests and mountain passes.

In practice, the application of keywords is often improvisational. If a character's profession keyword is "soldier," for instance, the player can apply that to any contest that involves the skills they successfully argue are part of that profession, like swordplay or horseback riding. Each keyword receives a numerical rating that is added to the result of a die roll in a unified resolution system—it works the same way for an arm-wrestling match, a philosophical debate, or a climb up a perilous cliff, with all the players working together

Hero Wars Narrator's Book, Issaries, Inc. and Moon Design, 2000 Robin D. Laws, Greg Stafford, and Roderick Robertson, Cover by Lee Moyer

HeroQuest, Second edition, Moon Design and Cubicle 7, 2011
Robin D. Laws, Cover by John Hodgson

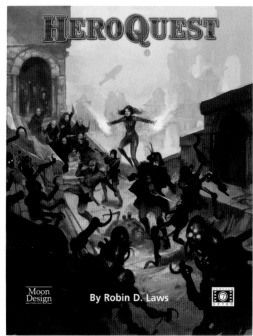

epics. But, the keyword mechanic is still important for many games, like *Dogs in the Vineyard.*

Hero Wars was rough around the edges when it came out. Further complicating matters, it was published as a series of digest-sized books, rather than the standard textbook size adopted by most RPGs at that time. The idea was to make the game more attractive to bookstores, but it didn't translate to sales—general audiences shrugged, and experienced players who only had eyes for A4 paper seemed not to notice the little books in the hobby shops. The digest size has since been popularized by the indie game scene, an indication that *Hero Wars* might have been ahead of its time.

The line continued until 2003, when a revised edition came out in partnership with Steve Jackson Games. This one features a textbook-sized rulebook and a new name: *HeroQuest.* Milton Bradley had let the trademark lapse, so Issaries snapped it back up. This rule set is more refined and polished, but the support

to describe the result of the die roll in terms of the shared story. Because the system is unified, the game easily scales from personal conflicts, like one-on-one combat, up to large military battles and on to cosmic events while resolution remains a "simple" die roll.

Comprehension becomes shaky when considering that vast variance in scale. From there, complexity gets layered on. One-on-one conflicts are easy enough to grasp, but group conflicts that consist of series of rolls can become dizzying. When the five different types of magic are accounted for, the vertigo really hits. This is a game that is interested in narrative but still bound to the basic framework of traditional RPGs. *Hero Wars* shows the vast potential of narrative gaming, and there is freedom in that revelation, yes, but that freedom is all too often paralyzing.

In a few short years, with the release of *Sorcerer*, the founding of the Forge, and the explosion of the storygame movement, that traditional framework finally falls away. Free of that, narrative-focused games clarify their own mechanics, usually centering on very specific experiences rather than sprawling, scaling

HeroQuest Glorantha, Moon Design, 2015
Jeff Richard and Robin D. Laws, Cover by John Hodgson

materials are scattershot. Where *Hero Wars* focused on developing the tribes of Sartar in Dragon Pass—a long awaited turn of events for Glorantha fans—*Hero-Quest* was splitting its attention between supplements for Sartarites, Praxians (who received the bulk of the original *RuneQuest* detail), and Lunar Imperials (the world's traditional antagonist), while the scenarios focused on the travails of Sartar. Those scenarios would never see their epic conclusion.

In 2004, the bust of the d20 System rippled through the industry, and Issaries ceased publication, licensing *HeroQuest* to Moon Design Publications (itself born out of the Reaching Moon Megacorp, a British Glorantha fan group), where it received a third edition. In a bizarre case of history repeating itself, this revised version was positioned as a generic system, suitable for any sort of setting.

As with Avalon Hill's third edition of *RuneQuest*, a gloss on Glorantha is included in the back, feeling like an afterthought. Unlike Avalon Hill, though, Moon Design followed the rules with a series of Glorantha sourcebooks and scenarios—*Sartar: Kingdom of Heroes* (2009), *Sartar Companion* (2010), and *Pavis: Gateway to*

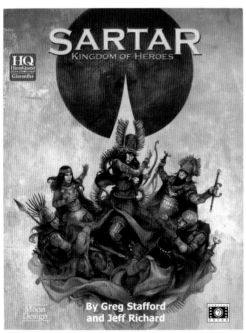

Adventure (2012)—that should be considered classics on the level of Chaosium's 1980s Glorantha box sets, like *Borderlands* and *Pavis: Threshold to Danger*.

In 2013, Stafford transferred all rights concerning Glorantha to Moon Design. A fourth edition, *HeroQuest: Glorantha*, appeared in 2015. As the name implies, it inextricably remarries the *HeroQuest* system to the world of Glorantha. By this time, the lines between Moon Design and Chaosium were increasingly blurry, a state of affairs that continues to this day. Two additional products for *HeroQuest: Glorantha* saw release, a sourcebook called *The Coming Storm* (2016) and *The Eleven Lights* campaign (2018), both published by Chaosium.

Finally, in 2020, Moon Design and Chaosium reached a deal to transfer the trademark for HeroQuest to Hasbro, who announced a new version of the classic board game the same year. Meanwhile, what used to be the *HeroQuest* RPG is now known as *QuestWorlds*. As of this writing, the only official releases under that name are a system reference documents and an open gaming license for third party designers to use in the making of genre packs for the system. Chaosium announced its intention to develop a line of packs in-house, as well. The first—a superhero-themed pack by *Sorcerer* designer, Ron Edwards.

De Profundis (2001)

There is something about the way that Lovecraft wrote about the *Necronomicon*, a tome of forbidden, mind-searing knowledge. There are the quotations, of course, like the famous couplet that opens the second act of "The Call of Cthulhu," one of his most famous stories: "That is not dead which can eternal lie, / And with strange aeons even death may die."

There are regular references to the book in his stories, both explicit and oblique, all of which are supported by his

SARTAR: KINGDOM OF HEROES, MOON DESIGN AND CUBICLE 7, 2012 GREG STAFFORD AND JEFF RICHARD, COVER BY JOHN HODGSON

DE PROFUNDIS: LETTERS FROM THE ABYSS, HOGSHEAD PUBLISHING, 2001
MICHAŁ ORACZ, COVER BY DENNIS DETWILLER

faux-historical essay on the history of its various editions. This seeming realness is magnified first by the use of the book by other contemporary authors in a sort of ad hoc shared fictional universe, then in pop culture, at large, as the book often pops up as an all-purpose grimoire of black magic. Its use in *Evil Dead II* (1987) is just one of many examples.

Pastiches abound, as do fan-made props (a limited-edition book called the *Al Azif: The Necronomicon*, written in a fake language, with an introduction by L. Sprague DeCamp, turned up in 1973) and hoaxes (author and paranormal "researcher" Colin Wilson was involved in the production of one in 1978). There is also some wishful thinking (if one can call hoping for an ancient pre-human book of sanity-melting knowledge wishful) in the occult community about the book.

Kenneth Grant, a disciple of Aleister Crowley, believed that Lovecraft's fiction was unwittingly inspired by a deeper metaphysical truth. That's the same hook on which "Simon" hung the most famous hoax *Necronomicon*. Their supposedly cursed grimoire full of Sumerian ceremonial magic was released as a mass-market paperback in 1980. Nothing says "eldritch lore" quite like a mass-market paperback.

The sum of all of these fabrications is that the *Necronomicon* feels less fictional than it ought. Perhaps because many readers first discover it during their adolescence, when the world seems particularly deceptive, the idea of a book supposedly containing the monstrous, secret truth of existence feels distinctly plausible. Lovecraft received many letters during his lifetime from readers inquiring after the book. I admit, I checked the card catalog at my local library for it when I was about 11 years old. Whatever the cause, this little glitch in reality lends a sense of credibility to the broader Cthulhu Mythos, that shared literary universe, and makes reality-subverting media, like *De Profundis,* not only possible, but also deliciously entertaining.

De Profundis is an epistolary horror RPG—that is, the play takes place through the mailed correspondence between players (usually two, but the game can scale up to accommodate more, or down to one for a solitaire experience). There is no game master, no combat, no dice, and no attributes. One player writes a letter, describing the spooky events befalling their character in a sort of fusion of roleplaying and creative writing. The other player receives the letter and replies in kind, advancing and developing the plot. The game's rules for the letter writing are practically non-existent. Most of the first edition (itself written as a series of letters) provides advice on structure and atmosphere. Players control all aspects of the action and mystery through their writing. As such, the game is almost entirely free form, collaborative, and improvisational.

The game takes its name from the title given posthumously to Oscar Wilde's letter to his former lover, Lord Alfred Douglas. Translated from the Latin, it means "out of the depths," which, in the context of Lovecraft, takes on a far more ominous feeling than in Psalm 130, where the term originates and where it expresses a cry of

278

existential anguish. There is an intimacy in letter writing that the game seeks to embrace, encouraging play to involve ink and paper, rather than emails and blogs (though, again, there is nothing about the game that forces one to handwrite). There is also a lack of surety. Who is reading what is sent? Who is writing what is received? Can any of this really be trusted?

Lovecraft only used the epistolary form a few times, notably in *The Whisperer in the Darkness* and *The Case of Charles Dexter Ward*, while the narrative of "The Call of Cthulhu," Lovecraft's most famous work, spins out of the examination and presentation of bits of research found in the possession of a late professor (which adds to the sense of plausibility and also, incidentally, surely inspired *Call of Cthulhu*'s enthusiastic embrace of cryptic clue handouts). Aside from Lovecraft, there are plenty of precedents for the fear-inspiring letter, both before— *Frankenstein* (1818), *Dracula* (1897)—and since—Stephen King's *Carrie* (1974), *World War Z* (2006). Even Nick Bantock's *Griffin & Sabine* trilogy (1991-1993), which incorporates actual envelopes and pull-out letters, taps into the uncanniness of correspondence.

So, too, does *De Profundis*. Whether players are pretending to be alternate versions of themselves or entirely different characters in different eras or places, the game encourages players to build an atmosphere of revelatory dread, which is created by reading, and escalates with each exchange (it is a game, of course, so a certain amount of one-upping is expected). It recalls, in a way, the Ouija board. Most folks at the board know that someone is moving the planchette, but the fun is pretending that isn't so, then acting scared in the hopes that the experience will *actually* become scary. Both games actively *invite* horror.

Although it's only of interest to players with a very specific set of predilections, *De Profundis* reinvents the RPG, which is

De Profundis, Second edition, Cubicle 7, 2010 Michał Oracz, Cover by Michał Oracz.

fitting for the game that ended up as the last entry in Hogshead Publishing's series of New Style RPGs, which first launched with *Baron Munchausen*. It is an entirely new form, with few rules or impediments. All that's needed to play is a pen, a piece of paper, a twisted imagination, and the price of postage.

This idea of writing as roleplaying has grown over time, with a number of epistolary games emerging from the indie space. A close solitaire-focused cousin, the journaling RPG, has also sprung up; the best example—*Thousand Year Old Vampire*—is similarly dedicated to horror and other gloomy themes. Broadly, it's another important star in the constellation of storytelling games that are dismantling preconceived notions about how and why RPGs are played. Like its inspirational material, so concerned with secret truths, *De Profundis* reveals something essential but previously hidden about how little structure a game needs to still be recognizable as something that can be played. Thankfully, though, that revelation lacks tentacles.

279

Sorcerer (2002)

Since its inception, the RPG industry has experienced moments of culmination, in which the threads spanning across previous years come together in a new and important way. It happened with dungeon design at end of the '70s, after which point RPG design exploded in all sorts of directions; It happened again at the end of the '80s with *Shadowrun*, a game that set the standard for most of the next decade; and it happens in 2002 with *Sorcerer*, an RPG that weaves together influences from a variety of offbeat games over the last two decades. *Toon, Pendragon, Ars Magica, Prince Valiant, Over the Edge, Fudge, Baron Munchausen, Hero Wars,* and more are all tributaries to this now roaring indie river.

Inspired by the indie comics scene—where creators, like Dave Sim (*Cerebus the Aardvark*, 1977-2004), Wendy and Richard Pini (*Elfquest*, 1978-present), and Colleen Doran (*A Distant Soil*, 1983-present) proved there was a viable market for creator-owned comic book series—Ron Edwards started out by selling a rough version of *Sorcerer* as a text file in 1996 and then as a computer-printed zine. By 1998, he'd upgraded to PDFs and adopted the shareware software distribution method: There was a light version of the rules available for free, while the full version cost $10 dollars.

Already, *Sorcerer* was blazing trails—back in 1996, not many RPGs were distributed online. *Fudge* was circulating on newsgroups, and a couple of publishers were issuing digital versions of rules, but that was about it. Over the next few years, though, PDFs and digital distribution, coupled with the founding of PayPal in 2000 and the launch of other e-commerce payment systems, would become crucial, inexpensive staples of indie RPG publishing and, eventually, the entire industry.

Around the same time, in 1999, Edwards was building a community, first on a site devoted to indie RPG designers called Hephaestus's Forge, which was reborn in 2001 as The Forge, a forum-focused site. There, self-publishers and designers tinkered with mechanics and debated design theory in a way that was reminiscent of *Alarums and Excursions*.

Two essays by Edwards are important to this nascent movement. "The Nuked Apple Cart" (1999) is a screed railing against traditional RPG publication and distribution methods. "System Does Matter" (originally published on The Outpost website in 1999 before later reposting on The Forge), meanwhile, asserts that there are three fundamental types of RPG player: Ones that want to use mechanics to simulate reality; ones that want to create contests that can be won; and ones that want mechanics to facilitate an entertaining story. Further, Edwards argues that a good system caters to one of these, rather than attempting to please all three—this would become a de facto design challenge for the early indie community. These two essays, combined with *Sorcerer,* which serves as an example of the ethos in practice, amount to a three-part manifesto for indie RPG design.

Beyond the high ideas, *Sorcerer* sets the template that many indie RPGs continue to embrace, more or less.

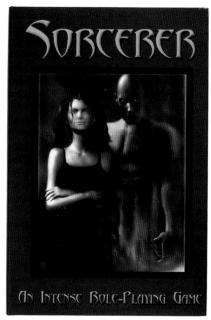

SORCERER, ADEPT PRESS, 2002
RON EDWARDS, COVER BY JEFF KROMER

For starters, as laid out in "System Does Matter," the game is narrow, both thematically and mechanically. It is a game about summoning and commanding demons, thus the mechanics are arranged around summoning and commanding demons. This narrow mechanical scope, coupled with the expansive power of the demons, brings focus to the philosophical and moral question that determines the narrative, Faustian beats of the game: "How far will you go to get what you want?"

If a player's interests lie outside of testing the extremes of personal desire, or if a player has no inclination to fall into a cycle of resisting then succumbing to temptation, the *Sorcerer* will most likely disappoint—not because it is intense or transgressive (though it can be) but because there is literally nothing else to do in the game. It aims for, and delivers, a singular experience.

The rules are lightweight. Skills and the powers of the player's demon are defined by keywords, in the mode of *Over the Edge* or *Hero Wars*. Conflict is resolved by rolling a pool of dice and comparing them with the single highest die determining the winner. Additional dice that beat the opponent's high die determine the degree of success, which helps the GM narrate the results.

Sorcerer also redistributes authority. Traditionally, players control their character and most of the things that "belong" to that character—a Ranger's animal companion, for instance, or a hired hand (until the morale rolls say otherwise, at least)—and the GM has broad jurisdiction over everything else.

In *Sorcerer*, players define their Kicker, which is an event that happens to their character just before play begins, and it forms a catalyst for that character's actions. In effect, the player is saying to the GM, "This is how my character's story

starts, and I'd like it to continue along these lines." Although players have broad authority in creating the demons under their character's control, the GM manages the demons in play. In retrospect, this small shift probably seems like a fairly tame alteration of responsibilities, but it inspired other games to radically re-imagine the power dynamics at the table. *Universalis* and *InSpectres* offer major reconfigurations the very next year.

Finally, *Sorcerer* is concerned with providing a way to play that is entirely unconcerned with *how* it is played. The game recognizes that every group is different and that there is no correct way to play. The Humanity attribute exemplifies this ambiguity. Trafficking with demons or engaging in terrible deeds—an easy task considering the game is built around summoning demons—results in the loss of Humanity points. Not so simple is regaining Humanity—at the discretion of the GM, noble acts, developments in the plot, and the banishment of powerful demons can net Humanity points. Dropping to zero Humanity means the GM gains control of the character. But, nowhere in the book is Humanity defined, nor is the loss of Humanity; what the loss of Humanity looks like and how it manifests are unclear. Those details are associated with a moral core of the game that must be determined by the group playing the game, not the game's designer.

The second supplement book for the game, *The Sorcerer's Soul* (2001) is entirely dedicated to pondering Humanity, but never commits to a concrete explanation of the concept. Resistance to definitive answers follows in just about every other aspect of the game. There are numerous options and ideas about what demons are and how magic works and what it all means for a sorcerer's inner life, but there is very little made explicit or mechanical. *Sorcerer* is the player's game, and they can do as they please; players will not only find the emotionally intense scenarios promised on the cover, but also find them tailored to fit their needs and desires. Creating these sorts of emotional experiences that directly address the wishes of a given table of players *on the fly* is a sought-after goal for many of the indie games that followed.

When fostering a school of game design that encourages the exploration of intense or potentially uncomfortable subject matter, it makes sense to provide tools that can help players avoid subjects they find genuinely upsetting. Ron Edwards tackled this topic in the supplement *Sex and Sorcery* (2003), which, as the title implies, contains guidelines for including sex and intimacy in a game of *Sorcerer*. At any table, there are going to be a spectrum of opinions regarding what is acceptable in the portrayal of sex in an RPG, so Edwards contrived Lines and Veils to manage those opinions.

The application of both tools is established by the group consensus and written down before play. Lines represent hard barriers that the narrative of the game shall not pass. Veils, on the other hand, obscure action that is obviously taking place, the equivalent of the camera in an old movie drifting toward the bedroom door and fading to black when two characters are clearly going to have sex.

Sorcerer only really applies Lines and Veils to sexual content, but they can be applied to any subject matter—one never really knows what might be weighing on someone's mind. After my dad died, most folks would think it natural that I didn't want to see dads dying in an RPG, but it might have surprised those same people to learn that I didn't want to hear any kind of story involving fatherhood. At the same time, generally, I found ultraviolence extremely cathartic. In light of that seeming paradox, I find Lines and Veils to be

valuable tools that can help a group support everyone's comfort level, especially when playing with relative strangers.

Recognizing that RPGs are supposed to be entertaining rather than upsetting, the use of safety tools has been on the rise since *Sorcerer* formalized the concept (though *The Whispering Vault*, 1993, previously, and the second edition of *Nobilis*, concurrently, discuss the notion of preserving player comfort).

Game designer John Stavropoulos came up with the X-Card, a physical card people can tap or show should something arise that makes them feel uncomfortable. Though it developed out of Stavropoulos's experiences with live action play, the X-Card has become a standard safety tool for all sorts of games—one comes packed in the *Star Crossed* box, for instance. Kira Magrann—designer of the card-based ode to David Lynch, *Something is Wrong Here* (2019)—came up with the O-Card, which does the opposite—players can tap it when they want more of something. Monte Cook Games provides a free PDF full of advice called *Consent in Gaming* (2019), and the *TTRPG Safety*

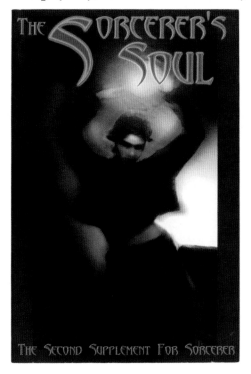

THE SORCERER'S SOUL, ADEPT PRESS, 2002
RON EDWARDS, COVER BY JEFF KROMER

Toolkit (2020), compiled by designers Kienna Shaw and Lauren Bryant-Monk, offers further resources.

These ideas, along with the notion of a pre-play Session Zero used to discuss them, aren't just for indie games, either. They've increasingly become a staple of play for all RPGs, especially for sessions run in public at conventions and among strangers online.

Universalis (2002)

Much of the history of RPGs is told through binaries: Storytelling or simulation, cultivated metaplots or emergent stories, unified (d20 System) or non-unified mechanics (*Shadowrun*, say), system light or system heavy, and on and on.

In 2002, the burgeoning indie movement is similarly represented by oppositional goals. On the one hand, there is Ron Edwards's *Sorcerer*, an exercise in specificity—play a sorcerer who can summon demons in a game where every mechanic is about being a sorcerer or summoning demons. On the other hand, there is *Universalis: The Game of Unlimited Stories*, which attempts to create a system that can do anything the players need it to.

Universalis throws out most of the conventions associated with tabletop RPGs. There is no prepared setting. Instead, everyone at the table creates it together; prepared work is actually counterproductive to the in-the-moment collaborative spirit of the game. There is no game master, either—everyone has a measure of control over the story. There is also no ownership of characters—a player may introduce one, but control and development are left to the entire group.

Building on *Baron Munchausen*'s simple ante system, coins are used for just about everything, which creates a sort of economic system reminiscent of resource management board games. Every player starts with 25 coins and spends them to establish facts about the world. Each fact

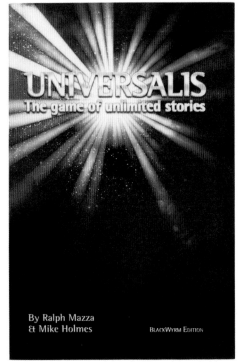

UNIVERSALIS, REVISED EDITION, RAMSHEAD PUBLISHING, 2012 RALPH MAZZA AND MIKE HOLMES, COVER BY JARI TUOVINEN

costs one coin, so establishing a scene in which a warrior breaks his sword fighting a foe on a wintery plain and is left defenseless would cost six coins (warrior, foe, fight, plain, broken sword, defenseless). Coins can also be spent to take control of a character, alter the scene, or even remove a character or item from the game.

The more facts attached to a *thing*, the more coins it takes to remove it, so in a strange but delightful twist, the more injured a character—each injury is a fact—the less likely it is they will be permanently removed from the game (this paradox jibes with certain genres, like pulp and hardboiled detective stories where the hero takes seemingly endless abuse but keeps crawling toward the story's climax). Complications are introduced by players in order to create conflict and potentially gain more coins. They're resolved with pools of 10-sided dice that match the number of facts involved, with the highest number of successes determining the victor—coins are rewarded in large numbers to the winner. If someone dislikes something introduced to the game—a silly plot point, for instance, or one that is too serious—there is a formal challenge system that uses a bidding mechanic to resolve disagreements.

There are many little, nuanced rules to provide structure to the game and adjudicate disputes, but those rarely crop up. *Universalis* is a game that wants to flow past mechanical hiccups as quickly as possible. As with playing pretend, it's usually possible and often preferable to handwave a solution that appeases all parties rather than looking up something in the book. The story is the focus, and keeping it going is paramount.

The pieces that make up *Universalis* aren't unique. *Baron Munchausen* is a clear forbearer, and many other RPGs have experimented with bidding mechanics: *Once Upon a Time* provided an early framework for collaborative storytelling; there is, perhaps, a relationship between the resource management here and the miracle system of *Nobilis*; further, assigning keywords mechanical weight is a feature of Robin D. Laws's games, *Over the Edge* and *Hero Wars*. None of these inspirations were widely imitated, however, but the combination of them into a new whole *was* unique.

Universalis is actually mind-blowing. It is a simple system that emphasizes creative collaboration and is versatile enough to handle literally any kind of story players can dream up. That is quite the accomplishment for a digest-sized RPG book. While it may be at the other end of the spectrum from *Sorcerer*, both games form a foundation that inspires dozens of indies in their wake.

InSpectres (2002)

In the wake of *Sorcerer* and the design community that formed around The Forge, there was an explosion of interesting indie games. *InSpectres*, by Jared A. Sorensen, is a good example of the design experiments that were going on at the time, primarily with the distribution of authority.

InSpectres, Jared A. Sorensen
Memento Mori Theatricks, 2002

The punny title (a regular feature of Sorensen's games) informs players exactly what to expect—inspecting spectres. Or, more accurately, players assume the roles of desperate employees of a franchise business dedicated to dealing with paranormal infestations, ranging from ghosts, to vampires, to far worse—it's a horror comedy and a send-up of entrepreneurialism and start-up culture. If it wasn't already obvious, there is much love here for the *Ghostbusters* films, but Sorensen also cites reality shows, like *Cops* and *The Real World*, as inspirations for key mechanics.

Like *Trail of Cthulhu*, *InSpectres* identifies a problem with how clues are handled in investigative games. Investigation is a matter of flow—if clues are too difficult to come by, progress slows, and the game becomes frustrating, but if clues are easy to find, the game speeds up and becomes an unchallenging narration by the GM. Both extremes lead to unfulfilling games.

InSpectres addresses this problem by taking management of the clues, traditionally the responsibility of the GM, and giving it to the players. This isn't like

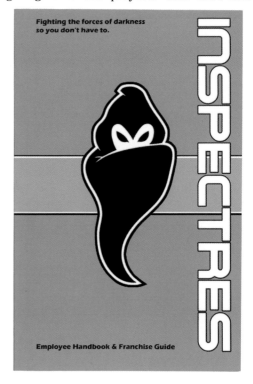

Fighting the forces of darkness so you don't have to.

Employee Handbook & Franchise Guide

reading the episode summary ahead of watching your favorite mystery show. It's more abstract than that. Basically, any time a skill roll is made, players narrate the successes, and the GM narrates the failures. High-quality successes (rolls of fives and sixes) net Franchise Dice, which act as the session timer—the job is over when the players accumulate twice the value of their franchise in dice. So, anything that nets Franchise Dice is narrated by the players and directly impacts the details of the story, including the finale. Much of the time in between rolls is spent trying to make up plausible explanations for the potentially ridiculous combinations of player-generated clues.

Then, there is the confessionals mechanic, an RPG version of the gimmick at the heart of *The Real World*. At any point in the game, a player can elect to directly address the metaphorical camera. Confessionals can have one of three amusing effects.

First, they can change other characters—if a player expresses their annoyance at one of their fellow players, say Steve, for, of all things, picking a fight in an IHOP parking lot before showing up at a haunted house, they can add "irritable" to Steve's player's traits on his character sheet. That keyword provides Steve's player a potential roleplaying cue and, if they use it, they earn an extra die for the franchise at the end of the game, giving the team more resources for future cases.

Second, a player can narrate in plot developments. "Little did we know that the IHOP waiter followed us to the haunted house—poor guy!" Narrations give raw material for other players to work with during their turns—in this case, the rest of the group now has an NPC that can meet a messy end.

Finally, anticipating a key mechanic in *Blades in the Dark*, confessionals can act as a flashback that alters the status quo. House haunted by a demon with a sweet tooth? Good thing a player grabbed extra packets of pancake syrup when picking up their IHOP to-go order, and they're in the van out front!

There are plenty of parallels between *InSpectres* and the *Ghostbusters* RPG—the latter involves setting up a local Ghostbusters franchise, has cool points, leans into the farcical, and only uses 6-sided dice—but the differences are more illuminating. *Ghostbusters* was one of the earliest forerunners of the cinematic style of play, which paved the way for the more narrative-focused games that influenced the indie movement. Despite that clear influence, both games play radically different from each other—a testament to how *new* indie design was in execution, despite emerging from similar sources.

Fate (2003)

Fate used to be *FATE*, which stood for *Fudge Adventures in Tabletop Entertainment* and then *Fantastic Adventures in Tabletop Entertainment*. Currently, it doesn't stand for anything, but the first acronym is illuminating: *Fate* is indeed derived from, and refines, *Fudge*. To the point that, until 2013, when the rules were rewritten from the ground up, the continued existence of *Fate* depended on *Fudge*'s open license.

The first rough edition was released through a dedicated Yahoo! Group in 2003 and a second, polished and complete edition was released online in the summer of the same year. The third edition doesn't exist as a stand-alone rulebook, but rather, like Gumshoe, it powers several games, like *Spirit of the Century* (2006) and the RPG adaptation of *The Dresden Files* (2010).

The fourth edition, born out of a massively successful, $433,000 dollar Kickstarter campaign in 2013 (one of the biggest hauls at the time), finally made it possible to release the game as a stand-alone ruleset in print, though even that milestone is a bit confounding—there's *Fate Core System*, which contains the full rules, *Fate Accelerated*, a streamlined version of

FATE CORE SYSTEM, FOURTH EDITION, EVIL HAT PRODUCTIONS, 2013
LEONARD BALSERA, BRIAN ENGARD, JEREMY KELLER, RYAN MACKLIN, AND MIKE OLSON, COVER BY KURT KOMODA

the game, and then there is the *Fate System Toolkit*, for hacking the game into new settings and genres. And, as if that wasn't enough, in 2020, Evil Hat released *Fate Condensed*, a streamlined version of the already aerodynamic *Fate Accelerated*.

Though the particulars shift around a bit, all of the various editions aim for the same goal: A straightforward, scalable universal system that favors roleplaying over dice rolling. While *Fudge* isn't really a game—it's an engine for making one's own game—*Fate* retains much of that open-ended toolkit-style utility (and thus makes it easy to hack and modify for other genres), but it replaces and adds to *Fudge* in ways that make it more playable from the start. The essential core remains, though: *Fudge* dice are used in an attempt to climb the adjective ladder and accomplish players' individual goals.

Beyond that core are many differences. There are no attributes, just skills (a choice embraced by *Gumshoe,* as well). The application of those skills comes in four actions—Attack, Defend, Overcome an Obstacle, or Create an Advantage.

Those advantages, and a good deal of the rest of the game, are defined through Aspects, which are freeform keywords or phrases—the book uses the example "manners of a goat," which is reminiscent of *Over the Edge* and *Hero Wars*.

Characters have Aspects, places have them, and they can be activated by spending a Fate Point for a bonus on a related die roll. In this way, Fate Points work similarly to a luck mechanic, but like *Universalis,* or the confessionals in *InSpectres,* they can be spent to exert control over (and gain the advantage of) a detail in the game. Similarly, the GM can use a character's existing Aspects to compel specific behavior in exchange for a Fate Point that can be used later (similar to how *Pendragon* characters can be ruled by their virtues and vices). In addition to all of these options, *Spirit of the Century* introduced the concept of Stunts, which act as predefined feats or powers, also activated by spending Fate Points.

Back in 1986, *GURPS* represented a kind of bird's eye view of a particular thread of RPG design that stretched back through *Champions*, *Fantasy Trip*, and ultimately, to *D&D*. *GURPS* universalized that thread, and through its constant expansion of rules, settings, and even systems, provided a generic benchmark for what RPGs were. In a way, it exists as a kind of simulation of every RPG experience available from 1986 through some point in the mid '90s, when RPG design started to push beyond the capabilities of *GURPS'* framework. Two decades or so later, *Fate* stands at a similar intersection, drawing from and synthesizing an array of contemporary design ideas, a kind of amalgamated avatar of the RPG industry, circa 2003, 2006, and 2013—and growing still.

Savage Worlds (2003)

After Pinnacle Entertainment Group, makers of *Deadlands*, went belly up, due to a variety of factors (including, ironically, the d20 boom—after publishing a d20 System version of *Deadlands*, players stopped buying the original game, which tanked the company's earnings), Shane Lacy Hensley founded a new company, Great White Games (though, after 2005, he reverted to the Pinnacle moniker).

Like the namesake shark, the game Hensley wanted to make was lean and mean. Thanks to d20, the majority of RPGs were, once again, increasing in complexity. Like the indie game movement, *Savage Worlds* constitutes a Newtonian reaction away from that rising complexity.

Savage Worlds is a generic system that prioritizes speed of play and low prep over everything else. In the game master section of the rulebook, Hensley explains that he was motivated to create this game because, "People have busy lives, and as much as everyone involved might love to play, they've still got to study for classes, take care of their children and otherwise live their lives."

Less time means fewer gains from playing complex games, so a more streamlined approach seemed logical. There's some irony in this goal, as *Deadlands* isn't exactly a simple game. Also, the direct ancestor of *Savage Worlds* is a miniature wargame, *Deadlands: The Great Rail Wars* (1997). Miniature wargames aren't usually noted for their lack of complexity either, but *The Great Rail Wars* was, in fact, a greatly pared down version of *Deadlands*. And, with just a bit of revision, it turned into *Savage Worlds*. Vestiges of the original systems remain—the "bennies" that can be spent to modify rolls in *Savage Worlds* are *Deadlands'* Fate Chips by another name, and the whole ruleset still works well as a wargame.

The system for players is straightforward. Characters are created by allocating points into attributes and skills, which are large umbrellas (as in the skill penumbra of *Unknown Armies* or *HeroQuest*) that encompass knowledge of the thing, as well as the ability to perform it—so, Computers can be used to use one, or build one, or find a tech to fix one, or maybe even to buy stock in a company that makes them.

The amount of points spent translates into specific sorts of dice, thus, getting a 4-sided die (the lowest) for Strength would cost nothing, while getting a 12-sided die (the highest) would cost four points. Rolling the highest value of the die is called Acing (another holdover from *Deadlands*) and allows a player to roll again, adding the results. Skills can be further enhanced by purchasing Edges, while players can gain additional points by taking on Hindrances. Attribute and skill checks are generally looking to beat a four—that low threshold for success indicates how fast and high-powered *Savage Worlds* can be.

The GM section of the rulebook runs just a handful of pages and encourages a GM to cut out as much work out as possible—keep it fast, furious, and fun, just like the cover says. The game's approach to campaign settings, begun with *50 Fathoms*

SAVAGE WORLDS, REVISED EDITION, PINNACLE ENTERTAINMENT GROUP, 2005
SHANE LACY HENSLEY, COVER BY JASON ENGLE

1970

1980

1990

2000

2010

SAVAGE WORLDS EXPLORER'S EDITION, PINNACLE ENTERTAINMENT GROUP, 2005
SHANE LACY HENSLEY, COVER BY CHEYENNE WRIGHT

(2003), uses what the designers call the Plot Point system. Similar to *Pathfinder*'s adventure paths, the system provides a main storyline, many side stories, and many more hooks and diversions, all presented in a concise way in order to make sessions as close to zero prep as possible.

The game's rules offer some advice to help players create their own savage world, and there are plenty of bespoke in-house settings, but with the second edition (2005) comes an interesting addition to the rules: Converting Settings. This revelation amounts to a page-and-a-half of advice, drawn from best practices developed by the game's fan community. I'm sure folks have used *GURPS* and generic systems to convert other game settings, and Steve Jackson Games even did it officially when it licensed the *World of Darkness* games for *GURPS* conversions, but I can't think of another instance where a game publisher amended their rules with a method for the practice.

That there was demand for such methodology vindicated Hensley's belief that busy people craved streamlined games. Many interesting game worlds that were saddled with complex systems

are now regularly mentioned in the same breath as *Savage Worlds*—*Skyrealms of Jorune, Shadowrun, Rifts*. That last one was such a popular fan conversion that Palladium Games and Pinnacle made the union official with *Savage Rifts* (2015). More recently, *Pathfinder for Savage Worlds* (2020) hit shelves, along with an adaptation of the first adventure path, *Rise of the Rune Lords* (originally published by Paizo in 2007).

Dogs in the Vineyard (2004)

Sorcerer kicks off the indie game movement, and *Universalis* expands the possibilities. *Dogs in the Vineyard* may be the first to generate a real sense of excitement and popularity. More than the others, it makes an important philosophical contribution to the scene, which would preoccupy indie designers for years to come.

Players take the role of members of God's Watchdogs, enforcers of religious doctrine in a place that resembles, but doesn't recreate, the Mormon Utah territory in the years before the Civil War. The Watchdogs travel from town to town, bringing news, delivering mail, preaching, and helping out when the need is great. In a perfect world, that would be all, but this one is sick with sin, so the Watchdogs also serve as six-gun inquisitors and exorcists—their word is final in matters of faith and their authority total.

Demons are alive in the world. So long as a town is free of sin, it is protected, but as soon as one person feels pride, the entire community is in peril. Pride leads to injustice, injustice to sin. Sin lets in the demons. Demons turn everything inside out, perverting the true faith into a false doctrine. Sorcery, hate, and murder are sure to follow, unless the Dogs can cut out the sinful rot. Therein lies the game: An excellent playground of moral and ethical quandaries.

Character creation is keyword based—not unlike *Hero Wars/HeroQuest*, which creator Vincent Baker calls "the grand-mother" of the indie movement. Every skill and attribute are assigned dice values. In conflict of any sort, the dice for the relevant skills and attributes are rolled, and the values of the dice are cashed in to move the action forward, using a poker-like mechanic of raises, until one side either gives voluntarily or runs out of dice.

Narration never stops, and the game encourages escalation—dice rolling contests can last for quite a stretch of real time. Getting nowhere with an argument? Punch the jerk and start the process over with an ongoing fist fight. If that doesn't go according to plan, pull a knife, or a gun, or set fire to the house. The character is a Watchdog of God, after all—who is going to say what they did was wrong?

There is a strong tension between the system, the setting, the moral requirements of the gameplay, and the sensibilities of the players, which almost certainly clash with the dominant, conservative social standards of the setting. Those tensions naturally fuel the escalation of the narrative—everything in the game is

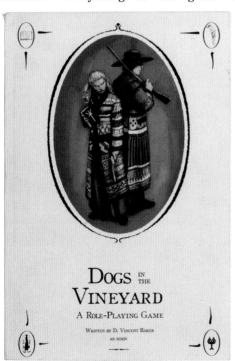

arranged around aggressively interrogating what the characters do and believe and how their choices change them. The key is to convince the GM to stand back and let it happen. To that end, the game suggests two pieces of general advice.

First, always present situations, not resolutions. Every game begins with the Watchdogs arriving in a town. The GM sets the stage and hints at what might be wrong, but then leaves the narrative to the players. They go about, talking to people, rooting through their secrets, seeing sin and demons everywhere. *Dogs in the Vineyard* encourages GMs to let them. In this way, the players tell the GM what they'd like to see and frame out the game's drama.

Then, when players ask to *do* something, the second piece of advice comes into play: The GM must "Roll dice or say yes." To translate: If nothing is at stake, the GM should let the players succeed in their action in order to more quickly arrive at conflict that *does* require dice-rolling, which is where the stakes are and when events rapidly spiral out of control—the heart of the game. *Dogs in the Vineyard* is at its best when the GM is constantly pushing the players back into the mesh of tensions and problems they have created for themselves. "Say yes" is one more way to encourage that drama.

This advice became central to many design philosophies in the indie space, to the point that it has become a rule of thumb within the broader hobby, known as "Vincent's Admonition." It doesn't work for every game all of the time—an investigative game, like *Call of Cthulhu*, for instance, is built around no-stakes skill checks and dead ends. But, it doesn't have to be! "Say yes" is a fundamental part of the Gumshoe system in which basic clues are gained automatically, and rolls determine the overall quality of the information. Vincent's Admonition represents a massive shift from the old school, where dice determine everything

DOGS IN THE VINEYARD, LUMPLEY GAMES, 2004
D. VINCENT BAKER, COVER BY DREW BAKER

and randomization is king. Say yes. Keep it interesting. Find the wildest consequences and run right up to them, but try not to fall in.

It should be noted that, unlike the vast majority of RPGs in this digital age, *Dogs in the Vineyard* is no longer offered for sale. Despite its success, Baker decided to pull the game because of his broad dissatisfaction with the setting, saying on Twitter, "Westerns are my favorite but they have to decolonize or go to hell, *Dogs in the Vineyard* very much included." A variant of the original game by Baker using another genre or setting is a possibility in the future.

Castles & Crusades (2004)

In the wake of the d20 System's precipitous collapse, several surviving companies abandoned the d20 trademark but, thanks to the terms of the Open Gaming License, stuck with the underlying mechanics. Troll Lord Games took this approach with *Castles & Crusades* (*C&C*), an RPG that would spark a surprising movement.

As a game, *C&C* is a stripped-down version of *Dungeons & Dragons'* Third Edition, derived from that game's System Reference Document and developed with an eye toward emulating the feel of the original *Dungeons & Dragons*. In service of that goal, classes are pared back to just include Fighter, Wizard, Cleric, and Rogue, while races are limited to human, elf, dwarf, and halfling. The game retains the basic mechanics of the Third Edition, including ascending armor class, but jettisons feats and skills. In their place is the Siege Engine (get it?), which is used to resolve all non-combat actions.

In short, each class has a primary attribute—for a Fighter, it's Strength; for a Wizard, it's Intelligence, and so on. All of the other attributes are considered secondary. When a player wants to pursue an action where success is not guaranteed, like climbing a wall, or reading a dead language, they roll a 20-sided die, add in any bonuses or penalties based on the situation and the attribute value. To succeed, the total needs to meet or beat a 12 (for a situation that tests a primary attribute) or an 18 (for a secondary attribute). Saving throws are determined in the same way, with different sorts of attacks keyed to different attributes—Strength saves against paralysis, charm spells use Charisma, and so on.

The Siege Engine goes a long way toward streamlining the complexity of the Third Edition and makes all of the attributes equally valuable. In the past, Charisma, which had little mechanical impact on the game, was often used as a dumping ground for the worst attribute value, producing lots of *D&D* heroes with amazing abilities and the personalities of a piece of driftwood. On a mechanical level, this system worked out so well that it served as a clear inspiration for the save system in the Fifth Edition of *D&D*.

The legacy of *Castles & Crusades* doesn't lie with 5E, though. Rather, it is *C&C*'s pursuit to evoke the *feel* of the original *D&D* that secured its place in RPG history.

The yearning for an older time went beyond just the play. The name of the game, for instance, is a reference to the Castle & Crusade Society, the chapter of the International Federation of Wargaming, founded by Gary Gygax and Rob Kuntz in 1970. Then, there's the packaging. Though standard size books came a little later, the original publication of the *C&C* rules took the form of three digest-sized books, packed in a white box, mimicking the later printings of the original *D&D*.

Soon after the game's release, Gygax and Kuntz were working on Castle Zagyg, a resurrection of their Castle Greyhawk dungeons, for use with the system. Support of *Castles & Crusades* from Gygax,

CASTLES & CRUSADES, BOX SET, TROLL LORD GAMES, 2004
DAVIS CHENAULT AND MAC GOLDEN, COVER BY PETER BRADLEY

Kuntz, and other *D&D* veterans, like James M. Ward, gave rise to the notion that the game is a spiritual successor to the older *D&D*, the game that might have been the Second Edition of *D&D* had Gygax never left TSR.

The old school spirit was already haunting the d20 era. For instance, Goodman Games' series of Dungeon Crawl Classics modules, complete with trade dress that mimicked the look of the old TSR publications, launched in 2003 with *Idylls of the Rat King*. Even though it had the retro vibe, it was still a module for the Third Edition of *D&D*, and it was saddled with the complexity of that system.

Castles & Crusades was built with the d20 System, but it *played* like an older *D&D*. It was faster. It favored rulings over rules, and, in so doing, it encouraged creativity and improvisation in play. "The rules are your servant, not your master," says the first booklet under the header, "Rule One." It felt fresh and free when compared to the ever-growing mountain of reference books available for the mainline *D&D*. If Troll Lord Games could use the Open Gaming License this way, what's to stop someone from using the OGL to simply reprint those old rules in their entirety?

The answer: Nothing at all. Thus, the Old School Revival was born.

Blue Rose (2005)

As *D&D* professionalized, the illustrations became increasingly standardized. With the Third Edition, these visual standards became the norm. This standardization is clearest in the game's approach to dragons. Previously, each artist put their own spin on dragons, often determined by the mood of the piece—there were crocodilian dragons and chubby dragons and cat-like dragons. For the Third Edition, artist Todd Lockwood was commissioned to rethink the dragon, giving them plausible and consistent anatomies while maintaining a cer-

tain amount of distinction between the various colors or breeds. *Draconomicon: The Book of Dragons* (2003), enshrined Lockwood's redesigns, and *D&D* dragons have matched that look ever since. Subsequent editions have aggressively embraced ever-narrower art direction.

Perhaps this impulse is a natural side-effect of the way RPG mechanics often demand neat taxonomies. Perhaps the lionization of "Appendix N"—a list essentially representing one man's taste in reading—contributes, as well; Gygax draws primarily from pulp-rooted sword and sorcery stories that have similar preconceptions of what fantasy ought to be. And even then, as time has gone by, the influence of Gygax's stranger inclusions—the trippy stuff by Roger Zelazny and Michael Moorcock—are clearly fading away. The strongest currents of *D&D* come from a specific place—lone wolf sword and sorcery stories translated into wargame-derived mechanics—which ensures *D&D* delivers a specific experience—and combat-oriented adventures arranged around self-enrichment; these two facts have become increasingly self-reinforcing.

There are other branches on the tree of fantasy, however. Take, for instance, romantic fantasy, which began to flower around the same time as RPGs, with books like Katherine Kurtz's *Deryni Rising*

BLUE ROSE, GREEN RONIN PUBLISHING, 2005
JEREMY CRAWFORD, DAWN ELLIOT, STEVE KENSON, AND JOHN SNEAD, COVER BY STEPHANIE LAW

(1970) and Mary Stewart's *The Crystal Cave* (1970). Inspired by chivalric romances, these novels (most often written by women) laid a foundation for Mercedes Lackey's *Valdemar* novels (1987-2022), Tamora Pierce's *The Immortals* series (1992-1996), and more.

Where the sword and sorcery subgenre favors loner heroes, martial prowess, and quests for glory and riches, the heroes and heroines of romantic fantasy seek social connection and emotional wealth. Instead of carrying on by themselves, they find belonging in a community and a purpose larger than themselves. Magic and psychic abilities are often in-born talents; intelligent animals speak; and societies are egalitarian. This is the sort of fantasy that *Blue Rose* seeks to explore.

It's another game that emerges after the precipitous collapse of the d20 System. As with Troll Lord Games, Green Ronin Publishing was an early advocate of the d20 System and was hesitant to abandon it entirely, so they, instead, hacked it, creating True20. The modifications temper the complexity of d20 and work to bring the mechanics in line with a play experience tuned to hopefulness, inclusivity, and the occasional tragedy.

There are only three classes in *Blue Rose*, no experience points (leveling

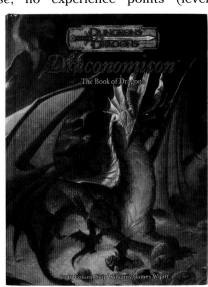

occurs automatically every few sessions), and no ability scores (players just log the modifier). That last is a great simplification that's since been adapted elsewhere, including in the Fifth Edition of *Dungeons & Dragons* (no surprise considering co-designer Jeremy Crawford wound up at Wizards of the Coast as their principal designer). Rather than rootless mercenaries, the characters in *Blue Rose* often start off as important people (or talking animals, which are a staple of fairy tales and fantasy stories, but rarely show up in RPGs, for some reason) within the community, and the game centers more on intrigue, both political and interpersonal, than exploration. I find it slightly odd that the overall system, being derived from *D&D*, is so combat-focused; this seems like a missed opportunity to develop the sort of social mechanics that were emerging among indie RPGs.

The broad strokes portray a world that is essentially good, and most of the various societies that populate it are invested in maintaining or building upon that inherent goodness—mostly. There is a lich king and some forces of wickedness, and villains abound, but in focusing on the positives, *Blue Rose* actively resists many of the stereotypes and clichés on which fantasy RPGs reflexively fall back.

Most RPGs strongly imply that players can play whomever and whatever they want to, while in practice, they only explicitly offer a handful of optimal configurations keyed to profession and often display problematic conceptions of race (see page 220). Up to this point, the various configurations of gender and sexual orientation were left unmentioned in nearly every RPG. When they are mentioned, they're often asserted to have no mechanical impact on the game (more rarely, the mentions are outright sexist, like the Charisma bonuses for a female character's physical attributes outlined in the *Arduin Grimoire*). *Blue Rose* not only directly addresses gender and sexual ori-

Draconomicon: The Book of Dragons, Wizards of the Coast, 2003. Andy Collins, Skip Williams, and James Wyatt, Cover by Todd Lockwood

1970

1980

1990

2000

2010

entation, but it also weaves both deeply into the fabric of the game—it is a game of romance, after all.

Four brief but powerful paragraphs lay out the game's stance. Inhabitants of the world accept marriage "between two or more legal adults." The arrangement of these relationships is seen as extremely flexible—characters in the world of *Blue Rose* have "types of people [they] are attracted to" and among them are those they "tend to fall in love with." No matter what those types and tendencies may be, there are no prejudices surrounding them. All possibilities are accepted. In this approach to romance, *Blue Rose* was and, in many ways, is still ahead of its time.

Like other games in this period, though, its prescience wasn't necessarily beneficial. It was aimed at an untapped audience for the industry, but it didn't succeed in cultivating it, at least not single-handedly—the initial line only saw two more releases, a companion rulebook and a guide to the world of Aldea. But the game *did* made RPGs more approachable to folks who weren't already entrenched in the hobby. The years since have proven the importance of *Blue Rose*, summarized in the following text from the 2015 Kickstarter campaign:

> Most important, we feel that games like *Blue Rose* are needed. Awareness of the importance of representation and inclusion in the hobby and the industry has grown in recent years. Now publishers need to follow-through on that increased awareness and deliver games that help to fulfill its promise.

That Kickstarter, for a second edition of *Blue Rose* powered by the Adventure Game Engine (developed for Green Ronin's tabletop adaptation of the *Dragon Age* videogame series), demonstrated a renewed interest. Following its release in 2017, the game has been supported by further RPG material, a line of fiction, and even a sourcebook that converts the setting for use in *D&D* 5E, indicating that this game of romantic fantasy that sought a once-elusive audience has finally found it.

Dread (2005)

Horror is tough. Laughter around the gaming table is almost inevitable. Players gather around it together to have fun, after all, not that being scared together isn't fun. But, creating the atmosphere necessary to play a horror RPG is difficult—dim lighting makes it hard to read the character sheet, mood music either drowns out conversation or gets buried by it—and the ambiance is even more difficult to maintain. One food delivery, one bathroom break, one silly joke, and the tension all evaporates. Even when executed perfectly, the spookiness is *still* fleeting. Horror RPGs don't usually scare, so much as they invite players to ponder the idea of being scared.

Unless the game is *Dread*.

Dread is a collaborative horror storytelling game with a novel core mechanic. The GM sets the framework of the story and provides players with a character creation questionnaire. Everyone then works together to flesh out characters and the world, immediately, so every game of *Dread* is unique and improvisational. As with *The Extraordinary Adventures of Baron Munchausen*, the freeform nature of the game can be just as intimidating as it is liberating, but the rulebook is largely dedicated to tool kits and essays that aim to support play and thaw any freeze-ups.

The novelty of *Dread*, and the way it earns its moniker, is the method the game uses to resolve conflict. Anytime a player wishes to do something when a positive result is not guaranteed, they remove a block from a *Jenga* tower. Pull it out without knocking over the tower, the character succeeds in the action. Knock over the tower, and the character fails the action and is out of the game (usually because they died as a result of the failure, though the game allows for deaths to be banked for a more dramatic departure when necessary).

In fact, if the tower is knocked over at all, any character can suffer a terrible doom. Or, occasionally, the character is just drawn away from the story—the book uses the example of collapsing the tower when translating an old book. Unless it is the *Necronomicon*, reading isn't usually a life-threatening exercise, so the rules suggest that if no other narrative twist presents itself, the character receives a phone call informing them of a death in the family and to come at once. It's silly, but sometimes, that's the way it goes. Once the doom (or deus ex machina) is resolved, the tower is re-stacked and play continues.

Is the *Jenga* tower a gimmick? Absolutely. But it's one that actually works. RPGs so rarely have physical stakes presented at the gaming table (another RPG that dabbles with such immediacy is *Ten Candles*, 2016). By tying success and failure to something so precarious as a *Jenga* tower, *Dread* introduces very real, very terrifying causes and effects for players to navigate (somewhat ironically, *Star Crossed*, 2018, leverages the same emotions evoked by the *Jenga* tower to very different ends in its portrayal of doomed romance). It removes characters from the abstract of attributes and dice rolls and puts their lives quite literally in the hands of the players.

Sure, there are shortcomings—*Dread* is a one-shot game, requiring improvisation that can make players freeze, and it only excels at very specific types of horror—but the fact that players are almost guaranteed, *by design*, to have a physical manifestation of fear is an achievement that makes up for nearly any deficiency. Horror at the game table is challenging to concoct, but *Dread* makes it seem easy.

Dread, The Impossible Dream, 2005
Epidiah Ravachol and Nathaniel Barmore. Cover by Nathaniel Barmore

Retroclones (2006)

While the way a person explains game mechanics can definitely be copyrighted, the mechanics themselves are not afforded that protection. This fact is clearly laid out (for legalese, anyway) in Title 17 of the U.S. Code of Laws, section 102, part b, which says:

> In no case does copyright protection for an original work of authorship extend to any idea, procedure, process, system, method of operation, concept, principle, or discovery, regardless of the form in which it is described, explained, illustrated, or embodied in such work.

So, the exact prose Gary Gygax used to describe how to make a saving throw? It's copyrighted. All of the made-up names of specific monsters, characters, and places, like illithids and Drizzt and Sigil? They're copyrighted. The name *Dungeons & Dragons*? Verboten—it's a registered trademark, so if it appears anywhere on a product, even just to say it is compatible, its use, most likely, represents an infringement, which is why all of the clones and hacks make clever references to "the world's best known fantasy adventure game" and such. But, the mechanics themselves? They belong to everyone.

This is the legal justification that allowed for Hong Kong toy manufacturers to create off-brand knock-offs of *D&D* products back in the '70s and '80s, and now, it rationalizes a whole host of off-brand knock-off games. As with the original Dragonriders of the Styx line (which closely reproduced some designs directly from the *Monster Manual* while the official *D&D* toys often looked nothing like monsters from the game), some of these imitations would display a keener understanding of the material than the original designers.

The mechanics the Open Gaming License claims to release into the public domain were already there. What the OGL really does is signal that Wizards of the Coast won't file a frivolous and expensive lawsuit in an attempt to bully a game company out of using mechanics to which they have a right.

Given TSR's reputation and track record—nicknames like T$R and They Sue Regularly don't just develop spontaneously—these sorts of suits posed a reasonable fear throughout the later twentieth century (though, it should be noted, that while TSR demanded changes to the original *Arduin Grimoire*, they didn't actually file suit, and *Arduin* was among many products that had a lengthy *D&D*-adjacent existence). The OGL wasn't a gift to the roleplaying industry, but claiming it was has, nevertheless, made for good PR for Wizards of the Coast.

In reality, the OGL had many unintended side-effects. When the industry abandoned the d20 System, many companies continued to produce material that was compatible with *Dungeons & Dragons* under the OGL. When *Castles & Crusades* did so, while trying to emulate the style of

play of the original *Dungeons & Dragons*, an intriguing hypothetical emerged in its wake: Why emulate the original, *when you can just use the original?*

OSRIC (2006), which is short for *Old School Reference and Index Compilation*, is one of the first attempts at what is now known as a retroclone, in this case, of the First Edition of *Advanced Dungeons & Dragons*. Judging from the introduction (penned by Matthew Finch, who previously worked on *Castles & Crusades*), its makers were nervous about finding themselves in legal pickle because of the book—there are lots of references to rules being non-copyrightable and much discussion about the pains the writers took to remove the "artistic presentation" of the original TSR books.

The idea here was to take the entire contents of the three core rulebooks—*Players Handbook*, *Dungeon Masters Guide*, and the *Monster Manual*—strip them of their original explanatory text, write new explanatory text, then release them and the OSRIC brand as an open-source system, similar to how third-party companies previously used the d20 System. Doing so would enable designers to publish old school material and allow readers to identify that material through the use of a shared trademark.

OSRIC wasn't a commercial release—initially the compendium was only available as a free download. In 2009, the option for print-on-demand physical copies became available. It isn't even clear that the authors of *OSRIC* intended for players to use the book at the table—the assumption on the part of *OSRIC*'s compilers was that players would continue to use their original rulebooks—this was less a system for play and more a mechanism to encourage new development for an old system. Almost immediately, material for *AD&D* surged into print.

All of the other iterations of *D&D* received their own clones soon after. Chris Gonnerman's *Basic Fantasy* (2007)

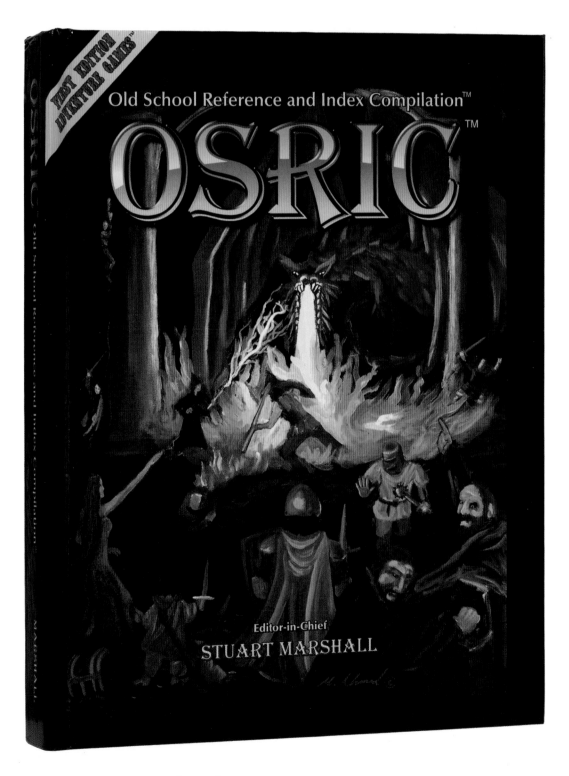

OSRIC, Second edition, First Edition Society, 2009
Matthew Finch, Stuart Marshall, and Dyvers Hands, Cover by Mark Ahmed

These clones paved the way for the larger OSR movement. Like the movement itself, the meaning of OSR is nebulous. For *OSRIC*, it stood for "Old School Reference." There was a time when designers and player said it stood for Open-Source Rules. These days, in both marketing copy and comments online, the OS generally stands for Old School, with folks using Revival or Renaissance interchangeably for the "R."

As the movement coalesced, it did so primarily around *Dungeons & Dragons*, despite all of the other retroclones in circulation. In retrospect, this focus was probably an inevitability born from the fact that the OGL spun out of *D&D* to begin with, and, due to *D&D*'s primacy in the industry over the years, most of the folks interested in making OSR content grew up playing *D&D*. Many of the foundational tenets of OSR play grew out of the aesthetics established in the first decade of the game.

Matthew Finch summarized four primary pillars in "A Quick Primer for Old School Gaming" (2008). First, rulings are more important than rules. Players shouldn't use their character sheets to see if they're able to do something; instead, players should concoct a plan and explain it to the GM, who, then, determines whether or not it's possible, making up rules on the spot, if necessary.

Finch's second pillar nests within the first—player skill is more important than character abilities. That is, adventures are meant to test the ingenuity of the players, rather than allowing them to rely on skill checks and other mechanics to overcome and/or succeed in sticky situations—that clever scamp Odysseus is the model OSR player. Third is an emphasis on the heroic, rather than the super heroic: High-level characters are collections of experiences, not superpowers. Finally, Finch's fourth pillar argues against the need for game balance in old school games; the possibility of players finding themselves

and Daniel Proctor's *Labyrinth Lord* (2007) came next. Both are slightly modified clones of the 1981 *Basic* and *Expert Sets*. Like *OSRIC*, they initially circulated online before print-on-demand copies became available. *Labyrinth Lord* also introduced the *Advanced Edition Companion* that converted material from *AD&D* into the *B/X* system, which laid the foundation for what would eventually lead to *Old-School Essentials*. The original white box got the treatment with Troll Lord Games' *Swords & Wizardry* (2008), also by Matthew Finch, while the *AD&D* Second Edition had to wait a couple of years to be cloned in *For Gold & Glory* (2010).

Many other retroclones popped up, as well. *Basic Role-Playing* saw one in *GORE: Generic Old-School Roleplaying Engine* (2007); *Mutant Future* (2008) used *Labyrinth Lord* as a basis to return to *Gamma World*; *DoubleZero* (2007) cloned *James Bond 007,* and *4C System* (2007) recreated the FASERIP system used in *Marvel Super Heroes*.

out of their depth is a benefit, adding high stakes and danger to the game.

As one might imagine, the OSR is often a contentious scene. Consider the moment of inception: Since 1999, Wizards of the Coast and *Dungeons & Dragons* has been owned by Hasbro, a multinational conglomerate. Corporate ownership could certainly chafe the hobbyist who defined the industry. In that context, the OSR reads as a return to independence, to the DIY ethic, to products made with heart and soul, rather than an overriding devotion to profit margins (this clarion call, perhaps, requires a naive view of the past that ignores the greed and the lawsuits for which T$R was so often mocked).

At the same time, the Third Edition of *D&D* was opening up the hobby to a new generation of players, which sometimes made the OSR embrace of "the old ways" sound like reactionary gatekeeping: *Kids today, with their rules for everything and their feats of heroism. Why, back in my day, you were lucky to get to second level!* These sorts of lines have persisted in some corners of the OSR and have grown louder as Fourth and Fifth Editions of *D&D* were perceived to be further diluting the game.

OSR was born out of a deep nostalgia. The proof is in the movement's quixotic pursuit of aesthetic over anything that could be remotely described as concrete. OSR is a feeling. It emerges from a mist of memory. Whatever edition of *D&D* a person played as a teen, during that period they had the most free time and the least responsibility, that was *The Best One*. From that hazy place is where the idea of "good OSR material" so often derives, but those experiences, which feel *so* powerful, are often confused as being universal when, in fact, they are deeply personal—the result of chance and cir-

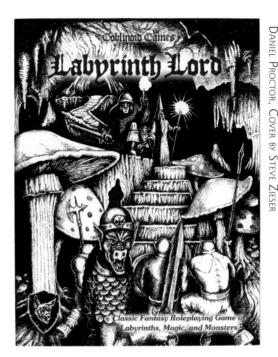

LABYRINTH LORD, REVISED EDITION, GOBLINOID GAMES, 2011 DANIEL PROCTOR, COVER BY STEVE ZIESER

cumstance (ironically, two things lionized in old school design).

There has *never* been any uniformity to *D&D*, despite Gygax's best efforts. The larger RPG hobby was created because many people's first impulse when confronted with the original *D&D* rules was to "fix" them with various tinkering. And, in the era before the internet, play was entirely decentralized. Outside of some vague notions from the guy who ran our local comic shop and some ideas from some folks' older brothers, my group in the '90s had no idea if we were playing the "right way," and we didn't spend a minute worrying about it. Every table was different, and many played in ways entirely counter to Finch's pillars (which, because of their focus on *D&D*, already discounted the experiences of large swaths of early RPG players).

That the idea of a monolithic Old School aesthetic as a mirage is self-evident, partly because of all of the fighting about it on message boards, like Dragonsfoot Forums, and partly because it started to mutate almost at once, pulling the movement in countless directions.

1970

1980

1990

2000

2010

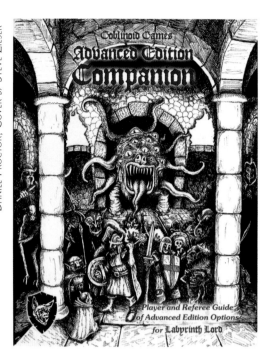

ADVANCED EDITION COMPANION, GOBLINOID GAMES, 2010
DANIEL PROCTOR, COVER BY STEVE ZIESER

Over the next few years, thanks to an increasing embrace of the "gonzo" ideas that color modern perceptions of early RPG play, games like *Dungeon Crawl Classics* (2012) emerge, and a general cross pollination of OSR design philosophies with those of storytelling games and indie sensibilities becomes more common. Games, like *Ultraviolet Grasslands* (2019) and *Electric Bastionland* (2020), feel like a continuation of this trend, to the point that, as a term, "Old School Revival" has been stretched so far that it is almost without meaning, if it ever had one. Now, for most players, it's primarily "*D&D*, but not Fifth Edition." Whatever *that* might mean.

Trail of Cthulhu (2008)

In *Call of Cthulhu* and other investigation-focused games, the core of play is in using skills to find clues. These, then, lead to more clues, and so on, until enough information has been accumulated, and the central mystery can be unraveled.

There is a fly in the ointment, though—a failed skill roll breaks the chain and prevents the players from unearthing what might be the pivotal clue. While this kind of dead end parallels many detective shows (and real-world investigations, where cases are often cracked by going over statements and evidence again and again until something shakes loose), it is frustrating for everyone when a game that's supposed to be fun hits the investigatory doldrums.

To fix this issue, Robin D. Laws designed the Gumshoe System in 2006. Unlike most RPGs, there is no standalone core rulebook for Gumshoe. Rather, different variants of the system have been used to create discrete games, mostly by Pelgrane Press (a notable exception is the excellent teen detective game *Bubblegumshoe*, 2016, released under the Open Game License by Evil Hat Productions).

The first Gumshoe game was *The Esoterrorists* (2006), which pits a good occult secret society against an evil occult secret society (who, amusingly, are frustrated that esoteric magic is so difficult and are looking for mystical methods that will give them powers along the lines of a *Dungeons & Dragons* Magic-User). A variety of other games have appeared since—*Fear Itself* (2007) is straight horror; *Night's Black Agents* (2012) tackles vampires and spies; *The Yellow King* (2017) is a sprawling examination of Robert W. Chambers's cosmic horror masterpiece, *The King in Yellow* (1895), across four eras. The centerpiece of Gumshoe, though, is *Trail of Cthulhu*, which is a direct attempt to repair perceived mechanical issues with *Call of Cthulhu*.

Gumshoe divides skills into two types: Investigative ones and everything else. Investigative skills are bought using a pool of points determined by the number of players and the game itself. *Esoterrorists*, as a more action-oriented game, has larger point pools to assign than the bookish *Trail of Cthulhu*, but *Trail's* points spend differently depending on character occupations. Other skills are bought from a separate supply of points that vary from game to game—in this case, *Trail* gets slightly more than *Esoterrorists*, simply because there are slightly more skills from which to choose. These parameters go toward establishing tone.

In both cases, these points, which generally range from one to four, don't represent prowess as they do in most other games. Rather, they form a pool that represents a personal capacity that depletes over the course of the day and is refreshed periodically, usually by rest. For non-investigative abilities, like driving or fighting, which run the risk of failure, the pool points are spent to modify a simple die roll.

Investigative skills work similarly, except they always succeed: A player always gets the core clue associated with that skill. Here, the pool of points can be spent in order to gain more information. These additional clues aren't mission critical, but they generally make the investigation easier or provide some other sort of benefit proportional to their cost, similar to the degree of success rules for the interrogation skill in *James Bond 007*.

At this point, most of the steps that mark the transition from a focus on simulation to a focus on narrative have already been made, but Gumshoe shows what falls through the cracks.

TRAIL OF CTHULHU, PELGRANE PRESS, 2008
KENNETH HITE, COVER BY JÉRÔME HUGUENIN

While the broad strokes are the same—mind-bending lore, cosmic gods, general horribleness—*Trail of Cthulhu* offers some additional modifications to the *Call of Cthulhu* formula. For starters, it moves the action from the fancy-free 1920s to the grim 1930s. The Great Depression is certainly a better fit, tonally, for a game of nihilistic horror.

Trail also offers three tunings for play (accomplished by adjusting the number of points for skills and by using a set of specialized rules). The default closely matches the feel of *Call of Cthulhu* (and "Call of Cthulhu"). A smaller point pool results in a "purist" game, which aims to match the feel of Lovecraft's later, cerebral horror stories in which horror consumes seekers of knowledge indiscriminately. The "pulp" option comes with a larger point pool and takes more of the "punch-it-before-I-die" vibe of Robert E. Howard's horror stories.

Most interesting is how the game handles the mental strain of confronting supernatural horrors. The system is divided into several layers. At the top is stability. This attribute functions like *Call of Cthulhu*'s sanity attribute; in other words, like mental hit points.

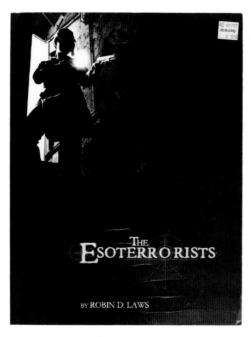

THE ESOTERRORISTS, PELGRANE PRESS, 2006
ROBIN D. LAWS, COVER BY JÉRÔME HUGUENIN

Beneath that is *Trail of Cthulhu*'s version of sanity, which is the numerical representation of a character's belief in consensus reality. The Cthulhu Mythos, being the corrosive truth at the heart of existence, is the only thing that erodes sanity, either by a character encountering the horrible truth and having their stability reduced to zero, or, interestingly, by using their Cthulhu Mythos skill. Apparently, just thinking about the Great Old Ones is enough to drive a character around the bend. Stability returns over time, but once lost, sanity never recovers.

Characters also have a drive, a powerful motivating energy at the core of their identity. This defines many of their actions. Just why is Professor Brookdale looking for forbidden artifacts and ancient ruins? Her drive compels her—literally, the GM gets to use character drives to force characters to act contrary to the interests of their players. Drives can be denied, but at the cost of stability. Along these lines, in the opposite direction, are pillars of stability. For every three points of sanity, a character has a person or thing that sustains them. Should those be destroyed, they will be shaken; should they lose sufficient sanity, they'll cease to care.

All of this mechanical nuance demonstrates an awareness of sanity mechanics that were developed in the years following *Call of Cthulhu*, particularly *Unknown Armies*. They all lead to the same place—mental trauma and irrevocable insanity—but they arrive using systems that attempt to connect these consequences to the intrinsic qualities of the characters they affect, rather than just rolling for a new mental illness on a random chart. The sanity systems of *Trail* likely influenced the much-improved version of sanity in the seventh edition of *Call of Cthulhu* (2014), as well as the bonds and downtime of Arc Dream's standalone *Delta Green* RPG (2016). And then back to *Trail of Cthulhu*, via the *Trail*-based *Fall of Delta Green* (2018): It's Cthulhu all the way down.

Fiasco (2009)

The fourth game by Jason Morningstar is a tragi-comical farce about crimes gone terribly wrong. It's basically Coen Brothers: The RPG. It tells a lot about the game, I think, that nearly every time I go to write *Fiasco*, I accidentally type *Fargo*.

The design springs directly out of Morningstar's first game, *The Shab-al-Hiri Roach* (2006)—a single session game with no GM; instead, each player has expansive authority in setting scenes during highly structured turns. Unlike its predecessor, though, *Fiasco* lacks cards; the rules are far more straightforward, and there is more room in the theming—*Roach* is hyper-specifically about a college campus under attack by a parasitic, Lovecraftian bug. While *Fiasco* is a game about criminal misadventures, it isn't particular about the details.

This openness sets the stage for one of *Fiasco*'s key features: Playsets. Four are included in the main book—a nice southern town, a town in the Wild West, a suburb, and McMurdo Station in Antarctica—but there are scads more, created by fans, available free on the Bully Pulpit site, or published in a series of companion books. Each playset comes with relationships, needs, objects, and locations, each in six sets of six, for players to, well, play with. Playsets are scaffolding that help players build their narrative and act as support to fall back on for creative fuel in the heat of improvisation.

Unlike most games, characters in *Fiasco* aren't defined by anything intrinsic, like attributes, but rather by their relationships with others. The components of the playset are used to define relationships with fellow players. For example, one player might be the boss of the player to their left and they could both share a need to get even with someone. It then falls to both players to work out the details of that relationship.

Play is broken into two acts; in each act, each character is the focus of two scenes. The active player can either establish the scene (picking who is there and why) or resolve it (determining the result of a scene), but not both—an arrangement that keeps everyone at the table invested while divvying the creative labor.

Scenes are ended when the resolving player chooses a die—white for a positive resolution, black for a negative—and passes it to the next player. There are no mechanics for conflict resolution. Everything is determined collaboratively. In between the two acts is the Tilt, a randomly determined, two-parted twist that must be worked into the second act's scenes—someone freaks out, a mysterious stranger shows up, a bad plan works perfectly, someone dies.

At the end, a player's accumulated number of dice in each color determines how the story concludes for their character. There's a chart for figuring out the Aftermath; for a pool with a majority of black dice, the chart uses a scale from zero to "awesome," while white dice results range from zero to "fan-fucking-tastic."

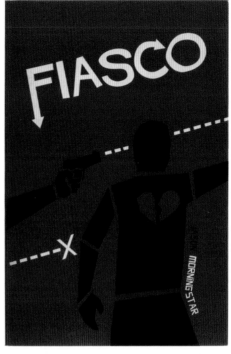

Fiasco, Bully Pulpit Games, 2009
Jason Morningstar, Cover by John Harper

Fiasco attempts to balance the improvisation of a story game with the mechanical support of a traditional RPG. Despite the formal structure of the turns and the helpfulness of the various items in the playsets, it focuses on narrative. As with other storytelling games, it has some points that can be intimidating, particularly the cold open at the beginning, which feels exactly like eyeing up a cold pool to jump into on a hot day—the refreshment comes only after the initial shock—and the implementation of the Tilt, which can sometimes feel artificially mechanical.

Beyond the trickiness of improvisation, *Fiasco* is a fine-tuned possibility engine. The system allows for players to do absolutely anything, be it violent, silly, or bizarre. Even the horrible deaths of other players are fine! The mechanics exist to facilitate storytelling and nothing else. Say something ridiculous, decide the consequences, and ramp up the tension. It's the best sort of RPG—one where the only limits are one's imagination (and, perhaps, one's appetite for comedic cruelty).

1970

1980

1990

2000

2010

Pathfinder (2009)

Grousing about the new edition of *D&D* is a pastime that is just about as old as *D&D* itself, but there is something different about the tenor of complaints that marked the transition from the Third Edition to Fourth.

Some folks were pissed from the very first announcement, long before the new system saw the light of day. Some felt that it was too soon. The First Edition lasted about 12 years, and the Second around 11. The Third had been around only seven years when players found out that it was being retired. Others felt a sense of financial betrayal, that somehow the expensive books they had bought were rendered useless, though it wasn't as if the words were going to suddenly fall out of them—there were no laws against continuing to play the Third Edition once the Fourth came out.

Just as it was back in 2000, when the d20 System scheme first launched: The real money was in core rulebooks, while the returns from everything else diminished over time. In retrospect, the only surprise about the Fourth Edition was that the megacorporation waited as long as it did before launching it.

Still, the more information that came out about Fourth Edition, the more contentious the reaction. And it wasn't just players who were complaining. Companies that had been publishing *D&D* material for the d20 System license or with the Open Gaming License were appropriately skittish. There was reason to be wary, thanks, in part, to Wizards of the Coast's poor stewardship of those initiatives in the past. But, there were also signs from the start that the Fourth Edition version, the Game System License, was going to be a disaster.

Restrictive provisions, like requiring that all derivative products refer to the core *D&D* rulebooks (essentially preventing the development of new games using Fourth Edition mechanics and limiting products to fantasy themes) and preventing publishers from using the Open Gaming License in the future, led nearly all of the established publishers to bail on creating material for the Fourth Edition. The first company to do so was Paizo.

Paizo took over publishing both *Dragon* and *Dungeon* magazines back in 2002, so surely, they knew something was amiss when Wizards of the Coast didn't renew the license in 2007. Paizo continued publishing its popular adventure paths—epic campaigns serialized monthly—in a new periodical called *Pathfinder Adventure Path*, which launched in August of 2007. In March of the following year, the company announced they were developing the *Pathfinder Roleplaying Game* as their own continuation of 3.5E *D&D*.

Nicknamed 3.75, *Pathfinder* is a clarified and slightly hacked version of 3.5E. Every system was re-examined, tweaked, and generally presented in a way that minimized misconceptions. For the most part, the two systems are compatible; the prime difference between the two is a higher power level in *Pathfinder*, which spins out of a driving concern about the basic character classes.

In the Third Edition, there is little reason for players to stick with the basic classes and their humdrum abilities through the higher levels when there is no shortage of prestige classes with exciting powers to defect to. Pathfinder has prestige classes, as well, but it ensures the base classes have enough bells and whistles to compete—everyone gets one new power, bonus, or ability at every level. This increase in power means other systems were rebalanced—there are more hit points to go around, for instance—but it generally plays like a highly polished version of 3.5.

Much of the gleam in that polish comes from the fact that Paizo developed *Pathfinder* in full view of the gaming public through a massive open playtesting period. This gave folks a chance to try the game out well before its release, to flag problems for correction, and to tinker with experimental systems—it turns out that the best way to excite players is to let them play a game as soon as possible. The resounding success of this method was not lost on Wizards of the Coast, who used a similar scheme in the development of *D&D*'s Fifth Edition.

On its own, *Pathfinder* has experienced robust success for a dozen years, equal to the amount of time the First Edition of *Advanced Dungeons & Dragons* was on store shelves. During certain periods between 2011 to 2014, it was the best-selling RPG, dethroning *D&D*, a feat no other roleplaying game has ever managed (although there is some anecdotal evidence that *Vampire: The Masquerade* outsold *D&D* for a bit in the early '90s). Even with Fifth Edition back in the top spot, *Pathfinder* is still one of the most played RPGs according to the virtual tabletop reports. Those who thought ending the Third Edition was premature were correct—combined, people have been playing the Third Edition and *Pathfinder* for over 20 years and show no signs of stopping.

Paizo also introduced a science fiction ruleset, *Starfinder* (2017), and rolled out a second edition of *Pathfinder* (2019), both of which were met with griping from certain segments of players—all variations of the same old edition wars' moaning. This sort of complaining about new editions of tabletop games, a key reason *Pathfinder* exists at all, is as much a part of the pas-

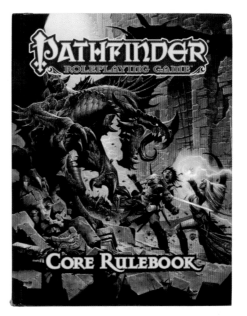

PATHFINDER ROLEPLAYING GAME, PAIZO, 2009 JASON BULMAHN AND DYVERS HANDS, COVER BY WAYNE REYNOLDS

time as the games themselves. There's even a term of variable endearment for it: "Grognard." Possibly coined by Napoleon Bonaparte, the French word means "grumbler" and applied to members of his Old Guard Grenadiers, valued veteran soldiers who, in recognition of their loyal service, were allowed to express their discontent at military life without consequence. The term was adopted by wargamers, themselves often preoccupied with Napoleonic conflicts in their games, and then embraced by the old guard in tabletop RPGs, who often feel entitled to the same candor afforded to Napoleon's favorites. Thus, the more things change in an RPG, the more likely a grognard can be found somewhere groaning about it.

THE 2010S

In which RPGs experience a renaissance.
D&D captures mainstream audiences while the zine
scene inspires beautiful experiments that captivate a new guard.
Previously unimagined horizons foretell the dawn of a new golden age.

STARS WITHOUT NUMBER, REVISED EDITION, SINE NOMINE PUBLISHING, 2017
KEVIN CRAWFORD, COVER BY NASA

Stars Without Number (2010)

Back in the '70s, Judges Guild changed the way RPGs approached wilderness exploration. *Wilderlands of High Fantasy* provided the GM a tool kit of random tables to use in generating the features of terrain hexes. Often expanded and imitated, the basic concept is simple: Travel to a new hex, roll the dice, find out what's there and in what shape it's in—hijinks ensue.

Stars Without Number takes this framework and uses it to create a vast galaxy, a hexcrawl in space. Or, more accurately, it gives the GM the tools to create their own. It then applies that system to everything else they might need to create. In this way, *Stars Without Number* is an RPG in its own right, but it also becomes a metatext about RPGs and how they work.

Stars Without Number takes an unusual approach to its world building—the goal is to create a rich and exciting sandbox galaxy to explore, but only in the direction the players are metaphorically facing. After a bit of basic prep work, nested random tables allow GMs to dial in the necessary level of detail in real time, as the players are interfacing with it, instead of creating a great deal of material during downtime in hopes that players will find it. This forward focus reduces the amount of labor for the GM, and channels the energy of the game toward the present moment at the table—no one knows what's around the corner, because the corner doesn't exist yet. That's exciting for everybody at the table!

The GM does set the stage ahead of time, defining the galaxy, of which only a sliver concerns the players, a grid of hexes eight-wide by ten-high called a sector. A number of initial stars are placed randomly by rolling an 8-sided die and a 10-sided die, using the results to plot the coordinates. Additional stars are added in order to connect clusters—the "spike drive" technology that powers interstellar travel can only jump three hexes, so anything beyond that range would be inaccessible to a campaign.

Each solar system has one planet of note (initially, anyway), which is defined by a pair of randomly generated tags (from a table of 100) that establish the tone. The result could be a Cybercommunist planet that also has some kind of Forbidden Tech, for instance. Each tag comes with five additional categories of prompts: One for Enemies, Friends, Complications, Things, and Places; so, one Cybercommunist complication is "planning computers can't handle the increasing population." None of the options under Forbidden Tech specifically solve that problem, but all of the mentions of "maltech" and out-of-control artificial intelligences imply many possibilities.

Planets then receive atmospheres, temperatures, biospheres, populations, and tech levels, all rolled randomly, each adding a bit of detail to the implied reality. There's more—fine grain detail for the starting world, then politics, factions, and trade routes at the sector level. All the while, the text emphasizes the different relationships and connections between the data points, encouraging the GM to start hanging stories on them. Often, this is the point at which a rulebook congratulates itself on a job well done and, after offering increasingly vague advice, leaves the rest of the world building to the GM. *Stars Without Number*, however, keeps going, applying the random tables to adventure creation, as well.

In 1895, Georges Polti published *The Thirty-Six Dramatic Situations*, an analysis of classical Greek and contemporary French literature that attempts to categorize every possible circumstance that might appear in fiction. Each established category is followed by a brief synopsis, the requisite elements, and examples of variations—all presented in bulleted lists.

Polti's language and analysis often feel too broad, to the point that his categories frequently verge on meaninglessness; but at the same time, it is also, perhaps, impossible to point to something he didn't account for. In many ways, Polti's book feels like an RPG sourcebook; key the entries, get a 36-sided die, and a GM is in business. *Stars Without Number* attempts something similar with a set of nested tables for problems, people, and places. These can generate many more than 36 situations, and there are 100 paragraph-long plot seeds besides.

And there's still more! There are tables for aliens, creatures, robots, and still more. Then there's the faction system, which allows GMs to assign a set of attributes to any and all groups, major and minor, within the game sector. Once assigned, the GM can, in the downtime between sessions, see what these fictional entities all do. Almost every GM has a story about how their players surprised them, but few can pinpoint a time in which the story or the world of their game held a shocking twist—it is difficult for the conductor to be startled by the performance when they're directing the orchestra. By removing much of the decision-making about the state of the galaxy from their purview, the faction system aims to make the setting surprising for the GM. As with all of these systems, they make for surprisingly satisfying solo games.

The underlying mechanics of *Stars Without Numbers* draws mostly from early *Dungeons & Dragons*—it's a self-identifying Old School Revival game. Character attributes are the same; there are saving throws, and the combat system functions pretty much identically. Other areas of the game are quite different.

D&D-style classes are secondary to occupation-based backgrounds, which convey skills in an echo of *Traveller*. There are only four classes—Warriors, Psychics (who wield the robust psionic abilities that take the place of magic), Experts (who are skill-focused), and Adventurers (who combine a bit of all three). Like *Metamorphosis Alpha*, power and prowess

result from good equipment rather than inherent powers; ship-to-ship combat has each player staffing a different battle station, à la *Star Trek*. The system is solid enough, but the real beauty of *Stars Without Numbers* is as a toolkit for the creation of interstellar sandboxes—it remains unmatched in both its depth and its potential application.

Apocalypse World (2010)

If *Dogs in the Vineyard* is a serious-minded period drama with an eye on an Oscar nomination, *Apocalypse World* is a post-apocalyptic B-movie with buckets of blood and the promise of excessive nudity. It revels in the grand tradition of schlock, like *The New Barbarians* (1983), *Exterminators of the Year 3000* (1983), and other classic "good-bad" movies that popped up in the wake of the box office success of *The Road Warrior* (1981).

Players choose from a group of sufficiently over-the-top archetypes. There are Battlebabes and cult leaders and psychics. These are each defined by an unusual set of attributes—Cool, Hard, Hot, Sharp, and Weird. Sharp, for instance, aligns with a character's percep-

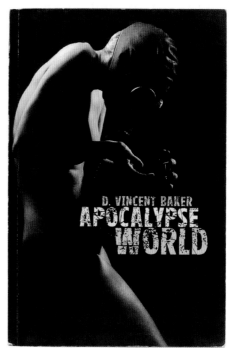

APOCALYPSE WORLD, LUMPLEY GAMES, 2010
D. VINCENT BAKER, COVER BY IVAN BLIZNETSOV

tion, Hard with their violent capabilities. On top of that, every player character has History with each player character, which increases during play and contributes to Experience and character improvement.

The method for resolving actions and conflicts is standardized. Every roll uses two 6-sided dice and adds in any modifiers. Ten and up is a success; six or lower is a failure, which gives the GM the chance to act, similar to *InSpectres*. In the middle is a partial success or hard choice—the player gets a little and loses a little. The mixed result captures some of the drama of action movies: Nothing ever goes smoothly; there's always a complication.

There are other neat features. The setting of *Apocalypse World* is implied by the character classes and their abilities and fleshed out through play. The GM is encouraged to come to the session with nothing prepared in order to ensure the experience is truly collaborative. The concerns of the game and the details of the world are laid out in a worksheet that is designed to motivate players to ask questions that the narrative can answer. The game also introduces the idea of using countdown clocks to manage threats and

other factors outside of the players' control—these become a central mechanic for *Blades in the Dark*. Set times for when the threat changes—at 5 p.m., the patrol will return and reinforce the fort—advance the clock as play progresses.

However, all of these mechanics pale in comparison to *Apocalypse World*'s major innovation: The way it handles actions.

Back in the '80s, IBM-compatible personal computers ran on DOS (literally "disk operating system"), and one of the major limitations of DOS was that it could only do one thing at a time. Need to use a calculator? Close that word processor first!

To circumvent this limitation, programmers used what is called a terminate-and-stay-resident (TSR) program—basically, when a user launched their program, the terminate-and-stay-resident program would install a bit of code that allowed the program to re-launch with a special key combination, essentially letting it lurk in the background. Amusingly, terminate-and-stay, abbreviated TSR, also fittingly describes the death and resurrection of *D&D* in the late '90s.

TSRs were an early form of macroinstruction (more commonly known as a "macro") that have since developed into a kind of user interface shortcut—bind a series of commands to a single keystroke and automate the process. For instance, as part of the preparation for printing, all of the photographs in this book need to be sharpened in image editing software, a process that occurs in several steps. Rather than perform those steps manually for every photograph, I can record them and bind them to a button in the program interface, thus reducing several steps to just one click of the mouse.

This bundling is what *Apocalypse World* does to RPGs with the introduction of the

APOCALYPSE WORLD, SECOND EDITION, LUMPLEY GAMES, 2016
D. VINCENT BAKER AND MEGUEY BAKER, COVER BY ALESMUNT

Moves mechanic, and it marks an important milestone for RPG design.

A Move is a collection of actions that are deployed and resolved within the context of a situation. Take, for example, a situation in which a group of player characters is inside an abandoned building with raiders shooting at them from the outside. The group needs to get the walkie-talkie that is *just over there* to fix it and call for back up. In most RPGs, doing so would likely require several discrete mechanical actions—a Dodge or Dexterity roll to get the walkie-talkie, a Repair roll to fix it, and maybe a Luck roll to make sure someone is listening on the other end of the line.

In *Apocalypse World*, all of these actions are handled by the Move called Act Under Fire, which, like all Moves, is resolved by a single die roll. And while the name implies that someone is shooting at the character using the Move, it can apply to any high stress situation—looking at a map while in a car chase or getting to the alarm button while in a physical struggle with someone.

Moves accomplish several things at once: First, they take a situation that would be mechanically daunting and sweep it up into a single roll, which makes the game easier, particularly for new players; they put mechanical training wheels on what would otherwise be a freeform narrative game, thus solving the problem of improvisational paralysis that has haunted story-oriented games since *Baron Munchausen*. Despite this framework, *Apocalypse World* retains much of the feel and freedom of story games, because the utility of Moves was intended to be open to interpretation and applied broadly—basically, players can riff around the table until they hit something that specifically triggers a Move. Finally, because a Move contains clear cause and effect, it makes tackling intense or difficult subject matter, which might otherwise make players feel uncomfortable, seem less daunting.

Apocalypse World applies an R-rating to itself for language, sex, and violence, and it is well-earned. For instance, owing to the desperate, "tomorrow may never come" tone of the setting, each class has its own sex Move that imparts particular bonuses and effects, thus encouraging the sorts of romantic (or convenient) entanglements audiences are accustomed to seeing in action movies (as famously laid out in the *Speed* films).

Each character is a collection of Moves called a Playbook. Some of these are basic and shared by all characters, like Act Under Fire. Others are specific to the character's class, as with the Brainer's In-Brain Puppet Strings, which plants a psychic command in another character's head. The sex Moves are all unique to their respective classes. Not to be left out, GMs have their own set of mechanic-free moves, designed to mimic plot developments and keep the action moving.

Because of the way Moves streamline play and how a set of Playbooks naturally implies a world to collaboratively flesh out and play in, *Apocalypse World* has become a popular system to hack, to the point that these hacks have become a category unto their own: Powered by the Apocalypse, or PbtA. There are dozens of them, if not hundreds, and they reflect the spectrum of RPG experiences, both conventional and strange.

Dungeon World (2013), translates the *D&D* experience into PbtA. There's *The Warren*, in which players take the role of rabbits, similar to *Bunnies & Burrows*. There's funny science fiction (*Farflung*, 2017) and serious science fiction (*Uncharted Worlds*, 2015), and cyberpunk (*The Sprawl*, 2016). There's the gritty action of '70s pop culture (*Spirit of '77*, 2015) and teen superheroes (*Masks*, 2016).

Monsterhearts is about teenage monsters in love (or, at least, they *think* it's love). *Brindlewood Bay* (2020) pits characters similar to *The Golden Girls* against the cosmic horror of Lovecraft. *World Wide Wrestling* (2015) takes the concept of Moves literally. Even older games are getting in on the action—the latest edition of *Kult* (2018) is PbtA. Sometimes, they're difficult to quantify, like the gorgeous, psychosexual *Bluebeard's Bride* (2017), in which players each take control of a fragment of the titular bride's personality as she explores the haunted rooms of her murderous husband's castle.

PbtA excels at facilitating these sorts of tightly constrained, emotionally charged games that ultimately focus on the mess of interconnected relationships. In a few short years, they mutated so rapidly and thoroughly that they began to stand on their own, resulting in *Blades in the Dark* and its own family of hacks, which have been jokingly referred to as being powered by the post-apocalypse.

Microscope (2011)

Ben Robbins makes what I consider meta-RPGs, games that utilize characters and stories to investigate the concepts *behind* those characters and stories. Why do players think a particular sort of character or plot is exciting? Does a player's proximity to a story matter, or the order in which it is told? Can a historical timeline be as compelling as an intensely personal internal monologue? Can players *play* through either of those extremes? Questions like these often arise from Robbins's games, though rarely do definitive answers follow—that ambiguity is actually part of the fun.

Microscope was his first RPG, and it is an unusual one: It's a collaborative, GM-less, zero prep, non-linear game about exploring the history of a fictional society. While that might sound complex, it isn't. Robbins's games may feature heady ideas, but the mechanics are almost

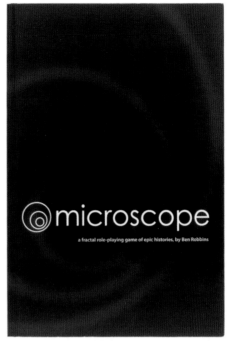

MICROSCOPE, LAME MAGE PRODUCTIONS, 2011
BEN ROBBINS

always approachable. In a nutshell: The players decide what the game is about; they set the starting and ending points, say, the rise and fall of a glorious king. The point at which he earns the throne might be the start, and his death would be the natural ending. Everything in between is the playing field.

Players take turns setting a focus for exploration. During a round, each player's additions to the timeline touch on the selected theme. A player might focus on the betrayal of the king's greatest champion, creating a period called "Sir Spearsome's Madness" and expand on it with an event about Spearsome murdering some folks. Accidentally? On purpose? Perhaps another player will decide. The next player, though, might leap ahead on the timeline to create an event that shows how Spearsome's madness affects the kingdom, or slide back on the timeline to reveal the prophecy that foretold all of this, or drill further down in the first player's event to roleplay a scene that answers a specific question about the betrayal: Did love drive Spearsome mad?

Once everyone has added something regarding Sir Spearsome to the timeline,

1970

1980

1990

2000

2010

KINGDOM, LAME MAGE PRODUCTIONS, 2013
BEN ROBBINS, COVER BY CAROLINE HOBBS

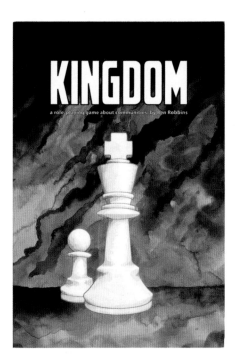

the next player chooses a new focus. Foci can be absolutely anything; the only rule is that facts established on the timeline can't be contradicted. In this way, players can move from what is essentially a collaborative character study to, say, a travelogue of many characters scouring the land for a misplaced cup or a mystery about a mischievous rogue who hides magical weaponry in unusual places. Play can conceivably continue on in this way forever.

Microscope takes on massively complicated concepts, like time and history, and provides elegant rules for navigating them in a way that is both thought provoking and fun. My initial reaction to the game was that of wonder. It didn't seem possible for the mechanics to be so simple and versatile, nor did it seem that an elaborate timeline could give way to stories that surprised everyone at that table. Yet, that's exactly what *Microscope* does.

Kingdom is Ben Robbins's second meta-RPG and, while it isn't a follow-up to *Microscope*, it explores many of the same

ideas about how history and storytelling intertwine. It also includes rules for fusing the games together, though I admit I find that prospect intimidating.

Kingdom is about communities at a pivotal moment in their history. Together, players create the broad strokes of their kingdom; it can be anything: A neighborhood, a law firm, a barony, a seed ship. They then create characters, their main problems, and their relationships with each other. Each character has a meta role—Power characters decide what the Kingdom does; Perspective characters can foresee the consequences of those actions, and Touchstones reflect the wishes of the people.

Players next create the Crossroads, a pivotal moment in the Kingdom's history in which their characters will play a crucial role. The players explore the Crossroads through a series of scenes, using their roles to define the story, building events to a point of decision or crisis. Thus, when the Touchstone character says the people are ready to rise up, it is true, until another Touchstone says it isn't; only a Power character can move to quell the uprising, but even then, it is the Perspective character who decides the outcome.

This arrangement uncouples the traditional relationship of cause and effect in RPGs. While the rules elegantly account for any eventuality in the broadest sense, the result is a story that no single player can ever fully control or predict. Building an engine for storytelling that routinely surprises the storyteller is quite an accomplishment.

There is, of course, much more happening, but the rules rarely feel overwhelming. Players learn the rules collaboratively by passing the book around and reading entries aloud; a full half of the book is devoted to thoughtful advice for the game and starting ideas for Kingdoms.

These and Robbins's other published games feel very much like their own sub-genre: Idiosyncratic explorations of specific elements of play put together by one designer that also happen to be fun for other people to play. They're fully fledged games, but they're also tools—players can use *Microscope* as a way to collaboratively create a campaign setting, and *Kingdom* can help work through the repercussions of major events in a game world.

Mostly, Robbins's games expand the definition of "tabletop roleplaying game" into newer, stranger territory. In some ways, they set the stage for the growing genre of world building games, like *A Quiet Year*, but that seems like more of a happy accident for these restrained and graceful experiments.

Monsterhearts (2012)

There are many, many RPGs that are Powered by the Apocalypse. One of the earliest is *Monsterhearts*. In many ways, it's the first game that shows what the Apocalypse Engine is capable of, embracing the way it encourages complicated interpersonal relationships, then pushes them into emotionally fraught territory. It's right there on the cover: "A story game about the messy lives of teenage monsters."

Players each pick a Skin, which is their secret identity that lurks under the veneer of teen angst. Most of these are monsters—Werewolves, Vampires, Ghosts, and on—but players can also play a Mortal, a Witch, or even a Buffy-esque monster hunter, the Chosen.

Whatever the archetype, each Skin serves as a channel for a particular kind of teenage pettiness. Witches silently judge (and make characters feel it with their hexes), Fae extract promises under duress and punish those who don't keep them, and the Chosen is plagued by self-doubt. As with *Apocalypse World*, the types of characters dictate the play—a game with a Chosen and a Mortal is natu-

rally going to be very different than one in which every character is undead. Players collaborate to create the school and the town. There's some menace skulking just out of view that needs to be defined and a homeroom seating chart to fill. But, if players are expecting a garden variety CW-style, supernatural romance, like those in *Buffy the Vampire Slayer*, they're in for a shock.

The game is arranged around the idea that teens are bundles of confusing, conflicting emotions, betrayed by the world and their developing, hormone-filled bodies. They're impulsive and make bad decisions and indulge in questionable behavior. The game characterizes them as *feral*. That can become literal rather quickly: Each Skin has a Darkest Self, their inner monster run wild, each with its own trigger and means of escape. There's also plenty of shitty teen manipulation. Each character has a web of connections between themselves and other characters called Strings—they represent leverage from some misstep and can be pulled mercilessly.

315

And then, of course, there's sex. As with *Apocalypse World*, every Skin has a unique sex Move that reaps special rewards and potential consequences. Nearly every mechanic in the game (including, uncomfortably, the manipulation mechanic) has a sexual component.

The most interesting of them is Turn Someone On, the first basic Move described in the book. All of the characters have it, and it is the only Move in the whole game that can be initiated at any time. All of the game's other Moves are triggered by narrative events, they're reactions, but not Turn Someone On, that's proactive—a player can just decide their character looks really good standing there, doing nothing, and make another character roll—*any* character. This distinction is purposely designed to remove the player's control over their character's sexuality and give it over to the dice.

It's a clever move. "The dice are going to be the ultimate referees of what is and isn't sexy for these characters," explain the rules. "Their own sexuality will confuse and surprise them; it'll show up in unexpected places and unlikely situations." This approach gives sexual attraction in *Monsterhearts* a sense of bewilderment and experimentation—even if the player of a cishet monster keeps abiding by cishet expectations in the narrative, the players can see the swirl of feelings they're experiencing through the rolls and the mechanics. The book spends two pages arguing for players to embrace queer content in their game (and they should!) but in play, the queerness of *Monsterhearts* is self-evident.

Monsters have long served as a metaphor for queerness—the social stigma, the duality, and the trauma of being closeted can all lead to a natural identification with the monstrous, not the villain, but the misunderstood, unfairly judged outsider. Evidence of this alignment can be seen as far back as *The Bride of Frankenstein* (1935). Directed by the openly gay James Whale, the film rewards queer readings. In more recent, RPG-related fare, this queering of the monstrous can be seen in the growing popularity of games centered on gay orcs.

In the past, RPGs have made room for queer-focused play. The various *World of Darkness* games (particularly *Changeling*), *Kult*, and *Over the Edge* all seem primed to be queer-centric, should players desire it. *Blue Rose* was ridiculed in some circles for welcoming all types of romance and for de-stigmatizing queerness in its setting material.

None, however, had been so explicitly organized around queerness, from the telling of queer stories to encouraging players to actively experiment with queerness. This shift is significant, partly because the creation, distribution, and play of RPGs have all historically been dominated by straight white men and partly because, to my eye, that dominance has rapidly waned in recent years, with queer-identifying players constituting a growing demographics in the hobby.

Monsterhearts is an important gateway, and it represents a massive step forward in diversifying the hobby.

Dungeon Crawl Classics (2012)

Goodman Games was old school long before anyone thought to revive the old school. In 2003, the company launched the Dungeon Crawl Classics line of modules for the d20 System with *Idylls of the Rat King*. That adventure module, with its yellow and purple trade dress and retro fonts, is an unmistakable throwback to the style of early '80s TSR products.

It's apparent just by looking at some of the subsequent titles of Goodman modules—*The Lost Vault of Tsathzar Rho* (2003), *The Iron Crypt of the Heretics* (2006), *The Sinister Secret of Whiterock* (2007)—that the company lovingly draws on vintage *D&D* aesthetics. Over the years, this love affair grew weirder,

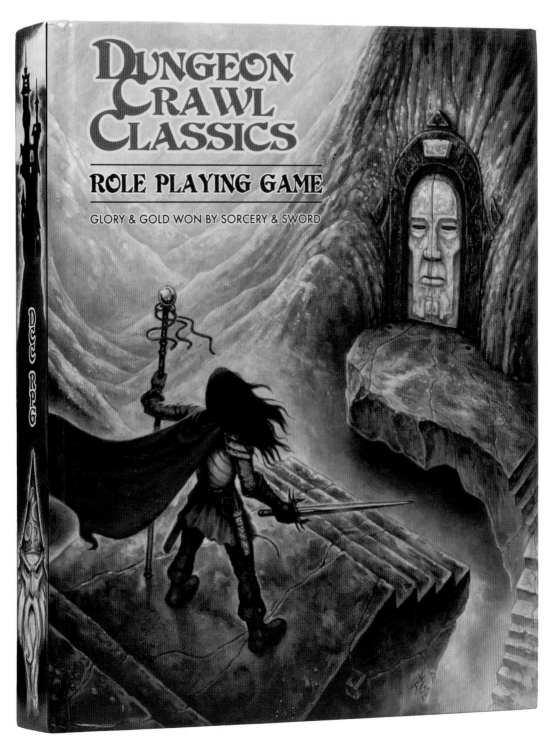

DUNGEON CRAWL CLASSICS, GOODMAN GAMES, 2012
JOSEPH GOODMAN, MICHAEL CURTIS, HARLEY STROH, AND DEITER ZIMMERMAN, COVER BY DOUG KOVACS   **317**

THE CHAINED COFFIN, SECOND EDITION, GOODMAN GAMES, 2019
MICHAEL CURTIS, COVER BY KEN KELLY

eventually producing the *Dungeon Crawl Classics* RPG (*DCC*), which marks the pinnacle of the Old School Revival movement and, perhaps, the birth of something completely new, as well.

Like *Castles & Crusades*, *DCC* is a version of the d20 System, heavily modified in order to capture the feeling of an earlier style of *D&D* play. Much of this "old-schoolification" is accomplished by tossing stuff out—feats, prestige classes, and skills—though ascending armor class, the simplified saving throws, and the unified d20 mechanics remain. Like *B/X D&D*, race is treated as class. Beyond that, well, here be dragons.

Of Matthew Finch's four pillars of OSR design (see page 295), *DCC* is most concerned with the fourth, which dismisses the necessity of game balance. *Dungeon Crawl Classics* doesn't just dismiss balance, it nukes balance from orbit and wages a relentless war on the straggling survivors. Randomness rules here.

The chaos manifests in two primary ways. The first is the funnel, *DCC*'s method of character creation, which may as well be named the meat grinder. Players begin by rolling up their character's attributes in order, using just three 6-sided dice. There is no point distribution, no re-arranging, no funny methods to gain higher results. Instead of one character to pin all hopes on, players are rolling up two to four zero-level characters, trusting the dice to make something that functions, keeping the results even if they don't. Then, the player marches them, along with everyone else's two to four bakers, stable hands, and whatever other vastly unqualified tradespeople, into a dungeon where they mostly get murdered. A player's last character standing is the one they play going forward.

Over the decades, character creation has moved towards the artisanal, favoring player choice and bespoke uniqueness. A player should get to play what they want, right? Nope. With the funnel system, *DCC* created something more dedicated to chance than even the games of the '70s were willing to consider. In passing through the funnel, players find that many of their preconceived notions about character, plot, and heroic destinies are stripped away. Ridiculous truths are revealed: The wholesale slaughter of player characters is hilarious, and wanton mayhem is a delight. RPGs need not be realistic at all, and, in fact, they may even excel at being unapologetically, bombastically unrealistic.

The second is the magic system. As with an attack using a sword, casting a spell requires the roll of a 20-sided die to determine success. Unlike a sword, magic in *DCC* is a tricky beast, so each spell has an individual table that determines the result of the roll, which can range from being a catastrophic failure to becoming a conduit for arcane energies far beyond expectation.

Take Feather Fall, a straightforward, classic *D&D* spell that slows the target's descent, should they, say, tumble over the edge of a cliff. Most results on the *DCC* chart offer degrees of success, ranging from taking slight damage to gaining the temporary ability to glide to, at the highest level, being totally immune to any additional effects of the fall, like burning up upon re-entry into the atmosphere after falling off of the moon.

A small range results in no effect and the spell being lost. A fumble can lead to physical changes, like the caster's hair permanently standing on end, as if they are perpetually falling, or terrible misfires, like accelerating instead of slowing the descent. Further complicating the magic system is spellburn (the option to burn off ability points to power spells), the risk of physical corruption, and the fickle impulses of supernatural patrons. The sum is a magic system that is totally unpredictable and prone to power surges. Every time a mage casts a spell, they risk blowing their face off, annihilating their party, or cracking the world in half, should they roll badly.

All of this (and other rules, too) create a play environment in which anything can happen, often does, and that is entirely the point. If players want a game that encourages character development, sprawling stories, or rewarding exploration, look elsewhere. Longevity isn't the point—short campaigns and glorious, improbable deaths are. *DCC* is about grabbing that old stick of dynamite, shaking it vigorously, and laughing maniacally while waiting to see if it explodes.

I often feel like *Dungeon Crawl Classics* is shouting at me. Part of this is physical—the narrow page margins and the large fonts make the text feel like it is leaping off of the page, swinging a wild haymaker. Then, there are the numerous doomed adventurers in the illustrations, silently screaming as they get eaten, stabbed, and otherwise dispatched.

It's in the prose, too, in which the boundless enthusiasm for the old ways

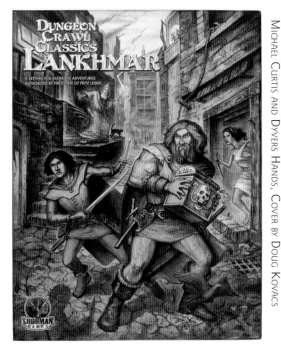

Dungeon Crawl Classics: Lankhmar, Box set, Goodman Games, 2019 Michael Curtis and Dyvers Hands, Cover by Doug Kovacs

can sometimes become grating. Early on, there is a page listing the qualifications potential readers must meet in order to peruse the book. Most of the requirements are fine and lighthearted, like a pledge recited to gain access to a tree house, but there are sour notes, like when it beseeches readers to liken Gary Gygax, Dave Arneson, and a list of other early designers to gods. The page is obviously meant to be taken with my tongue planted firmly in my cheek, but I find it difficult to keep from rolling my eyes.

Words aside, there is nothing but sweetness in the art. Pure joy leaps from the numerous pages of illustrations, all of which are in the black-and-white, old-school style, much of it by actual old-school artists, like Erol Otus, Jeff Dee, Russ Nicholson, Jim Holloway, Jim Roslof, Jeff Easley, Clyde Caldwell, and many more. They're joined by new hands, like Doug Kovacs, Peter Mullen, and Stefan Poag, who all push that traditional aesthetic to new and exciting places. For as many horrible deaths as that art depicts, they're also often silly and cartoonish. It is in the art that the true Dungeon Crawl Classics experience is mapped out for players.

1970

1980

1990

2000

2010

Joseph Goodman's primary stated inspiration for *Dungeon Crawl Classics* is Gygax's suggested reading list, "Appendix N," from the *Dungeon Masters Guide*. Goodman makes the case that *DCC*, through its embrace of "Appendix N," aims to create an RPG that taps a kind of proto-spirit of fantasy. *D&D* first appeared in a world where the strictures of fantasy were far less hardened than they are today. *DCC* wants to reach further back, to a time when, at least in retrospect, the possibilities seemed endless in order to shatter the pre-conceived notions of the modern era. He writes:

> To the many and varied OSR publishers, I offer one comment […] the OSR has re-published a plethora of variants on the core *D&D* concepts. The target customer is offered no shortage of retro-clones, adventures centered on goblin raiders, excursions into the underdeep and genre-based campaign settings. I started work on the volume you hold in your hand because I believe the time has come to break the chains of *D&D* convention and step back one era further, to the original inspiration of "Appendix N," beyond the confines of genre assumptions […]. I ask you to consider moving past the boundaries of "TSR mimicry." The time has come to offer our shared customer something both new *and* old-school.

In one way, *DCC* attempts to go further back through sheer gonzo energy, energy that outstrips even the weirdest of 1970s funhouses. More recently, that wildness was poured into *Mutant Crawl Classics* (2018), which takes the *DCC* system and applies it to a post-apocalyptic landscape in the style of *Gamma World*.

In another, quieter way, Goodman Games has expanded the DCC line with campaign settings based on the worlds described by "Appendix N" authors. *Lankhmar* (2019), based on Fritz Leiber's stories, *Empire of the East* (2021), based on Fred Saberhagen's novels, and *The Chained Coffin*, which evokes the work of Manly Wade Wellman, all dial down the wackiness in favor of exploring different styles of fantasy in ways that the various flavors of *D&D* have always struggled to achieve. They showcase the versatility of *DCC* and promise more experiments in substance and tone in the future.

Ehdrigohr: The Roleplaying Game (2012)

Ehdrigohr: The Roleplaying Game is a single book RPG—everything needed to play, from the system (a modified version of *Fate Core*) to the lore of the world, is under the cover. At a glance, the outline of that world seems fairly standard. A great war has just ended in an uneasy stalemate. Powerful magics are at work, and terrible creatures come out at night, leaving the survival of humanity a persistent uncertainty. While all of this might seem familiar, the specifics of *Ehdrigohr* feel fresh and new, even a decade later, thanks to the perspective from which it emerged.

Author Allen Turner is Black, Lakota, and Irish, and each of these ancestries inform *Ehdrigohr* in ways that distinguish the game and its world from the usual RPG fantasy fare. From the first page, the difference is apparent: There isn't even a hint of Euro-centric medievalism. Rather, *Ehdrigohr* explores a world where people are organized into nine tribes, each of which roughly correlates to a real-world tribal culture, primarily Native American tribes, like the Lakota, Cheyenne, Aztec, and the Pueblo peoples, though cultures from abroad, like the Bedouin and the Celts, are also represented.

With *Ehdrigohr*, Turner imagines a world without colonizers. In embracing a variety of tribal and indigenous outlooks, the game presents a set of priorities in play that are completely different from most other RPGs. The lore of *Ehdrigohr* is set unapologetically in the foreground to underscore this uncolonized reality—the detailed cosmology, the rich histories of its tribes, the web of their interactions, echoing *RuneQuest*, all inform the mechanics of the game. It is impossible to play *Ehdrigohr* without engaging a different kind of mindset.

These distinct priorities are most apparent in the character concepts. Only a handful align with the sorts of character frameworks that have become the default in RPGs—the Solitary is a wandering warrior, and the Thief is a thief; both speak to the dominant notion in sword and sorcery stories of a selfish loner adventuring for their own personal gain.

The majority of *Ehdrigohr*'s other character concepts are defined by societies that serve important functions for their communities. The Dove Society are spiritual guides who ensure the dead stay dead, for instance, while the Society of Crows stands in direct opposition to the Sorrows, the spiritual forces of darkness that seek to breach the walls of reality, and the Jay Society seeks to reunite the tribes in order to prepare for the next Age.

More prosaic professions, like guards, scouts, farmers, and traders, also exist and are contextualized through their usefulness to the whole of their communities, not their individual desires: Soldiers protect; scouts seek knowledge of the world; farmers provide food; traders bring goods. Their functions, if successful in play, encourage the growth of the community, which is as much a rebuke of the forces of evil as the thrust of a Crow warrior's sword. In structuring character concepts this way, *Ehdrigohr* presents a world that is dark, but a game that is about surviving in the face of that darkness. It seeks to overcome through fellowship.

A clear contrast emerges when comparing *Ehdrigohr*'s themes of tribal community with the lore of games, like *Dead-*

EHDRIGOHR: THE ROLEPLAYING GAME, COUNCIL OF FOOLS, 2012
ALLEN TURNER. COVER BY VALERIE XANOS

lands, which shares the similar overarching plot of invading extradimensional horrors. Both *Deadlands* and *Shadowrun* use the Ghost Dance, a ceremony developed in the late 1800s by several Native American tribes (including the Lakota) as a spiritual expression of (usually peaceful) resistance in the face of cultural genocide perpetrated but the United States government. In both of those games, the Ghost Dance is a plot device, deployed to cataclysmically change the colonizers and land-stealers' way of life by reintroducing magic to the world.

In *Deadlands*, the Native Americans who perform the ritual are robbed of agency, as they are dupes manipulated by outré forces. In *Shadowrun*, the Ghost Dance is described as the equivalent of a spiritual nuclear weapon, and its deployment leads to the united Native American Nations ascending to the world stage as a Western-style corporatist kleptocracy. These sorts of portrayals of indigenous cultures seem like ill-informed caricatures when they're lined up with the tribal groups seeking harmony and strong community in *Ehdrigohr*. They aren't primitive or vengeful or envious; rather, the people of *Ehdrigohr* are optimistic. It's a game about holding on to hope.

The Quiet Year (2013)

RPGs, as a hobby, are actually made of many smaller constituent hobbies. There's the playing, of course, which is primary for most folks and takes up the most time, but many of the activities that fall under the collective umbrella of "game prep" are satisfying pursuits in their own right. Simply reading RPG books is enough for some people while others pass the time by painting miniatures, writing campaign diaries, and drawing character portraits. Of them all, though, map making has, perhaps, the most powerful mystique.

For one, making maps of imaginary places is largely unique to RPGs. They're objects that are both aesthetic and semi-mechanical, where space is defined to please the eye and facilitate play. With a good map, a GM can see the flow of play and the potential action taking place, even without looking at the keyed entries. Maps use their own secret language, too—the possibilities laid out in Diesel La Force's cryptic map legend in the *Basic Set* fired the imagination of many a young mind. Some graph paper and a pencil (maybe a couple of colored pencils for the ambitious) is all a GM needs. Whole campaigns can spring out of an intriguing map!

It's no surprise, then, that someone would eventually craft a game where map making *is* the game. The first is *The Quiet Year* by Avery Alder, a collaborative map making game that uses playing cards to drive the narrative. The game, on the cover, calls itself "a map game about community and struggle," but I find the description on Alder's website cuts to the heart of it: "part roleplaying game, part cartographic poetry."

The Quiet Year is set in a post-apocalypse of vague aspect, just after a period of prolonged strife. Rather than focusing on particular characters, players guide an entire community through, as the title implies, a year of relative peace and reconstruction. In the winter, though, the Frost Shepherds will come, ending the game on an enigmatic note.

Play is broken up into 52 weeks, each represented by a playing card; four suits, one for each season. Spades represent winter, and the Frost Shepherds arrive whenever the king is drawn. Each card has story prompts or special events, which the active player reads then resolves at the start of the turn. They, then, have three potential actions.

Discover Something New allows the active player to add something to the map—a site to explore, a threat to deal with, a person of note within the community. Like the printed events on the cards, this action is designed to complicate the game. Start a Project allows players to interact with the map and the ongoing narrative. Players can hunt down those raiders or build a pen for the sheep—the length of time these projects take is determined by the group, and they're tracked using a 6-sided die that ticks down as the required weeks pass. Finally, Hold a Discussion, invites each player to share one thought on a topic in turn.

This last action underscores the way in which *The Quiet Year* seeks to complicate communication (and reveals the double

THE QUIET YEAR, BURIED WITHOUT CEREMONY, 2013
AVERY ALDER, COVER BY ARIEL NORRIS

The Quiet Year

a map game about community and struggle
by Avery Alder

meaning in the game's name). As the players embody an entire community, rather than the individuals within it, the game fosters imprecision in how players talk to each other. Chatter is discouraged. When required, the game urges players to be terse.

When a Discussion is Held, everyone weighs in, but nothing is resolved—that is for someone else to do when their turn comes around, using the other two actions, unilaterally and possibly in defiance of the consensus. As the rules state, conversation on a community scale is "untidy and inconclusive."

Details are filled in on the map as necessary. Inevitably, as priorities shift, tensions rise, and, if a player feels their interests are being ignored, they can take a Contempt token, which can be cashed in to act selfishly or even to split the community. Of course, Contempt often breeds more Contempt, so using the tokens often indicates serious fractures in the community.

The Quiet Year is an experimental game, and it is not for everyone. Limiting discussion is an unusual constraint that pushes against the social norms of the gaming table. While it reflects the messiness of communication within a community, around the table it seems designed to stoke resentments and foster Contempt—after all, there is nothing binding what the players say to what they actually do, at any point in the game. Pettiness is bound to drown out more serious problems in the fictional community, and feelings among the players are likely to be contentious. Those potentially emotional reactions are the real soul of the game—rebuilding after the end of the world isn't meant to be a pleasant experience.

While *The Quiet Year* is likely born, in some primal way, out of the tables for randomly generating worlds in products, like *Wilderlands of High Fantasy* and *Stars Without Numbers*, it also has a kinship to games, like *Dread* and *Ten Candles*, that use unusual physical mechanics to foster a sense of the precarious in the game's narrative. Many other games built around or including collaborative cartography have appeared in its wake, like *Beak, Feather & Bone* (2020) and *Beyond the Wall* (2013), and it is an important part of a growing movement for creating games devoted to the act of world building, which started earlier with *Microscope*.

Mutant: Year Zero (2014)

In 1982, Äventyrsspel released the first Swedish RPG, *Drakar och Demoner* (or *Dragons and Demons*), which was a sort of potpourri of Chaosium products. At its core was *Basic Role-Playing*, but it also incorporated the Magic World material from *World of Wonders* (1982) and the anthropomorphic ducks from *RuneQuest*.

The company's second game, *Mutant* (1984), was also based on the *BRP* system, but instead of a fantasy setting, it featured a *Gamma World*-inspired post-apocalyptic Scandinavia populated by human survivors, robots, and mutants, hence the name. A number of editions of *Mutant* appeared over the course of the '80s and '90s, including one that crossed over with *Kult*; it also spawned a spin-off

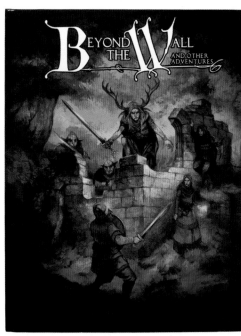

BEYOND THE WALL AND OTHER ADVENTURES, FLATLAND GAMES, 2013
JOHN COCKING AND PETER S. WILLIAMS; COVER BY JOHN HODGSON

MUTANT: YEAR ZERO, FREE LEAGUE PUBLISHING, 2014
TOMAS HÄRENSTAM, COVER BY OLA LARSSON

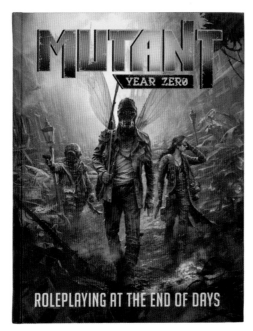

ROLEPLAYING AT THE END OF DAYS

game called *Mutant Chronicles* (1993). Äventyrsspel, later called Target Games, went out of business in 1999; a licensed revival of *Mutant* appeared in 2002, after which the game seemed destined for obscurity. Then, in 2014, came *Mutant: Year Zero* from Free League Publishing.

Year Zero, like its *Mutant* predecessors, owes a debt to games, like *Gamma World* and *Aftermath!* (1981). In tone, it sits somewhere between the two, neither as wild as *Gamma World* nor as realistic as *Aftermath!*. Unlike those games, the apocalypse is known to be a devastating plague. What follows—ruination, scarcity, struggle—feels familiar. The world, at least, painted in hues of brown and gray, holds few surprises to those with experience in the genre.

The three central pillars of play are survival, exploration, and community building. The player characters are part of a small mutant community—the Ark—that exists near what was once either London or New York City—a wasteland now called the Zone. With supply stockpiles low, characters must venture out of the safety of the enclave in search of food, water, and bullets, which serve as both ammunition and currency.

FORBIDDEN LANDS, BOX SET, FREE LEAGUE PUBLISHING, 2018
TOMAS HÄRENSTAM AND DYVERS HANDS, COVER BY SIMON STÅLENHAG

Hazards in the Zone are plentiful—mutant beasts, raiders, cultists, predatory grass, wild weather, strange diseases, and more await the unwary. Success in the Zone allows characters to contribute to community projects, similar to *The Quiet Year*, that improve the quality of life for residents of the Ark. All of that might buy the players and their fictional community enough time to search for Eden, a rumored promised land that is the focus of the line's larger metaplot. Characters are in a race against their own worsening mutations, however—though they initially serve as boons and special abilities, over time, they become debilitating. In this way, *Mutant: Year Zero* is about making a character's actions count in the brief time that they have.

The way *Mutant: Year Zero* breaks new ground has less to do with the setting and far more to do with the system.

The engine has six core features. The intent was to design something that was easy to learn, first and foremost, so it uses pools of 6-sided dice to check skills, with each six counting as a success. The more sixes, the better the result. This simplicity leads to the second feature: Speed. The leanness of the system plays fast and

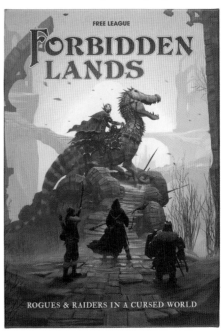

FREE LEAGUE

FORBIDDEN LANDS

ROGUES & RAIDERS IN A CURSED WORLD

pushes the action to its decisive moment as quickly as possible. In terms of pure mechanics, this pace makes Year Zero Engine (YZE) games dangerous and high risk, a fact that is exacerbated by the requirement of sixes to succeed in a roll.

The danger is somewhat mitigated by the option to re-roll the dice in exchange for a greater cost in the case of failure (which, in turn, heightens the game's risk). The Year Zero Engine generally considers the gradients of failure—and their ensuing complications—to be a more interesting way of pushing the story forward, rather than success. These stories are player-focused, with very few mechanical systems available to the GM for the handling of NPCs. Further, the engine uses a number of techniques inspired by storytelling games to encourage both players and the GM to drive the narrative to peaks of drama. Finally, the engine was designed to be adaptable and modular, providing support for many different kinds of themes and settings while maintaining a baseline of ease and approachability.

The versatility of the engine is on display in Free League's other games. Add a stress mechanic and focus on one-shot,

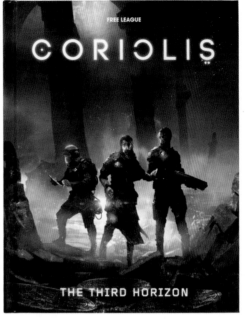

CORIOLIS: THE THIRD HORIZON, FREE LEAGUE PUBLISHING, 2017. TOMAS HÄRENSTAM AND DYVERS HANDS; COVER BY MARTIN BERGSTRÖM

cinematic play, and the result is *Alien*. Add spaceships and religions that, Glorantha-like, have a real mechanical impact on the story through a prayer system, and out comes *Coriolis* (2016). Add fantasy hex crawling to *Mutant: Year Zero*'s survivalism, and *Forbidden Lands* (2018) is born. Dial back the danger, add '80s nostalgia, and focus on the interpersonal dynamics between characters, and *Tales from the Loop* (2017) emerges. Yet, as different as these games are, they all feel familiar. There are character archetypes, a simple skill system, and damage tracked through traumas rather than hit points. Learning one of these games means, in essence, players have learned them all.

At Chaosium's height during the '80s, the company used *Basic Role-Playing* to crank out classic games and support materials that proved to be hugely influential to the hobby, at large. Mechanically and philosophically, the Year Zero Engine is *BRP*'s cousin and, in many ways, its spiritual successor. In just a few short years, Free League's suite of Year Zero Engine games have already been showered with ENNIE Awards and attracted a large community of players.

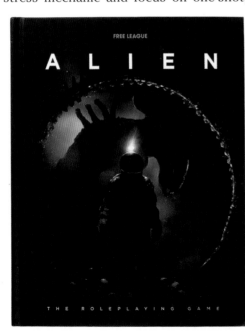

ALIEN: THE ROLEPLAYING GAME, FREE LEAGUE PUBLISHING, 2019. TOMAS HÄRENSTAM, ANDREW E. C. GASKA, AND DYVERS HANDS; COVER BY MARTIN GRIP

1970

1980

1990

2000

2010

Dungeons & Dragons Fifth Edition (2014)

Despite making money and bringing new players to the game, the Fourth Edition of *Dungeons & Dragons* never really emerged from under the shadow of the previous edition, thanks to the success of Third Edition's spiritual successor, *Pathfinder*. Support for the system was essentially abandoned after Wizards of the Coast announced the development of a new edition of *Dungeons & Dragons* in 2012.

The working title was "*D&D* Next," and it came along with a massive public playtesting process in which over 175,000 players took part. From the start, as with Third Edition, there was a sense of return, of going back to the primordial origins and correcting the mistakes of the previous edition. As if to underscore that objective, the first test packet contained a version of the Caves of Chaos from *The Keep on the Borderlands* for players to poke around. Many rules and mechanics were introduced, swirled around, then faded away. Wizards of the Coast's new edition promised something for players of every previous edition of *D&D*, yet the material in the packets never made clear how that was going to coalesce.

The first official published version of the game, presented in the abridged rule booklet contained within the *Starter Set*, remains strangely fuzzy, a summation of 40 years of *D&D* that somehow lacks any defining traits.

The system is lean and streamlined. There is something hearkening back to the First and Second Edition, an underlying buzz, but it's difficult to point to anything specific, what with everything polished so shiny and smooth. It retains the unified d20-centered system established with Third Edition. Despite unceremoniously abandoning the Fourth Edition, the push-button treatment of character abilities seems to spin directly out of it, as does the relentless pursuit of perfect mechanical balance that becomes apparent with the release of the *Players Handbook* (2014).

There are whiffs of other systems, as well—the practice of recording bonuses rather than attribute or skill values is borrowed from *Blue Rose*; the approach to saving throws derives from the Siege Engine in *Castles & Crusades,* and variations on the idea of advantage and disadvantage appear in many games, though Fifth Edition's approach most closely resembles *Apocalypse World.*

Strip away everything but the pure mechanics—forget the art, lore, campaign settings, and nostalgia, all of which are fraught, muddying topics—and the Fifth Edition *Player's Handbook* (2014) is the cleanest, most straightforward presentation of *D&D* to date. For players new to RPGs, I can think of no part of the system that needs improvement in terms of approachability. After the overly arcane First Edition, the bloat of the Second Edition, the endless byzantine detail of the Third and punishing balance of the Fourth, shepherding the game to this point seems like a nearly miraculous accomplishment. And the approach paid off, ushering a gob-smacking number of new players into *D&D.*

D&D STARTER SET, WIZARDS OF THE COAST, 2014
JEREMY CRAWFORD, MIKE MEARLS, AND DYVERS HANDS, COVER BY JAIME JONES

There has long been a rule of thumb in the industry: As *D&D* goes, so goes everyone else. If *D&D* is selling poorly, the industry is probably in trouble. If *D&D* is flying off shelves, then all of the smaller companies will be selling through stock, as well, because folks will naturally look to them to provide experiences that differ from *D&D*. This principle no longer seems to hold true, if it ever did.

Fifth Edition has very little in common with the games produced by the rest of the industry. *D&D* is owned and produced by a massive corporation (Hasbro) in partnership with a massive publishing house (Penguin Random House). It's a multimedia property, a brand with celebrity advocates, production infrastructure, and an audience of millions. Thanks to *Stranger Things* (2016-present) and streaming shows, like *Critical Role* (2015-present), *Dungeons & Dragons* is currently enjoying unprecedented mainstream success.

Despite the broad popularity of contemporary *D&D*, tabletop roleplaying was created by straight white men, and RPGs were almost exclusively made by straight white men. Over the decades, this dynamic created a sort of self-reinforcing structure that encouraged mostly straight white men to play because it appealed to and accommodated straight white men. The art demonstrates this dominance. Most obvious is the chainmail bikini phenomenon: Scantily clad women dressed in impractical combat garb increasingly appeared in *D&D* illustrations throughout the '80s and '90s, rewarding the gaze of straight white (mostly teen) males. The portrayal of non-white characters was usually confined to exoticized campaign settings, like *Oriental Adventures* and *Al-Qadim*. I can think of only one *D&D* rulebook illustration featuring a Black character before the turn of the millennium (*Tome of Magic*, 1991).

While efforts were made in previous editions, with the release of Fifth Edition, Wizards of the Coast made inclusivity a central pillar of the game and worked to make *Dungeons & Dragons* welcoming to all players, from the presentation down to the specifics of the system. Again, this change is most obvious in the art—women wear more reasonable clothes (and appear in larger numbers), and the first illustration in the *Player's Handbook* is of a Black man.

Fifth Edition's inclusion efforts aren't perfect—matters of inclusion seldom are—but it represented an awareness of the problem and an attempt to rectify it, at least back in 2014. In the years since, though, Wizards continued its efforts with mixed results. With the influx of new players has come an equal influx in the diversity of those players and a corresponding desire to see that diversity reflected in the game. Art alone isn't going to effectively depict and reflect such diversity. There are *systemic* problems.

D&D is still *D&D*, which means Fifth Edition is a set of rules for a particular sort of game, one primarily based on exploring dungeons and fighting monsters. Most of the character class abilities

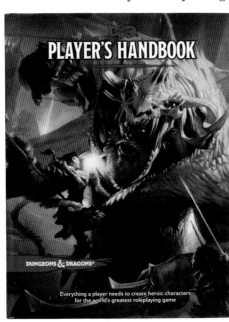

PLAYER'S HANDBOOK, WIZARDS OF THE COAST, 2014
JEREMY CRAWFORD, MIKE MEARLS, AND DYVERS HANDS.; COVER BY TYLER JACOBSON

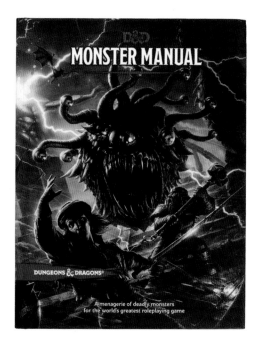

MONSTER MANUAL, WIZARDS OF THE COAST, 2014
JEREMY CRAWFORD, MIKE MEARLS, AND DYVERS HANDS, COVER BY RAYMOND SWANLAND

are centered on combat. The very idea of the dungeon crawl, the exploration by intruders into a settlement of Others with the express purpose of looting their treasure is inherently colonial. Race, as defined by fantasy conventions (dwarves, orcs, etc.), has a long history of being reductive and reinforcing casual stereotypes (see page 220).

A GM can certainly run a *D&D* game that minimizes these issues, but minimizing them only ignores or otherwise works around the existing structure that *is D&D*. A large number of people would like to see Wizards address these issues in a meaningful, substantive way. More than anything else, dismantling *D&D*'s systemic issues should occupy the brand in the coming years. There are positive signs in recent releases, like *The Wild Beyond the Witchlight* (2021), though how lasting those changes are will be a matter for posterity to judge.

Regardless, there are many games that are free of the structural issues that created the problems *D&D* now has to work to solve. They are designed specifically to appeal to people wanting to explore inclusivity, who don't want to resort to violence to solve their fictional problems,

who feel alienated by elaborate rules systems that often encourage gatekeeping and adversarial relationships between players and game masters. There are all kinds of games out there, for all kinds of players. Thanks to *Dungeons & Dragons*, these games exist. But because of *Dungeons & Dragons*, they exist in a tiny niche.

Audiences usually come into a medium at the broadest end and drill down to specifics as a matter of taste. "I like movies" leads to "I like fantasy movies" and from there to something specific, like "I like Arnold Schwarzenegger" or "My favorite movie is *Conan the Barbarian*." And there isn't an exclusivity associated with that; just because I like fantasy movies doesn't mean I won't watch a horror movie once in a while. With RPGs, the opposite is true. Far, far more people can say "I play *Dungeons & Dragons*" than can accurately say, "I play roleplaying games," plural. It's like a massive group of people clamoring for one single fantasy movie *and they don't even know horror movies exist.*

If it was true that as *D&D* goes, so goes everyone else, people would be pouring *out* of Fifth Edition and into games like *Monsterhearts, A Thousand Thousand Islands, Blue Rose, Tales from the Loop,* and dozens of zine-based games, all of which either address recent concerns stemming from *D&D* or avoid them entirely by providing vastly different experiences.

But there is no such firehose exodus. If folks are leaving, they're doing so in a trickle. Instead, contemporary *D&D* feels more like a walled garden, similar to the way Games Workshop has cloistered off its audience from the broader hobbies from which it grew. Separate. Remote. Perhaps *D&D* is now distinct from RPGs, a hobby unto itself.

20-something years later, it is easy to take the strange newness of a *Dark Sun, Planescape,* or a *Spelljammer* for granted. *Dungeons & Dragons* hasn't produced anything so weird or interesting since the death of Second Edition in 1999. *Eberron* (2004), a pulpy, steampunk-infused campaign setting for the Third Edition, is the only one that comes close.

The majority of Fifth Edition adventures, so far, are modernizations of classic *D&D* modules—*Tomb of Annihilation* (2017) riffs on *Tomb of Horrors, Princes of the Apocalypse* (2015) pays homage to *Temple of Elemental Evil, Curse of Strahd* (2016) updates *Ravenloft* and *Tales from the Yawning Portal* (2017), and *Ghosts of Saltmarsh* (2019) flat out converts classic vintage adventures to Fifth Edition. A surprising number of publications are aimed at synergizing the established worlds of *Magic: The Gathering* with *D&D*.

None of these modules break new ground. They can't, by definition and design. There is an aesthetic logic of safety that comes with that massive corporate budget. Again, there is evidence in the art. There are dozens of illustrators credited in the Fifth Edition *Monster Manual* (2014), but the art direction and the house style are so overwhelming that the book's illustrations appear to be painted by just three or four artists, at most. It all feels a bit flat, a bit unfinished.

Another clue: Flipping through the majority of books from the previous editions of *Dungeons & Dragons* will almost certainly reveal an illustration of adventurers in peril, grievously wounded, being eaten or just straight up dead—not so after 2014.

Critiques that call Fifth Edition a superhero game or liken play to being on a fantasy-inspired theme park ride seem needlessly snide, but there *is* something to them. In making an RPG that is broadly appealing, that finally captured the imagination of the general public, Fifth Edition, perhaps, transformed itself into something *D&D* never was before: A bit safe, a bit predictable, a bit boring.

Ten Candles (2015)

Ten Candles, by Stephen Dewey, is another game that builds on the idea of merging unusual mechanics with theme and narrative. Whereas *Dread* uses a *Jenga* tower to constantly remind players of physical precarity, and *Star Crossed* does the same with the emotional, *Ten Candles* uses lit votive candles as a central, and largely uncontrollable, game mechanic that represents the constant march (and cost) of time.

Like *Dread, Ten Candles* is a collaborative, zero prep storytelling game with a GM. Billed as a game of tragic horror, players go into this expecting a bad outcome. Endless night has fallen. The world is ending. Monsters are coming. *Ten Candles* is about hanging on, but only for a little bit longer.

To support this idea, there is a unique character creation process. Characters consist of two traits (a Vice and a Virtue), a Moment (which, if expressed in a scene, gives the character hope, in the form of a bonus die), and a Brink (a secret trait, used when all else is gone, that shows the character's essence).

Brinks aren't created by the character's player, but rather, by the player sitting to their right. They take the form of witnesses' statements. "I've seen you…" Do what? Anything—kill innocents, freeze in a crucial moment, give in to despair, indulge in dangerous escapism—the idea is to create a web of secret connections between the characters. In a twist, the last player, the one sitting next to the GM, gets to define a single fact about Them, the creatures pursuing the group.

Each of these pieces of character information are written on index cards. A player can invoke them in a scene to alter die rolls, but once used, they're burned— literally! Players use their votive to set the

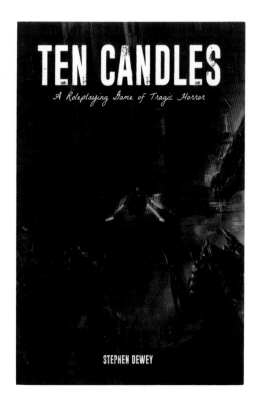

TEN CANDLES, CAVALRY GAMES, 2015
STEPHEN DEWEY, COVER BY J. C. PARK

card on fire and leave it smoldering in the burn bowl. These are the end times and surviving just another hour means leaving some part of yourself behind.

The game proceeds through up to ten scenes, created collaboratively with each character defining for it a single truth. Conflicts are resolved by rolling the communal dice pool—a six means success, while ones are removed from the pool for the rest of the scene, increasing the stakes. A scene ends in one of two ways: When a player fails a conflict roll and must blow out a candle, or when one or more candles go out on their own. When the final candle goes out, the game is over. A final scene plays out, but now, failed rolls result in the deaths of characters.

The march of time in *Ten Candles* isn't frantic, but it is inexorable. And like the *Jenga* tower, it's fragile—an errant draft could doom everyone. In tandem with the game's character-based narrative tools, the fire serves to create emotionally rich stories about desperation and sacrifice. Then, all that's left is darkness.

The Black Hack (2016)

No sooner had *Dungeons & Dragons* been born than folks set about trying to fix it—by hacking apart its systems, putting them back together again, replacing them, tossing whole sections out—every new configuration a new game.

The impulse is understandable because the original *D&D* rules are a mess: Rambling, poorly organized, and incomprehensible in some places—the intended combat system is in a whole other product! The mess was also a boon, because the folks who tried to fix *D&D* did so in public and in print, thus accidentally creating a whole RPG industry where, perhaps, there might never have been one. *Tunnels & Trolls*, *Bunnies & Burrows*, *Metamorphosis Alpha*, *The Arduin Grimoire*, and more all lay a foundation for one of the hobby's oldest traditions: Hacking.

The second edition of *The Black Hack* of the white box represents one of the purest refinements of a *D&D* hack ever to see print (the first edition is a lean, 20-page proof of concept, wildly expanded in the second edition). Developed by David Black (hence the name) as a homebrew re-imagining of the original *D&D* system with many modern RPG design ideas mixed in, he characterizes it as a reboot for modern players.

The book has much love for its source material, taking pains to rehabilitate the core rules of *OD&D* into something more streamlined and contemporary, with the arrangement intended to facilitate learning the game on the fly. These rules amount to about 30 pages that are so polished they're nearly slippery.

A lot of classic material is instantly recognizable (Fighter, Thief, Wizard, Cleric), but there are plenty of modernizations (advantage and disadvantage are in here), and clever rules created from whole cloth—the original *D&D* box's intended combat rules are entirely absent, so it seems appropriate that the *Black Hack* features a whole new combat system.

The game is fundamentally arranged around the players; everything that occurs results from a player's roll. So, instead of the GM rolling for monsters to attack, players make a defense roll when their character is targeted, only losing hit points if they fail. The armor attribute is a resource that can be spent to negate incoming damage. Even death is in the hands of the player. If their character is reduced to zero hit points, they roll on a random table to find out what happens—death is one outcome, being knocked unconscious is another, and various attribute reductions lurk in between.

The rest of the game follows this pattern. Every system is examined and renovated. Everything feels both familiar and new. For instance, Thieves have all of their usual sneaky abilities, like moving silently, but as with Fifth Edition, they're handled with Dexterity checks that they roll with advantage (two 20-sided dice, keeping the one that rolls the better result). Then, there are new perks, like: No matter what, a Thief can always produce a small throwing knife they had previously hidden on their person. There is no precedent for that roguish trick anywhere in any edition of *D&D*, but it feels so perfectly right, as if it's correcting a 40-year-old oversight.

The GM's section of the book, the bulk of its length, is even more impressive and energetic. Part workbook, part tool box, it's packed with tables, generators, and handy tips. It breaks down everything needed to run a game into easy-to-use, easy-to-comprehend chunks, then nudges the GM to mess around with them. *The Black Hack* has the spirit of those past activity books for children, brimming with puzzles, trivia, and drawing prompts, all tuned to keep the reader occupied for as long as possible. There are hooks and all sorts of small details that get a GM to reevaluate game conventions they take for granted, about monsters and dungeons and treasures. There are two pages

THE BLACK HACK, SECOND EDITION, BLACK LABEL, 2018
DAVID BLACK, COVER BY SKULLFUNGUS (KARL STJERNBERG)

of random tables for how to describe empty rooms. Nothing is left to reflex. One of the more difficult tasks for a GM is making game material up on the spot. The GM's section is primed to help by cueing up fresh ideas.

Like many other recent RPGs (*Dungeon Crawl Classics* and *Blades in the Dark*, for instance), *The Black Hack* seems to draw ideas from both the OSR and the indie design movements in equal measure, but, more than most, it walks a narrower line between the old and the new; it draws inspiration from the old, adopting a broad philosophy from early *D&D*.

The Black Hack embraces the OSR idea that there is plenty of merit in looking backwards—the past isn't just dusty old junk. At the same time, Black's willingness to play with these conventions defies the often closely-held notion that they are inherently sacred. The whole game is so elegant and smooth that it becomes a representation, not of what old school RPGs *are*, but rather what players wish them to be: Easy to pick up, fast to run, without an ounce of nonsense while remaining open and flexible enough for players to fill with whatever wild ideas they imagine. Glitteringly perfect, it's the rare oasis that isn't a mirage.

TALES FROM THE LOOP, FREE LEAGUE PUBLISHING, 2017
NILS HINTZE AND SIMON STÅLENHAG, COVER BY SIMON STÅLENHAG

Tales from the Loop (2017)

With *Tales from the Loop*, aesthetics lead the way. The RPG is based entirely on Simon Stålenhag's work, which was previously collected into a narrative art book with the same name (2015). Everything—the lore, the themes, the atmosphere—springs directly from his paintings.

The titular Loop is a huge, underground particle accelerator. In fact, there are two—one in Sweden and the other in the Colorado desert. The Loops promised technological marvels. There are some in the world—great sky ships that use the earth's magnetic field to stay aloft, robots to perform heavy labor—but much of that promise has been left unfulfilled. Steel rusts in the countryside, abandoned experiments lie in the woods, and strange, high-tech ruins become mysterious monoliths.

In Stålenhag's paintings, these wonders often serve as the backdrop for mundane domestic scenes—filling the car with gas, going for a walk, carrying in the groceries. The sky is usually overcast; the sun has just set, and the street lights have just come on, turning everything outside dark blue or gray. Stålenhag's world is an eternal, endless 1980-something. Kids are bored, misunderstood, and left to their own devices—sometimes, there is trouble to get into. Nostalgia drenches everything, but it is tinged with something else: Sorrow, regret, dread?

While *Mutant: Year Zero* debuts Free League's Year Zero Engine, *Tales from the Loop* showcases its versatility. It's a very different sort of game, but the mechanical underpinnings are essentially the same. Characters are archetypes, in this case, of the sorts of kids or young teens that might appear in *The Goonies* or similar kid adventure movies—Bookworm, Jock, Troublemaker, Weirdo, and so on. Attribute values and skills translate to a pool of 6-sided dice—the more dice, the better. To succeed in most tests, a player needs to roll a single six on one of the dice. Instead of hit points or the like, characters have four different conditions, like Scared or Injured, which negatively modify the pool total.

The rest feels quite different. Much of *Mutant: Year Zero* is arranged around survival, but in *Tales from the Loop*, while kids can be injured, they can never be killed (though, as with the mutation mechanic, kids can age out of play). The game plays out across a series of Mysteries, for which the rulebook provides ample, easy-to-use tools to create and manage. Like ABC's *Afterschool Specials*, the Mysteries provide opportunities to foreground the inner lives of the player characters. While the GM steers the overall course of a Mystery, the game turns on a concept called Trouble.

Trouble is anything that might prevent the kids from doing what they want to do, be it a booby-trap preventing entrance to a mad scientist's lair or a mom intent on enforcing curfew. Trouble is a collaboration between player and GM, much like a storytelling game. The GM wants Trouble that serves the overarching plot; players want Trouble that drives the development of their characters, and everyone wants Trouble that heightens the drama.

This arrangement pushes the players to constantly reevaluate their characters' relationship with the everyday world, for better or worse. It won't be long before navigating entanglements with parents, teachers, siblings, and bullies proves just as risky to the characters, and central to the players' experience, as trying to find out what happened with the time portal or dealing with a rampaging robot.

Stålenhag's paintings convey a very specific tone for *Tales from the Loop*. Nostalgic? Yes. But, there are deep veins of disappointment, squandered potential, and alienation. All of this high-tech weirdness hasn't made life easier. There are robots, sure, but bills still need paying. Adults are distracted, and kids aren't

OUT OF TIME, FREE LEAGUE PUBLISHING, 2019

RICKARD ANTROIA, NILS HINTZE, AND SIMON STÅLENHAG, COVER BY SIMON STÅLENHAG

taken seriously, even when they need to be. This isn't a nostalgic romp in the way that *Stranger Things* is, although that show is often mentioned in the same breath as *Tales from the Loop*. This world is too infused with melancholy—at least out of the box.

If a GM can replace robots and dinosaurs with ghosts and monsters (and they certainly can), they can also tweak the game to be whimsical or silly; but then it would become like every other trip down nostalgia lane. The appeal of *Tales from the Loop* is in Stålenhag's deep shadows and purple dusks. They hide the dangers and mysteries that often act an escape hatch, a way to avoid prosaic problems. But, that twilight also marks the far edge of the day and its freedoms. When the street lights come on, it is time to go home, no matter the adventure.

Blades in the Dark (2017)

John Harper's *Blades in the Dark* (*Blades*) is a heist game set in a sunless, pseudo-Victorian city plagued by ghosts. Inspiration seems drawn from a pool that includes Fritz Leiber's Lankhmar stories and videogames like *Dishonored* (2012), *Thief: The Dark Project* (1998), and *Fallen London* (2009), so it

should come as no real surprise that *Blades* is a game about scoundrels. Each player has a specific character, of course, but how they lock together informs the metacharacter of their Crew, which, in turn, largely defines how they will play. The Crew can be anything from a bunch of bruisers to a creepy cult.

Play centers on executing and dealing with the fallout of scores. There's no planning involved, though, because *Blades* is improvisational. Success and failure at skill checks not only determine the result of the action, but also often define the situation going forward—failures require consequences, meaning the GM needs to conjure all manner of complications out of thin air.

To facilitate this sort of improvisation, players have two tools. First, their equipment isn't determined ahead of time. They check items off as needed, when needed, up to a set limit. So, if the characters suddenly need to rappel down a wall, then the players can decide that someone happened to have packed some rope.

The second is the flashback. In exchange for Stress (which, coupled with Trauma, forms the game's damage system and encompasses both physical and psychological harm), players can narrate what they did before the heist to prepare for the situation that has just been presented to them. "Oh, see, I paid off Tom the Doorman so he won't give us any trouble; here's how it went." If this sounds ridiculous, that's because it is, but it is also fun and incredibly freeing. Good flashbacks get the adrenaline pumping just as effectively as standard swashbuckling derring-do.

The game's default position is that failure is inherently more interesting than success ("failing forward," while an inane bit of business self-help lingo, is an increasingly common modern RPG design philosophy) and is deployed to encourage recklessness. Characters can gain a bonus to their rolls if they take a Devil's

Bargain, which adds additional consequences, regardless of the result of the roll. Some of these can be narrative-focused—betray a friend, cause some collateral damage—or they can be mechanical—lose Reputation with another faction, add Heat (the mechanical measure of public exposure) to the Crew.

A player can also take a bonus for their character by pushing their limits, at the cost of Stress. Too much Stress results in Trauma, so during Downtime it is wise to allow characters to relax with their vices of choice, providing short-term relief and, inevitably, long-term problems. These factors conspire to shorten any individual character's life.

Thus, while *Blades* is immediately concerned with individual heists, there is a larger legacy component of the game that is preoccupied with the Reputation of the Crew and its holdings. With Reputation, the players accumulate turf, manage their criminal enterprises, establish front businesses, and generally measure themselves against their rivals. There are sheets to help track relationships with every faction in the city, which, in turn, bring the city to life and give players more material to draw from while improvising (and more resources for the characters to use). The life of a scoundrel is short, so this metagame gives the Crew a place in the world and a way for characters to cycle in and out while maintaining a rich continuity.

Although it's not obvious, *Blades in the Dark* is a hack of *Apocalypse World*. Once that fact is known, though, it becomes apparent in the same way the shape of an original building can be glimpsed under extensive renovations. Each class has their own abilities, for instance, and while they are presented as skills, like in any other RPG, they retain a specific feel and

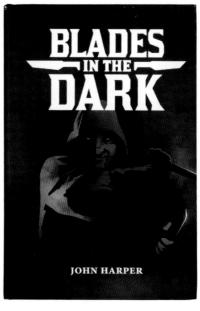

BLADES IN THE DARK, EVIL HAT PRODUCTIONS, 2017
JOHN HARPER, COVER BY JOHN HARPER

framing that resemble the Moves of *Apocalypse World*. The clocks are a dead giveaway, though. *Blades* uses countdown clocks for everything—impending trouble, long-term schemes, Crew building projects, *everything*. If it takes time, the GM can slap a clock on it.

This relationship between the two games is interesting. *Blades in the Dark* is different enough from *Apocalypse World* that it has inspired its own hacks, collectively known as Forged in the Dark games. Much of the difference stems from *Blades'* complexity. Each mechanic, on its own, is simple and easy to understand—most of them involve figuring out a small bonus or checking off the next box in a line—but the way they layer and flow together can feel complicated and overwhelming, especially as the focus zooms out wider from individual characters, to the Crew-as-character, to the management of the relationships that intertwine throughout the whole city.

For GMs, in particular, the game may feel daunting, in a way that hearkens back to earlier games, like *Shadowrun*—a curious development for a game that spun out of a narrative-focused indie. This tension seems to be part of a larger shift. Inklings of it are visible in games, like *Dungeon*

BLUEBEARD'S BRIDE, MAGPIE GAMES, 2017
WHITNEY "STRIX" BELTRÁN, MARISSA KELLY, AND SARAH RICHARDSON, COVER BY REBECCA YANOVSKAYA

Crawl Classics and *Tales from the Loop*, but increasingly, from this point on, there is a collision between indie sensibilities and older design philosophies, be they OSR or other systems with a retro appeal. Whether the result is a blurring of the lines, a muddying of the waters, or the emergence of something entirely new is yet to be determined. But, games, like *Blades* and *Troika,* and *The Black Hack* and *Ultraviolet Grasslands,* and *Thousand Year Old Vampire* and the growing zine scene, are linked despite their vast individual differences. Tweeter and occasional blogger, Layla Adelman (also known as @Pandatheist), discerned something similar in December of 2019. In her blog post titled "New School Revolution," she establishes criteria for a proposed classification of games by that name They feature: GMs (differentiating them from many indie RPGs), light rules that provide deadly stakes, strange settings, and a general focus on emergent storytelling and exploration. She writes,

No purity tests, no rules requirements, no us vs. them, just a brief list of stuff to help find games that match your taste. Think of this (with maybe the exception of the GM requirement) as a series of Venn diagrams […] Games like *Mothership*, *World of Dungeons*, *Troika* and *Into the Odd* have almost nothing in common if you just look at the mechanics. But drop someone who enjoys any one of those into a game of the other and they'll probably have a good time.

The only fault I can find with this proposal is that the criteria seem too narrow, that a wide array of design principles and game types and aesthetics have been reconfigured into a new fusion of play. Looking back, *Blades in the Dark* seems like an appropriate place on which to pin the genesis. Looking ahead, players will undoubtedly journey to still stranger destinations.

Bluebeard's Bride (2017)

According to the fairy-tale of Bluebeard, he is a rich and powerful lord who possesses a magnificent estate. He courts a poor farm girl and, despite some lingering questions regarding the number and dispositions of Bluebeard's previous wives, the two are married. Soon after, Bluebeard is called away on business.

Before he goes, he gives his wife the keys to every door in the castle but warns her not to open the one particular room that is unlocked by the smallest key on the ring. Alone, she spends her time in the sumptuous chambers of the palace, but she is blind to their pleasures because all she can think about is the small key and the door she must not open. Eventually, of course, she does open the forbidden door and discovers the corpses of her husband's previous wives. She soon joins them, once Bluebeard uncovers the trespass, though some versions of the tale have her briefly escape to a parapet, only to throw herself to the ground far below.

There are many other variants. The tale itself is, perhaps, inspired by the real-life Gilles de Rais, a one-time follower of Joan of Arc who was later accused of witchcraft and hundreds of child murders (the veracity of those charges are highly suspect). The RPG *Bluebeard's Bride* spins out of this mélange, saying,

The many versions of this lurid tale are a testament to the gripping quality of what is at its core. Violence. Sexuality. Death. [...] Some interpretations say it is a tale meant as an admonishment to women for their capricious nature. Others say it is a tale from women, for women, meant as a warning about men and their power.

In playing the game, it falls to players to develop their own versions and interpretations.

The game, which is based on the *Apocalypse World* engine, has players take on the role of the titular bride, as a GM, called the Groundskeeper, guides them through the castle. Rather than control the Bride's actions in turn, each player has control over a specific portion of her personality: The Animus is protective hostility, the Fatale embodies the way she can assert control through seduction, the Mother is her selflessness, the Virgin her vulnerability, and the Witch her ability to deceive. The dominant personality trait shifts depending on the situation and individual actions of the players. Embodying these five slivers of the Bride's psyche, players navigate from room to room, encountering wonders and Horrors that tell of Bluebeard, of his previous wives, and of the Bride herself.

The game, conceived and written by three women, is consciously feminine in its construction. The text addresses the reader as a woman, and the aspects of her psyche are referred to as Sisters. Bluebeard is irredeemable; the traumas that he and his legacy inflict are inherently masculine, and their targets are always feminine.

And still, despite the dangers, there is an allure. The illustrations, by Rebecca Yanovskaya and Kring Demetrio, present a rich, sensual decadence with their elaborate scroll work and gold foil. There is a dreaminess and unimaginable luxury. It is easy to understand why the Bride was tempted to reside in this manor, despite her husband's reputation and the Horrors that haunt its rooms.

As this is a game that is Powered by the Apocalypse, players have access to specific Moves. Some can be used at any time, by any player: Investigate, Take Stock, Care for Someone. Others can only be used by the active player, who risks taking trauma, a kind of psychic damage, for doing so: Shiver from Fear, Caress a Horror, Dirty Yourself with Violence, Cry Out for Help, and so on.

Individual personalities have their own specific Moves, as well. The Animus can be cruel to be kind, shielding another character from trauma by explaining how that trauma is actually the fault of that character. The Mother can offer another character forgiveness in order to take on some of their trauma. Every room is a psychological ordeal for the Bride to confront, and the players must struggle to find different ways to cope through the interactions of the various Moves. Once a room has been thoroughly reckoned with, the active player can Propose a Truth about it, solving its mystery and earning either a Token of Faithfulness or a Token of Disloyalty. A room can also prove too much, inspiring the active player to flee—but there is always a sinister, costly price for escape.

Depending on how players confront the truths they find, the Bride will move toward becoming fully Faithful or Disloyal; arriving entirely at either leads the Bride to the door of the forbidden room and her final fate. Sometimes, though, the Horrors may prove too great for the Bride, leaving all aspects of her personality Shattered. In that case, she becomes yet another Horror haunting the castle in Bluebeard's service, obsessed with either bettering herself for him or bettering his future brides.

THE DARK OF HOT SPRINGS ISLAND, THE SWORDFISH ISLANDS, 2017

JACOB HURST, GABRIEL HERNANDEZ, EVAN PETERSON, AND DONNIE GARCIA, COVER BY GABRIEL HERNANDEZ

Hot Springs Island (2017)

Wilderlands of High Fantasy essentially invented the hex crawl while *X1: The Isle of Dread* and *Griffin Mountain* popularized it. Heaps of adventures since have refined and experimented with the form in the ensuing years, and the Hot Springs Island campaign marks one of the current peaks in its evolution.

The campaign is split between two books: *The Dark of Hot Springs Island* (*The Dark*) for the GM and *A Field Guide to Hot Springs Island* for the players, an in-universe document written by an earlier explorer of the island. The fact that the player-facing book is nearly 250 pages indicates its level of detail—this wilderness is vast. In the distant past, the island was a leisure garden for debauched, now extinct elves. The ruins of their pleasure domes and their discarded baubles are scattered about the landscape, currently inhabited by singing statues and a strange, sentient orange sludge. The island's volcano (of course, there is a volcano) is home to an efreet and his extra-planar narcotics operation. Nearby is a tribe of ogres that aren't really ogres, who recently freed themselves from slavery under the efreet. There are vengeful nereids, lizard people, interdimensional cartels, party gods, and more lurking in the underbrush, or just beyond the shimmering veil of reality.

Hot Springs Island is one of those spots where all sorts of intelligences, terrestrial and otherwise, have an interest (even if they don't yet realize it). RPGs often present powers and principalities of the multiverse as remote and serious. Here, they seem driven in equal parts by unfettered capitalism and a desperate desire to fend off boredom—and surely, within the context of fantasy stories, in which divinity is often a goal and gods are merely greater versions of humans, it makes sense that immortals would be just as vapid and greedy. Moreover, this dissipation shows how the campaign undermines the expectations players likely have for a fantasy hex crawl. That subversion follows through to everything on the island: People, monsters, magic items, even the diabolical plots of the demonic-looking fellow who lives in the volcano—nothing is *quite* what players expect and certainly nothing is as it seems.

All of these interests and their histories form a web of imminent hostilities for the players to navigate. These connections reveal one of the campaign's central clever bits: It marries the hex crawl with the faction crawl. There are seven primary factions, loosely organized according to their overall goals, but with a seemingly unlimited number of sub-factions with their own desires, often at cross-purpose with the larger grouping. *The Dark* describes itself as black powder for an ongoing RPG campaign. The players ignite the factions of the island and explode a thundering flash of plots, attacks, desperate plans, confused retreats, betrayals, and more. The players act; the world reacts.

The Dark goes to great lengths to detail, not just the mysterious locations on the island, but also the wants, needs, and motivations of all of the major NPCs and those many groups lurking off stage. The result is a robust and vivid sandbox—thanks, in no small part, to the art of Gabriel Hernandez and the overland maps of Jason Thompson; both inject ample amounts of violence and mystery into the proceedings. Hex crawls are, by nature, plotless. The story emerges from the actions of the players, but the host of details in both books, as well as their illustrations, inspire and propel the action.

Of course, this information, which is plentiful, must be managed by the GM, usually resulting in a great deal of work. *The Dark*, like many recent RPG products, gives special attention to how it presents that information. The layout is uncluttered; key points are presented in bulleted

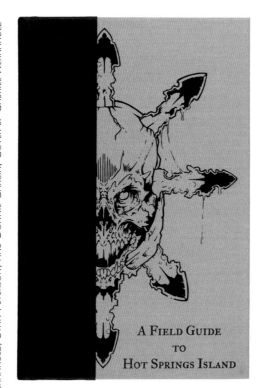

A Field Guide to Hot Springs Island, The Swordfish Islands, 2017

Jacob Hurst, Gabriel Hernandez, Evan Peterson, and Donnie Garcia, cover by Gabriel Hernandez

lists or easy-to-reference charts, and bold headers regularly break apart and summarize large sections of text. That text conveys characters and locales, leaving a clear impression long after even a single reading. The construction of the book helps the GM get the game to the table practically right after cracking the cover.

Finally, in acknowledgment of the proliferation of rule sets, hacks, and clones that continue to emerge from the OSR and indie scenes, Hot Springs Island is system agnostic (though, even without attribute blocks, it still feels, somehow, fundamentally and philosophically suited for some flavor of *Dungeons & Dragons*). There have been agnostic RPG products before, but they were generally limited to cities or settings. Agnostic scenarios are historically rarer, especially ones as lengthy or well-developed as Hot Springs Island. That's still generally true, though some adventures that do include systems for play, like *Ultraviolet Grasslands* (2019) and *Silent Titans* (2019), don't require those systems. With the increasing popularity of system agnostic material, particularly

among the makers of zines, *Hot Springs Island* will likely be remembered as one of the first games to take that step.

A Thousand Thousand Islands (2017)

A Thousand Thousand Islands (*ATTI*) is a series of zines detailing a fantastical version of Southeast Asia, particularly the islands of Malaysia, Indonesia, and the Philippines. In the real-world, these islands share in many social, cultural, and folkloric traditions, while each region, or even each island retains their own distinctions—so too with *A Thousand Thousand Islands*.

There are eight zines as of this writing (supplemented by two zines of artwork and a volume of essays and fiction examining supernatural creatures from Malaysian folklore), each unique but part of a greater whole. Mr-Kr-Gr is a kingdom ruled by crocodiles where travelers may not spend the night. Kraching is a region where cats are holy and protective of their secrets. Andjang is a trek up a mountain to find a haunted palace and the horrible parasitic queen who rules there (though, in truth, all royalty are parasites, no?). Stray Virassa is the fourteenth hell, the island where the spirits of the drowned dead of Mu think they must linger.

Each volume details places of interest, notable people, and goods worth seeking out. Players will encounter sorcerous snakes, anthropomorphic monitor lizards, and knights whose human heads have been replaced by the prows of war boats. There are random tables—for what characters find in the market stall, for what the god leech steals instead of a character's blood, for what pattern is woven into the scarf. If it weren't for the tables, a reader would hardly realize the zines are for RPGs at all; they read more like wistful travel journals rather than sourcebooks, though *everything* is a sourcebook if desired.

MR-KR-GR

THE DEATH-ROLLED KINGDOM

———

A THOUSAND THOUSAND ISLANDS

MR-KR-GR: THE DEATH-ROLLED KINGDOM, CENTAUR GAMES, 2017
ZEDECK SIEW AND MUNKAO, COVER BY MUNKAO

KRACHING: THE PLACE OF THE PAW, CENTAUR GAMES, 2017
ZEDECK SIEW AND MUNKAO, COVER BY MUNKAO

In fact, its incongruence with RPGs is one of the series' most beguiling features. It is powerfully written and full of poetry—that's something I don't think I can say about any other RPG book whose prose is too often preoccupied with adhering to the extremes of being weird or useful. Here, Zedeck Siew weaves song-like narratives that often feel personal in addition to being useful to an RPG. These narratives can also slip into surprisingly modern language—cut down a tree at the edge of Upper Heleng and the "forest shuts like a refrigerator door." A languorous sort of sexuality surfaces on occasion, as well; in searching for Stray Virassa, "Compasses spin like ceiling fans, constellations wobble like drunks; scrying spells leak like weak ejaculations."

All the while, artist Munkao instills the poetry with gravitas through detailed landscapes and emotive portraits. I get as lost in his illustrations as easily as I do in Siew's words. Together, they create a world that feels strange, vibrant, and enticing. No matter how many volumes come out, I'm left feeling like I've only caught a glimpse and that there is so, so much more to see.

UPPER HELENG: THE FOREST BELOVED BY TIME, CENTAUR GAMES, 2019
ZEDECK SIEW AND MUNKAO, COVER BY MUNKAO

In addition to its aesthetic qualities, *A Thousand Thousand Islands* is important in another way. In *The Hero with a Thousand Faces* (1949), Joseph Campbell argues that all human stories originated from a single, archetypal monomyth he dubbed "the hero's journey." In the years since its publication, this notion has increasingly dominated Western storytelling, particularly those stories in the fantasy genre—*Star Wars*, *Lost*, the videogame *Journey*. Practically every Disney movie and comic book hero draws, in some way, upon Campbell's theory, making it something of a self-fulfilling prophecy. However, despite Campbell's compelling argument, there are plenty of stories that don't fit so neatly into his monomyth—unsurprisingly, the farther from the seats of Western culture a person travels, the more often they'll encounter exceptions to Campbell's rules.

A Thousand Thousand Islands is the clearest defiance of Campbell's theory in RPGs. It consciously seeks to disconnect from Western conceptions of fantasy, which tend to be synonymous with the

culture, history, and folklore of Europe, from around the Medieval period to the early Renaissance. This vision so thoroughly dominates our shared conception of fantasy and, by extension, the aesthetics of fantasy RPGs, that it feels inescapable. This dominance is evident in the fantasy aesthetic of Japan, where the influence of Western fantasy media, like Tolkien or *Dungeons & Dragons*, can be seen in *Record of Lodoss War* (1988), *Berserk* (1989), and *Dark Souls* (2012), and is just as prevalent as more homegrown aesthetics.

For residents of southeast Asia, who grew up with the same legends as Siew and Munkao, who are touched by their cultures every day, I suspect *ATTI* feels like a reflection of themselves and their lives in a way that Western fantasy could never capture. Siew says,

There is a strong strain in a place like Southeast Asia (by its very name a periphery) to actively reject our own specificity. Give Western markets what we think they want: a Tolkienesque epic, wearing a reskin of exotically-shaped swords and syllables. The siren song to write our own stories according to the Monomyth blueprint—because Campbell is white, therefore aspirational; if we are to have value, we must follow white-people rules. Our nationalist myths insist on calling Malacca or Srivijaya "empires" (even though that word really doesn't mean anything, in this geography), because the empires of Europe are the yardstick, and we have to prove to ourselves that our histories measure up in glory.

ATTI is consciously a rejection of empirical, Campbellian yardsticks. An attempt to *not Other ourselves*. Munkao and I are pretty picky; everything in the zines—a narrative hook, a piece of jewelry, the way a character's gender/personhood is emphasized, how a god is or isn't

ANDJANG: THE QUEEN OF DOG MOUNTAIN, CENTAUR GAMES, 2019 ZEDECK SIEW AND MUNKAO, COVER BY MUNKAO

defined—has to "taste" like our context. Things have to feel specific, I guess? Otherwise we rework it, or leave it out.

I would like to think that other folks (SEAsian or not) can taste that mouthfeel, too.

As beautiful and evocative as *A Thousand Thousand Islands* is, it might be difficult to see how to translate its ideas into something playable. While not explicitly connected to the zine series, *Lorn Song of the Bachelor* (2019), written by Zedeck Siew and illustrated by Nadhir Nor, stands as an excellent companion work that puts a similar setting into action. Like the zines, it is essentially a system agnostic scenario with hints of *D&D*-esque attributes in the text. The scenario itself consists of a little bit of wilderness exploration, a little bit of dungeon crawling, and a whole lot of metaphysical strangeness.

The bachelor is a monstrous crocodile based on the legend of Bujang Senang, from the Iban people of Borneo. A brave

343

LORN-SONG OF THE BACHELOR, HYDRA COOPERATIVE, 2019
ZEDECK SIEW, COVER BY NADHIR NOR

warrior is killed trying to stop bandits from murdering his wife. In death, he asks the gods for revenge, and they turn him into a gigantic white crocodile. He terrorizes the descendants of the bandits, *Jaws*-like, from around 1940 until 1992, when the white croc was shot and apparently killed. Not all folklore is old, it seems.

In the adventure, the crocodile is magical—a reflection of the land. To wound it is to wound the land. Some of the local villagers believe they can help it transcend into godhood, but the regional trading company (an avatar of the very real specter of colonialism in Southeast Asia) wants the croc gone so it no longer disrupts shipping. And the dungeon? It is both an ancient ruin and the insides of the crocodile. And there is a demon made of hands, and golems made of teeth. The region and its factions are arranged to guarantee that no easy solutions are available to fix the problem of the bachelor, meaning players will likely become overwhelmed before they understand the situation, requiring them to spend time trying to clean up the messes they've made.

Harlem Unbound (2017)

H. P. Lovecraft was a virulent racist, and his views on race permeate many of his most famous and influential stories. Even beyond the explicit specifics, like the name of a certain black cat, there are whiffs of poisonous ideas throughout. The terror at the heart of cosmic horror, the style of horror that he formalized and popularized, turns on the nihilistic idea that the full scope of the universe is unknowable and our fates are determined by entities that don't care about us and don't even realize we exist.

The revelation that all of our works and ambitions are less than dust is supposed to be a mind-breaking experience:

> We live on a placid island of ignorance in the midst of black seas of infinity, and it was not meant that we should voyage far. The sciences, each straining in its own direction, have hitherto harmed us little; but some day the piecing together of dissociated knowledge will open up such terrifying vistas of reality, and of our frightful position therein, that we shall either go mad from the revelation or flee from the deadly light into the peace and safety of a new dark age.

Whiteness, as an identity, is often defined by knowing and exploiting, so a universe that is unknowable and unconquerable (most likely) represents the height of terror to a white person from Lovecraft's era.

In *The Ballad of Black Tom* (2016), Victor LaValle revisits H. P. Lovecraft's story "The Horror at Red Hook." Lovecraft wrote the story during a period of culture shock when he left his sheltered existence in Providence to live in a New York City teeming with immigrants and people of color. His wife later recalled that, when he found himself in a racially mixed crowd, Lovecraft would nearly lose his mind with rage.

344

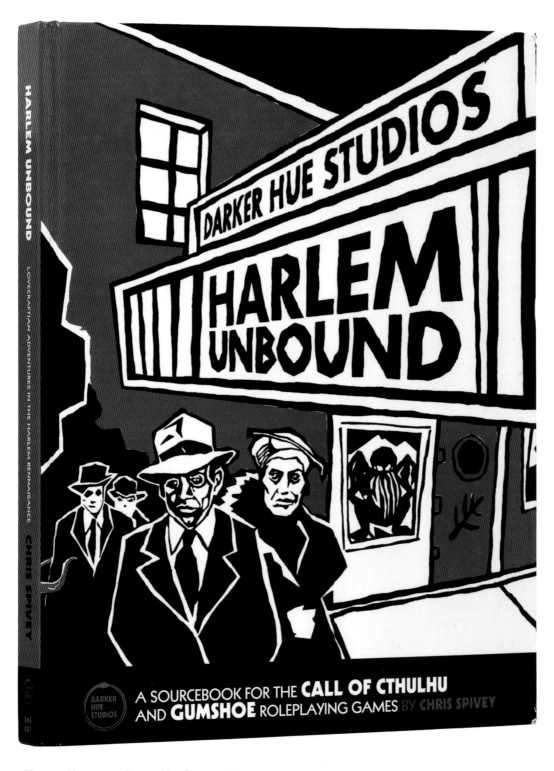

HARLEM UNBOUND, DARKER HUE STUDIOS, 2017
CHRIS SPIVEY, COVER BY BRENNAN REECE

HARLEM UNBOUND, SECOND EDITION, CHAOSIUM, 2020
CHRIS SPIVEY, COVER BY BRENNAN REECE

The resulting fiction is easily the man's most hysterically racist work. LaValle, a Black author, retells the story through the perspective of Tommy Tester, a Black man. The beats may be familiar, even without reading Lovecraft: A rich, old white man named Robert Suydam attempts to use forbidden magic to remake the world, and plans go terribly wrong. When they do, it is Tommy, not Suydam, who stands at the center, supernaturally transformed and vengeful.

LaValle hews closely to the structure of the original story and is adept at deploying outré chills in Lovecraft's mode, but the cosmically indifferent entities that lurk on the edges of the page pale in comparison to the raw horror of the everyday racism that Tommy experiences when he becomes embroiled in Suydam's schemes. When Suydam tries to recruit Tommy, he attempts to instill in him an awe for that cosmic indifference (again, what does a rich white man fear more than being ignored?). For Tommy, though, living in the New York City of the 1920s, where being Black means being considered less than human, fear is a constant passenger *every day.* As Tommy says after police unjustly murder his father—a gut-wrenching moment that channels the anguish of the murders of Michael Brown and Eric Garner and so many more Black men at the hands of police officers—"Indifference would be such a relief."

In *Harlem Unbound,* Chris Spivey explores many of the same ideas about the Cthulhu Mythos as *The Ballad of Black Tom,* but does so in the context of the RPGs that are inspired by it. The first edition was a sourcebook for both *Call of Cthulhu* and Gumshoe; the second edition, published by Chaosium, features expanded rules and additional scenarios for *Call of Cthulhu,* at the expense of support for the Gumshoe system.

Both games downplay any inherent racism in the source material. While many scenarios acknowledge and confront Lovecraft's racism, many more simply ignore it. Even when racism is part of the story and the historical setting, player characters are primarily white people of privilege. Cops, professors, and dilettantes abound—racism isn't something they experience, it's something they have the opportunity to confront (and feel good about in doing so).

Harlem Unbound flips that script. During the Harlem Renaissance, Harlem is a hotbed of creativity and Black prosperity. At the same time, the Tulsa massacre occurred in 1921, and the Ku Klux Klan posed an unrelenting threat to Black existence and accomplishment. It's into this world that *Harlem Unbound* drops players, with characters who are all assumed to be Black. Thanks to the booming art and jazz scenes, player characters can still be of independent means and conduct investigations, but no matter how well off they are, they will have to contend with the human evil of racism while struggling against the alien horrors of the Cthulhu Mythos.

As in *The Ballad of Black Tom*, the two strains of horror complement and contrast with each other. To emphasize this more terrestrial horror, Spivey introduces a lightweight Racial Tension system to ground the game's storytelling. In short, it provides an uneven playing field reflective of the time. In *Call of Cthulhu* the difficulty increases one step when rolling skill checks that involve characters of different races; in *Trail of Cthulhu*, the point spend increases by one.

Harlem Unbound is one of the best setting books I've encountered in recent years; it's rich in historical detail, extremely readable, and it's popping with ideas. But, its treatment of race feels *Important*, especially as more players from diverse backgrounds find their way into the hobby. Can white folks play Black characters? Spivey answers with an emphatic "yes," so long as care is taken to avoid accents and stereotypes. In fact, he argues that avoiding playing Black characters,

> doesn't help change the environment at the gaming table. It does not help create a welcoming and safe space for others. […] It's on you to battle that feeling of insecurity and fear of what other white people may think of you, and run games by diverse creatives. Promote diverse creatives. Talk about the issues presented and become an advocate for a better gaming world. That active choice may help make it easier on the next non-white heterosexual cisgender man who wants to play.

How do players portray prejudice and use its language at the table without being hurtful? The answer here is very much dependent on the tolerances of the group, but Spivey argues that players should always avoid using racist language and focus on the portrayal of racism through actions, explaining in an example that, "Using actions to portray the plantation owner's racism (rather than words, and

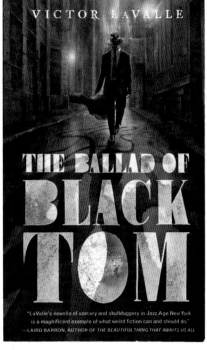

THE BALLAD OF BLACK TOM, TOR BOOKS, 2016 VICTOR LAVALLE, COVER BY ROBERT HUNT

more specifically the N-word) provides a strong alternative that allows the Keeper to use third-person to illustrate the scene." *Harlem Unbound*'s chapter on storytelling, which provides guidance on these matters of race and more, both in game and around the table, should be required reading for everyone running an RPG.

There is a sidebar in *Harlem Unbound* titled, "What Does it Mean to Be Black in America?" and it reads, "Submit! Submit! Plainly stated: life is 'FUCKED!' Apologize! Smile more! You're too aggressive! Know your place! Respect my badge! Serve! Submit! Submit! Submit! This is the message constantly played to African-Americans. Being Black in America means an unending struggle of enduring racism. Bring them to heel!"

P. Djéli Clark's *Ring Shout* (2020) follows monster hunter Maryse Boudreaux as she wields her magic sword against the demons who hide in the flesh and the robes of the Ku Klux Klan. They serve an

1970

1980

1990

2000

2010

347

RING SHOUT OR HUNTING KU KLUXES IN THE END TIMES, TOR BOOKS, 2020
P. DJÈLÍ CLARK, COVER BY HERNY SENE YEE

entity, the Grand Cyclops, that feeds on hate. A representative of that creature presents Maryse with a Faustian bargain: If she gives in to her own hate and anger, the Grand Cyclops will raise her and all of her people up to the seats of power and give them the whip handle. Maryse is sorely tempted but in the end,

> The words of the girl, my other self from the dream place, strikes me with a sudden understanding. The places where we hurt. Where *we* hurt. Not just me, all of us, colored folks everywhere, who carry our wounds with us, sometimes open for all to see, but always so much more buried and hidden deep. I remember the songs that come with all those visions. Songs full of hurt. Songs of sadness and tears. Songs pulsing with pain. A righteous anger and cry for justice.
>
> But not hate.
>
> They ain't the same thing. Never was. These monsters want to pervert that. Turn it to their own ends. Because that's

what they do. Twist you all up so you forget yourself. Make you into something like them. Only I can't forget, because all those memories always with me, showing me the way.

With that decidedly un-Lovecraftian revelation reveleted, Maryse proceeds to put her flaming sword to work on those racist demons with all the ass-kicking delight of any pulp hero, Black or white. That kind of exhilaration fuels the brilliant flip side of *Harlem Unbound*—it recognizes that stories about Black pain often overshadow stories about Black joy.

Harlem during the Renaissance is all about that joy—for music, art, dance, literature, and theater—and players can use *Harlem Unbound* to learn about it by using it as a rich backdrop for their game without having to plumb the depths of America's racist history. The racial tension mechanic is optional, after all.

Perverse though it may seem, cosmic horror is fun. There's a pleasure in being scared, in general, and it's enjoyable to see characters get eaten by monsters with tentacles and too many eyes. It's cathartic to leave behind real-world problems in exchange for supernatural ones. Lovecraft's work has long been synonymous with cosmic horror, despite the absurdity of something as limitless as the universe being contained within the ideas of just one deeply flawed man. In recent years, many creators have expanded the definition of cosmic horror beyond him. LaValle, Clark, and Spivey are all using Lovecraft's tricks to tell stories that Lovecraft would not have written, that he could not have written. It's matter and antimatter touching, a big bang rippling out to create a new cosmos that can be more than just indifferent—where rich, old white men and Outer Gods alike can know fear.

Honey Heist (2017)

Grant Howitt's one-page RPGs likely wouldn't exist if not for Patreon, an online service that directly connects creators with a paying audience through a subscription model. In Howitt's case (at the time of this writing), an individual signs up for one of two tiers: $5 dollars provides a digital copy of each game, while $15 dollars merits the mailing of a physical copy with bonus content on the reverse side.

Once a month or so, Howitt releases a game, patrons get charged, they receive their games, and Patreon takes their cut. Would Howitt be making a new game every month without Patreon? Possibly, but he might have a much more difficult time reaching an audience and, more importantly, being paid to do so. This fiscal conundrum is similarly true for makers of many other small and quirky games whose existence is facilitated by the patron model.

As the name implies, one-page RPGs are rather brief (though it is surprising how many systems can be smushed into the space). They're part of a growing impulse begun, perhaps, with *The Extraordinary Adventures of Baron Munchausen*, in which designers experimented with just how little information a game needed to consist of while still remaining a game. RPGs on pamphlets, postcards, and business cards, which have started to appear in recent years, are extensions of this enthusiastic minimalism. There's even an annual contest for 200-word RPGs. This chapter is already longer than that!

Brevity is a radical shift for RPGs. Big boxes, arcane rulebooks, and sprawling product lines were once signifiers of serious gaming, but they are also significant barriers to entry, for players and designers alike. In the '90s, there was a popular mindset that equated the thickness of the book with, if not the quality of a game, then its worthiness of consideration. Small games, on the other hand, are fast—

to make, to learn, to play. Get it to the table, try it out, and have some laughs. The costs are low, so the expectations are notably relaxed. Small games simply don't have the space to waste on purple prose or pointless digression. In fact, the constraint encourages a wanton embrace of wit and whimsy.

Howitt's games have wit and whimsy in spades. According to the Rowan, Rook, and Decard site, the most popular is "The Witch is Dead," in which players take the role of a familiar bent on revenge for the murder of their mistress. Next is "Crash Pandas," which is about a number of raccoons attempting to drive a car. "Pride and Extreme Prejudice" is, according to the product listing, "about proper ladies of a marriageable age and their giant robots powered by a malign eldritch intelligence."

A personal favorite is "Dead Channel," in which players find themselves trapped in a schlocky, randomly generated, straight-to-video horror movie. The bonus content for it introduces rules for changing the channel in the middle of the action, so they can start in a horror movie, but then crash into syndicated sitcoms, infomercials, and more, with the monster murderer thing hot on their heels—it's brilliant.

If there is a perfect archetype for Howitt's one-page RPGs, my money is on "Honey Heist," a heist game in which players are bears (or, in rare cases, a badger). The game is reproduced in its entirety on the next page. There are two primary attributes—Bear and Criminal. Both of these are ever-changing, depending on player behavior and how the heist is going. Should the Bear value ever reach six, the character goes full bear and loses interest in the job. If Criminal ever gets to six, the character loses interest in honey and turns into a criminal mastermind. There is a random table for hats, in case a player wants their bear to wear a hat, which seems likely now that I mention it. The bonus content on the other side of

HONEY HEIST.

A GAME BY GRANT H (2017) WITH THANKS TO ALL OUT OF BUBBLEGUM, 3:16 AND, WEIRDLY, POLARIS.

IT'S HONEYCON 2017. YOU ARE GOING TO UNDERTAKE THE GREATEST HEIST THE WORLD HAS EVER SEEN. TWO THINGS:

ONE: YOU HAVE A COMPLEX PLAN THAT REQUIRES PRECISE TIMING.

TWO: YOU ARE A GODDAMN BEAR.

Roll 3D6 to determine your descriptor, your role, and your bear type.

DESCRIPTOR:	BEAR TYPE (AND SKILL):
1: Rookie	1: Grizzly (Terrify)
2: Washed-up	2: Polar (Swim)
3: Retired	3: Panda (Eat anything that looks like bamboo)
4: Unhinged	4: Black (Climb)
5: Slick	5: Sun (Sense honey)
6: Incompetent	6: Honey Badger (Carnage)

ROLE:

1: Muscle	4: Hacker
2: Brains	5: Thief
3: Driver	6: Face

Name your bear, if you want. You're not a talking bear, per se, but you can sort of mangle human speech through your bear mouth, maybe? (You CAN talk to each other, though.)

STATS:

You have two stats: BEAR and CRIMINAL. Both start at 3. Use BEAR to: maul stuff, run and climb, shrug off damage, scare people, and generally do bear stuff. Use CRIMINAL to: do anything not directly related to being a bear.

ACTIONS: and the outcome is in doubt

When you act, roll a D6. If it's equal to or under the relevant stat, you succeed. If it's over the stat, you fail. If you're using your bear species skill, or doing something covered by your role, roll 2 dice and pick the lowest.

(BONUS HAT TABLE IF YOU WANT YOUR BEAR TO WEAR A HAT:)
1: TRILBY 2: TOP 3: BOWLER 4: FLAT CAP
(D8) 5: COWBOY 6: FEZ 7: CROWN 8: ROLL TWICE

CHANGING STATES

Hey GM! When a player rolls dice and the lowest dice they roll is a 6, introduce a twist or unseen complication into proceedings.

FRUSTRATION: When the plan fails and you run into difficulty, move one point from CRIMINAL into BEAR.

GREED: When the plan goes off without a hitch, move one point from BEAR into CRIMINAL.

You can voluntarily move one point from BEAR to CRIMINAL by doing a flashback scene in which you and the other bears plan out the heist over coffee and cigarettes in the back room of a seedy bar. You can voluntarily move one point of CRIMINAL into BEAR by eating a load of honey.

THE END

If your CRIMINAL stat ever reaches 6, you are lured into a life of crime and betray the party. If your BEAR stat ever reaches 6, you flip out bear-style and lose it, presumably to be picked up by animal control in half an hour or so.

RANDOM TABLES TO SET UP THE ADVENTURE:

HONEYCON IS BEING HELD IN A:

1: Creepy	1: Lakeside Camp
2: Busy	2: Fishing village
3: Run-down	3: Metropolitan city
4: Beautiful	4: Convention centre
5: Dangerous	5: Truck convoy
6: Lavish	6: Wilderness retreat

ASIDE FROM LOADS OF HONEY, THE PRIZE IS:

1: Ultradense megahoney from especially posh bees
2: A briefcase of pure manuka extract worth over $5m
3: The Queen of All Bees, Once Exiled, Now Returned
4: Black Orchid Honey, which turns anyone who eats it into a goth
5: Abraham Lincoln's beehive, thought to be haunted by his ghost
6: Miss Universe 2017, an especially attractive bee

SECURITY FEATURES (roll twice):

1: Armed guards
2: Electronically-locked doors
3: Laser tripwire grids
4: CCTV network
5: "Impenetrable" vault
6: Poison Gas

CONVENTION ORGANISER:

1: Cunning and sly
2: Greedy and wicked
3: Clueless and exploitable
4: Maybe too obsessed with honey
5: A spoilt trust-fund kid
6: Ruthless and corrupt

BUT LITTLE DO THE BEARS KNOW (GM, keep this secret!):

1: This place is rigged to blow!
2: The cops are en route!
3: Look - a rival team of bears!
4: They've been set up!
5: The prize is a fake!
6: The bees are angry!

HONEY HEIST, 2017
GRANT HOWITT, game reproduced via Creative Commons license

the sheet introduces a whole magic system, divided into six schools. It's absurd beyond any reasonable usc of the word—and wonderful. Get that honey!

Troika! (2018)

Let it never be said that weirdness is one size fits all. Rather, it is a strange, tittering rainbow overhead, a spectrum of surreal variety. For example, if *Dungeon Crawl Classics* is all maniacal laughter and chaotic shouting, *Troika!* is one too many googly eyes in an M. C. Escher landscape that periodically melts into iridescence.

Where the chassis of *DCC* is the third edition of Dungeons & Dragons, *Troika!* is a hack of the system originally used in the Fighting Fantasy gamebooks, resulting in a game that is very light. Characters are defined by three stats; I assume this is why the game is named "troika," a Russian word for a sleigh pulled by three horses.

Skill is a catchall value for a character's ability to do stuff, Luck is a resource that can be tested and spent to alter outcomes and Stamina is a measure of health — run out and the character is dead. Once the attributes are in place, players roll for a

Fronds of Benevolence, Melsonian Arts Council, 2019
Andrew Walter. Cover by Andrew Walter

background. This is the point that it becomes apparent that players are in for something very odd.

The backgrounds are loosely sketched, evocative and not at all what you expect to play in an RPG (*Electric Bastionland* takes a similar approach). Take, for example, the Befouler of Ponds, a priest of a toad god. Their background specialty is pissing in ponds and drinking stagnant liquids (though, presumably not the pissed in pond water).

Troika! features the best Dwarves, too – they are genderless, eat gems, sweat their excrement, smell terribly and reproduce by carving new Dwarves out of stone. There are boring things as well, like Burglars. Even more prosaic backgrounds are made strange, though. Take the Necromancer, for example: "The least popular of the magical practitioners, Necromancers are shunned by the major centers of learning, left to their own devices on the edges of society, passing on knowledge in the time-honored master-student dynamic. The loneliness encourages students to make their own friends."

Troika! Numinous Edition, Melsonian Arts Council, 2018
Daniel Sell. Cover by Andrew Walter

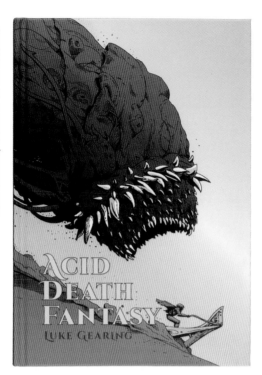

ACID DEATH FANTASY, MELSONIAN ARTS COUNCIL, 2020
LUKE GEARING, COVER BY DAVID HOSKINS

Backgrounds often come with special skills (the rating of which is added to the value of the character's Skill in a test), unique items (the Necromancer gets to choose between a zombie, a ghost and the skull of their master; regardless of the choice, the character has formed a codependent relationship with their "friend") and sometimes a special rule (Befoulers of Ponds are immune to diseases transmitted through stagnant liquid). Further, they're accompanied by an abstracted portrait in Dirk Detweiler Leichty's signature, geometrically dizzying style.

Taken all together, the backgrounds imply a strange and slippery world that verges on the nonsensical (in a good, delightfully British way—*Troika!* often feels like something Douglas Adams might have come up with under the influence of strong hallucinogens). Putting together a party and figuring out how they are all connected does a lot of worldbuilding necessary for the game, which then expands and contracts as characters die and are replaced.

It should be noted that characters die rather frequently. The combat system seems designed specifically to encourage this outcome. It resolves normally—rolling to hit, doing damage—but turn order is determined by drawing chips from a bag. Every player puts two chips in, every opponent gets two chips and they are joined by a chip that signifies the end of the round. The GM pulls a chip out of the bag to determine who acts next. If it is the end of round chip, that's it, start over.

Removing the certainty that a character is going to act in a combat round is a mischievous embrace of chaos on its own, but coupled with the fact that a character dies if they are at zero stamina at the end of a round makes this especially perilous. It also adds a strange sense of befuddlement to a fight—I love the idea of just a portion of the involved characters taking swings while the others stagger around in confusion or are otherwise paralyzed into inaction.

This makes a certain amount of sense. Only a handful of backgrounds seem like they should be capable when confronted by a physical altercation. That said, even the monsters are prone strange behavior. Each stat block is accompanied by a random table containing six miens, so players shouldn't be alarmed if they encounter goblins who are more inclined to gossip than fight.

It's absurd. But also charming in its way. Expect one-shots and very short campaigns that leave players shaking their heads in puzzlement. Andrew Walter's scenario *Fronds of Benevolence* (2019) is an excellent object lesson in how *Troika!* works, should bewilderment linger after reading the core rules.

The focus on backgrounds has led to a bustling business in zines and books that add to the base game. They're regularly encountered on Kickstarter and in online indie RPG storefronts. Some actively work to expand the theming of the implied world. An official expansion, *Acid Death Fantasy* (2020) by Luke Gearing and David Hoskins, brings in vast deserts, strange sultans, plastic people, and giant sand worms (and actually, as a setting, feels more classically ordered than the implied world of the core rulebook). Others add to the chaos—all manner of pop culture properties have outposts in the realms of *Troika!* now, though many with the serial numbers carefully filed off. *Seinfeld*, music subcultures, transforming robots, cats, friendly dinosaurs, and more have been *Troika!*-fied—many more will undoubtedly come.

Dialect (2018)

Every time I think I have a firm grip on what an RPG can be, something comes along and surprises the hell out of me. That's just what *Dialect* did.

Dialect is a collaborative, card-driven storytelling game focused on a language created by the players and how it eventually dies.

Words are powerful. *Dialect* pushes players to think about how and why we use words. That might sound intimidating, but in execution, it is easy to grok. The idea is that the characters are somehow isolated. That isolation can be literal, as in a colony on Mars, or metaphorical, like a clique in high school, and all of the other necessary bits are laid out in the included playsets, à la *Fiasco*.

Randomly drawn cards define key points of pressure on the community, which spur the creation of new words— these are fashioned by combining a root and affixes picked from a chart. Players aren't creating an entirely new language, like the Elvish of Tolkien, but a sort of specialized jargon.

Longtime players should be comfortable with the concept. It's a staple to define make-believe worlds with make-believe words (I bet most folks reading didn't second guess my use of Robert Heinlein's neologism "grok" a few lines up), but closer to home, the role-playing hobby uses many words non-players don't understand—"grognard,"

Dialect: A Game About Language and How it Dies, Thorny Games, 2018
Kathryn Hymes and Hakan Seyalioğlu, Cover by Jill DeHaan

"munchkin," and "metagaming" aren't slang; they have a greater utility in how games and play are communicated. Why and how these sorts of words develop is the phenomenon *Dialect* explores.

Each player has a unique character that both molds and reacts to the new language. Play continues through three eras (again, loosely defined—it could be a tour of duty on an off-planet mining facility or a series of school semesters), with new events (determined by cards) pushing the language to change in unexpected ways. The game culminates with the legacy phase during which players are prompted to narrate the aftermath of the events of play. At this point in the narrative, the formative isolation is likely over, and the language it created no longer needed.

Interestingly, play in *Dialect* mirrors the narrative one-to-one. The narrative is, of course, truncated and abstracted, in the same way a novel solely focuses on events that audiences need to know, rather than relaying a second-by-second record of events. But, to create the narrative, the players have to become it: They develop the language; they use it in their communication; they watch it grow and transform, and, at the end of the session, they abandon it forever.

Dialect isn't an easy game. Despite the brief rules, which are clear and extremely supportive of play at every step, it suffers, somewhat, from the intrinsic problems of storytelling games: Shy folks, those with stage fright, and people who are methodical, rather than improvisational in their thinking, will likely struggle.

Beyond that, though, playing with language is challenging. Much of how we communicate—word choice, sentence structure, tone—involves reflexes. Thinking about how reflexes work often messes them up.

Whatever awkwardness lurks in the valley, *Dialect*'s peak offers something unique. How often do players make something together in an RPG? Or make something at all? And then *use* it? RPGs are inherently collaborative, but *Dialect*'s mechanics crystallize that collaboration and give it weight, turning it into something that resembles a community. Every RPG up to this point is concerned with simulating experiences, but *Dialect* actually serves up the shared experience the game is about.

Leaving that shared experience behind has a whiff of melancholy about it. *Dialect* is intended to be a single session game, and the climax is always the same—the isolated community is no longer isolated and, in rejoining the larger whole, it and its language are destroyed. It was a moment in time, just like the game session. Players push back their seats and part ways—they'll continue on, but they'll never get back to that table, on that day, in the same way, again.

Mothership (2018)

What is a zine? Like so many other cultural classifications (punk, OSR, pornography, the concept of "indie"), a zine is physically easy to recognize, but its intrinsic traits are difficult to define.

Are zines made up of photocopied collages crudely stapled together? Sure! Is "zine" another word for "chapbook?" Sure! Are zines weird and countercultural? Probably! Do hippies and comic artists and punks and riot grrls and *Star Trek* fans make zines? Yes! And so do RPG designers and a lot of other people.

For the purpose of this book, zines are short, stapled, digest-sized booklets or chapbooks that are inexpensively produced in short runs, often, but not always, by one person, often but not always containing material that appeals to a niche or otherwise non-commercially viable population. In other words, zines are where to find the awesome weird shit.

A certain do-it-yourself, zinester aesthetic was baked into RPGs from the start. *D&D* was originally issued in stapled, digest-sized booklets that look similar to the science fiction fanzines from the same period, fanzines that gave many *D&D* artists their start. The success of *D&D* encouraged other publishers to stick with the format. There's *The Arduin Grimoire*, of course, with its photocopied, typewrit-

MOTHERSHIP, TUESDAY KNIGHT GAMES, 2018
SEAN MCCOY, COVER BY SEAN MCCOY

354

ten pages. The digest-sized first edition of *Traveller* feels a bit too professional, but it inspired many scrappy amateur zines. Even larger format products, like those from Fantasy Games Unlimited, Judges Guild, early Chaosium, and Flying Buffalo retain a certain small press feel, not to mention the amateur press association *Alarums and Excursions*, which is essentially a group of monthly zines bound together.

Then, as now, zines give enthusiasts an inexpensive way to participate in the larger hobby and to put their ideas into the world. Examples abound. *The Oracle* (originally from the early '80s, but recently compiled and republished by The Play Generated Map & Document Archive) is an excellent example of the periodical-style zine, full of homebrew adventures, editorials, and reviews. There's *Droids* (1983), an odd set of rules for a robot-based roleplaying game that doesn't really work as a standalone game but probably should have been a rule's expansion for *Traveller*. There's *Duel Arcane* (1980), a striking zine from Gamelords that offers rules for using the shapeshifting spell duel from the Disney animated film *The Sword in the Stone* (1963) in a fantasy RPG. There are likely countless more, circulated among friends, sold at conventions, lining the consignment shelf of local stores, given away, shared, and lost to time.

In recent years, access to high quality design software and increasingly affordable full-color digital printing (and the rediscovery of the eccentric risograph process) helped steadily advance the production value of zines. As attractive as they have become (and they are often very, very pleasing to the eye and hand), RPG zines have remained a bastion for the weird, the experimental, and the niche.

Dead Planet, Tuesday Knight Games, 2018. Donn Stroud, Fiona Maeve Geist, and Sean McCoy, cover by Sean McCoy

RPGs have always offered a creative space, but as *D&D* brings more people into the hobby, it simultaneously feels increasingly like homogenized output from a monolithic corporation. Alternatively, the zine scene feels like the beating heart and soaring soul of the hobby—diverse, idiosyncratic, beautiful, and unrestrained.

Sean McCoy's *Mothership* didn't start this revolution—it had been turning for years—but something about it grabbed the attention in that "right time, right place" kind of way. It didn't exactly bring people into the hobby like the *Fighting Fantasy* books, the *HeroQuest* board game, and the *D&D* coloring book did, but it offered a similar kind of gateway that inspired a re-commitment from many players whose interests were otherwise starting to drift. *Mothership* said to many of them that they could make game zines (and postcard games, pamphlet games, and little games that fit onto business cards), too. The game showcased the potential of the zine, and the emergence of *Mothership* coincides with a massive

A POUND OF FLESH, TUESDAY KNIGHT GAMES, 2019

SEAN MCCOY, DONN STROUD, AND LUKE GEARING, COVER BY JAN BURAGAY

swell of momentum in indie RPGs that has since grown exponentially.

Mothership is a science fiction horror RPG. Taking a curious page from videogame development, the game is in "alpha" as of this writing, meaning that current zine editions are still undergoing tweaks for a forthcoming definitive edition in a more traditional printed form (ferried along by a massively successful Kickstarter campaign). The in-progress nature of the zine gives the game and its increasing number of official and third party supplements a sprawling, experimental feel, with folks figuring out what works and what doesn't on the fly. In some ways, it is reminiscent of the open playtesting of *Pathfinder* and the Fifth Edition of *D&D*.

There are strong thematic cues here from films, like *Alien* (1979) and *Event Horizon* (1997), as well as the videogame, *Dead Space* (2008), and other similar claustrophobic, isolated outer-space horror stories. If a player likes those things, they're probably going to like *Mothership*. In fact, *Mothership* is arguably

the best option available to run something like them—this pressure cooker genre is strangely underrepresented in the spectrum of horror RPGs (well, it was, until the recently released *Alien* RPG, 2019).

Mothership is class-based—Scientist, Teamster, Android, and Marine. Each gets their own specialties, but each also deals with pressure differently. For instance, Marines have the best armor save, but when they Panic, it's contagious, and everyone else needs to make a Fear check. The system is based on 10-sided dice, and there are little bits that can be identified from other games—advantage and disadvantage is a key component; there are hit locations and nested skills. There are numerous random tables— some offer immediate utility while others, like the tables for uniform patches and trinkets, are merely aesthetic, although delightful. There are also lots of fidgety bits. The mechanics are essentially familiar, but they're applied in ways that feel slightly unexpected.

Taken all together, it's a little tricky to internalize how all of the mechanics mesh and stack, but this complexity also gives them the range necessary to ratchet up tension appropriate to this sort of horror game. A player who stops to pause and refresh themselves on the various methodologies parallel's the narrative, in a way—thinking through the complexity of the game mechanics simulates dealing with the sort of complicated systems characters might find on a starship. Nevertheless, players will have a decent grasp on the game by the time they're done reading the 40-page zine. And if they get stuck, there are flow charts to help.

The real novelty of the system is Stress and Panic, both of which interrupt the flow of the actions. Failed save rolls gain a player Stress, as do encounters with hostile creatures, seeing friends die, when the ship takes damage, going without sleep, and basically anything else that would normally freak a person out or set their nerves on edge. Too much Stress risks Panic, which results in negative effects. The system is an awful lot like the sanity system from *Call of Cthulhu* and similar horror RPGs, but instead of mucking about with depictions of mental illness, the Panic effects feel like plausible reactions to situational pressure. Some of them are even positive, resulting in focused or energetic action. The Stress and Panic mechanics are elegant, overall, and terribly punishing.

The core rules presented in the *Mothership* zine provide good bones, and the modules that followed built the house. Nearly every mechanical question I had about the core rules was resolved by reading *Dead Planet* (2018) and seeing their application.

Dead Planet is a scenario about, well, a dead planet. Something on it causes an anomaly that pulls ships out of hyperspace, stranding them in orbit. The longer people are there, the more they find themselves compelled to create strange sculptures. Eventually, the right sort of sculpture is made, forming a gate from which horrible monsters pour out, every hour on the hour (there are strong *Dead Space* vibes here).

There are more random tables—for nightmares, for salvage, for mutations. There's an absolutely brilliant method for generating random layouts for derelict ships. There are a number of venues for exploration, as well: A drifting research ship with a dead crew and an ancient artifact pulled from the planet's surface, a colony of self-cannibalizing survivors on the planet's moon, a ruined military facility, a gate to the Dead Dimension, and more. Each comes with a plethora of horrible fates and terrible solutions to the problem of being stranded.

GRADIENT DESCENT, TUESDAY KNIGHT GAMES, 2020
LUKE GEARING, COVER BY SEAN MCCOY

Dead Planet shows how the game system will test, and probably kill, players, and it does so exquisitely. *A Pound of Flesh* followed in 2019 and lays out a sleazy backwater space station that can act as the central hub of an ongoing campaign, or the focus of one, as there are several horrible fates that can befall it— all at the same time, in the hands of a particularly evil GM.

Gradient Descent came out in 2020 and provides an awful megadungeon for players to explore, filled with android ghosts and bizarre artifacts, along with a hostile, godlike artificial intelligence, all of which are brought to a terrible half-life with Nick Tofani's haunted artwork. All three of these zines provide additional rules and modular systems while illustrating different ways to play.

And thanks to *Mothership*'s specificity of tone and an open license, third party creators have had much success in contributing their own zines to the line. Along with *Mörk Borg* and *Troika!*, *Mothership* also boasts exciting and consistent creator community. *The Black Pyramid* (2020) has players investigating a very

Egyptian anomaly in space; *Blood Floats in Space* (2020) provides an analogue to the *Warhammer 40,000* universe, and *Primeval* (2020) is a terrifying jungle hex crawl. Together with the official *Mothership* publications, they're not only exploring a rich galaxy of terror, they're also laying out a whole new community-focused way to create and play.

Spire: The City Must Fall (2018)

In *D&D*, the drow are emblematic of a kind of racial essentialism that enables the game's underlying power fantasy—the entire dark-skinned, subterranean, spider-worshiping race is known to be inherently evil, so players can attack and kill them without upending their moral compasses (see page 220). *Spire: The City Must Fall* takes all of those assumptions *D&D* players might have about drow (and regular elves and the hyena-like gnolls, too) and throws them right out the window.

The titular Spire is a massive vertical city, once ruled by drow and now held by aelfir, the masked, decadent, sun-worshiping high elves who have subjugated the native population. Aelfir propaganda says that the drow were once aelfir themselves, but transgressed against the sun gods and were subsequently cursed with a debilitating allergy to daylight. Of course, for the aelfir, the weakness is proof of the drow's lesser status and justifies their subjugation. Some drow naturally disagree—players take the role of drow who are members of a secret society intent on overthrowing the aelfir occupation by any means necessary, which generally leads to an excess of revolutionary violence (shades of *Underground* abound).

The game is built around causing and sustaining damage—inflict every bit of suffering back onto the unjust system that caused it, and then some, no matter the cost. This recklessness is central to the mechanics, which use five Stress attributes to gauge a character's health—Blood (tracks physical damage), Mind (mental strain), Silver (physical resources), Shadow (the secrecy that protects a character's double life), and Reputation (a character's standing in their communities).

Any time a character fails a skill check, they gain Stress, and every time they gain new Stress, they roll against their total to find out if they experience Fallout. Fallout is a physical manifestation of Stress and is proportional to the amount of Stress a character has when they experience the Fallout. So, three points of Blood Stress might result in the Bleeding Status, while nine points might leave a character Dying. Severe Shadow Fallout might lead NPC collaborators to be dragged into the street and shot while severe Silver Fallout might encourage escape from the Spire to avoid the loan sharks keeping a character afloat.

Stress and Fallout accrue rapidly, ensuring that characters are fragile and situations are uncertain, while also keeping players fully aware of how much a character has left to give. Once a player notches that eighth point of Stress, they might want to start thinking about the best way to go out in a blaze of glory.

Spire dramatically re-imagines drow. Aside from being averse to sunlight, there is little that connects them to their *D&D*

ancestors, which is good. All of the available classes explore some aspect of this new vision of drow society while also naturally positioning characters on a path of radical opposition against the ruling aelfir elites. Many of the classes are bizarre—players can take the role of a merchant, a vigilante, or a freedom fighter, sure, but how about a drow/spider-hybrid Midwife devoted to protecting drow eggs (yes, drow are hatched, apparently), or a Vermissian Sage who can travel the city's vast, failed interdimensional mass transit system? I expect players will be hard pressed to read through the classes without devising dozens of ideas of how to run a character.

The idea-stoking extends to the city itself—there are no shortages of unexpected, inspirational concepts in the sourcebook section. Adrian Stone's setting-defining art further unifies the game, capturing the violence and the strangeness of the world with a style that evokes firebrand political art.

In *D&D*, drow are evil by default, a psychotic caricature, mad dogs to be put down so the players can feel powerful. In *Spire*, there is no moral certainty. The drow are under the heel, sympathetic and driven to extremes by desperation and poverty to reclaim their lands. Player characters regularly perform both wonderful and terrible deeds in the service of noble goals, but no matter their successes, no matter how wounded the system of oppression is, it persists while the characters burn up in their resistance.

Old-School Essentials (2019)

I get a perverse sort of pleasure in wanting to buy something I already own. I have a clear recollection of the day I bought *Muswell Hillbillies*, the 1971 LP by The Kinks, perhaps because I was on vacation at the time. I plucked it out of the crates at the Record Exchange in Salem and bought it on a lark—I knew exactly one song on it, the delightfully

OLD-SCHOOL ESSENTIALS RETRO ADVENTURE GAME, BOX SET, NECROTIC GNOME, 2019
GAV N NORMAN, COVER BY ANDREW WALTER

staggering "Alcohol," and spending $5 bucks on the assumption that the rest of the album would rise to that level seemed like a good bet. I played it on a little portable record player that I had in my hotel room, and it turned out that I was right. It doesn't crack my top ten, all-time favorite albums, but it is perfect for a lazy Sunday afternoon; that quality, coupled with the fond memory of the purchase itself, has left me with the strange impulse to buy it again whenever I see it in a store. I suppose my brain, acting on reflex, thinks doing so will somehow recreate that pleasant day. While I've never actually bought it again—what would I even do with another copy?—the urge remains.

I suspect a similar feeling fuels both the production and market for clones and hacks of the various older iterations of *Dungeons & Dragons*. For many, a glimpse of the original *Player's Handbook*, or the basic box sets, awakens a host of warm, nostalgic memories.

It seems much of the OSR movement is arranged around recapturing those experiences, and the many hacks and clones allow for players to re-enact that first RPG purchase. There's more to it, of course. To

OLD-SCHOOL ESSENTIALS CLASSIC FANTASY GENRE RULES, NECROTIC GNOME, 2019
GAVIN NORMAN, COVER BY ANDREW WALTER

continue the musical simile, a good hack or clone is like a cover song—each designer puts their own spin on well-known material, favoring this, downplaying that, introducing clever tweaks along the way, smoothing rough spots out for a different sort of audience. Every once in a while, there is a cover song that becomes a monster hit and just totally wipes out the original, sounding completely new despite being utterly familiar. Take Tiffany's version of "I Think We're Alone Now" (originally by Tommy James & the Shondells in 1967) or Soft Cell's "Tainted Love" (a banger originally by Gloria Jones in 1964). *Old-School Essentials* (*OSE*) is that kind of cover song.

The books call themselves a restatement of 1981 *Basic* and *Expert* box sets, which is essentially true. There are a handful of clarifications of ambiguities, expansions, and one optional rule (the inclusion of ascending armor class, first introduced in the Third Edition of *D&D*). All of these tweaks are meticulously recorded in the appendices, along with the reasoning behind them. With those few exceptions, this is a work of extensive renovation. The rules are buffed, polished, and streamlined to the point that it is difficult to see the original. It's all there, mechanically, but the refinement is so total that the result feels like a whole new game.

The feeling of newness is a testament to two elements: First, Gavin Norman's relentlessly clean, uncluttered layout, and second, the punishing chaos of the original booklets (which, admittedly, improved upon their predecessors). Those with an unfettered love of the original box sets have likely flipped through them so often that they might be blind to the disorder, but skimming the various *OSE* books will dispel that illusion.

For instance, using the old *Basic Set* to make an Elf character, a player turns to page eight for the experience table and page nine for the basic class information. Saving throws are on page 26, the attack table on page 27, and the Elf special ability for detecting secret doors on page 21. And that's not even getting into the Elf's ability to cast spells.

Compare all of that page turning to the two-page spread in *Old-School Essentials* that presents all of the relevant Elf-creation information in one convenient dashboard of sorts that displays the clear visual hierarchies that convey their relative importance. The text is precisely worded for maximum clarity. It practically beams *D&D* directly into a player's brain.

The form of the books is important, as well. Rather than being textbook-sized compendiums, *Old-School Essentials* opts for digests, which feel more intimate and take up less space. The rules are spread across five modular volumes—*Core Rules*, *Genre Rules* (character generation), *Cleric and Magic-User Spells*, *Monsters*, and *Treasures*—available separately or together in a box, so players only have to buy and lug around the rules they need. Alternately, there is a collected rules tome (good for reference when a GM is writing adventures) and a player tome that places all of the character-facing information under one cover. Admittedly, these options can be a bit confusing at the point of purchase, but the flexibility is ultimately a benefit that supports the line's overall focus on usability.

That usability makes *Old-School Essentials* special. No other set of rules, including the current iteration of *Dungeons & Dragons*, is so clear or easy to reference. Reading *OSE*, along with similarly brief books, like *Ultraviolet Grasslands* and *Electric Bastionland*, makes reading other RPGs, even the relatively user-friendly rulebooks, like the seventh edition of *Call of Cthulhu,* with their narrated prose rules encased in long blocks of text, seem more difficult. I hope that a bullet point revolution is in the making.

The *Old-School Essentials* line also includes a four-volume *Advanced Fantasy* expansion—*Genre Rules*, *Druid and Illusion Spells*, *Monsters*, and *Treasures*.

Unlike the core *Old-School Essentials*, these books are not a restatement of the *Advanced Dungeons & Dragons* rules. Rather, similar to *Advanced Labyrinth Lord*, they are a streamlined conversion that brings in much of the *AD&D* material, among them most of the playable races and classes (including those from *Unearthed Arcana*, like drow and deep gnomes), albeit in a form that is less powerful than *AD&D* players might be used to.

Then, there are optional rules to further bring *OSE* in line with *AD&D* expectations, should the GM be so inclined. The major one untethers race from class, a key point of difference in the original systems—the *Advanced* game treats class and race as separate, while the *Basic* game treats race *as* a class, so an Elf Fighter/Magic-User in *AD&D* is just an Elf in *Basic*. Now, a player can have a character who is an Elf *and* a Druid, or a Ranger, or whatever they like.

While this expansion finally addresses the perplexing historical disconnect

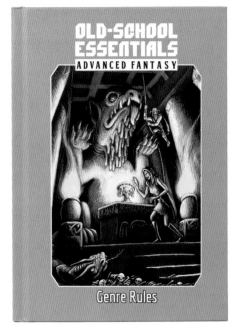

OLD-SCHOOL ESSENTIALS ADVANCED FANTASY GENRE RULES, NECROTIC GNOME, 2019
GAVIN NORMAN, COVER BY STEFAN B. POAG

between *Basic* and *Advanced Dungeons & Dragons*, the *Advanced Fantasy* rules are also exciting because they are instructional. They take something familiar—*AD&D*-specific classes, for instance—and show players how they should work within the *OSE* framework. With that, the sky is the limit; players can make this system do anything they want it to do.

Both of these flavors of *D&D* are predictable at this point. It seems to me that, in a way that is similar to *Troika!*, the classic qualities of *OSE* are designed to provide a firm, thoroughly understandable bedrock upon which other creators can build strange and beautiful things.

Take, for instance Gavin Norman's own forthcoming *OSE* campaign setting, the much-anticipated Dolmenwood. It was originally developed for *Labyrinth Lord* and was laid out intermittently in the *Wormskin* zine (2015-2018). Dolmenwood is an exceedingly weird place (not *Troika!*-level weird, but then so few games are), and the setting will include similarly unique classes, races, magic items, spells, and monsters. And, while all of that is likely to be entertaining in its own right, it, too, will teach players new ways to customize *OSE*.

FUNGI OF THE FAR REALMS, MELSONIAN ARTS COUNCIL, 2019
ALEX CLEMENTS AND SHUYI ZHANG, COVER BY SHUYI ZHANG

Fungi of the Far Realms (2019)

Fungi of the Far Realms proves that tabletop RPGs are in the midst of a wildly creative renaissance. Easily guessed from the title, it is a field guide to imaginary varieties of fungus. It's pure magic.

This golden moment is due to a confluence of factors. The hobby has always fostered a do-it-yourself ethic that has led to near-constant experimentation since the introduction of *D&D*. Add to the equation affordable prices for high quality printing, the introduction of increasingly diverse voices into the hobby, and the use of the internet to keep folks connected, and stir briskly. It may be a small renaissance, especially when compared to the corporate behemoth in whose shadow it sits, but size isn't the point. This community has developed an appetite for strange, beautiful what's-its, and the whole hobby is richer for it.

538 people pledged funds on Kickstarter to make *Fungi of the Far Realms* possible. It is hard to imagine most publishers taking a risk on a book this niche, this in-depth, this rules-ambivalent, and this physically lovely without the benefit of a crowd-funding campaign—a fact that has continued to change the face of the hobby.

The book is written in an in-universe style and purports to be a reprint of a rare but definitive tome on exotic, and often magical, fungi—218 of them, in fact. All are lavishly illustrated in watercolors by Shuyi Zhang in the style of a botanical text. The brown matte boards and the color scheme of the cover art (individually screened by hand on each copy) is reminiscent of a certain kind of science field guide aimed at young readers during the '50s or '60s.

Details on the fungi include habitat, appearance, mouthfeel/taste, and aroma. For example, the mindsnatcher mushroom grows in high mountainous terrain, tastes like oats, smells faintly of fermentation, and, despite the sinister name, is a harmless, hearty snack. Others are poisons, aphrodisiacs, contraceptives, hallucinogens, soul prisons, and more. Eating one pale gray cap can untether a player's shadow while another is sought by clowns to be used as false noses.

The vast majority of these 'shrooms provide just a bit of narrative flavor for a game, though some have practical applications for the rules. Which rules? Whichever rules; *Fungi* isn't picky. The obvious ones are left to the GM's discretion, while a handful of others—like the hypermushroom that exists simultaneously in multiple dimensions—are detailed in a brief appendix at the back of the book. There are also guidelines on how to run mushroom foraging in games. The authors clearly have a deep fascination with fungi.

It's unlikely that a player will use this book in every session of a fantasy game, although it will likely provide a richer, deeper experience in one foraging-centric session. The book is highly specialized material, but, like the trinkets in *Mothership*, these fine details often make a game session memorable or otherwise special. As of this writing, there is nothing else quite like *Fungi of the Far Realms* available, but with luck (and maybe some Kickstarter backers), that won't be true for long.

Thousand Year Old Vampire (2019)

The greatest hurdle to playing RPGs is the need for a group. No group? No game. *Tunnels & Trolls* recognized this barrier early on and created solo adventures, which eventually grew into adventure gamebooks, like the Fighting Fantasy series.

These consist of navigating through a branching narrative arranged in random, numbered passages, using a light system primarily for combat (though inventory and magic also come into play). For a long time, this was the only style of solitaire RPG experience available and,

THOUSAND YEAR OLD VAMPIRE, PETIT GUIGNOL, 2019
TIM HUTCHINGS, COVER BY TIM HUTCHINGS

though enjoyable enough, there's a large gap between a gamebook and playing at a table.

The idea of a more fulfilling solo RPG has remained a tantalizing one. In recent years, perhaps spinning out of the unique diary method of character creation in *Castle Falkenstein*, or the solitaire rules for the letter writing game *De Profundis*, a number of designers began experimenting with solo writing games. *Quill* (2016) and its many derivative letter-writing solo games were likely the best known examples for a time, but Tim Hutchings's *Thousand Year Old Vampire* recently raised the bar. Journaling, of course, isn't the only solution for more engrossing solitaire play, as *Disciples of Bone and Shadow*, demonstrates.

Most journaling RPGs are zines or print-on-demand booklets—low-cost products aimed at a small niche group of players. *Thousand Year Old Vampire* is a handsome hardcover book, designed to look like a Mysterious Old Book with a leather spine, marbled end papers, and evocative collages of ephemera inside.

This sort of skeuomorphism is a risky gambit—the majority of the Third Edition *D&D* books pretended to look like mystical grimoires of various designs, with the results ranging from puzzling to cringeworthy. *Thousand Year Old Vampire* fares better—the aesthetics of a weeded library book, cast aside, and stripped of its context, is far more than decoration; it's a visual metaphor of the game's themes.

A vampire is a collection of keywords. These are Skills (which can be used once in the narrative), Resources (Dracula had a castle, perhaps this vampire has a ship?), Characters (who regularly die of old age), and Marks (physical manifestations of their curse). Most of all, though, vampires have Memories. They have space for five Memories, each made of three Experiences (in practical terms, Experiences are single evocative sentences that, when collected, describe one moment, event, object, or person of importance). Once those spaces are full, they can offload up to four Memories into a diary.

All of these assets are at the mercy of the numbered prompts. A player starts at number one and then uses dice to navigate their way through the rest, subtracting the result of a 6-sided die from the result of a 10-sided die; a positive result moves that many entries forward, a negative result moves back. Prompts take many forms. Most often, they explain something then ask the player a question about it. Answering that question creates an Experience, which must immediately be logged.

Sometimes, prompts give—the first prompt burdens a player with the skill "bloodthirsty." More often, they take—instructing a player to kill Characters, use Skills, abandon Resources. After a little while, even when the prompts give, they take away. If every prompt creates an Experience, the player is soon full of memories; at that point, they have to choose what to forget.

Forgetting is the central torture of the game. Crossing out Memories—the product of play and the chronicle of a player's vampire's Experience—is an unexpected agony. There are horrible traumas that happen during the course of *Thousand Year Old Vampire*, but there are beautiful moments too, as well as dramatic, happy, and tragic ones. The prompts are sometimes untidy, like real-life, leading to momentary fancies and puzzling dead ends that never yield resolutions. Other times, the narrative draws tight, like a vise, with all themes and happenstance aligning to pummel the player's emotions. Surrendering to the tides of the prompts is necessary for the flow of the game, but when the player makes it through a chapter of the vampire's history only to start chipping away at those new Memories, it sometimes feels like the game asks too much. Worse yet is when it happens all at once. Fate can rob a vampire of their diary and, with it, all the Memories it contains. A loss of that magnitude feels like, well, being stabbed in the heart.

All things fade in time. The prompts erode all of the vampire's keywords and Memories. When they're all gone, the game is over, and the vampire's ultimate fate is revealed. Most often it is death, or some similar oblivion, and it is a relief.

Disciples of Bone and Shadow (2019)

Where *Thousand Year Old Vampire* largely does away with traditional RPG mechanics to solve the riddle of solitaire play, *Disciples of Bone and Shadow* embraces them for an exploration-focused experience that feels closer to solo play options for board games than it does an adventure gamebook.

The game is randomly generated, ensuring it is familiar, yet different every time it is played, which is reminiscent of dungeon crawler videogames, like *Rogue* (1980) and *Hack* (1982). Two sets of random generation rules facilitate the

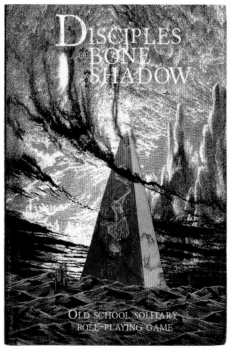

DISCIPLES OF BONE AND SHADOW, BLACKOATH ENTERTAINMENT AND EXALTED FUNERAL, 2019
ALEX T. COVER BY DAVID LOPEZ

exploration of the world, one for the overland hex map and one for interior spaces on a traditional grid. Both work similarly and draw on traditions established in the early days of the hobby. Hexes are populated in tables that resemble those used in *Wilderlands of High Fantasy*. Dungeons are created room by room in a way that is similar to the dungeon generator from the *Dungeon Masters Guide*.

Every step the character takes, the player creates the world, determining its features, and discovering its perils by consulting the random tables—there is even a table for quests that might be given to characters along the way. It plays very fast and maintains a consistent level of challenge—not knowing what lies ahead, because it doesn't yet exist, presents an endless test of the player's ability to improvise and survive. Similarly, when an important roll fails, there is a distinct disadvantage to not having a GM on the other side of the screen at which to aim pleas of mercy.

The system is recognizably traditional and pared down. There are no classes, but there is an archetype system that echoes them without being confining—as with *Warhammer Fantasy Roleplay*, there are basic archetypes and advanced ones into which characters can graduate given time and experience. Players can improve their characters further by using enhancement points to purchase additional skills. The most unusual feature of the game is Corruption, which is a ticking time bomb for characters who mess around with magic—hit the character's max value and that's it; their quest for arcane power turns them into a puddle of goo.

In a surprising twist for a solitaire game, a player controls a party of two characters! Because the systems are so lightweight, this isn't an onerous task, and it greatly increases the sorts of encounters a player can handle and the tactics they can employ.

Thank goodness. Even in the context of fiction, it is difficult to imagine exploring the Fractured Dominion alone. The game describes the world as scorched, demon-haunted, and desolate. Arcane nightmares, known as Tyrants, rule the perpetual twilight from their remote citadels. Horrors roam the wastes. Metal is scarce, luxury unheard of. The few people who have not been reduced to the state of wild beasts cower in their ramshackle settlements and scrape out their existences. If *Mörk Borg* is a doom metal RPG and *Ultraviolet Grasslands* is a psychedelic metal RPG, *Disciples of Bone and Shadow* brings the shrieking distortion of black metal to the table.

The problem with tables is that they're a finite resource. Play leads to familiarity and eventually they become exhausted. To mitigate this limitation, *Disciples of Bone and Shadow* has a second volume, the *Narrative Playbook*, that radically expands how the game is played.

The playbook encourages players to run a single character made with new creation rules. They're tougher, have access to more skills, and gain a few additional points of definition. Advantages and Disadvantages explain more about them, while Flaws dictate how they act in certain contexts. The former have no mechanical impact but provide color and roleplaying cues for the character. The latter, however, work a bit like Aspects in *Fate* or Passions in *Pendragon*, in that once triggered, they compel the character's behavior unless overcome with a roll of the dice.

Play takes place in scenes, which the player sets, defining the characters and the location. Beyond that, tables are used to randomly generate the responses that would otherwise be provided by a GM. The key table is the Augur, which functions as a sort of Magic 8 Ball, answering "yes" or "no" questions. A second table potentially adds a qualifier—"and," "but"—which is revealed on a third table devoted to complications.

A matrix of additional tables takes on all manner of GM duties, from generating missions, to describing actions, to doling out rumors. The name Augur is appropriate—the tables give just enough information to be evocative and to move the action along, but are open-ended enough to allow for a good deal of interpretation, thus giving the player a share of narrative control as they poke around the entrails that the dice lay out, seeking their fortune and their future.

It is imperfect, but that is usually true of anything situated on a frontier. *Disciples of Bone and Shadow* is way out there, experimenting with mechanics for solo play that few others are working with (but for which there is a sudden increase in demand because of the pandemic).

Alex T's subsequent design, *Seekers Beyond the Shroud* (2021), an urban horror game, incorporates many more options, allowing for a variety of mission-based activities in an occult underground. *Across a Thousand Dead Worlds*, his forthcoming horror-in-space game, is sure to push the boundaries even further.

Mörk Borg (2019)

If there is a perfect expression of the link between RPGs and heavy metal, it's *Mörk Borg* (Swedish for "Dark Fort"). The truth of this is self-evident when flipping through the book. Moody landscapes, splatters of gore, skulls, and inverted crosses abound—there is enough material here for a dozen album covers and as many band T-shirts. The back cover purports it to be a "doom metal album of a game." This is an accurate description, although it is somewhat subverted by the use of blinding yellow and Day-Glo pink in the graphic design.

The world is ending, which, on the one hand, is good, because it's an awful place, and its existence is a blight; but, on the other hand, it's bad, because the characters live there. *Mörk Borg* is about what player characters do in the last days—speed them up, work to stop them, or just try to get rich and enjoy themselves before the lights go out. Answering this central question is facilitated by a system of the extremely stripped-down *D&D* variety—rich in atmosphere and light on rules. It may seem odd, perhaps, to pair the aesthetics of transgressive heavy metal with an extremely easy and welcoming system, but these are strange times. That very juxtaposition is perhaps subversive, as well, as is the decision to drench the game in hard-to-read graphic design that requires a one-page, cleanly formatted rules document to reference.

The setting, naturally, is very grim. A *Mörk Borg* campaign lasts only as long as it takes for seven prophecies to come true, at which point the world ends, and players are encouraged to burn the book. That might seem like an extreme overreaction, but this exhortation hints at the solid core of silliness buried deep in the

Mörk Borg, Ockult Örtmästare Games and Stockholm Kartell, 2019. Pelle Nilsson and Johan Nohr. Cover by Johan Nohr

game's unhallowed heart. Still, the world is corrupt and beyond redemption. Nothing is worth saving, and it is rapidly filling with monsters, primary among which are a pair of two-headed basilisks that are marching the world to its end. Everything is blackened.

There is a sliver of hope, though. The basilisks are the source of the prophecies. Two bodies, four heads, all bickering—Verhu only speaks the truth, Gorgh resents Verhu's accuracy, Lusi is in denial, and Arkh always lies (or does she?). In that bickering, there is, perhaps, a way through the dooms foretold, should a player want to try to trick obscene entities of that size and power, of course.

That tiny dram of hope makes everything else taste all the more bitter. *Mörk Borg*'s appeal lies in the perverse desire to know what it feels like to welcome the apocalypse. An ending really does seem to be the only sensible option. So inevitable is this doom that the game is wishy washy about whether players should bother naming their characters. No other game is quite so delighted by its own nihilism.

FERETORY, FREE LEAGUE PUBLISHING, 2020
MÖRK BORG CULT, COVER BY JOHAN NOHR

This is not to say the game is a joyless affair. The book itself, as an object, is sublime. The layout and design work are aggressive, to the point that players might consider leaving it on the shelf instead of bringing it to the gaming table; the one-page, visually-minimal rules reference card is much more approachable.

While the game is certainly rules-light, that nomenclature slightly undersells the difficulty of navigating the ornate typesetting. Every spread is visually rich with chaotic font choices and gnarly splatter art. Even the ribbon bookmark has text, and the spine has a hidden message that only reveals itself in darkness. There are also foil mirrors and different types of paper.

It's a physically intense book, beautifully ugly, and remarkably consistent, thanks to the talents of artist and designer Johan Nohr. Looking through the book is an experience in itself. One commenter on Reddit reacted to the book saying, "I don't even care about the game at this point, just looking at the book makes me want to set it on fire," which prompted Nohr to ask if they could use the quote for marketing purposes (they could, and they did).

This is another example of the game's aforementioned sense of humor. It is very specific, draped in the trappings of death, black, and doom metal, but it's there, pushing those trappings to ridiculous extremes and struggling to maintain a straight face under the corpse paint. *Mörk Borg* is often cool and hilarious at the same time. It's apparent immediately upon picking up the book—the creep on the cover evokes a sort of Russ Nicholson-style of evil and violence, but inside the cover, that same creep has been reduced to a pile of bones with its own sword stuck in its head.

A thriving creator community has grown around the game, thanks to its open third party development license, and it shares that sense of humor—*Bork Borg*, for instance, is a brief supplement that "drastically increases the quantity and variety of dog options" while *Dukk Börg* is a parody that combines *Mörk Borg* and Disney's *DuckTales*.

Honestly, if you can't laugh at the end of the world, what *can* you laugh at?

The Ultraviolet Grasslands (2019)

Like comic books (which have always been an adjacent industry), RPGs are closely entwined with music, particularly underground rock, punk, and heavy metal. In the early days, this proximity was less a reflection of the interests of designers than it was a pairing discovered by players—*D&D* and Iron Maiden just go together well.

On a lark, I asked James M. Ward if he was a Devo fan, because there seemed to be a natural kinship between the mutants of *Gamma World* and the de-evolution originally cooked up by band members Gerald Casale and Bob Lewis. Artist Erol Otus placed the logo of the band Dead Kennedys prominently on the GM screen for *Gamma World*, so I hoped to learn Ward was an old punk or that he was an early Devo fan, an association that would

UVG FUNERAL EDITION, WIZARDTHIEFFIGHTER STUDIO AND EXALTED FUNERAL, 2019
LUKA REJEC, COVER BY LUKA REJEC

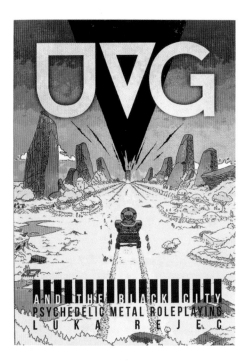

UVG AND THE BLACK CITY, REVISED EDITION, WIZARDTHIEFFIGHTER STUDIO AND EXALTED FUNERAL, 2021
LUKA REJEC, COVER BY LUKA REJEC

make *Gamma World* a bit cooler to me. His full response: "That is a very strange question. No."

Ward's response makes sense! There are some similarities between the early punk scene and the RPG scene, tied mostly to the unpretentious DIY ethos they both shared. Despite that, the philosophical crossover is rather limited. When Ward was working on *Deities & Demigods* in 1979, he was married, had three kids, and a day job teaching English in a Wisconsin town with a population of about 5,000. There is nothing countercultural about any of that. But, the early industry was full of folks whose backgrounds were like Ward's: White, middle class, Midwestern; their lives were portraits of small-town America, and they just happened to have nerdier than usual hobbies. In retrospect, it is probably far more likely that members of Devo played *Gamma World* than Devo's bizarro art punk influencing the RPG.

It's easy to lose sight of that fact, especially since I've observed, over the decades, that countercultures, anti-authoritarians, and general weirdos have flocked to RPGs in large numbers, often

growing up with them. The shift is visible in designers who came to define the later '80s and early '90s—subculture music and its trappings are obviously important to the people who made games like *Shadowrun*, *Nightlife*, *Kult*, *Underground*, and *Vampire: The Masquerade*.

The growing mutual interest between RPGs and musical subcultures produced some interesting collaborations. Games Workshop famously allowed the band Bolt Thrower to use the cover art to *Warhammer 40,000: Rogue Trader* (1987) on their 1989 album *Realm of Chaos* (that title itself is a reference to a *Warhammer* sourcebook, and the band's name is the same as an in-game siege engine), inadvertently making grindcore the unofficial soundtrack of the game. In 2000, White Wolf released a compilation album called *Music from the Succubus Club*, with bands from the goth scene, like Bella Morte and Mission U.K., contributing theme songs for each of *The Masquerade*'s vampire clans—Paralysed Age's theme for the Tzimisce, "Bloodsucker 2000," captures the strange mix of silliness and assured nonchalance that characterized that particular moment.

In recent years, music has more directly inspired some RPGs (and it is no longer limited to rock subcultures—as of this writing, two RPGs, *Boy Problems*, 2019, and *Black Heart*, 2019, draw from the works of pop chanteuse Carly Rae Jepsen). *Mörk Borg* clearly embraces the aesthetics of extreme metal, and the influences of the zine-based *Glam Metal Monster Hunter* (2020) are right there in the name. A Kickstarter recently ran for an RPG based on *The Real Thing* (1989) by Faith No More, with input from the band. *Ultraviolet Grasslands and the Black City*, meanwhile, is subtitled "Psychedelic Metal Roleplaying" and opens with a quote from "Burnin' for You," by Blue Öyster Cult. Paging through the book is like stepping into Arik Roper's painting for the re-issue of Sleep's classic album

Dopesmoker (1996 originally, 2012 for the reissue), which depicts a caravan of sci-fi nomads trekking through a *Dune*-like desert. This RPG's got riffs.

Ultraviolet Grasslands is a road trip game, and players travel a surreal landscape in weathered caravans and strange machines. The book is a gazetteer of settlements, environments, and mysterious locations arranged between the Violet City in the east and the mysterious Black City in the far west (what players will find there, if they make it, is, well, dangerously transcendent). Plenty of factions, all with their own strange wants and agendas, populate the world, as well.

While the book is arranged in a way that implies ceaseless forward motion, players aren't required to make the Black City their ultimate destination. There are plenty of adventures to be had going back and forth along the merchant routes and by becoming embroiled in local disputes.

Organizationally, *Ultraviolet Grasslands* and *Hot Springs Island* are quite similar. Care is taken to present information clearly, so it can be used and applied easily. The many random tables add character. What happens when characters party in an unfamiliar city? What unlucky event befalls them in the Forest of Meat? The dice hold the answers. Unlike *Hot Springs*, though, this is not a powder keg set to explode. There are adventures to be had, sure, but they emerge from the interaction between the portrayal of the landscape and the decisions of the players, rather than a choreographed module-style structure. *UVG* aligns with the experience of real-world travel—players see cool things, meet interesting people, and sometimes, something wild happens.

Much of this awe comes out of Luka Rejec's enigmatic landscapes. The strange color combinations and surreal features—

monolithic hands, biomechanical tumor trees, disorienting elements of Frank Lloyd Wright architecture, sci-fi pyramids, Bronze Age caravans, American-style RVs—invite and entice the traveler. Yes, danger probably lurks, but beauty also abounds—poke around, plumb the mysteries, breathe that purple air.

As a travelogue, *Ultraviolet Grasslands* makes for an excellent example of a pointcrawl, a modern variant of the old school hexcrawl. They're both ways of presenting players with an open wilderness sandbox, but they have different priorities. Hexes feel open and encourage hard, step-by-step exploration, the sort characterized by swinging machetes. Pointcrawls function under the assumption that roads or paths exist and that, in following them, nothing terribly interesting happens as a matter of course. Instead, it's what the paths link—the points—that are interesting.

Pointcrawls do away with much of the nitty gritty forward movement of hexcrawls. While there is always the chance of a random encounter, players don't need to worry about hauling equipment and rations, or where to camp or how to ford a river. The focus is on the destinations. With hexcrawls—where a hex can just as often contain empty wilderness as it does an adventure site—the exploration *is* the destination, filling the blank hex with the icon for the dominant terrain is the reward. So, in a way, hexcrawls are about space, while pointcrawls are more interested in time, or at least traversal.

Ultraviolet Grasslands comes packed with a light, flexible system called SEACAT (named for the six attributes: Strength, Endurance, Agility, Charisma, Aura, and Thought). Like other contemporary systems, it feels like a synthesis of both old and new notions arranged in a fresh configuration. The campaign itself is mostly system agnostic—creatures and people that characters encounter are given a level and a single word description (lazy, feral, among others) that, in most cases, is enough to map them to the GM's *D&D* hack or clone of choice. The few systems from SEACAT that are integral to *UVG*'s psychedelic road trip are easy to bolt on to other existing game systems. One of these is the concept of Hakaba (a sort of intertwining in the individual of body, soul, and personality) that supports some of *UVG*'s more existential elements.

For the most part, the system doesn't really matter when playing *UVG*. The journey is the destination, the forward motion is the thing, and the *soundtrack*—the discovery of mind-altering vistas deserves a sick mix rumbling in the background.

Electric Bastionland (2020)

The first curious thing about *Electric Bastionland* is that, despite the size of the hardcover rulebook (333 pages), it is a game devoted to aggressive minimalism. I've often wondered how little system a game can have while still functioning like a traditional RPG, and I might have my answer here. The entirety of the rules, a restatement of McDowall's earlier *Into the Odd* (2015), takes up two pages with another two devoted to character creation; together, this ties the page count of the equipment list. Peering at these scant rules long enough, I can see the basic shape of *Dungeons & Dragons* (Strength, Dexterity, Charisma, saving throws), but it's stripped to the bone and practically unrecognizable. Calling this a hack seems slanderous.

The system is largely beside the point. The primary function of the rules is to provide just enough tooth for the world to stick to while the players interface with it, and no more. The world is the focus, which leads to the second curious thing about *Electric Bastionland*: Everything else.

As with many other RPGs, players take the role of treasure hunters. Unlike most other RPGs, no one in Bastion actually wants to be a treasure hunter. A player's character would not be one if not for the fickle hand of fate and the nefarious debt they've accrued, which is shared by the entire party, giving the group a common purpose and an implied common past in one fell swoop.

In this way, the character isn't defined by who they *are*, but rather by who they *used to be*. Thus, instead of character classes, *Electric Bastionland* has Failed Careers—lots of them—the majority of the book is devoted to them. They run the gamut from mundane (Bartender) to strange (Cryptohistorian) to colorful (Pie Smuggler) and are united in the fact that none offer a typical RPG experience.

Comparisons to *Troika!* are unavoidable, but the approach here is slightly less intentionally bizarre and a bit more fleshed out. Each career has starting equipment and two tables, one keyed to the character's hit points, the other to their starting money. Taken all together, they give clues about a character and their past. For example, every Corpse Collector gets an axe and a wheelbarrow (which probably tells more about the job than a player may ever have wanted to know).

If a Corpse Collector starts with two bucks, the answer to the question, "What is the last thing you found on a corpse?" is "A crawling hand that follows basic instructions with something of a bad atti-

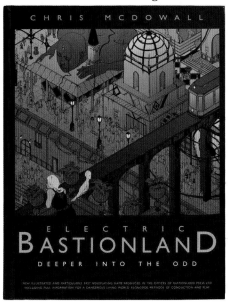

ELECTRIC BASTIONLAND, BASTIONLAND PRESS, 2020
CHRIS MCDOWALL, COVER BY ALEC SORENSEN

tude." The second table asks, "What was your job on the side?" If a player's Corpse Collector has six hit points, they were a tile fixer and get to add a tub of grout to their inventory. Surely that will come in handy?

All of these odd questions and answers work to imply the world at every turn. For the players, their careers paint a thin but vivid slice of existence in the city. For the GM, all of the careers that aren't in play form a reservoir of inspiration, plot hooks, and embellishments for the world.

The art, by Alec Sorensen, serves a similar purpose. The illustrations never show too much that is concrete, but taken together, it's impossible not to piece together a picture of the place—a little Art Deco, a little Art Nouveau, a little Victorian, a little psychedelic, and a lot dangerous. The only color in the book is yellow, but rather than brightness and sun, it saturates everything with a sense of noxious decadence.

When it comes down to it, the city of Bastion is the main character of the game. The player characters are tools used to explore the city, to define it, to tease out its mysteries, and to goad it into violence. Poke and prod, and see what happens. Then, they brace themselves to find the city utterly changed the next time they play—nothing in Bastion is permanent, and what lurks behind the next corner is never expected.

The first maxim of the game (one of many, laid out in clear bullet points) is that the world has no maps. This is as true for the GM as it is the players. Random tables abound, conjuring details that are relevant only for the moment in which they are rolled before rapidly decaying into inaccuracy as they are overwritten by new information. The charts are there to inspire—both the GM and the players—to summon a new Bastion into existence during every session, one defined by chance and fancy. As the book says, "This is a world discovered at the table, not inside a book."

Necronautilus (2020)

For years, Adam Vass has been churning out non-traditional and experimental RPGs on a near-monthly basis. Books, zines, postcards, story maps, newspaper broadsheets, sealed envelopes with secret instructions—no form is too strange or too small. *Necronautilus* is World Champ Game Co.'s wildest ride yet. It stands at the edge of something: An abyss? A frontier? An expanse of limitless potential? An unknown future? It's difficult to know for sure.

Like *Spelljammer* with a doom metal soundtrack, in *Necronautilus*, players take the role of sentient clouds of poison gas and soul stuff, exploring a dimension in which everything that ever died now resides, from bugs to dinosaurs to people to stars. These clouds travel the dead yet paradoxically living galaxy in a nautilus ship, enforcing the will of Death, who empowers them. Yet, they also seek answers about their own lost history— they were something else once, alive, autonomous, with hopes and desires. What happened? The only thing they remember is the reason they became an agent of Death.

The very light system is based on Words of Power—every character starts with three and writes them, appropriately, in the eye socket of the skull on the character sheet. Characters can collect up to nine additional, unused words; they're stored in the other eye socket and can be used to upgrade the ship or by the GM in the creation of planets to explore.

The beginning value of a Word of Power is six, and it can be invoked by rolling under that value with two 6-sided dice. With a success, the power manifests in the way the player narrates—it can be as specific or as abstract an application of the word as the player desires. Thus, "Fire" can start one, burn the flesh, inflame the heart, discharge a gun, or manifest four building-sized letters; so long as there is some connection between

NECRONAUTILUS, WORLD CHAMP GAME CO., 2020
ADAM VASS, COVER BY SHEL KHAN

the Word and the effect, no matter how tenuous, it happens.

Through its use, the Word is exhausted and removed from the sheet, but the player may then take a word from their collection and turn it into a Memory. Memories can be used in a similar way to a Word of Power—to give the character Life. Accumulate 30 points of Life and a player's character will be restored to a semblance of it—and then, in the inverse of most RPGs, removed from the game.

Rolling over the Word's value results in no manifestation of power. The word then changes—affixes, letters, or whole words are added to it, making it more specific and less versatile—but its value increases by one—making it more effective. Rolling the exact same number as the value overcharges the Word, the GM gets to narrate the effect, and the word fractures. The player then removes letters, making two words, a new Word of Power and a new Word for the Collection.

Agents go from planet to planet, speaking, learning, and collecting words, resolving missions, and tending to their ship. All of that—planets, inhabitants, and missions are generated using random tables and words from the characters' collections.

The Words are the heart of the game. They don't have to be spelled or pronounced correctly to work. The player using the word gets to say what's right or wrong about it, and define its meaning. A bit like *Dialect*, *Necronautilus* scratches at the way players communicate and the slippery, dynamic nature of meaning—for words and for people, too; after all, the Death Agents are searching for their personal meanings, too. And these games, they're just words, too—ever-mutating, shifting from person to person and table to table, spoken into the world for the first time, every time, to form a new story, over and over again.

Zines of Note

Though part of tabletop roleplaying from the very beginning, the definition of what makes a zine remains nebulous, although the original *Dungeons & Dragons* booklets seem to fit. Zines continued to percolate throughout the 2010s, and Kickstarter's annual Zine Quest promotion, begun in 2019, cemented RPG zines as the preeminent format for delivering a dizzying and vibrant variety to the hobby. When Kickstarter didn't hold a Zine Quest in February of 2022, as expected, independent designers started Zine Month (ZiMo) to promote projects while also experimenting with different crowdfunding platforms.

Zines are a showcase for artists and a proving ground for bizarre mechanics or off-beat concepts. The astonishing success rate of Kickstarter's Zine Quest campaigns has proven that no topic is too niche—there's an audience for everything, no matter how unexpected. It's the preconceptions of the larger publishers that are too narrow. RPGs don't need to be encased in giant hardcovers, thereby making it cheaper and easier for players to experiment with their roleplay.

Put simply: Zines are the brave new future of RPGs.

Goblinville Gazette (2019) is a punchy and fast, rules-light RPG in four volumes that puts players in control of a party of weirdo goblins. In most other fantasy games, goblins are usually cannon fodder, deployed to make players feel powerful, but *Goblinville* explores their quirky lives and society. Players venture out nearby, bringing back treasure and resources in order to improve the town of Goblinville. The stakes are both high and humorous, with a focus on managing inventory, light, and health, which reminds me of the grueling survival RPG *Torchbearer* (2013). It's more forgiving though—failure in *Goblinville* is often more fun, and funnier, than success.

There are numerous little intriguing mechanics. Combat is particularly neat: There are no hit points. Rather, goblins have a set of conditions they check off as they are injured while monsters have a number of moves (bite, claw, energy ray)

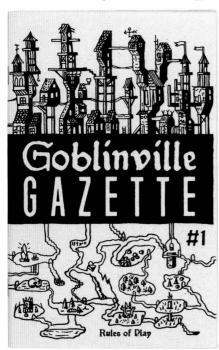

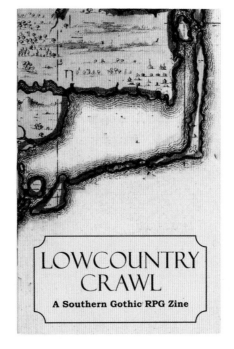

LOWCOUNTRY CRAWL, LAWFUL NEUTRAL AND TECHNICAL GRIMOIRE, 2019
JOHN GREGORY

that are removed by successful attacks. When a goblin checks off all of their conditions, they're dead; when a monster's moves are all removed, the same is true.

Expeditions are all in service of town building; items and treasure are used to construct and upgrade specialty buildings in town. Want tougher goblins? Build a fighting pit, and so on. The town building is a bit reminiscent of the turf mechanics of *Blades in the Dark*. *Goblinville* adds a humorous wrinkle: Any time the characters return to town, there is a chance that the townie goblins have mucked up something that players will need to fix.

It's all entirely delightful and easy to pick up and play. With clear goals and rewards built right in, thanks to the quirky character generation and the town building mechanic, it's challenging without being frustrating, funny, and surprising. After reading, players might think twice about smearing a party of goblins in their other games.

GOBLINVILLE GAZETTE #1: RULES OF PLAY, NARRATIVE DYNAMICS, 2019
MICHAEL DUNN-O'CONNOR AND ERIC SWANSON. COVER BY ERIC SWANSON

Lowcountry Crawl (2019), the first in a series, has a unique mission. 20 percent of the proceeds from sales go to the Penn Center, an organization dedicated to South Carolina's Gullah cultural heritage.

The zine seeks to fictionalize the coastal Lowcountry and Sea Islands of South Carolina, using *D&D* and OSR campaigns as means of exploring the region's nineteenth century folklore. The first issue presents a series of barrier islands, full of pirates, giant crabs, fish men, a wizard's tower situated in a lighthouse, and a mysterious fellow known as the Low Tide Merchant, who always has what characters want, though not necessarily at a price they're willing to pay.

There are charts for rolling up new, random islands, and there are new monsters, including the delightful Tommy Rawbones, a decapitated undead corpse in search of his head. Everything described holds on to a certain southern vibe. There's magic chewing tobacco, colonels, and forts. But, it is surprisingly easy to picture a group of standard fantasy adventurers roaming these dunes. This sort of aesthetic elasticity appeals in the same way as the mix of sci-fi and fantasy in *Expedition to the Barrier Peaks*.

According to a marketing line for the Fifth Edition *D&D* campaign book, *Baldur's Gate: Descent into Avernus* (2019), "It's like *Mad Max: Fury Road* in hell." Then the book came out, and the *Road Warrior* aspect seemed small and like an afterthought. Disappointed? Never fear, there's a zine that'll fix that.

Inferno Road (2018) is the real deal. By Wayne Snyder and Doug Kovacs, it's a stand-alone module for *Dungeon Crawl Classics*. Characters start as grubs in hell, with an infernal patron and an infinite hunger for souls. They've been dropped onto the Inferno Road to capture Satan's doom wagon and steal his wives. Each character has two past lives that they can use to manifest special, related items. They can also eat souls to gain physical upgrades and new forms (but if they're killed, a character will find themself as a sub-grub, which is an edible soul for other devils, including fellow players). Players need to get out there, burn rubber, and murder their way to glory!

Snyder and Kovacs cram all sorts of details in here. The different devil forms are gross and scary, and, since they are determined using a spinner, the random combinations result in some interesting party compositions. There are plenty of random charts, too—for past lives, icky physical upgrades, hell prince generation, mini bosses, and, perhaps most importantly, vehicle generation.

These vehicles are crazy death machines roaring through hell (and some devil forms have built-in wheels, adding to the gnarl). The main point of the game is to crash through this infernal destruction derby forever. Players might not realize it at first, because of all the mayhem, but they can't ever catch the doom wagon. They're just trapped in an endless cycle of carnage and destruction—after all, hell is *supposed* to be a punishment.

Nate Treme makes small TTRPG zines. They are adorable, every single one of them. The first one I saw, *Temple of the Bat Serpent*, is a dungeon laid out on a single sheet of paper, folded in thirds. Something about the cover design just spoke to me, so I joined his Patreon—the Highland Paranormal Society—and have been receiving similar little dungeons and adventures in the mail every month or so since; I have a membership card and everything. This sort of arrangement—supporting a designer directly and receiving bespoke RPG items in return—was unimaginable even five years ago, but it is a model that is increasingly funding independent creators.

The covers for *The Lost Isle* (2019), *The Moldy Unicorn* (2019), and *The Eternal Caverns of Urk* (2019) have such an appealing look, like little gemstone confections, showcasing a little bit of the old school forbidden aura, a little bit of psychedelia, and a whole lot of quirk. I see them, and I want to pick them up and flip through them again—proof that good visual design is priceless.

THE LOST ISLE, HIGHLAND PARANORMAL SOCIETY, 2019
NATE TREME, COVER BY NATE TREME

All of Treme's work is small, modular, and handy to have around to stick into an ongoing game (and thanks to the anthology *Haunted Almanac*, published by Games Omnivorous in 2021, now largely collected under one hardcover). Most of them marry cuteness with a distinct sense of menace. Players will likely have a good laugh as they're suffering horrible fates.

RPG zines are important because they afford creators the opportunity to create products that might not fit anywhere else. Do players need a whole book on horrible bugs for RPG games? I mean, maybe, but that is going to be a niche publication. But a zine? That's cheaper, shorter, and doesn't overstay its welcome (*Fungi of the Far Realms* is a peculiar and delightful outlier here). Those put out by Games Omnivorous are sure to be lovingly designed and printed. The company has a devotion to the craft of chapbook-making, and the results feel good, look gorgeous, and are a total aesthetic treat.

TEMPLE OF THE BAT SERPENT, HIGHLAND PARANORMAL SOCIETY, 2019
NATE TREME

THE INSECTIARY, GAMES OMNIVOROUS, 2020
ANDRE NOVOA AND PIPO KIMKIDUK, COVER BY PIPO KIMKIDUK

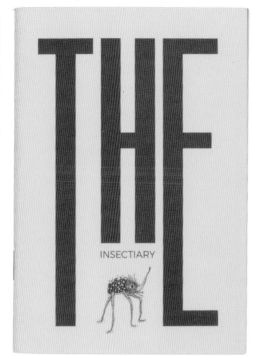

The Insectiary (2020) is a system agnostic collection of nasty bugs. Andre Novoa writes the words, and Pipo Kimkiduk does the ghastly (in a good way) illustrations. The whole zine is done in eye-smacking red and yellow. Every illustration has a little magnifying glass icon and a percentage, letting readers know how small the bugs are while all of the words explain how awful the bugs are. It's a perfect zine, delivering exactly what it promises in 40 pages then letting a reader get on with their day.

A Visitor's Guide to the Rainy City (2020) is pure setting; there are no rules, no scores, just lots of evocative detail on the titular city where it does, indeed, rain every day, year-round. This unrelenting weather has required the residents to adapt in unusual ways—the rain only lightens up enough to allow the burning of fires for part of the year, so there are many surprising culinary adaptations, for instance—alchemical boiling salts are a

must. Instead of rats, the vermin of choice are oozes and slimes. There are also way more umbrellas than the usual fantasy RPG setting. In fact, the entire culture of the city is defined by dampness and (depending on a character's level of wealth) its avoidance. Oh, and there are pirates who live on a floating island made of shipwrecks that have been bound together.

It could be called whimsical, for lack of a better word—it gets into a neighborhood similar to Neil Gaiman's or Susanna Clarke's. There are light elements of steampunk, too. But it never becomes cloying or overwhelming. Much of the appeal comes from Bill Spytma's art, which somehow channels the aesthetics of both medieval woodcuts and Victorian engravings, simultaneously.

It strikes a balance similar to *Planescape*. This resonance is appropriate, because the Rainy City seems to be at the center of all universes, and those other universes have started to collapse in on themselves. As a result of this off-stage cataclysm, refugees from other worlds are washing up by the shipload, making a strange world even more bizarre, which is saying something considering there are giant newt-drawn carriages driven by intelligent octopuses, and fish can survive out of the water for a quarter of the year.

All told, it is an impressive feat of world building, in which many of the details of the world are rendered in inference and implication, rather than tediously spelled out. This approach results in multiple imagination-stoking ideas on every page.

There are so many more zines: Ben Laurence's gorgeous *Through Ultan's Door* series, inspired by the fiction of Clark Ashton Smith, the Day-Glo attitude of *Mystic Punks*, the surreal metaphysics of

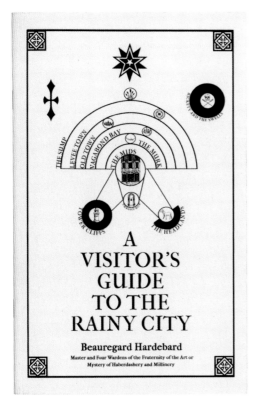

A VISITOR'S GUIDE TO THE RAINY CITY, SUPERHERO NECROMANCER PRESS, 2020
RICH FOREST, COVER BY ANDREW DEVENNEY

Icy City, the seemingly endless *Troika!* zines, and the player-made zines fostered by both *Mothership* and *Mörk Borg*. The zine scene grows stranger and more exciting as each month passes, with new ideas expanding the definition of what RPGs can be while charting a new future along a myriad of different radii.

The original *D&D* was three zines in a box. The first edition of *Tunnels & Trolls* from 1975 was a stack of photocopied, hand-stapled pages. That same year, Lee Gold founded *Alarums and Excursions*, an amateur press association, and acting as the central mailer, sends out a monthly collection of zines to subscribers. The form has been with the hobby since the beginning.

That's also true of the content. Much of the initial writing in *Alarums and Excursions* was dedicated to tweaking or modifying *Dungeons & Dragons*, before it gave way to experimentation in completely new and different systems. There is a long tradition of players publishing their own house rules and mechanical musings any way they could—many of the games in this book started as a "what-if," laid out in the pages of *Alarums and Excursions*. Every designer starts out as a player and, for many, their first form of expression is through zines or other forms of amateur publishing.

In this way, the modern zine revolution doesn't represent a new trail being blazed. Rather, it represents a rediscovery of the heart and soul of the hobby, reborn in new and ever stranger permutations.

Acknowledgments

As I mentioned in the introduction, my mom, Patricia Horvath, was apprehensive about *D&D* in the mid '80s. Mom always believed that more books are never a bad thing, though, and since RPGs were books, that impulse eventually (thankfully) won out. Decades of rewarding play have followed, and for that I am grateful. "More books" is also central to the thanks I give to my wife, Daisy DeCoster, who never raises an eyebrow at all of the packages I receive in the mail and who is always enthusiastically supportive of the games I play, even when I make the dubious claim that it is "work." She's pretty good at playing them, too, even if she claims otherwise. Her spinster librarian Hyacinth somehow managed to survive all the way through our *Masks of Nyarlathotep* campaign, though towards the end she was more often lugging a can of kerosene around rather than a stack of books. And then there is my son, Jeremiah, who, as of this writing, is almost five years old and has told me on multiple occasions, "I want to play all your games, Dad, but when I am a little bit taller." I don't think he understands the scale of what he's getting himself into, but I'm more than willing to take him up on that anyway.

This book wouldn't exist if not for Ed Park. I always thought the posts on the @VintageRPG Instagram feed were notes for *something*, but Ed's gentle cheerleading led me to figure out what that was. Sometimes the internet throws together strangers with shared interests and magic happens. Speaking of magic, most of it that manifests in The Vintage RPG Podcast is thanks to my co-host, John McGuire, who practically dragged me to the microphone to get it started. The podcast has been key in building an audience for this book and also for me literally talking through my thinking about many of the games that appear within it. It's also fun! Thanks for twisting my arm on that, Hambone.

An equal share of thanks is owed to Orrin Grey, whose line editing assured me that the book made sense and was at least modestly informative and entertaining; to Joe DeSimone, who checked all the facts to make sure they were, indeed, correct; to Alexander Saify, whose sensitivity read helped thread some of the RPG world's thornier issues; to Jamie Springer for her exhaustive copy editing, which polished my rough prose into a blinding gleam; and to Noah Springer at MIT Press for buying the book and having faith in it beyond any practical measure. Derek Kinsman's layout and Kyle Patterson's illustrations tie the whole thing up with a nice bow and honestly make something that I am painfully familiar with look new and exciting to my jaded eyes.

Sara Clemens, Ed Coleman, David Shimomura, Levi Rubeck, Ian Gonzales, Yussef Cole, Zac Bir, and Skull Dixon all deserve a round of applause for reading this book in various stages of completion, offering advice and generally keeping the writing on course and approachable. Jess Carrier and the folks at Noble Knight

Games were crucial in helping me get my hands on many of the products covered in here. Many thanks to all of the people who answered my questions along the way, as well. Most of them are noted in the text, but several providing context without being quoted. So, a hearty thanks to Colin Marco, who helped me understand the inner working of the RPGA's Living campaign worlds, and to Casey W. Christofferson, who provided insight into the early days of the Old School Revival. Chaosium's president, Rick Meints clarified some of Greg Stafford's thinking. Lawrence Schick, Chaosium's executive editor James Lowder, and Steve Jackson of Steve Jackson Games were also kind enough to confirm factoids in passing conversation. Special thanks to Simón D. Sotelo, who dug up amazing sources for the *Star Trek* chapter.

Thank you to all the folks who follow along daily on the @VintageRPG Instagram account, the generous gaggle who contribute to the Patreon, the people who make the Vintage RPG Discord such a pleasant place to hang around, and, of course, to *you*, for reading this book.

A number of references were critical in the writing of this book. First among them is Shannon Appelcline's four-volume history, *Designers & Dragons* (Evil Hat Production, 2014). Those books were an invaluable resource for getting my facts straight and should be the first stop for anyone desiring to read about the history of the RPG hobby. Another book that was always close at hand was Lawrence Schick's *Heroic Worlds* (Prometheus Books, 1991), a truly astounding and acerbic catalog of RPG products from their inception through the book's publication date. *Defining a Galaxy* (Rogue Genius Games, 2018) by Bill Slavicsek and the James Lowder-edited duology *Hobby Games: The 100 Best* (Green Ronin Publishing, 2007) and *Family Games: The 100 Best* (Green Ronin Publishing, 2010) were broadly informative, not just on specific games, but also in how designers think about them. *One Potato, Two Potato: The Folklore of American Children* (W. W. Norton & Company, 1976) is foundational to a lot of my thinking about how play develops, evolves, and disseminates.

Rounding out the reference shelf are *Fantasy Role Playing Games* by J. Eric Holmes (Hippocrene Books, 1981), *Board Games in 100 Moves* by Ian Livingstone and James Wallis (DK Publishing, 2019), and *Playing at the World* by Jon Peterson (Unreason Press, 2012). Many online resources made research, particularly of fine details, much easier. *RPG.net*, Wayne's Books (*waynesbooks.com*), and The Acaeum (*acaeum.com*) are all in my bookmarks. Also of periodic help were The Alexandrian (*thealexandrian.net*) and Grognardia (*grognardia.blogspot.net*).

My ongoing personal education on inclusion and representation has been a long one and is most often characterized by listening and gleaning insights, here and there, over many years, so it is difficult to compile an exhaustive list of works that might have contributed to my thinking. That said, two essays merit explicit mentioning. The first is "How *Dungeons & Dragons* Appropriated the Orient," by Aaron Trammell (*analoggamestudies.org/2016/01/how-dungeons-dragons-appropriated-the-orient/*), which greatly informed my chapter on *Oriental Adventures*. The second is "Orcs, Britons and the Martial Race Myth," by James Mendez Hodes (multiple parts, found on *jamesmendezhodes.com*), from which I derive many of the specifics of my thinking around regarding RPGs, colonialism, and race. Both essays, specifically, as well as Hodes's blog and the Analog Game Studies site, generally, should be considered required reading for those of us who hope to see an ever more diverse and equitable future for tabletop roleplaying games.

Glossary

Ability: Something unusual that a player's character can do, like cast spells, turn into a werewolf, or fly. It differs from skills, which are usually prosaic.

Adventure: A unit of play. Published adventures (often called adventure modules or scenarios) generally consist of a self-contained story that can be played in one or more sessions.

Adventure Seed: A brief, evocative sentence or two, meant to inspire a GM to create an entire adventure. Plant them and they grow into stories! Random tables are often arranged to generate adventure seeds.

Attributes: Often improperly called statistics or stats, these are generally a numerical representation of a character's fundamental physical and mental traits. The number of character attributes often (but not always) correlates to the game's overall complexity. *Dungeons & Dragons* has six: Strength, Dexterity, Constitution, Intelligence, Wisdom, and Charisma.

Campaign: An ongoing series of adventures. If an individual adventure is an episode of a TV show, then a campaign is the show's entire run.

Campaign World: The persistent setting of a campaign. It could be utterly fantastic, or it might not differ much from our world. Either way, it usually contains much lore.

Canon: a term derived from Biblical studies, denoting material that is considered part of the scripture, as opposed to non-canonical Apocrypha. In fiction, it is an often ambiguous, mercurial indication that material is official, considered part of the current storytelling continuity or otherwise acknowledged by the creators. Changes to canon are often met with strong reactions from fans.

Check: Also referred to as a Test. Any action with an uncertain result where dice are used to determine the outcome.

Chit: A small cardboard square placed on a play map to indicate something existing in the game environment: A character, a unit of troops, a hazard. Common in wargames, RPGs tend to use paper standees or three-dimensional miniatures instead.

Class: An abstraction of trade, training, and combat role, all of which are defined loosely for a character at inception. Class-based characters of a type progress predictably, unlocking the same abilities at the same levels as they accumulate experience. Thus, all Tightrope Walkers receive access to Seemingly Levitate when they reach Level Three.

Crunch: A synonym for the mechanics of a game, which become crunchier as they increase in complexity. It's the concrete, almost tactile opposite of fluff.

Dice Nomenclature: A common set of dice is made up of the Platonic solids (4-, 6-, 8-, 12-, and 20-sides) and two 10-sided dice (rolled together, they produce a percentile result). RPG books generally indicate the number of dice to be rolled, then a "D," then the value of the die, then any modifiers. Thus, 2D6+2 indicates that the player should roll two 6-sided dice and add two to the sum.

Experience Points (XP): A numerical abstraction of personal growth. In many games, experience points are accumulated primarily through successful combat encounters. Once a certain amount is attained, new skills and abilities are unlocked.

Fluff: A catch-all term for everything in a game that doesn't have a mechanical impact—the art, the vibes, the lore, the stories, the colorful flavor quotes. Fluff is the mystery that makes a player want to explore a world and play the game. It is the opposite of crunch.

Generic: A generic system is one that has no mechanics tying it to a specific style or genre, thus allowing it to be used to run any style or genre. Despite some game design theory hair-splitting, it is essentially the same as a universal system.

Game Master (GM): The person who runs the game. They control the world, the non-player characters, and the fickle winds of chance. They guide players through the stories. The intended mien of a GM has changed much over the years, ranging from adversarial to collaborative. Indie games often don't include a GM at all.

Hit Locations: Games concerned with realistic depictions of combat usually divide a body up into sections that can be damaged separately. A basic hit location scheme is the limbs, torso, and head—the idea being that you can destroy an arm and still survive—maybe. The more complicated the system, the more hit locations.

Hit Points (HP): The numerical representation of health, depleted by damage, which can be further complimented by a hit location system. The basic idea of health-as-resource isn't limited to physical measures. Sanity systems often use depleting point pools, and some games have experimented with managing social standing ("cool") with similar systems.

Indie Game: As with indie music, it is a combination of a business model (one independent of established game publishers) and an aesthetic consciously outside the mainstream. The indie RPG movement coalesced around the online message board, The Forge, from 1999 to 2001, and initially produced designs focused on storytelling, specificity of theme, and difficult moral choices.

Level: One of the most overworked words in RPGs. Level can refer to a character's accumulated experience, the power of a spell, or the various floors of a dungeon.

Lines: As a safety tool, players determine their lines before play, usually in a Session Zero, they're usually accompanied by veils. They represent sensitive subject matter the player doesn't want to see appear in the game.

Lore: Deep setting information, usually with a historical or philosophical bent, that is often fun, even compulsive to read, while also being of dubious usefulness in play. Some folks buy RPG books primarily to learn the lore, and lore is one of the key draws for many roleplaying videogames.

Metaplot: An overarching narrative continuity for a game world (or comic book multiverse or cinematic universe) advanced through new products. For example, a setting book that describes a kingdom being followed by a series of adventure modules that result in its fall.

Murder Hobo: A term coined in 2007 to describe a style of play, usually in *D&D*, in which the play loop centers on rootless wanderers killing everything in their path in order to secure ever more loot. There is a precedence for this behavior in much of the fantasy fiction that precedes RPGs.

Non-Player Character (NPC): Any character controlled by the GM, from inconsequential passersby to supporting cast to the villains of the piece.

Old School: A nebulous "good old days" period of gaming, usually defined as starting in 1974 and ending by 1989. The term has, in the context of the Old School Revival (OSR), increasingly become synonymous with older versions of *D&D* and their conventions.

Player: While everyone at the table is technically a player, the term is reserved for folks who are running individual characters. They play, while the GM administrates, adjudicates, or narrates.

Race: As in many examples of fantasy and science fiction, a spurious, pseudoscientific biological encoding of culture, community, and ancestry. Race in RPGs usually comes with specific, universal bonuses and penalties for character attributes. It is sometimes interchangeable with Class. As a mechanical concept, it is, thankfully, falling out of favor.

Rails: Like an amusement park ride, when a game is on rails, the action is largely pre-ordained. As this style of play minimizes player agency and choice, it is usually seen as a negative. It is the opposite of a sandbox.

Retroclone: A restatement or reworking of an older set of RPG rules, for use by modern players and made possible by the fact that game mechanics can not be copyrighted (though the descriptions of how they work can). Retroclones made way for the Old School Revival, though they often feature tweaks that bring clunky older systems into line with modern conventions of play.

Rule Weight: A theoretical gauge ranging from light to heavy. Light games have a small number of systems, each of which takes care of many of the tasks, while heavy games have lots of systems that are often highly specialized. As with numerous other sorts of RPG taxonomies, this one is highly subjective.

Sandbox: An open-ended style of play in which there is little to no narrative structure and players drive the action through their choices. It is the opposite of a game that is "on rails."

Session Zero: The game session occurs before the game starts, in which everyone sets their expectations, makes characters, and defines safety tools, like lines and veils. It's a modern practice.

Skills: Actions characters can take. These are usually available, in some regard, to all characters. Some are natural, like climbing; others are learned, like languages. All can be enhanced through training. Skills are distinct from abilities, which are often supernatural and unique.

Storytelling Game: As the name implies, an RPG that favors narrative above all else. These sorts of games are often collaborative, lack a GM, and feature open-ended, improvisational mechanics.

Unified: A unified system uses the same underlying mechanic to resolve everything in the game.

Universal: A universal system is one that has no mechanics tying it to a specific style or genre, thus allowing it be used to run a game of any style or genre. Despite some game design theory hairsplitting, it is essentially the same as a generic system.

Veil: A safety tool—players determine their veils before play, usually in a Session Zero and usually accompanied by lines. veils represent subject matter that is acceptable for play so long as it isn't explicit.

Appendix A: The Games

The 1970s

Abrams, Stephen, and Jon Everson. *Cities.* San Diego, CA: Midkemia Press, 1979.

Arneson, Dave. *Dungeons & Dragons Supplement II: Blackmoor.* Lake Geneva, WI: Tactical Studies Rules, 1975.

Bledsaw, Bob. *Tegel Manor.* Decatur, IL: Judges Guild, 1977.

Bledsaw, Bob, and Bill Owen. *City State of the Invincible Overlord.* Decatur, IL: Judges Guild, 1976.

Carr, Mike. *B1: In Search of the Unknown.* Lake Geneva, WI: Tactical Studies Rules, 1978.

Gorey, Edward, and Larry Evans. *Gorey Games.* San Francisco, CA: Troubadour Press, 1979.

Gygax, Gary. *B2: The Keep on the Borderlands.* Lake Geneva, WI: Tactical Studies Rules, 1979.

———. *D1: Descent into the Depths of the Earth.* Lake Geneva, WI: Tactical Studies Rules, 1978.

———. *D2: Shrine of the Kuo-Toa.* Lake Geneva, WI: Tactical Studies Rules, 1978.

———. *D3: Vault of the Drow.* Lake Geneva, WI: Tactical Studies Rules, 1978.

———. *Dungeon Masters Guide.* Lake Geneva, WI: Tactical Studies Rules, 1979.

———. *G1: Steading of the Hill Giant Chief.* Lake Geneva, WI: Tactical Studies Rules, 1978.

———. *G2: Glacial Rift of the Frost Giant Jarl.* Lake Geneva, WI: Tactical Studies Rules, 1978.

———. *G3: Hall of the Fire Giant King.* Lake Geneva, WI: Tactical Studies Rules, 1978.

———. *Monster Manual.* Lake Geneva, WI: Tactical Studies Rules, 1977.

———. *Players Handbook.* Lake Geneva, WI: Tactical Studies Rules, 1978.

———. *S1: Tomb of Horrors.* Lake Geneva, WI: Tactical Studies Rules, 1978.

Gygax, Gary, and Brian Blume. *Supplement III: Eldritch Wizardry.* Lake Geneva, WI: Tactical Studies Rules, 1976.

Gygax, Gary, and Dave Arneson. *Dungeons & Dragons.* Lake Geneva, WI: Tactical Studies Rules, 1974.

Gygax, Gary, and Greg Irons. *The Official Advanced Dungeons & Dragons Coloring Album.* San Francisco, CA: Troubadour Press, 1979.

Hany, Daryl, and Frank Chadwick. *En Garde!* Normal, IL: Game Designers' Workshop, 1975.

Holmes, Eric J. *Dungeons & Dragons Basic Set.* Lake Geneva, WI: Tactical Studies Rules, 1977.

Hume, Paul, and Bob Charrette. *Bushido*. Jericho, NY: Fantasy Games Unlimited, 1979.

Jackson, Steve. *The Fantasy Trip: Melee*. Austin, TX: Metagaming Concepts, 1977.

———. *The Fantasy Trip: Wizard*. Austin, TX: Metagaming Concepts, 1978.

Jaquays, Jennell. *Dark Tower*. Decatur, IL: Judges Guild, 1979.

———. *The Caverns of Thracia*. Decatur, IL: Judges Guild, 1979.

Kerestan, Peter, and Judy Kerestan. *Palace of the Vampire Queen*. El Segundo, CA: 1976.

Kuntz, Robert J., and James M. Ward. *Gods, Demi-Gods & Heroes*. Lake Geneva, WI: Tactical Studies Rules, 1976.

Miller, Marc W. *Traveller*. Normal, IL: Game Designers' Workshop, 1977.

Owen, Bob, and Bob Bledsaw. *Wilderlands of High Fantasy*. Decatur, IL: Judges Guild, 1977.

Perrin, Steve. *Superworld*. Ann Arbor, MI: Chaosium, 1983.

Perrin, Steve, and Dyvers Hands. *Worlds of Wonder*. Ann Arbor, MI: Chaosium, 1982.

Perrin, Steve, and Greg Stafford. *Cults of Prax*. Ann Arbor, MI: Chaosium, 1979.

Perrin, Steve, and Ray Turney. *RuneQuest*. Ann Arbor, MI: Chaosium, 1978.

Pimper, Jeff, and Steve Perrin, editors. *All The Worlds' Monsters*. Ann Arbor, MI: Chaosium, 1977.

———. *All The Worlds' Monsters, Volume Two*. Ann Arbor, MI: Chaosium, 1979.

Simbalist, Edward E. *Arden (Chivalry & Sorcery)*. Jericho, NY: Fantasy Games Unlimited, 1979.

Simbalist, Edward E., and Wilf Backhaus. *Chivalry & Sorcery*. Jericho, NY: Fantasy Games Unlimited, 1977.

St. Andre, Ken. *Tunnels & Trolls*. Scottsdale, AZ: Flying Buffalo, Inc., 1975.

Stafford, Greg, and Dyvers Hands. *Cults of Terror*. Ann Arbor, MI: Chaosium, 1979.

Stafford, Greg, and Rudy Kraft. *Snakepipe Hollow*. Ann Arbor, MI: Chaosium, 1979.

Ward, James M. *Metamorphosis Alpha*. Lake Geneva, WI: Tactical Studies Rules, 1976.

Ward, James M., and Gary Jaquet. *Gamma World*. Lake Geneva, WI: Tactical Studies Rules, 1978.

Wiseman, Loren K. editor. *Journal of the Travellers' Aid Society*. Normal, IL: Game Designers' Workshop, 1979.

The 1980s

Acres, Mark, and Tom Moldvay. *SF2: Starspawn of Volturnus*. Lake Geneva, WI: Tactical Studies Rules, 1982.

Abrams, April. *The City of Carse*. San Diego, CA: Midkemia Press, 1980.

Allston, Aaron, Steven Peterson, and Michael Stackpole. *Justice, Inc*. San Mateo, CA: Hero Games, 1984.

Amthor, Terry K., and Pete Fenlon. *The Iron Wind*. Charlottesville, VA: Iron Crown Enterprises, 1980.

Amthor, Terry K., Coleman Charlton, Pete Fenlon, and Dyvers Hands. *Rolemaster*. Charlottesville, VA: Iron Crown Enterprises, 1982.

Baker, Stephen. *HeroQuest*. East Longmeadow, MA: Milton Bradley, 1989.

Boomgarden, Karen S. *City System*. Lake Geneva, WI: Tactical Studies Rules, 1988.

Breault, Mike, with Jon Pickens. *WG7: Castle Greyhawk*. Lake Geneva, WI: Tactical Studies Rules, 1988.

Campbell-Robson, Keri. *Hawkmoon*. Ann Arbor, MI: Chaosium, 1986.

Charrette, Bob. *Valley of the Mists*. Jericho, NY: Fantasy Games Unlimited, 1982.

Chick, Jack. *Dark Dungeons*. Ontario, CA: Chick Publications, 1984.

Charlton, Coleman. *Middle-Earth Role Playing*. Charlottesville, VA: Iron Crown Enterprises, 1984.

Charlton, Coleman, Kurt H. Fischer, and Pete Fenlon. *Arms Law*. Charlottesville, VA: Iron Crown Enterprises, 1980.

Charrette, Bob, Paul Hume, and Tom Dowd. *Shadowrun*. Chicago, IL: FASA Corporation, 1989.

Cook, David "Zeb." *Advanced Dungeons & Dragons Second Edition*. Lake Geneva, WI: Tactical Studies Rules, 1989.

———. *Bullwinkle and Rocky Roleplaying Party Game*. Lake Geneva, WI: Tactical Studies Rules, 1988.

———. *CB1: Conan Unchained!* Lake Geneva, WI: Tactical Studies Rules, 1984.

———. *Dungeons & Dragons Expert Set*. Lake Geneva, WI: Tactical Studies Rules, 1981.

———. *Dungeon Master Guide*. Lake Geneva, WI: Tactical Studies Rules, 1989.

———. *Time of the Dragon*. Lake Geneva, WI: Tactical Studies Rules, 1989.

Cook, David "Zeb," and Tom Moldvay. *X1: The Isle of Dread*. Lake Geneva, WI: Tactical Studies Rules, 1981.

Costikyan, Greg. *Toon: The Cartoon Roleplaying Game*. Austin, TX: Steve Jackson Games, 1984.

———. *Star Wars: The Roleplaying Game*. New York, NY: West End Games, 1987.

Crossby, N. Robin. *Hârn Regional Module*. Blaine, WA: Columbia Games, 1983.

———. *Hârnmaster*. Blaine, WA: Columbia Games, 1986.

Davis, Graeme, Jim Bambra, and Phil Gallagher. *Shadows Over Bögenhafen*. Nottingham, UK: Games Workshop, 1987.

Denning, Troy. *Galaxy Guide 4: Alien Races*. New York, NY: West End Games, 1989.

DiTillio, Larry, and Lynn Willis. *Masks of Nyarlathotep*. Ann Arbor, MI: Chaosium, 1985.

DiTillio, Larry, Kevin Freeman, Mark L. Gambler, and Arno Lipfert. *Demon Magic: The Second Stormbringer Companion*. Ann Arbor, MI: Chaosium, 1985.

Dowd, Tom. *Street Samurai Catalog*. Chicago, IL: FASA Corporation, 1989.

Dunnigan, James F. *Dallas: The Television Role-Playing Game*. New York, NY: Simulations Publications, Inc., 1980.

Dyvers Hands. *The Monstrous Compendium, Volume One*. Lake Geneva, WI: Tactical Studies Rules, 1989.

Eastland, Kim. *SFAC3: Zebulon's Guide to Frontier Space, Volume 1*. Lake Geneva, WI: Tactical Studies Rules, 1985.

Gascoigne, Marc, and Pete Tamlyn. *Dungeoneer*. London, UK: Puffin Books, 1989.

Gordon, Greg. *Q Manual: The Illustrated Guide to the World's Finest Armory*. New York, NY: Victory Games, 1983.

Greenwood, Ed. *Forgotten Realms Campaign Set*. Lake Geneva, WI: Tactical Studies Rules, 1987.

———. *Manual of the Planes*. Lake Geneva, WI: Tactical Studies Rules, 1987.

———. *Marvel Super Heroes Advanced Set*. Lake Geneva, WI: Tactical Studies Rules, 1986.

———. *Spelljammer*. Lake Geneva, WI: Tactical Studies Rules, 1989.

Grubb, Jeff, and Steve Winter. *Marvel Super Heroes*. Lake Geneva, WI: Tactical Studies Rules, 1984.

Gygax, Gary. *S3: Expedition to the Barrier Peaks*. Lake Geneva, WI: Tactical Studies Rules, 1980.

———. *Unearthed Arcana*. Lake Geneva, WI: Tactical Studies Rules, 1985.

———. *WG7: Castle Greyhawk*. Lake Geneva, WI: Tactical Studies Rules, 1988.

———. *The World of Greyhawk*. Lake Geneva, WI: Tactical Studies Rules, 1980.

Gygax, Gary, Francois Marcela-Froideval, and David "Zeb" Cook. *Oriental Adventures*. Lake Geneva, WI: Tactical Studies Rules, 1985.

Halliwell, Richard, Rick Priestly, Graeme Davis, Jim Bambra, and Phil Gallagher. *Warhammer Fantasy Roleplay*. Nottingham, UK: Games Workshop, 1986.

Hargrave, David A. *The Arduin Trilogy*. Concord, CA: Grimoire Games, 1981.

Hickman, Tracy. *DL1: Dragons of Despair*. Lake Geneva, WI: Tactical Studies Rules, 1984.

Hickman, Tracy, and Laura Hickman. *DL8: Dragons of War*. Tactical Studies Rules, 1985.

———. *I6: Ravenloft*. Lake Geneva, WI: Tactical Studies Rules, 1983.

———. *I10: Ravenloft II: The House on Gryphon Hill*. Lake Geneva, WI: Tactical Studies Rules, 1986.

Hickman, Tracy, and Michael Dobson. *DL4: Dragons of Desolation*. Lake Geneva, WI: Tactical Studies Rules, 1984.

Jackson, Steve. *Fighting Fantasy: The Introductory Role-Playing Game*. London, UK: Puffin Books, 1984.

———. *GURPS*. Austin, TX: Steve Jackson Games, 1986.

———. *In the Labyrinth*. Austin, TX: Metagaming Concepts, 1980.

———. *Steve Jackson's Man to Man*. Austin, TX: Steve Jackson Games, 1985.

———. *Tollenkar's Lair*. Austin, TX: Metagaming Concepts, 1980.

Jackson, Steve, and Ian Livingstone. *The Warlock of Firetop Mountain*. London, UK: Puffin Books, 1982.

Jackson, Steve, and Warren Spector. *Orcslayer*. Austin, TX: Steve Jackson Tames, 1985.

Jaquays, Jennell, and Rudy Kraft. *Legendary Duck Tower*. Decatur, IL: Judges Guild, 1980.

Kern, Robert. *Thrilling Locations*. New York, NY: Victory Games, 1985.

Keyes, William R. *RuneMasters*. Ann Arbor, MI: Chaosium, 1980.

Kinney, Gregory L. *World Action and Adventure*. Dana Point, CA: M.S. Kinney Corporation, 1985.

Klug, Gerard Christopher. *James Bond 007 Basic Set*. New York, NY: Victory Games, 1983.

Kraft, Rudy, Jennell Jaquays, and Greg Stafford. *Griffin Mountain*. Ann Arbor, MI: Chaosium, 1981.

Leker, Andrew, and Miles Teves. *Skyrealms of Jorune*. Berkeley, CA: SkyRealms Publishing, 1985.

McCready, Anne Gray. *RS1: Red Sonja Unconquered*. Lake Geneva, WI: Tactical Studies Rules, 1986.

McLimore, Guy, Greg Poehlein and Davide Tepool. *Star Trek: The Role Playing Game*. Chicago, IL: FASA Corporation, 1983.

———. *The Triangle*. Chicago, IL: FASA Corporation, 1985.

Mentzer, Frank. *Dungeons & Dragons Set 1: Basic Rules*. Lake Geneva, WI: Tactical Studies Rules, 1983.

———. *Dungeons & Dragons Set 2: Expert Rules*. Lake Geneva, WI: Tactical Studies Rules, 1983.

———. *Dungeons & Dragons Set 3: Companion Rules*. Lake Geneva, WI: Tactical Studies Rules, 1984.

———. *Dungeons & Dragons Set 4: Master Rules*. Lake Geneva, WI: Tactical Studies Rules, 1985.

———. *Dungeons & Dragons Set 5: Immortal Rules*. Lake Geneva, WI: Tactical Studies Rules, 1985.

———. *IM1: The Immortal Storm*. Lake Geneva, WI: Tactical Studies Rules, 1986.

Miller, Marc W. *MegaTraveller*. Normal, IL: Game Designers' Workshop, 1987.

———. *The Spinward Marches Campaign*. Normal, IL: Game Designers' Workshop, 1985.

———. *Traveller: Starter Edition*. Normal, IL: Game Designers' Workshop, 1985.

Moldvay, Tom. *Dungeons & Dragons B/X*. Lake Geneva, WI: Tactical Studies Rules, 1981.

Nesmith, Bruce, and Douglas Niles. *Lankhmar: City of Adventure*. Lake Geneva, WI: Tactical Studies Rules, 1985.

Niles, Douglas. *Darkwalker on Moonshae*. Lake Geneva, WI: Tactical Studies Rules, 1987.

———. *Dungeoneer's Survival Guide*. Lake Geneva, WI: Tactical Studies Rules, 1986.

———. *Knight Hawks*. Lake Geneva, WI: Tactical Studies Rules, 1983.

O'Toole, Peter. *Dragonroar*. Hertfordshire, UK: Standard Games, 1985.

Perrin, Steve. *Superworld*. Ann Arbor, MI: Chaosium, 1983.

Perrin, Steve, and Dyvers Hands. *Borderlands*. Ann Arbor, MI: Chaosium, 1982.

———. *Worlds of Wonder*. Ann Arbor, MI: Chaosium, 1982.

Petersen, Sandy. *Call of Cthulhu*. Ann Arbor, MI: Chaosium, 1981.

Petersen, Sandy, and Dyvers Hands. *Cthulhu Companion*. Ann Arbor, MI: Chaosium, 1983.

———. *Cthulhu Now*. Ann Arbor, MI: Chaosium, 1987.

———. *Fragments of Fear*. Ann Arbor, MI: Chaosium, 1985.

Petersen, Sandy, and George MacDonald. *Champions: The Super Hero Role Playing Game*. San Mateo, CA: Hero Games, 1982.

Petersen, Sandy, and Lynn Willis, with Greg Stafford. *Ghostbusters*. New York, NY: West End Games, 1986.

Pondsmith, Mike. *Cyberpunk*. Kirkland, WA: R. Talsorian Games, 1988.

Rabe, Jean. *LC1: Gateway to Ravens Bluff, The Living City*. Lake Geneva, WI: Tactical Studies Rules, 1989.

Rolston, Ken. *Black Sword*. Ann Arbor, MI: Chaosium, 1985.

Sargent, Carl. *Power Behind the Throne*. Nottingham, UK: Games Workshop, 1988.

Sechi, Stephen Michael. *A Naturalist's Guide to Talislanta*. Aptos, CA: Bard Games, 1987.

———. *The Talislanta Handbook and Campaign Guide*. Aptos, CA: Bard Games, 1987.

Slavicsek, Bill, and Curtis Smith. *The Star Wars Sourcebook*. New York, NY: West End Games, 1987.

St. Andre, Ken, and Steve Perrin. *Stormbringer*. Ann Arbor, MI: Chaosium, 1981.

Stafford, Greg. *King Arthur Pendragon*. Ann Arbor, MI: Chaosium, 1985.

———. *Prince Valliant: The Story-Telling Game*. Ann Arbor, MI: Chaosium, 1989.

Stafford, Greg, and Lynn Willis. *Basic Role-Playing*. Ann Arbor, MI: Chaosium, 1980.

Stern, Michael. *Galaxy Guide 3: The Empire Strikes Back*. New York, NY: West End Games, 1989.

Sustare, B. Dennis, and Scott Robinson. *Bunnies & Burrows*. Jericho, NY: Fantasy Games Unlimited, 1982.

Sutherland III, David C., with Gary Gygax. *Q1: Queen of the Demonweb Pits*. Lake Geneva, WI: Tactical Studies Rules, 1980.

Tweet, Jonathan, and Mark Rein-Hagen. *Ars Magica*. Northfield, MN: Lion Rampant, 1987.

Turnbull, Don, editor. *Fiend Folio*. Lake Geneva, WI: Tactical Studies Rules, 1981.

Varney, Allen. *Deluxe City Campaign Set*. Lake Geneva, WI: Tactical Studies Rules, 1989.

Ward, James M., and Robert J. Kuntz. *Deities & Demigods*. Lake Geneva, WI: Tactical Studies Rules, 1980.

Willis, Lynn, and Dyvers Hands. *Thieves' World*. Ann Arbor, MI: Chaosium, 1981.

———. *Thieves' World Companion*. Ann Arbor, MI: Chaosium, 1986.

Winter, Steve, editor. *Star Frontiers*. Lake Geneva, WI: Tactical Studies Rules, 1982.

Wujcik, Erick. *After the Bomb*. Westland, MI: Palladium Books, 1986.

———. Road Hogs. Westland, MI: Palladium Books, 1986.

———. *Teenage Mutant Ninja Turtles & Other Strangeness*. Westland, MI: Palladium Books, 1985.

Wulf, Dick. *DragonRaid*. Colorado Springs, CO: Adventure Learning Systems, Inc., 1983.

The 1990s

Baas, Walter, and Kira Glass. *LC3: Nightwatch in the Living City*. Lake Geneva, WI: Tactical Studies Rules, 1991.

Bridges, Bill, and Andrew Greenberg. *Fading Suns*. Atlanta, GA: Holistic Design, Inc., 1996.

Bridges, Bill, Andrew Greenberg, and Dyvers Hands. *Fading Suns Players Companion*. Atlanta, GA: Holistic Design, Inc., 1997.

Browder, Dustin. *Milwaukee by Night*. Stockholm, SE: White Wolf Publishing, 1992.

Brown, Timothy B. *Dragon Kings*. Lake Geneva, WI: Tactical Studies Rules, 1992.

Brown, Timothy B., and Troy Denning. *Dark Sun Boxed Set*. Lake Geneva, WI: Tactical Studies Rules, 1991.

Chadwick, Frank, and David Nilsen. *Traveller: The New Era*. Normal, IL: Game Designers' Workshop, 1993.

Charlton, Coleman, Pete Fenlon and Dyvers Hands. *Gorgoroth*. Charlottesville, VA: Iron Crown Enterprises, 1990.

Costikyan, Greg (as Designer X). *Violence*. London, UK: Hogshead, UK: 1999.

Chup, Sam, and James A. Moore. *Necropolis: Atlanta*. Stockholm, SE: White Wolf Publishing, 1994.

Cook, David "Zeb." *Planescape Campaign Setting*. Lake Geneva, WI: Tactical Studies Rules, 1994.

Cook, Monte. *The Planewalker's Handbook*. Lake Geneva, WI: Tactical Studies Rules, 1996.

Detwiller, Dennis, Adam Scott Glancy, and John Tynes. *Delta Green*. Columbia, MO: Pagan Publishing, 1997.

Faughnan, John, Boy F. Petersen, Jr., and Michael Stackpole. *Sprawl Sites*. Chicago, IL: FASA Corporation, 1990.

Garvin, Lee, Nick Atlas, and John Huff. *Tales from the Floating Vagabond*. Baltimore, MD: Avalon Hill, 1991.

Gorden, Greg. *Earthdawn*. Chicago, IL: FASA Corporation, 1993.

———. *Torg: Roleplaying the Possibility Wars*. New York, NY: West End Games, 1990.

Greenwood, Ed. *The City of Ravens Bluff*. Lake Geneva, WI: Tactical Studies Rules, 1998.

———. *Drow of the Underdark*. Lake Geneva, WI: Tactical Studies Rules, 1991.

———. *Forgotten Realms Campaign Setting*. Lake Geneva, WI: Tactical Studies Rules, 1996.

———. *The Ruins of Undermountain*. Lake Geneva, WI: Tactical Studies Rules, 1991.

Greenwood, Ed, and Steven Schend. *City of Splendors*. Lake Geneva, WI: Tactical Studies Rules, 1994.

Greenwood, Ed, Douglas Niles, and R.A. Salvatore. *Menzoberranzan*. Lake Geneva, WI: Tactical Studies Rules, 1992.

Grubb, Jeff. *Al-Qadim: Arabian Adventures*. Lake Geneva, WI: Tactical Studies Rules, 1992.

———. *The Legend of the Spelljammer*. Lake Geneva, WI: Tactical Studies Rules, 1991.

Hensley, Shane Lacy. *Deadlands*. Chandler, AZ: Pinnacle Entertainment Group, 1996.

Hensley, Shane Lacy, and Steve Miller. *Fritz Lieber's Lankhmar: The New Adventures of Fafhrd and Gray Mouser*. Lake Geneva, WI: Tactical Studies Rules, 1996.

Herber, Keith. *Arkham Unveiled*. Ann Arbor, MI: Chaosium, 1990.

———. *Return to Dunwich*. Ann Arbor, MI: Chaosium, 1991.

Hickman, Tracy, and Laura Hickman. *House of Strahd*. Lake Geneva, WI: Tactical Studies Rules, 1993.

Johnson, Harold, and Dyvers Hands. *Tales of the Lance*. Lake Geneva, WI: Tactical Studies Rules, 1992.

Jonsson, Gunilla, and Michael Petersén. *Kult*. Folsom, PA: Metropolis, Ltd., 1993.

Kubasik, Christopher, and Ray Winninger. *Streets Tell Stories*. Chicago, IL: Mayfair Games, 1993.

Lambert, Richard, Andrew Rilstone, and James Wallis. *Once Upon a Time*. St. Paul, MN: Atlas Games, 1994.

McDevitt, Bradley K., L. Lee Cerny, and Walter H. Mytczynskyj. *Nightlife*. London, UK: Stellar Games, 1990.

McKenzie, David. *The Lawnmower Man Virtual Reality Role Playing Game*. Pasadena, CA: Leading Edge Games, 1993.

Mobley, Blake, and Timothy B. Brown. *WGR1: Greyhawk Ruins*. Lake Geneva, WI: Tactical Studies Rules, 1990.

Moore, Christian Scott, and Owen M. Seyler. *Aria: Canticle of the Monomyth*. Philadelphia, PA: Last Unicorn Games, 1994.

———. *Aria: Worlds*. Philadelphia, PA: Last Unicorn Games, 1994.

Nakazono, Barry. *Phoenix Command*. Pasadena, CA: Leading Edge Games, 1996.

Nakazono, Barry, and David McKenzie. *Bram Stoker's Dracula Role Playing Game*. Pasadena, CA: Leading Edge Games, 1992.

———. *Aliens Adventure Game*. Pasadena, CA: Leading Edge Games, 1991.

Nesmith, Bruce, and Andria Hayday. *Ravenloft: Realm of Terror*. Lake Geneva, WI: Tactical Studies Rules, 1990.

O'Sullivan, Steffan. *Fudge*. Randolph, MA: Grey Ghost Press, 1992.

Petersen Jr., Boy F. *Seattle Sourcebook*. Chicago, IL: FASA Corporation, 1990.

Pearcy, Derek. *In Nomine*. Austin, TX: Steve Jackson Games, 1997.

Pondsmith, Mike. *Cyberpunk 2020*. Kirkland, WA: R. Talsorian Games, 1990.

———. *Castle Falkenstein: High Adventure in the Steam Age*. Kirkland, WA: R. Talsorian Games, 1994.

Pondsmith, Mike, and Dyvers Hands. *Night City*. Kirkland, WA: R. Talsorian Games, 1991.

Pryor, Anthony. *Dune Trader*. Lake Geneva, WI: Tactical Studies Rules, 1992.

Rabe, Jean. *LC2: Inside Ravens Bluff, The Living City*. Lake Geneva, WI: Tactical Studies Rules, 1990.

Rabe, Jean, and Skip Williams. *LC4: Port of Ravens Bluff*. Lake Geneva, WI: Tactical Studies Rules, 1991.

Rein-Hagen, Mark, with Robert Hatch and Bill Bridges. *Werewolf: The Apocalypse*. Stockholm, SE: White Wolf Publishing, 1994.

Rein-Hagen, Mark, Graeme Davis, Tom Dowd, Lisa Stevens, and Stewart Weick. *Vampire: The Masquerade*. Stockholm, SE: White Wolf Publishing, 1991.

Ross, Kevin A. *Escape from Innsmouth*. Ann Arbor, MI: Chaosium, 1992.

———. *Kingsport: The City in the Mists*. Ann Arbor, MI: Chaosium, 1991.

Sargent, Carl. *From the Ashes*. Lake Geneva, WI: Tactical Studies Rules, 1992.

Siembieda, Kevin. *The Mechanoids*. Westland, MI: Palladium Books, 1992.

———. *Rifts*. Westland, MI: Palladium Books, 1990.

———. *Vampire Kingdoms*. Westland, MI: Palladium Books, 1991.

Siembieda, Kevin, and Peter Murphy. *Federation of Magic*. Westland, MI: Palladium Books, 1997.

Stolze, Greg, and John Tynes. *Unknown Armies*. St. Paul, MN: Atlas Games, 1998.

Tweet, Jonathan. *Everway*. Renton, WA: Wizards of the Coast, 1995.

Tweet, Jonathan, and Robin D. Laws. *Over the Edge*. St. Paul, MN: Atlas Games, 1992.

Tynes, John editor. *The Unspeakable Oath Issue 7*. Columbia, MO: Pagan Publishing, 1992.

Wallis, James. *The Extraordinary Adventures of Baron Munchausen*. London, UK: Hogshead Publishing, 1998.

Winninger, Ray. *The Nile Empire*. New York, NY: West End Games, 1990.

———. *Underground*. Chicago, IL: Mayfair Games, 1993.

Wujcik, Erick. *Amber Diceless Role-Playing*. Detroit, MI: Phage Press, 1992.

———. *Shadow Knight*. Detroit, MI: Phage Press, 1993.

The 2000s

Baker, D. Vincent. *Dogs in the Vineyard*. s.l.: Lumpley Games, 2004.

Balsera, Leonard, Brian Engard, Jeremy Keller, Ryan Macklin, and Mike Olson. *Fate Core System*. Silver Springs, MD: Evil Hat Productions, 2003.

Bulmahn, Jason, Monte Cook and Dyvers Hands. *Pathfinder Roleplaying Game*. Redmond, WA: Paizo Inc., 2009.

Chenault, Davis, and Mac Golden. *Castles & Crusades*. Little Rock, AR: Troll Lord Games, 2004.

Collins, Andy, Skip Williams, and James Wyatt. *Draconomicon: The Book of Dragons*. Renton, WA: Wizards of the Coast, 2003.

Cook, Monte. *Book of Vile Darkness*. Renton, WA: Wizards of the Coast, 2001.

Cooke, Monte, Jonathan Tweet, and Skip Williams. *Dungeons & Dragons Third Edition*. Renton, WA: Wizards of the Coast, 2000.

———. *Dungeon Master's Guide*. Renton, WA: Wizards of the Coast, 2000.

———. Williams. *Monster Manual*. Renton, WA: Wizards of the Coast, 2000.

———. *Player's Handbook v. 3.5*. Renton, WA: Wizards of the Coast, 2003.

Crawford, Jeremy, Dawn Elliot, Steve Kenson, and John Snead. *Blue Rose*. Seattle, WA: Green Ronin Publishing, 2005.

Edwards, Ron. *Sorcerer*. Chicago, IL: Adept Press, 2002.

———. *The Sorcerer's Soul*. Chicago, IL: Adept Press, 2002.

Finch, Matthew, Stuart Marshall, and Dyvers Hands. *Old School Reference and Index Compilation*. s.l.: First Edition Society, 2006.

Gonnerman, Chris. *Basic Fantasy Role-Playing Game*. s.l.: n.p., 2008.

Hensley, Shane Lacy. *Savage Worlds*. Chandler, AZ: Pinnacle Entertainment Group, 2003.

———. *Savage Worlds Explorer's Edition*. Chandler, AZ: Pinnacle Entertainment Group, 2005.

Hite, Kenneth. *Trail of Cthulhu*. London, UK: Pelgrane Press, 2008.

Hollian, Gary, Frederick Weining, Erik Mona, and Sean K. Reynolds. *Living Greyhawk Gazetteer*. Renton, WA: Wizards of the Coast, 2000.

Laws, Robin D. *Hero Wars*. Arcata, CA: Issaries, Inc., 2000.

———. *The Esoterrorists*. London, UK: Pelgrane Press, 2006.

Laws, Robin D., and Greg Stafford. *HeroQuest: Roleplaying in Glorantha.* Arcata, CA and Austin, TX: Issaries, Inc. and Steve Jackson Games, 2003.

Laws, Robin D., Greg Stafford, and Roderick Robertson. *Hero Wars Narrator's Book.* Arcata, CA: Issaries, Inc, 2000.

Mazza, Ralph, and Mike Holmes. *Universalis.* s.l.: Ramshead Publishing, 2002.

Moran, Jenna K. *Nobilis.* London, UK: Hogshead Publishing, 2002.

Morningstar, Jason. *Fiasco.* Chapel Hill, NC: Bully Pulpit Games, 2009.

Oracz, Michał. *De Profundis: Letters from the Abyss.* London, UK: Hogshead Publishing, 2001.

Quinn, Jeffrey. *Idylls of the Rat King.* Santa Clara, CA: Goodman Games, 2003.

Ravachol, Epidiah, and Nathaniel Barmore. *Dread.* s.l.: The Impossible Dream, 2005.

Sorensen, Jared A. *InSpectres.* New York, NY: Memento Mori Theatricks, 2002.

The 2010s

Alder, Avery. *Monsterhearts.* s.l.: Buried Without Ceremony, 2012.

———. *The Quiet Year.* s.l.: Buried Without Ceremony, 2013.

Antroia, Rickard, Nils Hintze, and Simon Stålenhag. *Out of Time.* Stockholm, SE: Free League Publishing, 2019.

Baker, D. Vincent. *Apocalypse World.* s.l.: Lumpley Games, 2010.

Beltran, Whitney "Strix," Marissa Kelly, and Sarah Richardson. *Bluebeard's Bride.* Albuquerque, NM: Magpie Games, 2017.

Black, David. *The Black Hack.* s.l.: Black Label, 2018.

Cocking, John, and Peter S. Williams. *Beyond the Wall and Other Adventures.* Greensboro, NC: Flatland Games, 2013.

Clemente, Alex, and Shuyo Zhang. *Fungi of the Far Realm.* Dagenham, UK: Melsonian Arts Council, 2019.

Crawford, Kevin. *Stars without Number.* Sterling Heights, MI: Sine Nomine Publishing, 2010.

Crawford, Jeremy, Mike Mearls, and Dyvers Hands. *D&D Starter Set.* Renton, WA: Wizards of the Coast, 2014.

———. *Monster Manual.* Renton, WA: Wizards of the Coast, 2014.

———. *Player's Handbook.* Renton, WA: Wizards of the Coast, 2014.

Curtis, Michael. *The Chained Coffin, second edition.* Santa Clara, CA: Goodman Games, 2019.

———. *Lankhmar.* Santa Clara, CA: Goodman Games, 2019.

Detwiller, Dennis, Shane Ivey, and Dyvers Hands. *Delta Green Slipcase Set.* Chelsea, AL: Arc Dream Publishing, 2018.

Dewey, Stephen. *Ten Candles.* s.l.: Cavalry Games, 2016.

Dunn-O'Connor, Michael, and Eric Swanson. *Goblinsville Gazette #1.* s.l.: Narrative Dynamics, 2019.

———. *Goblinsville Gazette #2: Monsters & Mazes.* s.l.: Narrative Dynamics, 2019.

Forest, Rich. *A Visitor's Guide to the Rainy City.* Mount Pleasant, MI: Superhero Necromancer Press, 2020.

Gearing, Luke. *Acid Death Fantasy.* Dagenham, UK: Melsonian Arts Council, 2020.

———. *Gradient Descent.* Dallas, TX: Tuesday Knight Games, 2020.

Gregory, John. *Lowcountry Crawl.* s.l.: Technical Grimoire Games, 2019.

Goodman, Joseph, Michael Curtis, Harley Stroh, and Deiter Zimmerman. *Dungeon Crawl Classics.* Santa Clara, CA: Goodman Games, 2012.

Härenstam, Tomas. *Mutant: Year Zero*. Stockholm, SE: Free League Publishing, 2014.

Härenstam, Tomas, and Dyvers Hands. *Forbidden Lands*. Stockholm, SE: Free League Publishing, 2018.

Härenstam, Tomas, Andrew E.C. Gaska, and Dyvers Hands. Stockholm, SE: Free League Publishing, 2019.

Harper, John. *Blades in the Dark*. Silver Springs, MD: Evil Hat Productions, 2017.

Hintze, Nils, and Simon Stålenhag. *Tales from the Loop*. Stockholm, SE: Free League Publishing, 2017.

Hurst, Jacob, Gabriel Hernandez, Evan Peterson, and Donnie Garcia. *The Dark of Hot Springs Island*. Austin, TX: Swordfish Islands, 2017.

———. *A Field Guide to Hot Springs Island*. Austin, TX: Swordfish Islands, 2017.

Hutchings, Tim. *Thousand Year Old Vampire*. Beaverton, OR: Petit Guignol, 2019.

Howitt, Grant. *Honey Heist*. s.l.: n.p., 2017.

Howitt, Grant, and Christopher Taylor. *Spire: The City Must Fall*. London, UK: Rowan, Rook and Decard, 2018.

Hymes, Kathryn, and Hakan Seyalıoğlu. *Dialect: A Game About Language and How It Dies*. Washington, D.C.: Thorny Games, 2018.

Larkins, David, with Mike Mason and Lynne Hardy. *Berlin: The Wicked City*. Ann Arbor, MI: Chaosium, 2019.

Laws, Robin D. *HeroQuest, 2nd edition*. Ann Arbor, MI and Meath, UK: Moon Design and Cubicle 7, 2011.

McCoy, Sean. *Mothership*. Dallas, TX: Tuesday Knight Games, 2018.

McCoy, Sean, Donn Stroud, and Luke Gearing. *A Pound of Flesh*. Dallas, TX: Tuesday Knight Games, 2019.

McDowall, Chris. *Electric Bastionland*. Manchester, UK: Bastionland Press, 2020.

Mason, Mike, and Friends. *Call of Cthulhu Starter Set*. Ann Arbor, MI: Chaosium, 2018.

Mason, Mike, and Dyvers Hands. *Pulp Cthulhu*. Ann Arbor, MI: Chaosium, 2016.

Miller, Marshall. *The Warren RPG*. Chapel Hill, NC: Bully Pulpit Games, 2015.

Mörk Borg Cult. *Feretory*. Stockholm, SE: Free League Publishing, 2020.

Nilsson, Pelle, and Johan Nohr. *Mörk Borg*. s.l.: Ockult Örtmästare Games, 2019.

Norman, Gavin. *Old-School Essentials Advanced Fantasy Genre Rules*. Berlin, DE: Necrotic Gnome, 2019

———. *Old-School Essentials Classic Fantasy Genre Rules*. Berlin, DE: Necrotic Gnome, 2019.

———. *Old-School Essentials Retro Adventure Game*. Berlin, DE: Necrotic Gnome, 2019.

Novoa, Andrew, and Pip Kimkiduk. *The Insectiary*. Oeiras, PT: Games Omnivorous, 2020.

Richard, Jeff, and Robin D. Laws. *HeroQuest Glorantha*. Ann Arbor, MI: Moon Design, 2015.

Robbins, Ben. *Kingdom*. Seattle, WA: Lame Mage productions, 2013.

Robbins, Ben. *Microscope*. Seattle, WA: Lame Mage Productions, 2011.

Proctor, Daniel. *Labyrinth Lord*. s.l.: Goblinoid Games, 2011.

———. *Advanced Edition Companion*. s.l.: Goblinoid Games, 2010.

Rejec, Luka. *The Ultraviolet Grasslands*. Seoul, KR and Meridian, ID: WizardThiefFighter Studio and Exalted Funeral, 2019.

———. *UVG and the Black City*. Seoul, KR and Meridian, ID: WizardThiefFighter Studio and Exalted Funeral, 2019.

Roberts, Alex. *Star Crossed*. Chapel Hill, NC: Bully Pulpit Games, 2018.

Sell, Daniel. *Troika! Numinous Edition*. Dagenham, UK: Melsonian Arts Council, 2018.

Siew, Zedeck. *Lorn-Song of the Bachelor.* s.l.: Hydra Cooperative, 2019.

Siew, Zedeck, and Munkao. *Andjang: The Queen of Dog Mountain.* Kuala Lumpur, MY and Port Dickson, MY: Centaur Games, 2019.

———. *Kraching: The Place of the Paw.* Kuala Lumpur, MY and Port Dickson, MY: Centaur Games, 2017.

———. *Mr-Kr-Gr: The Death-Rolled Kingdom.* Kuala Lumpur, MY and Port Dickson, MY: Centaur Games, 2017.

———. *Upper Heleng: The Forest Beloved by Time.* Kuala Lumpur, MY and Port Dickson, MY: Centaur Games, 2019.

Snyder, Wayne, and Doug Kovacs. *Inferno Road.* s.l.: Aleph Null, 2018.

Spivey, Chris. *Harlem Unbound.* Alexandria, VA: Darker Hue Studios, 2017.

Stafford, Greg, and Jeff Richard. *Sartar: Kingdom of Heroes.* Ann Arbor, MI and Meath, UK: Moon Design and Cubicle 7, 2012.

Stroud, Donn, Fiona Maeve Geist, and Sean McCoy. *Dead Planet.* Dallas, TX: Tuesday Knight Games, 2018.

T., Alex. *Disciplines of Bone and Shadow.* Meridian, ID: Black Oath Entertainment and Exalted Funeral, 2019.

Treme, Nate. *The Lost Isle.* Shreveport, LA: Highland Paranormal Society, 2019.

———. *Temple of the Bat.* Shreveport, LA: Highland Paranormal Society, 2019.

Turner, Allen. *Ehdrigohr: The Roleplaying Game.* Chicago, IL: Council of Fools, 2012.

———. *Necronautilus.* Chicago, IL: World Champ Game Co., 2020.

Ward, James M. *Doom on the Warden.* Santa Clara, CA: Goodman Games, 2020.

Walter, Andrew. *Fronds of Benevolence.* Dagenham, UK: Melsonian Arts Council, 2019.

INTERIOR VIEW OF ANOTHER RESERVOIR, GIOVANNI BATTISTA PIRANESI, 1764

Appendix B: Stu's "Appendix N"

Perhaps the most influential part of Gary Gygax's *Dungeon Masters Guide* is "Appendix N: Inspirational and Educational Reading," way in the back, on page 224. It is a brief list of authors and stories that Gygax said, "were of particular inspiration." For many players, like myself, it was a gateway into a larger world of genre fiction.

Aside from exposing people to many new authors and stories, it has also inspired the creation of many similar lists. *Star Frontiers* has one, as does Moldvay's *Basic Set*. In the current era, it is not uncommon to see similar lists include music and a "ludography" of other games. And, living in an age where the availability of texts is no longer affected by physical scarcity, we might have ideas of "better" entries for the list, stories that are more representative of the *D&D* experience but which Gygax was perhaps unaware of or otherwise overlooked.

How could I resist the lure of including my own?

A few criteria. First, I need to own a copy—it doesn't seem right to claim something is essential reading if I haven't kept it loitering on my own shelves. Second, it must contribute to my own personal sustained interest in RPGs; the larger cultural influence isn't important here: this is a list that inspires *me*. Third, why limit it to books? Fourth, derivatives are excluded. Thus, you won't find TSR novels and the (excellent) *King of Dragon Pass* videogame here.

Books from the original "Appendix N" appear in **bold;** books from Moldvay's Basic Set are in purple, and *Star Frontiers'* entries are in blue.

» Douglas Adams: *The Hitchhiker's Guide to the Galaxy*
» *Alien* (1979 film)
» Lloyd Alexander: *The Prydain Chronicles*
» Dante Alighieri: *Inferno*
» *Alone in the Dark* (1992 videogame)
» **Poul Anderson: *The Broken Sword***
» *Ars Goetia* (preferably with illustrations by Louis Le Breton)
» Robert Lynn Asprin and Lynn Abbey, etc: *Thieves World*
» Nathan Ballingrud: "The Butcher's Table"
» Nick Bantock: *The Egyptian Jukebox*; *Griffin & Sabine* trilogy

» **John Belairs: *The Face in the Frost***; *The Dark Secret of Weatherend*; *The Figure in the Shadows*, et al.

» Peter Bebergal (editor): *Appendix N*

» *Beowulf*

» James P. Blaylock: *Paper Grail*, et al.

» Jorge Luis Borges: *The Book of Imaginary Beings*, et al.

» Barbara Ninde Byfield: *The Glass Harmonica*

» Robert W. Chambers: *The King in Yellow*

» P. Djeli Clark: *Ring Shout*, et al.

» Clutch: "The Guild of Mute Assassins," et al.

» Daniel Cohen: *A Natural History of Unnatural Things*, et al.

» *Conan the Barbarian* (1982 film, but also the Basil Poledouris score)

» *Conan the Destroyer* (1984 film, but also the Basil Poledouris score)

» Susan Cooper: *The Dark Is Rising Sequence*

» David Day: *Castles* (with Alan Lee), Tolkien literary criticism, particularly *A Tolkien Bestiary*

» Phillip K. Dick: *A Maze of Death*, *V.A.L.I.S.*, et al.

» *Dictionary of Imaginary Places, The*, by Alberto Manguel and Gianni Guadalupi

» *Dragonslayer* (1981 film)

» **Lord Dunsany**

» Umberto Eco: *Foucault's Pendulum*; *The Book of Legendary Lands*

» Johan Egerkrans: *Vaesen*; *The Undead*, et al.

» Brian Froud and Alan Lee: *Faeries*

» John Gardner: *Grendel*

» *The Gate* (1987 film)

» William Gibson: *Neuromancer*; *Burning Chrome*

» *The Goonies* (1985 film)

» Karen Elizabeth Gordon (with Nick Bantock and Barbara Hodges): *Paris Out of Hand*

» *Hack* (1982 videogame)

» Ray Harryhausen: the Sinbad movies; *Clash of the Titans*; *Jason and the Argonauts*

» Heimat der Katastrophe (dungeonsynth label): particularly Kobold, Gnoll, Kormorg

» Frank Herbert: *Dune*

» High on Fire: beginning with *Death Is This Communion*

» *The Hobbit* (1977 film)

» William Hope Hodgson

» **Robert E. Howard: Conan (particularly "Red Nails")**; *Solomon Kane*, et al.

» Iron Maiden: *Seventh Son of a Seventh Son*, et al.

» *Krull* (1983 film)

» Madeleine L'Engle: *A Wrinkle in Time*, et al.

» *Labyrinth* (1986 film)

» Sydney Lanier: *The Boy's King Arthur* (illustrated by N.C. Wyeth)

» David Larkin, Julek Heller, Carolyn Scrace and Juan Wijingaard: *Giants*

» Victor LaValle: *The Ballad of Black Tom*

» Ursula K. LeGuin: *The Earthsea Cycle*; *The Left Hand of Darkness*

» **Fritz Leiber: the Lankhmar stories**; *Our Lady of Darkness*, **et al.**

» *The Lord of the Rings* (1978 film)

» **H. P. Lovecraft**

» Christopher Manson: *Maze*

» Mike Mignola: *Fafhrd and the Gray Mouser*; *Corum*; *Hellboy*; *Baltimore*

- » **Michael Moorcock: the Elric stories**; von Bek
- » Neptune Towers: *Caravans to Empire Algol*; *Transmissions from Empire Algol*
- » Larry Niven; *Ringworld*; *Ringworld Engineers*
- » Tim Powers: *The Anubis Gate*; *On Stranger Tides*; *The Drawing of the Dark*; *The Stress of Her Regard*, et al.
- » *Red Sonja* (1985 film)
- » Mark E. Rogers: *Zorachus*; *The Nightmare of God*; the Blood of the Lamb series; Samurai Cat, et al.
- » Fred Saberhagen: *Berserker*; *The Dracula Tape*
- » Alvin Schwartz: the *Scary Stories to Tell in the Dark* series
- » Clark Ashton Smith: particularly the Zothique stories
- » The Sisters of Mercy
- » Simon Stålenhag: *Tales from the Loop*, et al.
- » Mary Stewart: the Merlin trilogy
- » Bram Stoker: *Dracula*
- » **Margaret St. Clair: The Shadow People; Sign of the Labrys**
- » *Temple of Apshai Trilogy* (1985 videogame)
- » *The Thing* (1982 film)
- » Time-Life Books: *The Enchanted World*
- » **J. R. R. Tolkien: *The Hobbit*; *The Lord of the Rings***
- » **Manly Wade Wellman**
- » Robert Anton Wilson: *The Illuminatus Trilogy*; *Masks of the Illuminati*
- » Gene Wolfe: *The Book of the New Sun*
- » **Roger Zelazny: the *Amber* series** (both Corwin and Merlin cycles); *A Night in the Lonesome October*, et al.
- » *Zork* (1980 videogame)

Annotations, Musings, and Justifications (in no particular order)

1. You can view several of my selections—*Inferno*, *Beowulf*, *Ars Goetia*, Clark Ashton Smith—as corrections to Gygax's Appendix N. They seem strange oversights whose influence on *Dungeons & Dragons* is self-evident.

2. I am fairly certain that if Gygax had read the Earthsea books, *AD&D* would have been a very, very different game.

3. Nathan Ballingrud's "The Butcher's Table," collected in *Wounds* (2019), while in no way a *D&D* story, just absolutely captures the vibes of *Planescape* in unexpected ways.

4. It is often lamented that John Bellairs never wrote a follow-up to his adult-geared fantasy novel, *The Face in the Frost*. At the same time, his young adult horror novels are often overlooked. They are a treasure trove of supernatural forces, quirky magic items, clever puzzles, and spooky atmosphere. I was a bit surprised, but very pleased, to discover Moldvay had included them on his list.

5. *Dracula* similarly gets overlooked in this sort of context because it is such a famous Victorian-period horror novel and is rooted in our perception because of that, but in terms of plot structure relative to tabletop roleplaying games, I think it is an excellent framework for the story beats and locale shifts of an ongoing campaign—also, Strahd.

6. Much of this list informs ideas that I think are interesting additions to a game master's toolbox (*A Maze of Death* to mess with reality, *Ringworld* for survival, *A Night in the Lonesome October* to handle factions, to name a few). I expect other players to have a completely different list that does the same for them. RPGs help people make stories, but they also help them understand stories, too.

7. Likewise, some of this stuff (Iron Maiden, Harryhausen movies, *Faeries*) just makes me want to play. Other folks probably have their own idiosyncratic list of those things, too.

8. Mark E. Rogers doesn't get enough credit—as an illustrator or a fantasy writer—and a collective effort should be made to rectify that.

9. John Gardner's *Grendel* should be in the back of every GM's mind when making a villain. Christopher Manson's *Maze* should be on their mind when they design a space to explore. *Paris Out of Hand* will give endless insight into cities.

10. Tolkien is an extremely obvious entry on this list, so focus on David Day's volumes of Tolkien criticism, which will challenge perceptions of Middle-earth while providing fantastic illustrations by the likes of Ian Miller, Alan Lee, and more. Or just ignore Tolkien entirely, that's OK, too.

11. A game of *Vampire: The Masquerade* (or *Shadowrun*, or *Cyberpunk*, or really any gothic, contemporary, or near-future game) that doesn't feature The Sisters of Mercy's "Lucretia, My Reflection" playing in the background, is doing something terribly wrong.

12. Dungeonsynth, a weird atmospheric derivative of black metal that draws inspiration from RPGs and low-bit videogames, likely deserves a dedicated book. The scene is rich and vibrant, let Neptune Towers and the artists on Heimat der Katastrophe be your entry into a wider world (though beware of the strains of fascism, racism, and blood-and-soil nativism that infect the fringes of the scene).

INTERIOR VIEW OF THE VILLA OF MAECENAS, GIOVANNI BATTISTA PIRANESI, 1764

Appendix C: Artists of Note

RPGs may take place in the theater of the mind, but they are nevertheless art-focused products. It's the cover painting that snags my eye and begs me to take the book or box down from the shelf. I flip through rulebooks in order to revisit the art—goodness knows the technical writing of the rules isn't the poetry of my heart

These drawings and paintings inspire my games and provide the raw materials for my imagination. Praise is heaped upon the designers, but it's the artists who make the games come to life in my mind before they take on a whole different sort of vitality at the table in play. And, they speak a language of fantasy much larger and older than what is contained in the worlds of RPGs. So, it feels appropriate to shine a spotlight on the most important of them, their work, and some of their forebears.

This listing is nowhere near exhaustive, and it is emphatically a matter of personal opinion. Major works follow in bold.

Early Masters of Illustration

» Giovanni Battista Piranesi (1720-1778): ***Carceri d'Invenzione (Imaginary Prisons)***; *Vedute (Views)*. Not strictly a fantasist, the archaeologist and master etcher nevertheless provides a foundation for visuals of mysterious subterranean spaces and monolithic ruins.
» Edmund Dulac (1882-1953): ***The Rubaiyat of Omar Khayyam***; *Stories from the Arabian Nights*; *Ali Baba*; *Sinbad the Sailor*; *Edmund Dulac's Fairy Book*.
» Henry Justice Ford (1860-1941): **Andrew Langs' Fairy Books**; *Tales of Romance*; *The Arabian Nights Entertainments*. A master of pen and ink work.
» Theodor Kittelsen (1857-1914): *Nøkken;* trolls; Norwegian folklore.
» Howard Pyle (1853-1911): *The Merry Adventures of Robin Hood*; King Arthur; **pirates**. Pyle laid out the modern conception of flamboyant pirate fashion.
» Arthur Rackham (1867-1939): Wagner's *The Ring*; English fairy tales. The great English illustrator is known for his detailed watercolor work.
» N. C. Wyeth (1882-1945): ***Treasure Island***; *The Boy's King Arthur*; *Kidnapped*. Wyeth is an unrivaled painter of moonlight.

Non-RPG Fantasists

» Yoshitaka Amano (born 1952): ***Vampire Hunter D***; Elric; *Final Fantasy* series; *Sandman: Dreamhunters*.
» Wayne Barlowe (born 1958): *Barlowe's Guide to Extraterrestrials*; ***Expedition***; *Barlowe's Guide to Fantasy*; ***Barlowe's Inferno***. Also a prolific concept artist for film.

» Hannes Bok (1914-1964): *Who Goes There?* by John W. Campbell; countless pulp magazine covers. A prolific pulp artist whose work has been unfairly overlooked since the '90s.

» Frank Brunner (born 1949): Conan; **Elric**; Alice in Wonderland. Brunner was a staple of Marvel comics in the '70s.

» Gary Chalk (born 1952): **Lone Wolf gamebooks**; *Talisman*; Brian Jacques's *Redwall* series.

» Richard Corben (1940-2020): **Den**; *House on the Borderland*; Poe adaptations; *Bat out of Hell*. Corben was an acknowledged master of horror comics.

» Guy Davis (born 1966): *Baker Street*; **The Marquis**; *B.P.R.D.*; *The Nevermen*. No one does monsters quite like Davis. Primarily a comic artist, he also did work for White Wolf's RPGs during their heyday.

» Virgil Finlay: (1914-1971): Lovecraft, particularly the cover for *The Outsider and Others*; *Roads* by Seabury Quinn. The artistic embodiment of pulp-era science fiction, fantasy, and horror, Finlay is under-recognized in the modern era, with the most recent collections of his work published in the '90s by Underwood-Miller.

» Chris Foss (born 1946): Countless paperback covers, including the Panther editions of Isaac Asimov's *Foundation* series. Perhaps the finest painter of spaceships to ever put brush to canvas.

» Frank Frazetta (1928- 2010): **"Death Dealer," Conan, John Carter of Mars**. The rare artist whose entire body of work seems so important and the scale of his influence so great that he's difficult to discuss without resorting to hazy superlatives.

» Brian Froud (born 1947): **Faeries**; *The World of the Dark Crystal*; *The Goblins of Labryinth*; *Lady Cottington's Pressed Fairy Book*. Froud's work for Jim Henson Studios is easily as influential as his published art.

» Gary Gianni (born 1954): *Prince Valiant*; *Monstermen*; Solomon Kane; *A Knight of the Seven Kingdoms*; *The Call of Cthulhu*.

» Bob Haberfield (born 1938): Painter of UK paperback covers in the '70s, primarily novels by Michael Moorcock.

» John Higgins (born 1949): *Grail Quest* gamebooks; *2000AD*. Higgins was also the colorist on *Watchmen*.

» John Howe (born 1957) Time-Life's *The Enchanted World* series; **Tolkien**; *Beowulf: A Tale of Blood, Heat, and Ashes*.

» Jeffrey Catherine Jones (1944-2011): Countless paperback covers (the Ace editions of Leiber's Fafhrd and the Gray Mouser stories are notable), *Idyl*, work for *Creepy* and *Eerie*. Frazetta called Jones "the greatest living painter."

» Alan Lee (born 1947): *A Golden Book of the Mysterious*; **Faeries**; *Castles*; **Tolkien**. The use of Lee's work in the production of Peter Jackson's Tolkien films has redefined how the world imagines Middle-earth.

» Mike Mignola (born 1960): *Fafhrd and the Gray Mouser*; **Hellboy**; *Baltimore*. Mignola's comic work has redefined the look of pulp horror and adventure, much the same way as Frazetta did for fantasy. His influence is inescapable.

» Moebius (1938-2012, real name Jean Giraud): *Blueberry*; **Arzach**; *The Airtight Garage of Jerry Cornelius*. Moebius provided countless concept designs for film.

» Earl Norem (1923-2015): Countless comic books and adventure magazines; **He-Man and the Masters of the Universe**. A tireless commercial artist, Norem's work on children-centered products and properties in the '70s and '80s captured the imagination of an entire nerdy generation.

» Noriyoshi Ohrai (1935-2015): Known primarily as a painter of movie posters, particularly the international poster for *The Empire Strikes Back* and many *Godzilla* films.

» Katsuhiro Otomo (born 1954): *Domu*; ***Akira***.

» John Jude Palencar (born 1957): **"The Black School"** and all his work for Time-Life's *The Enchanted World* series; *Eragon*; Octavia Butler; *A Song of Ice and Fire*.

» Bob Pepper (1938-2019): Ballantine Adult Fantasy; *Dark Tower* (board game); *Dragonmaster*.

» Rowena (1944-2021): One of the first women to become a prolific painter of genre paperbacks. Her cover paintings for the two 1978 Jove Lovecraft collections—*The Colour Out of Space* and *The Dunwhich Horror*—are magnificent.

» P. Craig Russell (born 1951): ***Stormbringer***; *Sandman*; ***The Ring of the Nibelung***.

» Walter Velez (1939-2018): *M.Y.T.H.*; ***Thieves' World***; *Mystara*. He was a prolific painter of genre paperback covers.

» Charles Vess (born 1951): *Sandman #19*; *Stardust*; ***The Books of Earthsea***

» Michael Whelan (born 1950): **"Lovecraft's Nightmare;"** Elric, ***The Gunslinger***, *The Dark Tower*.

» Barry Windsor-Smith (born 1949): **Conan, particularly Marvel's *Conan the Barbarian***; *Monsters*.

» Bernie Wrightson (1948-2017, previously Berni, to differentiate from the Olympic diver): *Swamp Thing*; *Cycle of the Werewolf*; ***Frankenstein***. The master of gloopy monsters and corpses.

RPG Artists of Note

» Janet Aulisio: *Weird Tales*; *Shadowrun*; *Vampire: The Masquerade*; *Dangerous Journeys*; ***Earthdawn***. A master of deep shadows and elaborate patterning.

» Tom Baxa: ***Dark Sun***; *Spelljammer*; *Earthdawn*; many covers of *Dragon* and *Dungeon Magazine*, particularly *Dungeon Magazine #29*.

» John Blanche (born 1948): *A Tolkien Bestiary*; *Fighting Fantasy*; **Games Workshop**. Blanche was the company's art director for many years and established the unique look of the various *Warhammer* universes.

» Tim Bradstreet (born 1967): ***Shadowrun***; ***Vampire: The Masquerade***; *Dark Conspiracy*; *Hellblazer*. During the early '90s, Bradstreet defined the gritty, streetwise look many RPGs were going for before transitioning into a career as a comic book cover artist.

» P. D. Breeding: **Talislanta**.

» Gerald Brom (born 1965): ***Dark Sun***, particularly the core box set and *Dragon Kings*; ***Deadlands***; *Nightbane*; *Darkwerks*. He has also penned a number of fantasy novels.

» Michael Bukowski: **Yog-Blogsoth**, *Monstrous Mythologies*. A prolific illustrator of monsters.

» Clyde Caldwell (born 1948): *Greyhawk Adventures*, the *Dragonlance Saga*, ***I6: Ravenloft***. Along with the other members of the "Big Four," a defining artist of the '80s for both *D&D* and fantasy.

» Liz Danforth (born 1953): Many illustrations for ***Middle-Earth Role Playing***; *Tunnels & Trolls*; *The Fantasy Trip*.

» Darlene (born 1954): *Dungeon Masters Guide*; *B1: In Search of the Unknown*; ***World of Greyhawk***.

» Gene Day (1951-1982): ***Call of Cthulhu***; *Stormbringer*. Day was primarily a comic artist, doing important work on *Master of Kung Fu*, the Marvel *Star Wars* comic series and his own graphic novel, *Future Day*.

» Dirk Detweiler Leichty: **Silent Titans**; *Super Blood Harvest*; *Bring Me Her Bones*; *Dancing With Bullets Under a Neon Sun*.

» Tony DiTerlizzi (born 1969): *Monstrous Compendium*; *Dragon Mountain*; **Planescape**, specifically the core box sets and *The Planewalker's Handbook*; *The Spiderwick Chronicles*, **Realms**. DiTerlizzi has gone on to become an award-winning author and illustrator of children's and young adult fiction.

» Jeff Easley (born 1954): The covers of the **"Orange Spine" Dungeons & Dragons rulebooks**; the *Dragonlance Saga*, *Dragon Magazine #138* and many other *D&D* products. With the other members of the "Big Four," a defining fantasy artist of the '80s.

» Jason Eckhardt: **Kingsport: The City in the Mists**; **Escape from Innsmouth**. The bulk of Eckhardt's work was for Necronomicon Press, a chapbook publisher specializing in Lovecraft studies, but his brief stint with Chaosium produced evocative illustrations of dreams and ruins.

» Les Edwards (born 1949): Conan; Discworld; Fighting Fantasy: **HeroQuest**, *Power Behind the Throne*; *Realm of Chaos*; **"The Croglin Vampire."** Edwards was a key artist establishing the grittier look of UK horror and fantasy in the '80s.

» Johan Egerkrans (born 1978): **Vaesen**; *Norse Gods*; *The Undead*; *Ruin Masters*.

» Larry Elmore (born 1948): **Set 1: Basic Rules**; **"Avalyne the Life-Giver;"** the *Dragonlance Saga*; *Star Frontiers*; *Shadowrun*; countless *D&D* products. Elmore, along with the other members of the "Big Four," defined the clean, heroic look of *D&D* in the '80s.

» Stephen Fabian (born 1930): *Manual of the Planes*; **Ravenloft: Realm of Terror**. A prolific pulp illustrator influenced by Hannes Bok and Virgil Finlay, his body of *Ravenloft* art work is a treasure trove of Gothic horror.

» Amanda Lee Franck: *You Got a Job on the Garbage Barge*; *Vampire Cruise*; *Mouth Brood*.

» Lisa A. Free: *Borderlands*; **Pendragon**; *Ringworld*.

» Earl Geier: *Dark Designs*; *Dark Conspiracy*; **Fatal Experiments**; **Outworlder**. A staple of *Call of Cthulhu* and other horror games in the '90s, his illustration of the King in Yellow in *Fatal Experiments* is cross-hatched perfection.

» Bodie H.: *Slowquest*.

» Trevor Henderson (born 1986): *They Feed on Fear*, *Campfire* and an Instagram full of cryptids and urban legends.

» James Holloway (died 2020): *Oriental Adventures*; *Chill*; **Paranoia**; **Dragon Magazine #88**; **Dragon Magazine #127**; *Tales from the Floating Vagabond*. A workhorse illustrator and one of the very few who could convey comedy in his art.

» Daniel Horne (born 1960): **"Saving the Best for Last;"** countless covers for *Dragon Magazine* and *Dungeons & Dragons* products.

» David Hoskins: *Acid Death Fantasy*, *The Isle of the Plangent Mage*; *Black Knights*.

» Jennell Jaquays (born 1956): *Dark Tower*, *Unknown Gods*; *Cults of Terror*, *Dungeon Magazine #24*; **Dragon Mountain**.

» Justine Jones: *Grave of the Nameless God*; Warlock; *Halls of the Blood King*.

» Peter Andrew Jones (born 1951): many UK genre paperback covers; **Warlock of Firetop Mountain** and other *Fighting Fantasy* gamebook covers; the Games Workshop edition of *Stormbringer* and many other Games Workshop publications.

» Doug Kovacs (born 1973): **Dungeon Crawl Classics**; *DCC: Lankhmar*, Hobonomicon; *Inferno Road*. The definitive Goodman Games artist, he is the central figure in the fusing of early RPG aesthetics with gonzo sensibilities.

» Jeff Laubenstein: **Shadowrun**; *Earthdawn; Battletech*.

» Todd Lockwood (born 1957): **"Orcus," Draconomicon**.

- » Kevin Long: scads of **Rifts** books; *Beyond the Supernatural*; *Robotech*. The definitive artist of Palladium's games—much of *Rifts'* over-the-top appeal derives from his art.
- » Sam Mameli: *Ten People You Meet in the Undergarden*; *Hibernation Games*.
- » Angus McBride (1931-2007): **Middle-Earth Role Playing**; *Rolemaster*. McBride's primary work was as an illustrator of military history and appears in many books by Osprey Publishing.
- » Ian Miller (born 1946): Lovecraft; **A Tolkien Bestiary**; *Warhammer*, particularly **Death on the Reik** and *Warhammer City*; *Fighting Fantasy*, particularly *Creatures of Havoc* and **The Citadel of Chaos**. A monstrous talent, blending the Gothic with the surreal.
- » Evelyn Moreau: *Marvels & Malisons*; *Very Pretty Paleozoic Pals*; *The Dee Sanction*, **Where the Wheat Grows Tall**.
- » Dean Morrissey (born 1951): Many *Dragon Magazine* covers; *Ship of Dreams*.
- » Peter Mullen: **Dungeon Crawl Classics** and Goodman Games' line of *Alphabet* supplements; *Old-School Essentials*. Mullen is one of several contemporary artists revitalizing the artistic stylings of the early days of the hobby.
- » Munkao (born 1982): *A Thousand Thousand Islands*.
- » Russ Nicholson: **Fiend Folio**; **Warlock of Firetop Mountain**; many other *Warhammer* and *Fighting Fantasy* titles. Perhaps the most delightfully gruesome of the early RPG artists.
- » Johan Nohr: **Mörk Borg**.
- » Erol Otus (born 1960): **Deities & Demigods**; *Dungeons & Dragons Basic Set, Dungeons & Dragons Expert Set* and many other *D&D* publications.
- » Keith Parkinson (1958-2005): **The Dragonlance Saga**; *Rifts*; "What Do You Mean We're Lost?;" "Gods of Lankhmar;" **"Lord Soth's Charge"** and many more pieces for *Dungeons & Dragons*. Along with the other members of the "Big Four," Parkinson helped define fantasy art in the '80s.
- » Stefan Poag: **Dungeon Crawl Classics**; **Death on the Warden**; many, many other OSR and *DCC* publications. Another prolific reviver of old-school aesthetics.
- » Randy Post (born 1968): **The Great Modron March** and *Planescape* generally; *Deadlands*; *The Star Wars Essential Guide to Alien Species*.
- » Luka Rejec: *Witchburner*; **Ultraviolet Grasslands**; *Longwinter*.
- » Adam Rex (born 1973): *Changeling: The Dreaming*; *Planescape* and a variety of *D&D* Third Edition publications. Rex has since embarked on a career of writing and illustrating children's literature.
- » Wayne Reynolds: *2000AD*; **Dungeons & Dragons Third Edition**; *Pathfinder*.
- » Jim Roslof (1946-2011): *S2: White Plume Mountain*; *Q1: Queen of the Demonweb Pits*, **B2: The Keep on the Borderlands** and various other *D&D* publications.
- » Skinner: *Necronomicon Pop-Up Book*; the music video for High on Fire's "The Black Plot;" countless painting and murals. While not an illustrator of RPGs themselves, Skinner is one of many contemporary artists whose work is heavily influenced by the vast body of RPG art.
- » Skullfungus: *The Black Hack*; *Night Yeast*; *Lorn Song of the Bachelor*. Skullfungus' cartoonishly gross cartography has become a staple of indie and OSR publications in recent years.
- » Simon Stalenhag (born 1984): **Tales from the Loop**; *Things from the Flood*; **The Electric State**; *The Labyrinth*.

» Tom Sullivan: *Shadows of Yog-Sothoth*; *Masks of Nyarlathotep*; *S. Petersen's Field Guild to Cthulhu Monsters*; *Arkham Horror* and many other pieces for Chaosium. His most famous creation, though, is the *Book of the Dead* used on screen in *The Evil Dead*.

» David C. Sutherland III (1949-2005): *Dungeons & Dragons Basic Set*; ***B1: In Search of the Unknown***; ***Monster Manual*** and countless other *D&D* publications.

» Miles Teves (born 1963): ***Skyrealms of Jorune***. Teves has had a long career doing concept and effects work for film.

» Dave Trampier (1954-2014): ***Players Handbook***; ***Monster Manual***; ***Gamma World***; *Wormy*. Often regarded as the most important *D&D* artist of the '70s.

» Nate Treme: ***Highland Paranormal Society*** publications; *The Incandescent Grottoes*.

» Timothy Truman (born 1956): *X1: The Isle of Dread*; *X5: The Temple of Death*; *Jonah Hex: Two-Gun Mojo*. Truman was also a concept illustrator for the LJN line of *Dungeons & Dragons* toys.

» Valerie Valusek: *Forgotten Realms*; *Dragonlance Legends*; *Rary the Traitor*; *Torg*; *Changeling: The Dreaming*.

» Andrew Walter: *Troika*; ***Fronds of Benevolence***; *Old-School Essentials* and many zines.

» Bill Willingham (born 1956): *L1: Secret of Bone Hill*; *C2: The Ghost Tower of Inverness*; *GW1: Legion of Gold* and many other TSR products. Willingham went on to create the successful comic book franchise *Fables*.

Appendix D: Dungeons

If there is one truly great creation that comes out of RPGs, it must be the idea of the dungeon—not the castle prison cell, but the chthonic realm of danger and treasure of our shared fantasies.

Gary Gygax and Dave Arneson laid out the basic requirements in the third booklet of the original *Dungeons & Dragon* box set, *The Underworld & Wilderness Adventures*. In doing so, they captured something elusive that has been haunting human imagination for millennia. For them, a dungeon is a subterranean space, spread across many ever-deeper levels and sub-levels. Each of these is non-linear and maze-like. They generally become more dangerous the further they are from the surface and are populated with monsters and deadly traps. No sane person would ever venture into one, except for the call of the treasure and magical artifacts of great power that wait in the darkness to be claimed by intrepid souls.

In dungeons, we get, not just a place to explore, but also the very soul of the first roleplaying game: Travel deep, fight monsters, find treasure. As a space, they are constrained, with narrow, claustrophobic rooms, allowing players limited choices for routes in the immediate term. In the long term, though, those choices string together into a vast, non-linear space, constructed, fractal-like, out of an infinity of twisting corridors.

There are no real-world equivalents to this kind of dungeon. It is an irrational, imaginary space, a broken mirror cobbled together out of shards of myth, snippets of fiction and slivers of our own fears. More than the dragons or the power fantasies, this great below captured the collective imagination. The dungeon speaks to something primal about the way human minds work, even if we can't quite understand its shadowy vastness. Perhaps that's exactly the reason we keep going below—not for treasure, but for meaning.

What follows is a brief list of pieces that, possibly, contribute to a hazy understanding of this world underneath the world.

Cave Systems: Naturally formed caves are an obvious inspiration for certain sorts of dungeons, particularly massive ones, like Mammoth Cave in Kentucky or the Sistema Sac Actun in the Yucatan. The latter, which is often underwater but also has archaeological signs of ancient human habitation, seems particularly noteworthy. Mineral deposits and erosion often make natural caves appear alien.

The Underworld: Nearly every cycle of the world's mythologies has an underworld, a shadowy place to which the souls of the dead depart—Mictlan, Duat, Hel, Alam Ghaib, Sheol, even the *Inferno* of Dante. In the West, one of the most vividly remembered is Tartarus of the Greeks and Romans, with its hungry ghosts, hazardous pomegranates, clever punishments, and occasional monster (Cerberus, for one). Many heroes, including Odysseus, Hercules, and Theseus, descend in search of wisdom, which is a sort of treasure. Virgil placed its entrance at Avernus, the steaming volcanic crater lake near Cumae.

Pyramids and Tombs: The oldest Egyptian pyramid, Zoser's at Saqqara, dates to 2600 BCE, and there are 117 more, all of which immediately call to mind notions of mummies, secret passages, untold treasures, nefarious grave robbers, and traps to foil them. Add to this the treasures discovered in Tutankhamun's tomb in 1922 and its supposed curse, and the basic template for something like *S1: Tomb of Horrors* begins to emerge.

The Labyrinth of Crete: Likely the earliest literary reference to something modern readers would recognize as a dungeon (going back to at least 1200 BCE), the Labyrinth remains the best example for thousands of years. The stories claim it was built by the inventor Daedalus as a prison for the monstrous Minotaur; it was a maze so clever even its creator had a hard time finding a way out.

Dunjon: A French word for the central keep or tower of a castle. It has little to do with the modern connotation of a prison or cell. It is rare to find a castle room purpose-built for imprisonment before the twelfth century. After that point, they were usually constructed in gatehouse structures, not placed underground.

Carceri d'Invenzione: A portfolio of 16 prints by Giovanni Battista Piranesi and published in 1750, these "Imaginary Prisons" depict vast, nightmarish spaces. There are vaults, twisting stairs, hanging chains, instruments of torture, and endless shadows. A second printing, in 1761, features small alterations that make the depicted architecture impossible. They are a clear precursor to the Gothic notion of dungeons. Further, during the *Planescape*-era, in an effort to distance the *D&D* multiverse from real-world mythologies, designers replaced Tartarus with an infinite prison-plane called Carceri, a nod to Piranesi.

Oubliettes and Torture Chambers: While torture chambers and prison cells undoubtedly existed, our modern conception of them is primarily a fever dream born out of nineteenth century literature. The idea of an oubliette—a room with a hatch in the ceiling through which a prisoner was lowered and subsequently forgotten—is a popular punishment used by villains in Gothic novels. The first mention of the word was in Sir Walter Scott's *Ivanhoe* (1819), but the rooms to which he referred were likely cisterns, storerooms, or latrines, not prison cells. Still, the idea of a subterranean complex of cells and torture chambers is one that lives in the popular imagination, stoked to this day by horror films and lurid wax museums.

Gardens of Bomarzo: A monumental garden populated with monstrous statues in Lazio, Italy, the so-called Park of Monsters was constructed in the sixteenth century in a valley below the castle of Orsini. Nothing here is underground, but the massive mouth of Orcus is about the closest thing to a real-world dungeon entrance in existence, even if there is only a smallish dining room inside.

The Hollow Earth: A theory suggested by Edmund Halley in the late seventeenth century and disproved by Charles Hutton in 1774. The idea that the Earth contains a significant interior space has a powerful legacy of capturing the human imagination. Inspired by the mythological underworld, a number of oddballs in the nineteenth century proposed expeditions to places, like the North Pole, to search for entrances to what they were sure was a populated inner earth. Jules Verne brought the concept to science fiction (creating an entire sub-genre) with *Journey to the Center of the Earth* (1864). In the late 1800s and early 1900s, Edward Bulwer-Lytton's novel, *The Coming Race* (1871), about a magically empowered subterranean culture, was embraced by some occultists and theosophists as truth.

"The Scarlet Citadel" (1933) and *The Hour of the Dragon* (1935): Two of Robert E. Howard's Conan stories, both see our favorite barbarian imprisoned in an underground dungeon that matches the nineteenth century idea of both prison and torture chamber. Upon his escape, he flees into a lightless maze full of monsters, which he battles while searching for an exit.

***The Case of Charles Dexter Ward* (1927):** H. P. Lovecraft's horror novel of family legacies, black magic, and subverted identities set in Providence during the 1920s might be a strange place to find inspiration for fantasy dungeons, but it is! The antagonist, an eighteenth-century sorcerer named Joseph Curwen, kept his laboratory in a warren of catacombs under a local cemetery. Within are oubliettes, horrible monsters, and some terrible truths, though no treasures. Lovecraft's Dreamlands stories (written between 1918 and 1932) also explore dungeon-like spaces—the necropolises of the ghouls and the nighted cities of Gugs.

***Babes in Toyland* (1934):** The Laurel and Hardy musical comedy, often referred to as *March of the Wooden Soldiers*, also seem like an odd inclusion, but the caves and bogs of Bogeyland, separated from Toyland by an imposing gate, visually anticipate the dungeon-spaces of the fantasy literature and *D&D* modules that appear in its wake. Furthermore, the monstrous, hairy bogeymen who live in those caves seem to have a common ancestor in George McDonald's goblins, who also inspired Tolkien's orcs.

***The Hobbit* (1937):** In summary, Tolkien provides a clear template for the concerns of a *D&D* adventure—a band of treasure hunters, equipped with a treasure map, embark to find an underground vault full of treasure (and guarded by a dragon). In execution, nothing in the book truly feels like a dungeon—the stronghold of Erebor seems rather tidy and trap free, while the twisting tunnels of Goblin-town

fly by before making much of an impression—but even so, it still feels like a fundamental piece of the puzzle.

Fafhrd and the Gray Mouser: Fritz Leiber and Otto Fischer's pair of knaves typify much of what would become encoded into *D&D*'s conception of fantasy adventure, which, in turn, trickles into the rest of RPGs. They explore many places filled with traps, other rogues, deadly magic, and the occasional monster. The novel, *The Swords of Lankhmar* (1968), and the story, "The Lords of Quarmall" (1964), both see the duo navigating underground labyrinths in search of riches. The trap house of "The Jewels in the Forest" (1939, also known as "Two Sought Adventure") also feels surprisingly dungeon-like, despite being aboveground.

***The Fellowship of the Ring* (1954):** The first part of Tolkien's *Lord of the Rings* trilogy provides two more dungeon-like environments. Moria, the abandoned city of the dwarves, is the big one, a vast underground labyrinth—its entrance guarded by a tentacle monster, its halls populated by orcs, and its throne occupied by one terrifying balrog. It is, in many ways, Tolkien's spin at being a horror author, and it is one of the most memorable passages he wrote, though for our purposes, it is disappointing that Moria was an accidental place to pass through rather than a destination to explore. Though far less expansive in area, the sinister mounds of the Barrow-downs, full of treasure and revenants, are more in line with our expectations of a dungeon.

***The Sign of the Labrys* (1963):** A post-apocalyptic novel by Margaret St. Clair in which most of humanity is wiped out by a plague of virulent yeast, and many of the survivors live in underground complexes. Mostly man-made, they range from dormitories to lab complexes to military office wings to a fake ocean and an underground forest. Traversal through the lettered levels ranges from normal (stairs and elevators) to bizarre (a secret door in the bottom of an autoclave). If any piece of fiction captures the unreal vibe of exploring an ever-weirder dungeon in play, it's this novel.

The Book of Three (1964): The first volume in Lloyd Alexander's *Prydain Chronicles*, notable here for its extended scene in the maze-like tomb catacombs of Spiral Castle, where the protagonists find a very important magic sword. *The Prydain Chronicles* take their framework from Welsh mythology, and Spiral Castle gets its name from Caer Sidi, a sort of mystic fort that serves as the storehouse of the cauldron of Annwn (or Annwn's oracular severed head). According to the poem *Preiddeu Annwfn*, King Arthur led three boatloads of men to that place to retrieve the cauldron in a disastrous expedition; the poem doesn't say what transpired in that otherworldly place, but only Arthur and six of his companions returned alive and empty handed, a very old school *D&D* result.

The Shadow People (1969): Another bizarro novel by Margaret St. Clair, this one sees a hippie explore a vast interconnected cave system populated by cannibalistic, color-coded elves, most of whom are addicted to hallucinogen-infused grain. The hippie is looking for his ex-girlfriend, who the elves kidnapped (to eat?), and he is also part-elf, and by the time he gets back to the surface, a techno-fascist regime has taken over Berkeley, California. The book really needs to be read to be believed, but it does an excellent job of conveying the scope of an unimaginable subterranean space.

Castle Greyhawk: In *The Underworld & Wilderness Adventures* booklet, Greyhawk Castle is described as having "a dozen levels in succession downwards, more than that number branching from these and not less than two new levels under construction at any given time. These levels contain such things as a museum from another age, an underground lake, a series of caverns filled with giant fungi, a

bowling alley for 20' high Giants, an arena of evil, crypts and so on." While the world never really got to see Gygax's dungeon, that brief summation set the template for a wide range of exploratory experiences, in particular, the concept of the massive mega-dungeon.

Temple of the Frog: The first *D&D* adventure, contained in *Supplement II: Blackmoor* (1975), the titular adventure site consists of the working temple, full of frog worshipers, and a two-level dungeon populated by frog people. If Castle Greyhawk was the model for both big and *really* big, "Temple of the Frog" showed GMs how to do small and medium.

The World Dungeon: Implied in the D-series modules but explicitly laid out under the name Underdark in the *Dungeoneer's Survival Guide*, the world dungeon is the marriage of hollow earth theories with *D&D*. Especially in the early days of the game, when wilderness and city exploration were rudimentary, the dungeon *was* the game world. As those other venues became richer, adventure design necessitated the places below to grow ever more threatening and enticing.

Maze (1985): As with many other aspects of RPGs, the hobby's notions about dungeons crept back into the greater pop culture ecosystem. Primarily, this occurred through videogames, but *Maze*, a puzzle book by Christopher Manson, bears mentioning. It initially had a cash prize attached to it, awaiting the first person to find the optimal path to the center of the labyrinth and back again while also solving a key riddle. The space, painstakingly illustrated by Manson, is deeply evocative of all of the enigmatic features of an RPG dungeon. It is full of enigmas, dizzying twists, and while there are no monsters, the narrator (who may very well be the Minotaur) doesn't exactly have the reader's best interests at heart.

***Labyrinth* (1986):** Jim Henson's musical adventure, starring David Bowie, Jennifer Connelly, and many, many Brian Froud-designed Muppets, is the prime manifestation of the dungeon in film. The visuals of the goblin maze absorbed RPG ideas about dungeons up to that point, then reflected them back, influencing the fantasy aesthetic for decades to come. The set designers, at least, were aware of RPGs—keen-eyed viewers can spot a copy of Games Workshop's *Judge Dredd: The Role-Playing Game* (1985), of all things, on a shelf in Sarah's room.

Dungeon as Design: In the present, dungeons have become a design theory, a way to construct a play experience. Because so much of RPG aesthetics is tied to the trappings of fantasy, it is easy to forget that not every dungeon needs to be carved from stone and be full of goblins. There is nothing to say that an office building, a city sewer, a starship, or more cannot be a dungeon. The only requirement is that an interesting place be confined in some way and connected by narrow pathways to other confined spaces. So, a submarine is a dungeon. The point crawl approach to overland traversal is dungeon-like—the "rooms" are points of interest strung together by literal paths. A battle field can be a dungeon with "walls" of combat pushing a person towards noteworthy events. What else can be a dungeon? A spirited argument? A desperate attempt to remember a crucial detail? The future will show us.

THE DRAWBRIDGE, GIOVANNI BATTISTA PIRANESI, 1761

Appendix E: Thoughts on Collecting

In a way, this book is the story of a personal collection, so it seems natural that readers might be curious about how to start their own. I encourage this! There is a whole world of RPG books out there, much wider and weirder than anything that can be cataloged in just one book. I've been collecting for years, and I am still regularly surprised and delighted by items I come across. As rewarding as it may be, though, the second-hand market for RPGs is not without its pitfalls.

Generally, printed matter is considered collectible because it is rare, because it is in good condition, and because it is are otherwise notable. In addition to RPGs, I also collect books published by Arkham House, the publishing company founded by August Derleth and Donald Wandrei to preserve H. P. Lovecraft's literary legacy. Arkham House books are a good demonstration of all three pillars of collectability. Nearly every title was issued in small editions, usually no more than 2,000 copies. Setting aside the usual ravages of time, some Arkham House dust jackets seem particularly prone to chipping and fading, so there are clear ways to appraise a given volume's condition. And, of course, many Arkham House publications mark their author's first time in hardcover, making them noteworthy for enthusiasts of genre fiction.

All of these criteria apply to collecting RPG books, but with the added wrinkle of speculators. As with the collecting booms in the comic book industry in the mid '80s and the early '90s, there is a class of RPG collector who is buying (and selling) because they see the books as an investment. Whether or not you agree with that notion (I don't, for the record), the increasing popularity of *Dungeons & Dragons* has led to a rapid rise in prices in recent years, often with little regard to a given title's actual level of scarcity. This bubble has seemed to be in imminent danger of bursting for several years now, but as of this writing, it is still intact.

That said, my first piece of advice is to remember that RPG books are worth what you're willing to pay for them and not a single penny more. Just because someone says something is valuable doesn't mean they are right. For instance, a copy of the first edition of *Deities & Demigods*, the 144-page version containing the Cthulhu and Melnibonean mythologies, recently surfaced on eBay with an astounding $900 dollar asking price. While yes, because of the rumors surrounding that particular book, it is always going to be desirable to collectors, there is no good reason to pay *that much* money for it. Even the "typical" price of around $300 dollars is absurd when you know that there are likely 15,000 copies of the book in circulation. But sure enough, though that seller is probably never going to find a rube to pay his $900 dollar price, they gave permission to everyone else selling a copy to up their prices while still looking like a bargain. The bottom line for a collector is that if the price tag on an RPG book is over three or four times the retail price, there better be a very good reason for it.

It is also good to get into the practice of being patient. There is always a better price to be found if a buyer is willing to wait. Skim all of the sites, get a sense of what the market is asking for a book, then wait for a copy to show that is half that price. Because the market is not to be trusted! The market wants big spenders! That book is probably sitting on the dusty back shelf of a comic shop, marked with a half-off sticker; the trick is waiting to find that shop, or for the right mom to clean out the right attic. One of the best tools to facilitate this sort of patience is flagging keywords on eBay so the service will notify you via email when a new matching listing is posted. Auctions are generally preferable to "buy-it-now" options. And, though there are never bargains to be found, the network of Facebook groups dedicated to trading and selling RPGs will almost always net the buyer a *fair* price.

That said, the books that are actually rare and desirable will not only continue to be so, but will increase in value over time. So, if you can afford it, buy them now! I wish I had bought Ray Bradbury's *Dark Carnival* (1947) when I first got into Arkham House in the late aughts. Bradbury was still alive then, so a copy could be found for $400 dollars. Now? The asking price is regularly four times that. The first Lovecraft collection, *The Outsider and Others* (1939), used to run an astonishing $1,200 to $1,500 dollars, the memory of which makes my eyes water when I see them listed for $7,000 dollars now. This isn't any less true of the original woodgrain *Dungeons & Dragons* box set.

Most of all, though, have fun, don't break the bank (if the bubble does burst, this stuff is going to be worth a whole lot less in the aftermath), and be ready to get more shelving before you know it.

VIEW OF THE PYRAMIDAL TOMB OF CAIUS CESTIUS, GIOVANNI BATTISTA PIRANESI, 1755

Appendix F: RPG Publishers

What follows is a collection of most of the RPG publishers mentioned in the book and their dates of operation. RPG companies that go out of business or otherwise cease publication often have strange half-lives, thanks to their connection to intellectual property that remains valuable, even if the company producing it is not. Defunct companies linger on as holding companies, licensors, or find themselves as part of other sorts of arcane business arrangements. I've no desire to untangle those webs, as other authors have already done so with great success, so I've only included the dates for a company's "first life."

» Adept Press (2001-Present)
» Adventure Learning Systems, Inc. (1984-date unknown)
» Arc Dream Publishing (2002-Present)
» Atlas Games (1990-Present)
» Avalon Hill (1952-Present)
» Bard Games (1982-1990)
» Bastionland Press (2019-Present)
» Blackoath Entertainment (2019-Present)
» Bully Pulpit Games (2005-Present)
» Buried Without Ceremony (2016-Present)
» Cavalry Games (2014-Present)
» Centaur Games (2017-Present)
» Chaosium (1975-Present)
» Columbia Games (1972-Present)
» Council of Fools (1995-Present)
» Cubicle 7 (2003-Present)
» Darker Hue Studios (2016-Present)
» Evil Hat Productions (2001-Present)
» Exalted Funeral (2018-Present)
» Fantasy Games Unlimited (1975-1991)
» FASA Corporation (1980-2001)
» Flying Buffalo Inc. (1970-Present)
» Free League Publishing (2011-Present)
» Game Designers' Workshop (1973-1996)

» Games Omnivorous (2020-Present)
» Games Workshop (1975-Present)
» Goblinoid Games (2006-Present)
» Goodman Games (2001-Present)
» Green Ronin Publishing (2000-Present)
» Grey Ghost Press (1995-Present)
» Grimoire Games (1979-1984)
» Hero Games (1981-Present)
» Highland Paranormal Society (2018-Present)
» Hogshead Publishing (1994-2000)
» Holistic Design, Inc. (1992-2006)
» The Impossible Dream (1999-Present)
» Iron Crown Enterprises (1980-2000)
» Issaries, Inc. (1997-2004)
» Judges Guild (1976-1983)
» Lame Mage Productions (2006-Present)
» Last Unicorn Games (1994-2000)
» Leading Edge Games (1982-1993)
» Lion Rampant (1987-1990)
» Lumpley Games (2001-Present)
» Magpie Games (2011-Present)
» Mayfair Games (1981-1997)
» Melsonian Arts Council (2014-Present)
» Memento Mori Theatricks (1997-Present)
» Metagaming Concepts (1975-1983)

» Metropolis Ltd. (1993-1996)
» Midkemia Press (1979-1983)
» Moon Design Publications (1998-Present)
» Narrative Dynamics (2019-Present)
» Pagan Publishing (1990-unknown)
» Paizo (2002-Present)
» Palladium Books (1981-Present)
» Pelgrane Press (1999-Present)
» Petit Guignol (2018-Present)
» Phage Press (1991-2005)
» Pinnacle Entertainment Group (1994-Present)
» Puffin Books (1940-Present)
» R. Talsorian Games (1984-Present)
» Ramshead Publishing (2001-Present)
» Rowan, Rook and Decard (2017-Present)
» RPGA Network (1980-2014)

» Simulations Publications, Inc. (1969-1982)
» Sine Nomine Publishing (2010-Present)
» SkyRealms Publishing (1984-1988)
» Standard Games (1981-1999)
» Steve Jackson Games (1980-Present)
» Superhero Necromancer Press (2018-Present)
» The Swordfish Islands (2017-Present)
» Thorny Games (2016-Present)
» Troll Lord Games (2000-Present)
» TSR (Tactical Studies Rules) (1973-1997)
» Tuesday Knight Games (2013-Present)
» Victory Games (1982-1989)
» Wee Warriors (1975-1978)
» West End Games (1974-1998)
» White Wolf Publishing (1986-2006)
» Wizards of the Coast (1990-Present)

MAUSOLEUM OF HADRIAN, GIOVANNI BATTISTA PIRANESI, 1756

Stu Horvath is a writer from New Jersey. He founded Unwinnable, an outlet for independent cultural criticism, in 2010. In 2017, a lifelong enthusiasm for (and a fiscally questionable investment in collecting) tabletop role-playing games led to the creation of the @VintageRPG on Instagram. The Vintage RPG Podcast followed in 2018. Despite devoting an awful lot of time to reading about and writing about RPGs, he hasn't had nearly enough time to play them, which points to a fundamental flaw in his master plan.

Kyle Patterson was born outside Seattle with pencils for fingers and paint in his veins. He took proper advantage of his mutant powers by jumping headfirst into an illustration career after graduating with a Painting & Drawing degree from the University of Washington in 2017. He has contributed art (namely monsters, magic, and assorted curios) to a number of tabletop RPG products and publications, and is thankfully thought of as only marginally freakish by friends and family.

Layout and Design: Derek Kinsman
Line Editor: Orrin Grey
Copy Editor: Jamie Springer
Fact Checker: Joe DeSimone
Sensitivity Reader: Alexander Saify

Index

Page numbers in *italics* refer to illustrations.